Capital cities of Australia and New Zealand
Capital cities of the states and territories
other cities
Outback

Pacific
Ocean

Indian
Ocean

Great Barrier Reef

Brisbane

Cairns

Darwin

Queensland

Northern Territory

Uluru

Western Australia

South Australia

Perth

Albany

Adelaide

A u s t r a l i a

Sydney

New South Wales

Canberra

Australian Capital Territory

Melbourne

Victoria

Tasmania

Hobart

Tasman Sea

N e w   Z e a l a n d

Auckland

North Island

Wellington

Christchurch

South Island

Queenstown

Milford Sound

1000 miles

750

500

250

0

1000 km

500

0

westermann

On Track ◀◀◀

Englisch als
2. Fremdsprache

4

von:
Jon Hird
Heather Jones
Marc Proulx
Adrian Tennant
Agnes Tennant
Patricia Wedler
Story von Marcus Sedgwick mit
Illustrationen von Pete Williamson

herausgegeben von:
Helga Holtkamp

Begleitmaterialien zum Lehrwerk:

Workbook ISBN 978-3-14-040913-1
Medienpaket ISBN 978-3-14-062773-3
Ferienlektüre ISBN 978-3-14-040884-4
Schulaufgabentrainer ISBN 978-3-14-040894-3

BiBox – Digitale Unterrichtsmaterialien
Nähere Informationen unter www.bibox.schule

Vokabel-Apps sind online erhältlich.

westermann GRUPPE

© 2022 Westermann Bildungsmedien Verlag GmbH, Braunschweig, www.westermann.de

Druck A[1] / Jahr 2022
Alle Drucke der Serie A sind inhaltlich unverändert.

Unter Mitarbeit von: Stacy Bentz und Udo Diekmann

Beratung durch: Claudia Maria Hugo (Lindau), Günter Fischer (Mitwitz),
Friedrich Frenzel (Bad Neustadt an der Saale), Dr. Mario Oesterreicher (Nürnberg),
Christian Schulze (Lindau), Eva Maria Veitenhansl (München), Juliane Lobischer (Berlin),
Margot Adami (Paderborn), Alexa Bradbury (Paderborn)

Redaktion: Dr. Martin Walter
Umschlaggestaltung: Detlef Möller, Paderborn
Coverfoto vorne: © Wim Wiskerke / Alamy Stock Photo. Sydney Opera House with Sydney Harbor Bridge
Coverfoto hinten: © Andrew Michael / Alamy Stock Photo. Surf school on Main beach, Byron Bay, NSW, Australia
Druck und Bindung: Westermann Druck GmbH, Braunschweig

ISBN 978-3-14-**040903**-2

How to use this book   Wie du dieses Buch benutzt

On Track 4 starts with a *Welcome* double-page spread. Then there are four regular workshops. Every workshop has the same three parts. Parts one and two teach you new things, and part three helps you practise what you learned. The activities and exercises have numbers and letters. Sometimes they have symbols, too.

On Track 4 beginnt mit einer *Welcome*-Doppelseite. Darauf folgen vier Hauptkapitel. Jeder Workshop besteht aus drei Teilen (*Parts*): In Teil 1 und 2 lernst du neue Dinge. In Teil 3 übst du, was du Neues gelernt hast. Die Aufgaben und Übungen haben Zahlen und Buchstaben. Einige haben auch Symbole.

Here is an explanation of the symbols   Hier findest du Erklärungen zu allen Symbolen:

audio	🔊 14))	Listen to a dialogue, a text, song or story. Höre dir einen Dialog, Text, ein Lied oder eine Geschichte an.
video	🎞 2	Watch a film. Sieh dir einen Film an.
partner work	👥	Work with a partner. Arbeite mit einem Partner / einer Partnerin.
group work	👨‍👩‍👧	Work with two or more partners. Arbeite mit zwei oder mehreren Partnern.
mediation	M	Help an English person to understand German or a German person to understand English. Hilf einer englischsprachigen Person dabei, etwas auf Deutsch zu verstehen. Oder hilf einer deutschsprachigen Person dabei, etwas auf Englisch zu verstehen.
AE	🇺🇸	American English (specific vocabulary or spelling) Amerikanisches Englisch (spezielle Wörter oder Schreibweisen)
revision	*	Grammar revision Grammatikwiederholung
step 1, 2, 3, ...	S1	Activities with this symbol help you with a more complex task – step by step. Aufgaben mit diesem Symbol helfen dir Schritt für Schritt beim Bearbeiten einer komplexeren Lernaufgabe.
grammar	→ G18	There is more information about this grammar topic in the *Appendix*: Look up grammar rule 1 ... 26. Zu diesem Grammatikthema findest du mehr Informationen im Anhang (*Appendix*). Schau die Grammatikregel Nummer 1 ... 26 dort nach.
webcode	@ WES-40903-004	There is a webcode on the left hand page of every workshop. This webcode helps you to find all the audio and video material. You also find transcripts of the audios and videos as well as solutions to the activities on the *Review* pages. In den Workshops steht jeweils auf der linken Seite ein Webcode, unter dem du alle Audio- und Videodateien findest. Hier stellen wir dir außerdem Transkripte der Audios und Videos sowie Lösungen zu den Aufgaben auf den *Review*-Seiten zur Verfügung.

How to use the webcodes   Wie du die Webcodes benutzt

A webcode is like a small website. All the *On Track* audio and video material that you need for class or homework is here: www.westermann.de/webcodes. There is also extra material. You can listen and watch online or download everything. Type in the code for the workshop (**WES-40903-001**) without the @ and click "Aufrufen". There is your page for *Workshop 1*. There are webcodes in your workbook, too.   Ein Webcode funktioniert wie eine kleine Webseite. Alle Audio- und Videodateien sowie Extramaterialien für die Arbeit in der Schule oder für Hausaufgaben sind hier www.westermann.de/webcodes. Du kannst online zuhören und schauen oder alles herunterladen. Gib den Code ohne @ ein (**WES-40903-001**) und schon bist du auf der Webseite von *Workshop 1*.

These are the webcodes in *On Track 4*:   Dies sind die Webcodes in *On Track 4*:

Welcome: @ WES-40903-000	Workshop 2: @ WES-40903-002	Workshop 4: @ WES-40903-004
Workshop 1: @ WES-40903-001	Workshop 3: @ WES-40903-003	Extra pages: @ WES-40903-005

Contents

* grammar revision

Contents

* grammar revision

Contents

* grammar revision

English around the world

Look at the two flags. One flag is for Australia and the other for New Zealand. The Union Jack in the top left corner represents the historical link to the UK. Which one is the Australian flag?

■ countries where English is an official or de facto official or national language (e.g. UK, USA, Ireland, Canada, Australia and New Zealand)

■ countries where English is an official but not primary language (e.g. Singapore, India, Rwanda, etc.)

 Do the quiz and see how many questions you can get right. Compare your results in class.

 Which answers surprised you the most? Which facts do you find most interesting? Explain why.

English language quiz

1. Approximately how many languages are there in the world?
A 6,500
B 380
C 4,200

2. Which are the two most commonly spoken languages on earth?
A English and French
B Mandarin and Spanish
C English and Spanish

3. Approximately how many English speakers were there in the world in Shakespeare's time?
A 5 – 7 million
B 15 million
C 2 – 3 million

4. Approximately how many people speak English as a second language?
A 51 million
B 200 million
C 510 million

5. What is the main reason why English spread and became a world language?
A British colonialism
B popular music
C Shakespeare

6. You hear someone say 'No worries, mate'. Which country are they probably from?
A Australia
B South Africa
C USA

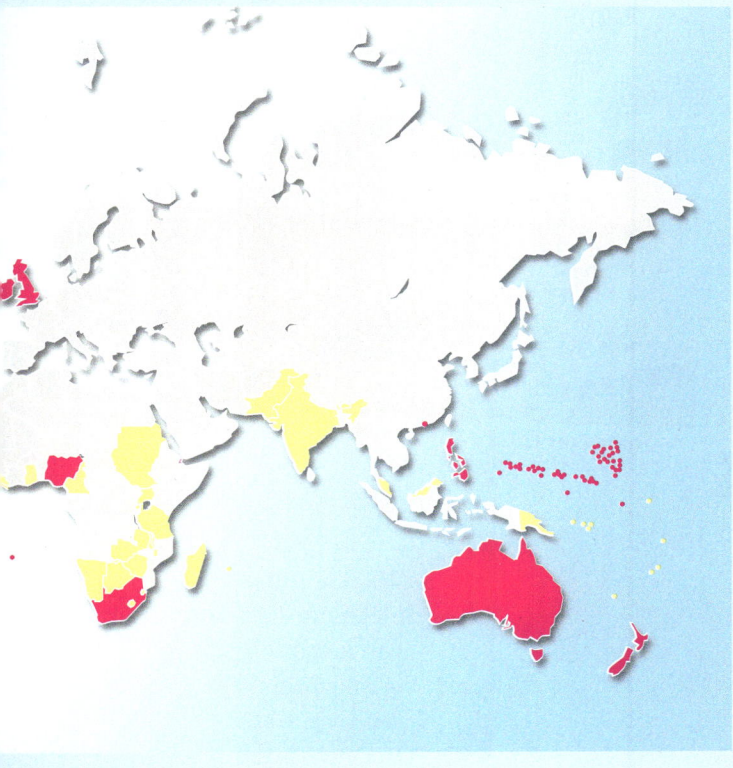

 1 Watch the slideshow and take notes. Compare your answers.

1 Why do most Australians speak English as their mother tongue?
2 What is the Commonwealth?
3 List the factors that helped make English a global language.

 Read and discuss what these teens say about different countries. Match them to these nations: *India, Australia, USA* and *South Africa*.

I said to a British friend, 'I like the color of your pants'. She looked horrified and replied 'Oh dear, are they showing?' That's when I realized we didn't speak the same language.

Brad

I told my friend we're having a braai just now and he said, 'Okay, let's go' and I said 'No, not now, just now'. He didn't seem to understand that 'just now' means 'later' where I come from!

Alain

When I first moved to this country, I often got confused by what people said. I remember standing at a bus stop one day and a boy saying 'How ya going?' When I answered, 'By bus', he looked at me as if I were crazy.

Sanjay

'It's hot! Grab your togs and let's hit the beach.' If you need me to translate that … well, what do you wear at a beach? Yep, your swimwear.

Nicole
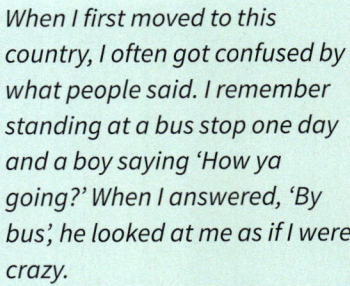

When I was visiting some relatives at my dad's birthplace, someone asked me, 'What's your good name, please?' I was really confused until I realized they just wanted to know my name. But when they asked if I had any doubts, I really hadn't got a clue.

Aesha

Aussies and Kiwis

 Do this mini quiz to see how much you already know about Australia.

1. Who were the first Australians?
   A Maoris
   B Aboriginal people and Torres Strait Islanders
   C Indians

The State Barrier Fence (the rabbit proof fence), Western Australia

Aboriginal culture show at Tjapukai Cultural Centre, Queensland

2. Who gave Australia its name?
   A The Aboriginal people
   B The British
   C The Dutch

3. What is Australia's nickname? And do you know why it is called this?
   A Down Under
   B Down South
   C Deep Down

4. What is Australia?
   A A continent
   B A country
   C A continent, a country and an island

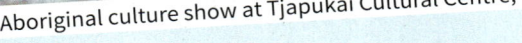
Kakadu National Park, Northern Territory

5. How big is Australia?
   A 12 times bigger than Germany
   B 16 times bigger than Germany
   C 22 times bigger than Germany

6. The population of Germany is about 80 million and of Australia ...
   A about 26 million
   B about 50 million
   C about 75 million

Aboriginal rock painting of the Rainbow Serpent, Kakadu National Park

Christmas on Bondi Beach, Sydney, New South Wales

7. What is the capital of Australia?
   A Sydney
   B Melbourne
   C Canberra

8. There are more kangaroos than people in Australia.
   A True
   B False

9. The interior of Australia is mainly desert and bush. What is its name?
   A The Territory
   B The Outback
   C The Billabong

10. The flight time from Brisbane to Christchurch, New Zealand is …
    A about 4 hours
    B about 6 hours
    C about 10 hours

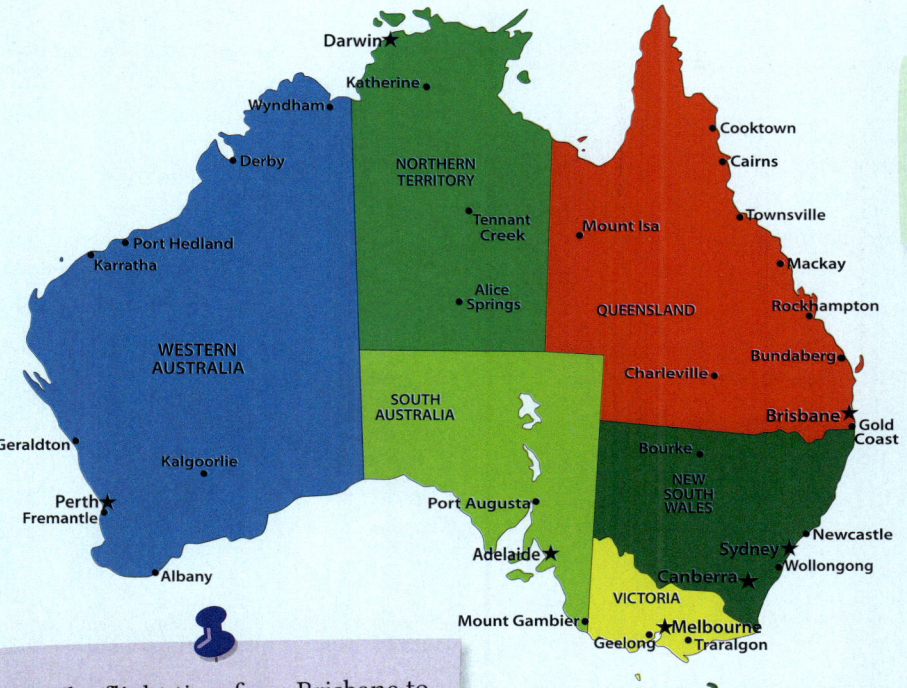

Darwin
Katherine
Wyndham
Derby
NORTHERN TERRITORY
Cooktown
Cairns
Townsville
Port Hedland
Karratha
Tennant Creek
Mount Isa
Mackay
Alice Springs
QUEENSLAND
Rockhampton
WESTERN AUSTRALIA
Bundaberg
Charleville
Brisbane
Gold Coast
Geraldton
SOUTH AUSTRALIA
Bourke
Kalgoorlie
NEW SOUTH WALES
Perth
Fremantle
Port Augusta
Sydney
Newcastle
Adelaide
Wollongong
Canberra
Albany
VICTORIA
Mount Gambier
Melbourne
Geelong
Traralgon

Launceston
TASMANIA
Hobart

Auckland
Hamilton
NEW ZEALAND
Wellington
Invercargill
Dunedin

Auckland is New Zealand's biggest city.

Watch the video to check your answers. You will find out more facts about this amazing country, so watch the video again and then make three questions for another pair.

Jason's choice

1 The big news

a Jason Turner is a student at Bayview High School in Melbourne. He plays on the school rugby team together with his friend Ricky Bates. Read the story, then do the tasks.

1 Explain how the rugby team players feel and give reasons for your answers.
2 Describe the choice that Jason faces.

b Decide whether these statements are true or false. Correct the false ones.

1 Ricky and Jason are both excited when they hear the news.
2 At the end of rugby practice, the whole team feels the same.
3 Jason's dad wants to know who will pay for the trip.
4 Jason's mum understands Jason's dilemma.

---

1 The players were breathing hard and sweating as they gathered around Coach Hansen. 'Nice workout, guys,' he said. 'Now, I've got some big news.'
Jason and Ricky exchanged puzzled looks.
5 'Our partner school in Christchurch has invited us to play in their rugby tournament. It starts at the end of their school term,' he announced. 'Who wants to go to New Zealand?'
There was silence, then the whole team jumped and
10 cheered. The noise echoed across the playing field and around the school campus.
'We're going to play against the Kiwis!' Jason said, giving Ricky a high five.
'Yeah, and we're going to *beat* them!' Ricky shouted.
15 When the coach announced the tournament dates, Jason's smile slowly disappeared. As they walked from the field, one thought kept going through his head: 'Nick and Eleni are celebrating their birthdays on 2 October'.

2 Sharing with a friend. Listen and do the tasks.

1 Describe what happens. Who is doing the sharing?
2 Compare how Jason and Ricky communicate with Eleni.
3 Choose one or more of these adjectives to describe Eleni's reaction: *happy, excited, shocked, supportive, uninterested, disappointed*.

3* Good friends

a Look at these sentences and the explanation in the box.

*You boys **have been playing** so well.*
*We**'ve had** a good season so far.*

Explain why the progressive form is used in the first sentence and not in the second.

b Complete the text. Sometimes two forms are correct.

Jason ___1___ (know) Ricky since primary school. They ___2___ (play) rugby together since they were both ten. Jason and Nick Kourakis ___3___ (be) friends for a long time, too. He ___4___ (work) part-time at the Kourakis' Greek deli for the past year. Since then Jason and Eleni ___5___ (spend) more time together.

Remember

● We use the present perfect to express that an action is completed or to emphasize the result. *I**'ve texted** my mum ten times today, but she **hasn't answered**.*

● We use the present perfect progressive with action verbs like *go, talk, play* or *try* to emphasize the length of the action. *The coach **has been trying** to organize a trip like this for a while.*

● With state verbs like *have, know, want* or *understand* we use the present perfect, not the present perfect progressive. *He **has always wanted** to take the team to play in New Zealand*

🔊)) **Words and phrases**

g'day   (AuE, NZeE) hello   **mate**   (BrE, AuE) friend   **puzzled**   not able to understand sth

At dinner Jason shared the news with his parents.
'That's brilliant, Jason!' his dad said. 'You boys have been
playing so well, I'm not surprised.'
'Yeah, we've had a good season so far,' Jason said.
5 'Christchurch, New Zealand? That's quite a trip,' his
mum said. 'Who's going to pay for it?'
'The school sports fund will pay for the plane tickets,'
Jason said. 'And we'll be able to stay with the families of
students from Papanui High School.'
10 'You don't look very enthusiastic. Is there a problem?'
Jason sighed. 'It's the same weekend when Nick's
parents invited me to go to Sydney with them. It's Nick's
and Eleni's sixteenth birthday.'
'Eleni?' his dad said.
15 'Nick's twin sister,' Jason's mum said.
'Ah, yes, the twins. Jason, I know Nick is your mate, but
the team needs you,' his dad said.
'I think Jason needs to decide for himself what's more
important,' his mum said. 'Eat up, Jason,' she added.
20 'Your film starts at 7.00, doesn't it?'
'It's OK,' said Jason. 'We're meeting at the cinema just
before 7.00. Nick's going to book the tickets online.'

4* **Planning to win**

a Look at the sentences and read the explanation
in the box. Why does Jason use the *going-to future*
in the first and the *will future* in the second?

We're going to play against the Kiwis.
The school will pay for the plane tickets.

Remember
- We use *going to* to talk about plans or to
  say what we have already decided to do.
- We use *will* to offer or promise to do
  something or when we decide to do
  something while we are speaking.

We use both tenses to make predictions:
- *going to:* when we see what's going to
  happen
- *will:* when we think we know what will
  happen (but don't know for sure)

We can also use present tenses to express
the future:
- We use the simple present to talk about
  timetables or programmes.
- We use the present progressive to talk
  about future arrangements.

b Jason is talking to his parents. Complete what
he says with the correct future forms.

Mr T.   Has your team started preparing yet?

Jason   Yes, the coach gave us a new schedule.
        We **1** (*have*) extra training at
        weekends from next week.

Mrs T. What do you know about your
        opponent?

Jason   Nothing yet, but we **2** (*meet*) them in
        a video call next week. I **3** (*try*) to
        find videos about the other school team
        on the internet. No matter what, we
        4 (*ask*) the coach to work out the
        best strategy for our team.

Mrs T. I bet he **5** (*do*) that! I hope you
        6 (*be able to*) go sightseeing in
        Christchurch as well. And how do you
        feel about the twins?

Jason   I know I **7** (*not be able to*) go to
        Sydney, but I am sure Nick and Eleni
        8 (*understand*). And they **9** (*have*)
        a barbie later in the year to celebrate
        their birthdays with everyone here.

5 **So far and so close.** Jason gets a phone call that
changes everything. Listen and do the tasks.

1 Describe what the rugby team has been
  getting ready for.
2 Explain why Ricky is so excited about the
  tournament.
3 Explain what Eleni's news means for Jason.

6 **It's your turn: A sporting expert**

a Which sport can you see in the
picture? Look at this list
(*Australian rules football, cricket,
netball, rugby*), choose a sport
and do some research. Then
prepare a two-minute talk.

b Find a partner with another
sport. Give your talks and ask
each other questions. What
didn't you know about your
partner's sport before?

Grammar and structures

Present perfect and present perfect progressive (revision) → **G1**
Eleni **hasn't known** about Aunt Koula's illness very long.
Her parents **have been waiting** for the right moment to tell her.

Future forms: *will* and *going to* (revision) → **G2**
The team **are going to** practise more so I believe we'll be able to win.

PART 1

PART 2

PART 3

1 **a** Did you know that the word 'selfie' originates from Australia? Australians love to add 'ie' or 'y' to words to make them informal. Can you guess what the words in the box mean?

> Aussie ■ brekkie ■ footy ■ lappy ■ prezzie

3 **b** Now go to the webcode and watch the video. See if you can find another word like the ones in the box.

2 Australian English has many informal words and phrases. Read Jason and Eleni's conversation and match the numbered words and phrases with the standard English ones in the box. The context will help you. Compare your answers with a partner.

> afternoon ■ barbecue ■ Don't worry ■ food ■ great ■ Hello ■ How are you? ■ lots ■ Thanks ■ Well done

Eleni   **G'day** (1), Jason.

Jason   Hi, Eleni! **How ya going?** (2)

Eleni   Oh, I'm fine. It's so hot today, though. I hope it won't be like this all weekend.

Jason   Aw, **no worries** (3). They say it's going to get cooler.

Eleni   That's good. Hey, we're having a **barbie** (4) at our house this **arvo** (5). Would you like to join us?

Jason   That sounds **ace** (6). I'd love to come. Shall I bring some **tucker** (7) with me?

Eleni   Aw, no need – we've already done the shopping. We've got **heaps** (8) to eat.

Jason   **Good on ya.** (9) **Cheers!** (10) Then I'll see ya later.

Eleni   See you then!

3 Here are some more Australian words. Guess or find out what they mean. Use some of these words or those in **1** and **2** to write a short dialogue. Then share your dialogue in class. Can the others understand it?

> beauty ■ chockers ■ mozzie ■ nana ■ pom ■ roo ■ sickie ■ swimmers ■ ta

4 **a** Read part of an interview with Coach Hansen for the Bayview High School newspaper. Use the *present perfect* or the *present perfect progressive* to complete the sentences.

Q: Coach Hansen, you ▢1 (*coach*) the boys' rugby team for eight years. What do you like about the job and what ▢2 (*change*) since you started?

A: I ▢3 (*always, have*) the full support of the school principal and the teaching staff. The students and the parents ▢4 (*believe*) in me too. When we started, the inter-school competition in Melbourne wasn't well organized, but it ▢5 (*get*) better every year, so that ▢6 (*be*) a positive change.

Q: Why do you think the boys' team ▢7 (*be*) so successful this year?

A: We've got an amazing team with players like Ricky Bates and Jason Turner. These boys ▢8 (*play*) rugby for at least five years, so they understand how to be effective on the field. Also, we ▢9 (*try*) different game plans, and now I think we ▢10 (*find out*) what works.

b Read the next part of the interview. Use *will* or *going to* to complete the sentences.

Q: The team has been invited to Christchurch in New Zealand to play against their rugby team. Could you tell our readers how you are preparing for this trip?

A: There are a lot of things we ▢1 (*need*) to organize. First, we ▢2 (*have*) a meeting with the parents soon where we ▢3 (*try*) to answer all the questions. The school sports fund ▢4 (*pay*) for the plane tickets and once we are there the players ▢5 (*stay*) with host families. I am sure they ▢6 (*have*) a great time and ▢7 (*have*) the opportunity for sightseeing.

Q: Do you think you ▢8 (*win*) against the Kiwis?

A: I think we have a good chance. We ▢9 (*have*) extra practice at the weekends and ▢10 (*learn*) as much as we can about our opponents. It ▢11 (*be*) hard work but lots of fun at the same time. And I am sure the parents ▢12 (*support*) us.

→ Workbook, page 11   **LISTENING AND VIEWING PRACTICE**

1 Look at the pictures connected to Australia. With a partner speculate what they show. Make notes.

2 Watch the slide show and check your ideas. What did you learn that you didn't know before?

3 **a** Put these events in the correct chronological order.

Aborigines arrive in Australia.   Captain Cook lands at Botany Bay.   Gold is discovered.

The Commonwealth of Australia is formed.   The Dutch 'discover' Australia.

The Eureka Rebellion takes place.   The first settlement is established at Sydney Cove.

b Watch the slide show again and check.

4 **a** Decide whether the <u>underlined</u> words and phrases are correct. Correct the wrong ones.

b Find ten factual mistakes in the text and correct them.

The first people to arrive in Australia were the Aborigine. They arrived between forty and sixty <u>thousands</u>[1] years ago. Then in 1506 a number of Dutch explorers 'discovered' Australia. They named this new land New Holland. In 1770 Captain James Cook <u>landed</u>[2] <u>by</u>[3] Sydney Cove. Sixteen years later the first colony <u>has been</u>[4] established at Sydney Cove with a lot of convicts sent from Britain. Between 1788 and 1868, around 64,000 convicts were transported <u>by the ship</u>[5] from Britain to Australia. In 1803, the Dutch explorer Mathew Flinders named it Terra Australis Incognita, which means 'unknown southern land'. In 1851, oil was discovered in New South Wales and thousands of free settlers arrived from around the world. In 1901, a competition <u>is hold</u>[6] to design a flag for the country. The Australian flag has four elements on a blue background. The first of these is the Union Jack in the top left corner showing that Australia was a British colony. Australia Day is celebrated on the first of January every year. This is the day that Australia became <u>independently</u>[7] <u>of</u>[8] Britain.

To move or not to move?

1 **Life in Australia.** Look at the picture. Speculate what is going on.

2 **Keira's email.** The Smiths are a family from the South of England. They have moved into the house next to the Turners. Keira, the daughter, is 15. She writes an email to her best friend back in the UK. Read the email, then do the tasks.

From: Keira Smith
To: Jasmine Roberts
Subject: Australia

Hiya,

So this arvo – that's Australian for afternoon –
we are going to go for a barbie (you can guess
what that means) with the Turners. They live
5 next door to the place we're staying in and
they've invited us round. I think Mrs Turner will
ask us how we are settling in. And I bet Mr Turner
will want to know if we are going to move to
Melbourne for good. I wonder if they'll ask us
10 what we kids think.
My dad says Fred and I have to like it here, too,
and it is our decision as well. My mum has just
told me not to worry, our opinion matters.
I'm not sure. I love it here. The weather is great,
15 and the people are really friendly, but if I am
asked, I will tell them that I don't want to leave
my friends.

Jazz, what do you think I should say to my
parents? I know they both love it here, but …
20 If we moved here, would you come over and
visit?

Love K.
xxx

---

1 Explain why Keira is writing to Jasmine.
2 Speculate who Fred is.

Reported speech

We use reported speech to talk about what other people say.

- We start with reporting verbs, expressions such as: *He says / She asks / wants to know / wonders / has told (me), will ask*, etc.
- When the reporting verb is in the present, present perfect or future tense, we do not change the tense of what we report.
  We love the area.
  *My dad **says / has said / will say** (that) we **love** the area …*
- When we report questions we change them into a statement after the question word:
  So how are you settling in?
  *She wants to know how we **are settling** in.*
- To report *yes/no*–questions we use *if* or *whether* and invert the subject and the verb.
  Are you going to move to Melbourne?
  *He wants to know **whether we are** going to move to Melbourne.*
- For orders and requests we use the infinitive form of the main verb with *to*.
  ***Don't worry.** → My mum tells me **not to worry**.*
- Be careful about the pronoun changes:
  *So do **you** think **you**'re going to move to Melbourne for good?*
  *Mr Turner has just asked **us** if **we** are going to move to Melbourne for good.*

🔊 **Words and phrases**

on your doorstep	very close to where you live
to **settle in**	to become familiar with a new way of life, place, job, etc.
to **switch**	to change from one thing to another

3 A life-changing decision

 a Listen to the conversation at the Turners' barbecue, then do the tasks.

1 Explain the big decision that the Smiths have to make. What do they have to think about?
2 Describe how Fred Smith feels and say why.

b Look at this question from Jason and Fred's answer. Report what they both say.

> Do you like sport, Fred? There are lots of sports clubs you can join.

> Wow. That's great.

4 Decision time

a Back home after the barbecue Mrs Smith, Fred and Keira carry on talking about the move. Read the conversation and do the tasks below. (You will need the blue words and phrases for activity **b**.)

Fred   What's wrong with you, Keira?
Mrs S. Please don't speak to your sister like that.
Fred   But mum! Why can't she decide?
Mrs S. I know you want to move here …
Fred   Yes, I do. Just think of all the things I can do outdoors and I can join the rugby team and …
Mrs S. Won't you miss your friends in England?
Fred   Sure, but I'll make new friends here.
Mrs S. It's a big decision for everyone, Fred. Be patient with Keira!
Keira   It's not easy …
Mrs S. No, it's not, Keira, but we don't have a lot of time. Can you think about it and make a decision by Wednesday?
Keira   Wednesday!? But that's only three days away.
Fred   I'll help you decide.

1 Explain why Fred is upset.
2 Analyse Keira's reaction to what Mrs Smith says.
3 Compare how Fred and Keira feel about the move.

b Keira is talking to her dad. Read the conversation again and complete what Keira tells him about it. The blue words in **a** can help you.

Mr S.   Are you OK?
Keira   Not really. Fred wants to know ___1___ and Mum has asked him ___2___.
Mr S.   So, you're not sure yet if you like it here?
Keira   No, but Fred is sure ___3___.
Mr S.   And what does your mother say?
Keira   Mum has told Fred ___4___. She wants me ___5___.
Mr S.   I'm sorry, I know it's hard for you. So, what are you going to do?
Keira   I'll talk to Fred. He has told me ___6___.

5 It's your turn: Going to Australia

a Think: Imagine you were going to spend a year abroad in Australia. How would you feel? What would you miss most? What would you be excited about? Makes notes.

b Pair: Tell ayour partner how you would feel if you were moving to Australia.

c Share: Report what yout partner says to the rest of the class.

Grammar and structures

Reported speech in statements and questions in the present, present perfect and future → G3

My dad **says** we **love** the area …
Fred **has told** me he **will help** me decide.

Mrs Turner **will ask** us how we **are settling in**.
My mum **has asked** Fred **not to speak** to me like that.

PART 1

1
🔊 6

a The day after the barbecue you see Jason and Keira in the shopping mall. Listen to their conversation and do the tasks.

1 Say what Jason and Keira are talking about.
2 Explain why Keira thinks it is a great idea to be introduced to Jason's classmates.

b While you are listening to Jason and Keira's conversation, a friend rings you. Report what you hear.

Jason says …   Keira admits that …   Jason wants to know …
Keira says that …   Now Jason has offered …
He thinks …   He also says …
Keira looks happy! She tells Jason …

PART 2

2 At the barbecue, Mr Turner invited Bob Smith to visit him at his workplace. The following week, Bob went to see Adrian Turner. While he is there, Wendy phones him and asks him about the visit. Read the conversation and correct the underlined mistakes.

Wendy   So, how is the visit with Adrian?
Bob   It is interesting. You remember he mentioned working at a big factory that bottles fruit juice …
Wendy   Yes, I know from Judith he has an important job there.
Bob   An important job! He owns the factory.
Wendy   Wow! Have you ask[1] him about that?
Bob   Yes, I have and he's[2] says he been[3] lucky as his dad started the company almost fifty years ago. He's just asked me what do I do[4] back in the UK and he seems to be happy that I am an electrician. He says that is great as he can always use electricians in the factory …
Wendy   What, you already have a job?
Bob   No, of course not. But I think if we decided to move over here for good, there might be a job waiting for me.
Wendy   That's wonderful news. What you[5] say to him if he asks?
Bob   I'll say I think[6] about it …
Wendy   Bob!
Bob   I'm joking, darling. I tell[7] him I'll be talk[8] to you and the kids more about moving to Melbourne …

PART 3

3 Jasmine discussed Keira's dilemma with her mum. Here are some of the things they said. Write an email from Jasmine to Keira in which you give her advice. Include some of the information and add your own ideas.

> Has Keira been in Melbourne long enough to get to know the place?

> Has she found anything she particularly likes?

> I am sure she'll make friends there quickly.

> You can use social media to keep in touch.

> You will go and visit her as soon as you can.

> What is the school system like there? – I think it's similar to ours.

> Keira can join a school club. She'll meet lots of people.

> Maybe she can start a blog about life in Australia.

→ Workbook, page 14 **PRACTICE B**

4 **a** Before they came to Australia Fred read this information leaflet. Read the leaflet and match the headings from the box to the paragraphs (A – F).

> Deadly wildlife ■ It's absolutely massive ■ It's not just cities ■ Learn the slang ■ Sport mad ■ Sun and snow

Moving to the Land Down Under

Moving to a new country is always a big deal and it can take time to settle in. Here is some information you might want to know if you are considering moving to Australia.

A

5 Deciding where to live can be tricky. Australia is about the size of Europe and the distance between Perth in the west and Sydney in the south-east is 3,290 km. It takes more than four hours to fly from one city to the other!

B

10 Most people think of Australia as scorching. Sure, it can get hot, but not everywhere all year round. In fact, it's possible to go surfing and skiing on the same day. When it's summer in the south, it's usually the wet season in the north, while Melbourne is known for having 'four
15 seasons in a day'.

C

Around 90 % of all Australians live in cities so there's a lot of empty space. There are more than five hundred National Parks, the world-famous Blue Mountains and
20 vast areas of outback to explore.

D

It's true that Australia has more than its fair share of deadly animals, but it's
25 often exaggerated. For example, there are only two species of deadly spiders in Australia and nobody has died from a bite since 1979! You're even quite safe in the sea. Stingrays
30 have only ever killed two people, and on average there is only one shark attack per year.

E

Although English is the official language, it can often be difficult to understand an Aussie when they speak. It's
35 not their accent that causes problems, but the amount of slang they use. Afternoon is *arvo*, when something is broken it's *cactus* and when you go for a *bogey*, it means you're going for a swim!

F

40 From Aussie Rules to cricket and rugby, everyone is crazy about sport. But these are not the only sports. Melbourne
45 hosts the Australian Open as well as one of the best known horse races in the world – the Melbourne Cup. Then, of course, there
50 are all the beach sports from beach volleyball to surfing. Australia is a paradise for any sports lover.

b Find words and phrases in the text to match the definitions.

1 very hot
2 extremely big
3 to hold a special event
4 important or special
5 difficult, needing attention
6 informal language usually spoken by a particular group of people
7 making something bigger, more important, better or worse than it really is
8 thinking about doing something

c Read the leaflet again and do the tasks.

1 Explain why the leaflet says deciding where to live in Australia can be tricky.
2 Analyse what is meant by the phrase: Melbourne is known for having 'four seasons in a day'.
3 Outline why there is so much empty space in Australia.
4 Illustrate why the leaflet claims that it's an exaggeration that Australia is full of deadly animals.
5 Explain why Australia would be a 'paradise for any sports lover'.
6 Comment on why, even if you spoke good English, you might find it difficult to communicate in Australia.

PART 1

PART 2

PART 3

1788

On January 26th, 1788 the First Fleet landed at Sydney Cove and established the first colony. The fleet consisted of 11 ships with 1480 people on board. Around half of these were convicts.

1851

In 1851 gold was discovered in Australia. A gold rush started with thousands of people arriving from different countries hoping to become rich. In just ten years, the population of Australia doubled!

1901

In 1901, the six territories joined together and formed the Commonwealth of Australia. A new flag was designed for the new country.

1956

In 1956, sports mad Australia held the 13th modern Olympic Games in Melbourne. Australia won 35 medals, 13 gold. The star was 17-year-old Iain Murray Rose who won three swimming gold medals!

2008

In 2008, the Parliament of Australia made a formal apology to Indigenous Australians for the forced removal of their children by Australian government agencies. The apology was delivered by Prime Minister Kevin Rudd.

1 **a** Look at the infographic on the left. Then listen to Jason talking to Fred about Australian history and complete the tasks.

1 Name the two events in the infographic which Jason mentions.
2 Explain why Jason laughs at one point during the conversation.

b Later on Fred makes some notes about what Jason told him. Listen to the conversation again. Read the notes and correct the mistakes.

> Australia used to be an American Colony.
>
> The first people from Europe arrived in 1856.
>
> The Olympic Games have been held twice in Melbourne.
>
> Australia has won a lot of medals in wrestling.
>
> Australia was set up as a penal colony.

2 **a** **Think:** Choose one event from the infographic. Carry out some internet research and make notes. Use your notes to structure a short talk.

b **Pair:** Find a partner who has chosen the same event. Prepare your talk together.

c **Share:** Find two pairs with different events. Take turns and give your presentation. The others ask questions and give feedback. Then decide which event is the most interesting. Give reasons and present it to the class.

3 Keira finds a book about the Aborigines that contains lots of information and also photos.
Listen to her describing one of the photos to her mum. Which one is she talking about?

4 a Choose two different photos each and do some research. Make notes about each photo and any information you can find.

b Describe your photos to your partner and use your notes to explain what they show.

c Compare your photos. Discuss what they have in common. What do they tell you about Aboriginal culture?

d Have you learned anything new about Aboriginal culture through the photos? Discuss the importance of Aboriginal customs and traditions for the Australian society.

PART 1

PART 2

PART 3

Understanding new words and phrases

S1 **Identifying main ideas.** Before you start reading a text, first look at the title and any pictures to get an idea of what the text is about. Discuss your ideas for the text below.

S2 **Working out the meaning of new words and phrases.** Read the text carefully. First look at the **blue** words. Then read the tips and work out what they mean.

> **TIP**
>
> **How to work out the meaning of new words**
> First decide if you need to know the meaning of the new word to understand the text. If you do, then follow these tips.
> - Is the word similar to a German or an international word?
> - Can you guess the meaning from the words before / after it? Or does the text give an explanation (often inside commas)?
> - Do you already know part of the word or another form of the word?

Before and after

Australia's first peoples were hunter-gatherers who lived in small family groups and were **semi-nomadic**, systematically moving from place to place following the changes of the seasons. Each group lived in a
5 defined **territory** with its own **distinct** history and culture. Although the hunter-gatherers didn't develop an **agrarian**, or farming, society, they managed the land and wild animals in various ways to make sure they had **predictable** supplies of food
10 and water.

When the British arrived in 1788, about 770,000 Aboriginal people were living in Australia, with **approximately** 260 different language groups and 500 **dialects**. How did colonization **impact** these communities? The most immediate **consequence** was a wave of epidemic diseases such as smallpox, influenza and measles. These diseases killed many indigenous people because they had no
15 **resistance** to them.

Many also died in **random** killings or organized **massacres**. Massacres often took the form of mass shootings or driving groups of people off **cliffs**. As a result, there was a drastic **decline** in the Aboriginal population. By 1900, it was estimated that only about 117,000 indigenous people were still living in Australia.

S3 **Using dictionaries to find the meaning of new words and phrases**

a Discuss these questions.

- How often do you use a dictionary? If not so often, why not?
- Do you use a printed dictionary or an online dictionary? Monolingual or bilingual? What are the benefits of each?
- What can you use a dictionary for? Make a list of your ideas and compare in class.

b Now look at the **red** words in the text in **2** and use a dictionary to find the right meaning in this context.

c You probably don't know the words *smallpox, influenza* and *measles*. Why is it not necessary to check what they mean?

d What does *looking for trouble* mean? Explain the cartoon.

→ Workbook, page 16   **WORKSHOP TASK**

Understanding texts on a new topic

S1 **Identify main ideas**

a Look at the title and the pictures. What do you think the text is about?

b Read and match the photos to the correct paragraphs.

Outback threatened by non-native species

Although much of Australia's interior is **arid** desert, it isn't empty of life. If you camp out in the outback, you'll hear the **howls** of dingoes, or wild dogs, **echoing** across the landscape. Dingoes were introduced into Australia around 4,000 years ago, and today they are both loved and **loathed**. They attack sheep and have
5 caused the decline of many native species. In spite of this, it's exciting to see them **roam around** wild in Australia.

But they are not the only non-native species that have become serious **pests**, causing enormous ecological damage to Australia. You'll also **come across** the world's largest herd of **feral** camels. Introduced from Arabia and India for
10 transport and work in the outback, they were **released** into the wild when they were no longer needed with the **advent** of powered engines. Other **invasive** species include foxes and rabbits, brought from Europe in the 19th century for sport hunting. They had few **predators**, so their populations **exploded**. Control **measures** have reduced their numbers, but they remain a big problem.

S2 **Work out the meaning of words and phrases.**
Use the tips on page **24** to help you work out the meanings of the **blue** words. Then match the correct words to these definitions. What words in the text helped you guess?

1 allowed to go free
2 an action to achieve a particular aim
3 an insect or an animal that destroys plants, etc.
4 sounding again and again
5 the sound a wild dog makes
6 to get bigger very quickly

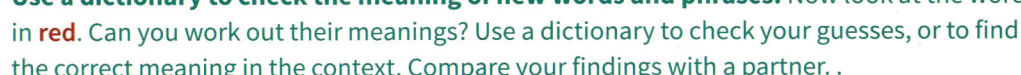

S3 **Use a dictionary to check the meaning of new words and phrases.** Now look at the words
 in **red**. Can you work out their meanings? Use a dictionary to check your guesses, or to find the correct meaning in the context. Compare your findings with a partner. .

S4 **Use different kinds of dictionaries**

a In groups of three, read the last paragraph of the text. Note down any words or phrases you don't understand. Look at the tips on page 24 again and work out as many meanings as you can.

b Now each use a different method to check the rest of the list: (1) a monolingual dictionary, (2) a bilingual dictionary and (3) an online dictionary. When you have finished, compare your results.

15 Australia's prolonged drought is now driving large groups of camels out of the desert onto farms and into towns. In their desperate search for water, the camels demolish fences and foul critical watering holes, polluting the water and making it undrinkable. In an effort to defend farm properties, hundreds of camels are culled a day, leaving thousands of dead animals to rot. The culls are controversial. There is little agreement on a long-term solution.

Discovering Australia

1 Famous sites

a Look at the title, photos and the introduction and discuss what you think the texts will be about. Then one of you reads text A and the other one text B. Make notes under these headings:

- Location
- Importance to Aboriginal people
- Creation legend

b Outline what you have learned to each other. Then decide which place you would most like to visit and why.

Sacred sites of Australia

Aboriginal and Torres Strait Islander nations have their own Creation or Dreamtime legends which have been passed down by the Elders from generation to generation. The whole continent is covered with sacred sites that are extremely important in Aboriginal tradition and folklore. Find out about two of them.

A Uluru (was once called Ayers Rock)

5 Uluru is one of the most sacred sites in Aboriginal folklore. It's a large rock formation located close to the exact centre of Australia and has been designated a UNESCO World Heritage Site.
The rock resumed its original name in 1985 when the land was given back to the local people, the Anangu, by the Australian Government. They now own the Kata
10 Tjuta National Park, which Uluru is part of. The Anangu had long wanted the title deeds to be returned. According to their leaders, 'this is how we can make sure the place is looked after properly for everyone'. Ancient Aboriginal paintings, which tell the story of the Dreaming, can be seen in caves in the rock.

Legend of Uluru according to the Anangu

15 Two tribes of ancient spirits were invited to a feast but didn't turn up. Their hosts were bitterly insulted. There was a great battle and many were killed. Uluru rose up to show that the land was deeply saddened by the bloodshed.

B Great Barrier Reef

The Great Barrier Reef is absolutely enormous. The size of about 70 million football fields, it's the only living thing on our planet that can be seen from space.
20 It stretches 2,300 kilometres along the coast of Queensland and is home to a huge variety of marine creatures, including fish, seabirds, whales, dolphins and sharks. Fishing has been practised here for thousands of years by Aboriginal and Torres Strait Islanders, who are the traditional owners of the Great Barrier Reef region. Tourism is very important, but it's carefully controlled to limit damage to the reef.

25 Legend according to Yindingi clan

This story tells of two brothers who went out fishing and were ordered by Bhiral, the Creator, not to hunt one particular kind of fish. One of the brothers disobeyed and speared the fish. Bhiral was extremely angry, so he threw lava and hot rocks down from the sky. The lava made the sea rise and when the lava had cooled, it formed what is now the Great Barrier Reef. The story is very similar to what scientists believe really happened.

2 For and against

a Tourism can have advantages and disadvantages. Together brainstorm a list of arguments for and against it.

For	Against
brings money for the local community	???

b Share your ideas with the class. Discuss: Should tourism be banned completely in some places?

Useful expressions:
On the one hand, … on the other hand, … / For example, … / However, … / First of all, … / In my opinion, … / I'd like to point out that … / You have a point, but … / I'm not sure if … / The reason for this is that … / Finally, …

9)) Words and phrases

to occupy a place   to live or stay in a place   **particular**   one thing and not a different one   **to stretch**   to cover a large area of land

3* What's most important?

a Read the information in the box on the right. Find more examples of passive sentences in the texts about Uluru and the Great Barrier Reef. Then decide why the passive was used. Choose from this list.

1 The person or object doing the action is not known or not important.
2 To avoid using vague subjects like *Someone, People, They*.
3 The focus of the sentence is on the action, not the agent.

b Uluru is a very popular tourist destination. Use Fred's notes to write a paragraph about Uluru and tourism. Where possible, use passive forms as in the example.

● big tour companies bring busloads of tourists every day
Busloads of tourists are brought in every day by big tour companies.

- many visitors expect allow climb rock
- tourists ban climb sacred site since 2019
- reason: totally unacceptable to Aboriginal owners
- alternative activities develop for tourists since ban
- visitors offer walking tours around base Uluru by experienced guides
- Anangu not want tourism ban
- reason: one of main sources of income
- tourism industry should give Aborigine bigger share profits

Remember
- We form the passive with a form of *be* and a past participle.
  *Each nation has its own Creation legends which **have been passed down** by the Elders.*
- When a verb is followed by a preposition, it stays in the same position in the passive.
- When a verb has two objects, the passive sentence can begin with either the direct or indirect object. Verbs that take two objects include *give, offer, promise, show*.
  The land was given back to the original owners OR
  The original owners were given back the land.
- We use the passive infinitive after modal verbs, and verbs like *expect, hope, like, need, want*.
  *Ancient Aboriginal paintings **can be seen** in caves in Uluru. They had long **wanted** the title deeds **to be returned**.*

4 A film trailer

a Your teacher is going to show you a trailer for the film *Walkabout*, which is set in the Australian outback. Look at the still from the film. What do you think the film will be about?

 b Watch the trailer and write a short summary. You can use the ideas below.

The film tells the story of a sister and brother …
The two children have to …
They are saved by …
Suddenly a white man …
The siblings and the aboriginal boy …

 c Watch again to check and add more details. What do you think happens at the end of the film? Present your ideas to the class.

Grammar and structures

Passive (revision) → G5

Passive with verb + preposition:	We can make sure the place **is looked after**.
Passive: verbs with two objects:	The land **was given back to** the local people.
Passive infinitive after *want, expect*, etc.:	The Anangu had long **wanted** the title deeds **to be returned**.
Passive infinitive after modal verbs:	Ancient Aboriginal paintings **can be seen** in caves in the rock.

PART 1

PART 2

PART 3

1 Look at the photos. What natural disasters do they show? Use a dictionary to find the English words you need. Then speculate how these disasters are connected to climate change and global warming.

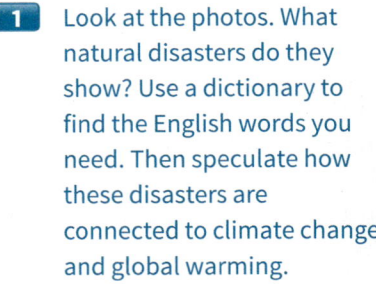

2 a Read the article to find out how climate change is affecting Australia and complete the text with the appropriate passive forms.

b Outline the main effects of climate change in your own words. Show how the writer gives examples to illustrate them.

3 a Jason's schoolmate Ricky is very concerned about climate change, so he and his friends are taking part in a demonstration. A radio journalist interviews them. Read the questions.

1 Why are they at the demonstration?
2 What are the aims of the Seed Mob movement?
3 Why is the land important to Aboriginal people?
4 What are the main causes of climate change in Australia?
5 How does climate change affect Aboriginal people?
6 What do they want the Federal Government to do?

b Listen and make notes on the questions in **a**. Compare with a partner, then listen again to check and complete your notes.

c Compare the situation in Australia with Germany. Describe the similarities or differences of the problems. Outline how Germany is affected by climate change and how the people react to it. Write about 150 words.

The climate reality

Australia is known for its stunning scenery, its fabulous beaches, and unique wildlife. Many animals such as koala bears, kangaroos, wombats **1** (can, only, find) in Australia. But scientists are warning that Australia is especially at risk from the
5 climate crisis. This is the climate reality:

Heat and drought
Australia is already a very hot and dry country and it's expected to get a lot hotter and drier if no action **2** (take) on climate change. In January 2018, temperatures in Sydney soared to over
10 47 degrees. It was the hottest day that the city had experienced in 80 years. Climate change is making heatwaves much more common, more severe and longer-lasting than they have ever been. More heat means more droughts.

Bushfires / Wildfires
15 Drought creates the perfect conditions for bushfires. Plants dry up and die, providing the ideal fuel for fires. Bushfires are becoming much more frequent and more extreme, especially in the south and east. In the last few years, there were nearly 200 fires in Queensland. Conditions like these **3** (never, see) in its history.

20 ### Farming
As Australia's climate changes, every type of farmer **4** (affect). The climate crisis is making it more and more difficult for farmers to grow food and raise livestock. Queensland is one of Australia's most populated states, where much of the country's food **5**
25 (produce). According to one farmer, 'Food security **6** (endanger) by climate change, there's no doubt about that.'

The ocean and the Great Barrier Reef
Our oceans are becoming warmer and more acidic. The Great Barrier Reef **7** (hit) incredibly hard by both factors.
30 It **8** (form) over many millions of years by tiny animals called polyps. But these are dying due to the rise in sea temperature, and the future of the reef is in doubt.

Australia has a lot to lose. The causes of climate change need **9** (tackle) urgently.

35 **WHO CAN CHANGE THIS? YOU!**
JOIN THE CLIMATE FIGHT AND TAKE ACTION.

Words and phrases

livestock	animals such as cows, sheep and pigs that are kept on a farm
stunning	very impressive or beautiful
to tackle sth	to try to solve a difficult problem
tipping point	the time when things start to happen in a situation, especially things that you can't change

@ WES-40903-001

1 How often do you read blogs? Talk about these questions:

- Where and how often do blogs appear?
- What kinds of topics can they cover?
- How are they structured?

- Who is the blogger's audience?
- What is a typical writing style for a blog (e. g. formal / informal, conversational, instructive, etc.)?

2 **a** Eleni is contributing to a website where teenagers post blogs about their home cities. Read her blog about Melbourne.

Melbourne is the place!
By Eleni Kourakis

Though I have lived in this magnificent city all my life, I can never get bored with it. If you asked me what I like about it most, I wouldn't know how to answer, there are so many attractions here. Let me take you on a virtual tour and show you the places I truly love. (If you ever come to visit, I am sure you'll love them, too.)

The narrow 'laneways' in the city centre are a good place to start. Do you
5 like cool cafés, amazing street art and buskers playing great music? If so, then you'll enjoy Centre Place and Hosier Lane. What about colourful outdoor markets? I love Queen Victoria Market – it's an awesome place for shopping, yummy street food and just hanging out. Getting around in the city centre is really easy, too: you can ride the trams for free, or do what lots
10 of people do – cycle! Cycling is my favourite way of exploring the city's back streets and hitting the beach at St Kilda. The list of cool and cheap things that you can do here goes on and on.

I've just mentioned St Kilda, so let me take you there. Do you want to soak up the sun on sandy beaches, cool down in the ocean or roller skate along
15 the promenade? Have a picnic or relax in a café – whatever you want, it's there. Or just gaze at the Melbourne skyline? If you are lucky, you might see skydivers landing on the shore. It's an unforgettable experience and the best birthday treat I've ever had! And make sure you stay till sunset if you want to see the penguins. Just follow the crowd to the end of the pier where
20 the sanctuary is.

Come check it out and this awesome city will win your heart, too.

b Say who the article is written for and explain what Eleni's aim is. Give examples of language she uses to achieve this. Include the line numbers.

c Look at the *TIP* box. Find examples in the article of the techniques that it lists. Compare and discuss with a partner.

d Write a blog entry (150 words or more) about your home, town or city. Select features you like and use techniques to persuade the reader to visit these places / to make your reader interested in these places.

> **TIP**
>
> Here are some useful techniques when you are writing to persuade your readers:
> - **Anecdotes** (short, personal stories) have an emotional effect.
> - **Comparisons** show that you are balanced and honest.
> - **Strongly positive or negative words** make the reader feel the same.
> - **Personal pronouns** like 'I', 'you' or 'we' speak directly to the reader.
> - **Direct questions** get the reader's interest and make him or her think.

🔊 **Words and phrases**

busker street musician

A New Zealand visit

1 **Away from home**

14)) **a** Paige Williams is in year nine at Papanui High School in Christchurch, New Zealand. She lives with her Aunt Christine and Uncle Tai. Look at the pictures and describe what they tell you. Listen, then describe the three scenes in more detail.

PART 2

14)) **b** Listen again and do these tasks.

1 List the topics Paige talks about in her video call.
- farm animals
- dad's health
- homesickness
- Paige's sister
- weather
- school
- Paige's aunt
- holidays

2 Explain why Paige lives with her aunt and uncle.
3 Name two things that their visitors find out during the conversation at dinner.

PART 3

2 **Life back home**

a Paige says: 'I love baby goats.' Her teacher says: 'You can talk about your farm in Kerikeri.' Now look at these sentences and the rules in the box.

*She said that she **loved** the baby goats.*
*My teacher told me I **could** talk about our farm in Kerikeri.*

> **Reported speech**
> - In reported speech, when the reporting verb is in the past, the tense in the part of the sentence we are reporting moves one step back in time.
>   *It's pretty cool and wet here.* → *She said that it **was** pretty cool and wet there.*
> - In reported speech you can leave out the word *that*.
>   *She told me **that** her subjects were tough.*
>   → *She told me her subjects were tough.*

b Later, Paige's dad told her more news from Kerikeri. Her aunt wants to know what he told her. Report what Mr Williams said. Remember: sometimes the pronouns change.

1 'Bella is doing a wonderful job with the vegetable garden.'
2 'Rachel texted me from Auckland yesterday. She texts at least every second day.'
3 'We've made the old shed into a guest house.'
4 'I can't come and visit now because of the sheep.'
5 'We'll be able to come in the summer.'

> **CULTURE CORNER**
>
> **Aussies and Kiwis – a special relationship**
> Relations between Australia and New Zealand have often been compared to those of siblings or cousins.
> Even though the countries share common experiences like fighting side-by-side in two World Wars, they don't always get along. They have different personalities and sometimes serious political differences. They also have a huge sporting rivalry – mainly in cricket, rugby and netball, and they like joking about each other.
> However, when they are out in the big world, they often team together, and when they describe their relationship, they speak of the respect and trust they feel for each other.

13)) **Words and phrases**

kinship	a feeling of being close or similar to another person
rivalry	a situation when people, countries, etc. compete for the same thing
sibling	a brother or sister
to **tip over**	(of a boat) to turn over in water
white water	river water that looks white because it is moving fast over rocks

3 South Island adventure

a Jason has been travel-blogging on social media. Look what he has posted. What do you find most interesting about each post? With a partner, compare and explain your thoughts.

b Think of a good heading for each post. Share your ideas.

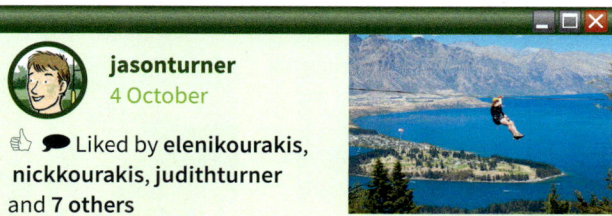

jasonturner
4 October

👍 💬 Liked by **elenikourakis, nickkourakis, judithturner** and **7 others**

This is my NZ blog! Today after rugby practice a few of us went to Christchurch Adventure Park. You take a chairlift up to the top of the Port Hills. Amazing views of Christchurch, along the coast and all the way to the Southern Alps! Then we rode the zipline. It's the longest in NZ – over 1 km. It's fast and scary. My heart was racing! I asked one of the guys to take this photo of us. 👍👍👍

jasonturner
5 October

👍 💬 Liked by **elenikourakis, judithturner** and **6 others**

Today we went to a place called Ko Tane. It's a interactive museum where Maori in costumes show how they lived before the Europeans came. We did the hongi greeting (nose to nose!), sang songs and watched this welcoming dance. Tai was such a great guide. We asked him what all the Maori words meant and he explained them. The best part was the hangi, a big meal cooked on hot rocks in the ground.

jasonturner
7 October

👍 💬 Liked by **elenikourakis, nickkourakis, judithturner** and **7 others**

The day after our game (they beat us by ONE point! 23 – 22 ☹), Coach Hansen organized a river rafting trip for us. 👍 The river was near some beautiful mountains where the Lord of the Rings trilogy was filmed! We practised paddling in the quiet part of the river, then we got to the white water. It was really moving fast! Our guide told us to paddle hard. We nearly tipped over once. At the end, we swam in the river in our wetsuits. Awesome!

4 An awesome trip

a Look at these examples from Jason's posts. What did Jason say directly to these people?

I asked one of the guys to take this photo of us.
We asked him what all the words meant.

Find one more example of indirect speech in Jason's posts and change it into direct speech.

> **Remember:**
> - To report *yes/no*-questions we use *if* or *whether* and invert subject and verb.
>   **Is Auckland** a big city? →
>   *I asked her **if Auckland was** a big city.*
> - For questions with a *wh*-question word, the order is the same as in statements.
>   **What do** the Maori **words mean?** →
>   *He asked **what** the Maori **words meant**.*
> - For orders and requests we use the infinitive form of the main verb with *to*.
>   *Could you **repeat** the question?* →
>   *She asked me **to repeat** the question.*

b Read these statements that other people made. What did Jason report to his parents?

Tai Show respect during the Maori rituals.
Guide Have you ever been rafting before?
Paige When are you going to visit us again?
Guide Keep your helmets on at all times.

5 It's your turn: A trip to Christchurch

a You and your partner are touring New Zealand and have two days in Christchurch. What will you do there? Form groups of four – **Pair A** and **Pair B**. Each pair should look at Jason's posts and do some more research about Christchurch. With your partner, discuss and agree on a plan.

b First **Pair A** presents their plan to **Pair B**. Then swap roles. Discuss the two plans and decide what you want to do in a group.

Grammar and structures

Reported speech in statements and questions in the past and in requests, offers, orders and advice → G6

Ricky **said** that he **wanted** to visit us again.
We **asked** Paige **to take** some photos.

They **asked** us **if** we **had enjoyed** the sightseeing.
Coach Hansen **told** us **not to be shy** on the river.

I **asked** them **where** the high school **was**.

Changes to adverbs of time and place in reported speech → G4

1 Do some research about five things or places that you find interesting, unusual or attractive about New Zealand. Get together in a group and discuss your choices. Rank them and present the top three to the class. Compare your results in class.

2 **a** Skim the text. Where would you find a text like this? Describe its function.

b Do these tasks.

1 Look at the map showing New Zealand on the front inside cover of the book. Find out which island the places are located on.
2 Outline what you learn about each place from the short programme description.

c **Think:** Collect ideas for a similar programme that looks at Germany. Include at least four places of interest and highlight one or two aspects of each place.

Pair: Compare your ideas and agree on a list of four places with highlighted aspects of each.

Share: Discuss and agree on a final list for your programme. Then, do a poster presentation of your places in class.

HOME | TV guide | Programs | Channels | Find a programme | 🔍

Two Islands Make a Nation
Starting Wednesday, September 19 at 9 pm

Amanda Nguyen and Shane Alcott visit our neighbours across the Tasman Sea to find out what makes New Zealand's North Island and South Island distinctive, what challenges they face, and what they each contribute to this unique island nation. The six weekly segments are:

- Part 1 **Auckland and Wellington** – why these cities matter and what makes each special
- Part 2 **Queenstown** – why this little town has become a hot spot and how it began
- Part 3 **Rotorua** – the town's natural wonders and its cultural significance
- Part 4 **Christchurch** – the city's regional importance and the challenges it has faced
- Part 5 **Coromandel Peninsula** – what makes this area such a magnet for visitors
- Part 6 **Milford Sound** – a national treasure, its biological diversity and how it is being protected

---

3 **a** One day, Paige turns on the radio and listens to an interview by Kiri Snow. She is interviewing the filmmaker Shaun Reed. Listen and choose the statement that sums up best what the filmmaker says.

1 The film looks at how rugby is organized in New Zealand.
2 The film shows why the All Blacks are the best rugby team in the world.
3 The film describes how the game helped New Zealanders find their identity as a country.
4 The film shows how rugby has united the country's older and younger generations.

b Tai comes home from work and Paige tells him about the interview. Listen again, then look at the following sentences. How does Paige report them?

Why don't we see a lot of rugby action in this film.
Kiri asked why we didn't see a lot of rugby in this film.

1 It's about our relationship to the game and how it has shaped us as a country. *Shaun said ...*
2 Please explain what you mean by that.
3 The game was brought here in the late 19th century when our country was still very young.
4 Why did rugby become so important?
5 Our team showed the world that this small island nation could be the best at something.
6 Do the younger generations today still identify with the game?
7 It's still very big, with team and league competition on every level, both boys and girls.

c Now answer questions 4 and 6 from **b**.

PART 1

PART 2

PART 3

4 **a** Ricky has found a tourist website with information about Maori culture. Read the text and do the tasks.

1 Explain why Maori culture is protected by law.
2 Describe how to say 'hello' in the Maori language.
3 Explain what *whanau* means.
4 Outline what New Zealanders think is 'essential'.

b Find words or phrases that mean:

1 having always lived in a place
2 a group of people who officially control a country
3 get better
4 say hello to somebody
5 part of the customs or way of life of a group
6 how people live

Maori culture

To understand New Zealand and its people, it's important to understand the influence of Maori culture. As New Zealand's second-largest ethnic group, Maori make up 16.6 per cent of the country's population. But more than that, they are the indigenous people of New Zealand and their rights, culture and
5 language have been protected by law since the country began in 1840. Although the government has not always respected those rights, relations between Maori and *Pakeha* (the Maori term for New Zealanders of European descent) have improved over time.

Today the acceptance of Maori culture is felt everywhere in New Zealand. In
10 everyday conversation, when someone says *kia ora*, he or she is greeting or thanking you; when people talk about *Aotearoa* ('Land of the Long White Cloud') they mean New Zealand; and when a Kiwi asks about your *whanau*, he or she wants to know how your family are doing. Official signs everywhere are in both Maori and English. The New Zealand national anthem is always sung
15 first in the Maori language, *Te Reo Maori*, then in English. The national rugby team, the All Blacks, famously perform the *haka* before each game, and variations of this traditional Maori dance are performed by both men and women at official and unofficial events all over the country.

Many believe that the Maori cultural influence is one reason for the success of New Zealand's multicultural society.
20 A survey reported that New Zealanders of every ethnic group see Maori culture as an 'essential' part of the New Zealand way of life.

New Zealand Prime Minister Jacinda Ardern exchanging a *hongi* – the traditional Maori greeting

The All Blacks rugby team performing the *haka*

5 **a** Look at these two pictures of New Zealand. Take turns to talk about one or both of the pictures. Make notes about what your partner says.

b Work with a new partner. Report what your previous partner said about the pictures of New Zealand.

16)) **Words and phrases**

anthem a song that has special importance for a country
influence the effect that somebody or something has on how people think and act
peninsula a large piece of land that sticks out into a lake or the sea

1 Read a newspaper article about climate change written by a teenager in New Zealand. Which paragraph does each picture on page **35** relate to? Give the line numbers.

Which paragraph does each picture on page **35** relate to?

What climate change means for New Zealand

A

As a Kiwi I'm really quite worried about climate change and what it will mean for me in the future. While New Zealand won't be as badly affected as other countries, particularly ones like the Pacific Islands, it will no doubt impact the way we live.

B

One reason for this is that two-thirds of people in New Zealand live within 5 km of the coast. As one consequence of climate change is increased sea levels, it's quite easy to understand that there will be an impact. We can already see results in some places like Moanataiari where the sea washed away parts of the road, and also in Kaiaua which experienced devastating floods. My aunt lives there and she told me it was the worst storm she had ever known, and she's lived there for over 40 years! One of the most surprising things was that they had no drinking water for ages. You'd think with so much water around it wouldn't be a problem, but apparently all the rain caused mudslides which contaminated the water in the reservoirs. Now, you might expect to have water shortages during a drought, and with climate change we are likely to experience more of those as well.

C

Hotter temperatures will lead to all sorts of problems. The elderly, the young and people with health issues are all likely to suffer as are people who have mental health issues. Why? Well, some people are already worried about climate change and, as the effects get worse, their anxiety levels will probably increase.

D

Higher temperatures have other consequences that people don't necessarily think about. For example, at the moment the climate in New Zealand is too cold for tropical diseases like malaria, but in the future that might not be the case. A warming climate also increases the frequency of extreme weather events such as storms, flooding, cyclones and forest fires. As many Kiwis love hiking in our beautiful nature, such events could really make a huge difference to the way we live and how we spend our leisure time.

E

However, it's not just the people who will bear the consequences of climate change. Many of our animals will also be at risk. I've already mentioned the threat of malaria from mosquitoes, but as temperatures rise the habitats where different animals live will also change. For example, at the moment it is too cold high up in the mountains for animals like rats, but as the snow melts then that might change. If it does, it will have a devastating impact on other animals that live there and don't have to worry about such predators yet.

F

Will everything connected to climate change be bad? Not necessarily. In the future, we may be able to grow crops that we can't at the moment. If you're like me and enjoy avocado on toast, then that might be good news! Recently, my best friend's uncle set up a touring company taking people out on boats in the new lake created by the melting of the Tasman Glacier on the West Coast. So, he's already making money from climate change. Sure, climate change will mean more challenges, but it could also mean some new opportunities.

2 Match the headings (1 – 6) to the paragraphs (A – F).

1 What about the people?   2 Not all bad

3 A Kiwi perspective   4 What about the animals?   5 Water – no water!   6 More extreme!

3 Find words or phrases in the text which have these meanings.

1 a powerful effect that something has on a situation or person
2 causing a lot of damage or destruction
3 to make something dirty or poisonous
4 a situation in which there is not enough of something
5 a feeling caused by worrying about something
6 to have to deal with something unpleasant
7 the natural environment in which an animal or plant usually lives
8 an animal that hunts, kills and eats other animals

4 Right, wrong or not in the text? Correct the false statements.

1 Other places will be worse hit by climate change than New Zealand.
2 Most people in New Zealand live in cities.
3 The writer's aunt lives in Kaiaua.
4 The elderly won't be affected by high temperatures.
5 New Zealand already has diseases like malaria.
6 The writer enjoys hiking in the mountains.
7 At the moment rats don't live high up in the mountains.
8 According to the writer, climate change could also have some positive effects.

5 Read the text again. Complete the tasks.

1 Explain why many people in New Zealand will be affected by rising sea levels.
2 Describe what happened to the writer's aunt.
3 Illustrate how people with health issues might be affected by climate change.
4 Describe what impact climate change might have on nature in New Zealand.
5 Comment on the last paragraph of the article. Do you agree with the writer?
   Say why or why not.

→ Workbook, page 26   **METHOD COACH**

Preparing to write an informative text

S1 **Researching a topic and evaluating notes**

a Your class has been asked to research and write an article about New Zealand for your international website. It should include information about New Zealand's history, geography, people and wildlife. Read the notes made by one student. Decide which information will be most useful and interesting for the readers.

b Do some online research of your own and make more notes. You can also look back at the quiz questions on pages **12 – 13** for ideas about the kind of information to look for.

- consists of two main islands — North Island and South Island
- 9th longest coastline in the world
- 600 smaller islands — largest = Rakiura island, also called Stewart Island
- first settled by the Maori people around 1300 — around 16% of population today
- first country to give women the vote in 1893
- unemployment 4%
- no snakes!

> **TIP**
>
> When doing research, use more than one source.
> Write short notes in your own words: don't copy or cut and paste. Bookmark your sources so can you find them again quickly.

S2 **Making a plan**

a Your text should have three main parts. Match the parts to their function and put them in the right order.

1 main body   2 introduction

3 conclusion

A summarizes key points or comments on the topic

B introduces the topic / purpose of the text

C provides the necessary information

b Organize the notes in **S1** into a logical sequence of paragraphs. The main body can be more than one paragraph.

S3 **Using an appropriate style.** Look at the *TIP* box below. Then look at the two extracts from a student's text. Describe and evaluate the style of each paragraph.

> **TIP**
>
> When writing an informative text:
> - choose the right style to suit your topic and audience, formal or informal, serious or chatty.
> - use a variety of sentence lengths and types, simple and complex.
> - include interesting facts to engage the reader.

What do you know about New Zealand? Can you find it on a map? Do you know which hemisphere it's in? Not sure? If you want to find out the coolest facts about this amazing country, read on!

As it is so remote, New Zealand has some very unusual wildlife that cannot be found anywhere else in the world. Nearly all the land animals are birds. Many of them lost the ability to fly as they had no predators.

@ WES-40903-001

Writing an informative text

S1 **Decide on a topic.** Look at the photos and tasks. Choose one of the topics to write about.

A

Write an informative article about High School exchange programmes for German students in Australia or New Zealand.

Divide your article into sections with headings to help the reader identify the key information. Headings could be typical questions which you give the answer to. Include this information:

- Reasons for going on a school exchange to Australia or New Zealand
- Organizations that arrange exchanges, what programmes they offer, their requirements (e. g. age, language level)
- What to expect at your High School – courses, after-school activities
- Benefits of staying with a host family
- Free time opportunities
- How to apply

TIP
- Use a chatty, personal style. Address your reader directly.
- Use adjectives like *great*, *exciting*, etc. to make your article more interesting and persuasive.

B

Write an informative report about climate change in New Zealand. Choose a good title, e. g. *Climate change reality in NZ* or *No time to lose*

Paragraph 1: Introduce the topic – concerns about climate change
Paragraph 2/3: Explain the main problems, causes and effects
Paragraph 3/4: Explain what's being done (by protesters / by the government)
Paragraph 4/5: Conclusion – say what's likely to happen in the future

TIP
- Include key facts.
- Write in a neutral and factual style.
- Don't include your personal opinion.

S2 **Research your topic.** Look at the tips on page **36** and make notes. Then make a plan and order your notes.

S3 **Write and edit your text.** Use a dictionary to help you improve your text and check it for mistakes.

S4 **Evaluate your texts**

a Form groups of three or four. Take turns explaining which topic you chose, and how you researched your topic.

b Exchange your written products. Read them and give each other feedback. Have your classmates followed the guidelines in the *TIP* box?

What's in a dictionary?
- the right meaning of a word (monolingual and bilingual dictionaries often give more than one meaning, so choose the one that is right for the context)
- the correct spelling of a word
- grammatical information (e.g. part of speech, plural forms, verb patterns, which preposition to use, etc.)
- synonyms

1 Ricky gives a talk to his teammates before their rugby match against Papanui High School. Later one of his teammates phones his parents. Read what Ricky said and complete what the teammate said to his parents by phone in your exercise book.

> *Hey guys! So, we are playing a match against Papanui High School. We know they are one of the best school teams in New Zealand, but we don't have anything to fear. Back home, we all practised really hard, and I am sure we can win. Remember, we've been playing together for over a year and we haven't lost any of our games. There is no reason this one will be any different. Do you agree?*

> *Last night Ricky gave a short speech. He started by reminding us that we were playing a match against Papanui High School. He said …*

2 **a** Read the story about the Rainbow Serpent and put the verbs into the appropriate tense.

The Rainbow Serpent
An Aboriginal tale from Australia

Australian aboriginal myths, also known as dreamtime stories, are traditionally told by the indigenous people of Australia. In one story, a group of Aboriginals **1** (*hunt*) in the outback. After they **2** (*hunt*) for many hours, they **3** (*decide*) to stop and rest. They **4** (*sit*) around, telling stories and warming their hands by the fire when one of them **5** (*look up*). There on the horizon was a beautiful multi-coloured rainbow. But the Aborigines **6** (*think*) that it was a serpent that **7** (*move*) from one waterhole to another, and they were frightened. They didn't want the huge serpent near their camp. They were grateful that he **8** (*not come*) too near their own waterhole.

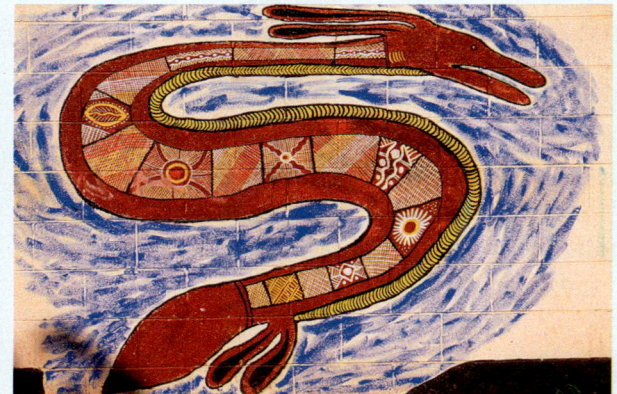

One young man wanted to know more about the Rainbow Serpent so when he **9** (*return*) home, he asked the old men of his tribe why the hunters **10** (*be*) scared of the Rainbow Serpent when they were out hunting.

b Listen to what one old man told Ricky about the Rainbow Serpent. Then explain who the Serpent was, what he had done and what he might do again.

3 Complete the talk with the words from the box and the correct form of the verbs in brackets.

> climate change ■ destruction ■ extinction ■ habitat ■ iconic ■ logging ■ to tackle

Today I'm going to talk about the ⬛1⬛ situation in Australia and the effect this ⬛2⬛ (*have*) on our unique wildlife.

In the last ten years, around 50% of the animals ⬛3⬛ (*wipe out*). If we ⬛4⬛ (*carry on*) like this, animals that only live in Australia face ⬛5⬛! Every year heatwaves, droughts and wildfires ⬛6⬛ (*report*) on the news, but what ⬛7⬛ (*cause*) this extreme weather?

One cause is deforestation. Trees are important for a number of reasons. One of these is that oxygen ⬛8⬛ (*release*) and CO_2 ⬛9⬛ (*capture*) by trees. Since the first European settlers arrived, more than half the trees ⬛10⬛ (*cut down*). A lot of this ⬛11⬛ is caused by ⬛12⬛. Another consequence of this is the loss of ⬛13⬛. A lot of experts say that around 45 million animals ⬛14⬛ (*kill*) each year because of logging! The situation ⬛15⬛ (*can, not, ignore*) and action ⬛16⬛ (*must, take*) ⬛17⬛ it soon. If nothing ⬛18⬛ (*do*), not only will temperatures increase, but we will lose some of our most ⬛19⬛ animals such as koalas and even our kangaroos!

4 Use the notes to write a short article about Christchurch for your school magazine in your exercise book.

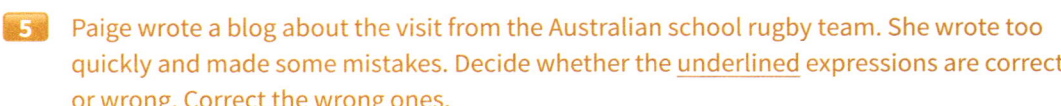

- largest city / South Island
- one of five 'gateway' cities / Antarctic exploration
- famous / street art
- tram or tourist bus / see the city
- street markets
- February 2011 earthquake / killed 185 / damaged or destroyed / buildings
- Hagley Park / third biggest / world
- slogan after earthquakes / 'Our city rocks!'
- southern Alps / 4-hour journey / film set 'Lord of the Rings'
- home / Canterbury Rugby Union team / most successful / New Zealand

5 Paige wrote a blog about the visit from the Australian school rugby team. She wrote too quickly and made some mistakes. Decide whether the underlined expressions are correct or wrong. Correct the wrong ones.

Last week a school rugby team from Australia came[1] to play against our school team. While they were hear[2], my Uncle Tai, took them out for a bit of an adventure and he asks[3] me to go with them. We visited most of the usual sides[4] – took the chairlift up the Port Hills, saw Ko Tane and did some withe[5] water rafting. One of the boys, Jason, told me he thinks[6] the hole[7] experience was awesome, so I told[8] him about my trip to Brighton last year. He asked me lot[9] of questions and seemed very interesting[10], but some of the questions were just silly. He asked me if I have meet[11] the Queen! I said him[12] I had[13] and he said[14] that he was jellous[15]. I don't know if he was joking or if he really tought[16] it was true! He asked me about the best part of the trip and I ansered[17] that apart from spending lots of time with Aimee, what I had enjoyed most was the visit to the *Mary Rose*.

M **Bernhard Holtermann**

a Anlässlich des australischen Nationalfeiertags im Januar möchte deine Schule eine Zeitung über Australien herausbringen. Die Schülerinnen und Schüler deiner Klasse schreiben dazu unter anderem Artikel über Deutsche, die nach Australien ausgewandert sind. Dir wurde Bernhard Holtermann zugeteilt. Benutze die abgedruckten Informationen, um über Holtermanns berufliche Tätigkeiten, seine Interessen und Anliegen und seinen Charakter zu schreiben (200 Wörter).

Bernhard Holtermann: Ein Leben mit vielen Kapiteln

Christoph Heins neues Buch *Australien 1872: Wie ein Deutscher sein Glück fand und Fotogeschichte schrieb* erzählt die Geschichte von Bernhard Holtermanns Leben und zeigt bisher
5 unveröffentlichte Fotos aus jener Zeit. Hein sprach mit André Leslie, dem Online-Editor des Goethe-Instituts Australien, über Holtermann und die Entstehung des Buchs.

Nachdem er mit Anfang 20 aus Hamburg nach
10 *Australien kam, scheint sich Bernhard Holtermann an zahlreichen Aspekten der australischen Gesellschaft aktiv beteiligt zu haben. Würden Sie ihn als Multitalent bezeichnen?*

Ja, er war sehr vielschichtig. Ich denke, Holtermann
15 wusste immer, wie er sich mit dem, was er tat, einen Vorteil verschaffen konnte, aber das ist in Ordnung, denn er tat wirklich viel zum Wohl der Allgemeinheit. Er wurde gewählter Politiker, setzte sich auf dieselbe Art, wie wir das heute tun könnten,
20 für Einwanderung ein und hatte sehr fortschrittliche Ansichten. In den 1880er Jahren spendete er einen Teil seines Vermögens für den Bau einer Brücke, die später die Sydney Harbour Bridge wurde. Ja, er achtete auf seinen eigenen Vorteil, aber er hatte
25 auch immer die Allgemeinheit im Sinn. Ich denke, das kann man heute mit Bestimmtheit sagen.

In Australien und insbesondere in Deutschland scheint es, als seien Holtermanns Leistungen etwas in Vergessenheit geraten. Würden Sie das auch so
30 *sehen?*

Ich sehe das absolut so. In Australien haben wir die Leute im Holtermann Museum in Gulgong und die in der Provinzstadt Hill End in New South Wales, die noch in diesem Geist leben. Es gibt zudem ein paar
35 neue, jüngere australische Künstler*innen, die mit den Fotos in der Holtermann Collection arbeiten.

In Deutschland ist Holtermann überhaupt nicht bekannt. So stieß ich beispielsweise in einem Hamburger Museum auf ein Fotoalbum mit Bildern,
40 die wahrscheinlich Bayliss für Holtermann machte. Sie hatten das Album zwar, aber niemand wusste wirklich, was es war oder wie es dorthin gelangt war.

Fotos scheinen für Holtermann sehr wichtig gewesen
45 *zu sein. Trotz der vielen verschiedenen Dinge, die er in seinem Leben machte, hat man den Eindruck, dass seine wahre Leidenschaft der Fotografie galt.*

Ich denke, das ist richtig. Holtermann scheint sehr an neuer Technologie interessiert gewesen zu sein,
50 er war Unternehmer. Er wollte die Nachricht davon, wie weit die Kolonie Australien damals entwickelt war, in die ganze Welt hinaustragen – und tat das auch buchstäblich. Australien war nicht mehr nur ein Ort für ehemalige Gefangene. Der beste Weg,
55 das zu zeigen, war damals über Fotos. Fotografie war für ihn das richtige Instrument, um von Australien zu erzählen, und das tat er auch. Er gründete zudem ein Pharmaunternehmen und war im Import-Export der neuesten Maschinen tätig.
60 Holtermann hatte immer einen guten Riecher für jede Chance, sich stärker zu profilieren. Er wurde berühmt, aber er wurde dadurch berühmt, dass er Australien dankte und der Welt zeigte, wie fortschrittlich das Land in den 1870er und 1880er
65 Jahren war.
Er und der berühmte australische Fotograf Beaufoy Merlin, der ebenfalls stets auf der Suche nach den neuesten Trends war, hatten eine großartige Partnerschaft. Die beiden arbeiteten gut
70 zusammen, sie waren Geistesverwandte. Holtermann freundete sich immer mit Leuten mit Fähigkeiten an, die er gerade brauchte. In dieser Hinsicht war er sehr clever.

Was, glauben Sie, können wir heute von Bernhard
75 *Holtermann lernen?*

Niemand kann sich heutzutage sein ganzes Leben
lang auf nur einen Beruf verlassen, es heißt, man
müsse bereit sein, alle fünf Jahre etwas anderes zu
machen. Holtermann wäre das perfekte Beispiel
80 dafür. Er war alles Mögliche, und er war im wahrsten
Sinne des Wortes ein Brückenbauer zwischen Europa
und Australien. Er war ein Mann mit vielen Talenten
und sehr mutig. Er wusste nie, ob er finanziellen
Erfolg haben oder verarmt sterben würde. Er verließ
85 Europa per Schiff, als er 20 Jahre alt war, ohne jede
Ahnung, ob er es nach Australien schaffen würde,
und er sprach damals kein Wort Englisch. Er stürzte
sich da einfach hinein. Sein berühmter Goldfund ist

ein gutes Beispiel. Sein
90 Geschäftspartner Louis
Beyers war nicht in Hill
End, als das Gold
ausgegraben wurde,
und Holtermann
95 schlief, als seine Leute
es fanden. Aber es war
immer als Holtermann
Nugget bekannt. Das ist
nicht ganz richtig. Sie
100 hätten es zumindest
Holtermann Beyers Nugget nennen sollen.

Taken and adapted from: https://www.goethe.de/ins/au/de/
kul/mag/21865525.html.

b Deine Mutter interessiert sich für den Artikel über Bernhard Holtermann und sagt, dass sie noch nie von dem
Mann gehört hat. Als sie dich fragt, ob er in Australien heutzutage noch bekannt ist, berichtest du ihr vom
Holtermann Museum in Gulgong. Du hast folgende Bewertungen im Internet gefunden. Deine Mutter möchte
wissen, was die Besucher über dieses Museum denken. Beantworte die Frage deiner Mutter und gib die Gründe
für die Bewertung der Museumsbesucher an.

Community museums rule! ★★★★★
This small museum is an inspiration. I was impressed by
the community working together to save two heritage
buildings in order to house the Holtermann Collection
of photographs and showcase Gulgong during the 1870s
Gold Rush. Really well displayed and engaging content
and brilliant staff. Really important stop if you visit this
heritage town.
July 2020

The Holterman Gulgong museum is first class.
★★★★★
This museum is well thought out with great touchscreens
if you want to dive deeper into Gold Rush life.
The photographers hired by Holtermann, i. e. Merlin and
Baylis, were masters of wet plate photography. The
clarity of the enlarged photographs is superb, giving a
great panorama of the gold fields. Well worth a visit.
June 2020

Excellent discovery! ★★★★☆
What history. It's all here and brilliantly presented.
Almost too much to take in. Just immerse yourself in
this snapshot of history in the goldfields, and then
delve into photos of Sydney and Melbourne in the
horse-drawn era.
June 2020

This UNESCO listed collection comes to life.
Enter the door! ★★★★☆
What an amazing collection, and the presentation is
stunning. Love that this significant historical collection
is so accessible. And also so relevant – standing in
Gulgong – it feels like you are back in history.
July 2020

Photography exhibition ★★★☆☆
An interesting photography museum primarily focused on the gold rush period. Rather small selection, but great photos.
Our kids got bored anyway.   September 2020

PART 1

PART 2

PART 3

Ready for Workshop 2?

1 **a** Look at these photos which are connected to the topics from this workshop.
Say what you can you remember about each of these topics.

Melbourne, Australia

Uluru

Australia / bushfire

Maori / Hongi

b Choose one of the topics from this workshop. Note down some information and use your notes to give a short (two-minute) talk to the rest of the class.

2 Complete the leaflet about the Great Barrier Reef with the correct form of the verbs from the box.

G1
G2
G5

> declare ■ hold ■ not take ■ post ■ set up ■ think ■ threaten ■ visit

The Great Barrier Reef is one of nature's wonders. It ▮1▮ that more than 1,500 species of fish live in the reef and it ▮2▮ a World Heritage site in 1981. Every year the Great Barrier Reef ▮3▮ by about two million people from around the world. Unfortunately, its very existence ▮4▮ by a number of issues connected to climate change.

If action ▮5▮ soon, it will be too late! A campaign ▮6▮ to help save the reef for future generations. A march ▮7▮ next Saturday. Information about the march ▮8▮ on different social media platforms, so come along and join us and help save the Great Barrier Reef.

→ Workbook, pages 32–34   **REVIEW**

3   Complete the conversation between Jack and Bruce with the correct form of the verbs in brackets.

50c

AUSTRALIA
Eddie "Koiki" Mabo 1936–92

G1	
G5	

Jack   Hi, Bruce. What are you reading?

Bruce It's a book about Eddie Koiki Mabo.

Jack   Who's he?

Bruce He **1** (*be*) a famous Aboriginal who **2** (*fight*) for the rights to land for his people.

Jack   Sounds interesting. So what have you learned?

Bruce He was born in the Torres Islands off the North Coast of Australia, but in 1959 he **3** (*move*) to Queensland. He **4** (*live*) there for 13 years when he tried to return to Murray Island. He **5** (*hope*) to visit his father, but the government wouldn't let Eddie go because he **6** (*not, live*) there for so long that they said he was a non-Islander.

Jack   Wow! That sounds terrible.

Bruce Yes, just six weeks later he **7** (*receive*) a message telling him his father **8** (*die*). After that he **9** (*spend*) the rest of his life trying to get equality for Aboriginal people in Australia.

Jack   And what happened?

Bruce Well in 1993 the Native Title Act **10** (*pass*) by the Australian Parliament. The Act said the land did belong to the Aborigine.

Jack   That was great. Eddie Mabo must have been happy.

Bruce Unfortunately, he **11** (*die*) the year before.

Jack   That's just so unfair. Can I borrow the book after you **12** (*read*) it?

Bruce Sure.

---

4   Read this text a German student wrote for a school magazine. Are the <u>underlined</u> words correct or wrong? Correct the ones that are wrong.

Earlier this year, I <u>have visited</u>[1] Auckland in New Zealand. We <u>had been</u>[2] on holiday in Australia for about a month when we decided to make the trip. <u>Interestingly</u>[3], Auckland is the largest city in New
5 Zealand, but it isn't the capital. We stayed in a small hotel downtown, which was great for sightseeing. One day we <u>were going</u>[4] to Auckland Domain which is the <u>cities</u>[5] largest park and is on the side of <u>a extinct</u>[6] volcano. We also visited the
10 iconic Sky Tower with <u>it's</u>[7] fantastic views of one of the two harbours. From <u>their</u>[8] we could see why Auckland <u>is known</u>[9] as 'the city of sails' because there are <u>thousands of yachts</u>[10] in the harbours. <u>I am</u>[11] a rugby fan since I first saw the All Blacks, New Zealand's national rugby team, <u>in TV</u>[12] a few
15 years ago. So, for me the best part of the trip was when <u>we went</u>[13] to Eden Park, which is the largest sports stadium in New Zealand. It was so <u>good visiting</u>[14] Auckland, and <u>I hope</u>[15] that next year I can go back and also visit the South Island.
20

---

5   After the rugby game between Bayview High School and Papanui High School, Jason phoned his parents and told them a few of the things Coach Hansen said. What did Jason say to his parents?

G3	
G4	
G6	

You played really well.

What would you change for the next match?

You can't win every game.

I know you practised really hard yesterday.

1 The narrator of the song writes from the perspective of the First Nation people. Read the text and summarize what is being said about his / her people (4 – 5 sentences).

2 **a** The vocabulary below will help you understand and talk about the text. Look the words up in a dictionary and explain what they mean in the context of the song.

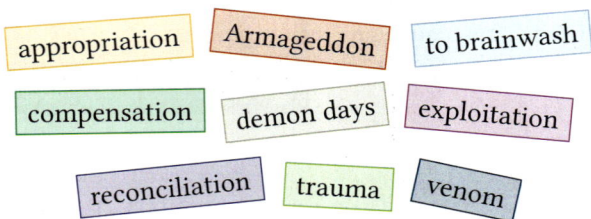

appropriation | Armageddon | to brainwash
compensation | demon days | exploitation
reconciliation | trauma | venom

b Find three more words you think are important to discuss the song. Give reasons for your choice.

3 **a** Do some online research and find out how the natives in Australia were treated by the white settlers.

b Work on these tasks related to the song in groups of four.

1 Discuss how the actions of the white men may have been justified and how they were perceived by the natives. Take notes and weigh positive and negative points.

2 Explain the idea of a 'nation within a nation'. What are they still waiting for?

3 Evaluate the four closing lines. Describe which view of the future the narrator has. Give reasons for your choice.

4 **a** Listen to the song. Comment on the music and how it supports the message.

18

b With a partner, talk about the emotions you had while you were listening.

Midnight Oil, 'First Nation' (2020)

First nation, first nation
First to deserve an explanation
First nation, first nation
Last to receive an invitation

5 First nation, first nation
When we gonna start the conversation?
When we gonna start the celebration?
When we gonna end the exploitation?
When we gonna say the word invasion?

10 Out loud, we're waiting
Still waiting, nation within the nation
Still waiting, nation within a nation

Earth black the church lacked the first fact
80 thou turned demon days and a dirt nap[1]
15 Generate the trauma that made a kid rage[2]
Now the ment' capat[3] be filled with all that
Fall back
Why my cousin commit?
Why my uncle locked up?
20 Why my aunty forget, how to put a glass cup down?
Fighting the fit
We done been[4] brainwashed into fighting the temptay[5]
Fought Armageddon and I be out the next day
Of course I'm a get 'em[6] till the spirit run empty[7]
25 My corpse full of venom outcome of the invade
How dare you try to put me up in grave

Strong vision, tradition
No ticket, no admission
No government indecision
30 No token[8] recognition
First nation, so ancient

Let's sit down and talk about appropriation
Let's sit down and talk about compensation
Let's sit down and talk about reconciliation

35 Out loud, we're waiting
Still waiting, nation within a nation
Still waiting, nation within a nation

Nation, nation within a nation
Nation, nation within a nation
40 Nation, nation within a nation

When will the light switch?
24/7 in the crisis
White noise killed black thoughts I sense
There's a shift, it'll come by the night's end
45 When will the light switch?
24/7 in the crisis
White noise killed black thoughts I sense
There's a shift, see the ship sink like this

---

[1] **dirt nap** (*sl.*) death (literally 'sleeping in the dirt') – [2] **to rage** *toben, wüten* – [3] **ment' capat** = mental capability = head / mind – [4] **we done been** (*sl.*) we have been – [5] **temptay** = temptation – [6] **I'm a get 'em** (*sl.*) I'm going to get them – [7] **to run empty** = to run on empty, losing enthusiasm or motivation (like a vehicle with low fuel) – [8] **token** *Geste*

Aaradhna, 'Brown Girl' (2016)

I'm more than the colour of my skin
I'm a girl that likes to sing
All I know is what's within
Not just a brown girl in the ring[1]

5 Go to school and learn their ways
Told how to think and what to say
While my mother says to pray
I pray for better days

God, please help them see
10 They ain't no different from me
Not above, not beneath
Teach them equality

I'm not just a brown girl in the ring
I'm a girl that likes to sing
15 I'm not just a brown girl in the ring
I'm a girl that likes to sing

I'm more than what they think of me
More than the colour tones that they see
More than urban, R&B[2], more than a slang[3] that I speak

20 Close your eyes, don't say your word
Don't speak about what you seen or heard
Let's pretend that it's OK
Just the way the devil likes to play

Look in my eyes, look in my eyes
25 I can't lie, I can't lie
All these years of my life
I'm judged from the outside

I'm not just a brown girl in the ring
I'm a girl that likes to sing
30 I'm not just a brown girl in the ring
I'm a girl that likes to sing

And if you don't know by now
Time will show you what I'm talking 'bout
Said if you don't know by now
35 Time will show you what I'm talking 'bout
I'm talking 'bout

I'm not just a brown girl in the ring
I'm a girl that likes to sing
I'm not just a brown girl in the ring
40 I'm a girl that likes to sing

5 **a** Listen, then do the tasks.

19

1 For the singer it is important to be 'more than...'. Find all the relevant lines and explain what they mean. Speculate which perspective for the future she develops.

2 In your own words, analyse her attitude towards education.

b Check the exact meaning of these words. Discuss to what extent they have a similar or a different meaning. Give reasons for your choices.

- prejudice
- stereotype
- discrimination
- bullying

c Find examples of the words in **b** from real life, either from your personal experience or from the news.

d Do some biographical research on the singer. Then prepare and give a two-minute talk.

6 Imagine you have just had a lesson on the German constitution. Your English teacher asks you to explain Article 3 to an exchange student from the USA:

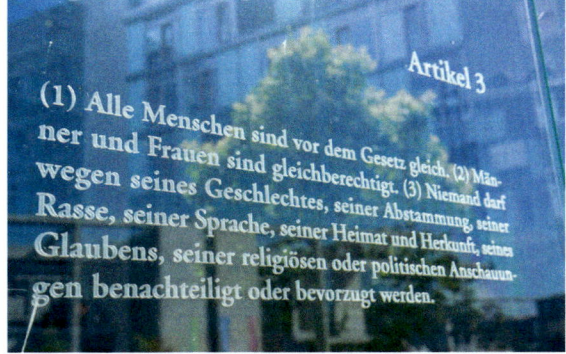

The law says ...
Relevant examples are ...
In my opinion ...

---

[1] **in the ring** (*idiom.*) referring to ring games that children play, in which one child is singled out and 'in the ring', surrounded by the other children–
[2] **R&B** = Rhythm and Blues, a music genre typically including elements of blues and African American folk music and marked by a strong beat –
[3] **slang** = informal language register, can be used in a regional or social sense, showing your origin and belonging to a region or affiliation to a group

20)) Marcus Sedgwick

Edgar and the Terrible Kidnappers

ONE

'What is the point of children?'

This is a question I have often asked myself, and when I say 'children', I mean, in particular: *small* children. Now, I know that someone reading this will
5 say – Edgar! Behave yourself! It's obvious; small children become big children, and with a little luck and a lot of food, big children become adults. And then the same person might talk about how from adults we get more small children, and they may even
10 mention something to do with the survival of the human species[1], and so on. But I'm not convinced that's such an important thing. So, I ask again: what is the point of small children? However, one day last year, something happened that made me see things
15 differently.

It all began on what we call Open Sunday. Every first Sunday of the month, we open the castle to visitors. We do not do this because we are nice. We do not do this because we like sharing history with people. We
20 do this because we are broke. Hard-up. What the man in the street might call 'skint'. In short, these are all ways of saying: we don't have much money. We are, I have to confess, poor. And we open the castle up to charge[2] people a little money to look at the suits of
25 armour[3], or inspect[4] the tapestries on the walls.

Heaven knows[5] why anyone would want to do that, but they do. They even pay for it.

There is a reason why we are poor, despite the fact that we live in a castle. We only live in a castle
30 because it came into the possession[6] of the Otherhand family some 300 years ago following an 'incident'. The 'incident' went like this: once upon a time, the castle was owned by a family called the Deffreeques. Then, the third Lord Otherhand came
35 along, and decided he really wanted to live in the castle. Then there was a short battle, and some 'nasty business'[7]. Since then, the Otherhands have lived in the castle, with an ever decreasing fortune. Not one penny has been spent on repairing the place since
40 the third Lord Otherhand moved his family in. So that's why we live in a castle, but I didn't tell you why we are poor. We are poor because Valevine and Minty, the parents of Solstice and Cudweed, Fizz and Buzz, the latest Lord and Lady Otherhand, are stupid.
45 Really, really stupid.

---

[1] **human species** Menschen – [2] **to charge sth.** etwas verlangen – [3] **suit of armour** Rüstung – [4] **to inspect** untersuchen – [5] **Heaven knows** weiß der Himmel – [6] **possession** Besitz – [7] **nasty business** schmutzige Angelegenheit

I may have told you before that Valevine is an inventor. And I may have told you before that his inventions come in two kinds: first, there are the things that might be a good idea, but simply don't
50 work. Then, there are the things that *do* work, but which are totally useless. Actually, now I think about it; there is a third type of invention that he makes – things that don't work *and* are also totally useless. Actually, now I think about it, *most* of his inventions
55 are of this third kind. For example, at the time this story starts, he was up in the tower where he has his laboratory. He was working on a machine that could clean itself. Needless to say; it wasn't working; this machine to clean itself, and (this is important) since
60 it had *no other function*, you may wonder what the use of it would be, even if it *did* work. Solstice tried pointing this out to her father and was sent to her room for the rest of the day for saying so.
Then there's Minty. Now, once upon a time, she had
65 been a witch, but she was no longer a witch, and people remembered that she was a bad witch, even
70 when she was one. By 'bad', I don't mean she was *evil*, or that she cast wicked spells[8] on people to turn them into post boxes,
75 or anything like that. I mean she was bad, as in, she was really, really terrible at making spells.
Since then, she has had a lot of children, of course,
80 and children are very time-consuming[9] things. Minty has four children, namely[10] Solstice, then Cudweed, and then, a bit later, the twins, Fizz and Buzz. Minty sometimes refers to the twins as 'my little accident' (I have no idea what that means) and this is where I
85 started, isn't it, because it is small children that I really have trouble understanding. I mean, what is the point? Not only that, but Fizz and Buzz are quite unusual. Even compared with other small children. They are always getting into mischief[11] of some kind
90 or other, and often get into dangerous situations, even though they themselves always survive unharmed[12]. They have, it's called, 'a charmed life'[13].

Anyway, this story starts (at last! I hear you cry) with the twins. It began on one of the Open Sundays. The
95 castle was open to visitors, who had each paid the ludicrously[14] small sum of £1.50 to look around. I keep trying to tell Minty she should charge more, but I think she feels guilty charging anyone at all, since her family stole the castle from the Deffreeques in
100 the first place.
On days like this, I like to hide. I go up to my cage in the Red Room which is in a part of the castle we never open, so we can have some peace even on Open Sunday. The day wore on[15], boring and slow as
105 Open Sunday always is, and finally, at five o'clock, the last of the visitors left the castle and the gardens, and we were alone again.

Minty counted up the day's takings[16]; it was barely[17] enough to pay for the electricity for another week,
110 but while Valevine and Minty were talking about that, Solstice came in.
'Er,' she said, 'er, has anyone seen the twins?'
'Fizz and Buzz?' said Valevine, as if he had many sets of twins.
115 'Exactly,' said Solstice. 'I've asked everyone and I've looked everywhere. I think …'
(Here she looked worried and her lip began to wobble[18].)
'… I think they might be missing.'
120 Minty blinked twice.
Valevine said, 'what, what?'
Cudweed said, 'I think so, too.'
And it was true. The twins were indeed missing.

---

[8] **to cast a wicked spell** einen bösen Zauber anwenden – [9] **time-consuming** zeitaufwendig – [10] **namely** und zwar – [11] **mischief** Unfug – [12] **unharmed** unversehrt – [13] **a charmed life** ein zauberhaftes Leben – [14] **ludicrously** lachhaft – [15] **to wear on (wore, worn)** sich hinziehen – [16] **takings** Einnahmen – [17] **barely** kaum – [18] **to wobble** wackeln

London: City of culture

Surprisingly, the City of London is the smallest city in the UK! It is a part of Greater London, but the City of London itself only covers 1.2 square miles and has a population of 7,500. Greater London covers more than 600 square miles with nearly 9 million people living within its boundaries! The population is very diverse and over 300 hundred languages are spoken.

The Houses of Parliament are an easily recognizable landmark in central London. As the home of the British government, they consist of the House of Commons and the House of Lords. In 1605, Guy Fawkes and twelve other men tried to blow up parliament in the 'Gunpowder Plot'. One misunderstanding is what the name 'Big Ben' refers to. It is actually the name of the bell behind the clock and not the tower itself, which is called the 'Elizabeth Tower'.

A

While London has lots of old buildings, there are many new ones, too. Visitors flying into London City Airport will immediately notice the skyscrapers at Canary Wharf. What used to be a run-down area is now home to some of the biggest multinational companies in London. In the East End, a lot of interesting buildings designed by famous architects have been built. They have names like 'The Gherkin' or 'The Shard'.

Look at the photos (A – F) and read the information. Write down what you have just learned.

21 Listen to three Londoners talking about their backgrounds. Are these sentences about Jack, Leroy or Amita?

1. ____ comes from a mixed background.
2. ____ describes the food he / she likes.
3. ____ hasn't visited the country his / her family originally came from.
4. ____ mentions how he / she speaks.
5. ____ talks about his / her grandparents' jobs.
6. ____ talks about where his / her parents met.
7. ____ was born in the City of London.

B

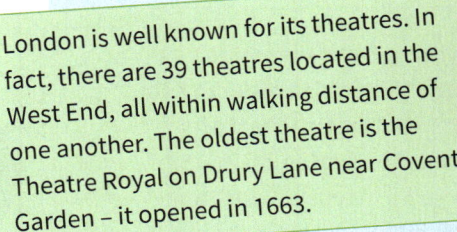
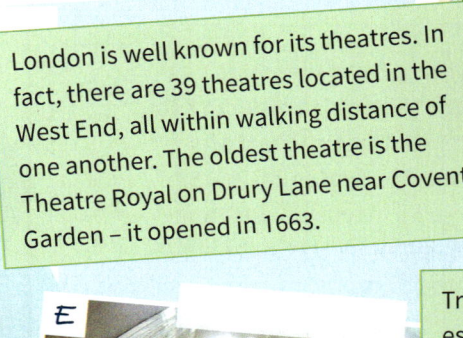

With over 100,000 visitors every weekend, Camden Town Market is a magnet for shoppers. The first market opened in 1974 with just 16 stalls, but today there are more than 1,000 stores and stalls, so there's plenty of choice for everyone!

C

D

London is well known for its theatres. In fact, there are 39 theatres located in the West End, all within walking distance of one another. The oldest theatre is the Theatre Royal on Drury Lane near Covent Garden – it opened in 1663.

British Museum

The Gherkin

St Paul's Cathedral

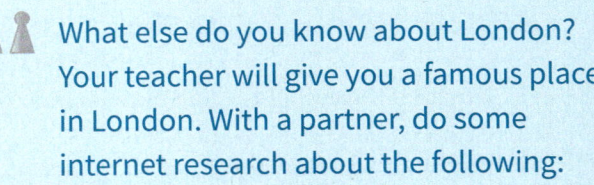

E

Travelling around London is easy, especially if you use the Underground, also known as the 'Tube'. There are eleven lines (all colour coded) and 270 stations. The first line opened in 1863 and ran from Bishop's Road, which is now called Paddington, to Farringdon Road. The most recent line is the Jubilee line, which was built to celebrate the Queen's 25 years on the throne in 1977, although it didn't open until 1979. Today, as many as two million people use the Tube on a daily basis!

The Shard

Tower Bridge

21))) Listen to the three young people again. List some of the similarities and differences between them.

What else do you know about London? Your teacher will give you a famous place in London. With a partner, do some internet research about the following:
- Why is your place famous?
- When was it built?
- How much does it cost to visit?
- What can you do or see there?
Make notes.

F

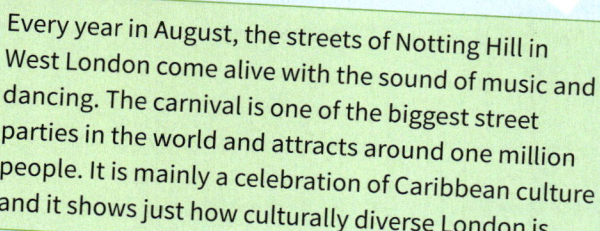

Every year in August, the streets of Notting Hill in West London come alive with the sound of music and dancing. The carnival is one of the biggest street parties in the world and attracts around one million people. It is mainly a celebration of Caribbean culture and it shows just how culturally diverse London is.

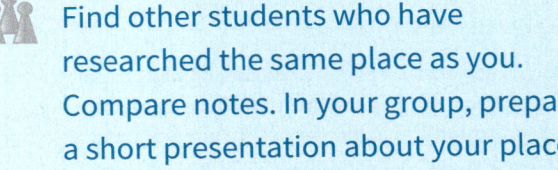

Find other students who have researched the same place as you. Compare notes. In your group, prepare a short presentation about your place and present it to the class.

The partnership

 Getting ready. Mrs Davidson, Deepak's form teacher, is talking to the class. Read what she says and do the tasks.

'As you all know, this year you will start your coursework in your GCSE subjects. In order to help you connect the theoretical studies to real-life experiences, we'll organize several study tours for
5 you to London, where you'll meet students from our partner school, Regent's Park High School. We are going to put you into groups according to your subject interests.
I hope you will all make the most of this great
10 opportunity. When I was younger, I used to live in Leeds, where I went to Allerton High School. We used to go on school trips of course, but these trips used to be more for fun than for study. They were not connected to subjects or course work. Our
15 exam preparation was very different to yours. We would go to the library to do research. We didn't use to have anything else apart from books and journals because there was no internet yet. Those of us who were preparing the course work for the
20 same subject would meet regularly and share our findings. I also remember we used to organize study trips to museums at the weekends with friends. We were very focused, we used to work hard but had lots of fun, too.
25 Anyway, I am sure you'll all find these tours with the students of our partner school useful. So, your first task is to …'

1 Describe the aim of the partnership between the two schools.
2 List what Mrs Davidson says about her preparation for the GCSE exams.
3 Speculate about the benefits of the programme she has introduced.
4 Think about what the students' first task could be.

CULTURE CORNER

GCSE is the General Certificate of Secondary Education. These are exams taken at the ages of 15 – 16 after two years of study in years 10 and 11. Most students take between 7 and 9 subjects, although some take as many as 12! All students have to take maths, English and science.

Used to

We can say *used to* + infinitive when we talk about states that were true in the past and actions that happened regularly, but don't happen now.
*When I was younger, I **used to live** in Leeds.*

We can use *would* + infinitive instead of *used to* + infinitive for repeated actions in the past, but NOT for states.
*We **would meet** regularly …*

When something wasn't true in the past but happens now, we use *didn't use to* + infinitive or *wouldn't* + infinitive.
*We **didn't use to have** anything else apart from books and journals.*

Words and phrases

cosmopolitan	having experience of many people or things from around the world
relevant	connected to, and useful for, something happening
to surround	to be everywhere around something or somebody
theoretical	based on ideas rather than practical realities
to underpin	to give support or a basic structure to something

2 **Past habits**

a Read the text again and find examples of *used to*. Which one(s) can you *not* replace with *would*?

b After the lesson, Deepak and Bex asked Mrs Davidson more about her life when she was their age. Complete the sentences with *used to* and *would*.

Deepak Mrs Davidson, did you go to the to the library a lot?

Mrs D. Yes, I did. I ▮1▮ live near the library. I ▮2▮ go to the library regularly for research.

Bex And how ▮3▮ (*you*) find the books you needed?

Mrs D. There ▮4▮ be a separate section with the catalogues of all the books in the library. All the students ▮5▮ go there to find the information they needed.

Deepak (*You*) mostly ▮6▮ work on your own?

Mrs D. No, for the projects we ▮7▮ work together in small groups. We ▮8▮ do our presentations together and share them in class.

3 **Getting prepared**

 a The students at Regent's Park High School are researching the permanent exhibitions on the Museum of London website. You can find the link to the museum's website under the *On Track* webcode. Work with a partner and choose an exhibition to research.

- Decide on a historical period you want to research. Note down the dates.
- Look at the exhibitions and agree on one which fits with your period and which you both find interesting / surprising / informative.
- Make notes on the details of the exhibition.

 b Find another pair who researched a different exhibition. Share what you found out.

 c In your group, draw a timeline and discuss which period of London's history you found most interesting and why. What questions do you have about it?

4 **It's your turn**

 a You were asked to prepare a museum tour for visiting students from the UK.

- Select a museum that has an exhibition about the history of the place where you live or the next big town.
- Make notes about the period the exhibition covers and the most important and interesting facts about the exhibition.

 b Present your findings to the class. Take a class vote on which museum your class thinks is best for your visitors. Give reasons for your choice.

Grammar and structures

Used to, didn't use to, would to describe past habits and states → G7

We **used to work** hard.
We **would go** to the library to do research.

PART 1
PART 2
PART 3

1 **a** Read the quotes. Explain what they mean.

> *When a man is tired of London, he is tired of life; for there is in London all that life can afford.* A

Samuel Johnson, 18th century English writer, poet and playwright

> *In London, everyone is different and that means everyone can fit in.* B

A Bear Called Paddington by Michael Bond

> *A person who is tired of London is not necessarily tired of life; it might be that he just can't find a parking place.* C

Paul Theroux, contemporary American travel writer and novelist

b Look at the words and expressions in the box and match them to the quotes. Which ones fit with A, B or C? Give reasons.

c With a partner, discuss what could be an appropriate description of your home town or city. Agree on one sentence. You can use the words from the box, but don't write more than 25 words.

> diversity ■ endless possibilities ■ multiculturalism ■ opportunities ■ transport ■ urban development ■ variety

2 **a** Listen to two interviews on a radio programme. What are the two guests talking about?

b Listen to the interviews again and complete the tasks.

1 Describe what Paul Turner would do as a young boy.
2 Explain where Paul lived as a young boy.
3 Outline the changes that have been made to Battersea Power Station.
4 List three things Mary says about her grandparents.
5 Explain why Mary is disappointed.

3 Read the text about Mary and decide whether the underlined parts are correct or wrong. Correct the wrong ones.

Mary would[1] live with her parents close to her grandparents. A few years ago, she moved in with her boyfriend. When she did, a lot of things changed in her life. Her boyfriend is very health conscious. Mary wouldn't[2] keep fit, but now she does yoga and Pilates. She used to[3] take the bus everywhere, but now she tries to cycle as much as possible. She used[4] eat lots of junk food, but now she is vegan. She didn't like staying in, so she would[5] go to lots of parties. In fact, Mary used to[6] go out every evening, but now she likes to spend time at home with her boyfriend. Mary used to be[7] happy with her new life and thinks the changes have made a lot of difference.

4 Look at the photos of London. With your partner talk about the changes these show about life in London.

@ WES-40903-002

→ Workbook, page 38   **LISTENING AND VIEWING PRACTICE**

1 You are going to watch a video clip which was shown at the 2012 London Olympics opening ceremony. Look at the picture on the right and describe it. Include the following in your description:

- the main focus of the picture
- the place and the time when it was taken
- the camera position
- what the people in the picture are doing

> **Useful words / expressions:**
> - *In the foreground / background, …*
> - *The camera shows a close-up / full view of …*
> - *The picture was taken from below / above …*

2 Watch the clip. Tell a partner about your first impressions and why you had them.

A The Queen and Bond walk down a corridor, out of the building and into a waiting helicopter.

B James Bond enters the front gate of Buckingham Palace in a London black cab.

3 Look at the summary of the plot and put the sentences in the correct order. Check with your partner.

C The helicopter passes Tower Bridge and the scene changes from day to night.

D As the helicopter flies over Parliament Square, an animated statue of Winston Churchill waves at it.

E A group of Brazilian children in the throne room see James Bond from the window.

F The helicopter flies across London, above crowds of cheering people.

4 **a** Watch the video again and focus on the interaction between Daniel Craig (James Bond) and the Queen. Pay attention to their body language and how they move. What do they tell you about the relationship between Bond and the Queen? How would you describe Bond's behaviour:

G The Queen and the Duke of Edinburgh, along with Jacques Rogge, are then introduced to the audience. The Queen is wearing the same dress she had on in the earlier scenes in the film, as if she had just arrived with Bond.

I Bond is taken to Queen Elizabeth II and escorts the Queen, who greets Bond with the words, 'Good evening, Mr Bond'.

H The film finishes with Bond and the Queen apparently jumping from a helicopter live above the Olympic Stadium with Union Jack parachutes.

- before meeting the Queen?
- with the Queen?

> **TIP**
>
> **How can you read the relationship between two people?**
> Non-verbal interaction reveals a lot about a people's relationship with each other. Pay special attention to body language, eye contact, facial expressions and movement. For example, a relaxed posture shows a close relationship and familiarity, while standing up straight shows respect. If someone maintains eye contact with someone, it usually means they're giving this person their full attention. A warm smile shows friendliness and walking slightly behind the other person shows your respect for their social rank.

b When we make a video or film, we use certain techniques to make it more interesting. Watch the video again and think about:

- the settings
- the camera shots
- the use of music
- the voice-over

c Discuss your ideas with a partner.

 Words and phrases

posture the way somebody stands or sits   **throne** a chair for a king or queen

In London

PART 1

1 **The second visit.** Deepak and the other students from Hill End School
are on a second visit to London to meet up with the students from
Regent's Park. Listen to the conversations and complete the tasks.

1 Explain why Deepak is excited about going to London.
2 Describe what will happen after they arrive in London.
3 Outline the advice that Mrs Davidson gives the kids.
4 Explain how they are travelling around London and why.

PART 2

2 **Different locations**

a The students split up and visit different important places around London. Speculate what kind of places
these are and what you could see or do there. Then research and write down their names.

PART 3

b Look at these signs. In which places from **a** do you expect to find them? Give reasons for your choice.

1
All bags will be searched at the entrance.

2
Souvenirs are available at the end of the exhibit area.

3
Photography of the works of art is not permitted.

4
Tickets for the next performance will go on sale soon.

c Discuss what each sign means and what other signs you might find in each location.

25)) Words and phrases

architecture	the style and design of buildings
debate	a serious discussion between two or more groups of people
possession	something that you own, that belongs to you
procedure	the way you have to do something
trade	buying and selling things

3 **Where are they?**

a Read the short conversations and match the students to the pictures of the places they are visiting. Then complete the tasks.

Deepak	Wow! I remember visiting the *Mary Rose* in Portsmouth. That was cool.
Amelia	I've been there, too, but I think this place is better. I've decided to write about it for my project.
Deepak	What's so special about it?
Amelia	It was used in the tea trade in the 19th century in order to sail across the ocean in a very short time. It was one of the fastest ships around.

Bex	You can't call that art! I think even I'm capable of doing better.
Logan	Oh, I quite like it. It's better than many of the dusty old paintings in some of the other museums.
Bex	I suppose so and I like the architecture. It's quite a cool building.

Mrs D.	Where's David?
Max	I think he stopped to take some photos.
Mrs D.	David, please stop taking photos. You're not allowed to take photos inside the church!
David	It's OK, Mrs Davidson. We can take photos in here, the rules were changed recently. But we are not allowed to use a flash or a selfie stick.
Max	But we've already taken some nice selfies outside.

1 Explain why Amelia thinks the *Cutty Sark* is important.

2 Interpret what Bex means by the words 'I'm capable of doing better'.

b In a group of three, act out the conversation between David, Max and Mrs Davidson.

c Look at the sentences from the third conversation. In which sentence did David do one thing and then do something else?

I think he stopped to take some photos.
David, please stop taking photos.

> **Remember**
> - Some verbs are always followed by the infinitive:
>   *I've decided to write about it.*
> - Some verbs are always followed by -ing:
>   *Let's leave early to avoid getting stuck in heavy traffic.*
> - Some verbs can be followed by the infinitive or -ing, but the meaning is different:
>   *I remember visiting St. Paul's.* – a memory of doing something in the past
>   *Remember to visit the Tower.* – don't forget to do something

4 **Amelia, Bex and Deepak continue chatting.** Complete their conversation with the verbs in the correct form.

Amelia	I know you wanted ▬1▬ (*visit*) the Globe Theatre, but we've decided ▬2▬ (*save*) that for the next time as there is so much to see in London.
Deepak	Oh no! That's a pity. Can't we try ▬3▬ (*go*) there later?
Amelia	I'm sorry, but there just isn't enough time. We tried ▬4▬ (*include*) it in the schedule, but it wasn't possible.
Deepak	Then we need ▬5▬ (*plan*) it for another trip.
Amelia	Exactly and I promise ▬6▬ (*make sure*) we visit the Globe then.
Bex	Great! I'm looking forward to ▬7▬ (*come*) to London again.

5 **It's your turn.** Plan a two-day trip around London. Make sure you include information such as ticket prices, how to get from one place to the next and what you can do or see in each place.

Grammar and structures

Gerund and infinitive (revision) → **G8**

He **stopped to take** some photos.
Please **stop taking** photos.
I've **decided to write** about it.
Let's leave early to **avoid getting stuck** in heavy traffic.

PART 1

PART 2

PART 3

1 **a** Read the information about visiting the Houses of Parliament in London. Write headings for each section. The first one has been done for you.

b Compare your headings and decide on the best one for each section.

Visitor information

Your safety is important to us. When you arrive, you will go through an airport-style system and your bag will be searched. This procedure can
5 take up to 45 minutes. The queues start outside the building, so make sure you are properly dressed for the weather.

1

Once you are inside the building, you will be
10 given a pass. You must wear this and make sure it is clearly visible. This allows you to go into all the public areas, such as the Central Lobby and the public galleries.

2

15 Only guide dogs are allowed inside the building. There is wheelchair access as well as facilities for the disabled throughout the building. However, there are no cloakrooms, so you need to keep your belongings with you at
20 all times. All bags must be smaller than 55cm x 36cm.

3

There are lots of different tour types available, including audio tours and guided tours. In
25 addition, there is a special year-round programme for schools. This often includes a question and answer session with the school's local MP.

4

30 Understanding everything you see is not easy. Although there are guided tours, you can also buy a useful 96-page book with stories about one of the most famous buildings in London. Learn about the history and what goes on
35 inside the building.

---

2 **a** Read an email that Deepak sent to his friend Jeff in Germany. Complete the email with the correct form of the verbs.

b Read the email again and complete the tasks.

1 Explain the purpose of the email.
2 Describe why Deepak was angry with Bex.
3 Explain what Deepak tells Jeff about the *Cutty Sark*.

Hi Jeff

I'm sorry I haven't written for ages, I've been really busy.
I remember __1__ (*mention*) to you that we were going to London again, but then I realized the other evening that I had forgotten __2__ (*tell*) you about it. So, here goes.

We took a coach from Durham down to London. During the journey, Bex kept on __3__ (*tease*) David and I got really angry with her. Bex thinks David is in love with Amelia. She denied __4__ (*say*) anything to her, but you never know with Bex.

Anyway, we were meeting up with Amelia to go and see the Cutty Sark. We had arranged __5__ (*meet*) next to the statue of Churchill in Parliament Square as the coach was parked near there.

I really liked the Cutty Sark. I got my phone out and tried __6__ (*take*) some photos, but we weren't allowed __7__ (*take*) pictures of everything. I suggested __8__ (*visit*) the Globe Theatre because it's nearby, but Amelia said we didn't have time.

Sorry, I need __9__ (*go*) now, my mum's calling me for dinner. I'll write more later.

Deepak

---

3 May visited the Science Museum. When she got back to the bus, she was really excited and spoke to Bex about what she'd seen and done. Put the conversation in the correct order. The first line has been done for you.

Bex   Wow! You look really excited, May.
May

K Wow! You look really excited, May.

A And was it good?

B Exactly. I designed a space rover and had to navigate across the surface of a distant planet.

C I bet you enjoyed that.

D It's a space full of inventions from the last two hundred and fifty years …

E Mmmm, that sounds like you actually do things rather than just look at them.

F That's the perfect place for you. What was the best part?

G The Object Gallery? What's that?

H Well, I thought I'd be most excited in the Object Gallery …

I Yes, it was amazing, but not as good as the Engineer Your Future stuff in the Interactive Gallery.

J Yes. I've just been to the Science Museum and it was fantastic.

4 Where would you find these notices?

1
The first performance starts at 6:45.

2
Please do not touch the exhibits.

3
Please keep off the grass!

4
Next home game: Saturday 3 p.m.

5
Do not feed the animals!

5 Do you know these places in London? Have you been there? What can you do there? Would you like to go there? Choose one place and carry out some research.

A

B

PART 1

PART 2

PART 3

1 **a** Look at these pictures of London sights. Do you know what they are? Describe what you can see.

b Read a short spoken presentation given by a tour guide about one of the sights. Which sight is being described?

King Henry the Eighth

The oldest part of this place was built by Henry VIII for one of his favourite people, Cardinal Wolsey, and the original building was completed in 1515. Sometimes Kings and Queens used to live here although the last king to do so was George II. The architecture is a mixture of Tudor and baroque. One
5 of the most famous things you can find in the garden is the maze. You can also find one of the oldest tennis courts in the grounds. Over the years, many films have been shot here and it was also the location of the Road Cycling Time Trials during the London Olympics in 2012.

c Read the presentation again. Say which information is included.

- When it was built
- The original use
- Anything it is famous for
- Who it was built for / who built it
- How much it costs to visit
- The number of visitors each year
- How to get there
- Other uses
- Why it was built

2 **a** Do some research and make notes about the information that is not included about the place in **1b**.

 b Use your notes to practise speaking about the place. Include the information you think is most important.

→ Workbook, page 42 **SPEAKING PRACTICE**

3 Now match the information (1 – 15) to the other three pictures.

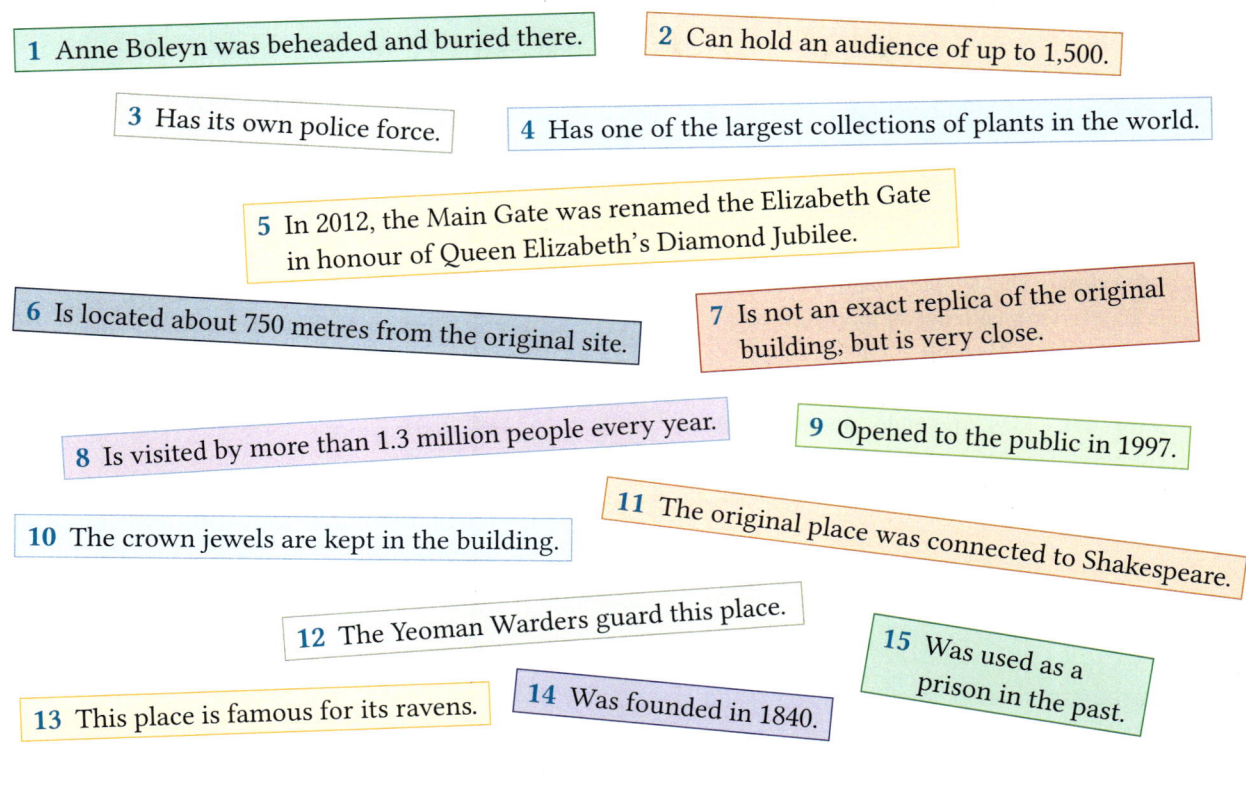

1 Anne Boleyn was beheaded and buried there.

2 Can hold an audience of up to 1,500.

3 Has its own police force.

4 Has one of the largest collections of plants in the world.

5 In 2012, the Main Gate was renamed the Elizabeth Gate in honour of Queen Elizabeth's Diamond Jubilee.

6 Is located about 750 metres from the original site.

7 Is not an exact replica of the original building, but is very close.

8 Is visited by more than 1.3 million people every year.

9 Opened to the public in 1997.

10 The crown jewels are kept in the building.

11 The original place was connected to Shakespeare.

12 The Yeoman Warders guard this place.

13 This place is famous for its ravens.

14 Was founded in 1840.

15 Was used as a prison in the past.

4 a Listen to an expert giving tips about how to give an effective presentation. Make notes and then complete the sentences.

1 An effective presentation is about ▬▬ as they listen to you.
2 Visual aids like ▬▬ help, but are not always necessary.
3 It's good to ▬▬ so you get enough air into your lungs.
4 It's important not to mumble and to try and ▬▬.
5 It will be obvious to your audience if you don't ▬▬.
6 Sequencing what you say in a ▬▬ helps people follow what you are saying.
7 Your audience will be interested if you sound ▬▬ about what you are speaking about.

A good presentation	
preparation	???
body language	???
voice	???
...	???

b Work in groups. Use your notes and answers to the tasks in **a** to design a checklist to use when you give or listen to a presentation.

5 **Think:** Choose one of the three remaining places in **1**. Carry out some more research.

Pair: With a partner, use the information from **2** to plan a presentation.

Share: Give your presentation. When you listen, use your checklist and tell your partners how well they presented.

PART 1

PART 2

PART 3

Choosing an idea for a documentary film

S1 **Brainstorm a topic for your documentary film**

a Read the information in the leaflet. Then choose one of the documentary types. Your film can be two to five minutes long.

> There are different types of documentary films. Here are two:
> **Interview** – This simple type of documentary is an interview with one or more subjects about a particular topic.
> *Example:* A student talking about her hobbies
> **Short doc** – This type of documentary is more complex. It looks at a topic using different techniques that may or may not include an interview.
> *Example:* A behind-the-scenes look at a school canteen

 b In groups of three or four, think about and discuss these questions to help you come up with ideas.

- What topics do you and your friends talk about a lot?
- What do you get excited or frustrated about?
- Are there topics or issues that you'd like to find out more about?
- Is there something that you feel isn't right or fair and that you want to try to change?

 c Now brainstorm some ideas. Write them on sticky notes or a big piece of paper. Collect as many as you can before you start analysing them.

TIP

You can find great **stories** in your own school, family or community, for example:
- Our school canteen
- Is our school green?
- An unusual hobby
- How inclusive is our school?

You could also choose a **concept** as your topic, for example:
- Friendship
- Work / School life

S2 **Choose the best idea for your film**

 a Go through your list of ideas. Talk about each topic and how you would make a film about it.

 b Make a shortlist of the three best ideas. Discuss their strengths and weaknesses. Agree on one idea that you think is the best.

S3 **Write a logline summary**

 a Look at these two different loglines for the same documentary film. Which do you think is better and why? Then discuss what makes an effective logline.

1 An interview with a teenager who works to help her family and also wants to go to university.
2 An ambitious student describes her conflict between following her dreams and helping the people she loves.

TIP

In the film industry, a *logline* is a very short summary of one or two sentences that describe what a film is about.

 b Write a logline for your film idea. Then share and discuss your loglines in your group. Agree on a logline that best describes your film and write the final version.

c Explain why it's a good exercise to write a logline when you're making a film.

S4 **Research and organize what you need for shooting**

 a **Information:** To make your film informative and interesting, research any background information about your topic that you need.

 b **Location:** Decide where you will shoot your film. If it's indoors, for example inside the school, find out if you need permission to film there.

 c **Subjects:** Find people for your film. Are they willing to participate? Some people are nervous or just boring when they get in front of a camera. To find out if somebody is right for your film, do a **screen test**, or a test interview on film. If the person doesn't 'come over well' on film, thank him or her and politely explain your decision. Then look for other subjects.

Creating a storyboard

S1 **Describe a storyboard**

a You've got your documentary film topic and you know the story that you want to tell. Now you will decide *how* you want to tell your story. Look at the example of a storyboard. Choose one of the shots and describe it.

Shot # 2			
Image	Image description	Camera	Audio
	trays of different hot foods on canteen buffet	close-up	background music

Shot #3			
Image	Image description	Camera	Audio
	kitchen manager sitting at table in empty canteen, speaking to interviewer (off camera)	medium shot	interview

b Look at the basic camera shots. Choose a shot. Describe what the camera shows and what kind of scene the shot might be good for.

 **1** long shot

 **2** medium shot

 **3** close-up

---

TIP

A storyboard visualizes each shot of the film. It's helpful during shooting as it gives you a visual overview of your story and the technical details about each shot. The pictures can be sketches or photos.

Film terms

to cut	to move quickly from one scene to another
lighting	the type of light and how it is arranged
prop	an object used by an actor or a subject in a play or film
voice-over	comments or information in a film spoken by a person who is not seen on the screen

---

S2 **Create your storyboard**

  a Follow the steps.

Step 1: Copy the storyboard above or photocopy the template that your teacher gives you. Keep a blank photocopy for further pages.

Step 2: Visualize and discuss how you want to tell your story with each camera shot. Think about the role of elements like props and voice-over if you plan to use them.

Step 3: After your discussion, choose a camera shot individually and make a plan for it.

Step 4: In your group, put the individual plans in order, shot by shot, as your story develops.

  b Share your finished storyboard with another group. Describe what happens and what the viewer sees in the film from one shot to the next. Make any changes or corrections that are needed.

Teenagers and consumerism

1 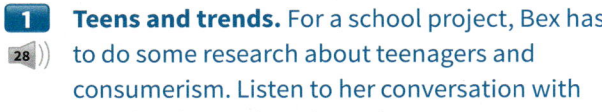 **Teens and trends.** For a school project, Bex has to do some research about teenagers and consumerism. Listen to her conversation with David and complete the tasks.

1 Explain why Bex is upset when David says 'Well, you know a lot about that with all the shopping you do!'
2 Illustrate how Bex tries to be ethically conscious when shopping.
3 Describe the role influencers have on what Bex buys.
4 Explain why Bex buys most of her clothes from second-hand shops.

2 **Label it!** Look again at these logos that are often found on different products. Do you know what each one means? Are there any labels you look for when you are shopping? If yes, what and why?

3 **Gen Z.** Bex wrote down the key ideas from an article she read online. Complete the notes using the words and phrases from the box.

> and where it comes from ■
> being health conscious ■ choice ■
> five times per week ■ GPS ■
> on social media ■ snack ■ to retailers ■
> value experiences ■ veganism

- Generation Z were born between the mid-1990s and the late 2000s.
- Key trends: convenience and `1`.
- Data available `2` shows what Gen Z buy.
- `3` is still an important factor.
- `4` can be used to track orders.
- 70% bought something they'd seen `5`.
- Gen Z `6` as much as products.
- 79% of teens `7` at least once a day.
- Gen Z want to know what's in the food they eat `8`.
- `9` is becoming increasingly popular with Gen Z consumers.
- Gen Z will go shopping up to `10` – no longer the once a week big shop.

4 **A report.** Now read a research report written by one of Bex's classmates. Find five factual mistakes and correct them.

Before researching the topic, I hadn't realized how important my generation were for companies. While carrying out the research, I found out lots of things I hadn't really known
5 before – I guess I'd just assumed these things. 'Gen Z', born after 2000, are technologically savvy and get much of their information from the internet and social media. However, buying something just because you've seen it on social
10 media is not common. There are two main trends that apply to Gen Z: convenience and a realization of how important health is. Using technology retailers are able to target consumers and analyse data to know about
15 their purchasing habits. Also, tracking orders

to find out when they will be delivered is easy with GPS. This is really useful as it means you don't have to wait at home for something to arrive. Convenience doesn't necessarily mean
20 buying things quickly. Gen Z people will often queue for hours to get something they want, as the product is more important than the experience. However, they like to do one big shop rather than lots of visits to stores during
25 the week. Ethical brands endorsed by influencers are usually the most popular. If asked about it, Gen Z would say that health is a major concern. I was amazed to find out that only 39% of teens snack more than once a
30 day – I snack a lot more frequently than that. Ingredients and nutritional information printed on products aren't so important, but whether something is organic is. Paying more for something because it is environmentally
35 friendly is very popular, which is one reason so many Gen Z people are becoming vegan.

Participle constructions help us to give information using fewer words. They are typically found in written English.

We can use the **present participle**:
- for simultaneous actions, carried out by the same person.
  *While **carrying out** the research, I found out lots of things I hadn't really known before.*
- in adverbial clauses of time (beginning with *before, after, while*).
  *Before **researching** the topic, I hadn't realized …*
- in adverbial clauses that give the reason for or the result of an action.
  __Paying__ more for something because it is environmentally friendly is very popular.

We can use the **past participle**:
- in reduced relative clauses when we shorten a defining or a non-defining relative clause.
  *Ethical brands **endorsed** by influencers are usually the most popular.*
- for shortening *if*-clauses, mainly when the verb is in the passive.
  *If **asked** about it, Gen Z would say that health is a major concern.*

Remember
- *-ing*: present participle, the *-ing* form of the verb (*staying, buying, …*)
- *-ed*: past participle, the 3rd form of the verb (*stayed, bought, …*)

---

5 **David's shopping habits.** After talking to Bex, David writes an email to his friend Jeff. Read his email and rewrite the underlined sentences using participle constructions.

Hi Jeff,

It was good to hear from you.
Last night I had a long conversation with Bex about our spending habits.
5 Bex and I spend our pocket money on different things. I guess it's because we have different interests. You remember that my number one passion is going to football matches. Fortunately, there are a few local teams. But it's an expensive
10 hobby. I support Durham City AFC, which means that I spend a big part of my money on a season ticket. And just like you, I still like cooking very much. I cook dinner every Saturday. It's not cheap, because I always buy organic ingredients
15 when I am cooking for the family. Do you still read fantasy novels? I am very much into them. I wish I could afford to buy every single book, but I have to be selective. I read online reviews about the new publications. They help
20 me to decide which books to buy. Then I wait till I find them in the second-hand bookshop. If I can't wait, I get them in digital format because I got an e-book reader for my birthday. But if I was asked about it, I'd say nothing beats the physical books.
25 I'd love to know what you spend your pocket money on.

Talk soon!
David

---

6 **It's your turn.** Look again at the key points Bex wrote and the report by her classmate. Does this reflect your habits and opinions about consumerism? Discuss your ideas in your group. Are they similar or different?

Grammar and structures

Participle constructions → G9
Using technology, retailers are able to …
Ethical brands **endorsed by** influencers …

→ Workbook, page 46   PRACTICE A

1 Look at the picture and do the tasks.

1 Discuss what it shows.
2 Explain the connection between the picture and digital consumerism. Discuss your ideas with your partner.

2 **a** Read the short text about digital consumerism and summarize it in one or two sentences.

The age of technology is here to stay. Many traditional retailers are finding that sales are plummeting and traditional shopping is no more. Unless a physical
5 shop also has an online presence, its very existence is under threat. Purely digital outlets are proving increasingly popular, especially among the digital savvy younger generations. However, just
10 being online isn't enough. You also need to be able to reach potential consumers and make them aware of what you do and sell. This is where popular video platforms and social media apps come
15 into their own, allowing companies to reach millions of people.

b Find words or phrases in the text which match the following definitions.

1 existing / being in place
2 falling / decreasing
3 having or showing practical knowledge and ability
4 only
5 possible when the necessary conditions exist
6 to be very useful in a particular situation

3 Listen to two conversations and do the tasks.

 29

1 Describe why Bex is upset.
2 Evaluate the advice May gives.
3 Explain Tariq's problem.
4 Describe why it might be a problem how Tariq paid for the app.

4 Complete the leaflet about consumer rights with the words and phrases from the box.

> entitled to compensation ■ if the digital content is faulty ■ If the fault can't be fixed ■ of your money back ■ once a download has started ■ to change your mind

Consumer rights for digital content

You have a 14-day right ▢1 and get a full refund. However, ▢2 you do not have this right if this was made clear before.

You are entitled to a repair or replacement ▢3 .

▢4 , or isn't carried out within a reasonable time, you have the right to get some, or all, ▢5 .

You may be ▢6 if the digital content has damaged your device.

5 Look at the sentences about online shopping. Shorten or link them to form participle constructions as in the example.

Before you choose a product, you should research it on the internet.
Before choosing a product, you should research it on the internet.

1 Products which are promoted on social media sites can reach a large audience.
2 Use familiar websites that you trust. It is usually the better option.
3 If a longer delivery time is chosen, it can save you money.
4 It is important to check the ingredients in a product, especially if you're allergic.
5 You can ask for a refund. It shouldn't be a problem.

1 **a** Get together in groups and read the results of a survey into teen shopping habits in the UK. Then do the tasks.

1 Discuss what surprised you.
2 Explain how relevant the questions are to your life.
3 Outline how you would answer the questions.

 b Conduct a teen shopping habits survey in your group. Choose questions from the survey and add others of your own. Record the results in a table. Then compare your results with the class.

> ### Teen shopping habit survey
>
> **How much money do you spend on average?**
> a) Teens spend an average of 60% of their money and save 40%.
> b) At the age of 15, the average amount spent is £25 per week.
> c) 4 out of 5 teenagers save every month.
>
> **What do you spend your money on?**
> a) 84% is spent on buying clothes and socializing (eating out, going to gigs or the cinema, etc.).
> b) 22% buy second-hand, using online sites and marketplaces.
> c) Girls spend 27% on clothes, while video games are the biggest expenditure for boys.
> d) Girls spend twice as much on books as boys.
> e) Spending on cosmetics and make-up has gone down in the last few years.
>
> **Where do you usually shop? (multiple answers possible)**
> a) Online-only shopping is done by 17% of the teenagers.
> b) Fewer teenagers than ten years ago buy products on the high street (24%).
> c) Many buy clothes from the websites of big chains (62%).
> d) Buying from independent / smaller shops has increased in the last few years.
> e) 39% of teens also shop at malls or big shopping centres.
> f) When shopping online, 78% use their phones.

2 **a** Read a letter written by a teenager to the editor in reaction to the survey. Does she agree with the survey results? Give reasons for your answer.

b Complete the letter with the phrases.

> In my opinion ■ I have to be honest ■
> I was amazed by the results ■
> some of the results did ring true ■
> some of your information doesn't match me at all ■
> I may be unusual

3 **a** Choose an issue about teenage life that you are interested in. Think about topics like *pocket money, eating meat, using social media* or choose a different topic. Do some research and make notes.

b Look at the phrases in the box, then include some of them in a letter or an email to a newspaper editor. Write between 120 and 180 words.

> Dear Editor,
>
> In a recent survey you published about teen shopping habits ⬛1⬛. As a teenager, I really do not think the results reflect my own attitude, or that of my friends, towards shopping.
> Of course, ⬛2⬛. I probably spend around 60% of my money most weeks, but not all the time. It is also true that I use my phone to shop online. However, ⬛3⬛. The survey results seem to indicate that girls spend most of their money on clothes, while boys spend a lot on video games. ⬛4⬛ and say I spend way more on video games than clothing and more than most of the boys I know. ⬛5⬛, but I love gaming as it is a great way to relax and meet people online. The problem with surveys like this is they often seem to show stereotypes. ⬛6⬛ that can be quite harmful.
>
> Emma Svenson (15)

Useful expressions
I believe it is important to …; In my view …; I am convinced that …; I think we should / we can do a lot …
I do not want to …; In my opinion, there is too much …; We could all reduce …

 Words and phrases

to ring true   to sound correct or accurate

Advertising and Generation Z

1 Ads and us

a May likes to blog, particularly about technology. Read her blog post and do the tasks.

1 Describe the decision May made when she started blogging. Explain why she made it.
2 List the different kinds of advertising that May mentions.
3 Outline how May as a user reacts to these different kinds of advertising.
4 Explain why, in May's view, teens react differently to advertising by vloggers.

b Look at the mind map and copy it. Find more words in the blog and add them to your mind map.

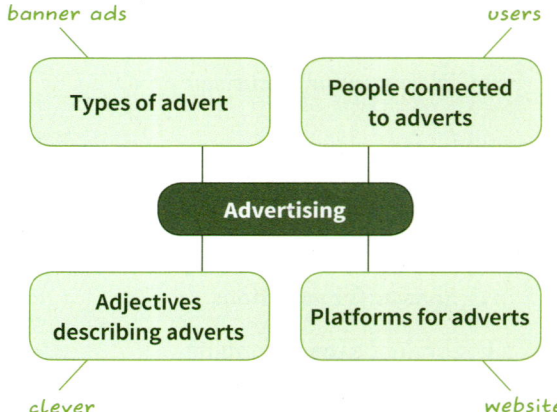

banner ads   users

| Types of advert | People connected to adverts |

Advertising

| Adjectives describing adverts | Platforms for adverts |

clever   website

| BLOG | ABOUT ME | GUEST BLOGGERS | COOL STUFF | ARCHIVE |

Media Geek

Ads and us
by May

Maybe you've noticed there aren't any ads on my blog site. Cool, right? When I first started, I did think about advertising space, but I decided not to because I can earn money in other ways that don't take away from the user experience. It does annoy me when you see adverts everywhere.

Need some statistics? The average teenager sees 400 to 600 ads daily. In the UK, companies spend around £1 billion
5 every year on marketing to teens. Businesses know that we, Generation Z, make up nearly a quarter of the population. So if they want to sell their product or service, they have to get our attention.

As 'digital natives' we socialize, shop and entertain ourselves online, and as users and consumers we're pretty savvy. We do know we're going to get blasted with ads for makeup, food, etc. every time we check our social media feeds. We see these banner ads and pop-up ads on webpages and blogs, too. Most of us scroll past them. Not once have I
10 clicked or tapped on one of those ads.

Advertisers use lots of tricks, though, to get onto our screens and into our heads. Think about the paid content at the bottom of news sites, blogs and posts – they do look like serious articles with attention-grabbing headlines. The video ads that they slip in between the content we watch on video-sharing sites can be more interesting. I click past most of them, but if the music is cool or the ad speaks to me personally, I'll watch it and even share it with friends.
15 This doesn't mean we go out and buy the product. What it means is that we enjoy clever content, even if it's advertising.

Some advertising is harder to separate from real content. When a film or TV show character is drinking a popular brand of cola or wearing stylish sneakers with a logo, they call this 'product placement'. Here's a tip: when you see or hear about a brand or product on social media or anywhere online, it's probably
20 sponsored. The vloggers we know and love are often sponsored, too, but they're a special case. Sure, we know that brands pay them a ton of money to influence our buying choices, but we still watch and listen to them. Maybe because we feel close to them and trust that they wouldn't sell a product they didn't believe in. Also, most are open about it – they'll say, 'I'm getting paid to do this'. It's casual
25 and personalized, and that makes it more authentic. The best vloggers don't really want to sell us anything. It's the advertisers who want our money.
Take my advertising mini-survey and leave a comment!

🔊 **Words and phrases**

banner ad	an advert that is placed on a webpage and that links to a website	**pop-up ad**	an online advert that suddenly appears in a window on your screen
brand	a type of product that is made by a particular company	**savvy**	(*infml.*) having practical knowledge or understanding about sth.
to get blasted with	to get hit with, bombarded with	**sponsored**	paid by a company for advertising reasons

2 The thing about ads

a Explain what advertisers need to do to get teenagers' attention. Do you agree with her?

b Think of other ways that advertisers try to influence you online. Make a list. Compare and combine your lists in class to make a single list.

c Write a short comment (100 words) to post under May's blog.

3 Let me emphasize

a Look at these examples from May's blog and complete the explanations in the grammar box.

*I **did** think about advertising, but I decided …*
*This doesn't mean we buy the product. **What** it means **is** that we enjoy clever content.*
*It's the advertisers **who** want our money.*

> • We use a form of when we want to emphasize a point we make.
> • We can start a sentence with or ___ to emphasize the subject or object.

b In a former draft of her blog post, May wanted to emphasize the underlined information. Rewrite the sentences using the words in brackets.

<u>Those ads blocking the content</u> are really annoying. (*What …*)
***What** are really annoying **are** those ads blocking the content.*

1 <u>All the paid content I saw on other sites</u> made me go ad-free. (*It …*)
2 The video ads <u>get</u> into your head. (*do*)
3 Advertisers should remember that <u>teenagers like ads that feel authentic</u>. (*What …*)
4 Influencers are good at <u>introducing you to cool stuff</u>. (*What …*)
5 It <u>annoys</u> me that adverts usually load faster than content. (*does*)

4 A mini-survey

a Answer the questionnaire that May has included with her blog post.

> _ □ ☒
>
> **Advertising and you**
>
> Hey! Let's find out how our experiences of online advertising compare. Just answer this questionnaire and I'll post the results in a few weeks. Thanks! May
> **1 Where do you notice advertising the most when you're online?**
> ❑ social media feeds ❑ websites and blogs
> ❑ video sharing portals ❑ shows and films
> **2 Which of these ad types attract your attention the most? Rank them from 1 (= most) to 6 (= least).**
> ❑ banners ❑ pop-ups ❑ paid content
> ❑ video ads ❑ product placement
> ❑ influencers
> **3 How often do you click on online ads?**
> ❑ at least once a day ❑ 1 – 2 times a week
> ❑ once every two weeks ❑ seldom / never
> **4 How much influence do online ads have on what you buy?**
> ❑ none at all ❑ not very much
> ❑ some ❑ a lot

b Combine your group's results, then compare and discuss them.

5 It's your turn: Asking about ads

a Write four questions you would ask someone about the ads they know. Use the prompts to help, but you can also add your own ideas.

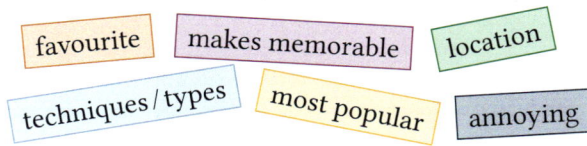

favourite   makes memorable   location
techniques / types   most popular   annoying

b Use your questions to interview a partner. Make notes about their answers.

c Get together in groups. Compare your results and draw conclusions.

Grammar and structures

Emphatic structures → G10

What it means **is** that we enjoy clever content.
They **do** look like serious articles.
It's the advertisers **who** want our money.

1 Look at the photos. What issues do they illustrate about body images? Discuss how much looks or physical appearance matter in today's society. Comment on these statements.

1 'Most teenagers do realize constant dieting is not good for your health.'

2 'I did worry about my looks a lot, but now I'm more relaxed about it.'

2 a Read the introduction to the article from a website that offers advice to teens. Then skim the rest of the text.

1 What is the article about?

2 What is the writer's purpose?

Teen Healthline

Body image: Avoiding the dangers

Teens often have an ideal body image that isn't realistic. There's so much pressure to be perfect and conform to the standards we see in the media. Many teens go on crash diets or take diet pills to be super-thin like their celebrity idols. Boys are increasingly using supplements to help them bulk up and look like their superheroes. But extreme
5 dieting and fitness supplements are bad for your health. Here are some tips on how to stay in shape AND healthy.

Dieting: Don't overdo it!

It's good to want to stay at a weight that's normal for your height – but it's dangerous to overdo it and go to drastic extremes trying to get super-model thin. The best way to achieve and maintain a healthy weight is to do regular exercise and follow a healthy eating plan.
10 Experts recommend that teens do 60 minutes of physical activity every day, such as jogging, swimming or dancing. Your diet should include lean meats, fruit, vegetables, whole grains and healthy fats. Avoid junk foods and fast food – they are full of bad fat and salt. Soda drinks contain large amounts of sugar and caffeine, so cut them out, too.

Body-building: It's not worth the risk!

15 It's good to do regular exercise, and strength training is an important part of physical fitness, but it can be dangerous if you don't practise it correctly or do too much. If you're under 16, your body is still developing. If you lift too much weight or lift weights incorrectly, you could injure yourself. Instead, build up your strength and fitness safely by following these simple tips. Check out your local gym and sign up for a strength training
20 class to learn the correct techniques. Steer clear of common fitness supplements, including steroids. Using steroids can raise your risk of heart disease or liver damage. Eat a well-balanced diet. Don't try to count your calories, load up on protein, or cut out carbohydrates – this can slow down your growth and development.

b Read the article again carefully and make notes, using your own words. Then do the tasks.

1 Describe what the best ways are to achieve and maintain a healthy weight.

2 Explain the dangers of strength training for teenagers.

3 Outline how teenagers can develop their physical fitness safely.

🔊 32 Words and phrases

lean meat meat with very little fat on it   **to steer clear of** to avoid
steroids a drug that increases your muscles, often taken illegally in sports

c Find words in the text to match these definitions.

1 to become bigger in size or weight
2 to do too much of something so it becomes dangerous
3 to increase something slowly
4 to eat a lot of
5 to stop eating something
6 to make something happen at a slower speed
7 to avoid something

3 At the end of the article there is a comment section. Add *do/did* to each comment to make it more emphatic. You might need to change the verb form.

1 I knew I shouldn't take steroids, but I took them anyway.
2 I exercise regularly, but not as much as some of my friends.
3 My sister took diet pills, but she doesn't now.
4 I think that adverts that play on the idea of a perfect body image should be banned.
5 I worry about my weight, but there's nothing I can really do about it!

4 a David wants to convince his friends to become vegetarians. Listen to him giving a talk to his class about what would happen if everyone stopped eating meat. List five results he describes.

b Listen again and note down the facts and figures David gives to support his argument.

1 There are ▆▆ vegetarians in the UK and nearly ▆▆ vegans.
2 Livestock produce over ▆▆ per cent of all greenhouse gas emissions.
3 Around ▆▆ per cent of deforestation in the Amazon is due to cattle ranching.
4 The proportion of farm animals raised on factory farms is ▆▆ in ▆▆.
5 Around ▆▆ per cent of the antibiotics used in the US are given to farm animals. This increases the risk of antibiotic resistance.
6 Meat-eaters are more likely to get diseases such as ▆▆, diabetes and heart disease.

c Do a survey of friends and family. Have any of them cut down on meat, become vegetarian or vegan? Ask them for their reasons why or why not.

5 Read the newspaper article and do the tasks.

While people do know that their weight is important, many people in the UK still don't take their own weight seriously. Obesity is a growing problem in the UK with one in four
5 adults now classed as obese – that is, very overweight.
Of course, obesity is not just about what you eat or how much you eat. One of the other contributing factors is the amount of physical
10 activity you do. Unfortunately, the majority of people in the UK don't do enough exercise. It is recommended that over a week an adult should be physically active for two and a half hours and children for at least one hour every day.
15 In the past thirty years, the problem has got far worse with the number of obese people increasing threefold. One of the biggest issues connected to obesity are the increase in deaths. While people don't die directly from being
20 overweight, they are more likely to get heart attacks, diabetes and high blood pressure.
So, what can you do to avoid becoming one of the statistics? Exercise, eat well and remember being healthy will make you happy.

1 Explain what the article is about.
2 Describe the two main causes of the problem.
3 Explain why it is such an issue.
4 Carry out some research to find out about the situation in Germany.

6 Are the underlined words and phrases correct or wrong? Correct the wrong ones.

D. Hey Bex, you do know[1] that eating a hot dog is bad for you, do you[2]? You didn't used to[3] eat fast food. Read this article about obesity.
B. I'm not fat.
D. I didn't say you were, but you eat too many junk foods[4]. Did you know that 25 per cent of the population in UK[5] is obese?
B. That's a lot. Does it say[6] why?
D. In a way. One reason is that people don't exercise too much[7]. The article also says the problem has got badder[8] and that there are now three times as much[9] obese people then[10] thirty years ago.
B. Do you want my hot dog?
D. Bex!

1 **a** You are going to read a short interview with a teenage girl about mental health. Write down six words you think will be in the text.

b Read the text and check your ideas.

A teen's perspective on mental health

Amelia Cohen is a student at Regent's Park High School in London. She spoke with us about mental health.

1

When I was in year 9 a friend of mine shared the news
5 that another close friend was feeling very low. I knew what depression was at the time, but I wasn't familiar with how best to deal with the situation. There was a teacher at school who a few of us were close to, so we directed our friend to speak with that teacher and a school counsellor. The experience of understanding my friend's thought processes
10 and going through that experience opened my eyes and made me consider questions like:
What are the best approaches to having a conversation with the least amount of stigma possible? What is the best approach to make sure people are well informed and have a way to start a conversation about the subject?

2

15 I'm involved with an organization called *YoungMinds*. I became a peer leader during year 10 and that motivated me to get more involved. I also learned more about the different projects they organize. I took part in a virtual run earlier this year and learned how important exercise is for someone's mental health. I've also been to a conference run by the organization.

3

20 I'm a bit biased, but I enjoyed the Mental Health panel that I was part of. The questions the audience asked were intriguing. There was one question from a lady who runs a youth mental health organization. She asked:
Is there anything we can do to support you?
The fact that mental health professionals in the community are ready to support us meant a lot.
25 There's only so much we can do as students to help children learn about mental health.

4

Organizations like *YoungMinds*, which focus on mental wellness, have the capacity to make a powerful impact in the community. As we work on mental health projects, it's important to think of the
30 target audience.
If changes need to be made so all cultural backgrounds have access to mental health support, then we should make these changes.

5

The best thing you can do is to get
35 involved about something you're passionate about. Don't wait for someone to tell you. For me it is youth mental health, but it can be anything. When you have a desire to get involved, then pursue your passion right away.

2 The text is an interview. Each paragraph is the answer to a question. Match the questions the interviewer asks Amelia to the paragraphs (1 – 5). There is one question you don't need.

a What should organizations working in mental health think about?
b Do you have any advice for young people on mental health challenges and wellness?
c Have you personally ever had any mental health issues?
d How did you end up as an advocate for mental wellness?
e What inspired your interest in youth mental health?
f What were the most important parts of the conference for you?

3 Find words in the text to match the definitions below.

1 Someone who is trained to listen to people and give them advice about their problems
2 A strong feeling of disapproval that most people in society have about something
3 To cause someone to do something
4 The fact of preferring a particular subject or thing
5 Very interesting because it is unusual
6 Has the ability to do a particular thing
7 Able to be reached
8 To follow someone or something to try and catch or reach it

4 Read the text again and do the tasks.

1 Describe what happened to Amelia to make her become passionate about mental health.
2 Outline the steps Amelia took to try and help her friend.
3 Describe how Amelia has become involved with helping people with mental health issues.
4 Explain why she was surprised by the question the lady on the panel asked.
5 Comment on Amelia's advice in the last paragraph.

5 Look at these comments by different people. Which ones do you agree with? Give reasons for your answers.

A Physical exercise often helps reduce mental health issues.

B The use of social media by young people often causes mental health issues.

D It's important to share and have someone to talk to. Keeping things to yourself only makes things worse.

C In the past, there were far fewer people suffering from mental health issues.

E Celebrities talking about their mental health really helps people realize that it's not something to hide, and anyone can have a problem.

PART 1

PART 2

PART 3

Preparing to shoot your film

S1 **Prepare for the shooting**

a Make a plan for your shoot. Read the information and make notes in your exercise book about your location, time of shooting and participants.

b Look at the example of a shooting schedule below. Answer the questions.

1 In what order is the film going to be shot? Why do you think this is the best order?

2 What will the filmmakers have to watch out for when filming the food buffet? Why?

3 When and where are they going to interview the kitchen manager? Why could this be?

4 Which parts of this shooting schedule would not be relevant for your shoot? Why not?

TIP

When you shoot your film, you need to have a detailed plan that includes:

● the location (where you are shooting your film, whether you need props and who is organizing these props)

● the time of day (When and how can you use natural light and, if you shoot outside your classroom, in any other location in the school, when is it the least crowded or least noisy?)

● participants (always let everyone know what your plans are)

Date	16.3 8.30 – 10.00	16.3 10.30 – 11.30	16.3 10.30 – 11.30	16.3 14.00 – 15.00
Scene	Scene 3: busy kitchen workers preparing food	Scene 1: canteen before lunch	1: canteen before lunch	2: interview with kitchen manager
Shot	Shot 4: kitchen worker from front or side — medium shot	Shot 1: canteen buffet — pan shot	2: canteen buffet — close-up	3: kitchen manager — shot medium
Location	school canteen — kitchen	school canteen — buffet area	school canteen — buffet area	school canteen — at dining table
What happens?	kitchen worker is putting food into serving pan; background kitchen sounds	buffet is ready with food selection before lunch; camera pans over buffet from left to right; no sound	camera shows hot food in serving pans; no sound	kitchen manager is sitting at table; she explains food preparation
Remember	• batteries charged? • Sound level not too high — kitchen is loud	• batteries charged? • lighting OK? • food ready? buffet full? • keep students out of picture	• lighting OK? • keep students out of picture	• batteries charged? • Canteen must be quiet — no voices, noisy plates etc. • check sound level

S2 **Plan and write your shooting schedule**

 a Review your storyboard. Discuss the following things in your group.

● Do you need to make any changes to your storyboard? Think about the order: does your plan allow continuous shooting?

● When will you shoot your film?

● Are there any conditions you need to think of, for example when a subject or a room is available?

Other thinks to check:

● batteries for your phone / camera

● any props you might need

● the furniture in the room – check if you need to move it

● necessary conditions – e.g. lighting (natural light works best!)

 b Complete your schedule.

● How should the people move?

● How are you going to move with the camera?

● What other things do you or your group members have to do when you are shooting?

 c Write a clean version and give it to every crew member.

Shooting and editing your film material

S1 **Shoot your film.** You've done all your preparation. Now it's time to shoot!

S2 **Evaluate your group's shots**

a After everyone in your group has shot their film, watch them together. Copy the planned sequence from your storyboard into the column on the left of the checklist below. Then use the checklist to help you review each film. Alternatively, review your own film. Ask yourself the following questions:

- Does the film show the planned steps?
- Is the sound clear?
- Is the light good enough?

Storyboard	Video	Sound	Light
1.			
2.			
3.			
....			

> **TIP**
>
> Before you start, check the location (props, light, space to move around with your phone or tablet). Make sure you shoot your film in one go. Remember that you won't have the opportunity to use any other footage.

b Make notes of what didn't go according to plan. Share your notes with your group and discuss what could / should have been done differently.

S3 **Edit your footage**

a You don't need expensive software to make basic edits on your film. Find advice on the internet about how to edit your film. The steps you need to take will depend on which company your phone was made by.

b Follow the instructions, edit and save your film.

S4 **Watch your documentary film**

 a Watch the edited films and agree on one that you want to share with the class.

 b Share your finished film with your class. Give feedback to each other, focus on the positives.

S5 **Reflect on the filming process**

 a Think back to all the steps and write a 'How to …' guide to help other students who want to make a similar film. Each choose a step in the process:
- finding the topic
- storyboard
- location / props / lighting / subjects
- filming
- editing

> **Useful words / expressions:**
> *Think about (how / when / why / …) …*
> *Make sure you always …*
> *Don't forget to …*
> *Be aware of …*
> *You must not / should not / should never …*
> *If … doesn't work, try …*
> *Don't panic if … Instead, …*

 b Put together the guide. Read it through and make changes if needed.

 c Share your 'How to ….' guide with the others.

1 Before they visited London, Tariq did some research. Complete the sentences with the correct words from the box. There are two words you don't need.

> architecture ■ attraction ■ commercial ■ congestion ■
> cosmopolitan ■ languages ■ lock ■ media ■ medieval ■
> modern ■ pollution ■ tourists

London is a ⬛**1** city where more than 300 ⬛**2** are spoken. In the past, ⬛**3** was a big issue in central London, but since the introduction of the ⬛**4** charge in 2003, the situation has improved.

You can see lots of different ⬛**5** in London, from old buildings like the Tower
5 of London to ⬛**6** places like the Shard. A lot of changes have taken place. Canary Wharf used to be full of ships, but now it is the ⬛**7** centre of London with lots of ⬛**8** companies.

London has always been a centre for ⬛**9**. A famous place for them to visit is Camden Market. More than 100,000 people visit it every weekend, making it
10 London's fourth-most popular ⬛**10**.

2 **a** Mary is sharing more about her grandparents who were a Pearly King and Queen. Complete what she says with *used to*, *didn't use to* or *would*. Sometimes more than one option is possible.

My grandparents ⬛**1** live in the same street as I do now, but it's changed a lot. My grandfather ⬛**2** own a small shop which sold everything you could imagine from tinned food to clothes pegs to
5 hang out your washing. He ⬛**3** make much money, but he said the shop was the best thing in his life after his family.

Everyone on our street ⬛**4** know each other and on special occasions they ⬛**5** hold a street party.
10 They ⬛**6** close the street to traffic and every family ⬛**7** cook a dish to share. The residents ⬛**8** bring out chairs and tables but they ⬛**9** decorate the street. The only time they did that was for the Queen's Coronation in 1953 and her
15 Silver Jubilee 25 years later. Now I don't even know my neighbours, let alone everyone who lives on the street. I think people ⬛**10** be a lot friendlier than they are now, but that's just my opinion.

b Read what Mary said again. Complete the tasks.

1 Think of reasons why the shop was so important to Mary's grandfather.
2 Describe what street parties used to be like.
3 Explain why Mary thinks people were friendlier in the past.
4 Speculate about what might have changed in the street and why.

3 Deepak and his mum are having a conversation. Complete it with modal verbs and the correct form of the verbs in bracket.

Mrs R. Deepak. Can you come here for a minute?

Deepak Sorry, Mum. I ⬛**1** go. I arranged ⬛**2** (*meet*) David and Bex.

Mrs R. You really ⬛**3** try ⬛**4** (*spend*) more time at home.

Deepak I know, but they asked me ⬛**5** (*help*) them with a project for school.

Mrs R. Why don't you try ⬛**6** (*tell*) them you're busy.

Deepak Mum! I'm not going to lie to them. Anyway, I like ⬛**7** (*spend*) time with them.

Mrs R. I know you do. Is the project about London?

Deepak Yes, it is. For some reason they think I ⬛**8** help them, but I'm not sure.

Mrs R. Okay, don't forget ⬛**9** (*be*) home by seven.

Deepak Seven? Why?

Mrs R. Your aunt promised ⬛**10** (*call*) then.

Deepak Okay, I really enjoy ⬛**11** (*talk*) to her. So, ⬛**12** I go?

Mrs R. Of course.

Deepak Bye. See you later.

PART 1

PART 2

PART 3

→ Workbook, pages 54-56   **MORE PRACTICE**

4   Read the text about advertising and consumerism. Decide whether the underlined expressions are correct or wrong. Correct the wrong ones.

Advertising would[1] be very different in the past, before social media and the internet. While advertise[2] on TV and radio still happens, it is a lot less important than it used to[3] be. In the US, which is the biggest market for advertisers, the amount of money being spent[4] on TV adverts has been steadily declining. Today
5 it makes up just 25% of all money spent[5] on advertising and marketing. Many experts think that to spend[6] lots of money on TV advertising doesn't actually make sense any more. However, there are some events such as the football World Cup, the Olympics and the Super Bowl in the USA, where it is still worth to invest and make[7] a commercial as it will be seen by millions of people.
10 Therefore, before spend[8] money on a TV commercial, it is essential to work out if the investment will lead to increased sales.

5   Read these comments by teenagers. What are they talking about? In your group, choose one comment you all agree with or make one of your own. Present your comment to the class supporting your choice with reasons and examples.

I don't even notice them anymore.

I do hate the fact that social media sites are full of the stuff.

What's annoying is that you can't avoid them.

It's worrying just how much they influence what you do or buy.

6   **a** May posted this blog on her website. Complete it with the phrases from the box and emphatic *do* and *did*.

are relatively new ■
I listed in my last blog ■
you all praised me for ■
you recognize

b Now rewrite the underlined sentences with *It's ...* or *What ...* for emphasis.

Hi everyone!
I wanted to catch up with you after you completed in my survey. I must say the number of you who responded ▉1▉ surprise me. Let me summarize the main
5 findings for you, which ▉2▉.
You all acknowledge that the advertisers who ▉3▉ ▉4▉ all look for an opportunity for free advertising. You also point out that some adverts are so unusual that they ▉5▉ get into our heads. However, we can all agree that we want to focus on the content, not the adverts. You also share my feelings
10 that personalized ads, which ▉6▉, ▉7▉ annoy us a lot. But we do not mind product placements in films.
Finally, I am proud that there are no ads on my blog site, which ▉8▉.

1 **Secret Food Tours**

M

a Dein Bekannter Karsten organisiert die Reise einer Gruppe von Hobbyköchen nach London und ist auf folgende Webseite gestoßen. Er weiß, dass du gut Englisch sprichst und hat dir ein paar Fragen zu der Webseite in einer E-Mail gestellt. Lies den Text und mach dir Notizen zu den Antworten, damit du Karstens Fragen in einem Telefongespräch beantworten kannst.

Hallo!

Wie du weißt, wollen meine Freunde vom Kochclub und ich einen Ausflug nach London machen. Bei der Planung bin ich auf diese Webseite gestoßen. Ich bin mir nur nicht sicher, ob die *Secret Food Tours* wirklich etwas für uns sind.

5 Anscheinend werden sie von den Teilnehmern recht gut bewertet, oder? Sind die *foodie guides* die Leute, die an den Touren teilnehmen? Am liebsten würden wir typisch englisches Essen kennenlernen, wenn wir schon einmal in London sind. Was meinst du, welche Tour da am besten für uns geeignet ist?

Geht man bei dieser Tour in ein bestimmtes Restaurant und isst mehrere
10 Gänge? Meinst du, wir sollten lieber an einer traditionellen Stadtführung teilnehmen? Eigentlich wollen wir ja auch etwas über London, v. a. seine Geschichte und Sehenswürdigkeiten, erfahren. Und wo muss man eigentlich die Tickets kaufen? Ich würde mich freuen, wenn du mir hier weiterhelfen kannst.

Danke und viele Grüße
Karsten

Tour information	Foodie guides	FAQs	Book now

Secret Food Tours London

We are truly passionate about showcasing mouthwatering and irresistible secret foods from all corners of the globe. Every year, our experienced, local, foodie guides show thousands of people the best and most delicious foods a city has to offer. Each tour is fun, highly rated (over 5,000 5-star reviews), and completely unique to its destination — no two tours are the same [...].

London Bridge Tour

First, your local guide will take you to the famous Borough Market where you will soak up the atmosphere and eat an English breakfast classic – the bacon and egg bap. Our second stop brings us to what is possibly Britain's most popular dish as we try award-winning fish and chips. Next up, we
5 sample the best traditional sausage roll in town. Your guide will give you 10 – 20 minutes to look around and give you a chance to buy gifts or sample some of the many delicious free tasters. He or she will explain the history of the market and the surrounding area, including Sir Francis Drake's Golden Hind, the Shard and Southwark Cathedral.
10 The tour will continue with a visit to a historic pub, where you'll try a selection of British cheeses, served with fruit, crackers and chutney. Moving on to the River Thames, you'll see the world-famous London and Tower Bridges, the Battleship HMS Belfast and the iconic London skyline.
Finally, we'll sit down for a classic English dessert, served with a pot of refreshing breakfast tea. Oh, and of course there's our delicious Secret Dish, too!

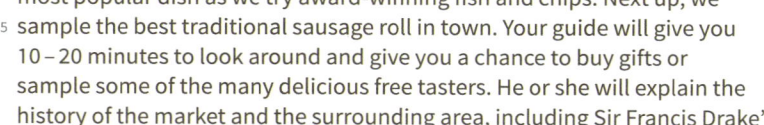

Indian Food Tour

By booking our award-winning Secret Indian Food Tour, discover and taste exciting curries, flavoursome dishes and learn about spices and Indian cuisine. This tour caters for all tastes and people, whether you are a seasoned curry fan and like them hot, or new to this type of food and need
5 an introduction to the varied tastes. Either way, we will show you a large variety of dishes from the Indian subcontinent, give you samples of authentic Indian sweets and savouries, inform you of the multitude of spices that make up Indian cooking, and take you off the beaten track for a truly authentic experience. There's a lot of food, so come hungry! [...]

| Tour information | Foodie guides | FAQs | Book now |

FAQs

How do I book?

That is very easy! Go to our 'Book Now' page, where we detail our tours. Select your tour and the time you prefer and book it! Are you looking for something special? Are you organizing an event? Just email us and we will do our best to arrange something that suits you. After your booking is made, we will send you an automatic email confirmation. If
5 you have any questions before the booking, please feel free to contact us via email or phone us.

Can I do private bookings?

Our delicious Secret Food Tours are perfect for any private event or celebration. Every experience caters to families, groups of friends, corporate events, corporate reward or incentive programmes, holiday celebrations, charity fundraisers, and more. For more information on our corporate packages please contact us.*

10 What if it rains or I change my plans?

Unfortunately, the weather is unpredictable in London. We do not issue refunds as per our terms and conditions. We also inform you that we never cancel a booking even if we have only 2 people! However we do reserve the right to cancel the tour if we feel the weather is extreme, and we cannot run the tour due to this. For more info see our terms and conditions.

* text adapted

b Karsten hat dir geschrieben und bittet dich noch einmal um Hilfe. Schreibe eine kurze E-Mail an die Veranstalter und stelle Karstens Fragen.

Hallo!

Das hört sich alles gut an! Danke für deine Hilfe!
Auf der Webseite befindet sich eine Kontaktadresse. Würdest du da bitte hinschreiben und noch Folgendes für mich klären?

- Gibt es Führungen auf Deutsch? Wenn wir uns zu zehnt anmelden, bekommen wir dann einen Gruppenrabatt?
- Dürfen eigentlich Hunde in englische Pubs und Restaurants? Einer unserer Kochfreunde hat nämlich eine Hundehaarallergie. Vielleicht kann man dies bei der Auswahl der Lokalitäten berücksichtigen.
- Was ist, wenn man kurzfristig erkrankt? Das Ticket muss man ja im Voraus kaufen. Kriegt man dann gegebenenfalls sein Geld zurück?
- Bekommt man die zu den Gerichten passenden Kochrezepte? Das fänden wir nämlich super! Dann könnten wir das, was uns geschmeckt hat, bei unserem nächsten Kochtreff nachkochen.

Danke!
Karsten

Ready for Workshop 3?

1 **a** Bex wrote a quiz about London. See if you can do it.

1 Nearly nine million people live in …
- **A** the city of London
- **B** the UK
- **C** Greater London

2 Big Ben is the name of …
- **A** the bell
- **B** the clock
- **C** the tower

3 There is a famous market in …
- **A** Canary Wharf
- **B** Notting Hill
- **C** Camden Town

4 Every day the Tube is used by …
- **A** nine thousand people
- **B** around a hundred thousand people
- **C** about two million people

London Quiz

5 The Globe is …
- **A** a royal palace
- **B** a theatre
- **C** a museum

6 Near to the Houses of Parliament, there is a statue of …
- **A** William Shakespeare
- **B** a Pearly King and Queen
- **C** Winston Churchill

b Choose a city in Germany. Carry out some research and write a quiz for another pair.

c Give your quiz to another pair. Do the quiz they give you and then check the answers together.

2 **a** After visiting London with his school, Deepak started a blog. Read one of his entries. Complete it with the correct form of the verbs from the box.

G5

build ■ call ■ enjoy ■ find (2x) ■
not even know ■ not realize ■ return ■
see ■ speak

b Read Deepak's blog again and find words to match the definitions below.

1 Very surprised
2 A place where people come to live
3 A very old story that is not always true
4 The earliest form of something
5 Something that belongs to a particular culture from the past, which is particularly important (often historically)

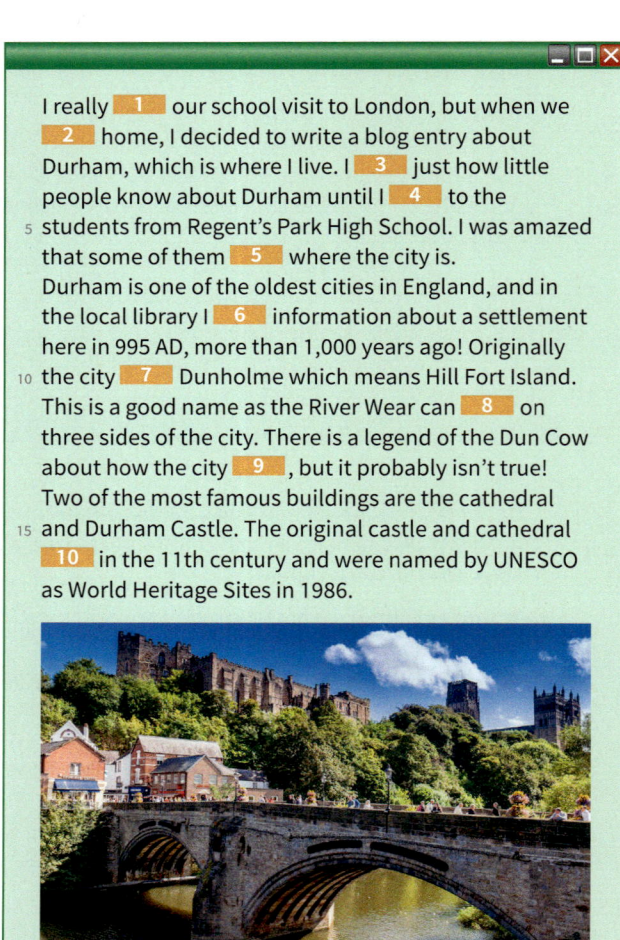

I really ⬚1⬚ our school visit to London, but when we ⬚2⬚ home, I decided to write a blog entry about Durham, which is where I live. I ⬚3⬚ just how little people know about Durham until I ⬚4⬚ to the
5 students from Regent's Park High School. I was amazed that some of them ⬚5⬚ where the city is.
Durham is one of the oldest cities in England, and in the local library I ⬚6⬚ information about a settlement here in 995 AD, more than 1,000 years ago! Originally
10 the city ⬚7⬚ Dunholme which means Hill Fort Island. This is a good name as the River Wear can ⬚8⬚ on three sides of the city. There is a legend of the Dun Cow about how the city ⬚9⬚, but it probably isn't true! Two of the most famous buildings are the cathedral
15 and Durham Castle. The original castle and cathedral ⬚10⬚ in the 11th century and were named by UNESCO as World Heritage Sites in 1986.

3 Listen to the conversation between David and Deepak and complete the tasks.

34

1 Explain why Deepak is surprised.
2 List some of the things David used to eat.
3 Describe why David made the decision to change what he ate.
4 Explain why David doesn't find it difficult to plan meals.
5 Comment on David's decision.

4 A German boy, Max, wrote a comment on his shopping habits on an English blog. Look at the <u>underlined</u> words and expressions and decide whether they are correct or wrong. Correct the wrong ones.

G1
G7
G8
G10

> Although I'm only fifteen, I <u>have shopped</u>[1] for a few years now. I don't spend all my pocket money, but <u>I do like</u>[2] to buy things for myself. I always <u>would</u>[3] go to the local shopping mall <u>buying</u>[4] things, but in the last year I've switched to shopping online. <u>Online shopping</u>[5] is so much easier than in stores as I have a lot more time to compare prices and products. One thing <u>I do find</u>[6] annoying are the pop-up ads that often appear on my screen. I can honestly say that <u>I've never been tempted</u>[7] by any of these ads, so I'm not sure how effective they are. My parents <u>used to</u>[8] worry about me <u>to buy</u>[9] things from the internet, but now they say that because I'm sensible they trust me and know I won't <u>waste</u>[10] my money on things I don't want or need.

5 **a** Use the information from this graphic to write a paragraph of between 100 and 150 words about teenagers' spending habits in the UK.

b Carry out some research to find out what the situation is like in Germany and write a short text comparing the situation in the UK with that in Germany.

6 **a** Choose one of the topics from the list below and prepare a short talk on why this aspect is important for teenagers today.

- cultural places
- diet
- social media
- advertising
- mental health

b Take turns to give your presentation.

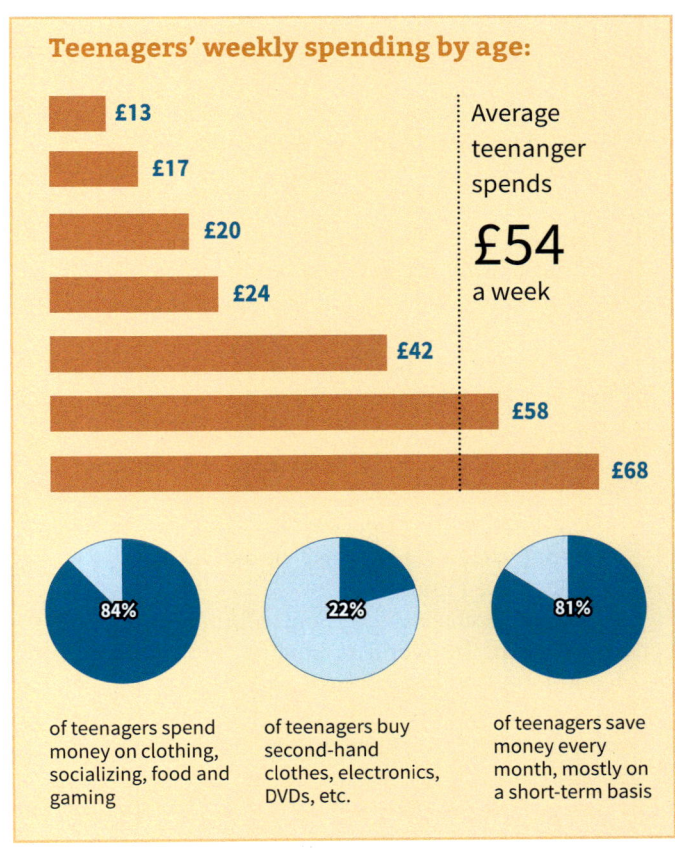

Teenagers' weekly spending by age:

£13
£17
£20
£24
£42
£58
£68

Average teenanger spends
£54
a week

84% of teenagers spend money on clothing, socializing, food and gaming

22% of teenagers buy second-hand clothes, electronics, DVDs, etc.

81% of teenagers save money every month, mostly on a short-term basis

The soup kitchen

When 16-year-old Paul takes on a part-time job in a soup kitchen, he learns that there's more to making and serving soup than just filling people's bellies. This is an excerpt from Walter Dean Myers's novel *All the Right Stuff*.

I was late for my first day at the soup kitchen because I couldn't find the place. It wasn't marked SOUP KITCHEN or anything like that. It was on the basement floor of a brownstone on 144th Street, and there was a
5 small sign over the bell that read ELIJAH JONES'S SOUP EMPORIUM[1].

I rang the bell and a small, bright-eyed man with gray hair answered.

'My name is Paul Dupree,' I said. 'And I'm supposed
10 to be working here four days a week.'

'Welcome, Mr. Paul Dupree,' he said. 'I'm Elijah Jones. Please come in.'

I followed him in, through a room with six long tables set up and into a large, airy kitchen. Mr. Jones sat
15 himself down at one end of the table in the kitchen and gestured toward the other stool. I sat down.

'Hand me one of those vidalias over there, please.' He pointed in my direction, then started cutting up vegetables for the soup we were making.
20 I looked over to where he was pointing and didn't see what he was talking about. The only things sitting on the bench were some onions.

'Some what?' I asked him.

He turned toward me. 'Give me your particulars[2]
25 again?'

'Paul Dupree,' I said. 'Sixteen years old and just finished eleventh grade.'

'Did you want to add anything in there about not knowing what a vidalia was?' he asked.
30 'Not really,' I said.

'Well, a vidalia is a sweet onion,' Elijiah said. 'I guess that's what the world is coming to today,' he said, turning back to his cutting board. 'We got wars going on, we got people robbing and shooting each other, and
35 we got young people like you don't even know what a

vidalia is. Do you think this might be the end of the world creeping up[3] on us?'

'No, sir, it's more about you dealing with onions and your vegetables, Mr. Jones,' I said. 'And if it was the end of the world, I don't think your onions would help too 40 much.'

'You'll call me Elijah,' he said.

'Sorry … Elijah,' I said.

'How about the soup? Do you think the soup would save the world? You never heard of anybody doing 45 anything really bad while they were having a bowl of soup,' he said.

Elijah told me he was eighty-four. He was dark, maybe five foot six or seven, and thin but not really skinny. He stood straight as an arrow and moved 50 around his kitchen almost as if he was dancing.

'So you're saving the world with your soup?' I asked.

'I hear the smile in your voice, Mr. Dupree,' Elijah said. 'I'm not trying to save all of it, just my little corner here in Harlem. If we could get everybody to save their 55 own little piece of this planet, then eventually we'd get the whole thing in pretty good shape.'

'Yes, sir.'

I watched Elijah make the soup of the day and get some vegetables ready for the next day's soup. At 60 twelve o'clock, the first people started drifting in, and he had me serve them.

For most of the afternoon, I cleaned anything that could be cleaned. This included the stove and the table and the floors. When everything was cleaned up, Elijah 65 sat down at his cutting board and rolled an onion – okay, it was a vidalia – over to me.

'I want you to stop past the butcher's shop on your way here tomorrow and pick me up ten pounds of veal bones. Do you think you can remember that?' 70

'Ten pounds of veal bones,' I repeated.

'The best soups start with a good liquid base[4],' Elijah said. 'The bones give some body to that base. People like soup made from a good stock[5].'

'People like any soup that's free,' I said. 'You're 75 making soup and giving it away for nothing. Naturally they like it.'

'I'm not just making soup,' Elijah said. 'I'm making good soup for the senior citizens on this block. Now, don't pay more than five dollars for those bones,' Elijah 80 said. 'And don't forget them because I'm running out of stock. And take that onion with you, Mr. Dupree, so you two can get acquainted[6].' […]

From: Walter Dean Myers, *All the Right Stuff*. New York: HarperCollins, 2012; pp. 13 – 17.

[1] **emporium** Laden – [2] **particulars** Personalien – [3] **to creep up** hinaufschleichen – [4] **base** Suppenfond – [5] **stock** Brühe – [6] **to get acquainted** sich kennenlernen

London has been an important city for musicians since the 18th century and many songwriters and bands have sung about its people, sights and sounds. Here are two songs about the city, one by the British rock band The Kinks and one by folk singer Reg Meuross.

The Kinks, 'Waterloo sunset' (1967) 35))

Dirty old river, must you keep rolling
Flowing into the night?
People so busy, make me feel dizzy
Taxi light shines so bright
5 But I don't need no friends
As long as I gaze[1] on
Waterloo sunset
I am in paradise

Every day I look at the world from my window
10 But chilly, chilly is the evening time
Waterloo sunset's fine

Terry meets Julie
Waterloo station
Every Friday night
15 But I am so lazy, don't want to wander
I stay at home at night
But I don't feel afraid
As long as I gaze on
Waterloo sunset
20 I am in paradise

Every day I look at the world from my window
But chilly, chilly is the evening time
Waterloo sunset's fine

Millions of people swarming[2] like flies 'round
25 Waterloo underground
But Terry and Julie cross over the river
Where they feel safe and sound[3]
And they don't need no friends
As long as they gaze on
30 Waterloo Sunset
They are in paradise
Waterloo sunset's fine
Waterloo sunset's fine

Text: Davies, Raymond Douglas,
© Carlin Music Corp. Musikverlag
Intersong GmbH, Hamburg

Reg Meuross, 'My name is London town' (2013) 36))

I've been struck[4] by the wind coming in from the east
That strips the grey river and stretches[5] your skin
I've been choked[6] by the engine and choked by the beast
Breathing fire and pollution and pleasure and sin

5 I'm the cry of the gulls[7] from St Katharine's Dock
I'm the cry of the Smithfield fishmonger[8] at dawn
I'm the sharp-suited[9] broker[10] who steals like a fox
To the stock exchange[11] floor to sell coffee and corn

My name is London Town
10 I'm your vision going up,
I'm your nightmare[12] coming down
I'm the Westminster fool, I'm the Pentonville clown
My name is London Town

I'm the bundle of rags[13] in the Oxford Street doorway
15 Matted[14] and ratted[15] and shivering with cold
I'm the homecoming sunset that lights up the westway
I'm the Union Flag, I'm the red, green and gold

My name is London Town
I'm your vision going up, I'm your nightmare coming down
20 I'm the Westminster fool, I'm the Pentonville clown
My name is London Town

I'm the dome of St Paul's, I'm the Regent's Park mosque[16]
I'm the Temple, the Arsenal and White Hart Lane
I'm the bomb in Victoria, the fire at Kings Cross
25 I'm the nine o'clock dole[17] queue and the ten o'clock train

My name is London Town
I'm your vision going up,
I'm your nightmare coming down
I'm the Westminster fool, I'm the Pentonville clown
30 My name is London Town

I'm the immigrant town, the city of night
Of carousel dreams of beauty and pain
My streets paved[18] with gold from the bold highway meters
Dick Whittington's ghost in a no turning lane

35 My name is London Town
I'm your vision going up,
I'm your nightmare coming down
I'm the Whitechapel murderer[19] making his rounds
My name is London Town
40 My name is London Town

Text: Meuross, Reginald Lawrence,
© 2013 BMG Rights Management GmbH, Berlin

---

[1] **to gaze** betrachten – [2] **to swarm** schwärmen, wuseln – [3] **safe and sound** wohlbehalten, gesund und munter – [4] **struck** to strike (stroke, struck) = treffen, stoßen – [5] **to stretch** strecken – [6] **to choke sb.** jmd. erwürgen – [7] **gull** Möwe – [8] **fishmonger** Fischhändler – [9] **sharp-suited** gut gekleidet – [10] **broker** Börsenmakler – [11] **stock exchange** Aktienbörse – [12] **nightmare** Albtraum – [13] **rags** Lumpen, Klamotten – [14] **matted** verfilzt – [15] **ratted** (*infml.*) betrunken – [16] **mosque** Moschee – [17] **dole** Arbeitslosengeld – [18] **paved** gepflastert – [19] **murderer** Mörder

TWO

What *is* the point of small children?
I understand (sort of) the point of the larger kind. For example: Solstice and Cudweed. I forget exactly how old they are now, but for some time I have had to
5 admit that they are actually quite fun. You can do things with them. For example, you can play games, like the game we play where they give me a rotten pear and then I fly high up into the air with the pear in my claws, and then drop it on whoever they point
10 at. I don't often hit anyone, but it's fun trying, and when I do, Cudweed and Solstice fall over from laughing too much. That's sweet.
And sometimes, large children, such as Solstice and Cudweed, can even be *useful*, which is a really
15 remarkable thing. For example, they sometimes clean my cage out (not that I ever spend much time in there – I don't like cages, and I only go in there when I am sulking, and on Open Sunday). And when we go on holiday, they carry my little suitcase. What does a
20 raven take on holiday, you ask? You'd be surprised!
Sunglasses, fancy¹ shirts, a book to read … In fact, anything *you* would take on holiday, with the
25 exception of sun cream. Ravens don't need sun cream.
Anyway, all this is
30 beside the point. The point is that I have never really understood the point of small children, and why adults seem to be so intent² on making new ones. So when the twins went missing³, I really didn't see what all the fuss was
35 about.
First of all, everyone ran all around the castle (which takes a really long time) looking for Fizz and Buzz. And everyone was really upset, especially Minty, who kept bursting into tears. I even think Valevine
40 was a bit upset too, because his eyebrows kept twitching and he said 'what, what?' about a hundred times every hour.

Because I know Fizz and Buzz well, I kept thinking that it was entirely possible that they were just having
45 a nap somewhere, probably inside a cannon. Or that they were hiding from us on purpose. But by dinnertime, even I had to admit it looked like they really were missing, because the twins do not miss dinner. Ever. That's one smart thing about them, at
50 least. As I said before, there is a way that big children become adults, and it is the same way that small children become big children. What you do is that you

give them food, and when you have done this for long enough, you will one day discover that they are big.
55 And the twins had really grown. They were no longer babies, only able to crawl about⁴ on hands and knees. These days they could walk; and even run (sort of), and I liked them even less since then, because they could chase me and try to pull my tail feathers out
60 much more easily than when they could only crawl. That now meant there were *three* creatures trying to pull my tail feathers; the twins, and Cudweed's awful pet monkey, Fellah. Although Fellah wasn't around just then; he'd been sent away to monkey training
65 school. This is just like those places where they get dogs to behave better, only for monkeys. I don't know why they bothered⁵, it was the fifth time he'd been sent there, it clearly wasn't working.

---

¹ **fancy** ausgefallen; originell – ² **to be intent on** auf etwas bedacht sein – ³ **to go missing** verschwinden – ⁴ **to crawl about** herumkrabbeln – ⁵ **to bother** sich bemühen

Anyway, there was a big argument about what to do
next.
Valevine thought we should just keep looking, but
Minty said we should call the police. Cudweed
thought that was a very good idea (although mainly, I
think, because he thought it would be exciting if a
police car came to the castle). Solstice came over to
me and asked if I could organize a search party[6] of
ravens, crows and possibly other very much less
intelligent birds (which is to say, all of them).
I said, 'Kronk', which meant 'well, I could do, but
maybe I could have dinner first?' because everyone
seemed to have forgotten all about eating. Everyone
ignored me.
There was even an argument about whether the
twins really were missing, and not just playing a
trick on us all[7]. But then everything changed.
Everything changed because Cudweed, who had
been searching for the twins in the kitchen came
back holding a letter. He also seemed to be chewing,
which made me suspicious about what he was really
doing in the kitchen.

'I was just walking back past through the hall, and I
saw this had been put under the front door,' he said,
waving the letter.
'What, what?' said Valevine, and Minty sighed.
She took the letter from her son and opened it.
Then she screamed, and then she fell backwards on
the floor.

Solstice grabbed the letter from her hand.
'It's a ransom note[8]!' she said. 'The twins have been
kidnapped! The kidnappers want a large amount of
money, and they say Edgar has to bring it to them,
alone, or we'll never see Fizz and Buzz ever again.'
Minty opened her eyes, sat up. Then she remembered
what had happened and fainted again.
Valevine's eyebrows rose up on his forehead as far as
I had ever seen them go.
'You say 'kidnappers',' he said to Solstice. 'What
makes you think there is more than one?'
Minty opened her eyes again, and sat up again.
'Do you think anyone could handle the twins on
their own?' she said.
'Good point,' said Valevine, and everyone nodded
thoughtfully.
Then Solstice said, 'Now we really have to call the
police!'
'Yes, you're right!'
Even Valevine agreed now, and went away to phone
the police, muttering[9] as he did, 'Scoundrels[10]!
Wicked villains[11]! Criminals!'
'Oh, what are we going to do?' cried Minty, and
Cudweed tried to comfort[12] her.
'Don't worry, Mother,' he said. 'The police will know
what to do. They *always* know what to do on TV.'
'Whoever the kidnappers are,' said Solstice, 'they
must have taken Fizz and Buzz during the time the
castle was open. Or maybe they were snatched[13] in
the gardens! It must have been some of the visitors
who did it!'
'Yes, you're right,' agreed Cudweed. 'If only we had
security cameras!'
'You know we couldn't afford them,' said Minty. 'And
now look what's happened! Oh! My poor little twins!
Will I ever see them again?'
Solstice said, 'Of course we will!'
And I said, 'Rork', which meant, 'are we really sure it
wouldn't be okay to leave them with the
kidnappers?'
But everyone ignored me.
Then Cudweed said, 'I'm going to search in the
kitchen again. Just in case.'
Bless him, he always eats a lot when he's worried.

---

[6] **search party** Suchtrupp – [7] **to play a trick on sb.** jmd. einen Streich spielen – [8] **ransom note** Erpresserbrief – [9] **to mutter** murmeln – [10] **scoundrel**
Schurke – [11] **villain** Bösewicht – [12] **to comfort** trösten – [13] **to snatch** schnappen

The USA, politics and social issues

A

There are five regions in the USA. Look at the map and the photos around it. Then read what each person says about their region. Match the photos (A–E) with the regions.

 What else do you know about the different regions? Choose one region and form a group for each one. Copy and do some internet research for the following:

Region: _____	
cities	???
famous landmarks / tourist attractions	???
foods	???
sports teams	???
well-known people	???
national parks	???

Hi, I'm Jermaine. I'm from Nashville, Tennessee. They call this place Music City. Music is a big part of life in this region. Country, Blues, Jazz and Rock & Roll music all started here. What else makes this region special? The warm, wet weather from the Atlantic Ocean and the Gulf of Mexico are good for growing cotton and tobacco. Also, the Florida beaches are great all year round.

Read what the teenagers say about politics.

I always try to stay informed about what goes on in the world. I think it's important.

Jackie

Teens want to be heard, and there are many political issues that teens are interested in. They want their opinions to be considered.

Luis

As a teenager, I don't really think about how the economy is doing or about healthcare because I'm not in charge of my own money or health insurance.

Jermaine

If there's no voice speaking for us in Congress or in the mayor's office, then why should we teenagers pay attention to politics?

Emily

Think: Whose opinion do you agree with most? Write down your reasons. If you don't agree with any, write your own comment.

 Pair: Discuss your choice / opinion with a partner. Give reasons and explanations.

 Share: Share your opinion with other students. Listen to how they feel about politics. Are their views similar or different to yours? Which opinion is shared by most of you?

I think people of my age often consider politics to be confusing, boring, or both.

Eric

Hey there! I'm Emily from San Francisco. I love the outdoors, and my region has lots of it! Washington has rainforests, Nevada has hot deserts, and Colorado has snowy mountains. California has all three of these – and sunny beaches, too. Earthquakes and forest fires are a real danger here, but you can chase your dreams in Las Vegas, Hollywood and Silicon Valley.

B

USA REGIONS

WEST

MIDWEST

NORTH EAST

SOUTHWEST

SOUTH EAST

C

My name is Luis. I live near Tucson, Arizona. It's very hot and dry here, but I don't mind. There's a desert climate so most people live in bigger cities like Phoenix in Arizona, Albuquerque in New Mexico, or Houston in Texas. I love the natural beauty of my region and the awesome landscapes like the Grand Canyon.

My name's Eric. Cedar Rapids, Iowa is my hometown. People call this part of the country 'America's Heartland'. It's a huge region with endless farmland. If you drive east from here, you will get to the Mississippi River. Further east and to the north of here are the Great Lakes. I've been to Lake Michigan and it's massive! Chicago, Illinois and Detroit, Michigan are the two main cities in the region.

E

D

Hi, I'm Jackie. My hometown is New York City. It's big and loud – but it's just one of several big urban areas between Boston and Washington, D.C. They say that more people live in this region than in any other part of the USA, but it's also the smallest region in size! It was part of the original 13 British colonies in the USA.

CULTURE CORNER

There are 50 states in the US. Each state has its own capital city, for example Austin is the capital city of the state of Texas, and Houston is a big city in that state. According to their geographical locations, the states are grouped into five regions.

A school trip to Washington D.C.

1* A capital project

🔊 39

a The students in Rochester are going on a school trip soon. Check the map at the back of your book and find Washington D.C. Listen to the conversation and complete the tasks.

1 Describe the purpose of the conversation.
2 Explain why Kelly knows so much about Washington D.C.
3 Explain why you think Kelly says 'Typical!'.
4 Outline what Mrs Golding wants the students to do and why.

b Read the sentences from the conversation. Then complete the rules in the box.

*The football team **are called** the Nationals …*
*Do you know when it **was built**?*

> **The passive (form)***
> In the simple present, we form the passive with ⬛ **1** and the past participle.
> In the simple past, we use ⬛ **2** or *were*.

2* Chris calls Mitch

🔊 40

a Listen and explain why Chris calls Mitch. Then say who is doing what.

1 Kelly   2 Mitch   3 Ava   4 Chris

🔊 40

b Chris tells Ava what he's talked about with Mitch. Listen again, then report Chris's and Mitch's conversation.

A. Hi Chris! Have you managed to talk to Mitch?
C. Hi Ava – yes, I have. I phoned him and asked him whether ⬛ **1** and why ⬛ **2** . He said ⬛ **3** . I also asked him ⬛ **4** and he told me ⬛ **5** . Then I asked if ⬛ **6** . He said ⬛ **7** and promised ⬛ **8** .

> **Reported speech***
> • If the reporting verb or expression is in the past, the tense in the reported part of part of the sentence moves one step back in the past.
>   *'Mrs Golding wants us to do some research.' He said that Mrs Golding wanted them to do some research.*
> • For *yes/no* questions, we use *if* or *whether* and we don't change the word order.
>   *She asked if I knew when Washington D.C. was built.*
> • For questions with a *wh*-question word, the subject and the verb are not inverted.
> • For orders, requests and offers, we use the infinitive form of the main verb with *to*.
>   *Ava asked Mrs Golding to repeat her question.*

3* The White House

a Mitch shares his research about the White House with the other students. Read what he found out on page 87 and match the words and expressions (1–5) with the definitions (a–e).

1 originally   2 federal
3 to lay something   4 a request
5 first-come first-served

a a form of governmental system in which several states form a unity but remain independent in internal affairs
b at first, in the beginning
c deal with people in the order they arrive
d put something down
e the act of asking for something

🔊 38

Words and phrases

basis	a particular method or system used for organizing something
laid	put in a position for a particular purpose
numerically	using numbers

to **permit**	to allow something to happen
public	relating to people in general and not a particular group

When George Washington became president in 1789, he decided to build a new capital city. Originally, the new city was called Federal City and in 1800 it became the home of the new government
5 of the USA. The government building – the Capitol Building – was built on one hill at one end of the city and the home of the president on another hill at the other end of the city.

The first stone for the White House was laid in
10 October 1792, and it took another eight years to complete. By the time it was finished, George Washington had died. He is the only president who never lived in the White House.

In 1805, the White House was opened for public
15 tours by President Thomas Jefferson. Today, the White House is visited by 100,000 people every month. People who want to visit the White House are asked to send a request to their Member of Congress. The tours are organized on a first-come
20 first-served basis. A limited number of places is available, so it's important to send your request in as early as possible. Video cameras, cell phones and tablets are not permitted inside the White House.

b Read the text again and find all the examples of the passive. Complete the rules in the box.

The passive (use)*
- We use the passive when we are more interested in ▮1▮ *happened* than ▮2▮ *did something*.
- If we want to say ▮3▮ did something, we add them with by.

4* **The Washington Nationals.** Complete the article Chris found with the correct form of the verbs.

The Washington Nationals are the eighth major league baseball team to play in Washington. The team ▮1▮ (*form*) in 1969 as the Montreal Expos. In 2004, the team ▮2▮ (*relocate*) to Washington and the following year the name ▮3▮ (*change*) to the Nationals. The Washington Nationals won the World Series in 2019 when they beat the Houston Astros 4-3. The World Series ▮4▮ (*play*) every year between the American League Champions and the National League Champions. The first ever World Series ▮5▮ (*hold*) in 1903 and ▮6▮ (*win*) by the Boston Americans.

CULTURE CORNER

A capital is a city or town where the government of a country or state is. A capitol is a building in which the parliament meets.

5 **Quiz time.**
🔊 41

The students from Rochester are taking an online quiz. Guess the answers to the quiz questions. Then listen and check.

1 What is the population of Washington D.C.?
  a about half a million   **b** about a million
  c about five million

2 Who attacked the White House in 1814?
  a the French   **b** the British
  c the Canadians

3 How are the names of the streets that run from north to south in the city organized?
  a alphabetically   **b** numerically
  c There is no organization.

4 The famous cherry trees were a gift from which country?
  a France   **b** Germany   **c** Japan

5 Who was the first president to live in the White House?
  a John Adams   **b** Thomas Jefferson
  c George Washington

6 **It's your turn: Historical buildings.** Work in groups. Choose an important building in Germany. Carry out some research about its history, what it was used for in the past and what it is used for now. Then write a paragraph of about 120 words about it. Indicate what sources you used.

Grammar and structures

Passive (revision) → G5
Video cameras, cell phones and tablets **are not permitted** inside the White House.
In 1805, the White House **was opened** for public tours.

Reported speech (revision) → G6
I phoned him and asked him whether he **was** okay.
He said he **had had to** look after his mother.

PART 1

PART 2

PART 3

1 Look at the picture. What do you think Ava is doing? Why? Then listen and check your ideas.

43))

2 The park where Ava and Chris meet the next morning looks terrible. Complete the conversation.

> break ■ collect ■ hold ■ ignore ■
> leave (2x) ■ make ■ spend

A. What a mess! What happened here?
C. A concert ⬛1⬛ here last night, and the park ⬛2⬛ like this afterwards.
A. I can see that, but is all of this litter just from last night?
C. I think so. I know litter ⬛3⬛ from the bins every day.
A. But what about from the ground? Look here! A glass bottle ⬛4⬛ and just left here. It's really dangerous. And what's this?
C. Oh! People often have barbecues here. The problem is that barbecues ⬛5⬛ unattended and fires can easily start.
A. This is a disaster. We should complain …
C. You can try, but lots of complaints ⬛6⬛ after the last event and they ⬛7⬛.
A. Ignored! Why?
C. Because a lot of money ⬛8⬛ on the concerts and the local council get a lot of it.

3 Chris and Ava have left the park and are walking to school. On their way, they walk past local amenities and notice different environmental problems. Read the conversation and use the prompts to complete it.

C. Look, Ava, this is my favourite restaurant, but you can hardly see it from the back.
A. Yes, there are so many dumpsters here you can't see the building. And they're all overflowing with leftover food from last night. *lots of food | waste | every day*. That's terrible.
C. I am not surprised at all. I read recently that *254 million tons | garbage | produce | US | every year*. I thought it was an exaggeration, but now I see it must be true.
A. Look, we've reached the fruit and vegetable market. I came here yesterday with my mom. You know what's great? *these apples | grow | locally*. They are not only tasty but *they | not transport | distant places*.
C. That's a really good way to reduce our carbon footprint. We should all eat locally grown produce, especially fruit and vegetables. Did you know that *last year | declare | the year of the vegan*?
A. Yes, of course. At home we are trying to cut down on meat. I've found some really good vegan recipes on the internet, so I cook vegan dishes for the family every weekend.
C. We're almost at the school. But see how bad the traffic is! Car after car … and it's not even rush hour.
A. Why are you surprised? Let me give you another fact: *1.1 billion | car trips | take | every day | US*. We have to do a lot better if we want to save the environment.
C. I agree. There is something to be proud of though: *these solar panels | install | our school | two years ago*. And we've introduced selective garbage collection and have cut down on the use of plastic bottles.

42)) **Words and phrases**

dumpster a large container used for trash

exaggeration saying that something is better, worse, bigger, more important, etc. than it really is

leftover remaining after you have used what you need or want

to overflow to come over the top of a container because it is too full

1 Ava has to write a report for the school magazine about the school trip to Washington D.C. Which of these topics do you think she will include?

- how they got from Rochester to Washington D.C.
- where they stayed
- what food they ate
- which places they visited
- what she bought
- who they met

2 Read her report and check your ideas. Which paragraph contains information that wasn't mentioned in **1**? What is the information about?

A school trip to Washington D.C.
by Ava Garcia

On Tuesday we went on a school trip to Washington D.C., our capital city. We left at 3 o'clock in the afternoon and 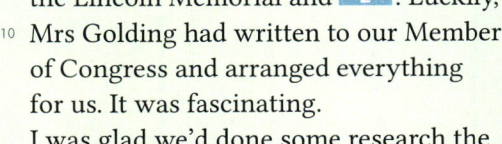. By the time we arrived I was exhausted. We stayed in a youth hostel
5 overnight. I shared a room with Kelly. In the morning we visited lots of landmarks. We saw the Capitol Building, the Washington Monument, the Lincoln Memorial and ` 2 `. Luckily,
10 Mrs Golding had written to our Member of Congress and arranged everything for us. It was fascinating.
I was glad we'd done some research the week before as it meant ` 3 `. Chris
15 complained the whole time because he wanted to visit the stadium where the Nationals play, but Mrs Golding told him it wasn't on the schedule for our trip.
In the afternoon, we were given some time on our own, but ` 4 `. We had to stay with a partner. Some of us decided to visit the parks nearby. Kelly and I went shopping as we both felt we had done
20 enough sightseeing to last us a lifetime! We bought some small souvenirs to remind us of the trip.

3 Complete the report with the extracts below. There is an extra one that you don't need.

a ... we already knew a lot about the history of the places we visited.
b ... it took almost seven hours to get from Rochester to Washington D.C. by coach.
c ... we had a list of questions we wanted to ask.
d ... we were asked not to go off alone.
e ... had a tour of the White House.

4 Write a report about a real or an imaginary school trip. Include the following aspects: *where, when, what* you did there and *why* you went. Write about 150 words.

The American political system

PART 1

PART 2

PART 3

1 **What do you know about American politics?**
The students in Rochester are going to watch a video presentation about the American political system. Look at the key words and phrases below. Match them with their definitions. There is one definition you don't need.

elections

the highest court in a country that deals with legal cases

President

the constitution

the leader of the winning party

the smaller upper assembly in the US

The House of Representatives

a change or an addition to the US Constitution

the lower house of the US Congress

The Senate

a set of political principles by which a state is governed

The Supreme Court

a national body in the US that makes the laws

Amendments

a time when people vote to choose someone for a political job

Congress

the highest political position in a country that is a republic (the elected head of a republican state)

Mount Rushmore National Memorial, South Dakota

The Supreme Court in Washington

2 **The political system.** Watch the first part of the video presentation and complete the tasks.

1 Explain what the role of the President is.
2 Outline the function of the American Constitution.
3 Describe the three best-known amendments to the American Constitution.

🔊 Words and phrases

to **allocate**	to give somebody a share of a total amount
branch	an office in a specific place that is part of a larger organization
to **cast**	to give the piece of paper with your vote on to an official
cycle	a series of events that happen in an order and are repeated; a period of time
to **enforce**	to do something to make people obey laws
to **ensure**	to make it certain that something will happen
framework	a system of ideas or rules that are used to plan or organize something

3 **The federal republic**

a Watch the second part of the video presentation and read the script. Fill in the gaps with the correct passive form of the verbs.

> There are 435 representatives in the House. The number of representatives for each state depends on its total population. States with more people get
> 5 more representatives. Representatives ☐1☐ (*elect*) every two years. They must be 25 years or older, have been a US citizen for at least seven years, and live in the state they represent.
> 10 The Senate has 100 members. Each state ☐2☐ (*represent*) by two senators. Senators ☐3☐ (*elect*) every six years. To become a senator a person must be at least 30 years old, have been a US citizen
> 15 for at least nine years, and must live in the state they represent.
> The Supreme Court is the highest court in the United States. The Judicial Branch of the government ☐4☐ (*make up*) of
> 20 judges and courts.
> Federal judges ☐5☐ (*not elect*) by the people. They ☐6☐ (*appoint*) by the President and then ☐7☐ (*confirm*) by the Senate.

b Are the statements true or false? Correct the false statements. Check with a partner.

1 Each state of the US has the same number of representatives in the Senate.
2 Only candidates who were born in the US can become senators.
3 The Supreme Court is independent from the government.
4 The President chooses the federal judges.

4 **Electing the President**

a Watch the last part of the video. With a partner, explain what the symbols of the main parties are and say why they use them.

b Complete the text about the American voting system with numbers from the video.

> Who becomes the President of the USA is not decided by the number of votes that each candidate gets. In fact, in ☐1☐ Hillary Clinton got ☐2☐ million votes, which was
> 5 ☐3☐ million more than Donald Trump, but she lost!
> The votes which are cast in each state are counted, and whoever wins the most votes in a state is declared the winner there.
> 10 Each state is allocated a number of electoral votes which is based on the population of the state. So, for example, California gets ☐4☐ electoral votes while Mississippi only gets ☐5☐.
> 15 To become President, the winning candidate needs to gain a total of ☐6☐ electoral votes. In 2016 Trump got ☐7☐ electoral votes, even though fewer people actually voted for him, but in 2020 Biden
> 20 won the electoral and the popular vote.

5 **It's your turn.** Choose one of the pictures **A** or **B** on page 90 and do some internet research. Give a short presentation about Mount Rushmore or the Supreme Court. In your presentation for **A** include the answers to these questions:

- Where does the name for the memorial come from?
- How long did it take to finish?
- What does it show? Who are the people?
- Why is there some controversy about it?

In your presentation for **B** include the answers to these questions:

- Who had the idea for this building and why?
- When was it first used?
- Where is it located?
- What can you find in the Great Hall?

Grammar and structures

Passive (revision) → G5
The number of representatives for each state **is decided** by their total population.
Representatives **are elected** every two years.

PART 1

1 Aimee received an email from Ava. Read the email and explain what Ava wants Aimee to do.

2 Aimee is talking to her dad. Listen and describe the purpose of their conversation. Say what Aimee is asked to do.

46))

Hi Aimee,

We've had an exciting time here at our school. Soon after the school trip to Washington D.C., we learned more about the American political system. There are so many things to remember – how the President is elected, how laws are made and how each of the states is represented in Congress – just to name a few. I'd like to know about your country – what is the political system in the UK like?

Bye,
Ava

PART 2

PART 3

3 **a** Aimee is writing a reply to Ava's email. She wants to tell Ava about the political system in the UK. Look at Aimee's notes about elections below and read her first paragraph. Choose one of the remaining nine topics from Aimee's notes and write a short paragraph.

Example:

> Elections: every 5 years;
> 650 constituencies (areas);
> one MP per constituency
> to parliament

Elections are usually held every five years in the UK. The country is divided into 650 constituencies. Each constituency is a geographical area. One candidate is elected as the MP that represents the constituency in parliament.

> 1 UK — constitutional monarchy
> — Head of State: King or Queen
> — no real political power

> 2 Head of UK government — Prime Minister: the leader of the party that wins the election

> 3 Political parties — candidates + programmes (manifesto) to vote for

> 4 Winning party: forms government;
> Opposition: the second biggest party

> 5 Role of PM: selects cabinet ministers who run government departments, makes action plans for the government, oversees the work of the government

> 6 UK Parliament (Westminster, London) — two parts: House of Commons + House of Lords

> 7 The House of Commons: 650 MPs (Members of Parliament) represent their constituents

> 8 House of Lords: peers — unelected, recommended by the Prime Minister, appointed by the monarch; sometimes inherited

b Work in groups. Share your paragraphs with each other. Ask questions to clarify anything you don't understand. Correct any mistakes.

> 9 Role of Parliament: making laws (House of Commons and House of Lords have to agree)

---

45)) **Words and phrases**

constituency a district that sends its own representative to parliament

peer somebody from a noble family

→ Workbook, page 68   **PRACTICE B**

4 Look at these comments. Which ones do you agree or disagree with?
Give reasons for your answers.

> *Young people today don't understand the importance of voting.*
> Bill, 56

> *I'm not interested in politics because politicians aren't interested in me.*
> Jasmine, 15

> *To get key ideas across to young people, politicians have to use social media.*
> Ellen, 42 – a local city politician

5 You are going to read an article about how social media has changed politics. Find words or phrases in the text which have these meanings.

- a period of time just before an important event
- to keep in contact or stay informed
- someone who takes messages between people who are unable or unwilling to meet
- describing something that quickly becomes very popular, particularly online
- to make something fit a particular situation or group of people
- to become or seem less connected with something

Why politics are different today

Thirty years ago, when your parents were teenagers, the relationship between the public and politicians was fairly simple. Politicians were interviewed on the radio, TV or by
5 newspapers. They would campaign, but usually only in the run-up to an election. In other words, the only people who had control over politicians' interactions with the general public were the politicians themselves or
10 people in the media. However, all of that has changed. So what exactly has changed?

The biggest revolution in the way politicians and voters interact with each other has been the rise of social media. Politicians can stay in
15 touch with the public directly and do not have to rely on the media as a go-between. In fact, the quickest way to spread a message now is to get other users to 'like' what they say and then share it with friends and online contacts. In
20 the past, a TV interview or political infomercial would reach a few million people who were watching at the time. Today, the same message can reach millions more people over a number of hours or days, especially if it goes viral.

25 Another way that social media has changed the face of politics is the ability to tailor a message to a specific audience. It's now fairly easy to find out who follows you on social media, what they are interested in and what
30 messages will appeal to them. This is partly because it is relatively easy to ask for feedback on social media. In fact, politicians will get feedback online even if they don't ask for it, so engaging with the public, even if that results
35 in negative feedback, is a must in today's world.

To sum up, politicians in the past were distanced from the public, but the existence of social media means this is no longer possible.

6 Read the article again. Complete the tasks.

1 Describe how politicians used to interact with the general public.
2 Explain two ways in which social media has changed the way politicians communicate their ideas and opinions now.
3 Describe how social media can help politicians send the right message.
4 Summarize the magazine article in about 100 words.

1 Ava, Kelly, Mitch and Chris take part in a school debate. Read the conversation and do the tasks.

Ava   Okay. I'll start. As far as I'm concerned there are far too many deaths in the US because of guns. In 2017, almost 40,000 died as a result of guns. To my mind, those numbers are crazy.

Mitch   I have no doubt that fewer guns would mean fewer deaths, but we also need to take into account the second amendment to the constitution.

Kelly   ⁵ Oh, come on! That was written more than 200 years ago and things change. From my point of view, guns should be made illegal.

Mitch   And what would happen to all those people whose jobs are connected to the gun industry? According to the figures, there are more than 300,000 jobs …

Chris   I see your point, but I have the feeling that someone who has lost a loved one because of gun ¹⁰ violence wouldn't really care about the loss of jobs. I agree with Kelly, things need to change.

Ava   I'd like to point out that we're in danger as well. You do know that there was a shooting at a school in Rochester recently? Did you know that since we started school there have been over 180 shootings at schools like ours?

Kelly   ¹⁵ Personally, these facts worry me. I don't think anyone has the right to put someone else in danger.

Chris   Absolutely!

Teacher   Well done. That was a very good debate. Mitch, are you okay? ²⁰ You probably had the hardest role.

Mitch   Yeah, I'm fine. It's just such a difficult issue. From a personal point of view, I can't see how anyone can argue in favor of guns.

1 Explain what the second amendment is.
2 Find phrases the students use to:
- express opinions
- introduce facts
- agree or disagree

3 Explain why the teacher thinks Mitch had the hardest role.

> **CULTURE CORNER**
>
> This is the original text from 1791 of the second amendment:
> 'A well regulated Militia, being necessary to the security of a free State, the right of the people to keep and bear Arms, shall not be infringed.'

2 **a** Ava and Chris spoke about some of the issues they feel strongly about. Look at these photos. What are the people protesting about?

A

B

C

🔊 47 **Words and phrases**

as far as I'm concerned in my opinion

b Read what some people said about the different protest issues and match each one to the correct protest in **a**.

A *Personally, I don't think it matters what I do. Why should I change my lifestyle unless everyone around the world does?*

B *In my opinion, it's just cruel. The animals don't get to choose.*

C *Honestly. It's crazy. These things kill not protect.*

D *It's important to understand that many of these animals wouldn't exist otherwise. They are bred and raised specifically for a purpose.*

E *Governments need to take action now before it's too late. It's our future we are talking about.*

F *You can't make guns illegal. It's a person's right to own a gun under the second amendment of the constitution.*

c Read again what the people said. For each issue say which argument you agree with. Give reasons for your opinion.

3 You are going to have a class debate about plastic waste. Choose one of the role cards below. Read the newspaper article and find information to support your role.

A
Your father works at a recycling plant. You think that if people recycled plastic there wouldn't be any problems.

B
You are an environmental activist. You are worried about the damage plastic is doing to the environment, especially wildlife.

C
During your summer holidays, you work in a factory that makes plastic bottles for drinks. You are worried about your job.

D
You volunteer every year to clear rubbish from the local park and beach. You often can't believe what you find.

A bad wrap!

Today we hear a lot about how bad plastic is for the environment, but is that the complete story? Synthetic materials such as plastic were originally invented to replace natural products that were in
5 short supply. For example, billiard balls used to be made from ivory, but are now usually made from a hard plastic. One reason why plastic became so popular was that it had many purposes.

Of course, it's impossible to deny that plastic waste is very bad. One of the biggest issues with plastic is 10 that it isn't biodegradable, so some plastic can last for up to 1,000 years. According to figures, about 500 billion plastic bags are used every year around the world. 60% of all the rubbish found on beaches is plastic, and it is estimated that by 2050 every seabird 15 species on the planet will have plastic in its diet, either directly or indirectly from the fish they eat. That also means that humans will be eating plastic! However, we must remember that plastic is essential today. Do you own a computer or a mobile phone? 20 We use plastic in most modern medicines, especially lifesaving equipment. Using plastic also helps us reduce our reliance on fossil fuels, which are one of the causes of climate change. Plastics are light, cheap and an important part of modern life. Maybe 25 plastic doesn't deserve the bad wrap it has got!

PART 1

PART 2

PART 3

Internet research

S1 **Search tips: keywords**

a For a school project, you have to write about this picture that was taken at an event on 21 October 2017. Read the questions below and make a list of keywords that can help you find information quickly.

1 Which state did the event happen in?
2 What was the purpose of the event?
3 What happened at the event?
4 Who are the men in the picture?
5 Is there a connection between the men?
6 Why is this picture very unusual?

 b Get together in groups and discuss your keyword lists. Decide which ones are most useful.

S2 **Reliable / Appropriate sources**

a There is a lot of information on the internet and not all of it is correct. It's important to choose the websites that will give you the information you need. Look at the descriptions of different kinds of websites. Which kind do you think:

1 is the most reliable?
2 is the least reliable?
3 can give helpful opinions and advice?
4 is mostly trying to sell something?
5 often has good information, but it should be checked?

b Which kind of websites would be your first choice for the questions about the event in **S1**?

S3 **Bookmarks and sources**

Bookmarks	Window	Help
Show Favourites		
Show Frequently Visited in Favourites		
Show Bookmarks		
Edit Bookmarks		
Add Bookmark		

a It's important to find your sources and refer to them again later. Every browser has a function to save a website to a 'Favourites' tab or 'Bookmarks' menu. If you don't know how to do this on your browser, search online and find out. Then bookmark some websites that you often use.

Description
A) .com at the end means this is a commercial website. Its purpose is to help sell a product, so the information might be factual, but it might only give you one side of the story.
B) .org at the end means this is a non-profit organization. Non-profits are not trying to sell something, so in most cases you can trust their information.
C) Wikipedia is a useful website, but many of its volunteer writers are not experts. It's a good idea to check the information.
D) Personal blogs and online forums, or message boards (discussion sites), are not the best places for reliable facts, but they're useful if you're looking for a personal point of view or an interesting anecdote.
E) Webnames with .edu at the end belong to educational institutions — usually colleges or universities. They're often good sources of accurate information.
F) .gov is used by official government websites. They have up-to-date statistics and other reliable information.

b If you already use the bookmark function, make notes on how to do it and be ready to explain to a partner how to use it.

Finding and evaluating sources

S1 Find the right sources of information

a Your family is planning to visit Washington D.C. this summer. You are interested in the city's history and you want to find out about:

1. how Washington developed into the city it is today
2. the US Capitol Visitor Center

You also want to check out:

3. fun things for teenagers in Washington
4. how to get around the city

b Which of the chain of key words from **a 1 – 4** cannot be used for your internet research? Why? How could you improve it?

S2 Evaluating search results

a Use key words to research Washington D.C.'s role in the American Civil War.

b When you're searching, make notes on the websites with information from:

1. a reliable factual source
2. a source that needs to be checked
3. a personal blog
4. a message board
5. a commercial organization
6. a social media site

c Which websites do you think are most useful for your research? Why? Choose three sources from your search results and bookmark them.

S3 Do your own research

a Now choose one of the other topics in **S 1**. Search for your keywords. Refine your search if necessary. Decide which websites are the most useful for your research and bookmark them.

b Your family is interested in history. Do some internet research and find out about:

- the name and location of the museums
- opening times
- exhibitions
- entry fee

A view of Britain

1 **A political poem**

a Ava has found a poem connected to British politics. Read the poem. Do you know what event it is about?

b Ava calls Aimee and asks her to explain the poem. Listen to the conversation and do the tasks.

1 State what Ava thinks of British history.
2 Briefly describe what happened on the day they are talking about.
3 Summarize how the date is celebrated today.

> Remember, remember
> the fifth of November.
> Gunpowder treason and plot.
> We see no reason
> 5 why gunpowder treason
> should ever be forgot.

2* **The British Monarchy**

a Here is an article Aimee emailed to Ava. Read the text and find words that match the definitions.

1 A king or queen
2 A title or position passed from parent to child as a right
3 A fight between armed groups of people
4 The period of time when a king or queen rules a country
5 A war fought between two groups of people living in the same country
6 To return something or someone to an earlier position
7 Complete and unlimited
8 To admire someone because they have good ideas or qualities

A brief history of the British Monarchy

According to historians, there have been 61 monarchs in England during the last 1,200 years or so. The monarchs are usually part of a 'House' and the position of King or Queen is hereditary. The first kings came from different houses, but they didn't rule the whole of England. Most historians believe that the modern monarchy started in 1066 with the Norman King **William the Conqueror**, who had defeated
5 Harold II at the battle of Hastings and who was the first king to be crowned at Westminster Abbey.

There have been lots of famous kings and queens over the years. For example, Richard I, known as Richard Lionheart, who took part in the crusades and Henry VIII, who had six wives, or Elizabeth I, who was one of the daughters of Henry VIII. After Elizabeth came James I who was also king of Scotland. During his reign, there was a union between the two countries and the gunpowder plot. The next
10 monarch could have been the last – Charles I. While he was king, there was a civil war and in 1649 the monarch was replaced by **Oliver Cromwell** and a republic.

However, in 1660, the republic came to an end and the monarchy was restored with Charles II becoming king. In 1688, after Charles' son had been forced from the throne, parliament asked William of Orange to become king. This was the start of 'The Glorious Revolution', which changed the absolute power of the
15 monarchy and gave parliament even more power. Since 1699 England has been a constitutional monarchy, meaning the monarch is more of a symbol than an actual decision-maker.
Today the monarchy is part of the House of Windsor. **Elizabeth II** became queen in 1952 and has been the longest serving monarch in history. In recent years, an increasing number of people have called for the end of the monarchy, but, overall, their popularity is still high. This is down to the respect for the current
20 Queen and the influence of the young royals in today's society. Will the monarchy survive for another 1,200 years? Probably not, but it is also unlikely that it is going to end any time soon.

Words and phrases

cellar	a room under a building often used to store things
contentious	involving or likely to cause argument or disagreement
to dominate	to have control over a place or a person
gruesome	extremely unpleasant and shocking, often connected to death

referendum	a vote in which all people are asked to decide between two options
slogan	a short easily remembered phrase
straw	the dried yellow stalks of crops like wheat often used for animals to sleep on

b Find examples for the rules in the text in **2a**.

Tenses*

- We use the **simple present** when we state facts that are (universally) true.
- We use the **simple past** when we
  – talk about events that happened in the past.
  – state facts that were true in the past.
- We use the **present perfect** when an event
  – started in the past and continues now.
  – in the past is connected with or has a consequence in the present.

- We use the **past perfect** when we show that one event happened before another event in the past.
- We use **future tenses** to talk about future plans or make predictions.
- We use the **passive form** of all these tenses when the focus is on the action and not on who does the action.

c Complete Ava's summary about the British monarchy with the correct form of the verbs.

England ▢1 (*be*) a monarchy for about 1,200 years. The kings and queens ▢2 (*come*) from different houses, the current monarch, Queen Elizabeth II ▢3 (*belong*) to the House of Windsor. The monarchy ▢4 (*experience*) several famous historical events, therefore some kings or queens ▢5 (*remember*) better than others. The political influence of the monarchy ▢6 (*change*), too. While before 'The Glorious Revolution' it ▢7 (*have*) absolute power, since 1699 the monarch, who is the head of state, ▢8 (*not have*) legislative power. This ▢9 (*call*) a constitutional monarchy. However, we cannot predict how long the monarchy ▢10 (*exist*).

A

3 A big issue!

a Chris is working on a school project about an important political event in the UK. Look at the pictures and discuss what his project could be about. Find captions for each picture.

b Chris listens to a podcast and then writes a short text for his project. Listen and correct the factual mistakes in his text.

On May 23rd, 2016 the population of England voted in a referendum on leaving the EU. After the votes were counted, 52% of the votes were for leaving and 48% in favor of remaining in the EU. The next day the Prime Minister resigned. Early in 2017 Theresa May, the new foreign
5 minister, gave a speech in which she said, 'A bad deal is better than no deal'. Over the next few years, Brexit came to dominate the political agenda in the EU parliament. In May 2019, Theresa May was forced to resign after losing the support of most of her party. She was succeeded by Boris Johnson. Later that year at the Conservative Party Conference
10 a new slogan was revealed: 'Get Brexit Over'. At midday on January 31st, 2020 the UK officially left the EU. After a twelve-month transition period, the agreement was finally signed but the event was overshadowed by the Corona pandemic.

B

C

Grammar and structures

Tenses (revision) → G11
The monarchs **are** usually part of a house. (simple present)
Elizabeth II **became** queen in 1952. (simple past)
Recently, some people **have called for** the end of the monarchy. (present perfect)

William became king in 1066 after he **had defeated** Harald. (past perfect)
Will the monarchy **survive**? (*will* future)
It is unlikely that it **is going to end** soon. (*going-to* future)
In 1649, the monarch **was replaced**. (passive)

@ WES-40903-003

1 Listen to a radio programme about the modern royal family and put
the events in the correct order.

51))

a Charles and Diana have a son. He is called William.

b Diana dies in a car crash in Paris.

c George VI becomes king.

d Edward VIII is in love with a divorced American woman, Wallis Simpson, and has to choose between her and remaining king.

e Elizabeth gives birth to her first child, Charles.

f Elizabeth's father dies and she becomes queen. She is crowned in Westminster Abbey.

g George V dies and his son, Edward VIII, becomes king.

h Prince Charles marries Lady Diana Spencer.

i Princess Elizabeth marries Philip Mountbatten.

2 Ava finds an article about the Duchess of Cambridge. Complete the text with the correct form of the verbs in the box. Use the adverbs in brackets and put them in the correct position.

admire ■ be ■ begin ■ broadcast ■ come ■ focus ■ gain ■ go ■ know ■ meet ■ play ■ represent ■ see ■ spend ■ support ■ take ■ take place ■ wear ■ work

The wife of Prince William, the Duchess of Cambridge __1__ (best) worldwide as Kate Middleton. Catherine, who was born in 1982, __2__ from an ordinary family. As a young child, Kate __3__ a few years abroad with her parents but __4__ to school and later to college in
5 England. After she __5__ a gap year abroad, she __6__ her studies at the University of St Andrews in Scotland in 2001. This is where she __7__ Prince William. They __8__ together for nine years when they got married in 2011. Their wedding, which __9__ in Westminster Abbey, __10__ all over the world and was watched by millions. The couple now
10 have three children.
As a royal, Kate __11__ hard to support the Queen in official engagements. Alongside Prince William, she __12__ the Queen on several overseas tours. She __13__ (actively) several charities that __14__ on young children's welfare. She __15__ (also frequently) at different sports events as sports __16__ (always) a big part in her life.
Kate __17__ (greatly) for her fashion style, too. She __18__ many followers, and the outfits she __19__ quickly sell out
15 from the shops. All in all, Catherine is a true representative of a 21st century royal.

3 a In 2016, young people were asked about the effects of Brexit on their lives. Read what they say and decide who supported Brexit, who was against it, and who was undecided.

1 If we want to make real changes in Britain, we need to leave.
2 We can trade with other countries without the restriction of the EU.
3 Freedom of going from country to country in the EU has been my privilege ever since I was born.
4 I think Brexit will be bad for me personally – Brexit can impact on how I pick my university.
5 It might change my prospects in the future in terms of jobs.
6 Having closed borders makes me a bit safer in a way.
7 I am hoping it's going to be good for me, but I am not sure.
8 The people we meet from the EU know different cultures and show us different ways of life and that makes us more open-minded.
9 I have multiple heritage – one parent from the UK, the other from an EU country – do I have to choose between being British or European rather than both?

b Do some research and find out which statements have become reality. Collect information on how Brexit has affected people's lives. Prepare a two-minute talk and present your findings.

1 **a** You are going to watch a video about a social issue in the world today. Look at the three pictures. Speculate what connects them and what you will hear about each one.

A

B

C

b Share your ideas with a partner.

2 **a** Watch the video and say what these figures refer to.

10

| 34% | 14.3 million | 14 million | 22,000 |

b Explain which fact(s) surprised you the most and why. Discuss your ideas together.

3 Watch the video again and find words or phrases that match these definitions.

10

1 A fact of not allowing someone to do or have something.

2 To give money or goods to help a person or an organization.

3 People who have nowhere to live, often because they are poor.

4 The fact that something is not available or there is not enough of it.

5 Not having the ability to do something or prevent something from happening.

6 A very poor and crowded area, particularly of a city.

7 Expecting something to be the case without realizing how lucky you are to have it.

8 An action or a situation that does not show respect for an important principle.

4 Complete the summary.

The video is about  1 in the world. The UN defines 2 as a denial of choices and opportunities and as a violation of 3. The video includes facts about the number of children who 4 every year because of poverty. It also says that poverty is not just about not having enough 5 but also lacking 6, education or not having a 7 so you can 8 enough money to buy food, clothes and pay for somewhere to live. The last part of the video suggests some 9 people can do to help solve the problem, such as giving money to 10.

5 Have you been involved in charities that fight poverty or have you taken part in protests? Collect ideas about what you can do to help fight poverty. Search the internet for activities and pictures and give a short presentation.

Plastic free

1 **Aimee at Glastonbury.** Listen to Aimee talking about her experience at the Glastonbury music festival in England. Which pictures show the events and other things that she mentions? Complete the tasks.

1 Describe what was different about Glastonbury this year.
2 Name the people who went to Glastonbury with Aimee.
3 Explain what Aimee did at the end of the festival and why.

2 **Glastonbury goes plastic free**

a Aimee shows Liam an article about Glastonbury. Skim the article and match the headings (A – H) to the paragraphs. There are two extra headings you don't need.

A The fight against plastic
B Looking back after the festival
C Just for the music
D Is it enough?
E What people think
F Recycle or reuse
G A message to the festival goers
H What can the organizers do?

b Scan the text and decide if the sentences are true, false or not in the text. Justify your answers by quoting the relevant lines.

1 Glastonbury had already banned the sale of plastic bottles before 2019.
2 People were not allowed to take their own plastic bottles to the festival in 2019.
3 Some charities said the organizers at Glastonbury had made a good start in dealing with single-use plastics.
4 The tents that are left after the festival are recycled.

Glastonbury goes plastic free

1 Two of the images that come to mind when people think of Glastonbury, and many other music festivals, are of people walking around in rubber boots and of fields covered in rubbish at the end of the festival.

5 2 Well, in 2019 the organizers tried to make some changes to this image. Of course, they couldn't really do anything about the weather. If it rained, it was going to get muddy, but they could try and tackle the mountains of rubbish.

3 One of the hottest topics in recent years has been single-use
10 plastics. In 2019, Glastonbury joined the fight by banning the sale of any single-use plastics, including bottles. This was quite a radical step to take because in 2017 festival-goers had got through more than 1.3 million plastic bottles!

4 One thing the organizers were unable to do was to stop
15 visitors bringing their own plastic bottles and leaving them behind at the end of the festival. However, people were asked not to bring any single-use plastics and were also urged to take all their rubbish away with them.

5 Organizations such as *Friends of the Earth* and *Greenpeace*
20 praised Glastonbury for the steps it was taking, but said more could still be done. They pointed out that people should also think about the food containers and cutlery they bring and their tents. Apparently, every year thousands of cheap tents are left in the fields at the end of the festival.

25 6 In fact, every year more than 1,000 volunteers stay behind after all the music has finished to help tidy up. The clean-up operation can take up to six weeks and lots of rubbish is collected including camping chairs, blow-up mattresses, cool boxes and lots of other things.

Words and phrases

blow-up mattress	the soft part of a bed which you sleep on; you blow air into it to make it inflate
concession	a reduction in the entrance price for some groups of people, e. g. children
discount	a reduction in the price of something (for everyone)
mountains of	a lot of something, often in piles

to praise	to say somebody is doing something well
radical	describing a new and very different way of doing something
to urge	to advise somebody very strongly about the action they should take

3 **After Glastonbury.** Aimee writes an email to Paige. Before you read it, list the topics you think she will mention. Then check your predictions.

Hi Paige!

I've got so much to tell you! As you know, I went to a festival this year. The festival was great and I had a really good time! I went with Holly and my
5 dad and we were there for eight days. I guess you might be surprised as the music only lasts for three days, but we stayed on after it finished to help clean up the site. You wouldn't believe how much rubbish people leave when they go home!
10 You know I'm very passionate about the environment and being green, so when I heard that you could volunteer to help, I asked my dad if we could. He wasn't too keen at first and he said he didn't have the time, but I managed to
15 persuade him.

I'd like to go to a festival every year, but it can be quite expensive. It's not just the cost of the tickets, you also need a tent and you need to buy food while you're there. One thing I really liked
20 about Glastonbury was the food. There was so much to choose from and a lot of choices for vegetarians too.

Have you ever been to a festival?

Love
25 Aimee

Articles

- When we mention something the first time we use the indefinite article *a/an*. Then when we mention the same thing again, we use the definite article *the*.
  I went to <u>a festival</u> this year. <u>The festival</u> was great and I had a really good time!

- When the noun is about something general and is uncountable we don't use an article – we call this the zero article. When we talk about something specific, we then use the definite article *the*.
  You need to buy <u>food</u> while you're there. One thing I really liked about Glastonbury was <u>the food</u>.

4 **Aimee and Paige.** Complete the short online conversation between Aimee and Paige with the correct articles. Don't forget the zero article. Then listen and check.

P. Hi Aimee! I'm glad you enjoyed Glastonbury. I went to **1** festival, too.
A. Really? Was it in New Zealand?
P. Yes, it was. **2** festival is called Hokitika Wildfoods festival.
A. Is that **3** music festival?
P. It does include **4** music, but the main attraction is **5** food.
A. Well, I know you like **6** food, so …
P. Ha ha. I even got **7** discount.
A. How much was **8** discount?
P. Ten per cent, so that was quite good.
A. It sounds great. I'd love to go one day.
P. Well, if you come to visit, we can go together.

5 **More about Glastonbury.** Listen to another conversation between Liam and Aimee. What did Aimee enjoy about Glastonbury?

TIP

When we talk about everyone in a group of people we use nominalized adjectives. We always use the definite article *the* to show this, for example, *the homeless*.
*We need to try and provide more places for **the homeless** to live.*

---

6 **It's your turn: Helping out.** Think about what you could do to help other people. Then complete the tasks and share your answers with a partner.

1 Explain what you think people can do to help the homeless.
2 Describe the help that is provided for the disabled in your town or school.

Grammar and structures

Nominalized adjectives → G12
The charity supports **the homeless**.

Definite, indefinite and zero articles → G13
I went to **a festival**. **The festival** was great.

PART 1

PART 2

PART 3

1 When she gets home Aimee tries to find out what she can do to help people like the homeless. She reads a short article on the internet. Complete the article with the definite article *the* or zero article (–).

Today many ▮1▮ young people wear wristbands to show the charities and causes that they support. Some of ▮2▮ most popular charities to donate money to are those that look after ▮3▮ elderly or ▮4▮ homeless. Of course, not all these people need financial support. There are many ▮5▮ elderly people who are quite well off. However, it isn't always ▮6▮ money that these people need. Sometimes these people need food or people to talk to. In other words, you don't need to be ▮7▮ rich to offer something to the charities that support these groups of people.

2 Aimee talks to her mum about helping a charity. Complete their conversation with the words from the box. There are two words that you don't need.

> homeless ■ poor ■ the homeless ■ the poor ■ the wealthy ■ the young ■
> wealthy ■ young

Aimee   Mum, I want to volunteer for a charity.
Mrs G. That's nice, Aimee. Are you going to do something for ResCom again with your uncle?
Aimee   No, I want to do something to help ▮1▮ .
Mrs G. Oh! That sounds nice, but you know we aren't ▮2▮ .
Aimee   I know that, but I don't have to give money. I could help out in a shop or …
Mrs G. Why don't you come and help me at the shelter?
Aimee   With ▮3▮ ?
Mrs G. Yes, they're usually ▮4▮ , that's why they are ▮5▮ .
Aimee   That's true. I also want to do something for the environment.
Mrs G. We all do. You know it's not only ▮6▮ who are worried about climate change.
Aimee   I know that, mum, but it's time for action and not just talking about the problems.

3 Before Glastonbury and at the festival Aimee and her dad are talking about different things. Look at the sentences and decide whether you need an article or not and which one.

Mr G.   I know you like ▮1▮ music. You'll enjoy Glastonbury.
Aimee   And what do you think of ▮2▮ music there?

Aimee   There are so many ▮3▮ people here.
Mr G.   But ▮4▮ people all look very happy.

Mr G.   You and Holly can share ▮5▮ tent.
Aimee   Don't you think ▮6▮ tent is too small?

Aimee   Look, I found ▮7▮ wallet.
Mr G.   You should take ▮8▮ wallet to lost property.

🔊 56)) **Words and phrases**

financial   to do with money

→ Workbook, page 77   **PRACTICE B**

4 Holly has written a blog post about her experience at the festival. Read her post and complete it with the definite, indefinite or zero article (-).

This post is about my first ever experience at 〔1〕 world-famous festival. Yes, you guessed it right – I was at Glastonbury. Let me tell you all about it.

As a special treat, my dad decided to take my sister Aimee and me to Glastonbury. 〔2〕 weather was glorious, 〔3〕 music wonderful – if you watched 〔4〕 broadcast about the event, this is not news to you.

5 I'd like to tell you about 〔5〕 things that happen in the background. Did you know that 〔6〕 festival supports 〔7〕 charities? The main ones are Oxfam, Greenpeace and WaterAid. I've found out that this year more than £2 million went to these charities alone. However, 〔8〕 smaller charities and organizations benefit from the profits, too. 〔9〕 charities that support 〔10〕 disadvantaged, 〔11〕 poor, 〔12〕 homeless all get their share.

Although there were thousands of people, the site was run efficiently. 〔13〕 volunteers gave out wristbands, helped
10 out at the kitchens and made sure that 〔14〕 rubbish was collected. I talked to some of them and they told me that there is 〔15〕 dedicated website where you can apply to be 〔16〕 volunteer. If you are chosen, you don't pay for 〔17〕 ticket. So this is my plan for next year …

5 **Think:** Read these quotes about charity. Decide which one do you think best describes your opinion.

> **A** *Your greatness is not what you have, it's what you give.*

> **B** *Charity isn't about pity, it's about love.*

> **C** *Be the change you want to see in the world.*

> **D** *We can't help everyone, but everyone can help someone.*

> **E** *Giving is not just about making a donation. It's about making a difference.*

Pair: Discuss your choice / opinion with a partner. Give reasons for your answer.

Share: In a group discuss your ideas and agree on one quote you all think is the best.

6 Write a blog post or an email to a friend about a time you went to a festival, a holiday camp, or on a trip with friends. Think about what you did and what you enjoyed most. Write 100 – 150 words.

57)) **Words and phrases**

pity   feeling sad about somebody else's situation or unhappiness
donation money or goods that are given to a person or an organization to help

PART 1
PART 2
PART 3

1 Complete the text about Winston Churchill with the sentences (A – H).

A As a young politician, he wasn't afraid of disagreeing with the Conservative leadership.

B The young Winston wasn't very good at school.

C During his time there, he was captured and was sent to prison.

D For almost a decade, Churchill found himself on the edges of politics in Britain.

E The collection also contains works from some of the most famous British artists like Turner and Constable.

F He won a second term as Prime Minister in 1951, but he would never be as powerful as before.

G At the time, Britain was losing the war against Germany and things looked bleak.

H Then, in 1924, Churchill once again switched parties, rejoining the Conservatives.

Sir Winston Churchill (1874 – 1965) is often regarded as one of the greatest Britons ever, but some people would question whether he deserves such a title. He was born at the family home, Blenheim Palace near Oxford, on 30th November 1874. His father, Lord Randolph, was a prominent Conservative politician and his mother,
5 Jennie Jerome, came from New York. _____1_____ Churchill was also very accident prone when he was young. He almost drowned in a lake in Switzerland, regularly fell off horses, crashed a plane when learning to fly, and was hit by a car when crossing 5th Avenue in New York.
In 1895, he graduated from the army college and joined the Queen's Own 4th Hussars.
10 He also worked in Cuba, India and Sudan as a war reporter. In October 1899, he went to South Africa as a war correspondent to write about the conflict between Britain and the Boer Republic. _____2_____ Somehow he managed to escape by climbing over a wall. Unfortunately, he didn't have a plan but was lucky enough to find his way to the house of a British coal mine manager who allowed him to stay for three days before hiding him on a train to Mozambique. From there Churchill was able to
15 make his way back to Durban. News of his escape reached Britain and it made him famous.
In 1900, he stood for election and became an MP (Member of Parliament) for the Conservative Party. He made his first speech in 1901, but as a result of a bad experience he had in 1904, he always used detailed notes when he spoke from then on. _____3_____ In fact, because he disagreed with their politics he joined the Liberal Party where he made his mark by becoming the youngest cabinet minister since 1866 in the 1908 government, which was
20 led by Prime Minister David Lloyd-George.
At the start of World War I, Churchill was responsible for the British Navy. Unfortunately for him, the navy lost some very important battles and he was forced to resign less than a year into the war. _____4_____ After becoming the Conservative MP for the seat of Epping, near London, he became Chancellor, the second most important position after Prime Minister in the UK. However, he again made a series of mistakes and in 1929, just three years
25 after the General Strike, Labour won the general election and Churchill was out of office once again.
_____5_____ All of that was to change in 1940 when he suddenly became Prime Minister. _____6_____ It was at this time that Churchill made what is probably one of his most famous speeches which included the lines, 'We shall fight on the beaches, we shall fight on the landing grounds, we shall fight on the fields … we shall never surrender' – meant to inspire the British people to fight Nazi Germany in the war.
30 Somehow, despite leading Britain to victory in the Second World War, Churchill managed to lose the election in 1945.
_____7_____ Churchill was both an accomplished artist and writer. He actually didn't start painting until he was in his 40s, but over a period of 48 years he produced more than 500 paintings. Some of his paintings are part of the National Trust
35 Collection. _____8_____ In 1953, while he was Prime Minister, he won the Nobel Prize for Literature, the only Prime Minister to date to do so.
On 24th January 1965 at the age of ninety, Winston Churchill died. Six days later, world leaders paid their respects to the great man as his coffin made its way through the streets of central London to St Paul's Cathedral for his funeral. He was laid to rest at his
40 ancestral home, Blenheim Palace, where he had been born 90 years earlier.

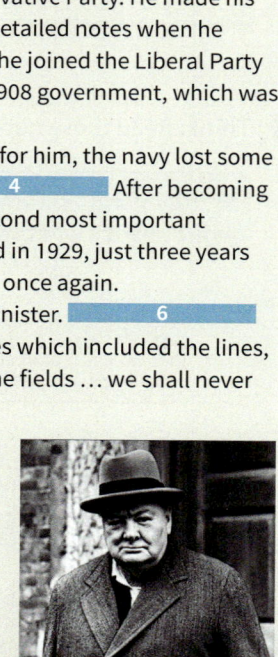

 Words and phrases

accident prone   likely to suffer or have lots of accidents

to switch   to change

2 **a** Find these expressions in the text. What do they mean? Use the context to help you.

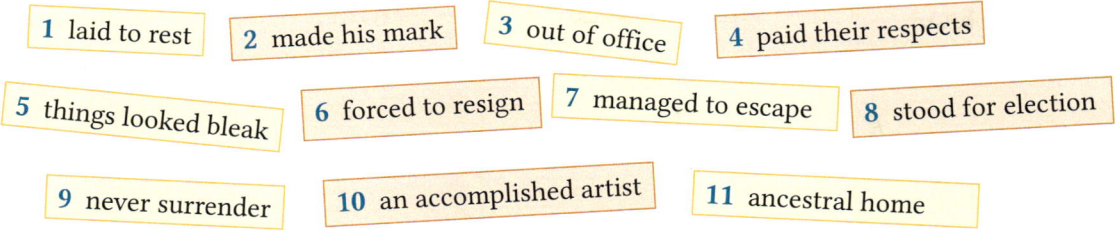

1 laid to rest   2 made his mark   3 out of office   4 paid their respects

5 things looked bleak   6 forced to resign   7 managed to escape   8 stood for election

9 never surrender   10 an accomplished artist   11 ancestral home

b Compare your ideas with a partner and check in a dictionary. Then share your ideas with the class.

3 Read the text again. Decide whether these statements are true, false or not in the text. Give the line numbers for true statements and correct the false ones.

1 Churchill's father was a member of the Conservative party.

2 He crashed while driving a car in New York.

3 After escaping from prison, he hid on a train.

4 He used notes when making his first speech in 1901.

5 He left the government shortly after the beginning of World War I.

6 Churchill made one of his most famous speeches in 1940.

7 He disagreed with the Conservative Party, so he joined the Labour Party.

8 He won the Nobel Prize for Literature for his first book.

9 He was in charge of Britain for most of World War II.

4 Read the text again and work on these tasks.

1 Outline Churchill's career before he entered politics.
2 Describe Churchill's role during World War I and II.
3 Assess the effect of Churchill's speech in 1940. Who did he appeal to?

5 Use these prompts to write statements about Winston Churchill.

1 born | 30th November 1874 | at Blenheim
2 worked | war reporter | in
3 1899 | escape | prison | Durban
4 became | MP | Oldham | 1900
5 1929 | lost | election
6 resigned | World War I | because
7 Prime Minister | 1940
8 died | 1965 | 90

Today, Blenheim Palace near Oxford is a tourist attraction.

PART 1

PART 2

PART 3

Researching and selecting information

S1   **Selecting relevant information.** Your teacher asks you to write an informative article about Hurricane Katrina on the Gulf Coast in America, including the information below. Read the extracts. Which source do you think will not be useful for your article? Why?

- When and where did the natural disaster take place?
- What happened (how the storm developed and moved)?
- What happened to the population, properties and how did the area recover from the disaster?

1 The Gulf Coast is situated on the southern part of the United States. It is about 1,900 kilometers long. The five US states along the shoreline – Florida, Alabama, Mississippi, Louisiana and Texas – are all famous for
5 their beaches, they attract tourists all year round. Apart from tourism, the main industries are petrochemicals, energy, aerospace, fishing and agriculture. Much of the year is warm or hot along the Gulf Coast. The three winter months are cooler, but
10 cold weather is very rare in the area.

2 On the evening of 25 August 2005, the category 1 hurricane, Katrina reached the shores of Florida. Trees were blown down by the wind. Although it weakened as it crossed Florida, it became stronger again, a category 3
5 hurricane, as it got to the Gulf of Mexico. On 27 August President George W. Bush declared a state of emergency in Louisiana, Alabama and Mississippi. The next day the mayor of New Orleans issued a mandatory evacuation order as the storm had strengthened further, now it was
10 classified as a category 5 hurricane.

3 More than a decade after the hurricane, New Orleans and the coastal communities that were hit hard by Katrina still haven't fully recovered. Some residents who were evacuated decided
5 not to return to their homes. Many people lost their homes. Lots of properties and businesses had to be rebuilt. The biggest issue was to design and construct new levees, structures that protect the city from flooding. The federal
10 government was criticized for the slow response in the emergency.

TIP

When you're researching:
- Use more than one source – and at least one English source.
- Skim the text for the main ideas.
- Select relevant information (for example *who, what, when, where, why*).
- Don't copy and don't cut and paste from the website.
- Write short notes in your own words.
- Write down the website details of your source immediately.
- Cite your sources.

Don't forget to bookmark or write down your sources, so you can refer to them again.

S2   **Make notes.** Compare extracts from two sets of notes for the article which were written by different students. Which set of notes is better? What is wrong with the other notes?

1

The hurricane that became category 5 in strength started over the Bahamas on 23 Aug 2005. It was named Katrina. It caused major destruction, destroyed properties so lots of people lost their homes. Cities like New Orleans had to be evacuated though there were people who refused to leave and instead found shelter in the Superdome Stadium. Unfortunately, there were people who couldn't be saved, but it could have been worse. As the hurricane battered the area, New Orleans got flooded. That's why after the hurricane the city needed new levees and new buildings. The US government gave financial support to rebuild the city.

2

Location and time
Started near the Bahamas on 23 Aug 2005 and lasted until 31 Aug. It became a category 5 hurricane on 28 Aug. The states most affected by Hurricane Katrina were Florida, Louisiana, Mississippi and Alabama.

Event
23 Aug 2005: Katrina, a tropical storm starts building over the Bahamas; 25 Aug: turns into a hurricane and hits Florida; 26 Aug: Mississippi and Louisiana declare a state of emergency; 28 Aug: people leave New Orleans or shelter in the Superdome Stadium; 29 Aug: heavy rains and winds – New Orleans is flooded; rescue efforts to save people and provide food and drinking water; 30 Aug: 80% of the city is underwater; 31 Aug – 5 Sept: more disruption, chaos but rescue attempts continue.

→Workbook, page 80

WORKSHOP TASK

Researching, writing and evaluating a short article

S1 **Choose a research topic.** Look at the pictures. Choose one of the topics you can see in the pictures. You are going to research and write an informative article about this topic for your school website.

C

Space Shuttle Challenger disaster

A

Washington D.C., Lincoln Memorial

B

A popular tourist destination in a region in the USA

D

A member of the Royal Family

S2 **Gather information**

a Decide on the keywords you will use for your search. Find and select the most useful websites. Look at the different types of websites on page **96**.

b Read the information you find on the websites and make notes. Follow the research tips on page **108**.

S3 **Write**

a Give your notes a clear structure so they'll be more useful for you when you're writing your text.

> **TIP**
>
> Think of a **title** that will get the reader's attention.
> The **opening paragraph** of your article should introduce the main point you want to make and get the reader interested. You can do this by using a question.
> The **middle paragraphs** should contain the main information. You can use **sub-headings** to show the content of each paragraph. Summarize your main points again in the **final paragraph**.

b Write the first draft of your article. When you have finished, check it through for mistakes. Then rewrite it and correct the mistakes.

S4 **Evaluate**

 a When you have finished, form small groups. Describe your topic and how you researched it. Take turns. What difficulties did you have? What new research strategies did you try? How successful were they?

 b Share your texts in your group and give feedback. Use the checklist to help you.

- Does the article have a clear structure?
- Does the writer use linking words to connect ideas, e.g.:
  - adding ideas: *and, also, in addition;*
  - contrasting ideas: *but, although, however;*
  - introducing causes and reasons: *so, because (of), as a result, That's why ...;*
  - introducing examples: *for example, for instance.*
- Is the grammar and spelling correct?

PART 1

PART 2

PART 3

1 Here are Kelly's notes about the Capitol Building. Complete her text and use the prompts in *italics* to write sentences in the passive.

1 Another famous building in Washington D.C. is the Capitol Building, which is the home of the US Congress. A competition was held and *a prize | $500 | offer | the best design.*

2 The *final design | choose | George Washington and Thomas Jefferson.*

3 On September 18, 1793 *the first stone | put in place | George Washington.*

4 Originally there was a law preventing any taller building from being built, but in 1910 this *law | change* and now the Capitol Building is only the fifth highest building in Washington D.C.

5 The *famous dome | not | add | until the 1850s.*

2 Ava is listening to a short radio programme about the history of Buckingham Palace. Listen and decide whether the following statements are true or false. Correct the false ones.

1 Buckingham Palace is in London, not in the City of Westminster.

2 Originally there was a town house on the site where Buckingham Palace is now.

3 John Sheffield built the original house for himself.

4 Converting the house into a palace was very expensive.

5 Queen Victoria was the first royal who lived in the palace.

6 The famous balcony and the east wing were built at the same time.

7 The state rooms can only be used by the monarch.

8 The whole palace is open to visitors in the summer months.

9 The flag flying on top of the palace indicates whether the monarch is in residence.

3 Aimee is telling her sister Holly about a recent conversation she had with Ava. Look at what Aimee told her sister and write what Ava actually said to Aimee.

A Ava said that she'd enjoyed the trip to Washington D.C.

B She agreed that the tour had been very well organized.

C She also told me that she'd been busy researching the British monarchy.

D I promised to answer all her questions.

E She asked me who Guy Fawkes was.

F I offered to send her weblinks where she could read about the royal family.

G She was wondering why British history was so gruesome.

H She also asked me not to laugh at her if she asked silly questions.

I She said she didn't understand what the difference was between an absolute and a constitutional monarchy.

4 Chris is talking to Ava. She is asking him about his recent project about Brexit. Use the prompts to make questions, then use the numbers to write the answers.

> 52% ■ June 23rd, 2016 ■ July 2019 ■ At midnight January 31st, 2020 ■ January 2017

1 referendum | held | ?
2 people | voted | to leave | ?
3 Theresa May | 'No deal is better than a bad deal.' | ?
4 Boris Johnson | Prime Minister | ?
5 the UK | officially | leave the EU | ?

5 Ava receives an email from Jeff about politics and social issues. Read his email. Decide whether the <u>underlined</u> phrases are correct or wrong. Correct the wrong ones.

Dear Ava,

I know you're fascinated by <u>politic</u>[1], but I have to say I'm <u>not particular interested</u>[2].
I think <u>one of the main problems</u>[3] is that politicians often do not consider young people or want to listen to <u>that what we have to say</u>[4]. I've seen this happen in the UK with Brexit, for example – so many young people <u>haven't been able to</u>[5]
5 vote and now they are directly affected by the consequences!
I'd also be interested to hear what you thought about the <u>in 2020 Presidential election</u>[6] in the US. How unusual that was! Did you feel like young people <u>were listened to</u>[7], even if they couldn't go out and vote?
That being said, <u>I'm very interested for</u>[8] social issues and <u>trying to involve</u>[9] as much as possible. My friend Jamila <u>has been</u>[10] vegan for over a year and I think I'm going to try to eat less meat. Last year, I <u>was taking part</u>[11] in a
10 sponsored run for a charity called ResCom. Last Christmas, I <u>volunteer</u>[12] at a local shelter for the homeless. My mum has been volunteering there <u>since a few years</u>[13].
Every year my family is involved in the local 'Park Clean' which is organized <u>from the local government</u>[14]. <u>There is</u>[15] many beautiful parks in Munich – one is even <u>calling</u>[16] the English Garden! – but people sometimes leave litter lying around, <u>also</u>[17] at Christmas we come and clean it up.
15 Anyway, as you can see, I do care about things, but just believe that politicians don't <u>hold young people's views for</u>[18] important, even when their policies will directly affect them. However, when I'm 18, I <u>vote</u>[19] because it could make a difference. Maybe my opinions <u>will be different</u>[20] then.

Jeff
xxx

6 Here are some notes about the Victoria & Albert Museum in London. Use these notes to write a short descriptive paragraph about the museum. You could start like this:

The Victoria and Albert Museum is devoted to art and design …

- World's largest museum devoted to art and design
- Officially opened: 1857, by Queen Victoria
- Located: Royal Borough of Kensington and Chelsea
- Collections: Art from 5,000 years ago until the present day
- Offers: educational tours with activities
- Open: Wednesday to Sunday, 10 a.m. – 5:45 p.m.

PART 1

PART 2

PART 3

M **Camp Adventure**

a Deine englische Freundin Sarah möchte die kommenden Sommerferien mit dir in Deutschland verbringen. Ihr möchtet zusammen in den Urlaub fahren und schaut euch eine Webseite an. Sarahs Deutsch ist nicht besonders gut. Beantworte ihre Fragen.

Sarah	Who is this man Jan Vieth?
You	…
Sarah	I guess it's his quote. What does he say?
You	…
Sarah	What else is special about these camps?
You	…
Sarah	I love adventures! I can understand the word pocketknife in the last paragraph. Do we all have to bring one along?
You	…
Sarah	OK. Is there anything else that is not allowed?
You	…
Sarah	Do these camps only take place in Germany?
You	…
Sarah	They often use the word 'camp'. Does that mean that we must go camping?
You	…
Sarah	I can understand that they organize camps for classes. Can we only take part with our classmates?
You	…
Sarah	OK. Can you tell me why you think that these camps could be a good choice for us?
You	…

Camp Adventure

Egal aus welchem Land oder aus welcher Kultur Kinder, Teenager oder Mitarbeiter*innen kommen – sie sollen sich alle gemeinsam wohlfühlen und eine einzigartige und unvergessliche Zeit im Camp erleben.

5 Jan Vieth, Gründer & Geschäftsführer von Camp Adventure

Camp Adventure ist eine Organisation des Gründers Jan Vieth, die seit 2002 die positiven Aspekte von deutschen Ferienfreizeiten mit denen kanadischer Sommercamps verbindet, um Kindern und 10 Jugendlichen aus aller Welt ein tolles Abenteuersport-Ferienlager zu bieten. Seit 2015 bieten wir auch erlebnispädagogische Klassenreisen in unserer Camp Adventure Academy in der Lüneburger Heide (Walsrode, Norddeutschland) an.

Camp Adventure ist auch Spezialist in Outdoor-Programmen 15 und Aktivitäten, die von Abenteuerflair, Naturerlebnis, Teamgeist und Selbsterfahrung geprägt sind. Als Experte auf dem Gebiet Abenteuer- und Erlebnisfreizeit können wir auch Hotels, Resorts und Freizeitparks speziell im Bereich der Programm- und Anlagengestaltung optimale Beratung bieten.

Was wir bieten

Internationale Sport- & Sprachcamps

20 Unsere Sport- & Sprachcamps vereinen das internationale und ganz besondere Camp Adventure Feeling. Sprachunterricht, praktische Projekte mit Fokus auf dem Erlernen neuer Fähigkeiten und die Mischung aus Campspielen und Sportarten aller Art führen zu fantastischen Erlebnissen und Erfahrungen. 25 Kommt und trefft viele neue Freund*innen in eurem Alter aus aller Welt in unseren internationalen Camps!

Erlebnispädagogische Klassenreisen

Unsere kreativen und abenteuerlichen Klassenreise-Programme zeichnen sich durch Ihre Programmvielfalt und gut abgestimmte erlebnispädagogische Inhalte aus. Unser Ziel ist es die 30 Klassengemeinschaft zu stärken und den Team Spirit zu wecken. Dies schaffen wir unter anderem durch eine individuelle Betreuung der Schüler*innen. ‚Back to nature' lautet eins unserer Mottos. Bewusst entscheiden wir uns dafür, mal ein paar Tage ‚offline' zu sein und zu entspannen.

Camp Adventure Academy

35 Als Spezialist in den Bereichen Erlebnispädagogik und Outdoor Sport, wurde die Academy bereits von vielen Schüler*innen und Profis genutzt, um ihre Fähigkeiten im faszinierenden Bereich der Outdoor Education zu erweitern und / oder als Team zusammen zu wachsen. Seit 2015 hat sie ihr festes Zuhause in der Lüneburger 40 Heide. Das Gelände ist durch seine Vielfältigkeit und Größe für eine Vielzahl von Aktivitäten und Veranstaltungen geeignet. Neben Klassenreisen und Jugendcamps bietet die Camp Adventure Academy auch die passende Location für Aus- und Fortbildungen, Firmenevents, Messen und Survival Kurse.

FAQs

Welche Sprachen werden im Camp gesprochen?

Die Hauptsprache in all unseren Camps ist zunächst Englisch. Dazu kommt die jeweilige Sprache des Landes, in dem das Camp stattfindet. Dadurch, dass wir unseren Hauptsitz in Deutschland haben, sind in allen Camps auch immer deutsche bzw. deutschsprachige Teamer dabei. Alle Ansagen und Erklärungen werden daher immer auf Deutsch und Englisch durchgeführt. Selbstverständlich stehen auch all unsere Teamer mit ihren unterschiedlichen Nationalitäten für einzelne Übersetzungen zur Verfügung.

Wie ist mein Kind im Camp untergebracht?

Im Adventure Camp Bayerischer Wald und in der Lüneburger Heide können die Juniors (7 – 12) und die Seniors (12 – 16) zwischen Zelt und Hütte wählen. Die Zelte sind mit einem Fußboden und einer Holz-Empore ausgestattet, pro Zelt werden 6 – 7 Personen untergebracht. Die Teilnehmer*innen können es sich mit Schlafsack und Isomatte gemütlich machen. Die Holzhütten sind mit Etagenbetten ausgestattet und bieten Platz für 4 – 8 Kinder. An den anderen Standorten werden die Teilnehmer*innen in Jugendherbergen, Sportzentren oder Internaten von Privatschulen in Mehrbettzimmern untergebracht. Ausführliche Informationen zur jeweiligen Unterbringung findet ihr auf den einzelnen Campseiten.

Gibt es verbotene Gegenstände?

Ja, die gibt es. Nicht erlaubt sind Taschenmesser, sämtliche Waffen, Feuerzeuge und Streichhölzer (Brandgefahr im Wald!). Drogen jeglicher Art, auch Alkohol und Zigaretten, gehören ebenfalls dazu.

b Auf der Webseite entdeckt ihr die Information, dass *Camp Adventure* eine Kooperation mit dem *Duke of Edinburgh's International Award* hat. Beim Recherchieren was das ist, betritt dein kleiner Bruder dein Zimmer. Er möchte wissen, was der *Duke of Edinburgh's International Award* ist. Du erklärst ihm, was das Hauptanliegen dieses Programms ist und worin die Verbindung zu *Camp Adventure* liegt.

What is the award?

The Duke of Edinburgh's International Award is a non-competitive, internationally recognized programme designed to encourage young people to develop positive skills and lifestyle habits.

The Award is about personal challenge and development and is adaptable according to each participant's interests and abilities. The strength of the Award is our ability to readily partner with other youth organizations through leader development and resource sharing. The Award concept is one of individual challenge. It presents young people a balanced, non-competitive programme of voluntary activities which encourages personal discovery and growth, self-reliance, perseverance, responsibility to themselves and service to their community.

The unique flexibility of the Award makes it ideally suited to easy adaptation and integration into different cultures and societies. The basic principles of the Award remain the same, but the activities and delivery continue to evolve and adapt to suit the changing demands of modern society and the varying needs of young people. The Award is now an international programme recognized and used by organizations working with young people throughout the world.

Ready for Workshop 4?

1 **a** Look at these photos which are connected to the topics from this workshop. What can you remember about each of these topics?

Washington D.C.

Winston Churchill

Royal Family

Plastic waste

b Choose one of the topics from this workshop and give a short (two-minute) talk to the rest of the class.

2 Jeff is talking to his grandfather about a conversation he had with Ava. Decide whether the underlined parts of the conversation are true or false. Correct the false ones.

G6

G11

Mr B.   So, what did you talk about with Ava?

Jeff   I was telling her my thoughts <u>from</u>[1] politicians and young people.

Mr B.   And what did she say?

Jeff   She said <u>she knew what I mean</u>[2], they have similar problems with youth engagement in the US, too.

Mr B.   Yes, I can imagine that. Did she mention the most recent election at all?

Jeff   Yes, she said she was <u>very anxious for it</u>[3], particularly when she <u>must</u>[4] wait such a long time for the results.

Mr B.   I can imagine.

Jeff   And the fact she <u>couldn't</u>[5] vote made it <u>very</u>[6] worse.

Mr B.   Yes, many young people felt like that with Brexit, too.

Jeff   We discussed Brexit <u>actually</u>[7]!

Mr B.   Really? What did she say?

Jeff   She said that even though the referendum was <u>already a long time</u>[8] now it <u>always still</u>[9] has a direct impact on national and global politics, as well as on the <u>life</u>[10] of young people. Or <u>something as this</u>[11], I can't quite remember!

Mr B.   Ah yes, sadly that's true. It's interesting she can see that all the way from America!

Jeff   Exactly. What do you think, <u>as a older person living</u>[12] in the UK?

Mr B.   I feel it <u>could had been</u>[13] the wrong decision.

3 The students in Brighton watched a video about the American political system. Afterwards, Liam wrote a short text about what he learned. Unfortunately, he made ten factual mistakes. Read the text and correct his mistakes.

> The election of the American president takes place every six years. There are usually two main candidates, one from the Republican Party and one from the Democratic Party. We say that someone is 'running for office' and that the 'presidential race is on'. A president can only be in office for one term of four years.
>
> 5 The American political system is based on the constitution. The first eight amendments were passed in 1891 and make up the Bill of Rights. One of the most famous of these is the first amendment. This amendment allows Americans to own guns.
>
> The judicial branch of the government is called Congress and it has two parts: The House of Representatives and the Senate. There are 100 congressmen and women in the first of these. Each
> 10 state has the same number of representatives who are elected every four years. They must be at least 25 years old and have been an American citizen for at least nine years.

4 Read the text about President Joe Biden that was written in February 2021. Complete it

G5

G11 with the correct form of the verbs from the box.

> be (2x) ■ become ■ campaign ■ elect (2x) ■ involve ■ kill ■ strike ■ win

> In November 2020, Joe Biden **1** to become the 46th President of the USA. Biden, who **2** in politics for fifty years, became one of the youngest people **3** a seat in the US Senate at the age of 29. Then tragedy **4** the family when his wife and
> 5 daughter **5** in a car accident and his two sons were seriously injured.
> During his time in politics, Biden **6** for some key issues including the Violence Against Women Act, which **7** law in
> 1994. He had run twice for the democratic nomination in 1988 and 2008 before he **8** as the
> 10 candidate in 2020. So, what is his presidency **9** like? With Covid-19 and real economic issues it is difficult to know for sure, but one thing that is likely is that it **10** different from the Trump years.

5 Use the information below to write an article about environmental issues in Germany. Add some ideas of your own and structure your article as you have learned in this workshop. Write about 120 words.

> • 2017 6.2 million tons of plastic waste produced.
> • 48% of the plastic waste collected / 38% recycled.
> • Famous 'Green Dot' recycling system introduced in 1991.
> • 40% energy from renewable sources in 2018.
> • Law agreed in 2019 after protests in over 500 towns and cities across the country.

Kamala Harris, *The truths we hold: An American journey* (2019)

Kamala Harris was born on October 20, 1964 in Oakland, California to an Indian mother and a Jamaican father. Her parents divorced when she was seven years old. In 2020, Harris became both the first female and first African-American vice president in the history of the United States. In this extract, she talks about her school years and what influenced her to become a lawyer.

My mother understood very well that she was raising two black daughters. She knew that her adopted homeland would see Maya and me as black girls, and she was determined to make sure we
5 would grow into confident, proud black women.

About a year after my parents separated, we moved into the top floor of a duplex[1] on Bancroft Way, in a part of Berkeley known as the flatlands. It was a close-knit neighborhood of working families who
10 were focused on doing a good job, paying the bills, and being there for one another. It was a community that was invested[2] in its children, a place where people believed in the most basic tenet[3] of the American Dream: that if you work hard and do
15 right by the world, your kids will be better off than you were. We weren't rich in financial terms, but the values we internalized provided a different kind of wealth.

My mom would get Maya and me ready every
20 morning before heading to work at her research lab. [...] She would kiss me goodbye and I would walk to the corner and get on the bus to Thousand Oaks Elementary School. I only learned later that we were part of a national experiment in desegregation[4],
25 with working-class black children from the flatlands being bused in one direction and wealthier white children from the Berkeley hills bused in the other. At the time, all I knew was that the big yellow bus was the way I got to school.

30 Looking at the photo of my first-grade class reminds me of how wonderful it was to grow up in such a diverse environment. Because the students came from all over the area, we were a varied bunch; some grew up in public housing and others were
35 the children of professors. I remember celebrating varied cultural holidays at school and learning to count to ten in several languages. I remember parents, including my mom, volunteering in the classroom to lead science and art projects with the kids. [...]
40
When Maya and I finished school, our mother would often still be at work, so we would head two houses down to the Sheltons', whom my mother knew through Uncle Aubrey, and with whom we shared a long-standing relationship of love, care, 45 and connection. [...]

When I would come home from the Sheltons', I'd usually find my mother reading or working on her notes or preparing to make us dinner. Breakfast aside, she loved to cook, and I loved to sit with her 50 in the kitchen and watch and smell and eat. [...] My mother cooked like a scientist. She was always experimenting – an oyster beef stir-fry one night, potato latkes[5] on another. Even my lunch became a lab for her creations: On the bus, my friends, with 55 their bologna[6] sandwiches would ask excitedly, 'Kamala, what you got?' I'd open the brown paper bag, which my mother always decorated with a smiley face or a doodle[7]: 'Cream cheese and olives on dark rye[8]!' I'll admit, not every experiment was 60 successful – at least not for my grade school palate[9]. But no matter what, it was different, and that made it special, just like my mother. [...]

Saturday was 'chores day,' and each of us had our assignments. And my mother could be tough. She 65 had little patience for self-indulgence. My sister and I rarely earned praise for behavior or achievements that were expected. 'Why would I applaud you for something you were supposed to do?' she would admonish if I tried to fish for compliments. And if I 70 came home to report the latest drama in search of a sympathetic ear, my mother would have none of it. Her first reaction would be 'Well, what did you do?' In retrospect[10], I see that she was trying to teach me that I had power and agency. Fair enough, but it still 75 drove me crazy.

---

[1] **duplex** an apartment with rooms on two floors – [2] **to be invested in sth.** to care about sth. very much – [3] **tenet** *Grundsatz* – [4] **desegregation** the process of ending the separation of groups, here, races – [5] **potato latkes** a kind of potato pancake – [6] **bologna** *Mortadella* – [7] **doodle** *Gekritzel* – [8] **rye (bread)** *Roggen(brot)* – [9] **palate** *Gaumen* – [10] **in retrospect** looking back

But that toughness was always accompanied by unwavering[11] love and loyalty and support. If Maya or I was having a bad day, or if the weather had been gray and depressing for too long, she would throw what she liked to call an 'unbirthday party,' with unbirthday cake and unbirthday presents. Other times, she'd make some of our favorite things – chocolate chip pancakes or her 'Special K' cereal cookies ('K' for Kamala). And often, she would get out the sewing machine and make clothes for us or for our Barbies. She even let Maya and me pick out the color of the family car, a Dodge Dart that she drove everywhere. We chose yellow – our favorite color at the time – and if she regretted having empowered[12] us with the decision, she never let on. [...]

Three times a week, I would go up the street to Mrs. Jones's house. She was a classically trained pianist, but there weren't many options in the field for a black woman, so she became a piano teacher. And she was strict and serious. Every time I looked over at the clock to see how much time was left in the lesson, she would rap my knuckles[13] with a ruler. Other nights, I would go over to Aunt Mary's house, and Uncle Sherman and I would play chess. He was a great player, and he loved to talk to me about the bigger implication of the game: the idea of being strategic, of having a plan, of thinking things through multiple steps ahead, of predicting your opponent's actions and adjusting yours to outmaneuver[14] them. Every once in a while, he would let me win. [...] I was happy just where I was. But when I was in middle school, we had to leave. My mother was offered a unique opportunity in Montreal, teaching at McGill University and conducting research at the Jewish General Hospital. It was an exciting step in advancing her career.

It was not, however, an exciting opportunity for me. I was twelve years old, and the thought of moving away from sunny California in February, in the middle of the school year, to a French-speaking foreign city covered in twelve feet of snow was distressing, to say the least. My mother tried to make it sound like an adventure, taking us to buy our first down jackets and mittens[15], as though we were going to be explorers of the great northern winter. But it was hard for me to see it that way. [...] I was sure to take my upbringing with me to Montreal. One day, Maya and I held a demonstration in front of our building, protesting the fact that kids weren't allowed to play soccer on the lawn. I'm happy to report that our demands were met. [...]. By the time I got to high school, I had adjusted to our new surroundings. I still missed home, my friends and family, and was always so happy to return during the summer and holidays, when we'd stay with my father or Mrs. Shelton. But I'd gotten used to most of it. What I hadn't gotten used to was the feeling of being homesick for my country. I felt this constant sense of yearning to be back home. There was no question in my mind I'd return home for college. [...]

During high school, I started thinking more concretely about my future – college and beyond. I'd always assumed I would have a career; I'd seen the satisfaction my parents derived from their work. I'd also seen a series of extraordinary women – Aunt Mary, Mrs. Wilson, Mrs. Shelton, and my mother most of all – leading in their respective fields of influence, and the difference they were making in others' lives.

Though the seed was planted[16] very early on, I'm not sure when, exactly, I decided I wanted to be a lawyer. Some of my greatest heroes were lawyers: Thurgood Marshall, Charles Hamilton Houston, Constance Baker Motley – giants of the civil rights movement. I cared a lot about fairness, and I saw the law as a tool that can help make things fair. But I think what most drew me to the profession was the way people around me trusted and relied on lawyers. Uncle Sherman and our close friend Henry were lawyers, and any time someone had a problem, within the family or the neighborhood, the first thing you'd hear was 'Call Henry. Call Sherman. They'll know what to do. They'll know how to make sense of this.' I wanted to be able to do that. I wanted to be the one people called. I wanted to be the one who could help. [...]

from: Kamala Harris, *The truths we hold: An American journey*. Penguin: New York, 2019.

[11] **unwavering** never changing – [12] **to empower** to give sb. freedom to do sth. – [13] **knuckles** where the fingers join on to the main part of the hand – [14] **to outmaneuver sb.** *jmd. ausbremsen* – [15] **mittens** *Fäustlinge* – [16] **to plant a seed** to lay the groundwork for sth.

THREE

The kidnappers' note asked for a lot of money. This was a problem, because, as I said earlier, the one thing the Otherhands do not have much of, is money.

'But we're not going to pay them anyway, are we?' asked Cudweed. 'That would be wrong.'

'It may be the *wrong* thing to do,' said his mother, 'but it might be the *only* thing to do! Just imagine if the police can't help.'

'I'm sure they can,' said Solstice, but I think she said that more to make Minty feel better than because she believed it herself. As it turned out, she was probably right about the police.

Before they arrived, Valevine kept checking the amount of money the kidnappers had asked for.

'One hundred thousand pounds ...' he said. 'Hmm. Minty, my dear, how much do we have?'

Minty blinked.

'You mean all the money we have in the world?'

'Yes, that's what I mean.'

'Well,' she said. 'We have today's takings from Open Day.'

'And how much is that?'

'About sixty-two pounds.'

'So, we're a little short then?' asked Valevine.

'Yes, dear,' said Minty. 'About a hundred thousand pounds short.'

'Children!' cried Valevine.

'Yes, father?' said Solstice and Cudweed.

'Go and check your piggy banks[1]. Right now! See if either of you have one hundred thousand pounds, will you?'

Everyone ignored Valevine, because he was clearly losing his mind.

'Don't worry,' said Solstice, 'the police will be here soon,' and just as she said that, the doorbell rang and it was, indeed, the police.

'Now everything will be all right,' she said, and went off to let them in.

A few minutes later Solstice returned with a policeman. Just one.

He was a short, skinny chap[2], so short that his uniform seemed to be too big for him. The bottoms of his trousers hung so low they dragged[3] on the floor, and his hat kept slipping down over his eyes.

'Where are the rest of you?' said Valevine.

'Hmm?' he said. It appeared that the police station had only sent one police officer. Not only that, they had sent one of their most stupid police officers. He took a notebook out of his pocket, and a pen, and began asking questions. But they were very stupid questions.

'So,' he said, thinking hard, 'Your twins have gone missing, am I right?'

'Yes, we told you that on the telephone!' said Minty.

'And you think they have been kidnapped? Why do you think that?'

'Because we have had a ransom note from the kidnappers! We told you that, too!'

The policeman looked rather sternly[4] at Minty.

'And you don't think, for one minute, that perhaps your little twins are just playing a trick on you, and sent you the note themselves?'

Minty lost her temper[5].

'No, I do not! They are four years old! They can't even spell their own names, do you think they can write a ransom note?'

The policeman looked unimpressed by this logic.

'When you've been a police officer as long as I have ...' he began, to which Valevine replied, 'Exactly how long have you been a police officer?'

The policeman looked confused.

'What day is it?' he asked.

'Sunday,' said Cudweed. 'Why?'

'In that case, three weeks,' he said. 'Still waiting for the right size of uniform.'

Valevine looked as if he was about to explode.

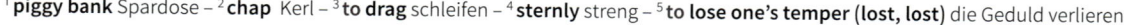

---

[1] **piggy bank** Spardose – [2] **chap** Kerl – [3] **to drag** schleifen – [4] **sternly** streng – [5] **to lose one's temper (lost, lost)** die Geduld verlieren

'Three weeks! What use is this idiot?'

90 'Now, sir,' said the policeman, 'I will ask you to watch your behaviour towards an officer of the law.'

'Poppycock[6]!' declared Valevine. 'Officer of the law? A cabbage would be more useful!'

Now, at least someone was talking about food, which 95 seemed a good thing to me, even if ravens only eat cabbage in an emergency; the sort of emergency where there is nothing else to eat.

Anyway, at this point, I started paying attention again, because maybe we could turn 'cabbage' into 100 'dried mouse', and then I really would feel like eating something.

None of this happened however, because just then, as Valevine was talking 105 about cabbages, the doorbell rang again. Solstice ran off to see who it 110 was, and then five minutes later (it's a long way to the door), she came running back, with another letter in her hand.

'It must have been the kidnappers again!' she said. 115 'They were right here!'

She looked at the policeman.

'Well? Aren't you going to chase after them and see if you can arrest them?'

'Maybe,' he said. 'In a while.'

120 'But the longer you wait, the more time they –'

'What does the note say?' he asked, interrupting.

Solstice read it.

'Oh my God!' the note said, 'How do you put up with them for five minutes? It's unbearable[7]. You can have 125 them back. You don't need to give us one hundred thousand pounds after all.'

'Hooray!' shouted Cudweed, but Solstice hadn't finished reading the note.

'You can have them back,' the note added, 'on one 130 condition. We will swap your children for the big raven. He can meet us on the old scary bridge in the forest at midnight.'

'Krark?' I said, which meant 'Raven? *Big* raven? Do they mean me? I've been on a diet recently.'

135 'Let me get this right,' said Valevine. 'The kidnappers originally wanted one hundred thousand pounds. But now, they're happy to forget all that if we give them Edgar instead? That doesn't make any sense!'

'No,' said Minty, 'maybe not, but it seems like a pretty 140 good deal to me.'

And then, everyone turned to look at me.

They didn't say anything, but they didn't have to. It was clear what they were thinking.

What I was thinking was, 'are we sure we can't just 145 let them keep the twins?'

But it was no good[8].

Solstice came over to me and looked into my eyes for so long I thought I might melt.

'Kruk,' I said, very quietly, which meant, 'okay, but I 150 am really not happy about this.'

So that was how I found myself sitting on the old scary bridge in the forest at midnight, waiting to meet the kidnappers.

---

[6] **poppycock** Schnickschnack; Unsinn – [7] **unbearable** unerträglich – [8] **it was no good** es hat nichts genützt

Youth matters

Young people around the world face lots of different issues. Look at the pictures and discuss what issues each one shows.

61)) Listen to six people talking about issues that affected them. Listen and match each speaker to one of the pictures.

A

'If they don't like you for being yourself, be yourself even more.'
Taylor Swift, US singer-songwriter

'Blood makes you related; love makes you a family.'
unknown

B

In a government survey in 2019, over 90 per cent of Canadian citizens said that they would be comfortable if a neighbour were gay, lesbian or bisexual, and 87 per cent would be comfortable if that neighbour were trans.
from an LGBT+ news website

C

'Every child is gifted. They just unwrap their packages at different times.'
Michael Carr, US author

'To me, beauty is about being comfortable in your own skin. It's about knowing and accepting who you are.'
Ellen Degeneres, US TV host

D

'Hating our bodies is something that we learn, and it sure as hell is something that we can unlearn.'
Megan Jayne Crabbe, British blogger

E

EQUAL RI SHOULD BE NOT FOUGHT

BLACK LIVES MATTER

'We are all different, which is great because we are all unique. Otherwise, life would be very boring.'
Catherine Pulsifer, US self-help author

'What I did in my youth is a hundred times easier today. Technology breeds crime.'
Frank Abagnale, US security consultant

F

61 Listen again and complete the sentences. Sometimes, you need more than one word.

The first speaker was thirteen when he first ⬛1⬛. The second speaker says his grandfather's views are rather ⬛2⬛. The third speaker is worried that her children might ⬛3⬛ when they are older. The fourth speaker's confidence is affected because she ⬛4⬛. The fifth speaker is surprised that ⬛5⬛ in the twenty-first century. The sixth speaker ⬛6⬛ to build his muscles faster.

Read the quotes. Discuss what makes people different.

We are family

1   Modern families

a   Read the introduction to the article (lines 1 – 13). Summarize how family structures have changed.

b   Read what Sadie and Mac say about their families and do the tasks.

1   Describe what kind of family Sadie and Mac each have.
2   List what difficulties each of them has experienced.
3   Explain what they think is the best thing about their families.

Families have changed!

Families are becoming increasingly diverse in English-speaking countries as well as in other parts of the world. For a long time a married couple and their children, who live in the same household have been referred to as 'a nuclear family'. Today
5   families can have many more different structures.
Up to half of marriages end in divorce, and many people get married again. This creates the blended family. In these cases, the children have to get used to living in a new unit.
Single-parent families, which may include a single mum or dad
10 and their children, are increasingly common.
Same-sex marriage, which was legalized in Canada in 2005 and in 2015 in the USA, has led to even more family diversity. The 2020 US Census was the first that allowed respondents to indicate they are part of a same-sex couple, either married or unmarried.

We asked two teens, one from Canada and one from the US, about life in their new-style families.

15 I was twelve when my mom and dad divorced. My two older brothers, who I've always been very close to, went to live with my dad, and me and my sister Kristen lived with my mom. I was upset about Mom and Dad splitting. But Dad made very clear that I'm still part of his family no matter what happens. Mom would always tell me the good parts of having two families so I didn't feel sad, like, 'You'll get two Christmas presents'. And I was just like, 'Oh
20 yeah', and I was really happy.
On weekends I'd go to my dad's house. When my friends, who had known me before my parents divorced, came over, they'd ask, 'Why don't you live at this house?' and I'd just tell them about exactly what I just said and they'd be understanding, they'd just be like, 'Oh, okay'.
Sadie, 16 (US)

25 Some people, who were brought up in traditional families, would probably think my family is a bit irregular, because I have two moms. As in – gay moms. But to me, my family, which gives me safety, is just normal. We do things that every other family does. We are friends with people who think we are just average. It's a very easy-going family, not very uptight, but the best thing is that it's loving.
30 A harder thing about being part of my family is the fact that I experienced teasing and bullying at school in the past. No one wanted to play with me because they were afraid they'd be bullied like me. Kids who came over would ask sometimes, 'Where's your dad?', and I'd have to explain. But my family has taught me to be accepting of everyone, no matter what race, skin colour, gender or really anything.
Mac, 15 (Canada)

🔊 62 Words and phrases

respondent	somebody who fills in a questionnaire
to tease	to make fun of somebody or to laugh at somebody in a playful, sometimes unkind way
uptight	strict, not very relaxed

2 **Giving information**

a Look at the information in the box. Then find more examples in the text.

Relative clauses

● **Defining relative clauses** give important information about a person or thing. If we left out the relative clause, the sentence would be incomplete.
*We do things **that** every other family does.*
*We are friends with people **who** think we are just average.*

● **Non-defining relative clauses** add extra information. We use commas to separate extra information from the rest of the sentence. If we remove the clause, the sentence is still grammatically correct.
*Single-parent families, **which may include a single mum or dad and their children**, are common.*
*My two older brothers, **who I've always been very close to**, live with my dad.*

---

b Which relative pronouns in the grammar box examples can be left out?

3* **Family matters**

a Complete the sentences with relative pronouns. Add any missing commas.

1 My family really matters to me, so I feel sorry for kids ▬▬▬ don't get on with theirs.
2 My mum and dad ▬▬▬ got divorced six years ago still meet regularly.
3 A nuclear family ▬▬▬ means a married couple plus children ▬▬▬ all live in the same household used to be the norm.
4 Same-sex marriage in Canada ▬▬▬ was legalized in 2005 is fairly common nowadays.
5 Children ▬▬▬ come from same-sex marriages sometimes experience bullying at school.

b Read the two texts. Decide which relative clause needs a comma. Explain your decision.

A Extended family
The extended family consists of cousins, aunts or uncles and grandparents who live together and who help to raise the children and carry out household duties. Children who are brought up
5 in such families often have a very close relationship to relatives other than their parents.

B Grandparent family
A growing number of children live with a grandparent or grandparents. Their parents cannot look after them for a variety of reasons. There are obvious difficulties with any
5 arrangement that asks a lot from everyone. Grandparents might struggle to keep up with young kids whose needs can be tiring.

---

4 **Family stories.** Valerie and Mike, two New Zealanders of immigrant descent, share their stories. Listen and do the tasks. Compare your answers with a partner.

1 Explain why Valerie's and Mike's relatives came to New Zealand.
2 Outline the difficulties Valerie's grandmother faced.
3 Illustrate how Valerie and Mike feel about their cultural heritage and identity.

5 **It's your turn: Talking about my family.**
Choose a different topic each. Make notes about your topic. Decide who starts as speaker A.
Student A: Speak about your topic for a minute.
Student B: Use phrases from the *TIP* box to show you're listening to your partner. Swap roles and do the task again.

● My grandparents / A grandparent
● Someone in my family who I am close to
● Family traditions
● What I like (best) about my family

TIP

Active listening can be used to encourage someone to speak, for example:
Go on. Tell me more. That's interesting.
Really? Wow! I know what you mean.

Grammar and structures

Defining relative clauses (revision) and non-defining relative clauses → **G14**

Mac's family are friends with people **who think they are just average**.
Single-parent families, **which may include a single mum or dad and their children,** are increasingly common.

→ Workbook, page 91   **PRACTICE A**

PART 1

PART 2

PART 3

1 **a Think:** Look at the cartoon. What gender expectations and roles are being challenged?

b Pair: Look at the list of typical household chores and activities. Draw a diagram like this and put them in the part of the diagram you think they belong to.

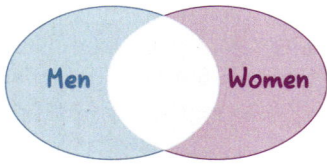

bake bread, cakes, etc. ∎ do the dishes ∎ do the grocery shopping ∎ do the ironing ∎ fix the computer ∎ mow the lawn ∎ prepare meals ∎ raise the children ∎ set up the internet ∎ take the rubbish out ∎ vacuum the house ∎ wash clothes ∎ wash the car

c Share: Compare your diagrams. Discuss the differences and similarities.

d Use your ideas after sharing and finish these sentences.

In the average family there are certain household chores and activities that are typically done by men and women.
- For example, men tend to …
- While women are often responsible for …, men …
- In some families, it is the men who … and the women who …

2 Read the extracts and identify:
- typical gender stereotypes for boys and girls.
- how gender roles are learned and reinforced.
- how / why things are changing today.
- what parents are doing to raise gender-neutral kids.

Raising children gender-neutral
We used to raise girls and boys based on gender stereotypes. We believed that being a boy or a girl dictated who you were and what you could do. But ideas about gender identity have
5 changed. More and more parents are raising their kids to be more gender-neutral. They are choosing clothes and toys that don't reinforce gender stereotypes. Some aren't even telling their children what gender they are. They want
10 to give their children the freedom to choose their own gender identity when they are old enough.

Gender expectations
Research shows that children start to understand gender expectations as young as four. They develop these ideas by watching and copying how the people around them behave.
5 So parents or carers who want to raise gender-neutral children should model what they want their kids to believe. For example, make sure household chores aren't gendered – i. e. mom cleans the house, dad mows the lawn; mom
10 looks after the baby, dad goes out to work. This can help kids understand that gender doesn't limit what tasks they do.

Popularity of gender-neutral names
New US data shows a huge rise in gender-neutral names since 1985. In 2018, 'Harper' (traditionally a boy's name) pushed 'Abigail' out of the top 10 girls' names for the first time in 17
5 years. Parents who don't want their children to conform to stereotypical expectations – 'boys climb trees and girls play with dolls' – are giving their children a unisex or genderless name. This could be helpful later when applying for jobs, as
10 gender bias still exists in the world of work.

🔊 64)) **Words and phrases**

to **reinforce**   to give support to an idea and make it stronger
to **conform to something**   to behave in a traditional way

WES-40903-004

→ Workbook, page 92

1 You're going to watch a video about a 14-year-old teenager called Tayler. What do you think the title *My genderation* refers to? Watch and find out about Tayler's journey.

2 Read what Tayler says and choose the correct meaning for the <u>underlined</u> parts.

1 I like <u>mucking around</u> outside.
   a spending time aimlessly, with silly things
   b cleaning the dirt off the outside path
   c playing in the mud

2 I never <u>identified with the girls.</u>
   a I never liked girls.
   b I never knew who the girls were.
   c I never felt I was a girl.

3 <u>Everything in my head clicked a lot more.</u>
   a I had a strange noise in my head.
   b I understood everything clearly.
   c My head hurt.

4 <u>It felt like a huge weight off my shoulder.</u>
   a I felt a lot better.
   b I put down the weight I carried on my shoulder.
   c My shoulder felt heavy.

5 It's trying to <u>conceal</u> something.
   a hide
   b ignore
   c deal with

CULTURE CORNER

LGBTQIA is an abbreviation used when referring to *lesbian*, *gay*, *bisexual*, *transgender*, *queer* (which is anyone who doesn't identify as heterosexual or 'straight'), *intersex* (that is people who have sex organs or hormones that don't match their gender) and *asexual* (a term for people who are not interested in sex). Together they are often seen as a group or community.

3 **a** Read the summary of Tayler's story, then complete it with the extra information below. Use relative clauses. Add commas when necessary.

> Tayler is a 14-year-old trans boy from Wales. Tayler decided he wanted to make the transition to become a boy. He is currently on hormone-blocker medication.
> 5 He was helped by Stonewall. Fox Fisher from Stonewall came to Tayler's school to give a talk and tell the other kids about him. Tayler felt very relieved after Fox's visit.
> His mum was surprised when Tayler first told
> 10 her that he felt like a boy trapped in a girl's body. She remembered how she had tried to make Tayler wear dresses. Finally, she accepted him for who he is and now she feels very proud of him.

1 Tayler likes skateboarding, drawing and playing on his video console.

Tayler is a 14-year-old trans boy from Wales, who likes skateboarding, drawing and playing on his video console.

2 He realized that he wasn't supposed to be a girl when he was 10 or 11.
3 This prevents puberty from starting.
4 Stonewall is an organization that supports LGBTQ people.
5 Tayler had been worried about telling everyone himself.
6 His mum didn't think she had forced gender roles on him.
7 This had made him angry because he'd only wanted to wear trousers.

b Write a letter to a magazine about gender issues (250 words). Use vocabulary from this workshop.

 Words and phrases

to muck about   (*infml.*) to behave in a silly way, especially when you should be doing something else

Schools and diversity

1 **A big decision**

 a Listen to the conversation between Deepak and his parents. Explain what they are discussing.

 b Listen again and do the tasks.

1 Outline why the Ramesh family might be moving to the USA.
2 Explain why Deepak is worried.
3 Outline the solution they agree on.

2 **Deepak's research**

a Deepak found a short article comparing the education systems in the UK and USA. Read it and outline the differences between the two education systems.

b Match these definitions with words from the article.

1 directed towards something
2 a standard
3 to study a particular subject or skill more than any others
4 following a particular order / one after the other and not at the same time

One language, two systems

The UK system is very exam orientated with Key Stage exams at the ages of 7, 11 and 14. At the end of Year 11 (equivalent to Grade 10 in the USA) students sit their GCSEs (General Certificate of Secondary Education), where each subject has a separate exam. In the USA, students study for their high-school diploma, which
5 they sit at the end of Grade 12. Different US states have their own systems, but often the criterion is to get enough credits from a range of subjects. In other words, in the UK the system is on specializing, while in the US it is geared towards generalization.
In the UK, there is a national curriculum, which all schools should follow. The
10 exception is Scotland, where the schools operate with a framework that focuses on the natural relationship between subjects rather than prescribing exactly what is taught and when.
In the USA, schools can often set their own curricula, or at least one is set at state or district level. Another big difference is that in the US subjects such as math and
15 science are taught sequentially. This means that in one grade students might study chemistry and in the following grade physics, but not both in the same grade.
At the end of high school, students can apply for college or university. Similarly to the UK, students pay tuition fees. The costs vary greatly in the US – while the average annual fee is comparable to that in the UK, famous universities such as
20 Harvard or Yale are much more expensive. A big difference here is that in the US universities often offer scholarships to students who excel at a sport or music. This is very unusual in the UK, although there are some scholarships offered to students from disadvantaged families.

3* **An email to Jeff.** Deepak is talking to Tariq about moving to the USA. Later, he tells Jeff about the possible move in an email. Write the mail using the underlined information and non-defining relative clauses.

T. So explain it to me again.
D. My father has been offered a job at Mass General. It's a hospital in Boston.
T. But why would he want to leave the job he's got here in Durham?

D. The job is connected to his research. It's a fantastic opportunity.
T. Where would you go to school?
D. Dad wants me to go to Boston Latin School. It's one of the best schools in Boston.
T. And what do you think?
D. I'm worried about my GCSEs at the end of this year. I want to pass them with good results.
T. What does your mum think?
D. Mum suggested we discuss the two school systems before we decide. She understands my concern.

 Words and phrases

to **excel (at something)**   to be superior or better than somebody else
scholarship   support given to a student by a college (usually money)

4 A special place

a Listen to a presentation on a radio programme from the USA. Say what it is about and outline what the speaker says about these topics.

No Child Left Behind Act   Mainstream schools
Special training   Monroe High School

b Look at the explanation in the box. Then combine the information below to create commenting sentences. Listen again and check.

> **Sentence commenting relative clauses**
> tell us something about the situation
> described in the main clause.
> *The most important point came with the
> passing of the 'No Child Left Behind Act',*
> **which was a real breakthrough**.

1 There are children from all sorts of ethnic backgrounds. I think that is really good.
2 I think all the children learn that they are all different and all special in their own way. It's a great lesson for life.

5 **A special school.** Use the comments below to complete the extract from the Monroe High School website. Sometimes, more than one answer is possible.

> this creates an inspiring learning
> environment ■ this guarantees that no
> child at Monroe is left behind ■ this helps
> to make the world a better place ■ this
> means there is a place here for everyone
> ■ ~~this means we do not receive public
> funding from the state~~

Monroe High School in Lexington is a non-governmental school, *which means we do not receive public funding from the state*. Our students come from diverse backgrounds, [1].
We provide the best education for all children whatever their background, ability or needs, [2], including children with special educational needs (SEN). Integration is one of our key strengths, [3]. Our students learn the importance of respect and tolerance, [4].

6 Special educational needs (SEN)

a In the programme, the woman spoke about different types of special educational needs. Read the explanations (1–4) and match them to the conditions (A–E). One condition isn't described.

A ADHD   B autism   C cerebral palsy
D dyslexia   E dyscalculia

1 People with this often have problems with numbers. They can also have problems with concepts like bigger vs. smaller, estimating time, counting money or understanding that the number 5 and the word *five* are the same.

2 This is a range of conditions, so not everyone will be the same. However, generally people with this will have challenges with social interaction, both verbal and non-verbal communication, and will often have repetitive behaviours.

3 People with this often have problems with tasks like reading, writing and spelling. They also have problems matching letters to sounds. Often people with this condition will develop strategies to cope or to hide it.

4 When someone has this condition, it can impact the way they behave. They are often hyperactive, find it difficult to sit still for long periods or to concentrate. In the past, children with this condition were often labelled as 'naughty'.

b Do some research on the condition that was not described in **a**. Write a simple explanation.

7 **It's your turn: Living with SEN.** Discuss what could be done to make life easier for students with SEN. Maybe you are one of these students or have a brother or sister or a friend who is. What do you think such students could benefit from? Come up with five suggestions.

Grammar and structures

Commenting clauses → G15
There are children from all sorts of ethnic backgrounds, **which I think is really good.**

PART 1

PART 2

PART 3

1
a Education is important, but what happens if you live hundreds of miles from the nearest school? Conny, who lives in a remote area of New South Wales, is talking about her school life. Look at the pictures and speculate about her life by finishing the sentences.

1 Conny doesn't go to a normal school because …
2 After breakfast Conny turns on the computer and waits for …
3 After her daily lesson, Conny …
4 Sometimes she gets help from …
5 All the learning materials are paid for by …
6 Twice a year Conny goes to a …

> **CULTURE CORNER**
>
> In some countries there are special SEN schools for students with learning difficulties. In New Zealand one such school for dyslexic students is the Summit Point School. In the UK there are several SEN schools offering specialized teaching.

 b Listen and compare. Which parts of her school life were you right about?

2
a Listen to the conversation between Graham and Mike. Explain what they are talking about and what Steven Spielberg, the famous film director, and Graham's son Tim have in common.

G. Hi! We're your new neighbours. We've just moved in.
M. Hi! I'm Mike.
G. I'm Graham and that's my son Tim over there. We moved here because Tim has a new school.

M. A new school? Why's that?
G. Well, Tim has dyslexia.
M. Right, and what does that mean?
G. People with dyslexia have problems reading.
M. When did you find out he had dyslexia?
G. When he started school, he had a few problems. Then, one of the teachers realized. She also has a son with dyslexia.
M. That was lucky.
G. Yes, it was. Now he goes to a special school nearby. He gets really good support there.
M. What does he want to do when he finishes school?
G. He's planning on going to university to study drama.
M. Even though he's got dyslexia?
G. Yes, there are special programmes designed to help people with dyslexia when they are studying.

M. And after university?
G. He has several options, but he wants to become an actor.
M. And how do they manage reading long scripts?
G. Well, Tim's hero is the famous film director Steven Spielberg. He didn't find out he was dyslexic until he was 60!
M. Wow! Well good luck and I hope you like your new house and Tim likes his new school.

b Mike is writing to a friend about the conversation he had with Graham. He typed too quickly and made twelve mistakes. Find and correct them.

> My new neighbour, who has just moved in, introduced me to his son, Tim who has dyslexia. When Tim started school, they thaught he wasn't clever because he had problems reading. Lucky, one of Tim's teachers who's son also has the condition realized why Tim had problems. Apperently Graham and his family moved here so Tim could go to a new school. At his new school, which is nearbye, Tim get really good supports. After he finishes school, he plans to go to university. There he will be in a special programme, which is desined to help people with Tims' condition to study. Tim who wants to become an actor, is hoping to follow in the footsteps of his hero – Steven Spielberg.

3 **a** Read the text about education in New Zealand and use the sentences in the box to complete it with relative clauses.

> Maori accounted for just 8% of the population in 1956 ■ It was originally based on the UK system ■ It's a shame ■
> The Maori language is now taught in most state schools ■ They are called *köhaga reo* ■
> It is a positive development

b Read the text again and do the tasks.

1 Name one reason why education in New Zealand has changed in recent years.
2 Describe how education has changed.
3 Assess the importance of the revival of the Maori language in terms of education.
4 Describe what further changes the writer would like to see in the future.

> Education in New Zealand, _____1_____, has gone through some radical changes in recent years. The biggest changes have been aimed at the indigenous Maori population. The number of Maori,
> 5 ____2____, has grown and now makes up 16% of the population of New Zealand. However, this increase is not the only reason for policy changes. While most Maori students are in mainstream education, there has been a shift in schools to focus
> 10 on helping them reach their potential. Centres for early learning, ____3____, are now quite common. There has also been a revival of the Maori language, ____4____ and, as a consequence, the number of Maori medium schools has increased. Also,
> 15 participation and attainment in schools among the Maoris has improved in recent years, ____5____. While these changes are welcome, the percentage of Maori going on to university is still extremely low, ____6____. It is hoped that the situation will
> 20 improve and all students in New Zealand will have the same opportunities.

4 **a** Rachel has started training to be a teacher at a SEN school. She is reading about ways of helping children with SEN. Complete her notes with the words from the box.

> aids ■ behaviour ■ breaks ■ copy ■
> extra ■ instructions ■ places ■ points ■
> real-life ■ schedule ■ steps ■ tasks

For students with autism
- Be consistent
- Stick to a ▮1▮
- Reward good ▮2▮
- Give them choices
- Find quiet ▮3▮

For students with dyscalculia
- Write out the problem
- Break tasks down into small ▮4▮
- Use ▮5▮ examples
- Review frequently
- Use visual ▮6▮ like graphs

For students with ADHD
- Seat them away from windows and doors
- Keep ▮7▮ short
- Try to do any difficult ▮8▮ first
- Use a variety of activities
- Have frequent ▮9▮

For students with dyslexia
- Provide ▮10▮ time to read or write
- Don't ask them to ▮11▮ from the board
- Use bullet ▮12▮

CULTURE CORNER

In the USA, two different grading systems are used in schools. One is numerical and the other is with letters, A, B, C, D and F. These letters are usually connected to a percentage score with anything below C regarded as a fail.

b Discuss with a partner which of the methods mentioned in **a** would help you be more efficient / happier / more relaxed in class.

5 Find out how much you can remember about the education systems in the UK and USA by doing this short quiz. Compare your answers.

1 What do the letters GCSE stand for?
2 Apart from at the end of Year 11, at what ages do children in the UK take exams?
3 When do students in the USA sit their high-school diploma?
4 What is one key difference in the approach to learning different subjects in the two systems?
5 What do all schools in the UK have to follow?
6 Who can get scholarships to go to college or university in the USA?
7 What do the letters SEN stand for?
8 What do people with dyscalculia have difficulties with?

PART 1

PART 2

PART 3

1 Describe what you can see in each picture. What's the connection between them?

A

B

C

D

2 **a** Marcus is an exchange student in the US. He's from Australia. Lindy, a reporter for her school's news website, interviewed him. Listen and number the photos in the order Marcus mentions them.

71))

71)) **b** Read Lindy's questions and listen again. How does Marcus answer them?

1 Can you please summarize the differences between the American and Australian school systems?
2 How would you describe a normal school day?
3 Can you choose your own electives?
4 If you want to go to college or university, what do you do?
5 What are your favourite aspects about being here?
6 What are you looking forward to during the rest of your exchange year?

c Compare your answers with a partner. Then list similarities and differences between the Australian school system and the German system. What do you think are the advantages and disadvantages of each system? Give reasons for your answers.

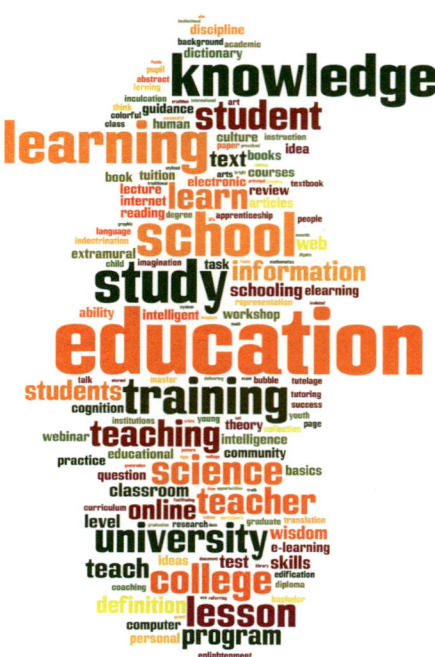

3 **a** There are a lot of SEN schools in the UK. Here are three with some of their key features. Choose one of the schools and carry out some research to give a two-minute presentation about the school. Make notes to help with your presentation.

Name of school	Abingdon House	Wilds Lodge	Greton
Location	London	Oakham, East Midlands	Cambridgeshire
SEN areas	Dyslexia, dyspraxia and communication problems	Social, emotional and mental health issues	Autism and Asperger's
Age range	5 – 17	5 – 19	5 – 19
Universal selling point	Integrated therapy approach focusing on mental health and integration.	Has designated specialists for all needs. Includes an 'eco-school' focusing on the environment.	Focus on life and social skills. Has a 'forest' school where students explore the outdoors.

 b Your teacher will put you in a group. Give your presentation in your group.

4 Look at these photos of special schools and read the text. Describe what each photo shows and discuss what you think is special about the students.

Autism is a neurological disorder that affects the way a person's body and brain works. People suffering from autism are able to speak and learn, but they may have trouble with:
- **expressing feelings and understanding the feelings of others.**
5   They might misunderstand other people's feelings or behaviour.
- **reading social cues.** They might not understand body language or facial expression.
- **handling sensory information.** Loud noises or crowds may bother them.
10 - **handling a new routine.** It might be hard for them to sit in a different seat or to react to people they don't know.

People with **Asperger's syndrome** have difficulties relating to others socially. Generally, people with Asperger's Syndrome can speak with others and can perform fairly well in their school work, but their
15 thinking patterns can be rigid and repetitive. Often, they develop specialized interests.

Cerebral palsy (CP) is a permanent moving disorder which includes difficulties in body movement and muscle coordination. For example, arms and legs can be stiff or forced into unusual positions.
20 Many people with CP have difficulties with tasks such as tying shoe laces or grasping objects.

Down syndrome is a genetic disorder. People with Down syndrome have an extra copy of chromosome 21 and are often mentally impaired. However, many students with Down syndrome are
25 educated in regular schools and some have a paid job in their later lives. Research has shown that children with this genetic disorder often learn better visually. For example, drawing may help with developing their reading or speaking skills.

Understanding diagrams (1)

S1 **Understanding the information.** Look at the line graph and the bar chart. How does each diagram present the information? Choose one diagram each and complete the description.

1 % children living with …

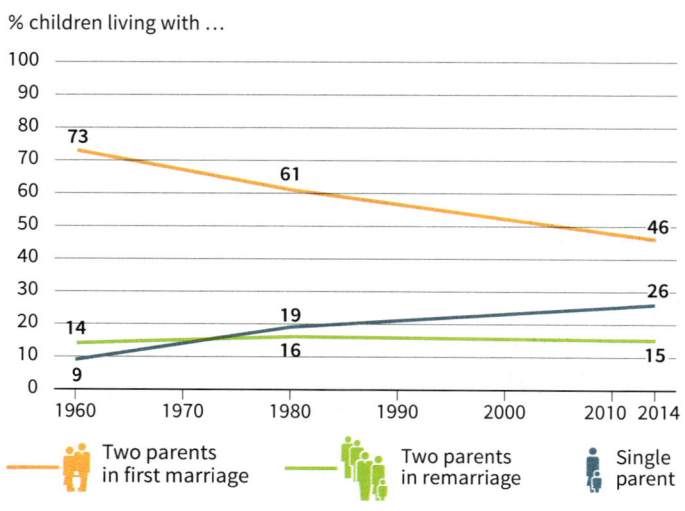

Two parents in first marriage — Two parents in remarriage — Single parent

The graph gives information about changes in family life in the USA. In 1960, 73% of all children were living in a family with two parents in their first marriage. By ⬛1, the number of children living in this type of family had declined to 61%. By 2014, the figure had fallen to less than ⬛2 (46%). By contrast, there has been a dramatic rise in the percentage of children living with single parents. In 2014, ⬛3 of children were living with one parent. The share of children living in a remarriage stood at ⬛4, a small ⬛5 from 14% in 1960.

2 % of people in 12 different countries who say over the past 20 years, equality between men and women in our country has …

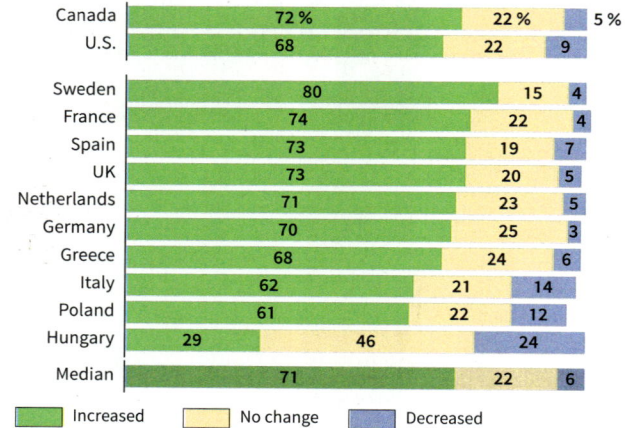

Increased · No change · Decreased

The chart compares the views of people in 12 countries on gender equality. It shows that a majority of people in all but ⬛1 of the countries surveyed believe that gender equality has increased over the past few years. The countries with the ⬛2 percentage holding this view are Sweden and France. In Sweden ⬛3 of people say it has increased, compared with a tiny minority who say it has declined. In contrast, fewer than a ⬛4 of Hungarians believe it has increased. ⬛5 say it has not changed and even ⬛6 say it has decreased.

Sources: (1) Pew Research Center, 2015; (2) Pew Research Center, 2020

S2 **Explaining the information.** Take turns to explain the information. Your partner should ask you to repeat and clarify if necessary.

TIP

Useful language for describing data

Describing the diagram:
The graph / bar chart is about … / shows … / gives information about … / figures for … / compares …

Describing / Explaining change:
By (date), the figure had fallen / declined / risen / increased to … / levelled off … / reached a peak.
There has been a (dramatic / rapid) rise / increase / fall / decline in (the number / percentage of) …

Comparing data:
The majority / A small / tiny minority of people think / believe that …
Less / More / Fewer than / Under (00)% / a half / a third think / believe that …
A smaller / larger / The highest percentage (of) … / 6 out of 10 / Smaller numbers of / Fewer (people) … compared with …
In contrast, …

Concluding:
Overall, … / In conclusion, … / In summary, …

Describing a diagram

S1 **Complete a description.** Look at the infographic. Explain what aspect of changing gender roles it illustrates. Read the description of the line graph and choose the correct words from the box. Refer to the *TIP* on page **132** to help you. You don't need all of the words. Mind the tenses!

> decline ■ decrease ■ fall ■
> fall below ■ fifth ■ higher ■
> increase (2x) ■ less than ■
> level off (2x) ■ lower ■
> more than ■ reach ■ rise ■
> stand at ■ third

S2 **Write a description**

a Look at the description of the line graph. What words and phrases are used to link the different paragraphs? Make a list and add at least three useful words or linking phrases.

b Look at the bar chart. Describe the information. Refer to the *TIP* on page **132** to help you with language.

- Introduction: Say what information the chart gives and what the survey is based on.
- Paragraph 2: Describe the highest statistics.
- Paragraph 3: Describe the lower statistics and those that show no change.
- Conclusion / Summary: Say what can be seen from the survey.

S3 **Edit your description.** Exchange your text with a partner. Your partner reads and edits it. Rewrite your report if necessary.

[1] % of mothers who are in the labor force with children …

The graph shows the ⬚1 in the number of mothers in the US labor force since 1975. It compares the percentage of working mothers with children under 3, 6 and 18.

As we can see, in 1975, ⬚2 half of mothers with children younger than 18 were in employment. Only 40% of those with children under 6 and about a ⬚3 of those with children younger than 3 years old were working outside of the home.

However, those numbers ⬚4 dramatically. By 2000, 73% of all mothers were in the labor force. Since 2000, participation rates of mothers ⬚5 and more or less ⬚6 a peak. Labor force participation in 2014 ⬚7 70% among all mothers of children younger than 18, and 64% of mothers with preschool-aged children.

In conclusion, we can see that the participation of mothers in the labor force has greatly increased since 1975. Although it ⬚8 since 2000, it is far ⬚9 it was four decades ago.

[2] % who say over the past 20 years …

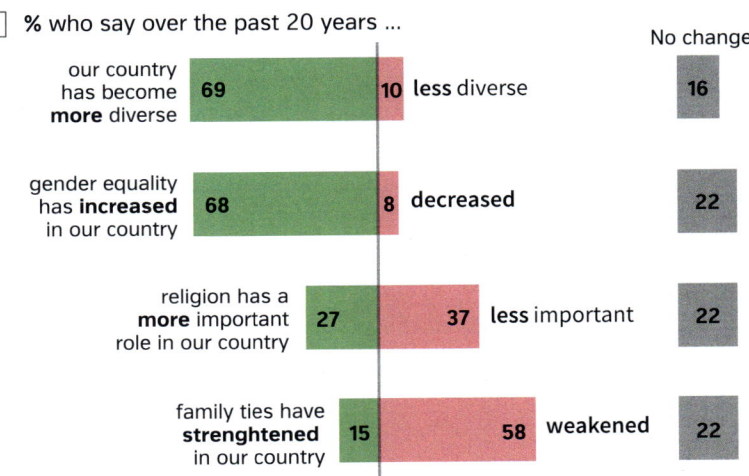

Sources: (1) California Cyrobank; (2) Office for National Statistics, UK 2020.

Applying for a job

1 **What's next?**

a *New Directions*, a career website for students and school leavers, has asked students to share their hopes and plans after they finish secondary school. Look at the options. Which seem most interesting or attractive to you? Rank them in order from 1 to 8 and explain the reasons for your ranking.

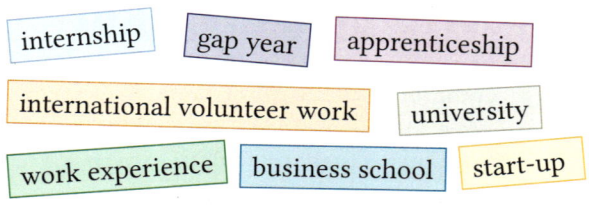

internship gap year apprenticeship

international volunteer work university

work experience business school start-up

b Read what five students have said. Match the options with the students – Amir, Daniela, Lauren, Ben and Sisi.

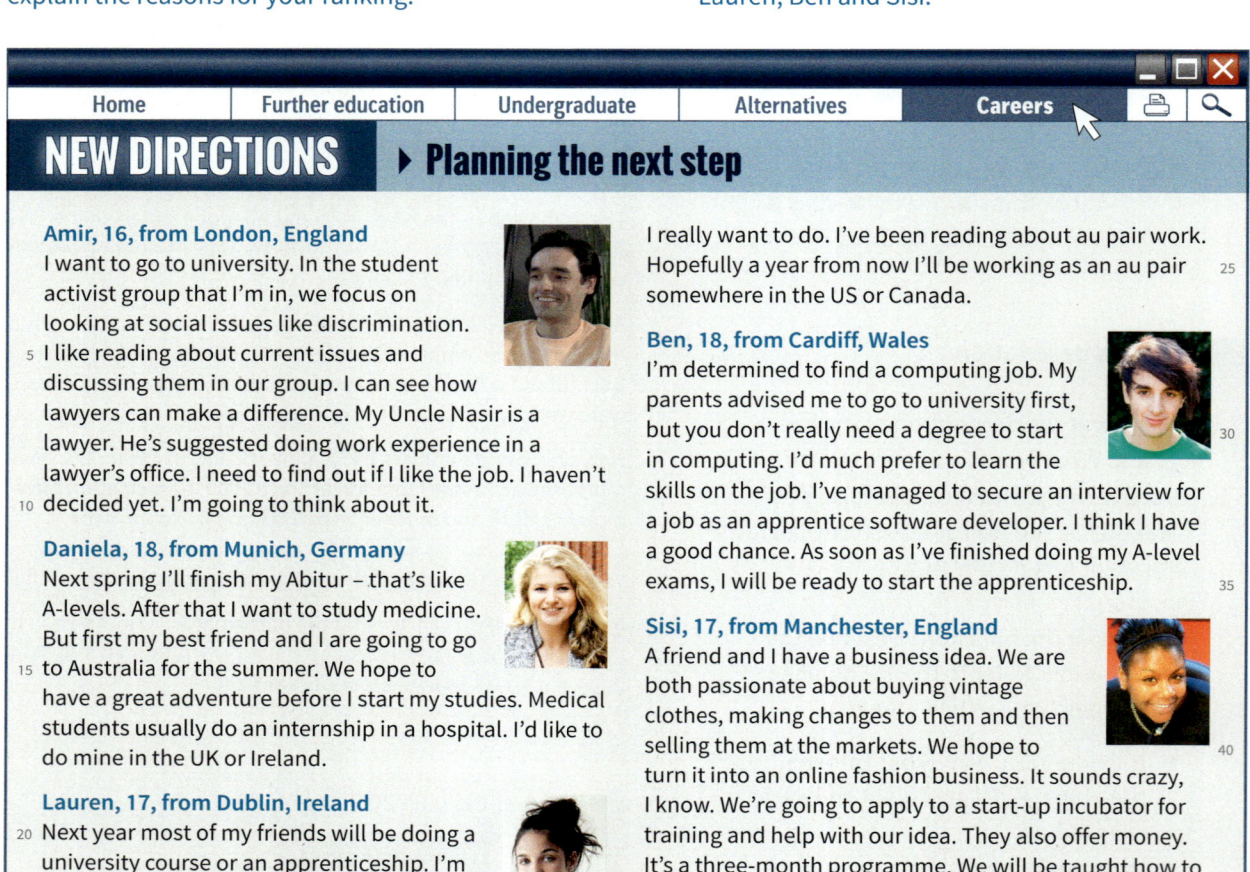

| Home | Further education | Undergraduate | Alternatives | Careers | |

NEW DIRECTIONS ▶ **Planning the next step**

Amir, 16, from London, England
I want to go to university. In the student activist group that I'm in, we focus on looking at social issues like discrimination.
5 I like reading about current issues and discussing them in our group. I can see how lawyers can make a difference. My Uncle Nasir is a lawyer. He's suggested doing work experience in a lawyer's office. I need to find out if I like the job. I haven't
10 decided yet. I'm going to think about it.

Daniela, 18, from Munich, Germany
Next spring I'll finish my Abitur – that's like A-levels. After that I want to study medicine. But first my best friend and I are going to go
15 to Australia for the summer. We hope to have a great adventure before I start my studies. Medical students usually do an internship in a hospital. I'd like to do mine in the UK or Ireland.

Lauren, 17, from Dublin, Ireland
20 Next year most of my friends will be doing a university course or an apprenticeship. I'm not ready for that yet. I'd like to take a gap year to work and get some ideas about what

I really want to do. I've been reading about au pair work. Hopefully a year from now I'll be working as an au pair 25 somewhere in the US or Canada.

Ben, 18, from Cardiff, Wales
I'm determined to find a computing job. My parents advised me to go to university first, but you don't really need a degree to start 30 in computing. I'd much prefer to learn the skills on the job. I've managed to secure an interview for a job as an apprentice software developer. I think I have a good chance. As soon as I've finished doing my A-level exams, I will be ready to start the apprenticeship. 35

Sisi, 17, from Manchester, England
A friend and I have a business idea. We are both passionate about buying vintage clothes, making changes to them and then selling them at the markets. We hope to 40 turn it into an online fashion business. It sounds crazy, I know. We're going to apply to a start-up incubator for training and help with our idea. They also offer money. It's a three-month programme. We will be taught how to build our website and also how to get started. If it 45 doesn't work, I'll probably go to business school.

c Complete the sentences in your own words.

1 Amir is interested in …
2 The first thing that Daniela wants to do is …

3 Lauren doesn't want to … yet.
4 Ben disagrees with his parents about … because …
5 Sisi and her friend are going to need …

🔊 72)) **Words and phrases**

degree	the qualification that you get when you finish college or university
gap year	a one-year break between secondary school and university
to **learn something on the job**	to learn the skills in a practical way
long-term	taking or lasting a long time
start-up incubator	a programme that helps people develop their business ideas

2 **Choices, choices**

a Choose the option that you identify with most – university, apprenticeship, gap year or own business. Explain your choices to your partner.

b Write a short text (150 – 200 words) about your choice to send to an advisor who works for *New Directions*. Include any questions you may have.

3* **A bright future.** Sisi is telling her class why she's applying to the local start-up incubator for training. Read what she says and complete the sentences with the correct form of the verbs.

> How did I become interested in ___1___ (*create*) something new and fashionable from vintage clothes? I was about 10 years old when I learned ___2___ (*do*) basic sewing from my grandmother. I remember ___3___ (*change*) the buttons on my dresses and ___4___ (*decorate*) my jeans with patches. Then I discovered a stall at the local flea market that sold vintage clothes. I got a beautiful dress from there and started ___5___ (*experiment*) with it. I enjoyed ___6___ (*work*) on it so much that I wanted ___7___ (*get*) more – and I did. Now I've decided ___8___ (*turn*) my hobby into serious business. That's why I am looking forward to ___9___ (*learn*) all the skills I'll need to make a living out of my hobby.

> **Remember:**
> Some verbs are always followed by a gerund (*having*) and others by a *to*-infinitive (*to have*). Some verbs can be followed by either a gerund or an infinitive. In these cases the meaning sometimes changes.
> * verb + gerund: *finish, imagine, practise*
> * verb + preposition + gerund: *carry on, look forward to, be interested in, believe in*
> * verb + infinitive: *agree, decide, learn, plan*
> * verb + gerund or infinitive with no change in meaning: *continue, hate, like, prefer*
> * verb + gerund or infinitive with a change in meaning: *forget, remember, stop, try*

4 **Work. Explore. Grow.**

a Listen to the *New Directions* podcast. Why do many school leavers choose to take a gap year? List at least three reasons. Compare your answers.

b Listen again. Are the statements true or false? Correct the false statements.

1 Lucy is planning to go to university in September.
2 She will need to save money for university.
3 In March Lucy plans to travel to the US.
4 Simon has already done work experience at a publishing company.
5 He preferred working at the publishing company to being a volunteer.
6 He hopes to get a place on a degree apprenticeship programme.

c Compare Lucy's and Simon's motivations for taking a gap year. Describe the similarities and differences.

5 **It's your turn: The next step**

a Interview your partner about his / her hopes and plans after finishing school. Make notes.

What ...? Where ...? How long ...?
How are you going to pay for it?
What will you do if ...?
What are you afraid of most?

b After two minutes, change partners and tell your new partner about your first partner's hopes and plans.

Grammar and structures

Different use of gerund and *to*-infinitive (revision) → G16

As soon as I've **finished doing** my A-level exams, I'll go travelling.
That's why I am **looking forward to learning** all the skills I'll need ... .

I **learned to do** basic sewing from my grandmother.
I **like reading** about current issues.
I **remember changing** the buttons on my dresses.

→Workbook, page 100 **PRACTICE A**

1 Discuss with your partner. If you could do work experience for a few weeks in any job or organization, what would it be? Explain why it would be important to you.

2 **a** Look at this job advert from a UK employment website. Do the tasks.

1 Describe the work opportunity that is being offered.
2 Outline the advantages described.
3 Explain how you can apply and how much you can earn.

Work experience placement

Putney Legal Advice Centre, London

Putney Legal Advice Centre is pleased to offer an unpaid work experience placement to a candidate
5 between 15 and 19 years old who shows an interest in one of the careers we offer.

This is a great opportunity to learn about the work of a legal professional and about how a legal advice centre protects the rights of people who cannot afford a
10 lawyer. We can also help you explore career options in the legal profession.

Apply in writing to Amanda.Cowley@putneylegal.co.uk.

---

b Decide which of the students from page **134** could be interested in the advert. Explain why.

3 **a** Amir has seen the advert and written an email about it to his Uncle Nasir. Complete his mail with the correct form of the verbs from the box.

> do ■ follow ■ get ■ look ■ search ■ show ■ talk

Hi Nasir,

I enjoyed 1 on the phone last week. Thanks for all your advice! You suggested 2 work experience to find out if I like legal work. I've
5 decided 3 your advice. I've started 4 at job ads. I want 5 you this advert I saw online. Have you heard of the Putney Legal Advice Centre? Do you think I should apply? Mum says I should, but I'd prefer 6 your opinion first.
10 For now I'll keep 7 the job ads!

Best, Amir

---

b Read Nasir's reply to his nephew. Look at the underlined phrases and decide whether they are correct or wrong. Correct the wrong ones.

Hi Amir,

Thank you for your email. I've looked at the job advert and I definitely think you should apply. I've heard a lot of good things about this legal
5 centre and I even remember to meet[1] lawyers who work there at a conference. They tried to persuade[2] me to go and work for them but as you know, I am happy at my firm. I can tell you they believe in helping[3] the community. The work they
10 do is very varied so if you'd like having[4] experience in different areas of the law then it's the right place for you.
If you do decide to apply[6] then remember including[7] all the articles you've read about social
15 issues. When you write the cover letter don't forget mentioning[5] what you are doing in the student activist group. I am sure they'll be impressed. I hope your application will be successful. But if I were you, I would try looking
20 for[8] other opportunities as well. Have a look at this link *Londonlawfirms.com*, you might find other similarly suitable positions. Good luck!

Nasir

---

4 Role-play a student and careers expert at a fair. Follow these steps:

1 Decide together who is the expert for traineeships and who is the expert for self-employment. Then read your text.
2 Close your books and do the role-play. One of you (A) is the expert, the other person (B) is the student. B asks specific questions about the topic, which the expert tries to answer. You can start like this:
A: *Hello. How can I help you?*
B: *Hello, I'm interested in finding out about …*
A: *Yes. What would you like to know?*
3 Swap roles and do the role-play again.

Traineeships	Self-employment
Traineeships are short, flexible education programmes for 16 – 23-year-olds who don't have the skills and experience to get a job or an apprenticeship.	Being self-employed means you run your own business. You are both the boss and the employee.

 **Words and phrases**

to boost   to increase or make better
failure   when sth doesn't succeed

1 Look at these pictures and describe the people in them. Pay attention to the body language. Speculate what the situation is in each picture. How do you know?

 A

 B

 C

2 **a** Estella, Lucas and Hailey are talking to their school counsellor about their part-time jobs. In groups of three, each of you should focus on one student. Copy the table, then watch the video and complete it.

	Estella	Lucas	Hailey
How is the job?	???	???	???
How is school?	???	???	???
How is the work-school-life balance?	???	???	???

 b Compare notes in your group.

1 Summarize what the three students have in common.
2 Explain in what ways they are different.

 c Find a partner from another group who also focused on your student. Compare your notes and your profiles. Then read the *TIP* box before you watch the video again. This time pay attention to non-verbal communication.

1 Are your answers similar or different? Talk about the differences.
2 How did your student's non-verbal communication help you reach your conclusions?

> **TIP**
>
> **Identifying attitudes through non-verbal communication**
> What a person communicates non-verbally is just as important as what he or she actually says. So what should we listen and watch for to learn about how somebody feels about something?
> - **Tone of voice:** Does the person speak loudly or softly? Fast or slowly? Does the intonation go up and down or is it flat and monotone?
> - **Eye contact:** Does the person look straight at you when speaking or being spoken to? Are his or her eyes fixed, or do they move around a lot?
> - **Facial expression:** Is the person's face relaxed or tense? Do his or her eyes, mouth or eyebrows move a lot or not? Are his or her facial expressions positive (e. g. smiling) or negative?
> - **Body language:** Are the person's shoulders relaxed or tense? Does he or she sit up with a straight back or slump in the chair? With crossed arms or legs? Does the person use hand gestures? If so, what kind of gestures?

 Words and phrases

monotone ≠ lively   to **slump** ≠ to sit straight   **tense** ≠ relaxed

Summer jobs

1 If I were older

 a Listen to Aimee and Liam's conversation and do the tasks.

1. Explain why Aimee is upset.
2. Summarize why Aimee is jealous of Holly.
3. State what kind of job Aimee is trying to find.
4. Explain why she hasn't succeeded.
5. Outline the advice Liam gives to Aimee.
6. List the jobs Liam is going to do and say what you think Liam did to get them.

 b Discuss the following questions:

1. Have you ever had a summer job?
2. If yes, what was it and how did you find it?
3. If no, what kind of job would you like to do?
4. Where would you look for a job?
5. If you found a job advertised in a paper or online, what would you need to do?

2 Looking for a summer job

Summer Job
Boy, 15, is looking for a summer job!
I am hard-working, reliable, good with animals, especially horses.
I am free every weekday and Saturday mornings.
If you can offer me any work, please contact me at summerjob@me.com or leave your contact details in the library.

Hi, my name is Chloe Burnstock and I'd really like to find some work in the summer holidays. I simply adore children, I have a young niece and she is so cute! Also, I am rather competitive when I play sports. My favourite is badminton. I'd prefer not to work at the weekend or start too early. I am willing to do anything if it's not too difficult and if it pays well. My number is 0863 244 9115. Call me!

a Read the summer job posts Liam found on the notice board in the library. Then discuss with a partner. Which one
- gives personal details?
- gives information about what the person is like?
- gives opinions?
- includes the person's availability?
- hints at what kind of work the person would like?
- sets conditions?
- is careful about giving out contact details?

b Which post do you think is more likely to get a reply? Why? Give reasons for your answer.

c Write Aimee's 'looking for a summer job' post. Include the following details:

> Age: 15 • good at swimming / table tennis • good / has experience with children and pets • available for 6 weeks (July – mid-August) but only weekdays

3 Do I need a CV?

a Brendan has found an advert for a job at a summer camp. He's applied and needs to send his CV (Curriculum Vitae) to the organizers. What should he include?

b Complete Brendan's CV on page **139** with the words from the box.

> Address ■ Education ■ Experience ■ Name ■ Qualifications ■ References ■ Skills

Words and phrases

to **adore**	to like something / somebody a lot, love
agency	a business that represents a person
to **boast**	to speak too proudly about something you have done or own
lifeguard	a person who works at a pool or beach and makes sure people are safe
stables (n.)	a place where you keep horses

Curriculum Vitae

1	:	Brendan Sullivan
Age:		14
2	:	36 Hillside Avenue
		Brighton B16 9OX
Phone number:		0896 312 6750
Email:		brendan1@me.com
3	:	King's Park High School, Brighton
		Year 10
4	:	Basic First Aid Certificate
5	:	Captain of the school football team
		Volunteer at Oaktree Primary School –
		assisting the Cubs (Junior Scouts)
6	:	Good organizational skills, team member,
		good with children, outgoing and approachable
7	:	Mr Butler, head teacher, King's Park High School
		Mr Sommersby, football coach, King's Park High
		School
		Mr Wilson, Cubs Leader

4* **From the USA.** Read the email Vivian writes to Aimee and complete the tasks.

> Hi Aimee,
>
> It was great to hear from you and I understand why you are so annoyed. I wanted to get a summer job as a model. Usually you have to be 16 or older, but
> 5 sometimes you can work for an agency when you're younger if your parents give you permission.
> I found an agency, so I asked my parents. My mother said I could, but my dad said 'no', so the agency said I wasn't allowed to work for them and to ask again
> 10 when I turn 16! My dad says I can get a job like dog walking or pet sitting, but I really don't want to. I really need to do something I'm interested in and I think it would be useful for my future career. I know it's too early to decide what I want to do after school,
> 15 but I think I have to make my own choices.
> Anyway, you shouldn't give up! I'm sure you will be able to find a great job. You may get lucky!
>
> Viv xxx

1 Explain why Vivian had to ask her parents' permission to work as a model.
2 Give two reasons why Vivian is upset.
3 Compare Vivian's situation with Aimee's.

Grammar and structures

Modal verbs → G17 – G22

Remember:
- We use *can* and *be able to* for ability: *I'm sure you will **be able to** find a job.*
- We use *can* and *be allowed to* for permission: *You have to be 16 to **be allowed to** work as a model.*
- We use *need to* and *have to* for necessity: *You **have to** be over sixteen.*
- We use *should* for advice: *You **shouldn't** give up!*
- We use *may* and *might* for possibility: *You **may** get lucky!*

5* **Advice from Mum.** Brendan has an interview for the summer camp job. He's asking his mum for advice. Complete the gaps with modals.

B. I have my interview tomorrow and I'm nervous. I don't know what it's like.
M. First, you **1** be there on time. Being late would give the wrong impression.
B. That's not a problem, I'll go straight after school. Oh, but then I **2** change.
M Brendan, wearing uniform is fine, but you **3** make sure your shirt is tucked in. First impressions matter, you know.
B. Got it.
M Listen carefully to the questions the interviewer asks you. You **4** be asked about details of your volunteer work with the Cubs, so you **5** be prepared for that. And if you don't understand a question, you **6** to ask for clarification, of course.
B. And what if I have any questions?
M I'm sure you'll **7** ask about anything you want to know. But you **8** wait till you are invited to ask questions.
B. Do you think I **9** ask about the pay?
M If the interviewer doesn't mention it, of course. You **10** know what you can expect if you get this job.

6 **It's your turn.** Consider what kind of summer job you'd like to do. Think about what's important to you, what your skills are and when you will be available. Write a short job post (80 words) like in **2**, but make sure you don't give your name. Then collect everyone's posts in a group. Mix them up, pick one and read it out. Is it well written or can it be improved?

1 Amelia, Larry, Chris and Paige have written short blog posts about their summer jobs.
Read the posts and and say which of the four students:

1 was offered a job at home?
2 had to apply for the position?
3 was saving up for a trip?
4 doesn't get paid?
5 works and lives at the same place?

6 thinks the job is useful to learn about a future career?
7 does hard physical work?
8 got to know new people?
9 doesn't know exactly what they will do in their job?

Amelia (London, UK)

I got this opportunity through my mum – she is the manager of a care home for the elderly in Chalk Farm. This is the first year I could volunteer there as you have to be 14 to be allowed to work in places like that. Even now,
5 I am only allowed to do certain things, for example serving food, making cups of tea or running errands for the staff or the residents. I love listening to their stories, they remind me of my grandparents. I want to be a nurse when I'm older so this is a good place for me to work.

Chris (Montreal, Canada)

When my mum told me that we couldn't go back home for the summer, I felt really disappointed. But then I saw an advert. The local golf club was looking for caddies for the summer months. I didn't think I had a chance, but I
5 filled out an application form just in case. I had a successful interview and got the position. It was the best decision ever! Now I can spend my days outside, I only have to look after one golfer at a time and the pay is really good. I may even get my own golf clubs.

Larry (Pretoria, South Africa)

I couldn't believe it when my father called me with the news that when I go back to South Africa I'll have a summer job! And not just any job – I'll be working at an animal rescue centre.
5 I know it isn't glamorous – quite the opposite. But I don't mind getting dirty or doing cleaning or heavy lifting. I love animals and I want to help them in any way I can.

Paige (Kerikeri, New Zealand)

In my summer break my dad offered me paid work at our farm, but I wanted to work somewhere else so nobody would think I was getting special treatment. Our neighbour has a huge orchard and was looking for fruit pickers. It was the ideal job for me as I could
5 work with young people from all over the world. I had to work hard to keep up with the others, but I didn't mind that at all. The good thing was that I didn't have to pay for meals and accommodation, so I was able to save up money towards a trip to England.

2 **a** To be good at certain jobs, you need to have the right personal qualities. Match the adjectives in the box with the definitions.

> confident ■ enthusiastic ■ fair ■
> friendly ■ hard-working ■ kind ■
> patient ■ punctual ■ reliable ■
> responsible ■ sensitive ■ strong ■
> team player ■ tidy

1 always does what is expected
2 always doing a lot of work
3 always on time
4 behaving in a nice way to someone
5 being able to wait
6 being good at working together with other people
7 certain of your abilities
8 helping other people
9 powerful
10 excited and interested in something
11 having everything arranged in the right place
12 the ability to make good decisions yourself
13 thinking about other people's feelings
14 treating someone in a way that is right

b Look at the adjectives and select the ones that describe Amelia, Larry, Chris and Paige. Give reason for your choices.

c What about you? How would you describe yourself?

🔊)) **Words and phrases**

errand	a short trip to do, or buy, something
glamorous	attractive in an exciting way
patient	able to wait and not get angry when something is difficult or takes a long time
sensitive	easily upset by what people say or do

→ Workbook, page 104   **PRACTICE B**

3   Read the article about teenage summer job opportunities and complete it with the correct modal verb. Sometimes there is more than one possibility.

Teenagers all around the world are looking for summer jobs, but wherever they live, they **1** find that their options are limited. They **2** do certain jobs as they are too young, for example, they **3** to work with machines or work in a dangerous environment. There are very few job adverts in the papers or on the internet the under 16's **4** apply for. Their best option is to ask family, friends or neighbours as they **5** need babysitters, dog walkers or help in the garden. Certain organizations **6** offer voluntary work where the young people **7** to have special qualifications. Youth clubs or summer camps always welcome help with activities too. It is true that not all these jobs are well-paid or paid at all, but teenagers **8** still benefit because they learn valuable skills.

4   **a Think:** Look at the four jobs teenagers can do and do the tasks.

1   Identify the jobs in the four pictures.
2   List the qualities needed for each job.
3   Describe what you have to do for each job.
4   Which job do you have the qualities for?

b Pair: Compare your answers. Which of the jobs would you like to do / not like to do? Give reasons for your answers.

c Share: Share your answers. Which is the most popular job in your group? Give the reasons why?

1 **a** You are going to read an article about work. Write down three things you think you will read about and compare your ideas with a partner.

b Skim the article and choose the best heading.

c Read the article in detail. Are all your ideas included? What does the article not mention? What had you not thought of?

1 The future of work   **2** The changing nature of work   **3** A job for life   **4** Women in the workplace

In the 1980s, when my parents were young, getting a job wasn't too difficult. Once you had a job that was often where you stayed for the rest of your working life, at least with the same organization or field of
5 work. The same cannot be said of the situation today. A recent survey revealed that it is taking young people two years longer to get their first job than it did twenty years ago. On top of that, they are likely to change jobs far more often than in previous
10 generations. In a recent poll 21% of millennials said they had changed jobs in the last year, while on average people will have had five different jobs by the age of 35! So, what does this all mean for young people today?
15 Firstly, it means they are often in an insecure position, at least in terms of finances. It is a lot harder to put money aside for those big-ticket items like a car, an apartment or a house. The lack of financial security also has an impact on starting a family, which may
20 explain why many people are waiting until much later than in the past. Secondly, living from pay-check to pay-check can have an impact on your mental health. For many youngsters, it is incredibly stressful not knowing if you'll have enough money to
25 pay the bills next month.
One consequence of this situation is that young people feel less loyalty towards their employers. Why should you give your all if you aren't sure you'll have a job in the future? Another consequence
30 is the idea of trying things out until you find something you like. For many, this isn't seen as a negative consequence, but actually something that is a positive.

I can remember a close friend of mine saying, 'My dad lived to work and he never really enjoyed his 35 job. Even though I work to live, if I don't like my job, I quit and look for another one.'
So, one question might be: How important is it that it's harder for young people to find work and to stay in the same job for long? It could be argued that 40 young people today have far more freedom as there isn't the expectation to leave school then get a job and settle down straight away. On the other hand, the uncertainty means that there is often little incentive to think of a long-term career. A result of 45 this might be that youngsters don't see the point in investing in a degree that has a narrow specific focus, but will choose something that has transferable skills, leaving them with more options later on.
Finally, while there are both obvious advantages and 50 disadvantages to the situation most youngsters find themselves in today when it comes to work, one thing can be said with certainty: the world of work and our attitude towards it have changed and continues to change. 55

2 **a** Read the text in detail and find words that match the definitions.

1 an area of activity or interest
2 a study in which people are asked their opinions
3 born in the 1980s or 1990s
4 lacking confidence, not fixed or safe
5 things that are expensive to buy
6 to stop doing something or leave a job or a place
7 what you believe or hope will happen (in the future)
8 that can be used in a different situation or for a different purpose

 b Write down all the words whose meaning you are not sure of. Compare your list with a partner. Are there any words you are both not sure of? Work out their meaning together. Check the tips on page **24**.

3 Read the article again and do the tasks.

1 Name two of the changes outlined in the article between the 1980s and nowadays.
2 Explain why young people are more likely to change jobs than previous generations.
3 Describe some of the consequences of not having a steady job.
4 Read lines 43–49 again. Comment on what the author writes. Do you agree with the statements made here? Say why or why not.

4 **a** Get together in groups of four or five and read the quotes about work. Choose a different quote each and spend two minutes preparing to explain it.

 b Explain the quote you chose to the rest of your group. Then discuss which one you can most identify with and why.

Your talent determines what you can do. Your motivation determines how much you're willing to do. Your attitude determines how well you do it.

Lou Holtz (*1937), former American football player, coach and analyst

Someday is not a day of the week.

Janet Dailey (1944 – 2013), American novelist

I haven't failed. I've just found 10,000 ways that won't work.

Thomas Edison (1837 – 1931), American inventor

If you don't design your own life plan, chances are you'll fall into someone else's plan and guess what they've planned for you? Not much!

Jim Rohn (1930 – 2009), American entrepreneur, author and motivational speaker

The only way to do great work is to love what you do. If you haven't found it yet, keep looking. Don't settle.

Steve Jobs (1955 – 2011), co-founder of Apple Inc.

5 **a** Look at these factors. Rank them from 1 – 8 in terms of which are the most important (1) to the least important (8) when considering a job.

- the pay
- adds value to the world we live in
- your colleagues
- you feel valued and appreciated
- it's something you love doing
- it's challenging
- there is a good work-life balance
- flexible hours

 b Compare your rankings in your group and try to agree on the top three.

c Share your top three. Give reasons for your choices and then vote as a class.

WES-40903-004

Understanding diagrams (2)

S1 **Understand the information.** Choose one diagram each and use the notes to write a short description and analysis of the information shown.

1 The pie chart gives us information about ▢1 in the US.

It is based on a sample of ▢2 in ▢3 . A tiny minority of teenagers ▢4 . Five times as many ▢5 as ▢6 . Just over a quarter ▢7 . The vast majority, almost ▢8 , stated that ▢9 .
Overall, we can see that bullying is ▢10 .

2 The line graph compares ▢1 by ▢2 in England and Wales in a period between ▢3 .

The number of young people who received sentences in 2010 was ▢4 in each age group at the beginning of this period. In 2010, just over ▢5 10 to 14-year-olds were sentenced. The figure for 15-year-olds (21,000) was about a ▢6 lower. The number in the other two age groups was between ▢7 and ▢8 .

Overall, this 10-year period saw a steady ▢9 in the number of convicted young people for each age group. The largest drop was for the number of ▢10 -year-olds, from over 30,000 to 5,000.

3 The bar chart shows which factors motivate teenagers to ▢1 .

While film stars are the ▢2 for both genders, they are more important for boys ▢3 .
The next most important factor for both boys and girls is ▢4 , but they ▢5 girls more than boys. Both genders agree, however, that print ads are the ▢6 motivating. This is followed by ▢7 and ▢8 for boys.

In conclusion, there is not a ▢9 difference in what motivates boys and girls to do physical exercise. However, almost ▢10 girls as boys list reading as an important factor.

Sources: (1) Cyberbullying Research Center, US 2016; (2) Ministry of Justice, UK 2020; (3) Journal of Clinical Nutrition and Dietetics, India 2018.

1 Bullied others in school and online (US, 12–17-year-olds, 2016)
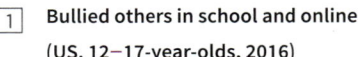
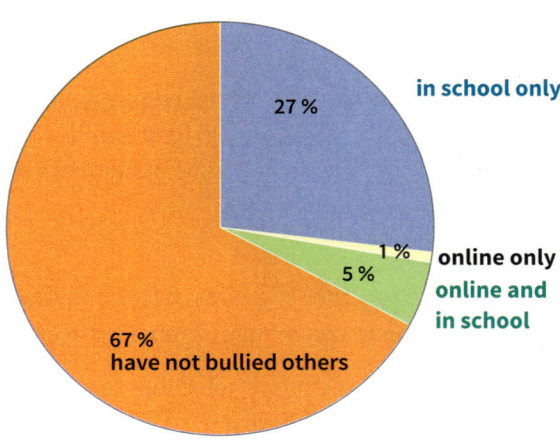

2 Number of children receiving a sentence by age (England and Wales)
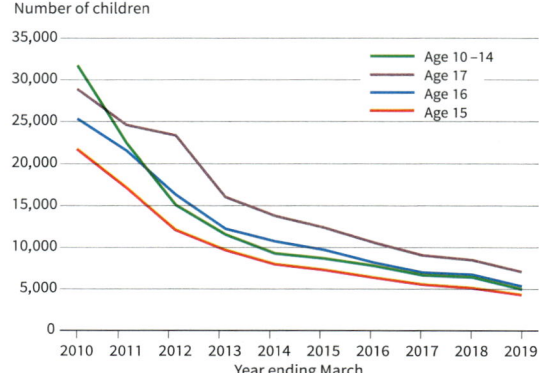

3 Factors motivating teens to do physical exercise
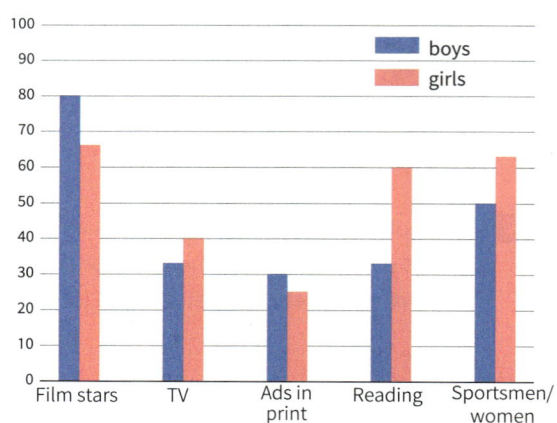

S2 **Discuss the data.** Think about the reasons behind the trends. Discuss and compare what you know about the same topics in Germany.

→ Workbook, page 107   **WORKSHOP TASK**

Presenting information from a diagram

S1 **Choose a diagram.** With a partner, discuss the two diagrams below and choose one to describe.
Refer to the *TIP* on page **132** for useful language and look at the descriptions on page **144**.

S2 **Write a description.** Organize your description into the following parts:
- Introduction: say what the diagram shows / is about
- Main body: explain and describe the key information
- Conclusion: summarize the main point(s) expressed in the diagram

1

Who influences children to decide which products to buy? (UK/US, 2019)
Based on a survey of more than 4,000 children aged 6–16, 50% in the UK, 50% in the US.

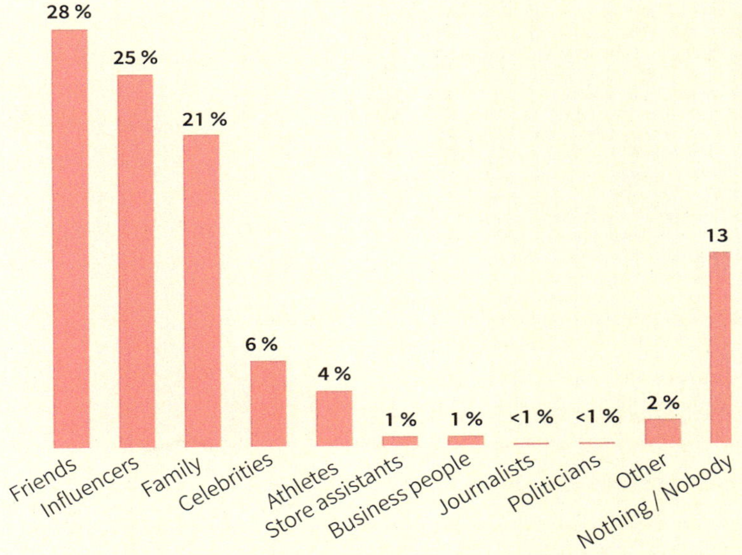

Friends 28 %
Influencers 25 %
Family 21 %
Celebrities 6 %
Athletes 4 %
Store assistants 1 %
Business people 1 %
Journalists <1 %
Politicians <1 %
Other 2 %
Nothing / Nobody 13

2

Cyberbullying statistics (England/Wales, 2020)
Frequency of online bullying experienced by children aged 10–15 in the previous 12 months (by type of behaviour).

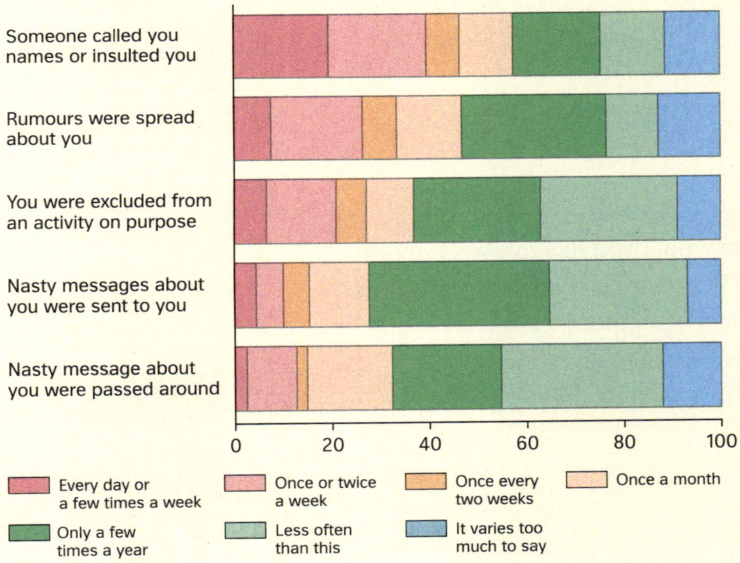

- Someone called you names or insulted you
- Rumours were spread about you
- You were excluded from an activity on purpose
- Nasty messages about you were sent to you
- Nasty message about you were passed around

0   20   40   60   80   100

- Every day or a few times a week
- Once or twice a week
- Once every two weeks
- Once a month
- Only a few times a year
- Less often than this
- It varies too much to say

Sources: (1) Wunderman Thompson Commerce; (2) Office for National Statistics, 2020

S3 **Edit another description.** Swap texts with a pair who looked at the other diagram. Give each other feedback, then correct and improve your original text.

S4 **Give a presentation.** Use your description to explain the data to the class. Prepare to comment on the data and start a discussion on the topic.

1 **a** Make a mind map about families and complete it with words connected to family. Look back at the workshop to help you.

b Complete the text about Sandie's family life with words connected to families. Use your mind map to help you.

After my parents got [1], we were a [2] family for a while. Then my mum met her new partner. Her name is Cathy and she has a son, a year younger than me. We moved in with them and now I am part
5 of a [3] family with two mums. At first I was worried that I'd get bullied, but all my friends accepted it. In fact, my best friend told me that his favourite uncle is in a [4] relationship with a guy called Tony, who I know from my community centre.
10 And my dad found a new wife, too. They have just had a baby so I guess, for now, they are a typical example of a [5] family.
For me the best time is when, on special occasions, I see my [6] family, the Chinese relatives on my
15 mother's side and also my dad's family.

2 **a** Do you remember the EDGEucation programme from last year? It is a different approach to learning. Complete the text with the phrases from the box.

are taught with this method ■ focus on the students' well-being ■ is a key to have success in later life ■ is tiring and feels unnatural ■ originated in Toronto, Canada

How would you like to walk around the classroom while you learn maths or skip along reciting poems? This special method, which [1],
5 would allow you to do just that. Students who [2] are not obliged to sit still for long periods of time, which [3]. Moving EDGEucation uses movement and social-emotional
10 learning techniques that [4]. This innovative approach can be used for all subjects and in all schools. It helps to develop creativity, confidence, and allows every student to perform to
15 their best ability, which [5].

b Find the opposites of these words. They are all in the text.

failure ■ inability ■
insecurity ■ old-fashioned

c Read the text again and do the tasks.

1 Compare the Moving EDGEucation approach to the way you learn at school.
2 Comment on whether you think this approach would work for you. Give reasons for your opinion.

3 After the careers fair, Leslie, a new adviser at the fair, writes a report for her manager.
Fill in the missing relative pronouns and put commas where necessary.

As I had never advised at the careers fair before I was amazed at just how many young people
1 visit the fair have no idea about their future plans. While I was preparing for the fair, I
read the reports **2** had been written by my colleagues in previous years. The fair, which is
attended by boys and girls from local schools, has clearly been growing in importance in recent
years. This event **3** was extended by one extra day this year, plays a crucial role in guiding
students **4** are searching for the right career path.
Before I actually spoke to anyone, I had the feeling from previous reports that the wish to study
is increasing. The tuition fees are very high **5** makes it rather surprising. My initial
impression **6** was confirmed during my discussions, highlighted the need to encourage
young people to really ask themselves what they wish to do with their degree. If you show
them other options and ask the right questions, those **7** were not really sure about studying
may reconsider their wish to go to university or think about choosing a path **8** will enable
them to gain more practical experience. In addition, if they are given a chance **9** enables
them to earn some money while they are studying, some of them rethink their original choices.

4 Emily found an advert on the website
youngjobs.co.uk. She decided to
apply for the apprenticeship. Read
the advert and write her cover letter.
Use the words and expressions from
the box.

additionally ■ applying for ■
basically ■ considering ■
have been ■ hearing ■ ideally
■ naturally ■ passionate
■ which you advertised
■ Yours sincerely

Apprentice wanted!   22 November

Are you passionate about horses? Do you want to earn while you learn?

We are a well-established, family-run riding school, catering for all
age groups.
5 We are currently looking for an enthusiastic, dedicated apprentice to
join our friendly, hard-working team.
The successful candidate will be assisting with the day-to-day
running of the yard, riding lessons and the daily care of the horses.
What we offer is a real job, with hands-on experience and a chance to
10 train while you work.
Interested? Send your CV and cover letter to
Penelope.Croxley@croxleystables.co.uk

The Grange
Horsham RH12 1AE
Surrey

Croxley Stables
Horsham RH12 4PX
Surrey

Application for apprenticeship   25 November 20

Dear Ms Croxley

I am 16 years old and a student at Thorton Lane Sixth Form College in Surrey. I am …

Emily Sullivan

1 **Summer jobs.** Dein amerikanischer Austauschpartner Elijah wird dich in den Sommerferien
M besuchen. Ihr wollt zusammen Geld für einen gemeinsamen Urlaub verdienen. Deshalb schaust
du dich nach Stellenangeboten für Jugendliche in deiner Gegend um. Auf der Internetseite eurer
Lokalzeitung hast du mehrere interessante Inserate gefunden. Elijah ist 15 Jahre alt und spricht
wenig Deutsch. Schreibe ihm eine E-Mail (120 Wörter), in der du ihm die Ferienjobs vorstellst.
Begründe, für welches dieser Jobangebote du dich entscheiden würdest.

Die Stadt Amberg vermittelt folgende Ferienjobs für Schülerinnen und Schüler und Studierende. Interessenten
melden sich bitte telefonisch bei Frau Gebhardt im Rathaus. Frau Gebhardt kann Ihnen weitere Fragen, u.a. zur
Bezahlung, beantworten.

Zeitungszusteller/in (m/w/d, Teilzeit, bis 20 h / Woche)

5 Für die Zeit vom 30. Juli bis 15. September sucht das Amberger
Stadtpanorama Aushilfen für die Zustellung der täglichen Zeitungen an
Privathaushalte. Die Zeitungen müssen am Zeitungsladen in der
Hauptstraße abgeholt und verteilt werden. Dafür werden mehrere Leute
eingesetzt, denen jeweils ein Stadtbezirk zugewiesen wird. Handwagen
10 werden gestellt. Die Zustellung erfolgt in den Morgenstunden bis 7 Uhr.

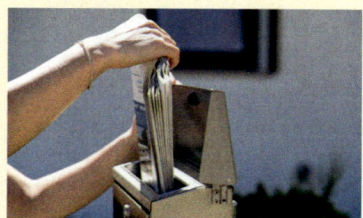

Helfer/in im landwirtschaftlichen Bereich (m/w/d)

Der Landwirtschaftsbetrieb Sievers in Raigering sucht für die Zeit der
Sommerferien nach Schülerinnen und Schülern, die ihren Hof unterstützen
möchten. Die Aufgaben reichen von einfachen Erntetätigkeiten (Obst,
15 Gemüse), Unterstützung bei der Weiterverarbeitung der Produkte bis zur
Mithilfe im Hofladen sowie Stallarbeiten. Vorerfahrung ist von Vorteil, aber
keine Voraussetzung. AG zahlt den gesetzlichen Mindestlohn.

Pizzaboten (m/w/d, 16 / Woche)

Die Pizzeria Pinocchio am Marktplatz ist auf der Suche nach Pizzaboten, die
20 telefonisch bestellte Speisen mit dem Fahrrad oder dem Roller ausliefern
können. Wichtig sind ein sicherer Fahrstil sowie Zuverlässigkeit und
schnelles Arbeiten. Die Arbeitszeit verteilt sich unter der Woche auf die
Abendstunden sowie am Wochenende sowohl mittags als auch abends.
Mitarbeiter/innen dürfen kostenlos in der Pizzeria essen.

25 Umfragen durchführen (je nach Bedarf)

Das Referat Jugend, Senioren und Soziales sucht nach jungen Leuten zur
Durchführung einer innerstädtischen Umfrage von Jugendlichen unserer
Stadt. Umfragebögen werden gestellt. Wer mithelfen möchte, wird in der
Fußgängerzone Personen zwischen 8 und 18 Jahren ansprechen und ihnen
30 Fragen zum Angebot unserer Stadt stellen. Ziel der Befragung ist es,
herauszufinden, ob es ein ausreichendes Freizeitangebot für Jugendliche
bietet, wie das bestehende Angebot genutzt wird und welche weiteren
Angebote sich junge Menschen wünschen.

Mitarbeit in Claudias Boutique (m/w/d, 10 h / Woche)

35 Claudia Menges ist auf der Suche nach zwei Personen, die sie in den
Sommerferien in ihrer Boutique unterstützen können. Die Boutique hat sich
auf klassische Mode und ausgefallene Schuhe und Accessoires spezialisiert.
Frau Menges braucht Hilfe beim Auspacken und Einräumen der Waren und
der Dekoration ihres Ladens.

→ Workbook, pages 111/112 **MEDIATION**

2 **The Holy Apostles Soup Kitchen.** Deine jüngere Schwester und du besucht eure Großeltern während der Sommerferien in New York. Eure Großmutter zeigt euch die Webseite einer Hilfsorganisation, für die sie arbeitet. Deine Schwester spricht noch nicht so gut Englisch und hat einige Fragen an dich. Beantworte sie.

The Holy Apostles Soup Kitchen

Founded in 1982, the Holy Apostles Soup Kitchen is currently the largest emergency feeding program in New York City and in the Episcopal Church nationally. Housed within the nave of the Church, the Soup
5 Kitchen serves over 1,200 meals every weekday and offers counseling and other support services to help the guests break the cycle of hunger, poverty, and despair. [...]

Our Mission
10 Feed the hungry, comfort the troubled, seek justice for the homeless, and provide a sense of hope and opportunity to those in need. [...]

Volunteer
Make a difference to the lives of New York's hungry and homeless.
Every weekday at 10:30 a.m., hundreds of hungry and homeless New Yorkers walk through the
15 doors of the Holy Apostles Soup Kitchen to get a warm nutritious meal and seek help in finding their way on to a better way of life. But 45 minutes beforehand, another crowd is gathering: 50–60 volunteers who will make sure that happens.
From greeting guests to serving food, cleaning tables to handing out haircut vouchers, it is our volunteers who enable us to be here for our guests every day. One of the most important things we
20 do is to treat our guests with dignity and respect, and as a volunteer this is part of your job, too. A warm smile or some friendly conversation can really help brighten our guests' days – and as a volunteer you might be surprised at how much this experience will brighten yours as well!
You can sign up to volunteer any weekday. You'll need to be available from 9:45 a.m. to 12:45 p.m. Many volunteers stay for lunch afterwards and, just like our guests, enjoy the community to be
25 found here.
Sign up and make a difference today!

from: Church of the Holy Apostles and the Holy Apostles Soup Kitchen, New York

Your sister	Was liest du denn da?
You	Auf dieser Website sind Infos über …
Your sister	Das ist also die Organisation, zu der Oma zweimal in der Woche geht? Was genau macht diese Organisation denn?
You	…
Your sister	Und du meinst, dass du dort auch helfen kannst? Die haben doch bestimmt feste Angestellte, die dort immer arbeiten.
You	….
Your sister	Was sind die Aufgaben der Helfer?
You	…
Your sister	Ach, das ist ja interessant. Vielleicht können wir dann ja zusammen hingehen. Aber haben wir dann überhaupt Zeit, uns New York anzusehen, wenn wir den ganzen Tag da helfen müssen?
You	…
Your sister	Dann lass uns mal zu Oma gehen und ihr sagen, dass wir mitkommen.

Ready for next level?

1 Use the clauses from the box to complete Sam's blog entry about his family. You will need to add the correct relative pronouns.

> are typical in many parts of the world ■ changed our lives completely ■ is famous for its diversity ■ is far from being traditional ■ makes him indigenous ■ makes the place really vibrant ■ shows you how unconventional my family is ■ was the only home I'd known

My name is Sam and I live in a city [1]. We have people from all over the world [2]. It also means that people are a lot more tolerant here. Diversity does not only mean lots of different nationalities, it
5 is also reflected in the family structures. Traditional families, [3], are almost rare here. My family, [4], is a good example to illustrate what I mean. My mother is a second-generation Chinese and my father is from a first nation tribe, [5]. However,
10 this is not all. Two years ago my parents made a decision [6]. They got divorced. We had to move out of the big house [7]. And then there was another change. I am going to tell you a story [8].

2 Read the email from Deepak to a local newspaper. Rewrite it with the information in the sentences below. Use relative clauses.

G14

- The article was published on the website.
- I felt the general statements about teenagers were unfair.
- The journalist seems to think all teenagers do is sit around playing computer games.
- The public service adverts should focus on issues that concern my generation.
- Blaming teenagers is what the journalist seemed to do.

Dear Editor,

I'm writing in response to a recent article in your newspaper. In the article, there were lots of general statements about teenagers. The journalist suggested that in the future there
5 would be a public health crisis because of lifestyle choices. However, she failed to realize that many of these choices are made because of the constant advertising targeted at teenagers. If there were more public service adverts, I think we would all be better informed and would be able to make
10 better choices. Rather than blaming teenagers for everything, it would be better to look at the real causes of the problems.

Yours truly,
Deepak Ramesh

3 **a** Deepak is organizing his notes about the UK and US educational systems. Copy the table and complete it with his notes. Then fill in the last column for Germany.

	UK	US	Germany
Curriculum	???	???	???
Exams	???	???	???
Science	???	???	???
Certificates	???	???	???
Scholarship	???	???	???

- Set nationally
- Common
- Excel in sports, music
- Separate for each subject
- At the end of Year 11
- High school diploma
- Credits
- Taught sequentially
- GCSE
- Set by state or district
- At the end of Grade 12
- Disadvantaged students
- Unusual

b Argue why it would be easy or difficult for Deepak to continue his studies in the US. Give reasons for your answer.

c Compare the German school system to that of the UK and US. Outline which of the two is closer to the German one. Give reasons for your answers.

4 Tina is in youth court because she has been accused of shoplifting and punching a security
guard who tried to stop her. Here is a newspaper report about what happened in court.
Rewrite the report without the emphatic *do / does* or *did*.

G10

As our readers will know, we do pride ourselves at the Echo about reporting on local news stories. This one is about Tina, a local teenager accused of shoplifting and punching a security guard. In court she admitted she had behaved badly. She said at the time she didn't think she was wrong but that
5 she does see it now. She said she had gone to the shopping centre with two friends and that when they said nobody would get hurt, she did believe them. However, everything went terribly wrong, and now she does need to take responsibility for her actions. Tina admitted that she did punch the security guard in the face and said she would like to apologize to him.
10 Finally, she did promise that it would never happen again and that she wouldn't give in to peer pressure in the future.

5 Read the two online texts asking for advice. Decide whether the underlined words and phrases
are correct or wrong. Correct the wrong ones.

I'm a 15-year old girl from Tulsa, in the USA. I need some advices[1] about bullying.
There are some girls at my school which tease me[2] about the clothes I wear. I come
from a single-parent family, because my parents got divorced[3] when I was young. My
mom does her best, but money is always a problem. She has two jobs and usually gets
5 home lately[4]. The priorities are food and pay the bills[5]. So, most of my clothes are
second-hand. What should I do[6]?
Kathryn

My name's Tom and I'm sixteen. I spent[7] a lot of time to play[8] games on my computer
and surfing the web. However, recently I was experiencing[9] online bullying. I've been to
10 a website about cyberbullying and tried to follow[10] the advice, but it hasn't had much
effect. Of course, one suggestion was not to go online, but I don't want giving up[11]
my hobby. Do you have any advice[12] for me?
Tom

6 Read these comments by teenagers. What are they talking about? Choose one comment
you all agree on – or come up with your own. Present your comment to the class. Support
your choice with reasons, examples, etc.

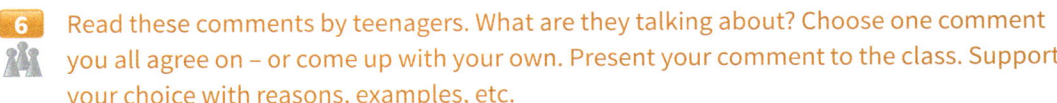

A *I don't even notice them anymore.*

B *I do hate the fact that social media sites are full of the stuff.*

C *What's annoying is that you can't avoid them.*

D *It's worrying just how much they influence what you do or buy.*

Karen McManus, *One of us is lying* (2019), Chapter Twenty

One of us is lying. Who? Only one? To whom? Why? Four teenagers at Bay View High are confronted with these questions as they try to find out how their schoolmate Simon could have been murdered while they were all together in detention. Now prime suspects, the secrets each of them has been hiding are slowly revealed and values such as true friendship are put to the test. One of the four is Cooper, who is aspiring to become a professional baseball player. As events unfold, he has to face the consequences of deceiving others as well as himself. He is sitting at dinner with his dad.

Tuesday, October 16, 5:45 p.m.

'Pass the milk, would you, Cooperstown[1]?' Pop[1] jerks his chin at me during dinner, his eyes drifting toward the muted television in our living room, where college
5 football scores scroll along the bottom of the screen. 'So what'd you do with your night off?' He thinks it's hilarious that Luis posed as me after the gym yesterday. I hand over the carton and picture myself answering his question honestly. Hung out with Kris,
10 the guy I'm in love with. Yeah, Pop, I said guy. No, Pop, I'm not kidding. He's a premed[2] freshman at UCSD who does modeling on the side. Total catch[3]. You'd like him. And then Pop's head explodes. That's how it always ends in my imagination. 'Just drove around for
15 a while,' I say instead. I'm not ashamed of Kris. I'm not. But it's complicated. Thing is, I didn't realize I could feel that way about a guy till I met him. I mean, yeah, I suspected. Since I was eleven or so. But I buried those thoughts as far down as I could because I'm a Southern
20 jock[4] shooting for an MLB[5] career and that's not how we're supposed to be wired. I really did believe that for most of my life.

I've always had a girlfriend. But it was never hard to hold off[6] till marriage like I was raised. I only recently
25 understood that was more of an excuse than a deeply held moral belief. I've been lying to Keely for months, but I did tell her the truth about Kris. I met him through baseball, although he doesn't play. He's friends with another guy I made the exhibition rounds
30 with, who invited us both to his birthday party. And he is German. I just left out the part about being in love with him. I can't admit that to anybody yet. That it's not a phase, or experimentation, or distraction from pressure. Nonny[7] was right. My stomach does flips
35 when Kris calls or texts me. Every single time. And when I'm with him I feel like a real person, not the robot Keely called me: programmed to perform as expected. But Cooper-and-Kris only exists in the bubble of his apartment. Moving it anyplace else scares
40 the hell out of me. For one thing, it's hard enough making it in baseball when you're a regular guy. The number of openly gay players who are part of a major league team stands at exactly one. And he's still in the minors. For another thing: Pop. My whole brain seizes[8] when I imagine his reaction. He's the kind of good old
45 boy who calls gay people 'fags[9]' and thinks we spend all our time hitting on straight[10] guys. The one time we saw a news story about the gay baseball player, he snorted in disgust and said, Normal guys shouldn't have to deal with that crap in the locker room.
50 If I tell him about Kris and me, seventeen years of being the perfect son would be gone in an instant. He'd never look at me the same. The way he's looking at me now, even though I'm a murder suspect who's been accused of using steroids[11]. That he can handle.
55 'Testing tomorrow,' he reminds me. I have to get tested for steroids every damn week now. In the meantime I keep pitching[12], and no, my fastball hasn't gotten any slower. Because I haven't been lying. I didn't cheat. I strategically improved. It was Pop's idea. He wanted
60 me to hold back a little junior year, not give my all, so there'd be more excitement around me during showcase season[13]. And there was. People like Josh Langley noticed me. But now, of course, it looks suspicious. Thanks, Pop. At least he feels guilty about
65 it. I was sure, when the police got ready to show me the unpublished *About That* posts[14] last month, that I was going to read something about Kris and me. I'd barely known Simon, only talked with him one-on-one a few times. But anytime I got near him I'd worry
70 about him learning my secret.

Last spring at junior prom he'd been drunk off his ass, and when I ran into him in the bathroom he flung an arm around me and pulled me so close I practically had a panic attack. I was sure that Simon – who'd
75 never had a girlfriend as far as I knew – realized I was gay and was putting the moves on me[15]. I freaked out so bad, I had Vanessa disinvite him to her after-prom party. And Vanessa, who never passes up a chance to exclude somebody, was happy to do it. I let it stand
80 even after I saw Simon hitting on Keely later with the kind of intensity you can't fake. I hadn't let myself think about that since Simon died; how the last time I'd talked to him, I acted like a jerk because I couldn't deal with who I was. And the worst part is, even after
85 all this – I still can't.

1 a Summarize the conversation at dinner time in three to five sentences.

b Describe the atmosphere. Speculate about Cooper's and his father's feelings.

c Examine the constellation of characters (family, friends, classmates) you read about in the excerpt. Make a mind map with Cooper in the centre and arrange the characters according to their closeness to the protagonist. Differentiate between emotional and physical distance.

d Collect the information you get from the text about Cooper's character and write a short characterization about him. Quote from the text in order to justify your statements. Make sure that you include descriptive adjectives.

e Analyse the relationship between father and son and evaluate it by comparing it to your understanding of a healthy parent-child relationship.

2 a With a partner, discuss the problems of coming out in today's society with a partner.

b Comment on one of the following statements:

> The truth may hurt for a little while, but a lie hurts forever.

> Better to be slapped with the truth than kissed with a lie.

> Three things cannot be long hidden: the Sun, the Moon, and the Truth.

3 Cooper's thoughts are written in the form of an interior monologue. He verbalizes all of his jumbled thoughts. Imagine yourself at a decisive point in your life. It might be happy or sad, something difficult you are afraid of or something you are looking forward to. Look at the text again and write down an interior monologue of your own in a similar style. Write between 150 – 200 words.

- **Step 1**: Collect adjectives that express your feelings.
- **Step 2**: Think of verbs that express what you might / could do or don't dare to do.
- **Step 3**: Then, think of three people that could be involved in your life at this point and describe their potential reaction to your situation.
- **Step 4**: Write the monologue.

Literary terms

- **Narrator:** the person who tells the story in a book or play (NOT the author!)
- **Plot:** the sequence of events that forms and unifies the main story of a novel, play or film
- **Point of view:** the perspective from which a story is told. The point of view of a first-person narrator like Cooper in this excerpt allows the reader to see through the narrator's eyes, to hear and listen through his ears, to read the thoughts in his mind.
- **Protagonist:** the main or most important character in a story of a book, play or film
- **Setting:** the time when and place where the events in a book or film happen

---

Interior monologue is the technical literary term for a character's train of thought and is usually found in a novel. For the reader it is like looking into a character's mind, gaining insights into the ideas and feelings in real time. The character's inner voice is speaking (self-talk) and often internal secrets are revealed.

---

[1] **Cooperstown / Pop** nicknames for Cooper and Cooper's father (from 'poppa' = dad) – [2] **premed freshman at USCD** Kris is a first-year-student at the University of California, San Diego. – [3] **catch** (*infml.*) a desirable person to start a relationship with ('a good catch') – [4] **jock** (AE, *infml.*) a student who practises a lot of sport but is less interested in or talented for an academic career – [5] **MLB** Major League Baseball, the American baseball league – [6] **to hold off** to delay sth. *here*: not to have sex before marriage – [7] **Nonny** = Grandma – [8] **my brain seizes** my brain stops working – [9] **fag** (AE, *slang*) taboo word for a homosexual man – [10] **straight** heterosexual – [11] **steroids** substances that should make your muscles grow and get stronger – [12] **to pitch** to throw the ball (in baseball) – [13] **showcase season** talent scouting: young players are keen to present their talents in order to be recruited for a well-reputed professional league club – [14] ***About That* posts** *About That* is a gossip app that Simon, one of the students at school, has been running, feeding it with ugly news and revealing secrets about his classmates until his death – [15] **to put the moves on somebody** to try and develop a (sexual) relationship with somebody you have a crush on

FOUR

79))

The second note from the kidnappers said two final things:
1 'The raven must come alone!'
And:
5 2 'No funny business[1]'
We weren't exactly sure what 'no funny business' meant, but we guessed it had something to do with 1; that I had to come on my own.
The policeman, whose name we finally found out
10 was Officer Slowfoot, had gone back to the police station. He didn't know what to do, and couldn't decide whether to do what the kidnappers said, or ignore them. He really was useless.
So, there I was, at midnight, sitting on the rail of the
15 old scary bridge in the middle of the forest. Waiting. They call it the 'old scary bridge', because that's exactly what it is. It's been there forever, and it looks as if it might fall down at any moment, but I had my instructions, so there I was: sitting on the bridge.
20 Solstice had told me I must do exactly what the kidnappers wanted. So I did.
Now, I would like to say that I wasn't very happy. Firstly, I still hadn't had anything to eat.
Secondly, I didn't see why I was being swapped for
25 the twins. I mean, I understood that the kidnappers were fed up with Fizz and Buzz. I mean, who wouldn't be? I can't spend more than three minutes in their company before I want to murder them. So that made sense. I just didn't see why the kidnappers
30 wanted *me* instead. And finally, I also didn't understand why the family thought it was just fine to hand me over to get the twins back. Solstice tried to explain that as soon as the twins were released[2], I would just be able to fly away, but something told me
35 it wouldn't be quite as simple as that. I wished they wanted Cudweed's monkey instead; that would solve another of my problems. But it seemed they wanted me, so there I was. I sat on the railing of the bridge, feeling grumpy and confused. And hungry.
40 And bored. Because although the kidnappers had said 'midnight', midnight had already come and gone. I know this because after a while Solstice and Cudweed suddenly appeared out of the forest. They ran up to me, looking worried.

45 'Are you still here?' Solstice said.
'It's nearly one in the morning!' said Cudweed. As well as worried, he also seemed quite excited at being awake at one o'clock in the morning. His eyes were wide, and he looked sort of frantic.
50 'Kark!' I said, which meant: what are you doing here? If the kidnappers see you …
'Yes,' said Solstice, 'we know, but we're over there, in the bushes, with Mum and Dad, just waiting. If …'
But she didn't finish what she was saying, because
55 we heard a vehicle approaching and saw headlights in between the trees.
'Kork!' I said, looking at the truck that was approaching, but when I looked back to the children, they had already disappeared again.
60 Then I heard a bush say something.
'Just remember to fly away!' said the bush, although I realized it was actually Solstice inside the bush. After a moment or two, the truck stopped on the bridge, but the engine stayed on.
65 At first, it was hard to see who was driving it, but then two figures climbed out of it.
They were a man and a woman, quite young. There was something odd about them, right from the start; they looked as if they didn't wash behind their ears

---

[1] **no funny business** keine faulen Tricks – [2] **to release** freilassen

70 very often, for one thing. For another thing, they looked strange next to each other: the man was very short and round; the woman was very, very tall, and thin.

Also, they were arguing. Constantly[3].

75 'I told you we should turn left at the castle,' said the woman.

'Ha! You don't even know left from right[4],' said the man.

'At least I know how to drive,' said the woman.

80 'I could learn if I wanted to,' said the man.

'Oh, you just don't want to, that's all.'

And on and on it went, until finally the man saw me and said, 'Look! There it is!'

It! He called me it! Horrible person.

85 While I was still thinking about that, the woman came up to me. She stared at me.

'Do you think it bites?' she asked the man.

'Why don't you find out?' the man muttered under his breath.

90 'What?' she snapped.

'Nothing, sister. Nothing. Shall we get on with it?' Sister! So they were brother and sister. But grown-ups.

95 I guessed they still lived together and had been arguing for approximately twenty-five years. They probably hated each other.

'Pull the truck forward,' said the man.

100 'You pull it forward,' said the woman, then added, 'Oh I remember now, you don't know how to drive.' She got in the truck again and drove it another ten metres forward, so that I was looking at the back, which was open.

105 Inside, there were two large cages.

One of the cages was empty, but in the other …

'Gar-gar!' I heard two little voices, both speaking at once.

It was Fizz and Buzz! They seemed rather pleased to

110 see me, which was almost sweet. Almost. They were locked together in one of the cages. I should explain that they don't speak the way other people do. They seem to have invented their own language, that no one else understands, and although they can speak

115 English, mostly they speak in what we call 'twinnish'. For example, they don't say 'Edgar'. They say 'Gar-gar'. Stupid children.

Then I saw that the thin woman was looking at me. 'So apparently you can understand English … Is that

120 right?'

I ignored her.

'And you can speak English, too?' she asked.

I ignored her again.

The woman turned and looked at Fizz and Buzz.

125 'Are you lying about this?' she asked them, looking very mean.

'No, no!' they said together. In English for once. They say everything together, at exactly the same time. It's very weird. 'Edgar!' they said. 'What goes in the top

130 of a bottle?'

Well, I was not in the mood to play games and I told them so.

'Kork,' I said, which means 'please behave yourselves for once'.

135 However, I may have said the wrong thing, because the woman turned to the man and said, 'See! He said 'cork'! He does speak English!'

'Right,' said the man. 'Let's get on with this[5].'

He opened the door of the empty cage.

140 'You get in the cage. See? Then, we let the twins go.'

'And good riddance[6],' said the woman. 'What awful children.'

'Kark,' I said, because we were in agreement about that, at least. But I did not want to get in the cage.

145 So much for Solstice's idea about just flying away.

'Please, please, Gar-gar!' said the twins, and the woman pointed at the door of the empty cage.

'In you go,' she said, 'then we let the children go.'

Well, I didn't like it, but there was no choice.

150 I flapped off the railing and into the cage and the woman quickly shut the door behind me! I was not happy.

'Right,' said the man, 'Let's get out of here! Help me with the kids.'

155 He climbed into the back of the truck and opened the door of the cage in which Fizz and Buzz were sitting. The second the door opened, they jumped out. Fizz bit the man's ankles, and Buzz started running towards the woman, who began screaming, 'Oh no!

160 Not again! Not again!'

There was a lot of fuss like this until finally the twins stopped attacking for long enough for the man and woman to jump into the truck and drive away. With me in the back!

---

[3] **constantly** ständig – [4] **to not know left from right** links und rechts nicht unterscheiden können – [5] **to get on with** weitermachen, fortfahren –
[6] **good riddance** gut, dass wir sie los sind

165 As the truck pulled away into the darkness of the trees, I saw Minty and Valevine, Solstice and Cudweed run out of their hiding places towards Fizz and Buzz. The family was reunited[7]!

Apart, that is, from me, who was driven off in the 170 middle of the night, for hours.

For some time, I tried to look out of the back windows of the truck, to keep an eye on where we were going. But then, it was very late, and, well, I fell asleep. When I woke up, I was in a very strange place.

175 It was a large room. It didn't seem to have any windows, and was quite dark, and I guessed we were in a basement[8]. But I could see it was full of stuff. All kinds of stuff. Weird stuff. Strange things. There was a dead crocodile on top of a grand piano; there was 180 an old motorcycle with no wheels leaning against a grandfather clock[9]. There was a human skeleton, with a top hat on its skull, standing by the door. There were piles of books all around, and boxes and boxes of who-knows-what?

185 Just as I was trying to work out where I was, I heard arguing.

'This had better work,' said a voice, as a door opened and in came the man and the woman. I was still in the cage, but already looking for a way out. It seemed 190 there was only one door.

'Of course it will work,' said the man.

'Why do you say 'of course'? None of your other ideas have worked!'

'*My* ideas? What about *your* ideas? Look around you! 195 This room is full of things you said we'd be able to sell for a fortune!'

'What about the things you stole? That crocodile, for example…'

'It looked like it was worth a lot of money!'

200 'It looked like rubbish! It still does!'

And on and on they went, arguing again, without stopping.

So! Two things were obvious to me.

First: they were thieves, and they stole things that 205 they thought they could sell again for money. And now they had me. And thought they could sell me for a lot of money.

Well, that was pretty clever, I admit, because I am an extremely special bird.

210 The second thing that was clear was this; if I didn't find a way to escape within twenty minutes, their arguing would drive me mad. The kidnappers didn't seem that dangerous. In fact, they seemed mostly harmless[10], and, apart from the idea about selling me, 215 very stupid. In fact, there was a third obvious thing – if this pair were kidnappers, they were terrible kidnappers.

'Are you sure it can speak?' said the man, peering[11] through the bars[12] of the cage at me. 'He only said 220 'cork'[13]. That could have been an accident.'

'If he can't speak, he's worthless[14]. We may as well get rid of him.'

Get rid of him? I didn't like the sound of that one bit.

225 The woman came up to the cage. She stared at me again.

'Good birdy, good birdy. Say something, will you, birdy?' She had a horrible fake smile on her face. She poked[15] her fingers through the bars of the cage a 230 little, trying to encourage[16] me to speak. Then the nasty smile dropped from her face, and she added, 'Or you're in big trouble.'

'Futhork,' I said. I was starting to get worried. Maybe they weren't as harmless as they appeared.

235 'What does that mean?' she said, turning to her brother. (It means something very rude, so rude I can't tell you what.) But while she wasn't looking, I took the chance to peck her fingers, very hard.

---

[7] **reunited** wiedervereinigt – [8] **basement** Keller – [9] **grandfather clock** Standuhr – [10] **harmless** harmlos – [11] **to peer** spähen – [12] **bars** Stäbe – [13] **cork** Korken – [14] **worthless** wertlos – [15] **to poke** durchstecken – [16] **to encourage** ermutigen

She screamed and I said 'kronk' – that's me laughing
240 – which only made her more angry.

'I don't think this bird can speak at all!' she yelled at
her brother. 'Another stupid idea of yours. We may as
well put some stones in the cage and throw him in
the river, right now.'

245 Stones?! The river?! Aaaaark! They might look
stupid, but they were dangerous after all. What evil
people! I had to escape, and soon. Or I was going to
be one drowned raven!

'Can't we just flush him down the toilet?' the man
250 was saying.

'Don't be stupid, he's too fat.'

Fat! Well, now I was more angry than scared, and I
decided to take matters into my own hands. Or claws.
You know what I mean.

255 As the woman tried
to poke me again,
I saw my chance!
I grabbed her
finger in my
260 beak and didn't
let go.
'Help!' she screamed,
'it's got me! Get it
off me!'

265 'Hang on!' said the man. 'I'll have to
open the cage door.'

'Well, just be careful. Make sure it doesn't …'
But he was too slow.
The moment he opened the door of the cage, I flew
270 out and began flying around the room at high speed,
so they wouldn't catch me again.

'Now look what you've done!' said the woman.
'It was your fault, you shouldn't have poked it.'
Now, while I was flying around the room, I saw
275 something. There was a log stove[17] in the corner of
the room, and I noticed three things about it.

One, it wasn't alight[18]. (This was important for my
plan.)

Two, the door was open.

280 And three, it had a chimney that led up through the
ceiling and one thing I know about chimneys is that
they always lead to open air.

The only problem was that the chimney pipe[19] was
quite narrow, but then, I told myself, no one has

285 given you anything to eat for at least 12 hours,
you've probably lost a little weight.

So, while the man and woman were still arguing, I
shot into the log stove and up the chimney like a
bullet in a gun.

290 I burst up into the air above
a small house in the middle
of the countryside.
I was free, but I had a
problem. I didn't know
295 where I was. They must have
taken me a long way in that
truck, because I know all the
forests around our castle and I
didn't recognize anything at all!

300 But then, just as I was worrying about how I was
going to find the way home, I saw something. There!
I looked down and saw three police cars, lots of
police officers, and the whole family: Minty and
Valevine, Solstice and Cudweed, and Fizz and Buzz.

305 'Look!' shouted Solstice, 'I told you he'd free himself!'
I landed on the roof of the nearest police car.
'Yes, you were right,' said Valevine. 'But how clever
of Fizz and Buzz to remember the way to the
kidnappers' house! Smart little things, eh?'

310 Fizz and Buzz had remembered the way? And told
the police?
Well, I was dumbfounded[20].
And, as the police went inside and arrested the
terrible kidnappers, I looked at Fizz and Buzz.
315 'Krark,' I said. Perhaps small children do have a point.
Sometimes.
I flapped over to them and, just to remind them
who's in charge, gave each of them a friendly peck
on the top of the head.

THE END

---

[17] **log stove** Holzofen – [18] **to be alight** brennen – [19] **chimney pipe** Kaminrohr – [20] **dumbfounded** verblüfft; sprachlos

Appendix

Grammatical terms

Appendix

> Here are some of the most important **grammatical terms** in English:

adjective	Adjektiv
adverb of frequency, manner, place, time	Adverb der Häufigkeit, der Art und Weise, des Ortes, der Zeit
adverbial	Adverbiale

clause
    if-clause
    main clause
    relative clause
    subordinate clause
	Teilsatz
	    Konditionalsatz / Bedingungssatz
	    Hauptsatz
	    Relativsatz
	    Nebensatz

comparative	Komparativ
conditional	Konditionalis / Konditionalsatz

future
    future with *going to*
    future with *will*
    future progressive
	Futur
	    Futur mit *going to*
	    Futur mit *will*
	    Verlaufsform des Futurs

gerund	Gerundium
negative	negativ, verneint
noun	Nomen, Substantiv
modals	Modale Hilfsverben
participle constructions	Partizipialkonstruktionen
passive	Passiv

past
    simple past
    past progressive
	Vergangenheit
	    Imperfekt, Präteritum
	    Verlaufsform des Imperfekt / Präteritum

past perfect (simple)	Plusquamperfekt
positive	positiv, bejaht

present
    simple present
    present progressive
	Gegenwart
	    Präsens
	    Verlaufsform des Präsens

present perfect
    present perfect (simple)
    present perfect progressive
	Perfekt
	    Perfekt
	    Verlaufsform des Perfekt

possessive pronoun, reciprocal pronoun, reflexive pronoun	Possessivpronomen, Reziprokpronomen, Reflexivpronomen
quantifiers	Numerale, Zahlworte
reported speech	Indirekte Rede
statement	Aussagesatz

subordinate clause
    subordinate clause of time
	Nebensatz
	    Temporalsatz

superlative	Superlativ

Grammar

> Do you have a question about grammar?
> The **grammar appendix** explains all the grammar that you learn in this book.

G 1 Present perfect and present perfect progressive (revision)

Workshop 1, pages 14 – 15

We form the present perfect with *has / have* + past participle.

	has / have		*past participle*	
I	**'ve**		**been**	*to Australia twice.*
But I	**haven't**		**been**	*to New Zealand.*
Jason	**has**		**known**	*Ricky since primary school.*
	Have	*you*	**seen**	*Bruce recently?*
The boys	**have**		**had**	*such a good season so far.*

We form the present perfect progressive with *has / have been + -ing*.

	has / have	*-ing*	
She	**'s been**	**coaching**	*the rugby team for ten years.*
We	**haven't been**	**living**	*here for long.*
How long	**have** *you* **been**	**waiting?**	
The boys	**have been**	**playing**	*really well.*

The present perfect connects the past and the present. An action or situation in the past is connected to or has a consequence in the present or something started in the past and continues in the present.

- We use the present perfect to express that an action is completed or to emphasize the result. We also use it when we are expressing 'how many times'.
  *Our partner school in Christchurch **has invited** us to play in their rugby tournament.*
  *I**'ve had** a go at surfing many times, but I just can't do it.*
  *I**'ve been** to the outback several times.*

- We use the present perfect progressive to emphasize the duration or repetition of an action.
  *The coach **has been trying** to organize a trip like this for a while.*
  *I**'ve been working** in the café for almost a year now.*
  *It**'s been raining** all day.*

There are some state verbs (e. g. *have, know, understand*) that we generally do not use in the present perfect progressive. With state verbs, we usually use the present perfect when we are expressing duration or repetition of an action.

*He**'s** always **wanted** to take the team to play in New Zealand.*
*Eleni **hasn't known** about Aunt Koula's illness very long.*
NOT ~~Eleni hasn't been knowing about Aunt Koula's illness very long.~~

Another difference between the present perfect and the present perfect progressive is that we can sometimes use the present perfect to express something that we see as more permanent or long-term and the present perfect progressive to express something that we see as temporary or short-term.

*I**'ve lived** here all my life.*
*I**'ve** only **been living** here for a couple of months.*

Examples

*I**'ve tried** to fix the computer, but I can't find the problem.*
*We**'ve known** each other since kindergarten.*
*I'm exhausted. We**'ve been driving** all day.*
*How long **have you been living** in Perth?*

G 2 Future forms: *will* and *going to* (revision) Workshop 1, pages 14 – 15

We can use *will* and *going to* to talk about the future. We use them to talk about intentions and decisions and also to talk about predictions.

Intentions, plans and decisions:
- We use *going to* to express future intentions or plans that were made before the time of speaking.
  *The team **are going to practise** more so I believe we'll be able to win.*
  *We'**re going to book** our plane tickets at the weekend.*

  Note that to avoid repeating *go*, we often omit *to go*.
  *I'**m going** ~~to go~~ to the gym this evening after rugby practice.*
  *We'**re going** ~~to go~~ shopping this evening.*

- We use *will* for decisions that are made at the time of speaking. This includes offers, promises and requests.
  *We've got a free hour or so. I think I'**ll do** some sightseeing. (decision made at the time of speaking)*
  *Are you ready to order? - I'**ll have** the vegetarian pizza, please. (request)*
  *I'**ll email** you the ticket as soon as I get it. (offer)*

Predictions:
- We use *going to* for predictions that are based on present evidence. In other words, there is something in the present that indicates something in the future.
  *The score's 25 – 10 after 75 minutes. We'**re going to lose**.*
  *I can't wait for the trip. It'**s going to be** great fun!*

- We use *will* for predictions that are based on personal feeling or opinion.
  *I am sure you'**ll have** a great time in Christchurch.*
  *Do you think you'**ll win** against the Kiwis?*
  *Do you want to wait. It **won't take** long to finish.*

G 3 Reported speech in statements and questions in the present, present perfect and future Workshop 1, pages 18 – 19

We sometimes report the person's exact words or the general idea.

Statements:
- We can use *say* and *tell* to report what someone says.
  *He **says** that he loves the area.*
  *Thomas **tells** me that you're going back to the UK.*

- We often use these reporting verbs in a present tense
  He says …
  She's wants to know…
  He's been asking …

- We can use *that* after *say* and *tell*. There is no rule about *that* and it is usually personal choice.
  *She **says** she's not hungry. OR She **says that** she's not hungry.*

- We use an indirect object (e. g. *me, us*) after tell.
  *He tells **me** they are hoping to set off at about 6.30.*

+ see next page!

- As well as *say* and *tell*, we can use the present tense of verbs such as *admit, agree, assure, claim, deny, inform, suggest, think* etc.
  He **admits** he's wrong.
  She **agrees** it's a good idea.

- When we use the present, the present perfect or the future with reporting verbs, we generally keep the information we are reporting in the same tense as the original comment. This is usually to show that something is still true, relevant or important.
  I'll be there in ten minutes. → *She says she'll be here in ten minutes.*
  It's Jenna's birthday today. → *Alice tells me it's your birthday!*
  I think Sam left about an hour ago. → *He thinks that Sam left about an hour ago.*
  We're going to the beach. → *Luke says they're going to the beach.*

- We sometimes need to change pronouns (*we* → *they*) and other words such as *here* → *there*, etc.
  I've lived here since I was 13. → *He says he's lived there since he was 13.*

Questions:

- We can report a question with verbs such as *ask, want to know* and *wonder*.
  Fred: Is everything OK? → *Fred wants to know if everything is OK.*
  David: When are we leaving? → *David's asking what time we're leaving.*
  Jessica: Where are we going next? → *She's wondering where to go next.*

- For a *yes/no*-question (without a question word) we use *if* or *whether*.
  He is asking me if I know his brother.
  Olga has asked me whether I could give her a surfing lesson.

- The word order is different from direct questions but the same as in statements.
  Where does he live? → *She wants to know where he lives.*
  When are we leaving? → *He keeps asking when we're leaving.*
  NOT ~~She's wants to know where does he live.~~ • ~~He keeps asking when are we leaving.~~

Examples   *Oliver **wants to know** if you can give him a lift to the airport.*
*The receptionist **is saying that** he's not expecting us until tomorrow.*
*Magdalena **tells me** you're applying for Australian citizenship.*

G 4   Changes to adverbs of time and place in reported speech

Workshop 1, pages 30–31

When we are reporting, we sometimes need to change adverbs of time and place.
I saw Anders yesterday. → *She mentioned she'd seen Anders the day before.*
I'll call you next week. → *She said she'd call me the following week.*
This is the first time I've been here. → *He said it was the first time he'd been there.*

Common changes include:
yesterday → *the day before*
tomorrow → *the next day / the day after*
last weekend / week / month / year → *the weekend / week / month / year before*
next weekend / week / month / year → *the following weekend / week / month / year*
here → *there*

G 5   **Passive (revision)**   Workshop 1, pages 26 – 27; Workshop 3, pages 86 – 87; 90 – 91

Use

- We often use the passive when we do not mention who does an action as we are more interested in what happens than who does the action. This is usually because who does the action is obvious, unknown or not important. The passive also means we can avoid using vague subjects like *someone, people* and *they*.
  *Canberra **was chosen** as the capital of Australia in 1908.*
  *The rugby world cup **is held** every four years. It **was** first **held** in 1987.*

- However, we can use the passive with *by* to say who does the action. This is often when we are giving new information about an existing topic. The passive enables us to put the existing information first and the new information second.
  *Each nation has its own Creation legends which have been passed down **by the Elders**.*
  *New Zealand was first settled **by the Maori people** as early as 1300 AD.*

Form

- We form the passive with the appropriate form of *be* + past participle.
  *Rugby Union **is played** by two teams of 15 players*
  *Relations between Australia and New Zealand **have** often **been compared** to those of siblings.*
  *The Olympics **were held** in Australia in 1956 and 2000.*
  *The museum **will be opened** by the Prime Minister.*

- We use *be* + past participle after modal verbs:
  *Ancient Aboriginal paintings **can be seen** in caves in Uluru.*
  *You **won't be contacted** unless you give us permission.*

- We use the passive infinitive *to be* + past participle after verbs that are normally followed by *to*-infinitive (e. g. *allow, ask, expect, hope, like, need, want*).
  *The Anangu had long wanted the title deeds **to be returned**.*
  *I hope **to be invited** to the opening ceremony.*

- We form a question by putting the subject after the auxiliary verb *be* or between the auxiliaries if there are two of them.
  *When **was** Parliament House **built**?*
  ***Has** the World Cup ever **been held** in Australia?*
  *What time **will** we **be collected** from the hotel?*

- When a verb is followed by a preposition, the preposition stays in the same position in the passive.
  *We can make sure the place **is looked after**.*
  *At the hotel, all diets are **catered for**.*

- When we use the passive in a relative clause, we can sometimes omit the relative pronoun and *be*.
  There are some amazing carvings (which are) made from wood, ivory and sandstone.
  I took part in a sponsored run for a charity (which is) called ResCom.

- When a verb has two objects, the passive sentence can begin with either the direct or indirect object. The direct object is usually a thing and the indirect object is usually a person. When we begin with the direct object, we use the preposition *to* or *for* before the indirect object.
  ***The land** was given back **to the original owners**. OR **The original owners** were given back **the land**.*
  ***Four seats** were saved **for us**. OR **We** were saved **four seats**.*

- Verbs that take two objects include:
  buy • find • get • give • offer • make • promise • send • show

Examples

*Australia **was** first **named** Terra Australis, which was later abbreviated to the current form.*
*Tasmania can **be reached** by boat in about ten hours from Melbourne.*
*They've arranged for us **to be met** the airport.*

G 6   Reported speech in statements and questions in the past and in requests, offers, orders and advice

Workshop 1, pages 30 – 31; Workshop 3, pages 86 – 87

Statements and questions

When reporting speech, we often use the past tense forms *said, told, asked, wanted to know, was wondering, assured, admitted, denied, suggested, promised* etc. We usually 'backshift' the tense (move the tense one step back in time) in the statement, comment or question we are reporting.

- present tense → past tense
  I work in Adelaide.   *She told me she worked in Adelaide.*
  What's wrong with you?   *Keira asked Fred what was wrong with him.*
  Ok, I admit I'm wrong.   *He admitted he was wrong.*

- past tense / present perfect → past perfect
  I didn't want to go.   *She told us she hadn't wanted to go.*
  We've just arrived.   *He said they'd just arrived.*

- will   would
  I'll call you later.   *She said she'd call me later.*

- can   could
  I can't find it.   *He told me he couldn't find it.*

- must   had to
  We must leave now.   *She said they had to leave.*

We sometimes use the past tense forms *said, told, asked, wanted to know, was wondering*, etc. and we do not change the tense. This is usually to show that something is still true, relevant or important.
Sam left about an hour ago. → *He said that Sam left about an hour ago.*
I'll be home in ten minutes. → *She said she'll be home in ten minutes.*
Where's Jamie going? → *She was wondering where Jamie's going.*

Requests, offers, orders and advice

- We can report a request with verbs such as *asked* and *want* + indirect object + *to*-infinitive.
  Can you wait here? → *She asked us to wait here.*
  Could you repeat the question? → *She asked me to repeat the question.*

- We can report an offer with *offer* + *to*-infinitive.
  I can give you a lift if you like? → *Maria offered to give us a lift.*
  I'll help you if you like. → *He offered to help us.*

- We can report an order or advice with *told* + indirect object + (*not*) + *to*-infinitive.
  You should apologize to them. → *She told me to apologize to them.*
  Don't be late again. → *He told me not to be late again.*

We can also use the present tense of the reporting verbs:
Gareth wants me to help him.
She's asking us to wait here.
Petra's offering to give us a lift.
The life guard is telling us not to swim here.

Examples   *He said he was from Wellington.* • *She said they were going to have a barbecue.* •
He asked me if I was OK. • *Olga asked me if I can give her a surfing lesson.* •
He wanted to know where I worked. • *Oliver wants me to phone him.* •
The receptionist asked us to wait a few minutes. • *I offered to help them with the tidying up.* •
The teacher told the children not to run in the corridors.

G 7 *Used to, didn't use to, would* to describe past habits and states

Workshop 2, pages 50 – 51

Used to
We use *used to* + infinitive to talk about past actions or situations that no longer exist. These could be:
- past actions, habits and routines
  *My dad **used to spend** an hour a day commuting to work.*
  *I **used to drive** to work, but these days I usually cycle.*
  *Do you do work in advertising? – No, but I **used to**.*

- past states
  *'Job hopping' is much more common than it **used to be**.*
  *There **used to be** a cinema here.*
  *I **didn't use to** go to the gym.*

Note that there is no final *'d'* in negatives and questions.
*I **didn't use to like** football.*
*What **did** people **use to do** before mobile phones?*
***Didn't** Jamie **use to work** in marketing?*

Would
We use *would* + infinitive to talk about past actions, habits and routines. *Would* is usually contracted to *'d* after pronouns.
*People **would commute** to the office every day.*
*In my old job, we**'d have** a meeting almost every day.*

We do not, however, use *would* to talk about past states.
NOT ~~'Job hopping' is much more common than it would be.~~

Frequency adverbs
Note that we can use frequency adverbs such as *never, always, usually, often, sometimes,* etc. with *would* and *used to*.
*I **never used to** play computer games.*
*I **sometimes used to wear** a tie in my old job.*
*He**'d often arrive** late for work.*

Examples
*My dad **used to** have a beard.*
***Didn't** there **use to** be a café here?*
*As a child, I**'d** spend hours climbing trees.*
*We**'d often stay up** all night when we were students.*

G 8 Gerund and infinitive (revision)

Workshop 2, pages 54 – 55

When one verb follows another verb, the second verb is usually either the gerund (*-ing*) or the *to*-infinitive. Here is an overview. See section G 16 for more explanation and detail.

- Some verbs are always followed by the gerund (*-ing*).
  I **hope** we can avoid getting stuck in traffic.
  She **suggested** go**ing** to the Tate Modern.

- Some verbs are always followed by the to-infinitive.
  Nobody **seemed to** like the film.

- Some verbs can be followed by the gerund (*-ing*) or the infinitive, but the meaning is different.
  I **tried** eat**ing** less meat.
  I **tried to** get some tickets, but they had sold out.
  I **remember** visit**ing** the Mary Rose in Portsmouth.
  Remember to visit Covent Garden when you are in London.
  I think he **stopped to** take some photos on his phone.
  Please **stop** tak**ing** photos. You're not allowed to take photos here!

- A very few verbs can be followed by the gerund (*-ing*) or the infinitive and there is no, or very little, difference in meaning. These verbs include: *begin, continue, intend, prefer, start*.
  I **started to play** the piano when I was ten.
  I **started playing** the piano when I was ten.

- Some prepositions are always followed by a gerund, not a *to*-infinitive. These include:
  after • against • before • by • without
  Have you done these activities **without** us**ing** a smartphone?

- Some combinations of adjectives, nouns and verbs with prepositions are also followed by a gerund. These include:
  capable of • to focus on • good at • importance of • interested in • reason for
  Some young people don't understand the **importance of** vot**ing**.

- A lot of nouns can be followed by a *to*-infinitive. These include:
  chance • idea • opportunity • plan • time
  It was **time to start**. • It's a good **idea to** check the information.

- We use the gerund after prepositions. This could be:
  verb + preposition
  I need to **carry on working** after dinner.
  Did they **apologize for being** later?
  Jake **insisted on paying** for the meal.
  I **congratulated her on getting** promoted.

  adjective or nouns + preposition
  She was **good at** playing basketball.
  Don't forget the **importance of recycling** plastics.

- A lot of nouns can be followed by a *to*-infinitive. These include:
  chance • idea • opportunity • plan • time
  It was time **to start**.
  It's a good idea **to check** the information.

Examples We **arranged to** meet at 6.30.
She **persuaded me to go** to the gallery with her.

See also Gerund + *to*-infinitive → G 16
Verb + gerund or *to*-infinitive with change of meaning → G 16
Verb + object + *to*-infinitive → G 16

G 9 Participle constructions instead of adverbial clauses (present, past and perfect)

Workshop 2, pages 62 – 63

There are two main types of participle:
- the present participle (the -*ing* form of the verb)
  *Before **arriving**, I received lots of information.*
  ***Wanting** to become a teacher, he volunteered in his local school.*

- the past participle (the regular -*ed* form or an irregular form).
  *I came across a fantastic workshop, **organized** by an Irish government agency.*
  ***Given** the opportunity, I would do it again.*

Other participle forms are:
- the perfect participle (e. g. *having done*)
  ***Having spent** eight wonderful weeks there, I can thoroughly recommend it.*

- the perfect passive participle (e. g. *having been done*)
  ***Having been cancelled** twice, the conference finally took place in December.*

To form the negative, we put *not* or *never* before the participle.
***Not wanting** to be late, they set off in plenty of time.*
***Never having been** to Ireland before, I was determined to do and see as much as I could.*

We can use present participle constructions:
- when two events happen at the same time or when one is immediately followed by another.
  *I fell asleep **watching** TV last night.*
  *Luke's in the library **researching** his assignment.*

- in clauses beginning with *before, after, while, since, when* etc.
  *Make sure you turn the computer off **before leaving**.*
  *She's worked here **since finishing** university.*
  *I came across a fantastic organization **while researching** internships abroad.*

- when we express the reason for or result of an action:
  ***Wanting** some hands-on experience before university, I contacted them.*
  ***Not earning** much at the factory, he took a second job working in a café.*
  *She did well in the exam, **passing** with grade A.*

Note that in the above present participle constructions, the events in both clauses are carried out or experienced by the same person.

- in reduced relative clauses when we shorten a defining relative clause. This can be:
  - in progressive tenses when we remove the relative pronoun and *be*.
    *I also met students at the hospital **already studying medicine**. (= I also met students at the hospital who were already studying medicine.)*
    *Who are the people **talking to Harry**?*

  - in place of a relative pronoun + simple tense that express a fact, state or permanent situation.
    *I work in an office **overlooking the river**. (= I work in an office that overlooks the river.)*
    *The students **living next door** are very friendly.*

+ see next page!

We can use past participle constructions
- in reduced defining or non-defining relative clauses. We remove the relative pronoun and the verb *be* in passive structure.
  *It's a local business, **run** by the same family for over 200 years. (= It's a local business, which has been run by the same family for over 200 years.)*
  *Have they found money **stolen** from the office?*
  *Cars **parked** here will be removed.*

- in shortened *if* clauses to give passive meaning, usually without *if*.
  *If **asked** about it, I'd say it was the prettiest place I've visited so far. (= If I was asked about it, …)*
  ***Given** the chance to take the exam again, I'd do it without hesitation. (= If I was given the chance to take the exam again, …)*

We can use perfect participle constructions when one event happens before another event. We use the perfect participle to emphasize that the first event is completed before the second or that there is a time interval between the two events.
***Having finally finished** their exams, they organized a big party.*
***Having met the staff**, he was even more keen to get the job.*
***Having overslept**, she was late for work.*
***Having managed** to work out where all the facilities were, I felt quite proud of myself.*

Note that beginning a sentence with a participle clause is more common in more formal writing and literary contexts.

Examples   *Louise is in the kitchen **making** a coffee, I think.* • ***After leaving** university, he got a job in a bank.* •
***Living alone**, Fred always looked forward to the few visitors he had.* •
***Having** suddenly **quit** his job, he now needed to look for something else.* •
*Bags **left** unattended will be destroyed.* • ***Given** the chance, I'd love to live abroad for a year or two.*

G 10 Emphatic *do / does, did*   Workshop 2, pages 66 – 67

We can use a form of the auxiliary verb *do* (*do, does, did*) to give emphasis to a statement.
In speaking, we stress *do, does, did*. We use *do* in this way for two reasons:

- to emphasize our feelings or emotions
  *I **do** wish I could turn the clock back.*
  *I **do** like Mexican food.*
  *Anna **does** have some great ideas.*
  *I **did** enjoy that film.*

- to emphasize a contrast
  *I don't do any sports, but I **do** like watching it on TV.*
  *He doesn't drive, but he **does** have a motorbike licence.*
  *I knew it was wrong to take them, but I **did** take them.*

With tenses and forms that already have an auxiliary verb, we stress the auxiliary verb to express emphasis in a similar way.
*I **am** looking forward to seeing them.*
*We really **have** had a great time, thank you.*

Examples   *I **do** agree with you.* • *Please believe me!* • *I **did** enjoy that meal. Did you?* • *It's not easy, but I **am** trying!*

G 11   Tenses (revision) Workshop 3, pages 98 – 99

Present tenses

Simple present

- We use the simple present to talk about something that happens all the time or that is always true.
  *My mum **works** as a nurse.*
  *I **love** my dog.*
  *We normally **watch** the football on Saturday afternoon.*

- We make negatives and questions with a form of *do*.
  *They **don't go** to the cinema very often.*
  *He **doesn't live** here anymore.*
  *Who **does** this dog **belong** to?*
  ***Don't** you **like** this movie?*

Present progressive

- We use the present progressive to talk about what is happening now when we are speaking.
  *They**'re playing** tennis now.*
  *We **aren't eating** lunch at the moment.*
  ***Are** you **reading** the newspaper or can I have it?*

- Some verbs do not have a progressive form, for example, *know, like, want* or *understand*.

Past tenses

Simple past

- We use the simple past to talk about things that happened at a time in the past. We often use expressions of time like *yesterday, last Thursday, two months ago,* etc. With regular verbs, we add -*ed* to the infinitive of the verb to make the simple past. We form the negative with *didn't* and questions with *did*.
  *We **stayed** in Australia for two months last summer.*
  *The British **arrived** in Australia in 1788.*
  *They **didn't treat** the Aboriginals respectfully.*
  *When **did** they **close** Uluru for tourists?*

- Some verbs don't add -*ed* in the simple past. They are irregular (see the list on page 179).
  *We **went** to the beach yesterday.* NOT *We goed to the beach.*
  *He **sent** me an email an hour ago.* NOT *He sended me an email.*

Past progressive

- We form the past progressive with *was / were* + -*ing*. We form the negative with *wasn't / weren't* + -*ing*. For questions, we put the subject between *was / were* and the -*ing* form.
  *My parents met when they **were living** in Spain.*
  *Sorry, I **wasn't listening**. What did you say?*
  ***Were** the others **waiting** when you arrived?*

- We often use the past progressive together with the simple past to give background information.
  *It **was raining** when I got up.*
  *While we **were cycling** home from training last week, I had an accident and fell off my bike.*
  *Jack went home from school early yesterday because he **wasn't feeling** well.*
  *What **were** you **doing** when I saw you in town last Saturday?*

+ see next page!

<u>Present perfect</u>

- We form the present perfect with *has/have* and the past participle. We form the negative with *hasn't/haven't* and the past participle. For questions, we put the subject between *has/have* and the past participle.
  *She **has called** several times.*
  *I **haven't seen** Morgan in school today.*
  *How long have you **lived** here?*

- We use the present perfect in two main ways.

  - To talk about something in the past which is connected with or has consequences in the present. We often use the present perfect in this way with *yet* and *already*.
    *I**'ve already** booked the tickets.*
    *I **haven't seen** the exhibition yet.*
    ***Has** she **given** her presentation yet?*

  - To talk about something that started in the past and continues now. We often use the present perfect in this way with *for* and *since*.
    *He**'s lived** in this house for ten years.*
    *We**'ve been** friends since we were seven.*

<u>Present perfect progressive</u>

- We form the present perfect progressive with *has/have + been + -ing*. We form the negative with *hasn't/haven't + been + -ing*. For questions, we put the subject between *has/have* and *been*.
  *I**'ve been playing** the guitar for three years/since I was 11.*
  *We **haven't been playing** very well since our trainer left.*
  *How long **have** you **been learning** English?*

- We often use the present perfect progressive to talk about an action or a situation which started in the past and continues to the present. We use it with *for*, *since* and *all* as well as in questions with *How long*.
  *I**'ve been living** here for years/since 20.. .*
  *The kids **have been playing** in the garden all afternoon.*
  *Sorry, I'm late. – Don't worry. We **haven't been waiting** long.*
  *How long **have** you **been working** here?*

<u>Past perfect</u>

- We form the past perfect with *had* and the past participle. We form the negative with *hadn't* and the past participle. For questions, we put the subject between *had* and the past participle.
  *I was late and the exam **had** already **started**.*
  *He **hadn't told** me he was Meg's friend.*
  ***Had** you seen the film before?*

- We use the past perfect to show that one event happened before another one in the past. We use the past perfect for the event that happened first and the simple past for the more recent event. We often use sequence adverbs such as *when, before, after* and *until* to link the two events.
  *A few hours after we **had started** along the trail, my father **fell** ill.*
  *We **had hoped** to reach this place sooner, but the bad weather **slowed** us down.*
  *The boy **had** just **had** his 8th birthday when he **fell** and **died**.*

- We also use the past perfect to show that something happened before a time in the past.
  *We**'d travelled** over 200 miles by 12 o'clock.*
  *I **hadn't met** him before the last concert in June.*

Past perfect progressive

- We form the past perfect progressive with *had + been + -ing*. We form the negative with *hadn't + been + -ing*. For questions, we put the subject between *had* and *been*.
  We'd been playing for 20 minutes when it started to rain.
  I hadn't been waiting long when the bus came.
  Had you *been looking for* an internship for long before you got one?

- We use the past perfect progressive to focus on the length of the earlier action and to show that it was in progress before the second action started.
  I'd been playing rugby for three years when I became captain.
  We hadn't been driving for long when dad realized that he didn't have his phone.
  How long *had* the others *been waiting* when you finally arrived?

Future tenses

Will future

- We use *will* to offer or promise to do something for somebody. The verb form always stays the same. For negatives we use *won't*.
  I'll help with your homework this evening.
  *There isn't any milk in the fridge. – Don't worry. I **won't forget** to buy some this afternoon.*

- We use *will* when we decide to do something while we are speaking.
  You look hungry. We'll buy a sandwich.
  *I'm tired, I **won't stay** up much longer.*

- We use *will* for predictions that are based on personal feeling or opinion.
  You'll love it in Canada!
  *It **won't take** long.*
  It'll take you longer than you think.

Going-to future

- We use *be going to* for decisions and future plans that were made before the time of speaking.
  I'm going to join the school drama club next term.
  *Have you packed? – No, I **am going to pack** after dinner.*
  We're going to book our train tickets at the weekend.

- We use *be going to* for predictions that are based on present evidence. In other words, there is something in the present that indicates something in the future.
  Look at the traffic. We're going to be late.
  It looks like it's going to be a lovely day.

The simple present

- We use the simple present to talk about future events when the statements are based on present facts, and when these facts are something fixed like a time-table, schedule or calendar.
  The bus leaves at 6.30, please hurry up.
  The soccer match starts at three o'clock on Sunday.

Present progressive
- We use the present progressive with a future time to talk about future arrangements.
  Next week, I'm seeing my cousin to discuss my internship.
  We're meeting at the pizzeria this evening.
  When *are* Chris and Jo *going* to the USA?

Future perfect

- We use the future perfect (*will have* + past participle) to talk about something already completed by a point in the future. We often use the future perfect with *by*.
  *The apprenticeship starts in September. I'll **have finished** my A-levels by then.*
  ***Will** you **have had** dinner by 8.30?*

- We can use the future perfect to talk about something not completed by a point in the future.
  *I'm afraid I **won't have finished** my report by Friday.*
  *I **won't have had** time to do much research before the interview.*

Future progressive

- We use the future progressive (*will be* + -*ing*) for an action in progress at a specific time in the future.
  *Next year most of my friends **will be doing** a university course or an apprenticeship.*
  *Hopefully by September I'**ll be working** somewhere in the US or Canada.*
  *This time tomorrow, I'**ll be having** my interview.*

The passive (all tenses)

- We use the passive in different tenses when we focus on the action and not on who does the action. We use *be* in the appropriate tense + past participle.

  Simple present (*am* / *is* / *are* + past participle)
  *The internet **is used** by billions of people every day.*
  *Today, most goods **are paid** for electronically.*

  Simple past (*was* / *were* + past participle)
  *It's hard to imagine life before electricity **was invented**.*
  *The first emails **were sent** in the 1970s.*

  Present perfect (*has been* / *have been* + past participle)
  *The way we communicate **has been revolutionized**.*
  *Today, many cashiers **have been replaced** by self-service check-outs.*

  Will (*will be* + past participle)
  *Autonomous drones **will be used** to deliver parcels to our doors.*
  *Many jobs **will be lost**.*

  Modal verbs (*can be* / *might be* / *had to be* + past participle)
  *Our homes will be full of smart appliances that **can be controlled** remotely.*
  *The new website **might be launched** soon.*
  *Until the early 20th century, all household chores **had to be done** by hand.*

G 12   Nominalized adjectives

Workshop 3, pages 102 – 103

We can use certain adjectives as nouns to refer to a group of people. We call these nominalized adjectives. We use *the* + adjective.

*There was even one that was collecting clothes for **the homeless**.*
*The law protects **the innocent** and convicts **the guilty**.*
***The elderly** are a growing section of the population.*
*There are special reduced rates for **the unemployed**.*
*The new tax laws help both **the wealthy** and **the poor**.*

! Be careful when using nominalized adjectives. Some people may take offence at being considered part of a group, especially when there is a possible negative connotation or meaning. It may be better to use phrases such as *unemployed people*, *homeless people*, etc.

G 13   Definite, indefinite and zero articles
Workshop 3, pages 102 – 103

There are a number of rules regarding the use of the definite, indefinite and zero article.

- We use the indefinite article (*a / an*) with countable nouns to talk about something non-specific. Either speaker or the listener (or both) does not know the exact thing.
  *As you know I went to **a festival** this year.*
  *Has your city got **a university**?*
  *Have you got **an umbrella**?*

  We use *a* before a consonant sound and we use *an* before a vowel sound.

- We use the definite article (*the*) to talk about something specific. Both the speaker and the listener know the exact thing because it has previously been mentioned or when there is only one of something.
  ***The festival** was great and I had a really good time!*
  *I saw **the film** when it finally came out in the summer.*

- We use no article (called the zero article) to talk about something in a general sense. Note that to talk about something in general in this way, we use the plural of a countable noun or an uncountable noun.
  *I love going to **festivals**.*
  *Most people stay in **tents** at the festival.*
  *I listen to **music** all the time.*

Examples   *I stayed in **a tent** with my friend. It was in **a big field**.*   •   *I wonder if there is **a café** near here?*

*One thing I really liked about Glastonbury was **the food**.*   •   *Let's meet at **the tent** when the band has finished.*   •   *Did you like **the café** we went to?*

*You need to buy **food** while you're there.*   •   *I like working in **cafés**.*

G 14   Defining relative clauses (revision) and non-defining relative clauses
Workshop 4, pages 122 – 123; 126 – 127

Defining relative clauses
- A defining relative clause defines, identifies or gives necessary information about a person or thing. A defining relative clause comes immediately after this person or thing and begins with a relative pronoun. We use *who* for people and *which* for things. We can use *that* for both people and things. We use *whose* to show possession.
  *Kids **who came over** would ask sometimes, 'Where's your dad?'*
  *Is this the book **which your parents gave you as a birthday present**?*
  *Mac and his family do things **that every other family does**.*
  *This is my friend **whose paintings I showed you**.*

- A relative pronoun can be the subject or the object of a relative clause.

	relative pronoun / subject	verb	object	
There's the man	*who*	*helped*	*us*	*yesterday.*

	relative pronoun / object	subject	verb	
There's the man	*who*	*we*	*helped*	*yesterday.*

- We can omit *who, which* or *that* when it is the object of the relative clause.
  There's the man (who) we helped yesterday. NOT *There's the man helped us yesterday.*
  Is this the picture (which) your parents gave you as a birthday present?
  Mac and his family do things (that) every other family does.
  Is this the café (that) Luke mentioned the other day?

Non-defining relative clauses
● A non-defining relative clause gives extra information about a person or thing. The non-defining relative clause comes immediately after this person or thing and begins with a relative pronoun. We don't use *that* in a non-defining relative clause. We always separate a non-defining relative clause from the main clause with commas.
*My two older brothers**, who I've always been very close to,** went to live with my dad.*
*Single-parent families**, which may include a single mother or dad and their children,** are common.*
*My best friend**, whose parents divorced when she was a baby,** was brought up by her mum.*
*He was born in Avalon**, which is a small town near Los Angeles.***

Non-defining relative clauses are used more common in writing and in more formal spoken contexts.

Where and *when*
We can use the relative adverbs *where* and *when* in relative clauses. We use *where* to identify a place and *when* to identify a time.
*The hotel **where we stayed** is in the city centre.*
*Thanksgiving is a day **when families and friends get together.***
*Carmel**, where we went the other week,** is one of my favourite places.*

Examples   *The girl **who is on the right** is my little sister.*
*The couple **that lives in the flat above us** is very noisy.*
*What's that game **we were playing** last night?*
*Mr Jones**, who also taught my mum,** is my maths teacher.*
*Christmas is usually a time **when families come together.***

G 15   Comment clauses Workshop 4, pages 122 – 123; 126 – 127

● We can use a non-defining relative clause beginning with *which* to comment on the whole of the previous clause. The comment clause is similar to a non-defining relative clause and is separated from the preceding clause by a comma.
*There are children from all sorts of ethnic backgrounds**, which I think is really good.***
*I was at a school reunion last weekend**, which was great fun.***
*The school became co-ed in the 1980s**, which was a major step forwards.***
*I missed the bus**, which was really annoying.***

● Whereas non-defining relative clauses are more common in writing and in more formal spoken contexts, comment clauses are quite common in spoken and more informal English.

Examples   *Maria offered to help**, which was very kind of her.*** ● *I found my phone**, which was a huge relief.*** ●
*The meal was €10**, which was quite cheap to be honest.***

G 16   Different use of gerund and *to*-infinitive (revision)

Workshop 4, pages 134 – 135

A gerund is the -ing form of a verb. A gerund followed by an object or an adverbial is called a gerund clause.

- We can use a gerund or a gerund clause as the subject of a verb. This is when the subject is an activity or action. We often use the gerund as a subject in signs and notices. To form the negative, we put *not* before the gerund.
  Spending a year abroad is very popular among young people.
  Not knowing what to study is a fairly common problem among teenagers.
  Parking here is forbidden.

- We can use a gerund or a gerund clause as the object of certain verbs. This is when the object is an activity or action.
  I don't mind waiting for you.
  I like seeing how people live here.
  I regret not going to the school prom.

- Sometimes we use two verbs together. The second verb adds information to what is expressed by the first verb. When one verb follows another verb, the second verb is usually the gerund (*-ing*) or the *to*-infinitive.

- We use the gerund (*-ing*) after certain verbs. These include:
  admit • avoid • consider • deny • don't mind • enjoy • fancy • feel like • finish • imagine • involve • keep (on) • mention • miss • practise • recommend • risk • spend time • suggest
  Did you enjoy reading the book?
  I miss seeing my old friends.

- We use the *to*-infinitive after certain verbs. These include:
  agree • aim • appear • arrange • can('t) afford • choose • claim • decide • demand • (be) determined • expect • help • hope • intend • learn • manage • need • offer • plan • pretend • promise • refuse • seem • tend • threaten • want • would like / prefer
  He hopes to get a place on a degree apprenticeship programme.
  I've decided to look for a new job.
  Did you manage to finish your assignment on time?
  Lucy is planning to go to university in September.

- Some verbs can usually be followed by the gerund or the *to*-infinitive with little or no difference in meaning. These include:
  begin • continue • hate • like • prefer • start

  I hate getting up early. OR *I hate to get up early.*
  I prefer studying alone. OR *I prefer to study alone.*
  I like reading about current issues. OR *I like to read about current issues.*

  However, we can sometimes use *like* + *to*-infintive to say that something is a good or sensible idea.
  I like to get my assignments finished before the deadline.
  I like to eat plenty of fresh fruit and vegetables.

- Some verbs can be followed by a gerund or the *to*-infinitive but there is a difference in meaning. These verbs include:

Try
We use *try* + gerund when we do something to see what the results will be.
*If you're unhappy at work, you should **try talking** to your boss.*
*I **tried turning** the computer on and off, but the program still didn't work.*

We use *try* + *to*-infinitive when we make an effort to achieve something.
*They **tried to persuade** me to go and work for them, but I am happy at my company.*
*I'm **trying to learn** the drums, so that I can join a band.*

Remember and *forget*
We use *remember / forget* + gerund to talk about memories.
*I **remember changing** my password.*
*Do you **remember going** to school for the first time?*
*I'll never **forget visiting** London. It was a wonderful trip.*

We use *remember / forget* + *to*-infinitive to say we do or don't do something.
*If you do decide to apply, then **remember to include** all the articles you've written about social issues.*
*Oh no! I **forgot to mention** my hobbies in my CV.*

Stop
We use *stop* + gerund to talk about something ending or stopping.
*I **stopped eating** meat ten tears ago.*
*I hope it **stops raining** soon.*

We use *stop* + *to*-infinitive to express the reason or purpose.
*Sorry I'm late. I **stopped to get** some petrol on the way here.*
*I was working, but I **stopped to watch** TV for a while.*

Go on
We use *go on* + gerund to say we continue to do something.
*Jack **went on studying** even though he wasn't really enjoying the course.*

We use *go on* + *to*-infinitive to say we do something new.
*When she didn't get a place to study medicine, Jen **went on to train** as a physiotherapist.*

- Some verbs are followed by an object + *to*-infinitive. These include:
advise • allow • ask • choose • encourage • expect • help • invite • need • order • persuade • tell • want • would like

*My boss **wants me to apply** for the new position.*
*Do you **need someone to help** you?*

Note that we can use some verbs (e. g. *ask, choose, expect, help, need, want*) without or with an object.
*We **expect to arrive** on Friday. We **expect them to accompany** us on Friday.*

Note that when these verbs are in the passive, they are followed directly by the *to*-infinitive.
*As a child, I **was** always **encouraged to work** hard.*

G 17   Modal verbs (form) (revision)   Workshop 4, pages 138 – 139

The modal verbs are *can*, *could*, *may*, *might*, *must*, *shall*, *should*, *will* and *would*. We also use modal substitutes *be able to*, *be allowed to*, *have to*, *need to* and *ought to*.

- A modal verb always has the same form. The ending never changes.
  She can speak English. NOT ~~She cans speak English.~~

- We use an infinitive without *to* after a modal verb.
  I will help you. NOT ~~I will to help you.~~

- To form a question, we put the modal verb before the subject.
  Can you help me? NOT ~~Do you can help me?~~

- To form a negative, we put *not* or *n't* after the modal verb.
  You mustn't do that. NOT ~~You don't must do that.~~

affirmative	*She can speak German.* • *It might rain.* • *They should go.*
negative	*She can't speak German.* • *It might not rain.* • *They shouldn't go.*
question	*Can she speak German?* • *Might it rain?* • *Should they go?*

See also   Can and *be able to* for ability → `G18`   Can and *be allowed to* for permission → `G19`
Need to, *have to* and *must* for necessity → `G20`   *Should* for advice → `G21`
May and *might* for possibility → `G22`

Examples   *I don't* **feel like studying** *today.* • *We* **hope to arrive** *around 6.30ish.*
I **hate being** *late for anything.* • *I* **tried to order** *online, but the website was down.*
Did *they* **ask** *Jack* **to go** *with them?*

G 18   *Can* and *be able to* for ability   Workshop 4, pages 120 – 121

We use *can* and *be able to* in a number of ways:

- to talk about general abilities and skills.
  Amir **can** *play the guitar.*
  I **can speak** *French and Spanish. But I* **can't** *speak Italian.*
  Some people **are able to** *speak several languages.*

- to talk about ability at a particular time.
  I **can't** *read this. The writing is too small.*
  I'm **not able to** *fix the problem, I'm afraid.*

The past tense of *can* is *could* and the past tense of *be able to* is *was / were able to*.
I **could** *speak some English when I was four years old.*
Unfortunately, I **wasn't able to** *find his office.*

We use *be able to* (not *can*) with *will* and the present perfect.
I'm sure you **will be able to** *find a great job.*
I've **been able to** *speak English since I was four.*

See also   Modal verbs (form) → `G17`

G 19 *Can* and *be allowed to* for permission
Workshop 4, pages 120 – 121

We use *can* and *be allowed to* to talk about permission. We use them:

- to talk about rules and laws.
  *You **can't** park here. But you **can** park over there.*
  *Are you **allowed to** wear jeans at work?*

- to talk about permission given by an individual.
  *You **can** leave when you have finished the report.*
  *I'**m not allowed to** stay up late on a school night.*

The past tense of *can* is *could* and the past tense of *be allowed to* is *was / were allowed to*.
*Sorry I'm late. I **couldn't leave** work any earlier.*
*In the UK, women **were** first **allowed to vote** in 1918.*

See also   Modal verbs (form) → `G17`

G 20 *Need to, have to* and *must* for necessity
Workshop 4, pages 120 – 121

We use *need to, have to* and *must* to talk about what is necessary or what is required.

- When they are used in this way, there is usually little difference in meaning, e.g. *I **have to** prepare for my interview. / I **need to** prepare for my interview. / I **must** prepare for my interview.* We use *must not* (or *mustn't*) to express a negative idea.
  *Education and work experience details **must** be included in your CV.*
  *Your information **must** be correct and up to date.*
  *You **need to** show some ID to get in the building.*
  *Does your dad **have to** wear a tie for work?*
  *You **mustn't** be late! You **need to** leave by 5.30 at the latest.*

- In more informal contexts, such as conversation, we can use *have got to*.
  *I'**ve got to** prepare for my interview.*
  *What time **have** we **got to** leave?*

- The past tenses are *needed to* and *had to*. We use *had to* as the past tense of *must*.
  *Sorry I'm late. I **needed to** stop at the shops on the way here.*
  *I **had to** stay at work later than usual today.*

- We use *don't have to* and *don't need to* to say that something isn't necessary.
  *We **don't need to** leave until midday. NOT ~~We mustn't leave until midday.~~*
  *In some countries, you **don't have to** give personal details in your CV.*
  *I **didn't need to** go to work today.*

See also   Modal verbs (form) → `G17`

G 21   *Should* for advice

Workshop 4, pages 120 – 121

> We use *should* and *shouldn't* to give advice and to say what we think is the best or correct thing to do.
>
> You **should** try to exercise at least once a week. • What **should** I do? • You **shouldn't** give up!

See also   Modal verbs (form) → G17

G 22   *May* and *might* for possibility

Workshop 4, pages 120 – 121

> We use *may* and *might* to say that something is possible or likely. *Might* is more common in informal contexts, such as conversation. The negative is *may not* and *might not*. We use them:
>
> - to say what is possible or likely in the future.
>   It **might** rain later.
>   I **might not** go to the meeting.
>   There **may** be a slight delay with your order.
>
> - to say what we think is possible or likely in the present.
>   This **might** be Nina's office. But I'm not sure.
>   She didn't answer the phone. She **might not** be at home.

See also   Modal verbs (form) → G17

Irregular verbs

infinitive	simple past	past participle	German
to **be**	**was / were**	**been**	sein
to **beat**	**beat**	**beaten**	schlagen
to **become**	**became**	**become**	werden
to **begin**	**began**	**begun**	beginnen, anfangen
to **bet**	**bet**	**bet**	wetten
to **bite**	**bit**	**bitten**	beißen
to **blow**	**blew**	**blown**	blasen
to **break**	**broke**	**broken**	brechen
to **bring**	**brought**	**brought**	bringen
to **build**	**built**	**built**	bauen
to **burn**	**burnt / burned**	**burnt / burned**	(ver)brennen
to **buy**	**bought**	**bought**	kaufen
to **catch**	**caught**	**caught**	fangen
to **choose** [u:]	**chose** [əʊ]	**chosen** [əʊ]	auswählen
to **come**	**came**	**come**	kommen
to **cost**	**cost**	**cost**	kosten
to **cut**	**cut**	**cut**	schneiden
to **deal**	**dealt**	**dealt**	handeln
to **dig**	**dug**	**dug**	graben
to **do**	**did**	**done**	machen, tun
to **draw**	**drew**	**drawn**	zeichnen
to **dream**	**dreamt / dreamed**	**dreamt / dreamed**	träumen
to **drink**	**drank**	**drunk**	trinken
to **drive** [aɪ]	**drove** [əʊ]	**driven** [ɪ]	fahren
to **eat**	**ate** [et], [eɪt]	**eaten**	essen
to **fall**	**fell**	**fallen**	fallen, stürzen
to **feed**	**fed**	**fed**	füttern

infinitive	simple past	past participle	German
to **feel**	**felt**	**felt**	(sich) fühlen, spüren
to **fight**	**fought**	**fought**	kämpfen
to **find**	**found**	**found**	finden
to **fly**	**flew**	**flown**	fliegen
to **forget**	**forgot**	**forgotten**	vergessen
to **forgive**	**forgave**	**forgiven**	vergeben
to **freeze**	**froze**	**frozen**	frieren
to **get**	**got**	**got / gotten (AE)**	bekommen, holen
to **give**	**gave**	**given**	geben, schenken
to **go**	**went**	**gone**	gehen, fahren
to **grow** [əʊ]	**grew** [u:]	**grown** [əʊ]	wachsen, anbauen
to **hang**	**hung**	**hung**	hängen
to **have (got)**	**had**	**had**	haben
to **hear** [ɪə]	**heard** [ɜ:]	**heard** [ɜ:]	hören
to **hide** [haɪd]	**hid** [hɪd]	**hidden** [hɪdn]	(sich) verstecken
to **hit**	**hit**	**hit**	schlagen
to **hold**	**held**	**held**	halten
to **hurt**	**hurt**	**hurt**	wehtun
to **keep**	**kept**	**kept**	(be)halten
to **kneel** [ni:l]	**knelt** [nelt]	**knelt** [nelt]	knien
to **know** [nəʊ]	**knew** [nju:]	**known** [nəʊn]	wissen, kennen
to **lead** [li:d]	**led** [led]	**led** [led]	führen
to **learn**	**learnt / learned**	**learnt / learned**	lernen
to **leave**	**left**	**left**	verlassen
to **lend**	**lent**	**lent**	leihen

infinitive	simple past	past participle	German
to **let**	**let**	**let**	lassen
to **lie**	**lay**	**lain**	liegen
to **light**	**lit / lighted**	**lit / lighted**	anzünden, anmachen
to **lose** [uː]	**lost** [ɒ]	**lost** [ɒ]	verlieren
to **make**	**made**	**made**	machen, herstellen
to **mean** [iː]	**meant** [e]	**meant** [e]	bedeuten
to **meet**	**met**	**met**	(sich) treffen, kennen-lernen
to **mow**	**mowed**	**mown / mowed**	mähen
to **pay**	**paid**	**paid**	bezahlen
to **put**	**put**	**put**	stellen
to **quit**	**quit**	**quit**	aufhören
to **read** [iː]	**read** [e]	**read** [e]	lesen
to **rebuild**	**rebuilt**	**rebuilt**	wieder aufbauen
to **rewrite**	**rewrote**	**rewritten**	umschreiben
to **ride**	**rode**	**ridden**	fahren, reiten
to **ring**	**rang**	**rung**	klingeln, anrufen
to **rise**	**rose**	**risen**	ansteigen, (sich) erheben
to **run**	**ran**	**run**	laufen, rennen, leiten
to **say** [eɪ]	**said** [e]	**said** [e]	sagen
to **see**	**saw**	**seen**	sehen
to **sell**	**sold**	**sold**	verkaufen
to **send**	**sent**	**sent**	schicken
to **set**	**set**	**set**	setzen, stellen, legen
to **shake**	**shook**	**shaken**	schütteln
to **shine**	**shone** [ɒ]	**shone** [ɒ]	scheinen

infinitive	simple past	past participle	German
to **shoot**	**shot**	**shot**	schießen
to **show**	**showed**	**shown / showed**	zeigen
to **sing**	**sang**	**sung**	singen
to **sink**	**sank**	**sunk**	sinken
to **sit**	**sat**	**sat**	sitzen
to **sleep**	**slept**	**slept**	schlafen
to **smell**	**smelt / smelled**	**smelt / smelled**	riechen
to **speak** [iː]	**spoke** [əʊ]	**spoken** [əʊ]	sprechen
to **spend**	**spent**	**spent**	verbringen, ausgeben
to **split**	**split**	**split**	sich trennen
to **spoil**	**spoilt**	**spoilt**	verderben
to **spread**	**spread**	**spread**	sich ausbreiten, etw. verteilen
to **stand**	**stood**	**stood**	stehen
to **steal**	**stole**	**stolen**	stehlen
to **stick**	**stuck**	**stuck**	kleben
to **sting**	**stung**	**stung**	stechen
to **swim**	**swam**	**swum**	schwimmen
to **take**	**took**	**taken**	nehmen, dauern
to **teach** [iː]	**taught** [ɔː]	**taught** [ɔː]	unterrichten
to **tell**	**told**	**told**	sagen, erzählen
to **think**	**thought**	**thought**	denken, glauben
to **throw**	**threw**	**thrown**	werfen
to **understand**	**understood**	**understood**	verstehen
to **wake up**	**woke up**	**woken up**	aufwachen
to **wear** [eə]	**wore** [ɔː]	**worn** [ɔː]	tragen
to **win**	**won** [ʌ]	**won**	gewinnen
to **write**	**wrote**	**written**	schreiben

Vocabulary

Here are all the words from the workshops. They are in the same order as in the workshop.

There is the page number and the activity.

A ▢ at the side is for words from the listening text. A ▇ is for words from videos.

Words in **grey** are important for one text or they are culture-specific. You don't have to be able to use them actively and you can always find them in the dictionary list at the end of the book

The phonetic transcription [ ] tells you how you say a word.

The example sentence shows you how we use a word.
= shows words with the same meaning
≠ shows words with the opposite meaning

❗ shows words with the same meaning in French, Latin or Spanish or it gives other interesting information about the word.

When you work with the *Vocabulary*, cover the German, look at the English word and the example and say the German word. You can also cover the German and the example sentences to practise the English.

page / exercise	Welcome Workshop		
10	to **represent** [ˌreprɪˈzent]	*I think Aimee should represent our class.* ❗ *Fr. 'représenter'*	vertreten
	approximately [əˈprɒksɪmətli]	*Approximately how many languages are there in the world?*	ungefähr; etwa
	commonly [ˈkɒmənli]	*Which are the two most commonly spoken languages on earth?*	gewöhnlich; häufig
	to **spread** [spred], **spread, spread** [spred, spred]	*What's the quickest way to spread a message?*	verbreiten
	colonialism [kəˈləʊniəlɪzəm]	*British colonialism helped to spread English around the world.*	Kolonialismus
	mate [meɪt]	*Nick is my mate, I've known him since kindergarten.* = *friend*	Kumpel
11	**slideshow** [ˈslaɪdʃəʊ]	*Watch the slideshow and take notes about the topic.*	Diaschau
	apart [əˈpɑːt]	*The USA and Australia are far apart.*	auseinander
	common [ˈkɒmən]	*What does the common language of the USA and Australia tell us about their history?* ❗ *Sp. 'común'*	gemeinsam; normal
	to **land** [lænd]	*The plane landed two hours late.*	landen
	decline [dɪˈklaɪn]	*Pollution can cause a decline in the insect population.* ❗ *Fr. 'décline' (m.)*	Rückgang
	to **gain** [geɪn]	*To become president, you need to gain a total of 270 electoral votes.* = *get*	bekommen; erreichen
	to **influence** [ˈɪnfluəns]	*Media pressure can influence people.* = *lead to believe* ❗ *Fr. 'influencer'*	beeinflussen

page	exercise	**Welcome Workshop**		
		trade [treɪd]	*Global trade is mostly done in English.*	Handel
		completely [kəmˈpliːtli]	*Should tourism be banned completely in some places?*	ganz; komplett
		mass [mæs]	*English became the language of entertainment for the masses.*	Masse
		status [ˈsteɪtəs]	*Its role in popular culture gave English a special status.* ⓘ Lat. 'status, -ūs' (m.)	Status
		golf [ɡɒlf]	*Popular sports that started in Britain and the US include golf, basketball and skateboarding.*	Golf
		to communicate [kəˈmjuːnɪkeɪt]	*I'm finding it difficult to communicate in French.* ⓘ Sp. 'communicar'	kommunizieren; etw. vermitteln
		lexicon [ˈleksɪkən]	*The lexicon of the digital world is in English.*	Wortschatz
		to publish [ˈpʌblɪʃ]	*When was the book published?* ⓘ Sp. 'publier'; Fr. 'publicar'	veröffentlichen
		slang [slæŋ]	*Young people often use slang that others don't understand.* = a language that consists of words, phrases and grammar that are very informal	Slang
		to identify [aɪˈdentɪfaɪ]	*Identify the differences of opinion between boys and girls.*	identifizieren
		pants [pænts]	*I like to wear pants with crazy colors.* ⓘ BE = trousers	Hose
		horrified [ˈhɒrɪfaɪd]	*She looked horrified and replied, 'Oh dear, am I late?'*	entsetzt
		swimwear [ˈswɪmweər]	*You see all sorts of swimwear at the beach.*	Badebekleidung
		doubt [daʊt]	*I have no doubts that he's a nice guy.*	Zweifel

page 12	exercise	**Workshop 1**		
		proof [pruːf]	*There is a rabbit-proof fence in western Australia.*	... sicher; undurchdringlich
		aboriginal [ˌæbəˈrɪdʒənl]	*What do the stories tell you about aboriginal culture?*	den Ureinwohnern Australiens zugehörig
		islander [ˈaɪləndə]	*The Torres Strait Islanders settled in the islands north of Australia about 10,000 years ago.* = somebody who lives on an island	Insulaner(in); Inselbewohner(in)
		nickname [ˈnɪkneɪm]	*What is Australia's nickname?*	Spitzname
		continent [ˈkɒntɪnənt]	*Australia is the only country in the world that covers an entire continent.* ⓘ Lat. 'continens, -entis' (f)	Kontinent
		times [taɪmz]	*How many times bigger is Australia than Germany?*	mal

page 13 exercise

Workshop 1

rainbow [ˈreɪnbəʊ]	When the sun shines while it's raining you can see a rainbow.	Regenbogen
serpent [ˈsɜːpənt]	= snake	Schlange
kangaroo [ˌkæŋgəˈruː]	Kangaroos live in Australia.	Känguru
interior [ɪnˈtɪəriər]	The interior of Australia is huge and very dry. ❗ Lat. 'interior, -oris'	Binnenland; das Innere
bush [bʊʃ]	In Australia, the bush is the land away from the big cities.	Busch
fascinating [ˈfæsɪneɪtɪŋ]	Australia has a long and fascinating history. = interesting	faszinierend
therefore [ˈðeəfɔːr]	The training was voluntary and therefore not considered as work.	daher; deshalb; darum
southern [ˈsʌðən]	The early European explorers set out to find this unknown southern land.	südlich
to nickname [ˈnɪkneɪm]	Can you guess why Australia is nicknamed 'Down Under'?	Spitznamen geben; nennen
equator [ɪˈkweɪtər]	Germany is north of the equator.	Äquator
hemisphere [ˈhemɪsfɪər]	There is a group of five stars that can only be seen in the night sky in the southern hemisphere.	Hemisphäre
to balance [ˈbæləns]	We added more weight in front to balance the load.	ausgleichen
remote [rɪˈməʊt]	They live in a remote wooded area. ❗ Lat. 'removere (removeo, removi, remotum)' = to remove	entfernt; abgelegen
platypus [ˈplætɪpəs]	If you want to see a platypus in the wild, you have to go to Australia.	Schnabeltier
koala [kəʊˈɑːlə]	Many animals such as koala bears, kangaroos and wombats can only be found in Australia.	Koala
creepy [ˈkriːpi]	It's a creepy fact that Australia has some very dangerous animals.	gruselig
deadly [ˈdedli]	There are deadly snakes in Australia.	tödlich
to unite [juˈnaɪt]	Australia's colonies united to create one nation. ❗ Sp. 'unir'	(sich) vereinigen
to form [fɔːm]	Thirteen British colonies formed the very first United States. ❗ Lat. 'formare (formo, faormavi, formatum'	gründen; bilden
tropical [ˈtrɒpɪkl]	There are tropical rainforests in the Northern Territory and snow-covered mountains along the East coast.	Tropen-
downhill [ˌdaʊnˈhɪl]	Skiing downhill can be dangerous when there are too many people.	bergab
neighbour [ˈneɪbə]	We see our neighbours in their garden.	Nachbar

page	exercise	**Workshop 1**		
14	1a	**workout** [ˈwɜːkaʊt]	*I do workouts every day to keep fit.*	Fitnesstraining
		puzzled [ˈpʌzld]	*Jason and Ricky exchanged puzzled looks.*	verblüfft; verwirrt
		silence [ˈsaɪləns]	*There was silence, then the whole team jumped and cheered.* ❗ Lat. 'silentium, -i' (n)	Schweigen; Ruhe
		to echo [ˈekəʊ]	*The noise echoed across the playing field and around the school campus.*	nachhallen; nachklingen
		to beat [biːt]	*Nothing beats our botanical gardens in New York.*	schlagen; übertreffen
	1b	**dilemma** [dɪˈlemə]	*Jason's mum understands his dilemma and wants to find a solution.*	Dilemma
	2b	**reaction** [riˈækʃn]	*What was her reaction? Was it good?* ❗ Fr. 'réaction' (f.)	Reaktion
		supportive [səˈpɔːtɪv]	*My mother has always been supportive and helped me.*	unterstützend
		nut [nʌt]	*There is a lot of protein in nuts.* ❗ Sp. 'nuez' (f.); Fr. 'noix' (f.)	Nuss
	3a	**to express** [ɪkˈspres]	*Every child has the right to express their opinions and adults must listen.*	äußern; etw. ausdrücken
15		**conflict** [ˈkɒnflɪkt]	*Talk about conflicts and how you solved them.*	Konflikt
	1a	**fund** [fʌnd]	*The school sports fund will pay for the plane tickets.*	Geldmittel; Fond
		to sigh [saɪ]	*Jason sighed, then took out the garbage as his mother had asked.*	seufzen
	3b	**deli** [ˈdeli]	*You can buy sandwiches and ready-made foods at a deli.*	Feinkostladen
	5	**godmother** [ˈgɒdmʌðər]	*My mother's best friend is my godmother.*	Patentante
		fanatic [fəˈnætɪk]	*I like the game, but I'm not a fanatic.* ❗ Lat. 'fanaticus, -a, -un'	Fanatiker(in); fanatisch
		netball [ˈnetbɔːl]	*Two of the biggest sports in Australia are netball and cricket.*	Netzball
	6	**sporting** [ˈspɔːtɪŋ]	*They have sporting events at my school every season.*	sportlich; Sport…
16	1b	**to slide on** [slaɪd ɒn], **slid, slid** [slɪd, slɪd]	*Slide on some sunnies to protect your eyes from the sun.*	*hier:* aufsetzen
	1a	**selfie** [ˈselfi]	*Did you know that the word 'selfie' originated in Australia?*	Selfie
		informal [ɪnˈfɔːml]	*Australian English has many informal words and phrases.*	informell
	1b	**to slip on** [slɪp ɒn]	*When you sit in the sun, slip on a shirt to protect your skin.*	rasch anziehen
		to slop on [slɒp ɒn]	*Slop on some sunscreen or you'll get sunburn.*	auftragen

page	exercise			
		Workshop 1		
		to **slap on** [slæp ɒn]	*When you go to the beach, be sure to slap on a hat.*	aufsetzen
		to **seek** [si:k]	*If the heat becomes too much for you, seek shade immediately.* = *look for*	suchen
		shade [ʃeɪd]	*In the afternoons we sit in the shade of the tree in the garden.*	Schatten
	2	**standard** [ˈstændəd]	*She speaks standard English, not a dialect.*	standardmäßig
		context [ˈkɒntekst]	*Find the right meaning for the word in this context.*	Kontext; Zusammenhang
		ace [eɪs]	*I would love to go. That would be ace!*	klasse
		heap [hi:p]	*We've got heaps to eat.*	Haufen
17		**fleet** [fli:t]	*The French had a big fleet of ships.*	Flotte
		convict [kənˈvɪkt]	*Convicts and their families were brought from Britain to settle Australia.*	Verurteilte
		prison [ˈprɪzn]	*During his time there, he was captured and sent to prison.* ❗ *Fr. 'prison' (f.)*	Gefängnis
		to **prove** [pru:v]	*They wanted to prove that you don't need to consume manufactured goods to have everything you need.*	beweisen
		uncommon [ʌnˈkɒmən]	*Fighting between the Aborigines and the settlers wasn't uncommon.*	ungewöhnlich; selten
		threat [θret]	*What is the biggest threat to the islands in the Pacific Ocean?* = *danger*	Gefahr
		to **double** [ˈdʌbl]	*In just ten years the population of Australia doubled.* ❗ *Fr. 'doubler'*	sich verdoppeln
		element [ˈelɪmənt]	*How many elements are there in the flag?* = *part*	Element
		unity [ˈju:nəti]	*Several states formed a unity.* ❗ *Lat. 'unitas, -atis' (f.)*	Einheit
	4b	**factual** [ˈfæktʃuəl]	*Find ten factual mistakes in the text and correct them.*	sachlich
19				

Aussie slang

ace [eɪs]	klasse		**nana** [ˈnænə]	Banane
arvo [ˈɑːvəʊ]	Nachmittag		**pom** [pɒm]	Brite / Britin
bogey [ˈbəʊgi]	Schwimmen		**prezzie** [ˈprezi]	Geschenk
brekkie [ˈbreki]	Frühstück		**roo** [ru:]	Känguru
chockers [ˈtʃɒkərz]	voll		**sunnies** [ˈsʌniz]	Sonnenbrille
footy [ˈfʊti]	Fußball		**sickie** [ˈsɪki]	Krankheitstag
g'day [gəˈdeɪ]	guten Tag		**tog** [tɒg]	Sachen; Zeug
lappy [ˈlæpi]	Laptop		**tucker** [ˈtʌkə]	Essen
mozzie [ˈmɒzi]	Mücke			

page	exercise	Workshop 1		
	3a	**cosmopolitan** [ˌkɒzməˈpɒlɪtən]	*London is a really cosmopolitan city.*	weltoffen; kosmopolitisch
		vibrant [ˈvaɪbrənt]	*It's a really vibrant city where lots of young people live.* ❗ *Fr. 'vibrant, vibrante'*	dynamisch; lebhaft
		drive [draɪv]	*It's an hour's drive from the city to the beach.*	Fahrt
		doorstep [ˈdɔːstep]	*If something is on your doorstep, it's very near.*	Türschwelle
		neighbourhood [ˈneɪbəhʊd]	*I love this neighbourhood because there are so many trees here.* ❗ *AE = neighborhood*	Nachbarschaft
		undecided [ˌʌndɪˈsaɪdɪd]	*I'm pretty much undecided about whether I want to move or not.*	unentschieden; unentschlossen
20	2	**electrician** [ɪˌlekˈtrɪʃn]	*I am an electrician and work in a factory.*	Elektriker(in)
21	4a	**deal** [diːl]	*Moving to a new country is a big deal.*	Geschäft; *hier:* Angelegenheit
		to settle in [ˈsetl]	*They moved to a new city but settled in really quickly.*	sich eingewöhnen
		tricky [ˈtrɪki]	*Finding a place to live when you can't pay much rent can be tricky.*	kompliziert
		scorching [ˈskɔːtʃɪŋ]	*Most people think of Australia as scorching hot.*	glühend
		to exaggerate [ɪgˈzædʒəreɪt]	*The number of deadly animals in Australia is often exaggerated.*	übertreiben
		species [ˈspiːʃiːz]	*There are only two species of deadly spiders in Australia and nobody has died from a bite since 1979.* ❗ *Lat. 'species, -ei' = view, look*	Spezies; Art
		stingray [ˈstɪŋreɪ]	*Stingrays are often seen in the Great Barrier Reef.*	Stachelrochen
		average [ˈævərɪdʒ]	*What's an average day like for you?*	durchschnittlich
		although [ɔːlˈðəʊ]	*Although English is the official language, it can often be difficult to understand Aussies when they speak.*	obwohl
		accent [ˈæksənt]	*It's not their accent that causes problems, but the slang they use.* ❗ *Fr. 'accent' (m.)*	Akzent
		cactus [ˈkæktəs], **cacti** [ˈkæktaɪ]	*There is a vast range of cacti in the desert.*	Kaktus
		paradise [ˈpærədaɪs]	*Australia is a paradise for any sports lover.* ❗ *Fr. 'paradis' (m.); Sp. 'paraiso' (m.)*	Paradies
	4c	**to outline** [ˈaʊtlaɪn]	*Outline the advice given to parents.*	umreißen; zusammenfassen
		to claim [kleɪm]	*He claimed that his dog ate his homework!* *= to allege*	behaupten
		exaggeration [ɪgˌzædʒəˈreɪʃn]	*I thought it was an exaggeration but now I see it must be true.* ❗ *Sp. 'exageración' (f.)*	Übertreibung

page	exercise	**Workshop 1**		
22	1a	**removal** [rɪˈmuːvl]	*The Parliament of Australia made a formal apology to Indigenous Australians for the forced removal of their children.*	Wegnahme; Entfernung
		agency [ˈeɪdʒənsi]	*Government agencies forced the removal of Indigenous children. = organization*	Agentur; Organisation
		penal [ˈpiːnl]	*Australia was set up as a penal colony.*	strafrechtlich
23	3	**didgeridoo** [ˌdɪdʒəriˈduː]	*A didgeridoo is a large bamboo or wooden trumpet of the Australian aborigines.*	Didgeridoo
24	S2	**hunter-gatherer** [ˌhʌntə ˈgæðərər]	*Australia's first peoples were hunter-gatherers who moved from place to place following the seasons.*	Jäger und Sammler
		systematically [ˌsɪstəˈmætɪkli]	*Semi-nomadic people systematically move from place to place following the changes of the seasons.*	systematisch
		distinct [dɪˈstɪŋkt]	*Each native group has its own distinct history and culture.* ⚠ *Lat. 'distinctus, -a, -um'*	eindeutig; eigenständig
		agrarian [əˈgreəriən]	*The hunter-gatherers didn't develop an agrarian, or farming, society.*	agrarisch
		predictable [prɪˈdɪktəbl]	*The future is not predictable.*	vorhersehbar
		colonization [ˌkɒlənaɪˈzeɪʃn]	*How did colonization impact these communities?*	Kolonialisierung
		immediate [ɪˈmiːdiət]	*The most immediate problem was providing housing and fresh water.*	unmittelbar; umgehend
		consequence [ˈkɒnsɪkwəns]	*One consequence of climate change is increased sea levels.* ⚠ *lat. 'consecutio, -onis' (f.)*	Folge; Konsequenz
	S2	**influenza** [ˌɪnfluˈenzə]	*There was an influenza epidemic in 1918.*	Grippe; Influenza
		measles [ˈmiːzlz]	*Measles infections have been increasing in the world.*	Masern
		resistance [rɪˈzɪstəns]	*Diseases killed many indigenous people because they had no resistance to them.* ⚠ *Fr. 'résistance' (f.)*	Widerstand; *hier:* Resistenz
		random [ˈrændəm]	*They died in random killings that were motivated by racism.*	zufällig, willkürlich
		mass shooting [mæs ʃuːtɪŋ]	*Massacres often took the form of mass shootings or driving groups of people off cliffs.*	Massenerschießung
		cliff [klɪf]	*Cliffs are high areas of rock with a steep side.*	Klippe; Felsen
		drastic [ˈdræstɪk]	*It's dangerous to go to drastic extremes to get super-model thin.* ⚠ *Sp. 'drástico, drástica'*	drastisch

page	exercise	**Workshop 1**		
		to **estimate** [ˈestɪmeɪt]	*Can you estimate what is going to happen?*	schätzen
	S3	**monolingual** [ˌmɒnəˈlɪŋgwəl]	*A monolingual dictionary gives definitions but no translations.*	einsprachig
		benefit [ˈbenɪfɪt]	*Speculate about the benefits of the programme she has introduced.* ≠ challenge	Vorteil
		smallpox [ˈsmɔːlpɒks]	*The biggest threat to the Aborigine were diseases like smallpox, which killed tens of thousands.*	Pocken
		cartoon [kɑːˈtuːn]	*When I was a child there were cartoons in newspapers.*	Cartoon
25	S1a	to **threaten** [ˈθretn]	*Climate change is threatening the lives of future generations.*	gefährden
		non-native [ˌnɒn ˈneɪtɪv]	*Native plants in the Outback are being threatened by non-native species.*	zugewandert
		howl [haʊl]	*The howls of wild dogs called dingoes can be heard in the Outback.*	Geheul
		dingo [ˈdɪŋgəʊ]	*The dingo is a kind of wild dog mainly living in Australia.*	Dingo
		to **loathe** [ləʊð]	*Dingoes came to Australia around 4,000 years ago, and today they are both loved and loathed.*	hassen; verabscheuen
		in spite of [ɪn spaɪt]	*We had a nice hike in spite of the rain!*	trotz
		to **roam** [rəʊm]	*You can see dingoes roam around wild in Australia.*	herumschweifen; durchschweifen
		pest [pest]	*This plant is now a pest that is causing enormous ecological damage in Australia.*	Plage; Schädling
		ecological [ˌiːkəˈlɒdʒɪkl]	*Non-native species are causing enormous ecological damage to Australia.* **!** *Lat. 'oecologicus, -a, -um'; Fr. 'écologique'*	ökologisch
		damage [ˈdæmɪdʒ]	*Was there a lot of damage?* **!** *Fr. 'dommage' (f.)*	Beschädigung
		feral [ˈferəl]	*You'll come across the world's largest herd of feral camels.*	wild
		camel [ˈkæml]	*In desert counties camels are used to ride on.*	Kamel
		to **release** [rɪˈliːs]	*The smartphone was released in 1994.*	veröffentlichen; auf den Markt bringen
		advent [ˈædvent]	*With the advent of engines, animals were no longer needed to do work.*	Beginn; Einführung
		to **power** [ˈpaʊə]	*Powered engines replaced animals in farming.*	antreiben
		invasive [ɪnˈveɪsɪv]	*Other invasive species include foxes and rabbits, brought from Europe in the 19th century for sport hunting.*	invasiv

page	exercise	Workshop 1		
		predator [ˈpredətər]	When there aren't any predators, a species can grow uncontrollably.	Räuber; Raubtier
		to **explode** [ɪkˈspləʊd]	They had few predators, so their populations exploded. ⚠ Fr. 'exploser'; Sp. 'explotar'	explodieren
	S2	to **achieve** [əˈtʃiːv]	You can achieve and maintain a healthy weight by exercising and eating healthily. ≠ fail	erreichen; schaffen
	S4	**prolonged** [prəˈlɒŋd]	A prolonged drought is creating multiple ecological problems.	anhaltend; verlängert
		drought [draʊt]	Drought creates the perfect conditions for bushfire.	Dürre
		to **demolish** [dɪˈmɒlɪʃ]	Before building the highway they had to demolish several houses.	abreißen; demolieren
		critical [ˈkrɪtɪkl]	In the desert, water supply is critical.	kritisch; *hier:* wichtig
		watering hole [ˈwɔːtərɪŋ həʊl]	Watering holes are important to the people who live in the Outback.	Wasserstelle
		to **pollute** [pəˈluːt]	Industry is polluting water all around the world.	verschmutzen; verseuchen
		to **defend** [dɪˈfend]	Be ready to defend yourself walking home alone at night. ⚠ Lat. 'defendere (defendo, defendi, defensum)'	verteidigen
		property [ˈprɒpəti]	The fire caused major destruction and destroyed properties.	Eigentum; Immobilie
		to **cull** [kʌl]	When there is a disease, animals are often culled to stop the spreading.	keulen
		to **rot** [ˈrəʊtə]	After they are culled, thousands of dead animals are left to rot.	verfaulen
		cull [kʌl]	The culls of animals are controversial.	Schlachten; Keulen
26	1a	**location** [ləʊˈkeɪʃn]	Many films have been shot in this location. ⚠ Lat. 'locus, -i' (m.) = place	Standort
		creation [kriˈeɪʃn]	Do you know the Aboriginal people creation legend? ⚠ Lat. 'procreatio, -onis, (f.)	Schöpfung
		dreamtime [ˈdriːmtaɪm]	Aboriginal myths, known as dreamtime stories, are told by the indigenous people of Australia.	Traumzeit
		elder [ˈeldə]	Creation or dreamtime legends have been passed down by the Elders for generations.	Älteste(r)
		folklore [ˈfəʊklɔːr]	The sacred sites are extremely important in Aboriginal tradition and folklore.	Folklore

page	exercise	**Workshop 1**		
		formation [fɔːˈmeɪʃn]	*Uluru is a large rock formation located close to the exact centre of Australia.* ❗ *Fr. 'formation' (f.);* *Sp. 'formación' (f.)*	Formation
		to resume [rɪˈzjuːm]	*The sacred rock resumed its original name in 1985 when the land was given back to the local people.*	übernehmen
		deed [diːd]	*They had long wanted the title deeds to the land to be returned.*	Urkunde
		according to [əˈkɔːdɪŋ tə]	*According to my grandmother, my family came from Ireland.*	laut
		bitterly [ˈbɪtəli]	*She cried bitterly when she hurt herself.*	bitterlich
		saddened [ˈsædnd]	*I was deeply saddened when I heard he was dead.*	betrübt
		bloodshed [ˈblʌdʃed]	*When a lot of people are killed, we call it bloodshed.*	Blutvergießen
		reef [riːf]	*The reef is home to many species and a tourist attraction.*	Riff
		variety [vəˈraɪəti]	*There is a variety of animals.*	Vielfalt; Auswahl
		creature [ˈkriːtʃər]	*Divers can see marine creatures, including fish, seabirds, whales, dolphins and sharks.* ❗ *Lat. 'creare (creo, creavi, creatum)' = to create*	Geschöpf; Lebewesen
		seabird [ˈsiːbɜːd]	*Many seabirds live near the reef.*	Seevogel
		limit [ˈlɪmɪt]	*Students are encouraged to push themselves to their limits.*	Grenze
		clan [klæn]	*Their clan has many legends about their people.*	Stamm
		creator [kriˈeɪtər]	*In many religions God is the creator of the world.*	Schöpfer(in); Erschaffer(in)
	2a	**disadvantage** [ˌdɪsədˈvɑːntɪdʒ]	*What do you think are the advantages and disadvantages of each system?* ≠ advantage	Nachteil
27	3a	**vague** [veɪɡ]	*Avoid using vague subjects like 'someone,' 'people' and 'they' in your description.*	unbestimmt; vage
		focus [ˈfəʊkəs]	*The focus of the sentence is on the action, not the agent.*	Fokus; Brennpunkt
		agent [ˈeɪdʒənt]	*The focus of the sentence is on the action, not the agent.* ❗ *Fr. 'agent' (m.)*	Handlungsträger(in); Handelnde(r)
		position [pəˈzɪʃn]	*Which position is he playing on?* = physical place	Position
	3b	**destination** [ˌdestɪˈneɪʃn]	*National parks are popular tourist destinations.*	Reiseziel

page	exercise	**Workshop 1**		
		busload [ˈbʌsləʊd]	*Big tour companies bring busloads of tourists every day.*	Busladung
		unacceptable [ˌʌnəkˈseptəbl]	*It was totally unacceptable to allow tourists to climb in the sacred site.*	inakzeptabel
		alternative [ɔːlˈtɜːnətɪv]	*Alternative activities, such as walking tours, were developed for visitors after climbing Uluru was banned.*	alternativ
		base [beɪs]	*We will meet at the base of the mountain after the hike.* **!** *Fr. 'base' (f.); Sp. 'base' (f.)*	Fuß; Basis
		experienced [ɪkˈspɪəriənst]	*He was an experienced engineer.* *= knowledgeable* **!** *Lat. 'experentia, -ae' (f.) = experience*	erfahren
		income [ˈɪnkʌm]	*Tourism is an important source of income for many countries.*	Einkommen
		profit [ˈprɒfɪt]	*Some organizations don't want to make a profit, they are non-profit.*	Profit; Gewinn
	4	**trailer** [ˈtreɪlər]	*I saw a trailer for a film that is set in the Australian outback.*	Trailer
	4b	**suddenly** [ˈsʌdənli]	*It felt like a huge weight was suddenly off my shoulders.*	plötzlich; auf einmal
		sibling [ˈsɪblɪŋ]	*The film tells the story of two siblings, a sister and brother.*	Geschwister
		harsh [hɑːʃ]	*The winter was harsh and many people died.* *= rough*	rau
		demanding [dɪˈmɑːndɪŋ]	*In some parts of Australia, nature is harsh and demanding.*	anspruchsvoll
		civilized [ˈsɪvəlaɪz]	*This place is no place for civilized people.* **!** *Lat.'civiv, -is' (m./f.) = citizen*	zivilisiert; kultiviert
28	1	**global warming** [ˌgləʊbl ˈwɔːmɪŋ]	*Speculate how these disasters are connected to climate change and global warming.*	Erderwärmung
	2a	**appropriate** [əˈprəʊpriət]	*What is the appropriate use of the money?* *= right* *≠ inappropriate*	angemessen
		reality [riˈæləti]	*The reality of climate change can really be felt in Australia.* **!** *Fr. 'realité' (f.); Sp. 'realidad' (f.)*	Realität
		stunning [ˈstʌnɪŋ]	*The views from the top of the mountain are stunning*	toll; atemberaubend
		wombat [ˈwɒmbæt]	*A wombat looks like a little bear.*	Wombat
		risk [rɪsk]	*Smoking raises your risk of getting ill.* **!** *Fr. 'risque' (m.)*	Risiko; Gefahr

page	exercise	Workshop 1		
		crisis [ˈkraɪsɪs]	*Scientists are warning that Australia is especially at risk from the climate crisis.*	Krise
		heatwave [ˈhiːtweɪv]	*Climate change is causing more and longer heatwaves.*	Hitzewelle
		severe [sɪˈvɪə]	*Climate change causes severe problems all over the world.* *= strong*	schwer; stark
		bushfire [ˈbʊʃfaɪər]	*Drought creates the perfect conditions for bushfire.*	Buschfeuer
		ideal [aɪˈdiːəl]	*Plants dry up and die, providing the ideal fuel for fires.*	ideal
		frequent [ˈfriːkwənt]	*It's good for children to take frequent breaks during the school day.* ❗ *Lat. 'frequens, -entis'*	häufig
		extreme [ɪkˈstriːm]	*All over the world, we are experiencing more extreme weather conditions.*	extrem
		livestock [ˈlaɪvstɒk]	*The climate crisis is making it more and more difficult for farmers to grow food and raise livestock.*	Viehbestand
		populated [ˈpɒpjuleɪt]	*Queensland is one of Australia's most populated states.*	bevölkert; besiedelt
		security [sɪˈkjʊərəti]	*Climate change is going to make food security a major issue in the future.* ❗ *Fr. 'securité' (f.)*	Sicherheit
		acidic [əˈsɪdɪk]	*Our oceans are becoming warmer and more acidic.*	sauer
		polyp [ˈpɒlɪp]	*Polyps are tiny animals.*	Polyp
		due to [djuː tə]	*Corals are dying due to the rise in sea temperature.*	wegen
		urgently [ˈɜːdʒəntli]	*We need to change things urgently.*	dringend
	3a	**schoolmate** [ˈskuːlmeɪt]	*Jason's schoolmate Ricky is very worried about climate change.* *= classmate*	Schulkamerad(in)
		concerned [kənˈsɜːnd]	*My parents were concerned that I have too much stress in school.*	besorgt
		demonstration [ˌdemənˈstreɪʃn]	*They are very concerned about climate change, so they're taking part in a demonstration.* ❗ *Sp. 'demonstración' (f.)*	Demonstration
		mob [mɒb]	*We call ourselves a mob movement because we organize lots of activities together to raise awareness.*	Mob, Leute
		federal [ˈfedərəl]		Bundes...
	3b	**faraway** [ˈfɑːrəweɪ]	*This isn't a faraway problem.* *≠ close*	fern
		listener [ˈlɪsnə]	*It's important to be a good listener.* *≠ talker*	Hörer(in)

page	exercise	**Workshop 1**		
		to **burn** [bɜːn]	*We light the wood, then the wood will burn.*	brennen
		exporter [ekˈspɔːtər]	*Australia is the world's biggest exporter of coal and gas.* ≠ *importer*	Exporteur(in)
		hurricane [ˈhʌrɪkən]	*Hurricanes and severe storms have become much more common.*	Hurrikan; Orkan
		to **frack** [fræk]	*When you frack, you open cracks in the ground to get out oil or gas.*	fracken
		homeland [ˈhəʊmlænd]	*Aboriginal people are being moved off their homelands.*	Heimat
		wheat [wiːt]	*Wheat is a plant we use for making flour for bread.*	Weizen
		renewable [rɪˈnjuːəbl]	*We want to encourage renewable energy sources, like the sun.* ⚠ *Lat. 'renovare (renovo, renovavi, renovatum)' = to renew*	erneuerbar
		bushland [ˈbʊʃlænd]	*People need to stop destroying forest and bushland.*	Buschland
		tipping point [ˈtɪpɪŋ pɔɪnt]	*We've only got a few years before we reach the final tipping point in climate change.*	Kipppunkt; Trendwende
29	1	to **structure** [ˈstrʌktʃə]	*How buildings are structured determines whether they can survive an earthquake.* ⚠ *Fr. 'structurer'*	strukturieren; aufbauen
		conversational [ˌkɒnvəˈseɪʃənl]	*I think about conversational topics before going on job interviews.*	Gesprächs…
		instructive [ɪnˈstrʌktɪv]	*The style of the video is instructive.*	instruktiv; lehrreich
	2a	to **contribute** [kənˈtrɪbjuːt]	*Eleni contributes to a website where teens write about their cities.* = *to give something*	mitarbeiten; beitragen
		to **post** [pəʊst]	*We are posting it on all the social media pages.* ⚠ *Fr. 'poste' (f.)*	posten
		magnificent [mægˈnɪfɪsnt]	*I live in a magnificent city, but I can get bored of it.* ⚠ *Lat. 'magnificus, -a, -um'; Fr. 'magnifique'*	großartig; herrlich
		virtual [ˈvɜːtʃuəl]	*Let me take you on a virtual tour and show you the places I love.*	virtuell
		truly [ˈtruːli]	*We are truly proud of you.*	wirklich
		laneway [ˈleɪnweɪ]	*There are many small 'laneways' in the city centre.*	Sträßchen
		busker [ˈbʌskər]	*Do you like cool cafés, amazing street art and buskers playing great music?*	Straßenmusiker(in)
		lane [leɪn]	*We are building more cycle lanes.*	Fahrbahn; Gasse

page	exercise	Workshop 1		
		market [ˈmɑːkɪt]	We buy our vegetables at the market. ❗ Fr. 'marché' (m.); Sp. 'mercado' (m.)	Markt; Börse
		to ride [raɪd]**, rode, ridden** [rəʊd, ˈrɪdn]	Getting around in the city centre is easy - you can ride the trams for free.	fahren
		sandy [ˈsændi]	I don't like laying around on a sandy beach in the sun.	sandig
		promenade [ˌprɒməˈnɑːd]	There are beautiful houses on the promenade close to the sea. ❗ Fr. 'promenade' (f.)	Promenade
		to gaze [geɪz]	You can relax on the beach and gaze at the ocean.	blicken; starren
		skyline [ˈskaɪlaɪn]	New buildings have changed the London skyline.	Skyline
		skydiver [ˈskaɪdaɪvər]	If you are lucky, you might see skydivers landing on the shore.	Fallschirmspringer(in)
		unforgettable [ˌʌnfəˈgetəbl]	I still remember the unforgettable story she told me.	unvergesslich
		pier [pɪər]	A lot of seaside towns have piers into the sea.	Kai
		sanctuary [ˈsæŋktʃuəri]	The bird sanctuary is home to thousands of migrating birds.	Schutzgebiet
	2c	**technique** [tekˈniːk]	Find examples in the article of the techniques that work well.	Technik
	T	**anecdote** [ˈænɪkdəʊt]	Anecdotes are short, personal stories that can have an emotional effect. = short story	Anekdote
		comparison [kəmˈpærɪsn]	Comparisons show that children have better grades when they are happy. ❗ Lat. 'comparatio, -onis' (f.)	Vergleich
30	1a	**humour** [ˈhjuːmə]	She's so funny, I like her sense of humour. ❗ Sp. 'humor' (m.)	Humor
		guy [gaɪ]	He's a good guy.	Kerl; Typ
		weed [wiːd]	Take out the weeds so the vegetables can grow better.	Unkraut
		organic [ɔːˈgænɪk]	You can show how much you know about animals and organic veggies.	biologisch
		veggie [ˈvedʒi]	I don't eat meat, I prefer veggies.	Gemüse
		drop kick [ˈdrɒp kɪk]	We worked on our drop kicks at rugby practice.	Dropkick
	1b	**homesickness** [ˈhəʊmsɪknəs]	I have homesickness whenever I'm away from home too long.	Heimweh
	cc	**relation** [rɪˈleɪʃn]	Talk about the impact that rugby has had on race relations.	Beziehung; Verhältnis
		personality [ˌpɜːsəˈnæləti]	They have different personalities and serious political differences. ❗ Fr. 'personalité' (f.); Sp. 'personalidad' (f.)	Persönlichkeit; Prominente

page	exercise	**Workshop 1**		
		rivalry [ˈraɪvlri]	*There is rivalry in sports such as cricket, rugby and netball.*	Konkurrenz, Rivalität
31	3a	**chairlift** [ˈtʃeəlɪft]	*You can take a chairlift up to the top of the mountain.*	Sessellift
		zipline [ˈzɪplaɪn]	*Riding the zipline down the mountain is great fun.*	Seilrutsche
		river rafting [ˈrɪvər ˈrɑːftɪŋ]	*River rafting can be dangerous.*	River-Rafting
		trilogy [ˈtrɪlədʒi]	*A trilogy consists of three parts.*	Trilogie
	4a	**to invert** [ɪnˈvɜːt]	*Sometimes you can invert the subject and verb in a sentence to form a question.*	umkehren; umstellen
	4b	**ritual** [ˈrɪtʃuəl]	*Please show respect during the Maori rituals.* = practice	Ritual
32	1	**attractive** [əˈtræktɪv]	*Which places in New Zealand are most interesting or attractive to you?* ❗ *Fr. 'attractif'*	reizvoll
		to rank [ræŋk]	*If you rank a list, you put it in an order.*	einordnen; in eine Reihenfolge bringen
	2a	**to skim** [skɪm]	*Skim the article and answer the questions below.*	überfliegen
		function [ˈfʌŋkʃn]	*Every browser has a function to save a website to a 'Favourites' tab.* ❗ *Fr. 'fonction' (f.)*	Funktion
		distinctive [dɪˈstɪŋktɪv]	*What makes New Zealand's North Island and South Island distinctive?* = special	unverwechselbar; ausgeprägt
		weekly [ˈwiːkli]	*We have a weekly meeting on Thursdays.*	wöchentlich
		segment [ˈsegmənt]	*The six weekly segments each focus on a different game.*	Segment; Abschnitt
		significance [sɪgˈnɪfɪkəns]	*The town's natural wonders are of great significance.* ❗ *Lat. 'significare (significo, significavi, significatum)' = to mean*	Bedeutung; Wichtigkeit
		regional [ˈriːdʒənl]	*The article highlights the city's regional importance and the challenges it has faced.*	regional
		peninsula [pəˈnɪnsjələ]	*Many rare and endangered water birds live on the peninsula.*	Halbinsel
		magnet [ˈmægnət]	*This town is a magnet for tourists.* ❗ *Sp. 'magneto' (m.)*	Magnet
		treasure [ˈtreʒə]	*His treasures are in a museum.* ❗ *Fr. 'trésor' (m.)*	Schatz
		biological [ˌbaɪəˈlɒdʒɪkl]	*The biological diversity of Australia is a national treasure.*	biologisch
		diversity [daɪˈvɜːsəti]	*Same-sex marriage, which was legalized in Canada and in the USA, has led to even more family diversity.*	Vielfältigkeit

page	exercise	Workshop 1		
	2c	**to collect** [kə'lekt]	We collect and recycle old plastic bags. ❚ Lat. 'colligere (colligo, collegi, collectum)'	sammeln; einsammeln
	3a	**filmmaker** ['fɪlm meɪkə]	Documentary filmmaker Shaun Reed is here in the studio to talk about his new film.	Filmemacher(in)
		phenomenon [fə'nɒmɪnən]	The new documentary film 'Beyond the Black', looks at the rugby phenomenon in our country.	Phänomen
		intense [ɪn'tens]	The film shows the intense rivalry between two schools. = strong	stark; ernsthaft
		talented ['tæləntɪd]	There are so many strong and talented players.	begabt; talentiert
		pride [praɪd]	The All Blacks are a source of pride for the whole nation – for Maori and non-Maori.	Stolz
33	4a	**essential** [ɪ'senʃl]	essential skills	wichtig; wesentlich
		ethnic ['eθnɪk]	The Maori are New Zealand's largest ethnic majority. ❚ Fr. 'ethnique'	ethnisch
		descent [dɪ'sent]	Two children of immigrant descent will share their stories.	Abstammung
		acceptance [ək'septəns]	The acceptance of Maori culture is felt everywhere in New Zealand. ❚ Fr. 'acceptation' (f.); Sp. 'aceptación' (f.)	Akzeptanz
		variation [ˌveəri'eɪʃn]	There are different variations of this traditional dance.	Variante; Variation
		multicultural [ˌmʌlti'kʌltʃərəl]	a multicultural society	multikulturell
34	1	**to relate to** [rɪ'leɪt tə]	Which paragraph does each picture relate to?	sich beziehen auf
		devastating ['devəsteɪtɪŋ]	This area has experienced devastating floods. = enormous	verheerend
		mudslide ['mʌdslaɪd]	The mountain sides were wet and the rain caused mudslides.	Schlammlawine
		to contaminate [kən'tæmɪneɪt]	The rain caused mudslides and they contaminated the water. ❚ Lat. 'contaminare (contamino, contaminavi, contaminatum)'; Fr. 'contaminer'	verschmutzen
		reservoir ['rezəvwɑːr]	The water reservoirs keep pur drinking water.	Reservoir; Behälter
		shortage ['ʃɔːtɪdʒ]	You can expect to have water shortages during a drought.	Mangel

page	exercise	Workshop 1		
		elderly [ˈeldəli]	The charity looks after elderly people.	älter
		to suffer [ˈsʌfə]	They suffer from breathing problems because of smoke from wildfires.	leiden
		anxiety [æŋˈzaɪəti]	Anxiety about climate change is growing in many countries. ❗ Fr. 'anxiété' (f.)	Sorge; Ängstlichkeit
		malaria [məˈleəriə]	Malaria is caused by mosquito bites.	Malaria
		frequency [ˈfriːkwənsi]	An adverb of frequency describes how often something is done. ≠ infrequency	Häufigkeit
		cyclone [ˈsaɪkləʊn]	A cyclone is a very bad tropical storm.	Zyklon
		leisure [ˈleʒə]	There is a time for work and a time for leisure. ≠ work	Freizeit
		habitat [ˈhæbɪtæt]	The habitats of wild animals are in danger.	Habitat
		avocado [ˌævəˈkɑːdəʊ]	Avodacos are healthy food.	Avocado
35	2	**perspective** [pəˈspektɪv]	Listen to this teen's perspective on mental health. ❗ Lat. 'spectare (specto, spectavi, spectatum)'	Aussicht; Perspektive
	3	**destruction** [dɪˈstrʌkʃn]	The floods caused major destruction. = damage	Zerstörung
		poisonous [ˈpɔɪzənəs]	Wearing boots in the jungle provides protection against bites from poisonous snakes.	giftig
36		**informative** [ɪnˈfɔːmətɪv]	This article is very informative, I've learned a lot.	informativ
	S1	**coastline** [ˈkəʊstlaɪn]	We walked for hours along the coastline and watched sea birds.	Küstenlinie; Küste
	T	**to bookmark** [ˈbʊkmɑːk]	Bookmark important websites on your browser.	markieren
	S2a	**purpose** [ˈpɜːpəs]	What is the purpose of the underlined clauses in these sentences?	Zweck
	S2b	**logical** [ˈlɒdʒɪkl]	Organize the notes into a logical sequence of paragraphs. ❗ Sp. 'lógico, lógica'	logisch; folgerichtig
	S3	**to evaluate** [ɪˈvæljueɪt]	Make sure you evaluate your sources.	bewerten
	T	**complex** [ˈkɒmpleks]	Complex topics need more detailed explanations.	komplex; schwierig
		to engage [ɪnˈgeɪdʒ]	Include interesting facts in your writing to engage the reader.	einnehmen
	S2	**to provide** [prəˈvaɪd]	You have to provide enough information. ❗ Lat. 'providere (provido, providi, provisum)'	zur Verfügung stellen; versorgen (mit)
37	S1	**requirement** [rɪˈkwaɪəmənt]	Think about the requirements of the school exchange programme.	Voraussetzung; Bedingung

page	exercise	Workshop 1		
		to apply [əˈplaɪ]	When you apply for jobs, employers can see everything. ❗ Fr. 's'appliquer'	sich bewerben
		concern [kənˈsɜːn]	My main concern for the future is climate change.	Sorge; Bedenken
	T	**persuasive** [pəˈsweɪsɪv]	Provide details to make your article more interesting and persuasive.	überzeugend
	S3	**spelling** [ˈspelɪŋ]	What is the correct spelling of 'famous'? F, A, M…	Rechtschreibung; Schreibweise
		pattern [ˈpætn]	These buttons used to be sewn in patterns that had a meaning.	Muster
38	2a	**horizon** [həˈraɪzn]	There on the horizon is a beautiful multi-coloured rainbow. ❗ Fr. 'horizon' (m.)	Horizont
		waterhole [ˈwɔːtəhəʊl]	Lakes are big waterholes.	Wasserstelle
	2b	**to shape** [ʃeɪp]	At last, when he had finished shaping the earth, the Rainbow Serpent crawled into a waterhole.	formen; gestalten
		to crawl [krɔːl]	= to move slowly ≠ to race	krabbeln; kriechen
		rainstorm [ˈreɪnstɔːm]	There was a rainstorm when we walked home and we got really wet.	Regenschauer; Gewitter
		to disturb [dɪˈstɜːb]	We had to be quiet, so we didn't disturb the adults.	stören
39	3	**extinction** [ɪkˈstɪŋkʃn]	Climate change is leading to mass extinction.	Aussterben
		to wipe out [waɪp aʊt]	In the last ten years around 50% of the animals have been wiped out. = to kill	auslöschen
		deforestation [ˌdiːˌfɒrɪˈsteɪʃn]	Deforestation is leading to climate change.	Abholzung
		oxygen [ˈɒksɪdʒən]	Trees capture carbon dioxide and release oxygen. ❗ Fr. 'oxygène' (m.); Sp. oxigeno' (m.)	Sauerstoff
		to capture [ˈkæptʃə]	The criminal was captured by the police. = to catch ≠ to release ❗ Lat. 'capere (capio, cepi, captum)'	einfangen; festnehmen
		loss [lɒs]	Job loss during the pandemic was a major problem.	Verlust
	4	**gateway** [ˈɡeɪtweɪ]	There are five gateway cities to Arctic exploration.	Zugang; Gateway
42	2	**to declare** [dɪˈkleə]	Do you know that this year was declared the year of the vegan?	ausrufen; verkünden
		existence [ɪɡˈzɪstəns]	The existence of social media brings politicians closer to the public.	Existenz
		march [mɑːtʃ]	A march will be helt next Saturday.	Marsch; Demonstration

page	exercise	Workshop 1		
43	3	**equality** [iˈkwɒləti]	He spent the rest of his life trying to get equality for Aboriginal people in Australia. 🔲 Fr. 'égalité' (f.)	Gleichberechtigung
		act [ækt]	The Act said the land did belong to the Aborigine.	Gesetz; Handlung
	4	**downtown** [ˌdaʊnˈtaʊn]	We stayed in a small hotel downtown, which was great for sightseeing.	Innenstadt
		yacht [jɒt]	The harbour is full of luxurious yachts.	Jacht; Yacht

page	exercise	Workshop 2		
48		**boundary** [ˈbaʊndri]	More than 9 million people live in Greater London. = border	Grenze
		recognizable [ˈrekəgnaɪzəbl]	The Houses of Parliament are a famous landmark in central London. 🔲 Sp. 'reconocible'	erkennbar
		to notice [ˈnəʊtɪs]	Have you noticed how Lara looks at Greg?	bemerken
		wharf [wɔːf]	Visitors flying into London City Airport will immediately notice the skyscrapers at Canary Wharf.	Werft; Anlegeplatz
		multinational [ˌmʌltiˈnæʃnəl]	What used to be a run down area is now home to some of the biggest multinational companies in London.	multinational
		architect [ˈɑːkɪtekt]	A lot of interesting buildings have been designed by famous architects. 🔲 Lat. 'architectus, -ti' (m.)	Architekt(in)
		gherkin [ˈgɜːkɪn]	Gherkins are a type of cucumber.	Gurke
		shard [ʃɑːd]	The glass broke and shards of glass went everywhere.	Scherbe
		jerk chicken [dʒɜːk ˈtʃɪkɪn]	Jerk chicken is a Jamaican dish.	in Gewürzen mariniertes und gegrilltes Hühnchen
		plantain [ˈplæntɪn]	Fried plantain is delicious!	Kochbanane
49		**shopper** [ˈʃɒpə]	Camden Town Market is a magnet for shoppers.	Käufer(in)
		stall [stɔːl]	The market opened in 1974 with sixteen stalls, but today there are more than 1,000.	Stand
		basis [ˈbeɪsɪs]	Today, as many as two million people use the tube on a daily basis.	Grundlage; Basis
		carnival [ˈkɑːnɪvl]	The carnival is one of the biggest street parties in the world and attracts around one million people.	Karneval
50		**partnership** [ˈpɑːtnəʃɪp]	There is a partnership between the two schools.	Partnerschaft; Kooperation
	1	**coursework** [ˈkɔːswɜːk]	You will start your coursework in your GCSE subjects this year.	Facharbeit

page	exercise	Workshop 2		
		theoretical [ˌθɪəˈretɪkl]	*theoretical studies and practical workshops*	theoretisch
	2	**habit** [ˈhæbɪt]	*Using technology, you can analyse consumer habits easily.*	Angewohnheit; Verhalten
52	1a	**quote** [kwəʊt]	*The quotes show what people said.*	Zitat
		playwright [ˈpleɪraɪt]	*Samuel Johnson was an 18th century English writer, poet and playwright.*	Dramatiker(in)
		contemporary [kənˈtemprəri]	*My parents don't listen to any contemporary music.*	zeitgenössisch
		novelist [ˈnɒvəlɪst]	*Paul Theroux is a contemporary American travel writer and novelist.*	Schriftsteller(in)
	1b	**endless** [ˈendləs]	*It's a huge region with endless farmland.* ≠ limited	endlos; unendlich
		multicultural-ism [ˌmʌltiˈkʌltʃərəlɪzəm]	*Big cities are centres for multiculturalism.*	Multikulturalismus
		urban [ˈɜːbən]	*It's just one of several big urban areas between Boston and Washington.*	städtisch; urban
	2a	**to fascinate** [ˈfæsɪneɪt]	*This book fascinates me. It's so interesting.* ⓘ Sp. 'fascinar'	faszinieren
		rundown [ˈrʌndaʊn]	*This area used to be fairly rundown, but now of course that's all changed.*	heruntergekommen; verwahrlost
		circus [ˈsɜːkəs]	*When I was a child I loved to go to the circus.* ⓘ Fr. 'cirque' (m.)	Zirkus
		eyesore [ˈaɪsɔːr]	*Some buildings from the 70s are real eyesores.*	Schandfleck
		to convert [kənˈvɜːt]	*The factory has been converted into flats.*	umwandeln
		to dominate [ˈdɒmɪneɪt]	*Skyscrapers dominate the skyline.*	dominieren; beherrschen
		turbine [ˈtɜːbaɪn]	*Turbines are huge engines that use air or water to generate energy.*	Turbine
		to sew [səʊ]	*She sewed clothes from deerskins.*	nähen
		to dream [driːm]	*She dreams of becoming a lawyer one day.*	träumen
	3	**conscious** [ˈkɒnʃəs]	*Bex tries to be ethically conscious when shopping.* ⓘ Lat. 'conscius, -a, -um'	bewusst
		junk food [dʒʌŋk]	*Avoid junk foods and fast food – they are full of bad fat and salt.*	Junk Food
		vegan [ˈviːgən]	*She used to eat lots of junk food, but now she is a vegan.*	vegan; Veganer(in)
53	1	**foreground** [ˈfɔːgraʊnd]	*Describe what you see in the foreground of the photo.*	Vordergrund
	3	**animated** [ˈænɪmeɪtɪd]	*As the helicopter flies over Parliament Square, an animated statue of Winston Churchill waves at it.*	animiert

page	exercise	**Workshop 2**		
		to **parachute** [ˈpærəʃuːt]	*He parachuted out of an airplane.*	Fallschirm springen
		to **escort** [ˈeskɔːt]	*Bond escorted the Queen.*	begleiten
		to **greet** [griːt]	*You say 'hello' when you greet someone.*	grüßen
	4a	**interaction** [ˌɪntərˈækʃn]	*Analyse the interaction between Daniel Craig and the Queen.* = communication ⚠ Fr. 'interaction' (f.)	Interaktion
	T	**verbal** [ˈvɜːbl]	*Verbal and non-verbal communication are both important.*	verbal; mündlich
		to **reveal** [rɪˈviːl]	*Non-verbal interaction reveals a lot about people's relationships.* = show ≠ hide	zeigen
		facial [ˈfeɪʃl]	*Pay special attention to body language, eye contact, facial expressions and movement.*	Gesichts-
		posture [ˈpɒstʃə]	*A relaxed posture shows that you feel good.*	Körperhaltung
		familiarity [fəˌmɪliˈærəti]	*She greeted everybody with familarity.*	Vertrautheit
		to **maintain** [meɪnˈteɪn]	*Try to maintain eye contact when you speak to people.*	pflegen; aufrechterhalten
		friendliness [ˈfrendlinəs]	*A warm smile shows friendliness.*	Freundlichkeit
		rank [ræŋk]	*If you rank a list, you put it in an order.*	Reihenfolge; Rank
	4b	**setting** [ˈsetɪŋ]	*The setting is the location and time in which a story takes place.*	Szene; Umgebung
54	1	to **split up** [ˌsplɪtˈʌp], **split, split** [splɪt,]	*The students split up and visit different places around London.* = to divide	(sich) trennen
		possession [pəˈzeʃn]	*He packed all of his possessions and moved away.* ⚠ Lat. 'possessio, -onis' (f.)	Besitz
	2b	**available** [əˈveɪləbl]	*Souvenirs are available at the end of the exhibit area.*	verfügbar; erhältlich
		to **permit** [pəˈmɪt]	*Taking photos of the work of arts is not permitted.* ⚠ Lat. 'permittere (permitto, permisi, permissum)' = to permit; to allow	erlauben
55	3a	**capable** [ˈkeɪpəbl]	*I think even I'm capable of doing better.* ⚠ Fr. 'capable'	fähig
		dusty [ˈdʌsti]	*This modern art is better than many of the dusty old paintings in some of the other museums.*	verstaubt
		flash [flæʃ]	*We are not allowed to use a flash or a selfie stick.*	Blitz

page	exercise	Workshop 2		
		to **interpret** [ɪnˈtɜːprət]	*Interpret what Bex's words mean.* *= try to explain* ❗ *Fr. 'interpréter'*	interpretieren
56	1a	**procedure** [prəˈsiːdʒə]	*This procedure can take up to 45 minutes.* ❗ *Fr. 'procédure ' (f.)*	Prozedur; Verfahren
		visible [ˈvɪzəbl]	*The batch has to be clearly visible.*	sichtbar
		lobby [ˈlɒbi]	*The lobby is the first room you enter.*	Eingangshalle; Lobby
		disabled [dɪsˈeɪbld]	*There is wheelchair access as well as facilities for the disabled throughout the building.*	Behinderte(r)
		cloakroom [ˈkləʊkruːm]	*There are no cloakrooms so you need to keep your belongings with you.*	Garderobe
		addition [əˈdɪʃn]	*in addition*	Zusatz; Ergänzung
		session [ˈseʃn]	*The meeting includes a question and answer session.*	Session ; Sitzung
	2a	to **deny** [dɪˈnaɪ]	*She denied saying anything to her, but you never know with Bex.* ≠ *admit*	leugnen
57	3	**rover** [ˈrəʊvər]	*Space rovers are used on the moon and Mars.*	Fahrzeug
		to **navigate** [ˈnævɪgeɪt]	*In the video game you have to navigate a robot through a city.* ❗ *Lat. 'navigare (navigo, navigavi, navigatum)' = to sail*	navigieren; lenken
		distant [ˈdɪstənt]	*They are not only tasty, they have not been transported from distant places.* *= far away*	weit entfernt
		engineer [ˌendʒɪˈnɪə]	*More women are becoming engineers.* *= train driver*	Ingenieur(in); Lokführer(in)
59		to **bury** [ˈberi]	*Anne Boleyn was beheaded and buried there.*	beerdigen
		to **rename** [ˌriːˈneɪm]	*The Main Gate was renamed the Elizabeth Gate in honour of Queen Elizabeth's Jubilee.* ❗ *Sp. 'renombrar'*	neu benennen
		to **guard** [gɑːd]	*This place is heavily guarded by security.*	bewachen
	4a	**aid** [eɪd]	*Use visual aids to help people understand your ideas.* ❗ *Fr. 'l'aide' (f.)*	Hilfe; Unterstützung
		lung [lʌŋ]	*The lung is a part of the body.*	Lunge
		to **mumble** [ˈmʌmbl]	*Speak clearly and try not to mumble or speak too quietly.*	murmeln

page	exercise	**Workshop 2**		
		to **underestimate** [ˌʌndərˈestɪmeɪt]	People often underestimate how difficult it is to give a good presentation. ⓘ Lat. 'aestimare (aestimo, aestimavi, aestimatum)' = to estimate	unterschätzen
		to **ramble** [ˈræmbl]	When you speak to a group of people, be sure not to ramble.	weitschweifend reden
		to **sequence** [ˈsiːkwəns]	Can you sequence the events?	in eine Reihenfolge bringen
60	S1b	**frustrated** [frʌˈstreɪtɪd]	What do you get excited or frustrated about?	frustriert
	S1c	**sticky** [ˈstɪki]	People put sticky notes with their names on some things like yoghurt.	selbstklebend; klebrig
	T	**inclusive** [ɪnˈkluːsɪv]	How inclusive is our school for kids with disabilities?	integrativ
		concept [ˈkɒnsept]	You could also choose a concept such as friendship as your topic.	Konzept; Begriff
	S2b	**weakness** [ˈwiːknəs]	Discuss their strengths and weaknesses. ≠ strength	Schwäche
	S3	**logline** [lɒglaɪn]	Look at these two different loglines for the same documentary film.	Logline; kurzer Text, der das Wesentliche zusammenfasst
	S4c	to **participate** [pɑːˈtɪsɪpeɪt]	Students participate in lectures and demonstrations. ⓘ Fr. 'participer'; Sp. 'participar'	teilnehmen
61	S1	**storyboard** [ˈstɔːribɔːd]	A storyboard shows each shot of the film.	Storyboard; Szenenbuch
	S1a	**buffet** [ˈbʊfeɪ]	The food is presented as a buffet. ⓘ Fr. 'buffet' (m.)	Buffet
	S1b	**basic** [ˈbeɪsɪk]	basic rights	Grund-; grundsätzlich; einfach
	T	to **visualize** [ˈvɪʒuəlaɪz]	You have to visualize the scene.	veranschaulichen
		overview [ˈəʊvəvjuː]	Get an overview before you start.	Überblick; Übersicht
	S2a	**blank** [blæŋk]	Keep a blank photocopy of the form to fill out next time. = empty	leer
	S2b	**correction** [kəˈrekʃn]	Make any changes or corrections that are needed.	Korrektur
62		**consumerism** [kənˈsjuːmərɪzəm]	Bex is doing research about teenagers and consumerism. ⓘ Fr. 'consumérisme' (m.)	Konsumverhalten
	1	**trend** [trend]	What are the latest trends?	Trend
		influencer [ˈɪnfluənsər]	Video influencers make money through product placement.	Influencer(in)
		cosmetics [kɒzˈmetɪks]	My sister spends a lot on cosmetics.	Kosmetik
		palm [pɑːm]	Palm oil is used in many cosmetics.	Palme
		brand [brænd]	When you see a brand on social media, it's probably sponsored.	Marke

page	exercise	**Workshop 2**		
	2	**cruelty** [ˈkruːəlti]	*If we stopped eating meat, we would end this terrible cruelty to animals.*	Grausamkeit
	3	**retailer** [ˈriːteɪlər]	*Many traditional retailers now have an online presence.*	Einzelhändler(in)
		veganism [ˈviːɡənɪzəm]	*Veganism means not eating animal products.*	Veganismus
		convenience [kənˈviːniəns]	*Today our homes are full of conveniences such as microwaves and fridges.*	Bequemlichkeit; zweckmäßiges Gerät
		increasingly [ɪnˈkriːsɪŋli]	*Families are becoming increasingly diverse.* = *more and more* ≠ *less*	zunehmend
		consumer [kənˈsjuːmər]	*Companies address consumers through adverts.* ⚠ Lat. 'consumere (consumo, consumpsi, consumptum)' = *to consume*	Verbraucher(in)
	4	**technological** [ˌteknəˈlɒdʒɪkl]	*technological developments*	technologisch
		savvy [ˈsævi]	= *clever* ≠ *stupid*	klug; schlau
		realization [ˌriːəlaɪˈzeɪʃn]	*There is a realization of how important it is to live a healthy life.*	Erkenntnis
63		**to endorse** [ɪnˈdɔːs]	*I endorse brands that are ethical.*	unterstützen
		nutritional [njuˈtrɪʃənl]	*The ingredients and nutritional information printed on products is important.*	ernährungs-
		simultaneous [ˌsɪmlˈteɪniəs]	*In order to get it to work, simultaneous actions were needed.* ⚠ Lat. 'simul'	gleichzeitig; simultan
		to shorten [ˈʃɔːtn]	*Shorten your sentences.* = *make shorter*	kürzen; abkürzen
	5	**passion** [ˈpæʃn]	*Because I've got a passion for nature, I'm involved in environmental activism.* ⚠ Fr. 'passion' (f.); Sp. pasión' (f.)	Leidenschaft
		fortunately [ˈfɔːtʃənətli]	*Fortunately, my family lives close.* ⚠ Lat. 'fortuna' (f.) = fortuna	glücklicherweise
		selective [sɪˈlektɪv]	*I wish I could afford to buy every single book, but I have to be selective.*	getrennt
		publication [ˌpʌblɪˈkeɪʃn]	*I read online reviews about the new publication.*	Veröffentlichung
		format [ˈfɔːmæt]	*Your CV should have a clear format and structure.*	Format
64	2a	**presence** [ˈprezns]	*This big shop also has an online presence.*	Präsenz
		purely [ˈpjʊəli]	*In the future, society will be purely digital.*	rein; völlig

page	exercise	Workshop 2		
		outlet [ˈaʊtlet]	*Digital outlets that don't have a physical shop are becoming popular.*	Markt
		potential [pəˈtenʃl]	*What are your potential career options?* *= possible*	möglich; potentiell
		aware [əˈweər]	*Talk to people and make them aware of what your group does.*	bewusst
	2b	**knowledge** [ˈnɒlɪdʒ]	*You should leave school with more than just basic knowledge.*	Wissen
	3	**refund** [ˈriːfʌnd]	*Why don't you just take it back to the shop and swap it or ask for a refund?*	Erstattung; Ersatz
	4	**entitled** [ɪnˈtaɪtld]	*You are entitled to a repair or replacement.*	berechtigt
		compensation [ˌkɒmpenˈseɪʃn]	*The victim is getting compensation.* ❗ *Lat. 'compensatio, -onis' (f)*	Entschädigung
		content [ˈkɒntent]	*What it means is that we enjoy clever content, even if it's advertising.* ❗ *Sp. 'contenido' (m.)*	Inhalt
		faulty [ˈfɔːlti]	*The computer is faulty and has to be replaced.*	fehlerhaft
		replacement [rɪˈpleɪsmənt]	*If it breaks, you are entitled to a repair or replacement.*	Ersatz; Austausch
		reasonable [ˈriːznəbl]	*The repairs should be carried out within a reasonable amount of time.*	angemessen; vernünftig
	5	**to promote** [prəˈməʊt]	*Influencers often promote brands.*	fördern
		delivery [dɪˈlɪvəri]	*Many gig workers are delivery drivers.*	Zustellung
		allergic [əˈlɜːdʒɪk]	*It is important to check the ingredients in a product, especially if you're allergic.* ❗ *Sp. 'alérgico, alérgica'*	allergisch
65	1a	**relevant** [ˈreləvənt]	*Which parts of the article are relevant for your research?*	wichtig
		to socialize [ˈsəʊʃəlaɪz]	*Teens spend 84% of their money on buying clothes and socializing.*	Kontakte pflegen
		gig [ɡɪɡ]	*I am working a few part-time gigs to top up my income.*	Gig; Auftritt
		marketplace [ˈmɑːkɪtpleɪs]	*As many as 22% of teens buy second-hand clothing using online sites and marketplaces.*	Markt; Marktplatz
		expenditure [ɪkˈspendɪtʃər]	*Video games are a big expenditure for boys.*	Ausgaben
	2a	**attitude** [ˈætɪtjuːd]	*I don't think the results of the survey reflect my own attitudes.* ❗ *Fr. 'attitude' (f.)*	Ansicht; Einstellung
		to indicate [ˈɪndɪkeɪt]	*You have to indicate what sources you used.*	angeben; zeigen
		stereotype [ˈsteriətaɪp]	*What are typical gender stereotypes for boys and girls?*	Stereotype; Klischee

page	exercise	**Workshop 2**		
		harmful [ˈhɑːmfl]	*The effect isn't good, it's harmful.* ≠ *beneficial*	schädlich
66	1a	**archive** [ˈɑːkaɪv]	*Articles written last year are still available in the archive.* ❗ *Sp. 'archivo' (m.)*	Archiv
		geek [giːk]	*My best friend is a geek and helps me with my homework.*	Geek; Spezialist(in)
		to annoy [əˈnɔɪ]	*It does annoy me when you see adverts everywhere.* ❗ *Fr. 'ennuyer'*	ärgern; aufregen
		billion [ˈbɪljən]	*In the UK, companies spend around £1 billion every year on marketing to teens.*	Milliarde
		to entertain [ˌentəˈteɪn]	*She entertained the whole group.*	unterhalten
		makeup [ˈmeɪk ʌp]	*My mother says I can start wearing makeup when I'm 14.*	Schminke
		banner [ˈbænə]	*We see these banner ads and pop-up ads on webpages and blogs too.*	Transparent
		trick [trɪk]	*Advertisers use lots of tricks to get onto our screens and into our heads.*	Trick
		stylish [ˈstaɪlɪʃ]	= *modern*	schick
		sneaker [ˈsniːkər]	*Many people buy sneakers because of the logo.* ❗ *BE = trainer*	Turnschuh
		placement [ˈpleɪsmənt]	*Product placement is when a popular brand appears in a movie or TV show.*	Platzierung
		ton [tʌn]	*They're paid a ton of money to influence us, but we still watch and listen to them.*	Tonne
		casual [ˈkæʒuəl]	*A text message is more casual than an article.*	locker; lässig
		to personalize [ˈpɜːsənəlaɪz]	*It's casual and personalized, and that makes it more authentic.*	personalisieren
67	2b	**to combine** [kəmˈbaɪn]	*In our school, classes combine students of different ages.* ❗ *Fr. 'combiner'*	kombinieren; mischen
	3b	**former** [ˈfɔːmər]	*In a former draft of her blog post, Mary emphasized different information.*	frühere(r)
		to block [blɒk]	*Those ads blocking the content are really annoying.*	blockieren
		to load [ləʊd]	*Some websites load very slowly.* ≠ *unload*	(be)laden
	4a	**portal** [ˈpɔːtl]	*You can post your film on the video sharing portal.* ❗ *Lat. 'porta, -ae' (f.) = door*	Portalseite
		pop-up ad [ˈpɒp ʌp]	*I hate it when pop-up ads open when I visit websites.*	Popup Anzeige
		seldom [ˈseldəm]	*We very seldom go out in the evening.*	selten

page	exercise	**Workshop 2**		
68	1	**constantly** [ˈkɒnstəntli]	*Most teenagers do realize that constantly dieting is not good for your health.*	ständig; konstant
		to diet [ˈdaɪət]	*My friends are always dieting, but it's important to eat healthy food.*	Diät
		realistic [ˌriːəˈlɪstɪk]	*Teens often have an ideal body image that isn't realistic.* ❗ *Sp. 'realista'*	realistisch
		to conform (to) [kənˈfɔːm tə]	*There's so much pressure to conform to the standards we see in the media.* *= to fit to*	(sich) anpassen (an); übereinstimmen (mit)
		crash diet [ˈkræʃ ˈdaɪət]	*Crash diets aren't effective and very unhealty.*	Crash-Diät
		pill [pɪl]	*Taking diet pills is bad for your health.*	Tablette
		celebrity [səˈlebrəti]	*Many teens want to look like the celebrities in the media.* ❗ *Lat. 'celebrare, celebro, celebravi, celebratum)' = to celebrate*	Prominente
		idol [ˈaɪdl]	*My idols have always been rock stars.*	Idol
		food supplement [ˈfuːd ˌsʌplɪmənt]	*There are lots of different kinds of food supplements, but many of them are not good for you.*	Nahrungsergänzungsmittel
		to bulk up [bʌlk]	*Boys are increasingly using supplements to help them bulk up and look like their superheroes.* *= build up*	Masse zusetzen; *hier:* Muskeln aufbauen
		superhero [ˈsuːpəhɪərəʊ], **superheroes**	*The comics are about six superheroes.* ❗ *Lat 'heros, -ois' (m.)*	Superheld
		to overdo [ˌəʊvəˈduː], **overdid, overdone** [əʊvədɪd, əʊvəˈdʌn]	*It's good to stay at a weight that's normal for your height – but it's dangerous to overdo dieting.*	übertreiben
		grain [greɪn]	*Your diet should include lean meats, fruit, vegetables, whole grains and healthy fats.*	Getreide
		soda [ˈsəʊdə]	*Soda drinks contain large amounts of sugar, so cut them out too.*	Limo; Sprudel
		caffeine [ˈkæfiːn]	*Tea and coffee contain caffeine.* ❗ *Fr. 'caféine' (f.)*	Koffein
		steroid [ˈsterɔɪd]	*Steer clear of common fitness supplements, including steroids.*	Steroid
		liver [ˈlɪvər]	*The liver is a vital organ.*	Leber
		calorie [ˈkæləri]	*You are active, so a high-energy breakfast with a lot of calories will give you energy.*	Kalorie
		protein [ˈprəʊtiːn]	*Foods such as eggs, fish, and meats are rich in protein.*	Protein

page	exercise	Workshop 2		
		carbohydrate [ˌkɑːbəʊˈhaɪdreɪt]	*If you want to loose weight, cut out carbohydrates.*	Kohlenhydrat
		growth [grəʊθ]	*Counting calories all the time can slow down your growth and development.*	Wachstum
69	3	**emphatic** [ɪmˈfætɪk]	*Add do or did to each sentence to make it more emphatic.*	emphatisch
	4a	**meat-eater** [miːt iːtər]	*My father is a meat-eater and likes barbecues.*	Fleischesser(in)
		greenhouse [ˈgriːnhaʊs]	*Sheep and cattle produce more greenhouse gases than cars.*	Treibhaus
		cattle [ˈkætl]	*Raising animals like sheep and cattle produces more greenhouse gases than driving cars.*	Rinder
		to set fire [set ə ˈfaɪər], **set, set** [set, set]	*They're also setting fires to clear the land, and that releases more greenhouse gases.* = *to burn*	in Brand stecken
		ranching [rɑːntʃ]	*Around 70% of deforestation in the Amazon is due to cattle ranching.*	Viehwirtschaft; Viehhaltung
		antibiotic [ˌæntibaɪˈɒtɪk]	*Antibiotic resistance is a big health problem.*	Antibiotikum
		farmed [fɑːmd]	*Factory farmed animals often suffer from diseases.*	gezüchtet
		bacteria [bækˈtɪəriə]	*Farmers give animals loads of antibiotics to fight bacteria.* 🛈 *Fr. 'bacteries' (f.); Sp. 'bacteria' (f.)*	Bakterie
		resistant [rɪˈzɪstənt]	*After a while, some bacteria become resistant to the antibiotics.*	resistent
		cancer [ˈkænsər]	*Smoking causes cancer.*	Krebs
		diabetes [ˌdaɪəˈbiːtiːz]	*Meat-eaters are more likely to get diseases such as diabetes.*	Diabetes
	4b	**proportion** [prəˈpɔːʃn]	*The proportion of young people donating money to charities has fallen.* = *number* 🛈 *Lat. 'proportio, -onis' (f.)*	Anteil; Proportion
	5	**obesity** [əʊˈbiːsəti]	*Obesity is a growing problem in the UK with 1 in 4 adults being too fat.*	Adipositas; Fettleibigkeit
		to class [klɑːs]	*A fourth of the British population is classed as obese.*	einordnen; klassifizieren
		obese [əʊˈbiːs]	*Did you know that 25% of the population in the UK is obese?* 🛈 *Fr. 'obèse'*	fettleibig
		overweight [ˌəʊvəˈweɪt]	*Overweight people weigh far too much.* ≠ *too thin*	übergewichtig

page	exercise	**Workshop 2**		
		majority [mə'dʒɒrəti]	*The majority of people in the UK don't do enough exercise.* ≠ minority	Mehrheit
		threefold ['θri:fəʊld]	*The number of obese people has increased threefold in the last thirty years.*	dreifach
70	1b	**depression** [dɪ'preʃn]	*I knew what depression was, but I didn't know how to deal with it.*	Depression
		process ['prəʊses]	*Understanding my friend's thought processes opened my eyes.* ❗ Fr. 'processus' (m.)	Prozess
		stigma ['stɪgmə]	*Stigma is a problem when treating mental disorders.*	Stigma
		peer [pɪə]	*I listen to my peers more than to adults.*	Peer; Gleichrangige(r)
		to motivate ['məʊtɪveɪt]	*What motivates teenagers to do physical exercise?*	motivieren; anregen
		conference ['kɒnfərəns]	*It's our school's first video conference.* ❗ Fr. 'conférence' (f.); Sp. 'conferencia' (f.)	Konferenz
		biased ['baɪəst]	*I'm a bit biased, but I enjoy the youth Innovation panel that I'm on.*	parteiisch
		panel ['pænl]	*There are many experts on the panel.*	Gremium; Forum
		intriguing [ɪn'tri:gɪŋ]	*The questions the audience asked were intriguing.*	faszinierend
		professional [prə'feʃnl]	*My mother is a doctor and a health professional.* ❗ Fr. 'professionnel, professionnelle'	Fachfrau; Fachmann
		capacity [kə'pæsəti]	*The concept has the capacity to make a powerful impact in the community.* = means	Fähigkeit
		passionate ['pæʃənət]	*You should get involved in something you're passionate about.*	leidenschaftlich
		desire [dɪ'zaɪər]	*When you have the desire to do something, you should act.* ❗ Lat. 'desiderium, -i' (nt.)	Wunsch
		to pursue [pə'sju:]	*It's important to pursue your goals.* = follow	verfolgen
71	2	**advocate** ['ædvəkət]	*How did you end up as an advocate for mental wellness?*	Fürsprecher(in)
	3	**disapproval** [ˌdɪsə'pru:vl]	*People used to have a feeling of disapproval for same-sex couples.*	Missbilligung; Missfallen
72	S1a	**participant** [pɑː'tɪsɪpənt]	*Who are the participants in the discussion?*	Teilnehmer(in)
	T	**detailed** ['di:teɪld]	*When you shoot your film, you need to have a detailed plan.*	detailliert; ausführlich
	S1a	**selection** [sɪ'lekʃn]	*We made our lunch selection and ordered food.* ❗ Lat. 'selectio, -onis' (f.)	Auswahl

page	exercise	**Workshop 2**		
73	S3	**footage** [ˈfʊtɪdʒ]	*You don't need expensive software to edit the footage of your film.*	Filmmaterial; Filmaufnahmen
74	1	**commercial** [kəˈmɜːʃl]	*Do you watch commercials on TV?* ▪ Sp. 'comercial'	Werbespot
		congestion [kənˈdʒestʃən]	*There is a lot of congestion leaving the city in the evenings.*	Stau; Stauung
	2a	**tinned** [tɪnd]	*When fresh produce wasn't available, they bought tinned fruit.*	Dosen-; in Dosen
		clothes peg [peg]	*Use clothes pegs to fix your clothes on the washing line.* ▪ AE = clothespin	Wäscheklammer
		coronation [ˌkɒrəˈneɪʃn]	*The queen was crowned during the coronation ceremony.* ▪ Lat. 'coronatio, -onis' (f.)	Krönung
75	4	**steadily** [ˈstedəli]	*The amount of money being spent on TV adverts has been steadily declining.*	stetig; ununterbrochen
		to invest [ɪnˈvest]	*We invested a lot of money.*	investieren
		investment [ɪnˈvestmənt]	*Before spending money on commercials, work out if the investment will lead to increased sales.*	Investition
	6	**to praise** [preɪz]	*Greenpeace praised the organizers for the steps they were taking.*	loben
		to acknowledge [əkˈnɒlɪdʒ]	*People acknowledge that advertisers look for an opportunity for free advertising.*	bestätigen; anerkennen
79	3	**cookbook** [ˈkʊkbʊk]	*I got a vegan cookbook as a present.*	Kochbuch
		spicy [ˈspaɪsi]	*It's a spicy cabbage dish from Korea.*	scharf; würzig
	4	**tempted: to be tempted by** [bi ˈtemptɪd baɪ]	*I can honestly say that not once have I been tempted by any of these ads.*	in Versuchung sein
	5a	**graphic** [ˈgræfɪk]	*The information is presented in a graphic.* ▪ Sp. 'grafico' (m.)	Grafik

page	exercise	**Workshop 3**		
84		**cotton** [ˈkɒtn]	*The warm, wet weather from the Gulf of Mexico is good for growing cotton.* ▪ Fr. 'coton' (m.)	Baumwolle
		tobacco [təˈbækəʊ]	*They are growing tobacco.*	Tabak
		economy [ɪˈkɒnəmi]	*What opportunities does the gig economy offers?* ▪ Fr.'économie' (f.)	Ökonomie
		healthcare [ˈhelθkeə]	*Healthcare is very important for a community.*	Gesundheitsfürsorge
		insurance [ɪnˈʃʊərəns]	*Everybody should have health insurance.*	Versicherung
85		**farmland** [ˈfɑːmlænd]	*It's a huge region with endless farmland.*	Ackerland

page	exercise	**Workshop 3**		
	CC	**geographical** [ˌdʒiːəˈɡræfɪkl]	The geographical locations determine the five regions.	geografisch
		to group [ɡruːp]	The states are grouped into five regions.	gruppieren
86	1a	**contestant** [kənˈtestənt]	There was a contestant on the show who knew all the answers.	Wettkämpfer(in); Teilnehmer(in)
	3a	**governmental** [ˌɡʌvnˈmentl]	A governmental system can be a federation.	Regierungs…
		internal [ɪnˈtɜːnl]	internal affairs	innen; inner…
		affair [əˈfeə]	The states are responsible for their own internal affairs. ❗ Fr. 'affaire' (f.)	Angelegenheit; Affäre
87		**cell phone** [ˈsel fəʊn]	Cell phones are not permitted inside the White House. = mobile phone	Handy
	4	**to relocate** [ˌriːləʊˈkeɪt]	The team relocated from Montreal to Washington. = move	umziehen
	5	**numerical** [njuːˈmerɪkl]	One is numerical and the other is marked with letters, A – D. ❗ Lat. 'numerus, -i' (m.) = number	numerisch
88	2	**afterwards** [ˈɑːftəwədz]	Afterwards, Liam wrote a short text about what he learned. ≠ before	danach
		unattended [ˌʌnəˈtendɪd]	The problem is that unattended barbecues can easily start fires.	unbeaufsichtigt
	3	**amenity** [əˈmiːnəti]	On their way they walk past local amenities.	Einrichtung
		hardly [ˈhɑːdli]	I can hardly recognize it, it looks so different.	kaum
		dumpster [ˈdʌmpstə]	There are so many dumpsters here you cannot see the building.	Müllcontainer
		to overflow [ˌəʊvəˈfləʊ]	The bins are overflowing with waste.	überlaufen
		leftover [ˈleftəʊvə]	The dumpsters are all overflowing with leftover food from last night.	übriggeblieben
89	2	**hostel** [ˈhɒstl]	Hostels are cheaper than hotels.	Hostel
		monument [ˈmɒnjumənt]	Washington is full of monuments to American history.	Monument; Denkmal
		memorial [məˈmɔːriəl]	The Lincoln Memorial is close to the White House. = monument	Denkmal
		luckily [ˈlʌkɪli]	Luckily, nobody died during the storms.	glücklicherweise
	4	**imaginary** [ɪˈmædʒɪnəri]	Write a report about a real or imaginary school trip. ❗ Sp. 'imaginario, imaginaria'	erfunden; fiktiv
90	1	**court** [kɔːt]	It is the highest court in the country that deals with legal cases.	Gericht

page	exercise	Workshop 3		
		upper [ˈʌpə]	The upper floor can only be reached using the stairs.	obere(r)
		representative [ˌreprɪˈzentətɪv]	The number of representatives for each state depends on the state's total population. ❗ Lat. 'repraesentator, -oris' (m.)	Vertreter(in); Abgeordnete(r)
		supreme [suˈpriːm]	The Supreme Court is the highest court in the country.	oberste(r, -s)
		amendment [əˈmendmənt]	There are 27 amendments to the constitution. = addition	Ergänzung
		republic [rɪˈpʌblɪk]	The United States is a Federal Republic with a union of 50 states. ❗ Fr. 'république' (f.)	Republik
		republican [rɪˈpʌblɪkən]	Is she republican or independent?	republikanisch
	2	**colleague** [ˈkɒliːg]	I am Jonas, and these are my colleagues, Kathy and Roger.	Kollege, Kollegin
		responsible [rɪˈspɒnsəbl]	Who is responsible for the running of the government? ❗ Fr. 'responsable'	verantwortlich
		to enforce [ɪnˈfɔːs]	The president is responsible for enforcing laws.	durchsetzen
		framework [ˈfreɪmwɜːk]	This written document is a framework for the federal government of the United States.	Rahmen
		to guarantee [ˌgærənˈtiː]	It protects the citizens and guarantees their basic rights.	garantieren
		to ensure [ɪnˈʃʊə]	The amendment ensures the freedom of speech.	sicherstellen
		evidence [ˈevɪdəns]	to give evidence in court	Nachweis; Beweis
		guilty [ˈgɪlti]	He was found guilty and went to prison.	schuldig
		crime [kraɪm]	Some say that technology breeds new types of crime. ❗ Fr. 'crime' (m.); Sp. 'crimen' (m.)	Verbrechen
91	3a	**senator** [ˈsenətə]	Each state is represented by two senators in Congress.	Senator(in)
		judicial [dʒuˈdɪʃl]	The judicial branch is made up of courts and judges. = having to do with the law	Justiz-
		to appoint [əˈpɔɪnt]	They are appointed by the president.	ernennen
		to confirm [kənˈfɜːm]	They are appointed by the president and then confirmed by the Senate. ❗ Fr. 'confirmer'	bestätigen
		legislative [ˈledʒɪslətɪv]	The legislative branch is the Congress, which includes the House of Representatives and the Senate.	Legislative; gesetzgebend
		executive [ɪgˈzekjətɪv]	The executive branch is one of three branches of government in America.	Exekutive; ausführend

page	exercise	**Workshop 3**		
		to **select** [sɪˈlekt]	*The members are selected by the president.* ❗ *Fr. 'selectionner'*	wählen; auswählen
		to **approve** [əˈpruːv]	*Members of the Supreme Court are selected by the president and approved by the Senate.* *≠ disapprove*	zustimmen; genehmigen
	4a	**donkey** [ˈdɒŋki]	*A donkey is an animal similar to a horse.*	Esel
		to **cast** [kɑːst], **cast, cast** [kɑːst, kɑːst]	*The votes which were cast in each state are counted.*	*hier:* abgeben
		to **allocate** [ˈæləkeɪt]	*Each state is allocated a number of votes based on the population of the state.* *= give*	zuordnen; zuweisen
		electoral [ɪˈlektərəl]	*To become president, the winner needs to get a total of 270 electoral votes.*	Wahl...
	5	**controversy** [ˈkɒntrəvɜːsi]	*Why is there controversy about sex education in schools?*	Kontroverse

92

Politics

cabinet [ˈkæbɪnət]	Kabinett	**monarch** [ˈmɒnək]	Monarch(in)
constituency [kənˈstɪtuənsi]	Wahlbezirk	**monarchy** [ˈmɒnəki]	Monarchie
court [kɔːt]	Gericht	**opposition** [ˌɒpəˈzɪʃn]	Opposition
electoral [ɪˈlektərəl]	Wahl...	**representative** [ˌreprɪˈzentətiv]	Vertreter(in); Abgeordnete(r)
executive [ɪgˈzekjətɪv]	Exekutive, ausführend	**republican** [rɪˈpʌblɪkən]	republikanisch
judicial [dʒuˈdɪʃl]	Justiz-	**republic** [rɪˈpʌblɪk]	Republik
legislative [ˈledʒɪslətɪv]	Legislative, gesetzgebend	**senator** [ˈsenətə]	Senator(in)

	2	**monarchy** [ˈmɒnəki]	*The UK is a constitutional monarchy with a king or queen as the head of state.* *= a country that has a king or queen*	Monarchie
		armed forces [ˌɑːmd ˈfɔːsɪz]	*The Queen is the Commander-in-chief of the armed forces.* *= military*	Streitkräfte
		monarch [ˈmɒnək]	*It is the Houses of Parliament that makes our laws, not the monarch.* ❗ *Fr. 'monarque' (m.);* *Sp. 'monarca' (f.)*	Monarch(in); Herrscher(in)
	3a	**constituency** [kənˈstɪtʃuənsi]	*The country is divided into 650 constituencies.*	Wahlbezirk; Interessengemeinschaft
		opposition [ˌɒpəˈzɪʃn]	*After the election, the opposition became the second largest party.* ❗ *FR. 'opposition' (f.);* *Sp. 'oposición' (f.)*	Opposition
		cabinet [ˈkæbɪnət]	*The cabinet ministers control the government politics.*	Schrank; Kabinett

page	exercise	Workshop 3		
		department [dɪˈpɑːtmənt]	*The cabinet ministers run the government departments.*	Abteilung
		to oversee [ˌəʊvəˈsiː]**, oversaw, overseen** [ˌəʊvəˈsɔː, ˌəʊvəˈsiːn]	*The Prime Minister oversees the work of the government.*	überwachen; beaufsichtigen
		constituent [kənˈstɪtʃuənt]	*The 650 Members of Parliament represent their constituents.*	Wähler
		unelected [ˌʌnɪˈlektɪd]	*The peers are unelected. They're recommended by the Prime Minister.* ≠ elected	nicht gewählt
		to inherit [ɪnˈherɪt]	*My parents inherited from my grandparents when they died.* ◼ Fr. 'heriter'	erben
		manifesto [ˌmænɪˈfestəʊ]	*Political parties have official manifestos.* = programme	Manifest
	3b	**to clarify** [ˈklærəfaɪ]	*Ask questions to clarify anything you don't understand.*	(etw.) klären
93	5	**unable** [ʌnˈeɪbl]	*They were unable to meet.* ≠ able	unfähig; nicht imstande
		to rely on [rɪˈlaɪ ɒn]	*Through social media, politicians address the public directly and do not have to rely on other media.*	sich verlassen auf
		infomercial [ˌɪnfəʊˈmɜːʃl]	*= a program that promotes something in an informative way*	Infomercial
		viral [ˈvaɪrəl]	*The message became viral and reached millions of people in a short time.* ◼ Sp. 'viral'	viral
		to tailor [ˈteɪlə]	*Messages are tailored to specific audiences.*	zuschneiden; anpassen
		partly [ˈpɑːtli]	*The success of our system is partly due to its use of technology.*	teilweise
		distanced [ˈdɪstənst]	*Because of social media, politicians are not distanced from the public.*	distanziert; abgeschieden
		to interact [ˌɪntərˈækt]	*Politicians and voters interact with each other.*	interagieren
94	2	**favour: in favour of** [ɪn ˈfeɪvə əv]	*Are you in favour of the law or against it?*	pro; für
95	4	**bad wrap** [ræp]	*Maybe plastic doesn't deserve the bad wrap it has got.*	schlechter Ruf
		synthetic [sɪnˈθetɪk]	*Synthetic materials such as plastic replaced natural products.*	synthetisch
		billiard ball [ˈbɪliəd]	*Billiard balls used to be made from ivory, but are now made from plastic.*	Billardkugel
		biodegradable [ˌbaɪəʊdɪˈɡreɪdəbl]	*One of the biggest issues with plastic is that it isn't biodegradable, so some plastic can last for up to 1,000 years.*	biologisch abbaubar
		medicine [ˈmedsn]	*My grandma takes a lot of medicine.* ◼ Lat. 'medicina, -ae' (f.)	Medizin

page	exercise	Workshop 3		
		lifesaving [ˈlaɪfseɪvɪŋ]	*We use plastic in most modern medicine, especially in lifesaving equipment.*	lebensrettend
		reliance [rɪˈlaɪəns]	*Recycling helps to reduce our reliance on fossil fuels.*	Abhängigkeit
96	S2	**reliable** [rɪˈlaɪəbl]	*Make a list of websites that are reliable sources of information.*	verlässlich
	S2a	**commercial** [kəˈmɜːʃl]	*A commercial organization makes money.*	kommerziell
		accurate [ˈækjərət]	*What are good sources of accurate information?* = *correct* ❗ *Sp. 'exacto, exacta'*	genau; präzise
97	S3a	**to refine** [rɪˈfaɪn]	*Refine your search if necessary.*	verfeinern
98	1a	**treason** [ˈtriːzn]	*Treason is a crime against the state.*	Verrat
	1b	**briefly** [ˈbriːfli]	*Explain briefly what they discuss.* = *in short* ❗ *Fr. 'brièvement'*	kurz
		gruesome [ˈɡruːsəm]	*She was wondering why British history was so gruesome.*	grauenvoll; abscheulich
		cellar [ˈselər]	*He was found in a cellar with lots of gunpowder.* = *basement*	Keller
		straw [strɔː]	*A model made of straw and dressed in old clothes is burned on the bonfire.*	Strohhalm; Stroh
	2a	**unlimited** [ʌnˈlɪmɪtɪd]	*Unlimited power has no restrictions.*	unbegrenzt; unbeschränkt
		to admire [ədˈmaɪə]	*It is nice to admire someone because they have good ideas or qualities.* ≠ *dislike* ❗ *Fr. 'admirer'*	bewundern
		hereditary [həˈredɪtri]	*The monarchs are usually part of a 'House' and the position of King or Queen is hereditary.*	vererblich
		crusade [kruːˈseɪd]	*The crusades were religious wars against Muslims.*	Kreuzzug
		to restore [rɪˈstɔː]	*Now the ship has been restored and looks like new.* ❗ *Fr. 'restaurer'*	wiederherstellen
		absolute [ˈæbsəluːt]	*The revolution ended the absolute power of the monarchy.*	absolut
		actual [ˈæktʃuəl]	*The monarch is more of a symbol than an actual decision maker.* = *real*	richtig; wirklich
		overall [ˌəʊvərˈɔːl]	*Overall, the British still like their monarchy.*	allgemein; im allgemeinen
		popularity [ˌpɒpjuˈlærəti]	*The popularity of the Queen is high.*	Popularität
99	2b	**universal** [ˌjuːnɪˈvɜːsəli]	*This is a universal truth all over the world.*	allgemein

page	exercise	**Workshop 3**		
	3b	**contentious** [kənˈtenʃəs]	*Brexit was a contentious issue.*	umstritten
		referendum [ˌrefəˈrendəm]	*In 2016, the UK held a referendum on whether to stay in the EU or leave.*	Volksentscheid; Referendum
		to resign [rɪˈzaɪn]	*The president had to resign.* ⚠ Fr. 'resigner'	zurücktreten
		resignation [ˌrezɪɡˈneɪʃn]	*Brexit lead to her resignation as Prime Minister.* ⚠ Sp. 'resignación' (f.)	Amtsniederlegung; Rücktritt
		influential [ˌɪnfluˈenʃl]	*Many celebrities are very influential.*	einflussreich
		transition [trænˈzɪʃn]	*the transition from one state to another* ⚠ Lat. 'transitus, -us' (m.)	Wechsel; Übergang
		to negotiate [nɪˈɡəʊʃieɪt]	*They negotiated a deal.*	verhandeln
		to rejoin [ˌriːˈdʒɔɪn]	*Some people want to rejoin the EU.*	wieder beitreten
		midday [ˌmɪdˈdeɪ]	*At midday on January 31st, 2020 the UK officially left the EU.*	Mittag
		to overshadow [ˌəʊvəˈʃædəʊ]	*The agreement was signed, but the event was overshadowed by the Corona pandemic.*	überschatten
		pandemic [pænˈdemɪk]	*The charity was founded during the Corona pandemic to help musicians.* ⚠ Fr. 'pandémie' (f.)	Pandemie
100	1	**tragedy** [ˈtrædʒədi]	*It was a tragedy that the children were seriously injured in the accident.*	Tragödie
	2	**worldwide** [ˌwɜːldˈwaɪd]	*The book was a worldwide success.*	weltweit
		engagement [ɪnˈɡeɪdʒmənt]	*As a royal, Kate works hard to support the Queen in official engagements.*	Engagement; Einsatz
		alongside [əˌlɒŋˈsaɪd]	*The gap between rich and poor grows alongside the rise in the UK's total wealth.*	daneben
		welfare [ˈwelfeər]	*She is passionate about the welfare of children.*	Wohl; Sozialhilfe
		outfit [ˈaʊtfɪt]	*The outfits she wears quickly sell out from the shops.*	Outfit; Kleidung
	3a	**restriction** [rɪˈstrɪkʃn]	*We can trade with other countries without the restrictions of the EU.* ⚠ Sp. 'restricción' (f.)	Einschränkung
		to pick [pɪk]	*After Brexit, I couldn't pick the universities I wanted.*	auswählen
		prospect [ˈprɒspekt]	*Going to university will change my prospects in the future.*	Aussicht; Möglichkeit
		open-minded [ˌəʊpən ˈmaɪndɪd]	*It's important to be open-minded about other cultures.*	aufgeschlossen
101	2a	**to take for granted** [teɪk fə ˈɡrɑːntɪd]**, took, taken** [tʊk, ˈteɪkən]	*We take it all for granted, but this might not be true.*	als selbstverständlich ansehen

page	exercise	Workshop 3		
		poverty [ˈpɒvəti]	We want to raise awareness about different social issues like food poverty. ❗ lat. 'paupertas, -tatis' (f.)	Armut
		violation [ˌvaɪəˈleɪʃn]	The UN defines poverty as a violation of human rights. ❗ Lat. violare (violo, violavi, violatum)' = to violate	Verletzung; Verstoß gegen etw.
		denial [dɪˈnaɪəl]	One of the biggest social issues today is the denial of opportunities.	Verweigerung; Leugnung
		slum [slʌm]	Millions of people live in slums near big cities in poverty.	Slum; Getto
		household [ˈhaʊshəʊld]	Three generations live in this household.	Haushalt
		homeless [ˈhəʊmləs]	In many cities we see the homeless sleeping on the streets.	obdachlos; Obdachlose(r)
		powerless [ˈpaʊələs]	We are not powerless to solve problems.	kraftlos; machtlos
		to **prevent** [prɪˈvent]	There are laws that prevent children from working.	verhindern; abhalten
102	1	**muddy** [ˈmʌdi]	After it rains it's really muddy.	schlammig; matschig
	2a	to **reuse** [ˌriːˈjuːz]	We should recycle and reuse as much as we can. ❗ Sp. 'reutilizar'	wiederverwenden
		organizer [ˈɔːgənaɪzə]	The organizers made some changes to the event.	Organisator(in)
		radical [ˈrædɪkl]	Our society has undergone some radical changes in recent years.	radikal; grundlegend
		to **urge** [ɜːdʒ]	People were asked not to bring any single-use plastics and were urged to take all their rubbish away.	dringend bitten
		container [kənˈteɪnə]	People should also think about the food containers and cutlery they bring to the event.	Behälter; Container
		mattress [ˈmætrəs]	We bought a new mattress for the bed.	Matratze
	2b	to **justify** [ˈdʒʌstɪfaɪ]	Justify your answers by quoting the relevant lines. ❗ Fr. 'justifier'; Sp. 'justificar'	rechtfertigen
103	4	**discount** [ˈdɪskaʊnt]	How much was the discount?	Rabatt; Nachlass
	5	**glamping** [ˈglæmpɪŋ]	Glamping is luxurious camping.	glamouröses Zelten
		glam [glæm]	I think the glam part is short for glamorous.	schick
		glamorous [ˈglæmərəs]	I like the glamorous world of show business.	glamourös
		to **benefit** [ˈbenɪfɪt]	You would benefit from taking the course.	profitieren

page	exercise	Workshop 3		
		to **exclude** [ɪkˈskluːd]	*The disabled should not be excluded from school and other activities.* 🛈 *Lat. 'excludere (excludo, exclusi, exclusum)'*	ausschließen
104	1	**financial** [faɪˈnænʃl]	*A lot of people need financial support to be able to survive.*	finanziell
105	4	**disadvantaged** [ˌdɪsədˈvaːntɪdʒd]	*There are scholarships for students from disadvantaged families.*	benachteiligt
		wristband [ˈrɪstbænd]	*The wristband shows that you are allowed on the festival grounds.*	Armband
	5	**greatness** [ˈɡreɪtnəs]	*Your greatness is not what you have, it's what you give.*	Großartigkeit
106	1	**bleak** [bliːk]	*When America entered the war, Britain was losing the war against Germany and things looked bleak.*	düster
		prominent [ˈprɒmɪnənt]	*His father was a prominent Conservative politician.*	bedeutend
		to **crash** [kræʃ]	*He crashed a plane.*	abstürzen (lassen)
		to **graduate** [ˈɡrædʒuət]	*They teach us what we need to know to get a job when we graduate.*	den Schulabschluss machen
		correspondent [ˌkɒrəˈspɒndənt]	*He wrote as a war correspondent about conflicts in South Africa.*	Korrespondent(in); Reporter(in)
		somehow [ˈsʌmhaʊ]	*Somehow he managed to escape by climbing over a wall.*	irgendwie
		strike [straɪk]	*The students went on strike.*	Streik
		labour [ˈleɪbər]	*The labour party won the election.* 🛈 *AE = labor*	arbeits...
		to **surrender** [səˈrendə]	*We shall never surrender, we will win.* = to give up	aufgeben; übergeben
		despite [dɪˈspaɪt]	*Despite leading Britain to victory he lost the election in 1945.* = although ≠ because of	obwohl; trotz
		victory [ˈvɪktəri]	*He led his team to victory against the other school.* 🛈 *Lat. 'victoria, -ae'*	Sieg
		coffin [ˈkɒfɪn]	*They burried the coffin at the funeral.*	Sarg
		funeral [ˈfjuːnərəl]	*When he died, his funeral was attended by many world leaders.* 🛈 *Lat. 'funus (-neris)' (n)*	Beerdigung
		ancestral [ænˈsestrəl]	*He was laid to rest at his ancestral home.*	zur Familie gehörend; den Vorfahren gehörend
108	S1	to **recover** [rɪˈkʌvə]	*The area has recovered from the disaster.* 🛈 *Lat. 'recuperare (recupero, recuperavi, recuperatum)*	(sich) erholen
		situated [ˈsɪtʃueɪtɪd]	*The Gulf Coast is situated on the southern part of the United States.*	gelegen

page	exercise	**Workshop 3**		
		shoreline [ˈʃɔːlaɪn]	The five US states along the shoreline are all famous for their beaches. = coast	Küste
		petrochemical [ˌpetrəʊˈkemɪkl]	Petrochemicals are an important industry.	Petrochemikalie
		aerospace [ˈeərəʊspeɪs]	The main industries are petrochemicals, energy, aerospace and agriculture.	Luftfahrt
		to weaken [ˈwiːkən]	The storm weakened for a while.	schwächer werden; schwächen
		mandatory [ˈmændətəri]	A mandatory order cannot be refused.	verpflichtend
		evacuation [ɪˌvækjuˈeɪʃn]	The mayor issued an evacuation order after the storm became stronger.	Evakuierung
		to strengthen [ˈstreŋkθn]	The storm strengthened over night. = become stronger ≠ weaken	stärker werden; stärker machen
		to classify [ˈklæsɪfaɪ]	The storm was classified as a category 5 hurricane. ❗ Fr. 'classifer'	etw. einstufen
		coastal [ˈkəʊstl]	The coastal communities that were hit hard by the storm still haven't fully recovered.	Küsten…; an der Küste
		to evacuate [ɪˈvækjueɪt]	They had to evacuate because of the flood. ❗ Fr. 'évacuer'	verlassen; evakuieren
		to construct [kənˈstrʌkt]	The biggest issue was to design structures that protect the city from flooding.	bauen; errichten
		levee [ˈlevi]	They built new levees, structures that protect the city from flooding. = dam	Deich
		response [rɪˈspɒns]	The federal government was criticized for the slow response in the emergency. ❗ Lat. 'responsum, -i' (n.)	Reaktion; Antwort
		to flood [flʌd]	As the hurricane battered the area, New Orleans was flooded.	überfluten
110	2	**balcony** [ˈbælkəni]	The royal family show themselves on the balcony. ❗ Sp. 'balcón' (m.)	Balkon
		residence [ˈrezɪdəns]	The flag indicates whether the Queen is in residence.	Residenz; Wohnsitz
		inner [ˈɪnər]	It is a popular destination, situated in the inner part of the city.	innere, -r, -s
		undoubtedly [ʌnˈdaʊtɪdli]	New York City is undoubtedly one of the best cities in the world.	zweifellos

page	exercise	**Workshop 3**		
		administrative [əd'mɪnɪstrətɪv]	*The Queen has many administrative duties.*	administrativ; verwaltend
		headquarters [ˌhedˈkwɔːtəz]	*The company's headquarters are in the centre of London.*	Hauptquartier
		to commission [kəˈmɪʃn]	*He commissioned John Nash as a builder.*	beauftragen
		transformation [ˌtrænsfəˈmeɪʃn]	*After the war, many countries saw fundamental transformations.* **!** *Fr. 'transformation' (f.)*	Veränderung; Verwandlung
		courtyard [ˈkɔːtjɑːd]	*The palace was built around the central courtyard.*	Innenhof
		to amount to [əˈmaʊnt tə]	*Nash did a magnificent job, but the cost of the building amounted to half a million pounds.* *= to come to*	betragen; ausmachen
		to authorize [ˈɔːθəraɪz]	*The building cost considerably more than the sum the parliament authorized.*	genehmigen; autorisieren
		unoccupied [ˌʌnˈɒkjupaɪd]	*The palace remained unoccupied until Queen Victoria came to the thrown in 1837.*	unbewohnt
		surgery [ˈsɜːdʒəri]	*Doctors work in a hospital or a surgery.*	Praxis; Sprechstunde
114	2	**anxious** [ˈæŋkʃəs]	*I'm anxious all the time and I know that isn't healthy for me.*	besorgt; ängstlich
115	3	**democratic** [ˌdeməˈkrætɪk]	*Of the two candidates, one was from the Republican and one from the Democratic Party.* **!** *Fr. 'de1mocratique'*	demokratisch
	4	**nomination** [ˌnɒmɪˈneɪʃn]	*You have to run for nomination before you can become the candidate.* **!** *Lat. 'nominatio, -onis' (f.)*	Ernennung
		presidency [ˈprezɪdənsi]	*The presidency is held for four years.*	Präsidentschaft; Vorsitz
	5	**dot** [dɒt]	*The famous 'Green Dot' recycling system was introduced in 1991.*	Punkt

page	exercise	**Workshop 4**		
120		**shoplifting** [ˈʃɒplɪftɪŋ]	*Shoplifting is a crime.*	Ladendiebstahl
		to bully [ˈbʊli]	*You should never bully other people.* *= intimidate*	mobben
		self [self]	*It's not just that the bullying makes me unhappy, it also affects my confidence and self-belief.*	selbst...
		gay [geɪ]	*Being gay and black means I face a lot of problems.*	schwul
		tolerance [ˈtɒlərəns]	*Society shows more tolerance to people who are different.* **!** *Fr. 'tolerance' (f.);* *Sp. 'tolerancia' (f.)*	Toleranz

page	exercise	**Workshop 4**		
		march [mɑːtʃ]	*Information about the march is posted on different social media platforms.*	Marsch
		obsession [əbˈseʃn]	*It started off just as a way of getting fit, but then it became an obsession.*	Obsession; Besessenheit
		songwriter [ˈsɒŋraɪtər]	*Taylor Swift is a US singer-songwriter.*	Texter(in); Liederkomponist(in)
		lesbian [ˈlezbiən]	*Lesbians continue to fight for basic rights, including the right to marry.*	lesbisch; Lesbe
		bisexual [ˌbaɪˈsekʃuəl]	*Most Canadian citizens said that they would be comfortable if a neighbour were gay, lesbian or bisexual.*	bisexuelle
		trans [trænz]	*Trans rights are human rights.*	trans...
		LGBT (lesbian, gay, bisexual, transgender) [ˌel dʒiː biː ˈtiː]	*LGBT is an abbreviation used when referring to lesbian, gay, bisexual and transgender people.*	LGBT
		gifted [ˈɡɪftɪd]	*Every child is gifted in his or her way.*	begabt
		to unwrap [ʌnˈræp]	*They just unwrap their packages all at once.*	auspacken
		package [ˈpækɪdʒ]	*My parents sent me a package.* ❗ *Fr. 'paquet' (m.)*	Paket
121		**consultant** [kənˈsʌltənt]	*Frank is a technology security consultant.*	Berater(in)
122	1	**nuclear** [ˈnjuːkliə]	*Nuclear engineering is a science.* ❗ *Fr. 'nucléaire', Lat. 'nucleus, -i' (m.) = core*	Atom...; Nuklear...
		unit [ˈjuːnɪt]	*My grandma, my mom and my little brother are my entire family unit.* ❗ *Lat. 'unitas, -atis' (f.)*	Einheit
		sex [seks]	*Same-sex marriage, which was legalized in Canada in 2005 and in 2015 in the USA, has led to even more family diversity.*	Geschlecht; Sex
		to legalize [ˈliːɡəlaɪz]	*Same-sex marriage was legalized in Canada in 2005.*	legalisieren
		census [ˈsensəs]	*The 2020 US Census allowed respondents to indicate they are part of a same-sex couple.*	Zensus; Volkszählung
		respondent [rɪˈspɒndənt]	*How many respondents were there in the census?*	Befragte(r)
		uptight [ˌʌpˈtaɪt]	*You should relax and not be so uptight.* ≠ *easy-going*	verklemmt
		gender [ˈdʒendə]	*My family has taught me to be accepting of everyone, no matter what race or gender they are.* ❗ *Sp. 'género' (m.)*	Geschlecht; Gender

page	exercise	**Workshop 4**		
123	2a	**incomplete** [ˌɪnkəmˈpliːt]	*Without the subject the sentence would be incomplete.* *≠ complete*	unvollständig
	3b	**extended** [ɪkˈstendɪd]	*There are cousins, aunts and uncles in the extended family.*	erweitert
		arrangement [əˈreɪndʒmənt]	*When you've made an arrangement, you should stick to it.* ❗ *Fr. 'arrangement' (m.)*	Vereinbarung
		to struggle [ˈstrʌgl]	*Grandparents might struggle to keep up with new technologies.*	sich anstrengen; sich bemühen
	4	**to immigrate** [ˈɪmɪgreɪt]	*Her parents wanted to give their daughter a better life than they had, so they immigrated to New Zealand.*	einwandern
		to descend [dɪˈsend]	*His family are directly descended from African slaves.*	abstammen
		to step up [step ʌp]	*After my father died, my grandma stepped up to take his place.*	vortreten
		to envy [ˈenvi]	*When I was younger, I used to envy my friends' families a lot.*	beneiden
124	1a	**to challenge** [ˈtʃælɪndʒ]	*We were challenged not to drink fizzy drinks for a week.*	herausfordern
	1b	**grocery** [ˈgrəʊsəri]	*At the weekend I have to buy groceries and tidy my room.*	Lebensmittel
		ironing [ˈaɪənɪŋ]	*My weeks are so busy, I have to do the ironing on the weekend.*	Bügeln
		to mow [məʊ]	*On Saturdays I mow the grass in grandma's garden.*	mähen
		lawn [lɔːn]	*We don't like to mow the lawn too often.*	Rasen
		to vacuum [ˈvækjuːm]	*I have to vacuum the house before I can hang out with my friends.*	staubsaugen
	1d	**to tend to** [ˈtend tə]	*When my mother was a child, men tended to work and women stayed home.*	zu etw. neigen
	2	**to reinforce** [ˌriːɪnˈfɔːs]	*Describe how gender roles are learned and reinforced.*	verstärken; bekräftigen
		to dictate [dɪkˈteɪt]	*Being a man or a woman long dictated what you could be in life.* ❗ *Lat. 'dictare (dicto, dictavi, dictatum)'; Fr. 'dicter'*	bestimmen; diktieren
		carer [ˈkeərə]	*Children who don't have parents are raised by carers.*	Betreuer(in)
		genderneutral [ˌdʒendə ˈnjuːtrəl]	*Many parents give their children genderneutral names.*	geschlechtsneutral
		gendered [ˈdʒendəd]	*Household chores aren't gendered.*	geschlechtsspezifisch
		stereotypical [ˌsteriəˈtɪpɪkl]	*I don't want to conform to stereotypical expectations.*	stereotypisch
		unisex [ˈjuːnɪseks]	*It makes a lot of sense to have unisex bathrooms that everyone can use.*	Unisex...; nicht geschlechtsspezifisch

page	exercise	Workshop 4		
		genderless ['dʒendələs]	Some people want to give their children a unisex, or genderless, name.	geschlechtslos
		bias ['baɪəs]	Gender bias still exists in the world of work.	Voreingenommenheit
125	1	to **muck around** [mʌk ə'raʊnd]	I like skateboarding and mucking around outside with my friends.	Spaß haben
		peace [piːs]	The war ended and there was peace. ≠ war ❶ Fr. 'paix' (f.), Lat. 'pax, pacis' (f.)	Frieden
		hormone ['hɔːməʊn]	He is currently on hormone treatments to stop the sex hormones that don't match his gender. ❶ Sp. 'hormona' (f.)	Hormon
		blocker [blɒkər]	I started on the treatment of hormone blockers which stop my male hormones.	Blocker
		to **conceal** [kən'siːl]	I no longer try to conceal my true gender.	verbergen
		tomboy ['tɒmbɔɪ]	They thought she was a tomboy because she was interested in things that boys generally like.	burschikoses Mädchen; Wildfang
		disgusted [dɪs'gʌstɪd]	The boy was disgusted when his mother fed him vegetables.	empört; angewidert
	2a	aimlessly ['eɪmləsli]	On weekends I like to spend time aimlessly, with silly things.	ziellos
		dirt [dɜːt]	Clear the dirt off the floor with the vacuum cleaner.	Dreck; Schmutz
	CC	transgender [trænz'dʒendər]	My uncle is transgender, so it's never felt unusual to me that people might not feel comfortable with their sex.	transgender
		queer [kwɪər]	Someone who is 'queer' doesn't identify as heterosexual or 'straight'.	schwul; queer
		heterosexual [ˌhetərə'sekʃuəl]	Most of my friends are heterosexual.	heterosexuell
		intersex ['ɪntəseks]	Intersex people have sex organs or hormones that don't match their gender.	Intersex
		organ ['ɔːgən]	The skin is the human body's largest organ. ❶ Fr. 'organe' (m.); Sp. 'órgano' (m.)	Organ
		asexual [ˌeɪ'sekʃuəl]	Asexual is a term for people who are not interested in sex.	asexuell
	3	currently ['kʌrəntli]	We are currently looking for an apprentice to join our team.	derzeit; gerade
		puberty ['pjuːbəti]	There are medications that can stop puberty from starting. ❶ Fr. 'puberté' (f.)	Pubertät
126	1a	compatible [kəm'pætəbl]	I have an old computer and hope that it's compatible with the software.	kompatibel

page	exercise	**Workshop 4**		
	2a	**orientated** [ˈɔːriənteɪt]	*The UK system is very exam orientated.*	orientiert
		equivalent [ɪˈkwɪvələnt]	*Year 11 is equivalent to grade 10 in the USA.*	entsprechend
		diploma [dɪˈpləʊmə]	*In the USA, students study for their high-school diploma.*	Diplom; Urkunde
		criterion [kraɪˈtɪəriən]	*There are a lot of criteria for getting into this university.*	Kriterium
		range [reɪndʒ]	*You need to get credits from a range of subjects, not just a couple.*	Angebot; Palette
		to gear: be geared towards [bi ɡɪər təˈwɔːdz]	*The UK system is geared towards specializing.*	auf etw. ausgerichtet sein
		generalization [ˌdʒenrəlaɪˈzeɪʃn]	*The US educational system focuses on generalization.* ⚠ *Sp. 'generalización' (f.)*	Generalisierung
		curriculum [kəˈrɪkjələm]	*In the UK, there is a national curriculum, which all schools should follow.*	Curriculum; Lehrplan
		exception [ɪkˈsepʃn]	*Powerful women in the world are the exception, not the rule.* ≠ *norm* ⚠ *Lat. 'exceptio, -onis' (f.)*	Ausnahme
		to prescribe [prɪˈskraɪb]	*The educational system here prescribes exactly what is taught.* ⚠ *Lat. 'praescribere (praescripto, praescribsi, praescriptum)'*	vorschreiben; festsetzen
		district [ˈdɪstrɪkt]	*Every state is divided into districts.*	Bezirk
		sequentially [sɪˈkwenʃəli]	*In the US subjects such as math and science are taught sequentially.* = *one after the other*	der Reihe nach
		tuition [tjuˈɪʃn]	*University tuition is very high in the USA.* ⚠ *used in the singular*	Studiengebühr(en)
		to vary [ˈveəri]	*The costs of an education vary greatly in different parts of the world.* ≠ *to stay the same*	variieren
		comparable [ˈkɒmpərəbl]	*The average annual fees for university in the USA are comparable to the fees in the UK.* ≠ *different*	vergleichbar
		scholarship [ˈskɒləʃɪp]	*Who can get scholarships to go to college or university in the USA?*	Stipendium
		to excel [ɪkˈsel]	*He wanted to excel in his geography test, but failed.*	sich selbst übertreffen; sich hervortun
127		**provision** [prəˈvɪʒn]	*An expert is talking about the special educational needs provision in schools in the USA.*	Maßnahme

page	exercise	Workshop 4		
		breakthrough ['breɪkθruː]	*The passing of the No Child Left Behind Act was a real breakthrough. = success*	Durchbruch
		assistance [ə'sɪstəns]	*The school provides assistance for special needs children.*	Unterstützung
		to require [rɪ'kwaɪə]	*We study and take the required tests.* ❗ *Lat. 'requiere (requiro, requisivi, requisitum)'*	erfordern; verlangen
		additional [ə'dɪʃənl]	*Often children are given additional support if they have dyslexia.*	zusätzlich; ergänzend
		dyslexia [dɪs'leksɪə]	*Dyslexia makes learning to read difficult.* ❗ *Fr. 'dyslexie' (f.)*	Legasthenie
		dyscalculia [ˌdɪskæl'kjuːlɪə]	*Children are given additional support in school if they have dyscalculia.*	Dyskalkulie
		autism ['ɔːtɪzəm]	*When working with students with autism, be consistent.*	Autismus
		cerebral palsy [sə'riːbrəl 'pɔːlzi]	*There is a girl with cerebral palsy in my class.*	zerebrale Kinderlähmung
	6	**repetitive** [rɪ'petətɪv]	*People with Asperger's Syndrome can perform fairly well in school but their thinking patterns can be repetitive.*	repetitiv
		to cope [kəʊp]	*Often people with this condition will develop strategies to cope with it.*	zurechtkommen
		hyperactive [ˌhaɪpər'æktɪv]	*They are often hyperactive and find it difficult to sit still for long periods or to focus their attention.*	hyperaktiv
128	CC	**dyslexic** [dɪs'leksɪk]	*With help, dyslexic children can be great students.*	legasthenisch
	1b	**streaming** ['striːmɪŋ]	*We've got the internet and live video streaming to help with long-distance learning.*	Streaming
		headset ['hedset]	*I've got a headset with a microphone so that I can actively take part.*	Headset; Kopfhörer
		to demonstrate ['demənstreɪt]	*Our teacher demonstrated some problems on the whiteboard.* ❗ *Lat. 'demonstrare (demonstro, demonstravi, demonstratum)'*	zeigen; vorführen
129	2a	**nearby** [ˌnɪə'baɪ]	*His new school is nearby, so he can walk there in the morning.*	in der Nähe
	3a	**to account for** [ə'kaʊnt fər]	*In 1956, Maori accounted for just 8 % of the population.*	ausmachen
	3b	**to aim** [eɪm]	*The biggest changes have been aimed at reducing pollution.*	zielen
		shift [ʃɪft]	*There has been a shift in schools to focus on individual learning.*	Veränderung
		revival [rɪ'vaɪvl]	*The revival of the Maori language in schools is important for New Zealand's culture.*	Wiederbelebung

page	exercise	**Workshop 4**		
		participation [pɑːˌtɪsɪˈpeɪʃn]	The participation of mothers in the labor force is increasing. ⚠ Fr. 'participation' (f.); Sp. 'participación' (f.)	Beteiligung
		attainment [əˈteɪnmənt]	Attainment refers to the highest level of education a student gets.	Leistungen
	4a	**consistent** [kənˈsɪstənt]	My teacher is consistent about classroom rules.	konsequent
		reward [rɪˈwɔːd]	Give your dog a reward when he learns something new.	Belohnung; Preis
		graph [ɡrɑːf]	Use visuals like graphs to help listeners understand information.	Diagramm
	4b	**efficient** [ɪˈfɪʃnt]	Which method of learning is most efficient for you? ⚠ Fr. 'efficace'	effizient; wirksam
	CC	**to grade** [ˈɡreɪdɪŋ]	The teacher graded my homework.	bewerten
		fail [feɪl]	In our school, a D or an F is considered a fail.	Durchfallen
130	2a	**polo shirt** [ˈpəʊləʊ ʃɜːt]	In most high schools students wear a white polo shirt.	Polohemd
		blazer [ˈbleɪzər]	In our school all students wear blazers.	Blazer; leichte Sportjacke
		badge [bædʒ]	We wear a blazer with the school badge on the top pocket.	Abzeichen; Plakette
		tuck shop [tʌk ʃɒp]	A tuck shop is a shop on the grounds of a school.	Laden; Geschäft
		elective [ɪˈlektɪv]	We have a lot of electives to choose from. ⚠ Lat. 'electio, -onis' (f.) = election	Auswahlfach
		production [prəˈdʌkʃn]	I'm taking theatre production – it's my favourite.	Produktion; Inszenierung
		cheerleader [ˈtʃɪəliːdə]	I enjoy being a cheerleader.	Cheerleader(in)
		sporty [ˈspɔːti]	I'm not very sporty, but I do like hiking. ⚠ Fr. 'sportif, sportive'	sportlich
		to experience [ɪkˈspɪəriənsɪŋ]	Talk to your parents if you experience cyberbullying.	erfahren; erleben
		homecoming [ˈhəʊmkʌmɪŋ]	Homecoming is a special week at school and includes a student dance.	traditionelles Event in der Highschool
131	3a	**therapy** [ˈθerəpi]	I have therapy twice a week now that my leg has healed.	Therapie
		specialist [ˈspeʃəlɪst]	There is a specialist for this problem at the hospital.	Spezialist(in); Expert(in)
	4	**neurological** [ˌnjʊərəˈlɒdʒɪkl]	Autism is a neurological disorder that affects the way a person's body and brain works.	neurologisch
		disorder [dɪsˈɔːdər]	Autism is a neurological disorder that affects the way a person's body and brain works.	Störung

page	exercise	Workshop 4		
		to misunderstand [ˌmɪsʌndəˈstænd]**, misunderstood, misunderstood** [ˌmɪsʌndəˈstʊd, ˌmɪsʌndəˈstʊd]	*They might misunderstand other people's feelings or behaviour.*	missverstehen
		cue [kjuː]	*You should learn to read social cues.* = tip	Hinweis
		to handle [ˈhændl]	*How did the teacher handle the problem?*	handhaben
		sensory [ˈsensəri]	*Some people have difficulties dealing with sensory information.* = relating to the five senses	sensorisch
		routine [ruːˈtiːn]	*I am pretty good at handling new routines.* ⚠ Fr. 'routine' (f.)	Routine
		Down syndrome [ˈdaʊn sɪndrəʊm]	*Children with Down syndrome often go to a mainstream school.*	Downsyndrom
		rigid [ˈrɪdʒɪd]	*Their thinking patterns can be rigid and inflexible.*	starr; rigide
		coordination [kəʊˌɔːdɪˈneɪʃn]	*Cerebral palsy is a permanent moving disorder which causes difficulties in body movement and muscle coordination.* ⚠ Sp. 'coordinación' (f.)	Koordinierung
		stiff [stɪf]	*Her legs were stiff and she couldn't move.*	steif; starr
		to tie [taɪ]	*He stopped walking and tied his shoes.*	binden; zubinden
		to grasp [grɑːsp]	*I grasped the cup when it fell.*	greifen; festhalten
		genetic [dʒəˈnetɪk]	*Down syndrome is a genetic disorder.*	genetisch
		chromosome [ˈkrəʊməsəʊm]	*Humans have 23 chromosomes.*	Chromosom
		mentally impaired [ˌmentəli ɪmˈpeəd]	*People with Down syndrome have an extra copy of chromosome 21 and are often mentally impaired.*	psychisch beeinträchtigt
132	S1	**remarriage** [ˌriːˈmærɪdʒ]	*Remarriage is common and results in blended families.*	Wiederverheiratung
		to decrease [dɪˈkriːs]	*The number of two-parent households decreased.* = to become less ≠ to increase ⚠ Sp. 'decrecer'	fallen; zurückgehen
		dramatic [drəˈmætɪk]	*There has been a dramatic rise in carbon emissions.*	dramatisch
		minority [maɪˈnɒrəti]	*Only a tiny minority of teenagers save their money.* ≠ majority ⚠ Fr. 'minorité' (f.); Sp. 'minoría' (f.)	Minderheit
	T	**to level off** [ˈlevl ɒf]	*The data on the graph levels off this year.*	sich ebnen; abflachen

page	exercise	**Workshop 4**		
		peak [piːk]	There was a peak in the middle of the last year.	Gipfel; Höhepunkt
133	S1	**labor force** [ˈleɪbə fɔːs]	The percentage of women in the labor force has increased in the past decades. ❗ BE = labour force	Arbeitskräfte; Arbeitnehmerschaft
		employment [ɪmˈplɔɪmənt]	Look at this job advert from a UK employment website. ≠ unemployment	Beschäftigung; Arbeit
		rate [reɪt]	The participation rates have increased.	Rate; Anteil
		preschool [ˈpriːskuːl]	It's difficult for mothers with preschool-aged children to work full-time.	vorschulisch, Vorschul...
	S2b	**bar chart** [ˈbɑː tʃɑːt]	The bar chart presents the findings of the survey.	Balkendiagramm
134	1a	**apprenticeship** [əˈprentɪʃɪp]	Some school leavers go to university but others start an apprenticeship. ❗ Fr. 'apprentissage' (f.)	Lehrstelle; Ausbildung
	1b	**undergraduate** [ˌʌndəˈgrædʒuət]	My sister will be an undergraduate at the university next year.	Student(in) (ohne Abschluss)
		discrimination [dɪˌskrɪmɪˈneɪʃn]	I am in a student activist group that deals with social issues like discrimination.	Diskriminierung; Ausgrenzung
		lawyer [ˈlɔɪə]	I can see how lawyers can make a difference.	Rechtsanwalt
		determined [dɪˈtɜːmɪnd]	I really want a job in computing, I'm determined to get one.	entschlossen
		apprentice [əˈprentɪs]	I've managed to secure an interview for a job as an apprentice software developer.	Auszubildende(r); Lehrling
		developer [dɪˈveləpər]	Software developers are always needed.	Entwickler(in)
		vintage [ˈvɪntɪdʒ]	I buy vintage clothes, make changes and then sell them at markets.	alt; klassisch; Vintage
		incubator [ˈɪŋkjubeɪtər]	We applied to an incubator for training and help with our idea.	Inkubator; Unterstützer von Start-ups
135	2b	**advisor** [ədˈvaɪzər]	The careers advisor suggested a gap year while I decide what to do.	Berater(in)
	3	**fashionable** [ˈfæʃnəbl]	I'm interested in creating something fashionable from vintage clothing. = trendy	modisch
		patch [pætʃ]	I like those jeans with colouful patches.	Fleck; Flicken
		flea [fliː]	I discovered a stall at the local flea market that sold vintage clothes.	Floh
	4a	**academics** [ˌækəˈdemɪks]	I'm taking a break from academics to travel and get work experience.	Wissenschaft

page	exercise	Workshop 4		
		publisher [ˈpʌblɪʃər]	*I worked in the marketing department of a book publisher.*	Verleger(in); Verlag
	4c	**motivation** [ˌməʊtɪˈveɪʃn]	*What's your motivation for taking a gap year?*	Motivation; Begründung
136	2a	**profession** [prəˈfeʃn]	*We can help you explore career options in the legal profession.* ❗ *Lat. 'professio, -ionis' (f.)*	Profession; Beruf
	3b	**nephew** [ˈnefjuː]	*My uncle has three nephews, two are my cousins.* ❗ *Fr. 'neveu' (m.)*	Neffe
		application [ˌæplɪˈkeɪʃn]	*I hope your application will be successful.*	Bewerbung
	4	**traineeship** [ˌtreɪˈniːʃɪp]	*Traineeships are short programmes for 16 – 23 year olds who haven't got a job or an apprenticeship.*	Praktikumsplatz
		flexible [ˈfleksəbl]	*Traineeships are short, flexible education programmes.*	flexibel
		self-employed [ˌself ɪmˈplɔɪd]	*Being self-employed means you run your own business.*	selbständig
		employee [ɪmˈplɔɪiː]	*New employees are shown around the workplace on the first day.* ❗ *Fr. 'employé' (m.)*	Angestellte(r)
137	2c	**profile** [ˈprəʊfaɪl]	*Write a profile for a job.*	Profil
	T	**tone** [təʊn]	*Pay attention to the speaker's tone of voice.* ❗ *Fr. 'ton' (m.); Sp. 'tono' (m.)*	Ton
		monotone [ˈmɒnətəʊn]	*When you speak in front of people try not to let your voice be monotone.*	monoton
		eyebrow [ˈaɪbraʊ]	*Do his eyes, mouth or eyebrows move a lot when he speaks?*	Augenbraue
		to slump [slʌmp]	*Does he or she sit up with a straight back or slump in the chair?*	abrutschen; zusammensacken
		gesture [ˈdʒestər]	*Does she use hand gestures when she speaks?* ❗ *Fr. 'geste' (m.)*	Geste
138	1a	**lifeguard** [ˈlaɪfgɑːd]	*Holly is starting a job as a lifeguard at the swimming pool.*	Rettungsschwimmer(in)
		hopeless [ˈhəʊpləs]	*It's important not to ever think that a situation is hopeless.*	hoffnungslos
		stable [ˈsteɪbl]	*I work at the stables looking after horses.*	Stall
	2a	**to adore** [əˈdɔː]	*I adore children; I have a young sister and she is so cute.* ≠ *hate* ❗ *Fr. 'adorer'; Sp. 'adorar'*	anbeten; bewundern
		niece [niːs]	*My sister's daughter is my niece.*	Nichte
		to hint [hɪnt]	*A person's hobbies hint at the kind of work the person would like.*	andeuten

page	exercise	**Workshop 4**		
		availability [ə,veɪlə'bɪləti]	*What is your availability next week?*	Verfügbarkeit
	3b	**reference** ['refrəns]	*Could you write me a reference for a job I'm applying for?*	Empfehlung
139		**to assist** [ə'sɪst]	*You will assist with the running of the yard and care of the horses.* = help	unterstützen
		organizational [,ɔ:gənaɪ'zeɪʃənl]	*I have good organizational skills and am never late.*	organisatorisch
		outgoing [,aʊt'gəʊɪŋ]	*I'm outgoing and work well with others.*	kontaktfreudig
		approachable [ə'prəʊtʃəbl]	*I am good with children, outgoing and approachable.*	aufgeschlossen
	4	**necessity** [nə'sesəti]	*Food and water are necessities.* ≠ extra ⚠ Lat. 'necessitas, -atis' (f.)	Notwendigkeit
	5	**to tuck in** [tʌk 'ɪn]	*Make sure your shirt is tucked in.*	einstecken
		clarification [,klærəfɪ'keɪʃn]	*The listeners should ask for repetition and clarification if necessary.*	Abklärung
140	1	**errand** ['erənd]	*After school I run errands for the staff and the residents.*	Besorgung
		caddie ['kædi]	*The local golf club was looking for caddies for the summer months.*	Caddie
		to lift [lɪft]	*They lifted the boat out of the water.* = move upwards ⚠ Fr. 'lever'	heben
		orchard ['ɔ:tʃəd]	*Our neighbour has a huge orchard with apple trees.*	Obstgarten
		picker ['pɪkə]	*I work as a fruit picker every summer.*	Pflücker(in)
	2a	**punctual** ['pʌŋktʃuəl]	*She's always punctual, never late.* = on time ≠ late ⚠ Fr. 'punctuel, punctuelle'	pünktlich
		sensitive ['sensətɪv]	*My father is responsible, sensitive and strong.*	einfühlsam
141	3	**voluntary** ['vɒləntri]	*Certain organizations offer voluntary work to young people.* ⚠ Lat. 'voluntarius, -a, -um'	freiwillig
142	1c	**poll** [pəʊl]	*The poll asked whether young people would consider a gap year.*	Umfrage
		millennial [mɪ'leniəl]	*In a recent poll 21% of millennials said they had changed jobs in the last year.*	Millennium-Generation
		insecure [,ɪnsɪ'kjʊər]	*Freelancers are often in an insecure position, at least in terms of finances.* ≠ secure	unsicher; instabil
		finances ['faɪnænsɪz]	*My mother looks after the family finances.*	Finanzen
		aside [ə'saɪd]	*It is harder to put money aside for those big-ticket items like a car.* = to one side	beiseite

page	exercise	Workshop 4		
		youngster [ˈjʌŋstər]	*Youngsters and teenagers have greater career choices nowadays.*	Jugendliche(r)
		stressful [ˈstresfl]	*I think life wasn't as stressful as it is now.* *≠ relaxing*	stressig
		loyalty [ˈlɔɪəlti]	*One consequence of gig work is that young people feel less loyalty towards their employers.*	Loyalität
		employer [ɪmˈplɔɪə]	*Who's your dad's employer?* *≠ employee* **!** *Fr. 'employeur, employeuse' (m., f.)*	Arbeitgeber(in)
		to quit [kwɪt]	*I should quit and look for another job.* *= to leave* *≠ to join*	kündigen
		uncertainty [ʌnˈsɜːtnti]	*Many young people feel uncertainty about their jobs.*	Unsicherheit
		incentive [ɪnˈsentɪv]	*When people aren't paid well they have little incentive to work harder.*	Anreiz; Antrieb
		transferable [trænsˈfɜːrəbl]	*Transferable skills like problem solving become more important.*	übertragbar
		certainty [ˈsɜːtnti]	*We can't say with certainty what will happen in the future.* **!** *Sp. 'certeza' (f.)*	Gewissheit
143	4b	**to determine** [dɪˈtɜːmɪn]	*Your talent and motivation determine what you can do.* *= decide* **!** *Fr. 'déterminer'*	ausmachen; bestimmen
		analyst [ˈænəlɪst]	*My father works as an analyst who looks at data about climate change.*	Analytiker(in)
		to fail [feɪl]	*Unfortunately, he failed again, but he didn't give up.*	scheitern
		founder [ˈfaʊndə]	*Steve Jobs was one of the founders of a famous computer company.* *= sink*	Gründer(in)
		entrepreneur [ˌɒntrəprəˈnɜːr]	*Are you a young entrepreneur with an outstanding and innovative business?* **!** *Fr. 'entrepreneur' (m.)*	Unternehmer(in)
		motivational [ˌməʊtɪˈveɪʃənl]	*The motivational speaker talked about the importance of self confidence.*	anregend; Motivations...
	5a	**to value** [ˈvæljuː]	*When someone thanks you for your work, you feel valued.*	wertschätzen
		to appreciate [əˈpriːʃieɪt]	*I appreciate your help.* **!** *Fr. 'apprécier'; Sp. 'apreciar'*	anerkennen; schätzen
144	S2	**analysis** [əˈnæləsɪs]	*Write a short description and analysis of the information.*	Analyse; Untersuchung
		sample [ˈsɑːmpl]	*Based on a sample of ten students, only a quarter thinks school lunches are good.*	Stichprobe

page	exercise	**Workshop 4**		
		sentence [ˈsentəns]	*The maximum sentence you can receive for theft is five years in prison.*	Strafe
		to convict [kənˈvɪkt]	*She was convicted for theft.*	verurteilen
		cyberbullying [ˈsaɪbəbʊliŋ]	*Cyberbullying is a serious issue in schools.*	Cyber-Mobbing
146	2a	**unnatural** [ʌnˈnætʃrəl]	*Working too late into the night is tiring and feels unnatural.*	unnatürlich
		to recite [rɪˈsaɪt]	*In English class we picked a poem to recite.*	aufsagen
		obliged: to be obliged (to) [bi ˈɒblɪgeɪtɪd]	*In the UK, you are not obliged to include a photo in your CV.*	müssen; verpflichtet sein
		innovative [ˈɪnəveɪtɪv]	*We are very innovative in our approach.* ⊞ *Sp. 'innovador, innovadora'*	innovativ
	2b	**failure** [ˈfeɪljə]	*Try hard and don't be afraid of failure.*	Misserfolg
		insecurity [ˌɪnsɪˈkjʊərəti]	*Food insecurity causes terrible stress for families.*	Unsicherheit
147	4	**to cater** [ˈkeɪtə]	*We are catering for all age groups.*	sorgen für; bedienen
		dedicated [ˈdedɪkeɪtɪd]	*We are looking for an enthusiastic, dedicated apprentice to join our team.*	engagiert
150	1	**unconventional** [ˌʌnkənˈvenʃənl]	*My family may seem unconventional to other people, but to me it's normal.*	unkonventionell
	2	**constant** [ˈkɒnstənt]	*I don't like websites with constant advertising.*	ständig
		to target [ˈtɑːgɪt]	*Advertising is constantly targeting teenagers.*	ins Visier nehmen; zielen auf
151	4	**to accuse** [əˈkjuːz]	*She was accused of shoplifting and is in court.* ⊞ *Lat. 'accusare (accuso, accusavi, accusatum)'*	beschuldigen; anklagen
		to punch [pʌntʃ]	*She punched her teacher and ran out of the room.*	schlagen
		guard [gɑːd]	*The shop is watched by security guards.* ⊞ *Fr. 'gardien'*	Wächter(in); Sicherheitsbeamte(r)

Dictionary: English – German

A

a lot, lots [lɒt] eine Menge; viel OT 1

abbey [ˈæbi] Abtei; Kloster OT 3

abbreviation [əˌbriːviˈeɪʃn] Abkürzung OT 2

able: be able [bi ˈeɪbl] fähig sein; können OT 2

abolitionist [ˌæbəˈlɪʃənɪst] Abolitionist(in); Sklavereigegner(in) OT 3

aboriginal [ˌæbəˈrɪdʒənl] den Ureinwohnern Australiens zugehörig **WS 1**, 12

about [əˈbaʊt] über; wegen; ungefähr; um ... herum OT 1

above [əˈbʌv] oben; oberhalb OT 2

abroad [əˈbrɔːd] im Ausland OT 2

to abseil [ˈæbseɪl] (sich) abseilen OT 2

absolute [ˈæbsəluːt] absolut **WS 3**, 98

   absolutely [ˈæbsəluːtli] absolut; wirklich OT 2

academics [ˌækəˈdemɪks] Wissenschaft **WS 4**, 135

accent [ˈæksənt] Akzent **WS 1**, 21

acceptance [əkˈseptəns] Akzeptanz **WS 1**, 33

access [ˈækses] Zugang OT 2

accessible [əkˈsesəbl] zugänglich; barrierefrei OT 2

accessory [əkˈsesəri] Zubehör OT 3

accident [ˈæksɪdənt] Unfall; Missgeschick OT 1

   Accident and Emergency [ˈæksɪdənt ənd ɪˌmɜːdʒənsi] Notaufnahme OT 1

   by accident [baɪ ˈæksɪdənt] versehentlich OT 2

accommodation [əˌkɒməˈdeɪʃn] Unterkunft OT 3

accompanied [əˈkʌmpəniːd] in Begleitung OT 3

to accompany [əˈkʌmpəni] begleiten OT 3

according to [əˈkɔːdɪŋ tə] laut **WS 1**, 26

accordion [əˈkɔːdiən] Akkordeon OT 2

account [əˈkaʊnt] Konto OT 3

to account for [əˈkaʊnt fə] ausmachen **WS 4**, 128

accurate [ˈækjərət] genau; präzise **WS 3**, 96

to accuse [əˈkjuːz] beschuldigen; anklagen **WS 4**, 151

ace [eɪs] klasse **WS 1**, 16

to achieve [əˈtʃiːv] erreichen; schaffen **WS 1**, 25

acidic [əˈsɪdɪk] sauer **WS 1**, 28

to acknowledge [əkˈnɒlɪdʒ] bestätigen; anerkennen **WS 2**, 75

acoustic [əˈkuːstɪk] akustisch OT 2

across [əˈkrɒs] auf der anderen Seite; hinüber OT 1

act [ækt] Gesetz; Handlung **WS 1**, 43

to act [ækt] sich verhalten; handeln; Theater spielen OT 1

   to act out [ækt aʊt] ausspielen OT 2

action [ˈækʃn] Aktion OT 2

   in action [ɪn ˈækʃn] im Einsatz OT 2

activity [ækˈtɪvəti] Aktivität; Beschäftigung OT 1

actor [ˈæktə] Schauspieler(in) OT 1

actual [ˈæktʃuəl] richtig; wirklich **WS 3**, 98

   actually [ˈæktʃuəli] eigentlich; um genau zu sein OT 3

to add [æd] hinzufügen; addieren OT 1

addition [əˈdɪʃn] Zusatz; Ergänzung **WS 2**, 56

additional [əˈdɪʃənl] zusätzlich; ergänzend **WS 4**, 127

address [əˈdres] Adresse; Anschrift OT 1

adjective [ˈædʒɪktɪv] Adjektiv OT 2

administrative [ədˈmɪnɪstrətɪv] administrativ; verwaltend **WS 3**, 110

to admire [ədˈmaɪə] bewundern **WS 3**, 98

admission [ədˈmɪʃn] Eintritt OT 2

to admit [ədˈmɪt] zugeben OT 2

to adore [əˈdɔː] anbeten; bewundern **WS 4**, 138

adult [ˈædʌlt] Erwachsene(r) OT 1

advanced [ədˈvɑːnst] fortgeschritten OT 3

advent [ˈædvent] Beginn; Einführung **WS 1**, 25

adventure [ədˈventʃə] Abenteuer OT 1

adventurer [ədˈventʃərə] Abenteurer(in) OT 3

adventurous [ədˈventʃərəs] abenteuerlustig OT 2

to advertise [ˈædvətaɪz] Werbung machen für OT 2

advertisement [ədˈvɜːtɪsmənt] Werbung; Reklame OT 1

advice [ədˈvaɪs] Rat OT 2

to advise [ədˈvaɪz] raten OT 3

advisor [ədˈvaɪzər] Berater(in) **WS 4**, 135

advocate [ˈædvəkət] Fürsprecher(in) **WS 2**, 71

aerospace [ˈeərəʊspeɪs] Luftfahrt **WS 3**, 108

affair [əˈfeə] Angelegenheit; Affäre **WS 3**, 86

to affect [əˈfekt] sich auswirken auf OT 3

to afford [əˈfɔːd] sich leisten OT 2

afraid [əˈfreɪd] ängstlich OT 2

African [ˈæfrɪkən] afrikanisch OT 2

after [ˈɑːftə] nach; hinter OT 1

afternoon [ˌɑːftəˈnuːn] Nachmittag OT 1

afterwards [ˈɑːftəwədz] danach **WS 3**, 88

again [əˈgen] wieder; gleich wieder OT 1

against [əˈgenst] gegen; gegenüber OT 1

age [eɪdʒ] Alter; Zeitalter OT 1

agency [ˈeɪdʒənsi] Agentur; Organisation **WS 1**, 22

agenda [əˈdʒendə] Tagesordnung OT 3

agent [ˈeɪdʒənt] Handlungsträger(in); Handelnde(r) **WS 1**, 27

agile [ˈædʒaɪl] beweglich OT 3

agrarian [əˈgreəriən] agrarisch **WS 1**, 24

to agree [əˈgriː] sich einig sein; Ja sagen; zustimmen OT 1

agreement [əˈgriːmənt] Vereinbarung OT 3

ahead [əˈhed] weiter vorn OT 2

aid [eɪd] Hilfe; Unterstützung **WS 2**, 59

aim [eɪm] Ziel OT 2

to aim [eɪm] zielen **WS 4**, 128

aimlessly [ˈeɪmləsli] ziellos **WS 4**, 125

air [eə] Luft OT 2

airport [ˈeəpɔːt] Flughafen OT 1

alarm [əˈlɑːm] Wecker; Alarm OT 2

album [ˈælbəm] Album OT 3

alcohol [ˈælkəhɒl] Alkohol OT 3

to alert [əˈlɜːt] alarmieren OT 2

alien [ˈeɪliən] Außerirdische(r); Alien OT 2

alive [əˈlaɪv] lebendig OT 2

all [ɔːl] alles; alle OT 1

allergic [əˈlɜːdʒɪk] allergisch **WS 2**, 64

to allocate [ˈæləkeɪt] zuordnen; zuweisen **WS 3**, 91

to allow [əˈlaʊ] erlauben OT 3

   be allowed to [əˈlaʊd] erlaubt OT 2

alone [əˈləʊn] allein OT 2

along [əˈlɒŋ] entlang; dahin OT 2

alongside [əˌlɒŋ'saɪd] daneben **WS 3**, 100

alpaca [æl'pækə] Alpaka OT 2

alphabet ['ælfəbet] Alphabet OT 1

alphabetical [ˌælfə'betɪkl] alphabetisch OT 2

already [ɔːl'redi] schon OT 2

alternative [ɔːl'tɜːnətɪv] alternativ **WS 1**, 27

although [ɔːl'ðəʊ] obwohl **WS 1**, 21

always ['ɔːlweɪz] immer; immer noch OT 1

amazed [ə'meɪzd] erstaunt; überrascht OT 3

amazing [ə'meɪzɪŋ] erstaunlich; unglaublich OT 1

ambitious [æm'bɪʃəs] ehrgeizig OT 3

ambulance ['æmbjələns] Krankenwagen OT 1

amendment [ə'mendmənt] Ergänzung **WS 3**, 90

amenity [ə'miːnəti] Einrichtung **WS 3**, 88

amount [ə'maʊnt] Betrag OT 2

to **amount to** [ə'maʊnt tə] betragen; ausmachen **WS 3**, 110

to **analyse** ['ænəlaɪz] analysieren OT 3

analysis [ə'næləsɪs] Analyse; Untersuchung **WS 4**, 144

analyst ['ænəlɪst] Analytiker(in) **WS 4**, 143

ancestor ['ænsestə] Vorfahr(in) OT 3

ancestral [æn'sestrəl] zur Familie gehörend; den Vorfahren gehörend **WS 3**, 106

to **anchor** ['æŋkəd] ankern OT 3

ancient ['eɪnʃənt] antik OT 2

and [ənd] und OT 1

anecdote ['ænɪkdəʊt] Anekdote **WS 1**, 29

to **anger** ['æŋgə] wütend machen OT 3

angry ['æŋgri] böse; wütend OT 1

animal ['ænɪml] Tier OT 1

animated ['ænɪmeɪtɪd] animiert **WS 2**, 53

ankle ['æŋkl] Knöchel; Fußknöchel OT 1

to **announce** [ə'naʊns] ansagen; bekannt geben OT 2

announcement [ə'naʊnsmənt] Bekanntgabe; Ansage OT 2

announcer [ə'naʊnsə] Ansager(in) OT 2

to **annoy** [ə'nɔɪ] ärgern; aufregen **WS 2**, 66

annoying [ə'nɔɪɪŋ] ärgerlich OT 2

annual ['ænjuəl] jährlich OT 3

another [ə'nʌðə] noch ein(e); noch eine(r, -s); ein(e) andere(r, -s) OT 1

answer ['aːnsə] Antwort; Lösung OT 1

anthem ['ænθəm] Hymne OT 3

antibiotic [ˌæntibaɪ'ɒtɪk] Antibiotikum **WS 2**, 69

anxiety [æŋ'zaɪəti] Sorge; Ängstlichkeit **WS 1**, 34

anxious ['æŋkʃəs] besorgt; ängstlich **WS 3**, 114

any ['eni] irgendein(e) OT 1

anybody ['enibɒdi] irgendjemand; jede(r, -s) OT 1

anymore: not anymore [ˌeni'mɔː] nicht mehr OT 3

anything ['eniθɪŋ] irgendetwas; alles OT 1

anytime ['enitaɪm] jederzeit OT 3

anyway ['eniweɪ] trotzdem; sowieso OT 1

apart [ə'paːt] auseinander **WW**, 11

to **apologize** [ə'pɒlədʒaɪz] sich entschuldigen OT 2

apology [ə'pɒlədʒi] Entschuldigung OT 3

apostrophe [ə'pɒstrəfi] Apostroph OT 3

app [æp] App OT 3

apparent [ə'pærənt] erkennbar; sichtbar OT 3

apparently [ə'pærəntli] anscheinend OT 3

appeal [ə'piːl] Aufruf OT 2

to **appear** [ə'pɪə] erscheinen OT 2

appearance [ə'pɪərəns] Aussehen OT 2

to **applaud** [ə'plɔːd] applaudieren OT 2

applause [ə'plɔːz] Applaus OT 2

apple ['æpl] Apfel OT 1

appliance [ə'plaɪəns] Gerät OT 3

application [ˌæplɪ'keɪʃn] Bewerbung **WS 4**, 136

to **apply** [ə'plaɪ] sich bewerben **WS 1**, 37

to **appoint** [ə'pɔɪnt] ernennen **WS 3**, 91

appointment [ə'pɔɪntmənt] Termin OT 3

to **appreciate** [ə'priːʃieɪt] schätzen; würdigen OT 2

apprentice [ə'prentɪs] Auszubildende(r); Lehrling **WS 4**, 134

apprenticeship [ə'prentɪʃɪp] Lehrstelle; Ausbildung **WS 4**, 134

approachable [ə'prəʊtʃəbl] aufgeschlossen **WS 4**, 139

appropriate [ə'prəʊpriət] angemessen **WS 1**, 28

to **approve** [ə'pruːv] zustimmen; genehmigen **WS 3**, 91

approximately [ə'prɒksɪmətli] ungefähr; etwa **WW**, 10

aquarium [ə'kweəriəm] Aquarium OT 2

aqueduct ['ækwɪdʌkt] Aquädukt OT 3

archaeological [ˌɑːkiə'lɒdʒɪkl] archäologisch OT 2

archaeologist [ˌɑːki'ɒlədʒɪst] Archäologe; Archäologin OT 2

archeology [ˌɑːki'ɒlədʒi] Archäologie OT 3

architect ['ɑːkɪtekt] Architekt(in) **WS 2**, 48

architecture ['ɑːkɪtektʃə] Architektur OT 3

archive ['ɑːkaɪv] Archiv **WS 2**, 66

arctic ['ɑːktɪk] arktisch; Arktis OT 3

area ['eəriə] Gebiet; Gegend OT 1

arena [ə'riːnə] Arena; Bühne OT 1

to **argue** ['ɑːgjuː] sich streiten OT 3

argument ['ɑːgjumənt] Streit; Auseinandersetzung OT 1

arm [ɑːm] Arm; Ärmel OT 1

armchair ['ɑːmtʃeə] Sessel OT 1

armed forces [ˌɑːmd 'fɔːsɪz] Streitkräfte **WS 3**, 92

army ['ɑːmi] Armee OT 2

around [ə'raʊnd] um; um ... herum OT 1

arrangement [ə'reɪndʒmənt] Vereinbarung **WS 4**, 123

arrival [ə'raɪvl] Ankunft OT 2

to **arrive** [ə'raɪv] ankommen; kommen OT 1

arrow ['ærəʊ] Pfeil OT 3

art [ɑːt] Kunst OT 1

artefact ['ɑːtɪfækt] Artefakt OT 2

article ['ɑːtɪkl] Artikel; Gegenstand; Geschlechtswort OT 1

artificial [ˌɑːtɪ'fɪʃl] künstlich OT 3

artist ['ɑːtɪst] Künstler(in); Könner OT 1

as [æz] als; wie OT 1

asexual [ˌeɪ'sekʃuəl] asexuell **WS 4**, 125

ash [æʃ] Asche OT 2

ashamed [ə'ʃeɪmd] beschämt OT 3

ashore [ə'ʃɔː] an Land OT 3

aside [ə'saɪd] beiseite **WS 4**, 142

to **ask** [ɑːsk] fragen; bitten OT 1

asleep [ə'sliːp] schlafend OT 2

aspect ['æspekt] Aspekt OT 3

assembly [ə'sembli] Versammlung; morgendliche Schulversammlung OT 1

assembly hall [ə'sembli hɔːl] Aula OT 1

to **assess** [ə'ses] beurteilen OT 3

assimilation [əˌsɪmə'leɪʃn] Assimilation; Anpassung OT 3

to **assist** [ə'sɪst] unterstützen **WS 4**, 139

assistance [əˈsɪstəns] Unterstützung **WS 4**, 127

astonishingly [əˈstɒnɪʃɪŋli] erstaunlicherweise OT 3

at [ət] an; in; bei OT 1

athletics [æθˈletɪks] Leichtathletik; Sport OT 1

atmosphere [ˈætməsfɪə] Atmosphäre OT 3

to **attach** [əˈtætʃ] befestigen OT 3

attack [əˈtæk] Angriff OT 2

attainment [əˈteɪnmənt] Leistungen **WS 4**, 128

attempt [əˈtempt] Versuch OT 2

attendant [əˈtendənt] Aufseher(in); Diener(in) OT 2

attention [əˈtenʃn] Aufmerksamkeit OT 2

to **pay attention** [ˌpeɪ əˈtenʃn] aufpassen OT 2

attic [ˈætɪk] Dachboden OT 2

attitude [ˈætɪtjuːd] Ansicht; Einstellung **WS 2**, 65

attractive [əˈtræktɪv] reizvoll **WS 1**, 32

audience [ˈɔːdiəns] Publikum; Zuschauer OT 1

audio [ˈɔːdiəʊ] Audio... OT 2

August [ɔːˈɡʌst] August OT 1

aunt [ɑːnt] Tante OT 1

auntie [ˈɑːnti] Tantchen OT 2

authentic [ɔːˈθentɪk] authentisch; echt OT 3

author [ˈɔːθə] Autor(in) OT 2

authority [ɔːˈθɒrəti] Autorität; Behörde OT 3

to **authorize** [ˈɔːθəraɪz] genehmigen; autorisieren **WS 3**, 110

autism [ˈɔːtɪzəm] Autismus **WS 4**, 127

autumn [ˈɔːtəm] Herbst OT 2

availability [əˌveɪləˈbɪləti] Verfügbarkeit **WS 4**, 138

available [əˈveɪləbl] verfügbar; erhältlich **WS 2**, 54

avatar [ˈævətɑː] Avatar OT 3

average [ˈævərɪdʒ] durchschnittlich **WS 1**, 21

avocado [ˌævəˈkɑːdəʊ] Avocado **WS 1**, 34

to **avoid** [əˈvɔɪd] vermeiden OT 3

awake [əˈweɪk] wach OT 2

award [əˈwɔːd] Auszeichnung OT 2

aware [əˈweə] bewusst **WS 2**, 64

away [əˈweɪ] weg OT 2

B

baby [ˈbeɪbi] Säugling; Baby OT 1

back [bæk] zurück OT 1

back [bæk] Rücken OT 1

backbone [ˈbækbəʊn] Rückgrat OT 2

backcountry [ˈbækkʌntri] Hinterland OT 3

background [ˈbækɡraʊnd] Hintergrund... OT 3

to **backpack** [ˈbækpæk] mit dem Rucksack reisen OT 3

bacon [ˈbeɪkən] Speck OT 1

bacteria [bækˈtɪəriə] Bakterie **WS 2**, 69

bad [bæd] schlecht; ungünstig OT 1

badge [bædʒ] Abzeichen; Plakette **WS 4**, 130

badminton [ˈbædmɪntən] Badminton; Federball OT 1

bag [bæɡ] Tüte; Beutel OT 1

to **bake** [beɪk] backen OT 1

baked beans [ˌbeɪkt ˈbiːns] weiße Bohnen in Tomatensoße OT 1

bakery [ˈbeɪkəri] Bäckerei OT 3

balance [ˈbæləns] Balance OT 3

to **balance** [ˈbæləns] ausgleichen **WS 1**, 13

balcony [ˈbælkəni] Balkon **WS 3**, 110

bald [bɔːld] kahl OT 3

ball [bɔːl] Ball; Kugel OT 1

to **ban** [bæn] verbieten OT 3

banana [bəˈnɑːnə] Banane OT 1

band [bænd] Band; Musikkapelle OT 1

bandage [ˈbændɪdʒ] Verband OT 2

bank [bæŋk] Ufer; Bank OT 3

banner [ˈbænə] Transparent **WS 2**, 66

bar [bɑː] Bar; Lokal; Riegel OT 1

bar chart [ˈbɑː tʃɑːt] Balkendiagramm **WS 4**, 144

barbecue [ˈbɑːbɪkjuː] Grillen OT 2

to **bark** [bɑːk] bellen OT 2

barn [bɑːn] Scheune OT 2

barrier [ˈbæriə] Barriere OT 3

base [beɪs] Fuß; Basis **WS 1**, 27

baseball [ˈbeɪsbɔːl] Baseball OT 1

based (on) [beɪst] basierend (auf) OT 3

basic [ˈbeɪsɪk] Grund-; grundsätzlich; einfach **WS 2**, 61

basically [ˈbeɪsɪkli] im Grunde OT 3

basics [ˈbeɪsɪks] Grundlagen OT 2

basin [ˈbeɪsn] Becken OT 3

basis [ˈbeɪsɪs] Grundlage; Basis **WS 2**, 49

basket [ˈbɑːskɪt] Korb OT 3

basketball [ˈbɑːskɪtbɔːl] Basketball OT 3

bass [beɪs] Bass OT 2

double bass [ˌdʌbl ˈbeɪs] Kontrabass OT 2

bat [bæt] Fledermaus; Schläger (Sport) OT 1

bath [bɑːθ] Badewanne; Bad OT 1

bathhouse [ˈbɑːθhaʊs] Badehaus OT 2

bathroom [ˈbɑːθruːm] Badezimmer; Toilette OT 1

battery [ˈbætri] Batterie OT 2

battle [ˈbætl] Schlacht OT 3

bay [beɪ] Bucht OT 2

to **be** [biː] sein OT 1

to **be into** [biː ˈɪntʌ] auf etwas stehen OT 2

beach [biːtʃ] Strand OT 1

bean [biːn] Bohne OT 1

bear [beə] Bär OT 1

beard [bɪəd] Bart OT 1

beat [biːt] Schlag; Takt OT 3

to **beat** [biːt] schlagen; übertreffen **WS 1**, 14

beauty [ˈbjuːti] Schönheit OT 3

because [bɪˈkɒz] weil OT 1

to **become** [bɪˈkʌm] werden OT 2

bed [bed] Bett; Grund; Beet OT 1

bedroom [ˈbedruːm] Schlafzimmer OT 1

bedtime [ˈbedtaɪm] Schlafenszeit OT 2

bee [biː] Biene OT 1

beef [biːf] Rindfleisch OT 2

beer [bɪə] Bier OT 1

before [bɪˈfɔː] vor OT 1

to **behave** [bɪˈheɪv] sich benehmen OT 2

behaviour [bɪˈheɪvjə] Benehmen OT 2

to **behead** [bɪˈhed] köpfen OT 3

behind [bɪˈhaɪnd] hinter; hinterher OT 1

being [ˈbiːɪŋ] Wesen OT 3

belief [bɪˈliːf] Glaube OT 3

to **believe** [bɪˈliːv] glauben OT 2

bell [bel] Glocke; Klingel OT 1

to **belong** [bɪˈlɒŋ] gehören OT 2

belongings [bɪˈlɒŋɪŋz] persönliche Gegenstände OT 3

beneficial [ˌbeniˈfɪʃl] vorteilhaft OT 2

benefit [ˈbenɪfɪt] Vorteil **WS 1**, 24

to **benefit** [ˈbenɪfɪt] profitieren **WS 3**, 103

berth [bɜːθ] Koje OT 3

best [best] beste(r,-s) OT 1

to **bet** [bet] wetten OT 1

better [ˈbetə] besser OT 1

between [bɪˈtwiːn] zwischen; unter OT 1

to **beware** [bɪˈweə] vorsichtig sein OT 2

beyond [bɪˈjɒnd] dahinter OT 3

bias [ˈbaɪəs] Voreingenommenheit **WS 4**, 124

biased [ˈbaɪəst] parteiisch **WS 2**, 70

bike [baɪk] Fahrrad; Motorrad OT 1

to **bike** [ˈbaɪk] Rad fahren OT 3

bilingual [ˌbaɪˈlɪŋɡwəl] zweisprachig OT 3

bill [bɪl] Gesetz; Rechnung OT 3

billiard ball [ˈbɪliəd] Billardkugel **WS 3**, 95

billion [ˈbɪljən] Milliarde **WS 2**, 66

bin [bɪn] Tonne OT 3

binoculars [bɪˈnɒkjələz] Fernglas OT 2

biodegradable [ˌbaɪəʊdɪˈɡreɪdəbl] biologisch abbaubar **WS 3**, 95

biofuel [ˈbaɪəʊfjuːəl] Biokraftstoff OT 3

biographer [baɪˈɒɡrəfə] Biograf(in) OT 3

biography [baɪˈɒɡrəfi] Biografie OT 3

biological [ˌbaɪəˈlɒdʒɪkl] biologisch **WS 1**, 32

biology [baɪˈɒlədʒi] Biologie OT 1

bird [bɜːd] Vogel OT 1

birth [bɜːθ] Geburt OT 2

  date of birth [ˌdeɪt əv ˈbɜːθ] Geburtsdatum OT 2

birthday [ˈbɜːθdeɪ] Geburtstag OT 1

birthplace [ˈbɜːθpleɪs] Geburtsort OT 2

biscuit [ˈbɪskɪt] Keks; Plätzchen OT 1

bisexual [ˌbaɪˈsekʃuəl] bisexuell **WS 4**, 121

bison [ˈbaɪsn] Bison OT 3

bit [bɪt] Stück OT 2

  a bit [bɪt] ein bisschen OT 1

bite [baɪt] Biss OT 2

bitterly [ˈbɪtəli] bitterlich **WS 1**, 26

bittersweet [ˌbɪtəˈswiːt] herb; halbbitter OT 3

black [blæk] schwarz OT 1

blackberry [ˈblækbəri] Brombeere OT 1

blackbird [ˈblækbɜːd] Amsel OT 1

blackboard [ˈblækbɔːd] Tafel OT 1

blank [blæŋk] leer **WS 2**, 61

blast [blɑːst] Tuten OT 3

blazer [ˈbleɪzə] Blazer; leichte Sportjacke **WS 4**, 130

bleak [bliːk] düster **WS 3**, 106

block [blɒk] Block OT 3

to block [blɒk] blockieren **WS 2**, 67

blocker [ˈblɒkər] Blocker **WS 4**, 125

blog [blɒɡ] Blog OT 1

to blog [ˈblɒɡ] bloggen; einen Blog schreiben OT 3

blogger [ˈblɒɡə] Blogger(in) OT 3

blonde [blɒnd] blond OT 1

blood [blʌd] Blut OT 2

bloodshed [ˈblʌdʃed] Blutvergießen **WS 1**, 26

to blow [bləʊ] blasen; pfeifen; wehen OT 2

blubber [ˈblʌbə] Walspeck OT 2

blues [bluːz] Blues OT 3

board [bɔːd] Tafel; Bord OT 2

boarding pass [ˈbɔːdɪŋ pɑːs] Bordkarte OT 2

boat [bəʊt] Boot; Schiff OT 1

boater [ˈbəʊtə] Bootsfahrer(in) OT 3

boating [ˈbəʊtɪŋ] Bootfahren OT 3

body [ˈbɒdi] Körper; Rumpf OT 1

bold [bəʊld] mutig; kühn; fettgedruckt OT 1

bone [bəʊn] Knochen; Gräte OT 1

book [bʊk] Buch; Heft OT 1

bookcase [ˈbʊkkeɪs] Bücherregal; Bücherschrank OT 1

booking [ˈbʊkɪŋ] Buchung OT 2

to bookmark [ˈbʊkmɑːk] markieren **WS 1**, 36

boot [buːt] Stiefel; Kofferraum OT 1

bored [bɔːd] gelangweilt OT 1

boring [ˈbɔːrɪŋ] langweilig OT 1

born: to be born [bi bɔːn] geboren sein OT 2

to borrow [ˈbɒrəʊ] (aus)leihen OT 2

boss [bɒs] Chef(in) OT 2

both [bəʊθ] beide OT 1

to bother [ˈbɒðə] stören OT 3

bottle [ˈbɒtl] Flasche OT 1

bottom [ˈbɒtəm] Boden; Fuß; unterster Teil OT 1

boundary [ˈbaʊndri] Grenze **WS 2**, 48

bow [bəʊ] Bogen OT 2

bowl [bəʊl] Schüssel; Schale OT 1

box [bɒks] Kiste; Karton OT 1

boy [bɔɪ] Junge OT 1

boyband [ˈbɔɪbænd] Boygroup OT 2

bracket [ˈbrækɪt] Klammer OT 2

brain [breɪn] Gehirn OT 2

to brainstorm [ˈbreɪnstɔːm] brainstormen OT 2

branch [brɑːntʃ] Ast OT 2

brand [brænd] Marke **WS 2**, 62

  brand new [ˌbrænd ˈnjuː] brandneu OT 2

brave [breɪv] tapfer; mutig OT 1

bravery [ˈbreɪvəri] Mut OT 2

bread [bred] Brot OT 1

bread roll [ˌbred ˈrəʊl] Brötchen OT 1

break [breɪk] Pause; Urlaub OT 1

to break [breɪk] brechen; zerbrechen OT 1

breakfast [ˈbrekfəst] Frühstück OT 1

breakthrough [ˈbreɪkθruː] Durchbruch **WS 4**, 127

breath [breθ] Atem(zug) OT 2

to breathe [briːð] atmen OT 2

breathless [ˈbreθləs] atemlos OT 3

breeches [ˈbrɪtʃɪz] Kniehose OT 3

breeze [briːz] Brise OT 3

bridge [brɪdʒ] Brücke OT 1

briefly [ˈbriːfli] kurz **WS 3**, 98

bright [braɪt] leuchtend; glänzend OT 1

brilliant [ˈbrɪliənt] genial; großartig OT 1

to bring [brɪŋ] bringen OT 1

British [ˈbrɪtɪʃ] britisch OT 1

broad [brɔːd] breit; weit OT 3

broccoli [ˈbrɒkəli] Brokkoli OT 1

brochure [ˈbrəʊʃə] Broschüre; Prospekt OT 1

broken [ˈbrəʊkən] gebrochen OT 1

brother [ˈbrʌðə] Bruder OT 1

brown [braʊn] braun OT 1

to browse [ˈbraʊz] das Internet durchsuchen OT 3

brush [brʌʃ] Bürste; Pinsel OT 2

bubble [ˈbʌbl] Blase OT 2

buddy [ˈbʌdi] Kumpel OT 2

to budget [ˈbʌdʒɪt] einplanen OT 3

budgie [ˈbʌdʒi] Wellensittich OT 1

buffalo [ˈbʌfələʊ] Büffel OT 3

buffet [ˈbʊfeɪ] Buffet **WS 2**, 61

to build [bɪld] bauen; aufbauen OT 1

building [ˈbɪldɪŋ] Gebäude; Bau OT 1

to bulk up [bʌlk] Masse zusetzen; hier: Muskeln aufbauen **WS 2**, 68

bullet [ˈbʊlɪt] Kugel OT 2

to bully [ˈbʊli] mobben **WS 4**, 120

to bump into [bʌmp ˈɪntə] anstoßen OT 2

bumpy [ˈbʌmpi] holperig; uneben OT 3

bundle [ˈbʌndl] Bündel OT 2

bunk bed [ˈbʌŋk bed] Stockbett OT 3

burger [ˈbɜːɡə] Hamburger OT 1

to burn [bɜːn] brennen **WS 1**, 28

to bury [ˈberi] beerdigen **WS 2**, 59

bus [bʌs] Bus OT 1

bush [bʊʃ] Busch **WS 1**, 13

bushfire [ˈbʊʃfaɪə] Buschfeuer **WS 1**, 28

bushland [ˈbʊʃlænd] Buschland **WS 1**, 28

business [ˈbɪznəs] Geschäft(e) OT 3

busker [ˈbʌskə] Straßenmusiker(in) **WS 1**, 29

busload [ˈbʌsləʊd] Busladung **WS 1**, 27

busted [ˈbʌstɪd] kaputt OT 3

busy [ˈbɪzi] beschäftigt; belebt OT 1

butter [ˈbʌtə] Butter OT 1

button [ˈbʌtn] Knopf; Taste OT 1

to buy [baɪ] kaufen; glauben OT 1

buzzard [ˈbʌzəd] Bussard OT 2

bye [baɪ] Tschüss! OT 1

C

cab [kæb] Taxi; Fahrerkabine OT 1

cabbage [ˈkæbɪdʒ] Kohl OT 1

cabin [ˈkæbɪn] Kabine OT 2

cabinet [ˈkæbɪnət] Schrank; Kabinett **WS 3**, 92

cable [ˈkeɪbl] Kabel OT 3

cactus ['kæktəs] Kaktus **WS 1**, 21

caddie ['kædi] Caddie **WS 4**, 140

café ['kæfeɪ] Café OT 1

cafeteria [ˌkæfə'tɪəriə] Cafeteria OT 2

caffeine ['kæfi:n] Koffein **WS 2**, 68

cake [keɪk] Kuchen; Torte OT 1

calendar ['kælɪndə] Kalender OT 1

call [teɪk ə kɔ:l] Anruf OT 2

    to **take a call** [teɪk ə kɔ:l] einen Anruf entgegennehmen OT 2

to **call** [kɔ:l] anrufen; nennen OT 1

called [kɔ:ld] namens; mit dem Namen OT 1

caller ['kɔ:lə] Anrufer(in) OT 2

to **calm down** [ka:m daʊn] beruhigen OT 2

calorie ['kæləri] Kalorie **WS 2**, 68

camel ['kæml] Kamel **WS 1**, 25

camera ['kæmərə] Fotoapparat; Kamera OT 1

camp [kæmp] Camp; Lager; Ferienlager OT 1

to **camp** [kæmp] zelten; campen OT 1

campaign [kæm'peɪn] Kampagne OT 2

camper ['kæmpə] Camper(in) OT 2

campfire ['kæmpfaɪə] Lagerfeuer OT 2

campground ['kæmpgraʊnd] Zeltplatz OT 2

campsite ['kæmpsaɪt] Zeltplatz; Campingplatz OT 2

campus ['kæmpəs] Campus OT 2

can [kæn] Dose OT 2

can [kæn] können; dürfen OT 1

canal [kə'næl] Kanal OT 3

canary [kə'neəri] Kanarienvogel OT 2

cancer ['kænsə] Krebs **WS 2**, 69

candidate ['kændɪdət] Kandidat(in) OT 2

candle ['kændl] Kerze OT 2

canned [kænd] Dosen... OT 2

cannon ['kænən] Kanone OT 3

canoe [kə'nu:] Kanu OT 2

canoeing [kə'nu:ɪŋ] Kanufahren OT 2

canteen [kæn'ti:n] Kantine OT 1

canvas ['kænvəs] Leinen OT 3

canyon ['kænjən] Schlucht; Canyon OT 3

cap [kæp] Mütze; Kappe OT 1

capable ['keɪpəbl] fähig **WS 2**, 55

capacity [kə'pæsəti] Fähigkeit **WS 2**, 70

capital ['kæpɪtl] Hauptstadt OT 1

captain ['kæptɪn] Kapitän(in) OT 3

caption ['kæpʃn] Bildunterschrift; Bildtext OT 2

to **capture** ['kæptʃə] einfangen; festnehmen **WS 1**, 39

car [ka:] Auto; Wagen OT 1

caravan ['kærəvæn] Wohnwagen OT 1

carbohydrate [ˌka:bəʊ'haɪdreɪt] Kohlenhydrat **WS 2**, 68

carbon ['ka:bən] Karbon OT 3

carbon dioxide [ˌka:bən daɪ'ɒksaɪd] Kohlendioxid OT 3

card [ka:d] Karte; Karton OT 1

care [keə] Betreuung; Sorge OT 2

to **care** [keə] besorgt sein OT 2

    I don't care! [aɪ dəʊnt keə] Das ist mir egal! OT 2

career [kə'rɪə] Karriere OT 3

careful ['keəfl] vorsichtig; sorgfältig OT 1

careless ['keələs] sorglos OT 2

carer ['keərə] Betreuer(in) **WS 4**, 124

caretaker ['keəteɪkə] Hausmeister(in) OT 1

caribou ['kærɪbu:] Karibu OT 3

carnival ['ka:nɪvl] Karneval **WS 2**, 49

car park ['ka: pa:k] Parkplatz OT 2

carpenter ['ka:pəntə] Zimmermann; Tischler(in) OT 3

carriage ['kærɪdʒ] Wagen; Beförderung OT 2

carrot ['kærət] Karotte; Möhre OT 1

cartoon [ka:'tu:n] Cartoon **WS 1**, 24

to **carve** [ka:v] schnitzen OT 2

carver [ka:v] Schnitzer(in) OT 3

carving ['ka:vɪŋ] Schnitzerei OT 3

case [keɪs] Koffer; Aktentasche; Tasche; Fall OT 1

cash [kæʃ] Kleingeld; Bargeld OT 1

to **cast** [ka:st] hier: abgeben **WS 3**, 91

castle ['ka:sl] Burg; Schloss OT 1

casual ['kæʒuəl] locker; lässig **WS 2**, 66

cat [kæt] Katze OT 1

to **catalogue** ['kætəlɒg] katalogisieren; erfassen OT 3

to **catch** [kætʃ] fangen; nehmen OT 1

category ['kætəgəri] Kategorie OT 3

to **cater** ['keɪtə] sorgen für; bedienen **WS 4**, 147

cathedral [kə'θi:drəl] Kathedrale; Dom OT 1

cattle ['kætl] Rinder **WS 2**, 69

caucus ['kɔ:kəs] Vorwahl OT 2

to **cause** [kɔ:z] verursachen OT 2

cautious [kɔ:ʃəs] vorsichtig OT 3

cave [keɪv] Höhle OT 3

ceiling ['si:lɪŋ] Decke OT 2

to **celebrate** ['selɪbreɪt] feiern OT 3

celebrity [sə'lebrəti] Prominente **WS 2**, 68

cellar ['selər] Keller **WS 3**, 98

cello ['tʃeləʊ] Cello OT 1

cell phone ['sel fəʊn] Handy **WS 3**, 87

census ['sensəs] Zensus; Volkszählung **WS 4**, 122

centimetre ['sentɪmi:tə] Zentimeter OT 2

central ['sentrəl] Zentral- OT 1

central heating [ˌsentrəl 'hi:tɪŋ] Zentralheizung OT 2

centre ['sentə] Mitte; Stadtmitte OT 1

century ['sentʃəri] Jahrhundert OT 2

cereal ['sɪəriəl] Cornflakes; Müsli; Frühstücksflocken OT 1

cerebral palsy [sə'ri:brəl 'pɔ:lzi] zerebrale Kinderlähmung **WS 4**, 127

ceremonial [ˌserɪ'məʊniəl] zeremoniell; feierlich OT 3

certainty ['sɜ:tnti] Gewissheit **WS 4**, 142

certificate [sə'tɪfɪkət] Zeugnis; Zertifikat OT 2

chain [tʃeɪn] Kette OT 3

chair [tʃeə] Stuhl; Vorsitz OT 1

chairlift ['tʃeəlɪft] Sessellift **WS 1**, 31

challenge ['tʃælɪndʒ] Herausforderung OT 3

to **challenge** ['tʃælɪndʒ] herausfordern **WS 4**, 124

chamber ['tʃeɪmbə] Kammer OT 2

champion ['tʃæmpiən] Champion OT 3

championship ['tʃæmpiənʃɪp] Meisterschaft OT 3

chance [tʃa:ns] Zufall; Möglichkeit OT 2

    by chance [baɪ 'tʃa:ns] zufällig OT 2

change [tʃeɪndʒ] Wechselgeld OT 1

to **change** [tʃeɪndʒ] ändern; sich verändern; wechseln OT 1

chapter ['tʃæptə] Kapitel OT 1

character ['kærəktə] Charakter OT 2

characteristic [ˌkærəktə'rɪstɪk] charakteristisches Merkmal OT 2

to **charge** [tʃa:dʒ] aufladen OT 2

charge: in charge ['ɪn tʃa:dʒ] zuständig; verantwortlich OT 1

charity ['tʃærəti] Wohlfahrtsorganisation OT 2

charming ['tʃa:mɪŋ] charmant OT 3

chart [tʃa:t] Hitparade OT 3

to **chatter** ['tʃætə] plaudern OT 2

chatty ['tʃæti] gesprächig OT 3

cheap [tʃi:p] billig OT 2

to **check** [tʃek] überprüfen; kontrollieren OT 1

checklist ['tʃeklɪst] Checkliste OT 2

cheeky ['tʃi:ki] frech OT 3

cheerful ['tʃɪəfl] fröhlich OT 2

cheerleader ['tʃɪəli:də] Cheerleader(in) **WS 4**, 130

to **cheer up** [ˈtʃɪə ʌp] jubeln; zujubeln; aufmuntern OT 1

cheese [tʃiːz] Käse OT 1

cheeseburger [ˈtʃiːzbɜːgə] Cheeseburger OT 3

chef [ʃef] Küchenchef(in); Koch, Köchin OT 1

chemical [ˈkemɪkl] Chemikalie OT 3

cherry [ˈtʃeri] Kirsche OT 3

chess [tʃes] Schach OT 1

chest of drawers [ˌtʃest əv ˈdrɔːz] Kommode OT 1

chest [tʃest] Truhe OT 1

chicken [ˈtʃɪkɪn] Huhn; Hähnchen OT 1

child [tʃaɪld] Kind OT 1

childhood [ˈtʃaɪldhʊd] Kindheit OT 3

chili [ˈtʃɪli] Chili OT 2

chimney [ˈtʃɪmni] Schornstein OT 3

chip [tʃɪp] Fritte; Kartoffelchip OT 1

choc-chip [ˈtʃɒk tʃɪp] Schokoladensplitter OT 1

chocoholic [ˌtʃɒkəˈhɒlɪk] Schokoladensüchtige(r) OT 3

chocolate [ˈtʃɒklət] Schokolade; Praline OT 1

choice [tʃɔɪs] Wahl; Auswahl OT 1

choir [ˈkwaɪə] Chor OT 1

cholera [ˈkɒlərə] Cholera OT 3

to **choose** [tʃuːz] auswählen; aussuchen OT 1

chopped [tʃɒpt] gehackt OT 2

chore [tʃɔː] Pflicht OT 3

chromosome [ˈkrəʊməsəʊm] Chromosom WS 4, 131

chronological [ˌkrɒnəˈlɒdʒɪkl] chronologisch OT 3

church [tʃɜːtʃ] Kirche OT 1

cinema [ˈsɪnəmə] Kino OT 1

circle [ˈsɜːkl] Kreis OT 2

circus [ˈsɜːkəs] Zirkus WS 2, 52

to **cite** [saɪt] anführen OT 2

citizen [ˈsɪtɪzn] Einwohner(in) OT 2

civilized [ˈsɪvəlaɪz] zivilisiert; kultiviert WS 1, 27

to **claim** [kleɪm] behaupten WS 1, 21

clan [klæn] Stamm WS 1, 26

to **clap** [klæp] klatschen OT 1

clarification [ˌklærəfɪˈkeɪʃn] Abklärung WS 4, 139

to **clarify** [ˈklærəfaɪ] (etw.) klären WS 3, 92

clarinet [ˌklærəˈnet] Klarinette OT 2

class [klɑːs] Stunde; Klasse OT 1

to **class** [klɑːs] einordnen; klassifizieren WS 2, 69

classic [ˈklæsɪk] klassisch OT 2

to **classify** [ˈklæsɪfaɪ] etw. einstufen WS 3, 108

classmate [ˈklɑːsmeɪt] Klassenkamerad(in) OT 3

classroom [ˈklɑːsruːm] Klassenzimmer OT 1

to **clean** [kliːn] putzen; reinigen OT 1

cleaner [ˈkliːnə] Reinigungsmittel OT 3

clear [klɪə] klar OT 2

clearly [ˈklɪəli] deutlich OT 3

to **click** [klɪk] klicken OT 3

cliff [klɪf] Klippe; Felsen WS 1, 24

climate [ˈklaɪmət] Klima OT 2

to **climb** [klaɪm] klettern; steigen OT 1

climber [ˈklaɪmə] Kletterer, Kletterin OT 2

climbing [ˈklaɪmɪŋ] Klettern; Bergsteigen OT 1

clip [klɪp] Ausschnitt OT 2

cloak [kləʊk] Umhang; Deckmantel OT 2

cloakroom [ˈkləʊkruːm] Garderobe WS 2, 56

clock [klɒk] Uhr OT 1

close [kləʊs] nah OT 1

to **close** [kləʊz] schließen; zumachen OT 1

closed [kləʊzd] geschlossen OT 1

cloth [klɒθ] Stoff OT 2

clothes [kləʊðz] Kleidung; Kleider OT 1

clothes peg [ˈkləʊðz peg] Wäscheklammer WS 2, 74

cloud [klaʊd] Wolke; Schatten OT 1

cloudy [ˈklaʊdi] wolkig; bewölkt OT 1

club [klʌb] Klub; Verein OT 1

clumsy [ˈklʌmzi] ungeschickt OT 2

co-ed [ˌkəʊˈed] gemischtgeschlechtlich OT 2

coach [kəʊtʃ] Reisebus; Eisenbahnwagen; Trainer(in) OT 1

coal [kəʊl] Kohle OT 2

coast [kəʊst] Küste OT 1

coastal [ˈkəʊstl] Küsten...; an der Küste WS 3, 108

coastguard [ˈkəʊstgɑːd] Küstenwache OT 2

coastline [ˈkəʊstlaɪn] Küstenlinie; Küste WS 1, 36

coat [kəʊt] Mantel OT 2

cobblestones [ˈkɒblstəʊns] Kopfsteinpflaster OT 3

code: in code [ɪn kəʊd] verschlüsselt OT 2

coffee [ˈkɒfi] Kaffee OT 1

coffin [ˈkɒfɪn] Sarg WS 3, 106

coin [kɔɪn] Münze OT 1

cold [kəʊld] kalt; unfreundlich OT 1

collar [ˈkɒlə] Halsband OT 2

colleague [ˈkɒliːg] Kollege, Kollegin WS 3, 90

to **collect** [kəˈlekt] sammeln; sammeln OT 1

collection [kəˈlekʃn] Sammlung OT 2

college [ˈkɒlɪdʒ] Hochschule OT 2

colonial [kəˈləʊniəl] kolonial OT 3

colonialism [kəˈləʊniəlɪzəm] Kolonialismus WW, 10

colonist [ˈkɒlənɪst] Kolonist(in) OT 3

colonization [ˌkɒlənaɪˈzeɪʃn] Kolonialisierung WS 1, 24

to **colonize** [ˈkɒlənaɪz] kolonisieren OT 3

colony [ˈkɒləni] Kolonie OT 2

colour [ˈkʌlə] Farbe; Gesichtsfarbe OT 1

coloured [ˈkʌləd] farbig; bunt OT 1

colourful [ˈkʌləfl] farbenfroh OT 3

column [ˈkɒləm] Säule; Spalte OT 1

comb [kəʊm] Kamm OT 2

combination [ˌkɒmbɪˈneɪʃn] Kombination OT 3

to **combine** [kəmˈbaɪn] kombinieren; mischen WS 2, 67

to **come** [kʌm] kommen; bevorstehen OT 1

to **come first / second / third** [kʌm ˈfɜːst / ˈsekənd / ˈθɜːd] den ersten / zweiten / dritten Platz belegen OT 2

comfortable [ˈkʌmftəbl] bequem; komfortabel OT 1

comic [ˈkɒmɪk] Comicheft; Komiker(in) OT 1

commander [kəˈmɑːndə] Kommandant(in) OT 2

commander-in-chief [kəˌmɑːndər ɪn ˈtʃiːf] Oberbefehlshaber(in) OT 2

commanding [kəˈmɑːndɪŋ] befehlshabend OT 2

to **commemorate** [kəˈmeməreɪt] gedenken OT 3

commemoration [kəˌmeməˈreɪʃn] Gedenken OT 3

to **comment** [ˈkɒment] bemerken; kommentieren OT 3

commerce [ˈkɒmɜːs] Handel OT 3

commercial [kəˈmɜːʃl] Werbespot WS 2, 74

commercial [kəˈmɜːʃl] kommerziell WS 3, 96

to **commission** [kəˈmɪʃn] beauftragen WS 3, 110

committee [kəˈmɪti] Kommission; Komitee OT 3

common [ˈkɒmən] Gemeindeland OT 3

common ['kɒmən] gemeinsam; normal **WW**, 11

commonly ['kɒmənli] gewöhnlich; häufig **WW**, 10

to **communicate** [kə'mju:nɪkeɪt] kommunizieren; etw. vermitteln **WW**, 11

communication [kə,mju:nɪ'keɪʃn] Kommunikation OT 1

community [kə'mju:nəti] Gemeinschaft OT 2

commuter [kə'mju:tə] Pendler(in) OT 2

commuter rail [kə,mju:tə 'reɪl] Pendlerbahn OT 2

company ['kʌmpəni] Unternehmen OT 1

comparable ['kɒmpərəbl] vergleichbar **WS 4**, 126

comparative [kəm'pærətɪv] Komparativ OT 2

to **compare** [kəm'peə] vergleichen OT 1

comparison [kəm'pærɪsn] Vergleich **WS 1**, 29

compass ['kʌmpəs] Kompass OT 2

compatible [kəm'pætəbl] kompatibel **WS 4**, 126

compensation [,kɒmpen'seɪʃn] Entschädigung **WS 2**, 64

to **compete** [kəm'pi:t] konkurrieren OT 2

competition [,kɒmpə'tɪʃn] Konkurrenz; Wettbewerb OT 1

competitive [kəm'petətɪv] konkurrenzorientiert OT 3

competitor [kəm'petɪtə] Konkurrent(in); Wettbewerber(in) OT 3

to **complain** [kəm'pleɪn] sich beklagen; sich beschweren OT 3

complaint [kəm'pleɪnt] Beschwerde OT 2

to **complete** [kəm'pli:t] vervollständigen OT 1

completely [kəm'pli:tli] ganz; komplett **WW**, 11

complex ['kɒmpleks] komplex; schwierig **WS 1**, 36

complicated ['kɒmplɪkeɪtɪd] kompliziert OT 3

to **compose** [kəm'pəʊz] komponieren OT 3

composer [kəm'pəʊzə] Komponist(in) OT 2

compost ['kɒmpɒst] Kompost OT 3

composting ['kɒmpɒstɪŋ] Kompostierungs- OT 3

computer lab [kəm'pju:tə ,læb] Computerraum OT 2

to **conceal** [kən'si:l] verbergen **WS 4**, 125

to **concentrate** ['kɒnsntreɪt] konzentrieren OT 3

concept ['kɒnsept] Konzept; Begriff **WS 2**, 60

concern [kən'sɜ:n] Sorge; Bedenken **WS 1**, 37

concerned [kən'sɜ:nd] besorgt **WS 1**, 28

concert ['kɒnsət] Konzert OT 1

concessions [kən'seʃnz] Gastronomie OT 3

conclusion [kən'klu:ʒn] Schluss OT 3

concrete ['kɒnkri:t] Beton OT 2

condition [kən'dɪʃn] Zustand OT 2

condor ['kɒndɔ:] Condor OT 3

to **conduct** [kən'dʌkt] durchführen OT 3

conference ['kɒnfərəns] Konferenz **WS 2**, 70

confidence ['kɒnfɪdəns] Selbstvertrauen OT 2

confident ['kɒnfɪdənt] selbstsicher OT 3

to **confirm** [kən'fɜ:m] bestätigen **WS 3**, 91

conflict ['kɒnflɪkt] Konflikt **WS 1**, 15

to **conform (to)** [kən'fɔ:m tə] (sich) anpassen (an); übereinstimmen (mit) **WS 2**, 68

confused [kən'fju:zd] verwirrt OT 2

confusing [kən'fju:zɪŋ] verwirrend OT 2

congestion [kən'dʒestʃən] Stau; Stauung **WS 2**, 74

to **congratulate** [kən'grætʃuleɪt] gratulieren OT 2

congratulations [kən,grætʃu'leɪʃnz] Glückwünsche OT 2

conjunction [kən'dʒʌŋkʃn] Konjunktion OT 2

connection [kə'nekʃn] Verbindung OT 2

connectivity [kə,nek'tɪvəti] Vernetzung; Verbindung OT 3

to **conquer** ['kɒŋkə] erobern OT 2

conquest ['kɒŋkwest] Eroberung OT 2

con [kɒn] Nachteil OT 2

conscious ['kɒnʃəs] bewusst **WS 2**, 52

consequence ['kɒnsɪkwəns] Folge; Konsequenz **WS 1**, 24

conservation [,kɒnsə'veɪʃn] Schutz OT 2

considerable [kən'sɪdərəbl] bedeutend; erheblich OT 2

to **consist** [kən'sɪst] bestehen aus OT 3

consistent [kən'sɪstənt] konsequent **WS 4**, 129

consonant ['kɒnsənənt] Konsonant; Mitlaut OT 1

constant ['kɒnstənt] ständig **WS 4**, 150

constantly ['kɒnstəntli] ständig; konstant **WS 2**, 68

constituency [kən'stɪtʃuənsi] Wahlbezirk; Interessengemeinschaft **WS 3**, 92

constituent [kən'stɪtʃuənt] Wähler **WS 3**, 92

constitution [,kɒnstɪ'tju:ʃn] Verfassung OT 3

constitutional [,kɒnstɪ'tju:ʃənl] konstitutionell OT 2

to **construct** [kən'strʌkt] bauen; errichten **WS 3**, 108

construction [kən'strʌkʃn] Bau OT 3

consultant [kən'sʌltənt] Berater(in) **WS 4**, 121

consumer [kən'sju:mə] Verbraucher(in) **WS 2**, 62

consumerism [kən'sju:mərɪzəm] Konsumverhalten **WS 2**, 62

contact ['kɒntækt] Kontakt; Berührung OT 1

to **contact** ['kɒntækt] kontaktieren OT 2

to **contain** [kən'teɪn] etw. enthalten OT 3

container [kən'teɪnə] Behälter; Container **WS 3**, 102

to **contaminate** [kən'tæmɪneɪt] verschmutzen **WS 1**, 34

contemporary [kən'temprəri] zeitgenössisch **WS 2**, 52

content ['kɒntent] Inhalt **WS 2**, 64

contents [kən'tents] Inhalt OT 2

contentious [kən'tenʃəs] umstritten **WS 3**, 99

contestant [kən'testənt] Wettkämpfer(in); Teilnehmer(in) **WS 3**, 86

context ['kɒntekst] Kontext; Zusammenhang **WS 1**, 16

continent ['kɒntɪnənt] Kontinent **WS 1**, 12

to **continue** [kən'tɪnju:] weitermachen OT 2

to **contribute** [kən'trɪbju:t] mitarbeiten; beitragen **WS 1**, 29

to **control** [kən'trəʊl] kontrollieren OT 3

control [kən'trəʊl] Kontrolle OT 2

controversial [,kɒntrə'vɜ:ʃl] umstritten OT 3

controversy ['kɒntrəvɜ:si] Kontroverse **WS 3**, 91

convenience [kən'vi:niəns] Bequemlichkeit; zweckmäßiges Gerät **WS 2**, 62 conversation [ˌkɒnvəˈseɪʃn] Gespräch; Unterhaltung OT 1

conversational [ˌkɒnvəˈseɪʃənl] Gesprächs... WS 1, 29

to convert [kənˈvɜːt] umwandeln WS 2, 52

convict [kənˈvɪkt] Verurteilte WS 1, 17

to convict [kənˈvɪkt] verurteilen WS 4, 144

to convince [kənˈvɪns] überzeugen OT 3

to cook [kʊk] kochen OT 1

cookbook [ˈkʊkbʊk] Kochbuch WS 2, 79

cooker [ˈkʊkə] Herd OT 3

cooking [ˈkʊkɪŋ] Kochen OT 1

cool [kuːl] kühl; besonnen; cool OT 1

to cool [kuːl] kühlen OT 3

cooling system [ˈkuːlɪŋ ˈsɪstəm] Kühlsystem OT 3

coordination [kəʊˌɔːdɪˈneɪʃn] Koordinierung WS 4, 131

to cope [kəʊp] zurechtkommen WS 4, 127

to copy [ˈkɒpi] kopieren; abziehen OT 1

corner [ˈkɔːnə] Ecke; Kurve OT 1

coronation [ˌkɒrəˈneɪʃn] Krönung WS 2, 74

correct [kəˈrekt] richtig; korrekt OT 1

to correct [kəˈrekt] verbessern; korrigieren OT 1

correction [kəˈrekʃn] Korrektur WS 2, 61

correspondent [ˌkɒrəˈspɒndənt] Korrespondent(in); Reporter(in) WS 3, 106

corridor [ˈkɒrɪdɔː] Korridor OT 2

corset [ˈkɔːsɪt] Korsett OT 3

cosmetics [kɒzˈmetɪks] Kosmetik WS 2, 62

cosmopolitan [ˌkɒzməˈpɒlɪtən] weltoffen; kosmopolitisch WS 1, 19

cost [kɒst] Kosten; Preis OT 1

to cost [kɒst] kosten OT 1

costume [ˈkɒstjuːm] Kostüm OT 2

cottage [ˈkɒtɪdʒ] Häuschen OT 3

cotton [ˈkɒtn] Baumwolle WS 3, 84

cougar [ˈkuːgə] Puma OT 2

could [kʊd] konnte; durfte; könnte(n) OT 1

counselor [ˈkaʊnsələ] Jugendbetreuer(in) OT 2

to count [kaʊnt] zählen OT 2

countable [ˈkaʊntəbl] zählbar OT 1

country [ˈkʌntri] Land; Landschaft OT 1

countryside [ˈkʌntrisaɪd] Land; Landschaft OT 1

coupon [ˈkuːpɒn] Gutschein OT 2

courier [ˈkʊriə] Kurier(in) OT 2

course [kɔːs] Kurs; Gang OT 1

of course [əv ˈkɔːs] natürlich OT 1

coursework [ˈkɔːswɜːk] Facharbeit WS 2, 50

court [kɔːt] Gericht WS 3, 90

courtyard [ˈkɔːtjɑːd] Innenhof WS 3, 110

cousin [ˈkʌzn] Cousin(e) OT 1

to cover [ˈkʌvə] abdecken OT 2

cow [kaʊ] Kuh OT 1

cozy [ˈkəʊzi] gemütlich OT 3

cracker [ˈkrækə] Cracker OT 3

cramp [kræmp] Krampf OT 2

cramped [kræmpt] beengt OT 3

crane [kreɪn] Kran OT 3

to crash [kræʃ] abstürzen (lassen) WS 3, 106

crash diet [ˈkræʃ ˈdaɪət] Crash-Diät WS 2, 68

crate [kreɪt] Kiste OT 3

to crawl [krɔːl] krabbeln; kriechen WS 1, 38

crazy [ˈkreɪzi] verrückt OT 2

cream [kriːm] Sahne; Rahm OT 1

to create [kriˈeɪt] schaffen; kreieren OT 2

creation [kriˈeɪʃn] Schöpfung WS 1, 26

creative [kriˈeɪtɪv] kreativ OT 2

creativity [ˌkriːeɪˈtɪvəti] Kreativität OT 3

creator [kriˈeɪtə] Schöpfer(in); Erschaffer(in) WS 1, 26

creature [ˈkriːtʃə] Geschöpf; Lebewesen WS 1, 26

credit card [ˈkredɪt kɑːd] Kreditkarte OT 1

creepy [ˈkriːpi] gruselig WS 1, 13

creepy-crawly [ˌkriːpiˈkrɔːli] Krabbeltier OT 2

cricket [ˈkrɪkɪt] Kricket; Grille OT 1

crime [kraɪm] Verbrechen WS 3, 90

crisis [ˈkraɪsɪs] Krise WS 1, 28

crisp [krɪsp] Kartoffelchip OT 1

criterion [kraɪˈtɪəriən] Kriterium WS 4, 126

critical [ˈkrɪtɪkl] kritisch; hier: wichtig WS 1, 25

to criticize [ˈkrɪtɪsaɪz] kritisieren OT 3

crop [krɒp] Getreide; Feldfrüchte OT 3

cross [krɒs] verärgert OT 2

to cross [krɒs] überqueren; übersetzen OT 1

cross country [ˌkrɒs ˈkʌntri] Querfeldein- OT 2

crowd [kraʊd] Menge; Menschenmenge OT 1

crowded [ˈkraʊdɪd] überfüllt OT 2

crown [kraʊn] Krone OT 1

to crown [kraʊn] krönen OT 1

cruel [ˈkruːəl] grausam OT 3

cruelty [ˈkruːəlti] Grausamkeit WS 2, 62

to cruise [kruːz] mit dem Boot fahren; eine Kreuzfahrt machen OT 3

cruise ship [ˈkruːz ʃɪp] Kreuzfahrtschiff OT 2

crusade [kruːˈseɪd] Kreuzzug WS 3, 98

crutch [krʌtʃ] Krücke OT 2

to cry [kraɪ] weinen; schreien OT 1

cub [kʌb] Junge(s) OT 2

cucumber [ˈkjuːkʌmbə] Gurke; Salatgurke OT 1

cuddly [ˈkʌdli] knuddelig OT 3

cue [kjuː] Hinweis; Stichwort WS 4, 131

cull [kʌl] Schlachten; Keulen WS 1, 25

to cull [kʌl] keulen WS 1, 25

cultural [ˈkʌltʃərəl] kulturell OT 3

culture [ˈkʌltʃə] Kultur OT 1

cup [kʌp] Tasse; Pokal OT 1

cupboard [ˈkʌbəd] Schrank OT 1

curious [ˈkjʊəriəs] neugierig; gespannt OT 3

curlew [ˈkɜːljuː] Brachvogel OT 2

curling [ˈkɜːlɪŋ] Curling OT 3

curly [ˈkɜːli] gelockt OT 3

current [ˈkʌrənt] aktuell OT 2

currently [ˈkʌrəntli] derzeit; gerade WS 4, 125

curriculum [kəˈrɪkjələm] Curriculum; Lehrplan WS 4, 126

curry [ˈkʌri] Currygericht OT 1

curtain [ˈkɜːtn] Vorhang OT 2

cushion [ˈkʊʃn] Kissen; Polster OT 1

custard [ˈkʌstəd] Vanillesoße OT 1

custom [ˈkʌstəm] Brauch OT 3

customer [ˈkʌstəmə] Kunde, Kundin OT 2

customs [ˈkʌstəmz] Zoll OT 2

to cut [kʌt] schneiden OT 2

cute [kjuːt] niedlich OT 3

cutlery [ˈkʌtləri] Besteck OT 3

cyberbullying [ˈsaɪbəbʊliŋ] Cyber-Mobbing WS 4, 144

to cycle [ˈsaɪkl] mit dem Fahrrad fahren; einen Kreislauf durchlaufen OT 1

cyclist [ˈsaɪklɪst] Radfahrer(in) OT 3

cyclone [ˈsaɪkləʊn] Zyklon WS 1, 34

D

dad [dæd] Papa; Vati OT 1

daffodil [ˈdæfədɪl] Osterglocke; Narzisse OT 3

daily [ˈdeɪli] täglich OT 2

damage [ˈdæmɪdʒ] Beschädigung
WS 1, 25

to **damage** [ˈdæmɪdʒ] beschädigen OT 3

dance [dɑːns] Tanz OT 3

dancing [ˈdɑːnsɪŋ] Tanzen OT 1

danger [ˈdeɪndʒə] Gefahr OT 2

dangerous [ˈdeɪndʒərəs] gefährlich OT 1

to **dare** [deə] wagen OT 2

dark [dɑːk] dunkel; finster OT 1

dark-haired [ˌdɑːk ˈheəd] dunkelhaarig
OT 3

data [ˈdeɪtə] Daten OT 3

date [deɪt] Verabredung OT 3

to **date** [ˈdeɪt] zurückgehen auf;
bestehen seit OT 3

daughter [ˈdɔːtə] Tochter OT 1

day [deɪ] Tag; Zeit OT 1

day out [deɪ ˈaʊt] Tagesausflug OT 2

one day [ˈwʌn deɪ] eines Tages;
später einmal OT 2

dead [ded] tot; taub OT 1

deadly [ˈdedli] tödlich WS 1, 13

deal [diːl] Geschäft; hier: Angelegenheit
WS 1, 21

to **deal with** [diːl wɪð] umgehen OT 2

death [deθ] Tod OT 2

date of death [ˌdeɪt əv ˈdeθ]
Todesdatum OT 2

decade [ˈdekeɪd] Dekade; Jahrzehnt
OT 3

to **decide** [dɪˈsaɪd] entscheiden;
beschließen OT 1

decision [dɪˈsɪʒn] Entscheidung;
Entschluss OT 1

deck [dek] Deck OT 3

to **declare** [dɪˈkleə] ausrufen;
verkünden WS 1, 42

decline [dɪˈklaɪn] Rückgang WW, 11

to **decorate** [ˈdekəreɪt] dekorieren;
schmücken OT 2

to **decrease** [dɪˈkriːs] fallen;
zurückgehen WS 4, 132

dedicated [ˈdedɪkeɪtɪd] engagiert
WS 4, 147

deed [diːd] Urkunde WS 1, 26

deep [diːp] tief; schwer OT 1

deer [dɪə] Hirsch OT 1

to **defeat** [dɪˈfiːt] besiegen OT 2

to **defend** [dɪˈfend] verteidigen WS 1, 25

defender [dɪˈfendə] Verteidiger(in) OT 3

to **define** [dɪˈfaɪn] definieren;
bestimmen OT 3

definite [ˈdefɪnət] eindeutig OT 1

definitely [ˈdefɪnətli] bestimmt;
definitiv OT 2

definition [ˌdefɪˈnɪʃn] Definition;
Schärfe OT 1

deforestation [diːˌfɒrɪˈsteɪʃn]
Abholzung WS 1, 39

degree [dɪˈɡriː] Grad OT 3

dehydrated [ˌdiːhaɪˈdreɪtɪd] dehydriert
OT 2

delegate [ˈdelɪɡət] Abgeordnete(r) OT 3

deli [ˈdeli] Feinkostladen WS 1, 15

delicate [ˈdelɪkət] empfindlich; delikat
OT 3

delicious [dɪˈlɪʃəs] lecker; köstlich OT 1

delivery [dɪˈlɪvəri] Zustellung WS 2, 64

demanding [dɪˈmɑːndɪŋ] anspruchsvoll
WS 1, 27

democracy [dɪˈmɒkrəsi] Demokratie
OT 3

democratic [ˌdeməˈkrætɪk]
demokratisch WS 3, 115

to **demolish** [dɪˈmɒlɪʃ] abreißen;
demolieren WS 1, 25

to **demonstrate** [ˈdemənstreɪt] zeigen;
vorführen WS 4, 128

demonstration [ˌdemənˈstreɪʃn]
Demonstration WS 1, 28

demonstrative [dɪˈmɒnstrətɪv]
Demonstrativbegleiter OT 1

denial [dɪˈnaɪəl] Verweigerung;
Leugnung WS 3, 101

dentist [ˈdentɪst] Zahnarzt, -ärztin OT 3

dentures [ˈdentʃəz] Gebiss OT 3

to **deny** [dɪˈnaɪ] leugnen WS 2, 56

department [dɪˈpɑːtmənt] Abteilung
WS 3, 92

to **depend** [dɪˈpend] abhängen OT 2

dependent [dɪˈpendənt] abhängig OT 3

depression [dɪˈpreʃn] Depression
WS 2, 70

to **descend** [dɪˈsend] abstammen
WS 4, 123

descendant [dɪˈsendənt] Nachkomme
OT 3

descent [dɪˈsent] Abstammung WS 1, 33

to **describe** [dɪˈskraɪb] beschreiben OT 1

description [dɪˈskrɪpʃn] Beschreibung;
Schilderung OT 1

descriptive [dɪˈskrɪptɪv] beschreibend
OT 3

desert [ˈdezət] Wüste OT 3

to **deserve** [dɪˈzɜːv] verdienen OT 2

designated [ˈdezɪɡneɪtɪd] vorgesehen
OT 3

designer [dɪˈzaɪnə] Designer(in) OT 3

desire [dɪˈzaɪə] Wunsch WS 2, 70

desk [desk] Schreibtisch; Empfang OT 1

desperate [ˈdespərət] verzweifelt OT 3

desperately [ˈdespərətli] verzweifelt
OT 3

despite [dɪˈspaɪt] obwohl; trotz
WS 3, 106

dessert [dɪˈzɜːt] Nachtisch; Dessert OT 1

destination [ˌdestɪˈneɪʃn] Reiseziel
WS 1, 27

to **destroy** [dɪˈstrɔɪ] zerstören OT 2

destruction [dɪˈstrʌkʃn] Zerstörung
WS 1, 35

detail [ˈdiːteɪl] Detail OT 2

detailed [ˈdiːteɪld] detailliert;
ausführlich WS 2, 72

to **determine** [dɪˈtɜːmɪn] ausmachen;
bestimmen WS 4, 143

determined [dɪˈtɜːmɪnd] entschlossen
WS 4, 134

determiner [dɪˈtɜːmɪnə]
Bestimmungswort OT 1

devastating [ˈdevəsteɪtɪŋ] verheerend
WS 1, 34

to **develop** [dɪˈveləp] entwickeln OT 2

developer [dɪˈveləpə] Entwickler(in)
WS 4, 134

development [dɪˈveləpmənt]
Entwicklung OT 3

diabetes [ˌdaɪəˈbiːtiːz] Diabetes
WS 2, 69

dialect [ˈdaɪəlekt] Dialekt OT 3

dialogue [ˈdaɪəlɒɡ] Dialog OT 1

diaper [ˈdaɪəpə] Windel OT 3

diary [ˈdaɪəri] Terminkalender;
Tagebuch OT 1

to **dictate** [dɪkˈteɪt] bestimmen;
diktieren WS 4, 124

dictionary [ˈdɪkʃənri] Wörterbuch OT 2

didgeridoo [ˌdɪdʒəriˈduː] Didgeridoo
WS 1, 23

to **die** [daɪ] sterben; eingehen OT 1

diesel [ˈdiːzl] Diesel OT 3

to **diet** [ˈdaɪət] Diät WS 2, 68

difference [ˈdɪfrəns] Unterschied OT 1

different [ˈdɪfrənt] unterschiedlich;
anders OT 1

difficult [ˈdɪfɪkəlt] schwer; schwierig
OT 1

difficulty [ˈdɪfɪkəlti] Schwierigkeit OT 2

to **dig** [dɪɡ] graben OT 3

digit [ˈdɪdʒɪt] Ziffer OT 2

digital [ˈdɪdʒɪtl] digital; Digital... OT 1

dilemma [dɪˈlemə] Dilemma WS 1, 14

dimension [daɪˈmenʃn] Abmessung
OT 2

dingo [ˈdɪŋɡəʊ] Dingo WS 1, 25

dining room [ˈdaɪnɪŋ ruːm] Esszimmer
OT 1

dinner [ˈdɪnə] Abendessen; Mittagessen OT 1

dinosaur [ˈdaɪnəsɔː] Dinosaurier OT 1

diploma [dɪˈpləʊmə] Diplom; Urkunde **WS 4**, 126

direct [daɪˈrekt] direkt OT 2

direction [təˈwɔːdz] Richtung OT 2

directions [dəˈrekʃnz] Wegbeschreibungen OT 2

dirt [dɜːt] Dreck; Schmutz **WS 4**, 125

dirty [ˈdɜːti] schmutzig; dreckig OT 1

disability [ˌdɪsəˈbɪləti] Behinderung OT 2

disabled [dɪsˈeɪbld] Behinderte(r) **WS 2**, 56

disadvantage [ˌdɪsədˈvɑːntɪdʒ] Nachteil **WS 1**, 26

disadvantaged [ˌdɪsədˈvɑːntɪdʒd] benachteiligt **WS 3**, 105

to **disagree** [ˌdɪsəˈɡriː] anderer Meinung sein; nicht übereinstimmen OT 1

disagreement [ˌdɪsəˈɡriːmənt] Uneinigkeit OT 3

to **disappear** [ˌdɪsəˈpɪə] verschwinden OT 3

disappointed [ˌdɪsəˈpɔɪntɪd] enttäuscht OT 2

disappointingly [ˌdɪsəˈpɔɪntɪŋli] enttäuschend OT 3

disapproval [ˌdɪsəˈpruːvl] Missbilligung; Missfallen **WS 2**, 71

disaster [dɪˈzɑːstə] Katastrophe OT 2

discount [ˈdɪskaʊnt] Rabatt; Nachlass **WS 3**, 103

to **discover** [dɪˈskʌvə] entdecken OT 2

discrimination [dɪˌskrɪmɪˈneɪʃn] Diskriminierung; Ausgrenzung **WS 4**, 134

to **discuss** [dɪˈskʌs] besprechen; diskutieren OT 1

discussion [dɪˈskʌʃn] Besprechung; Diskussion OT 1

disease [dɪˈziːz] Krankheit OT 2

disgusted [dɪsˈɡʌstɪd] empört; angewidert **WS 4**, 125

disgusting [dɪsˈɡʌstɪŋ] ekelhaft OT 2

dish [dɪʃ] Gericht; Schale OT 2

dishes [ˈdɪʃɪz] Geschirr OT 2

to **do the dishes** [ˌduː ðə ˈdɪʃɪz] den Abwasch machen OT 2

disinfectant [ˌdɪsɪnˈfektənt] Desinfektionsmittel OT 3

to **dislike** [dɪsˈlaɪk] nicht mögen OT 2

to **disobey** [ˌdɪsəˈbeɪ] nicht gehorchen OT 3

disorder [dɪsˈɔːdə] Störung **WS 4**, 131

disorganized [dɪsˈɔːɡənaɪzd] chaotisch OT 2

to **dispose** [dɪˈspəʊz] entsorgen OT 3

disrespectful [ˌdɪsrɪˈspektfl] respektlos OT 3

distance [ˈdɪstəns] Entfernung OT 2

distanced [ˈdɪstənst] distanziert; abgeschieden **WS 3**, 93

distant [ˈdɪstənt] weit entfernt **WS 2**, 57

distinct [dɪˈstɪŋkt] eindeutig; eigenständig **WS 1**, 24

distinctive [dɪˈstɪŋktɪv] unverwechselbar; ausgeprägt **WS 1**, 32

district [ˈdɪstrɪkt] Bezirk **WS 4**, 126

to **disturb** [dɪˈstɜːb] stören **WS 1**, 38

to **dive** [daɪv] tauchen; hineinspringen OT 3

diver [ˈdaɪvə] Taucher(in) OT 3

diverse [daɪˈvɜːs] vielfältig; verschieden OT 3

diversity [daɪˈvɜːsəti] Vielfältigkeit **WS 1**, 32

to **divorce** [dɪˈvɔːs] sich scheiden lassen OT 3

divorce [dɪˈvɔːs] Scheidung OT 3

to **do** [duː] tun; machen OT 1

doctor [ˈdɒktə] Arzt, Ärztin; Doktor OT 1

document [ˈdɒkjumənt] Dokument OT 3

documentary [ˌdɒkjuˈmentri] Dokumentation OT 2

dog [dɒɡ] Hund; Rüde OT 1

doll [dɒl] Puppe OT 2

dollar [ˈdɒlə] Dollar OT 1

dolphin [ˈdɒlfɪn] Delfin OT 1

dome [dəʊm] Kuppel OT 3

to **dominate** [ˈdɒmɪneɪt] dominieren; beherrschen **WS 2**, 52

to **donate** [dəʊˈneɪt] spenden OT 2

donation [dəʊˈneɪʃn] Spende OT 2

donkey [ˈdɒŋki] Esel **WS 3**, 91

door [dɔː] Tür OT 1

doorbell [ˈdɔːbel] Klingel OT 2

doorstep [ˈdɔːstep] Türschwelle **WS 1**, 19

dot [dɒt] Punkt **WS 3**, 115

double [ˈdʌbl] doppelt; zwei; Doppel... OT 1

to **double** [ˈdʌbl] sich verdoppeln **WS 1**, 17

doublet [ˈdʌblət] Wams OT 3

doubt [daʊt] Zweifel **WW**, 11

doughnut [ˈdəʊnʌt] Krapfen OT 2

down [daʊn] hinunter; herunter OT 1

downhill [ˌdaʊnˈhɪl] bergab **WS 1**, 13

to **download** [ˈdaʊnləʊd] herunterladen OT 3

to **downsize** [ˈdaʊnsaɪz] reduzieren; sich einschränken OT 3

downstairs [ˈdaʊnsteəz] im unteren Stockwerk; Parterre OT 1

down syndrome [ˈdaʊn sɪndrəʊm] Downsyndrom **WS 4**, 131

downtown [ˌdaʊnˈtaʊn] Innenstadt **WS 1**, 43

to **doze** [dəʊz] ein Nickerchen machen OT 2

draft [drɑːft] Entwurf OT 2

dragon [ˈdræɡən] Drache(n) OT 3

to **drain** [dreɪn] abgießen OT 2

drama [ˈdrɑːmə] Drama; Dramatik OT 1

dramatic [drəˈmætɪk] dramatisch **WS 4**, 132

drastic [ˈdræstɪk] drastisch **WS 1**, 24

to **draw** [drɔː] ziehen; zeichnen OT 1

drawer [drɔː] Schublade OT 1

to **dream** [driːm] träumen **WS 2**, 52

dream [driːm] Traum OT 2

dreamtime [ˈdriːmtaɪm] Traumzeit **WS 1**, 26

dress [dres] Kleid OT 1

to **dress** [dres] sich anziehen OT 1

to **dress up** [dres ʌp] sich verkleiden OT 3

drink [drɪŋk] Getränk; Drink OT 1

to **drink** [drɪŋk] trinken OT 1

to **drip** [drɪp] tropfen OT 3

drive [draɪv] Fahrt **WS 1**, 19

to **drive** [draɪv] fahren OT 1

driver [ˈdraɪvə] Fahrer(in) OT 2

driveway [ˈdraɪvweɪ] Zufahrt; Auffahrt OT 3

to **drop** [drɒp] fallen lassen; fallen OT 1

drop kick [ˈdrɒp kɪk] Dropkick **WS 1**, 30

drought [draʊt] Dürre **WS 1**, 25

to **drown** [draʊn] ertrinken OT 3

drum [drʌm] Trommel OT 3

drummer [ˈdrʌmə] Schlagzeuger(in) OT 2

drums [drʌmz] Schlagzeug OT 1

dry [draɪ] trocken OT 3

duchess [ˈdʌtʃəs] Herzogin OT 2

duck [dʌk] Ente OT 3

due to [djuː tə] wegen **WS 1**, 28

duke [djuːk] Herzog OT 2

dumpster [ˈdʌmpstə] Müllcontainer **WS 3**, 88

dust [dʌst] Staub OT 2

dusty [ˈdʌsti] verstaubt **WS 2**, 55

duty free [ˌdjuːti ˈfriː] zollfrei OT 2

duvet [ˈduːveɪ] Bettdecke OT 2

dwelling [ˈdwelɪŋ] Behausung OT 3

to **dye** [daɪ] färben OT 3

dyscalculia [ˌdɪskæl'kjuːliə] Dyskalkulie **WS 4**, 127

dyslexia [dɪs'leksiə] Legasthenie **WS 4**, 127

dyslexic [dɪs'leksɪk] legasthenisch **WS 4**, 128

E

eager ['iːgə] eifrig OT 2

eagle ['iːgl] Adler OT 2

ear [ɪə] Ohr OT 1

early ['ɜːli] früh; zeitig OT 1

earth [ɜːθ] Erde OT 1

earthquake ['ɜːθkweɪk] Erdbeben OT 2

east [iːst] Ost- OT 2

eastern ['iːstən] östlich OT 2

to **eat** [iːt] essen; fressen OT 1

to **echo** ['ekəʊ] nachhallen; nachklingen **WS 1**, 14

ecological [ˌiːkə'lɒdʒɪkl] ökologisch **WS 1**, 25

ecology [i'kɒlədʒi] Ökologie; Umweltwissenschaft OT 3

economy [ɪ'kɒnəmi] Ökonomie **WS 3**, 84

ecotourism ['ikəʊtʊərɪzəm] Ökotourismus OT 3

edge [edʒ] Rand OT 3

to **edit** ['edɪt] überarbeiten; schneiden OT 3

editor ['edɪtə] Redakteur(in); Herausgeber(in) OT 2

educational [ˌedʒu'keɪʃənl] Bildungs- OT 3

effect [ɪ'fekt] Wirkung OT 3

effective [ɪ'fektɪv] wirksam OT 3

efficient [ɪ'fɪʃnt] effizient; wirksam **WS 4**, 129

efficiently [ɪ'fɪʃntli] effizient OT 3

effort ['efət] Anstrengung; Mühe OT 3

egg [eg] Ei OT 1

eight [eɪt] acht OT 1

eighteen [ˌeɪ'tiːn] achtzehn OT 1

eighty ['eɪti] achtzig OT 1

either ['aɪðə] auch nicht OT 2

elbow ['elbəʊ] Ellbogen OT 1

elder ['eldə] Älteste(r) **WS 1**, 26

elderly ['eldəli] älter **WS 1**, 34

elective [ɪ'lektɪv] Auswahlfach **WS 4**, 130

elector [ɪ'lektə] Wahlmann, -frau OT 3

electoral [ɪ'lektərəl] Wahl... **WS 3**, 91

electric [ɪ'lektrɪk] elektrisch; spannungsgeladen OT 1

electrician [ɪˌlek'trɪʃn] Elektriker(in) **WS 1**, 20

electricity [ɪˌlek'trɪsəti] Strom OT 2

electronic [ɪˌlek'trɒnɪk] elektronisch OT 2

element ['elɪmənt] Element **WS 1**, 17

elementary school [ˌelɪ'mentri skuːl] Grundschule OT 2

elephant ['elɪfənt] Elefant OT 1

eleven [ɪ'levn] elf OT 1

else [els] sonst noch; andere(r,-s) OT 1

email ['iːmeɪl] Email OT 3

to **email** ['iːmeɪl] emailen OT 3

embarrassed [ɪm'bærəst] verlegen; peinlich berührt OT 3

embarrassing [ɪm'bærəsɪŋ] peinlich OT 2

emergency [i'mɜːdʒənsi] Notfall; Not... OT 1

emission [ɪ'mɪʃn] Ausstoß; Emission OT 3

emoji [ɪ'məʊdʒi] Emoji OT 2

emotion [ɪ'məʊʃn] Emotion OT 3

emotional [ɪ'məʊʃənl] emotional OT 3

emperor ['empərə] Kaiser OT 2

to **emphasize** ['emfəsaɪz] betonen OT 3

emphatic [ɪm'fætɪk] emphatisch **WS 2**, 69

empire ['empaɪə] Reich OT 2

employee [ɪm'plɔiiː] Angestellte(r) **WS 4**, 136

employer [ɪm'plɔiə] Arbeitgeber(in) **WS 4**, 142

employment [ɪm'plɔimənt] Beschäftigung; Arbeit **WS 4**, 133

empty ['empti] leer OT 1

to **encourage** [ɪn'kʌrɪdʒ] ermutigen OT 3

encyclopedia [ɪnˌsaɪklə'piːdiə] Enzyklopädie; Lexikon OT 3

end [end] Ende OT 1

end zone ['end zəʊn] Endzone OT 2

to **end** [end] enden; beenden OT 1

endless ['endləs] endlos; unendlich **WS 2**, 52

to **endorse** [ɪn'dɔːs] unterstützen **WS 2**, 63

enemy ['enəmi] Feind(in) OT 3

energetic [ˌenə'dʒetɪk] aktiv OT 2

energy ['enədʒi] Energie OT 3

to **enforce** [ɪn'fɔːs] durchsetzen **WS 3**, 90

to **engage** [ɪn'geɪdʒ] einnehmen **WS 1**, 36

engagement [ɪn'geɪdʒmənt] Engagement; Einsatz **WS 3**, 100

engaging [ɪn'geɪdʒɪŋ] ansprechend OT 3

engine ['endʒɪn] Motor; Lokomotive OT 2

engineer [ˌendʒɪ'nɪə] Ingenieur(in); Lokführer(in) OT 2

engineering [ˌendʒɪ'nɪərɪŋ] Ingenieurwesen OT 2

English ['ɪŋglɪʃ] englisch OT 1

to **engrave** [ɪn'greɪv] gravieren; eingravieren OT 3

engraving [ɪn'greɪvɪŋ] Gravur OT 3

to **enjoy** [ɪn'dʒɔɪ] genießen; sich schmecken lassen OT 1

enjoyable [ɪn'dʒɔɪəbl] angenehm OT 2

enormous [ɪ'nɔːməs] riesig; gewaltig OT 1

enough [ɪ'nʌf] genug; genügend OT 1

to **enslave** [ɪn'sleɪv] versklaven OT 3

to **ensure** [ɪn'ʃʊə] sicherstellen **WS 3**, 90

to **enter** ['entə] eintreten; eintragen OT 2

to **entertain** [ˌentə'teɪn] unterhalten **WS 2**, 66

entertainment [ˌentə'teɪnmənt] Unterhaltung OT 2

enthusiastic [ɪnˌθjuːzi'æstɪk] begeistert OT 3

entitled [ɪn'taɪtld] berechtigt **WS 2**, 64

entrance ['entrəns] Eingang; Eintreten OT 1

entrance hall ['entrəns ˌhɔːl] Eingangsbereich; Eingangshalle OT 1

entrepreneur [ˌɒntrəprə'nɜː] Unternehmer(in) **WS 4**, 143

entry ['entri] Eintrag; Einsendung OT 2

envelope ['envələʊp] Briefumschlag OT 2

environment [ɪn'vaɪrənmənt] Umfeld; Umwelt OT 2

environmental [ɪnˌvaɪrən'mentl] Umwelt-; ökologisch OT 3

environmentalist [ɪnˌvaɪrən'mentəlɪst] Umweltschützer(in) OT 3

to **envy** ['envi] beneiden **WS 4**, 123

epidemic [ˌepɪ'demɪk] Epidemie OT 2

equality [i'kwɒləti] Gleichberechtigung **WS 1**, 43

equator [ɪ'kweɪtə] Äquator **WS 1**, 13

equipment [ɪ'kwɪpmənt] Ausrüstung OT 2

equivalent [ɪ'kwɪvələnt] entsprechend **WS 4**, 126

errand ['erənd] Besorgung **WS 4**, 140

to **erupt** [ɪ'rʌpt] ausbrechen OT 2

escalator ['eskəleɪtə] Rolltreppe OT 1

to **escape** [ɪ'skeɪp] entkommen OT 2

to **escort** ['eskɔːt] begleiten **WS 2**, 53

especially [ɪˈspeʃəli] besonders OT 2

essay [ˈeseɪ] Aufsatz OT 3

essential [ɪˈsenʃl] wichtig; wesentlich WS 1, 33

to establish [ɪˈstæblɪʃ] etablieren; einführen OT 3

to estimate [ˈestɪmeɪt] schätzen WS 1, 24

ETA (estimated time of arrival) [ˌiː tiː ˈeɪ] geschätzte Ankunftszeit OT 2

ethical [ˈeθɪkl] ethisch; moralisch vertretbar OT 3

ethnic [ˈeθnɪk] ethnisch WS 1, 33

to evacuate [ɪˈvækjueɪt] verlassen; evakuieren WS 3, 108

evacuation [ɪˌvækjuˈeɪʃn] Evakuierung WS 3, 108

to evaluate [ɪˈvæljueɪt] bewerten WS 1, 36

even [ˈiːvn] sogar; selbst OT 1

evening [ˈiːvnɪŋ] Abend OT 1

event [ɪˈvent] Ereignis; Veranstaltung OT 1

ever [ˈevə] je; jemals OT 1

every [ˈevri] jede(r, -s) OT 1

everyday [ˈevrideɪ] alltäglich OT 3

everyone [ˈevriwʌn] jeder; alle OT 1

everything [ˈevriθɪŋ] alles OT 1

everywhere [ˈevriweə] überall; überallhin OT 1

evidence [ˈevɪdəns] Nachweis; Beweis WS 3, 90

to evolve [ɪˈvɒlv] sich entwickeln OT 3

ewe [juː] Mutterschaf OT 2

exact [ɪɡˈzækt] genau OT 2

to exaggerate [ɪɡˈzædʒəreɪt] übertreiben WS 1, 21

exaggeration [ɪɡˌzædʒəˈreɪʃn] Übertreibung WS 1, 21

exam [ɪɡˈzæm] Prüfung; Examen OT 1

example [ɪɡˈzɑːmpl] Beispiel OT 1

to excavate [ˈekskəveɪt] ausgraben OT 2

excavation [ˌekskəˈveɪʃn] Ausgrabung OT 2

to excel [ɪkˈsel] sich selbst übertreffen; sich hervortun WS 4, 126

excellent [ˈeksələnt] ausgezeichnet OT 2

except [ɪkˈsept] außer OT 2

exception [ɪkˈsepʃn] Ausnahme WS 4, 126

exchange [ɪksˈtʃeɪndʒ] Austausch; Wechseln OT 1

to excite [ɪkˈsaɪt] aufregen OT 3

excited [ɪkˈsaɪtɪd] begeistert; aufgeregt OT 1

exciting [ɪkˈsaɪtɪŋ] aufregend; spannend OT 1

exclamation [ˌekskləˈmeɪʃn] Ausruf OT 3

to exclude [ɪkˈskluːd] ausschließen WS 3, 103

to excuse [ɪkˈskjuːz] entschuldigen OT 1

to execute [ˈeksɪkjuːt] hinrichten OT 3

executive [ɪɡˈzekjətɪv] Exekutive; ausführend WS 3, 91

exercise [ˈeksəsaɪz] körperliche Bewegung; Übung OT 1

exercise book [ˈeksəsaɪz bʊk] Übungsheft; Schulheft OT 1

exhausted [ɪɡˈzɔːstɪd] erschöpft OT 3

exhausting [ɪɡˈzɔːstɪŋ] anstrengend; ermüdend OT 2

to exhibit [ɪɡˈzɪbɪt] ausstellen OT 2

exhibition [ˌeksɪˈbɪʃn] Ausstellung; Messe OT 1

to exist [ɪɡˈzɪst] existieren OT 3

existence [ɪɡˈzɪstəns] Existenz WS 1, 42

exit [ˈeksɪt] Ausgang; Abfahrt OT 2

to expand [ɪkˈspænd] wachsen; ausbauen WS 4, 127

to expect [ɪkˈspekt] erwarten OT 2

expectation [ˌekspekˈteɪʃn] Erwartung OT 3

expedition [ˌekspəˈdɪʃn] Expedition OT 2

expenditure [ɪkˈspendɪtʃə] Ausgaben WS 2, 65

expensive [ɪkˈspensɪv] teuer OT 1

experience [ɪkˈspɪəriəns] Erfahrung OT 2

to experience [ɪkˈspɪəriənsɪŋ] erfahren; erleben WS 4, 130

experienced [ɪkˈspɪəriənst] erfahren WS 1, 27

experiment [ɪkˈsperɪmənt] Experiment; Test OT 2

expert [ˈekspɜːt] Experte, Expertin OT 3

to explain [ɪkˈspleɪn] erklären OT 1

explanation [ˌekspləˈneɪʃn] Erklärung; Erläuterung OT 1

to explode [ɪkˈspləʊd] explodieren WS 1, 25

to exploit [ɪkˈsplɔɪt] ausbeuten OT 3

exploration [ˌekspləˈreɪʃn] Erforschung OT 3

to explore [ɪkˈsplɔː] erforschen; erkunden OT 1

exporter [ekˈspɔːtə] Exporteur(in) WS 1, 28

exposure [ɪkˈspəʊʒə] Aufdeckung OT 3

to express [ɪkˈspres] äußern; etw. ausdrücken WS 1, 14

expression [ɪkˈspreʃn] Ausdruck; Äußerung OT 1

extended [ɪkˈstendɪd] erweitert WS 4, 123

extinct [ɪkˈstɪŋkt] ausgestorben OT 2

extinction [ɪkˈstɪŋkʃn] Aussterben WS 1, 39

extra [ˈekstrə] Extra…; besonders OT 1

extract [ɪkˈstrækt] Auszug OT 3

extreme [ɪkˈstriːm] extrem WS 1, 28

eye [aɪ] Auge; Blick OT 1

eyebrow [ˈaɪbraʊ] Augenbraue WS 4, 137

eyelid [ˈaɪlɪd] Augenlid OT 2

eyepiece [ˈaɪpiːs] Okular OT 2

eyesore [ˈaɪsɔː] Schandfleck WS 2, 52

F

fabulous [ˈfæbjələs] fabelhaft OT 2

face [feɪs] Gesicht; Seite OT 1

facial [ˈfeɪʃl] Gesichts- WS 2, 53

facility [fəˈsɪləti] Anlage OT 3

fact [fækt] Tatsache; Wahrheit; Fakt OT 1

factor [ˈfæktə] Faktor OT 3

factory [ˈfæktri] Fabrik OT 3

factual [ˈfæktʃuəl] sachlich WS 1, 17

fail [feɪl] Durchfallen WS 4, 129

to fail [feɪl] scheitern WS 4, 143

failure [ˈfeɪljə] Misserfolg WS 4, 146

faint [feɪnt] schwindlig OT 2

to faint [feɪnt] ohnmächtig werden OT 2

fair [feə] gerecht; fair OT 1

fairground [ˈfeəɡraʊnd] Jahrmarkt OT 2

fairy tale [ˈfeəri teɪl] Märchen OT 1

to fall [fɔːl] fallen; stürzen OT 1
    to fall over [fɔːl ˈəʊvə] hinfallen; umfallen OT 2

familiar [fəˈmɪliə] vertraut; bekannt OT 2

familiarity [fəˌmiliˈærəti] Vertrautheit WS 2, 53

family [ˈfæməli] Familie OT 1

famine [ˈfæmɪn] Hungersnot OT 2

famous [ˈfeɪməs] berühmt; bekannt OT 1

fan [fæn] Fan; Ventilator OT 1

fanatic [fəˈnætɪk] Fanatiker(in); fanatisch WS 1, 15

fantastic [fænˈtæstɪk] fantastisch; toll OT 1

fantasy [ˈfæntəsi] Fantasy; Fantasie OT 2

far [fɑː] weit OT 1

far-off [ˈfɑː ɒf] fern OT 2

faraway [ˈfɑːrəweɪ] fern WS 1, 28

farmed [fɑːmd] gezüchtet WS 2, 69

farm [fɑːm] Bauernhof OT 1

farmer [ˈfɑːmə] Bauer, BNäuerin OT 2

farmhouse [ˈfɑːmhaʊs] Bauernhaus OT 2

farming [ˈfɑːmɪŋ] Landwirtschaft OT 2

farmland [ˈfɑːmlænd] Ackerland **WS 3**, 85

farmyard [ˈfɑːmjɑːd] Hof OT 2

to **fascinate** [ˈfæsɪneɪt] faszinieren **WS 2**, 52

fascinating [ˈfæsɪneɪtɪŋ] faszinierend **WS 1**, 13

fashion [ˈfæʃn] Trend; Mode OT 1

fashionable [ˈfæʃnəbl] modisch **WS 4**, 135

fast [fɑːst] schnell; fest OT 1

fat [fæt] Fett OT 2

father [ˈfɑːðə] Vater OT 1

fault [fɔːlt] Schuld; Fehler OT 2

to **fault** [fɔːlt] bemängeln OT 2

faulty [ˈfɔːlti] fehlerhaft **WS 2**, 64

favour: in favour of [ɪn ˈfeɪvə əv] pro; für **WS 3**, 94

favourite [ˈfeɪvərɪt] Lieblings... OT 1

fear [fɪə] Angst; Furcht OT 3

feat [fiːt] Meisterleistung OT 2

feather [ˈfeðə] Feder OT 2

federal [ˈfedərəl] Bundes... **WS 1**, 28

fed up: to be fed up [fed ˈʌp] satthaben OT 1

fee [fiː] Gebühr OT 3

to **feed** [fiːd] füttern OT 2

feedback [ˈfiːdbæk] Feedback OT 2

to **feel** [fiːl] (sich) fühlen; empfinden; fühlen; anfassen OT 1

feeling [ˈfiːlɪŋ] Gefühl OT 2

female [ˈfiːmeɪl] weiblich OT 2

fence [fens] Zaun OT 1

feral [ˈferəl] wild **WS 1**, 25

ferry [ˈferi] Fähre OT 3

fertilizer [ˈfɜːtəlaɪzə] Dünger OT 3

festival [ˈfestɪvl] Festival; Festspiele; Fest OT 1

few [fjuː] wenige OT 1

fictional [ˈfɪkʃənl] erfunden OT 2

field [fiːld] Feld; Acker OT 1

field trip [ˈfiːld trɪp] Schulausflug OT 2

fifteen [ˌfɪfˈtiːn] fünfzehn OT 1

fifty [ˈfɪfti] fünfzig OT 1

fight [faɪt] Kampf; Schlägerei OT 1

to **fight** [faɪt] kämpfen OT 1

fighter [ˈfaɪtə] Kämpfer(in) OT 2

file [faɪl] Datei OT 2

file card [ˈfaɪl ˌkɑːd] Karteikarte OT 2

to **fill** [fɪl] füllen; ausfüllen OT 1

film [fɪlm] Film OT 1

filmmaker [ˈfɪlm meɪkə] Filmemacher(in) **WS 1**, 32

final [ˈfaɪnl] endgültig; letzte(r, -s) OT 2

finally [ˈfaɪnəli] schließlich; endlich OT 1

finances [ˈfaɪnænsɪz] Finanzen **WS 4**, 142

financial [faɪˈnænʃl] finanziell **WS 3**, 104

to **find** [faɪnd] finden; feststellen OT 1

to **find out** [faɪnd aʊt] herausfinden OT 2

fine [faɪn] gut; prima OT 1

finger [ˈfɪŋgə] Finger OT 1

fingernail [ˈfɪŋgəneɪl] Fingernagel OT 2

to **finish** [ˈfɪnɪʃ] abschließen; beenden; aufhören OT 1

fire [ˈfaɪə] Feuer OT 2

to **fire** [ˈfaɪə] abfeuern; schießen OT 2

firefighting [faɪəfaɪtɪŋ] Brandbekämpfung OT 2

fireplace [ˈfaɪəpleɪs] Kamin OT 1

fireworks [ˈfaɪəwɜːks] Feuerwerk OT 3

first [fɜːst] erste(r, -s) OT 1

at first [ət ˈfɜːst] zuerst; anfangs OT 2

first aid [ˌfɜːst ˈeɪd] Erste Hilfe OT 2

fish [fɪʃ] Fisch OT 1

to **fish** [fɪʃ] fischen OT 3

fisherman [ˈfɪʃəmən] Fischer OT 2

fish finger [ˈfɪʃ ˌfɪŋgə] Fischstäbchen OT 1

fishing [ˈfɪʃɪŋ] Fischerei OT 3

fit [fɪt] in Form; geeignet OT 2

five [faɪv] fünf OT 1

to **fix** [fɪks] korrigieren OT 2

fizzy [ˈfɪzi] kohlensäurehaltig OT 2

flag [flæg] Flagge; Fahne OT 3

flagship [ˈflægʃɪp] Flaggschiff OT 3

flamingo [fləˈmɪŋgəʊ] Flamingo OT 2

flash [flæʃ] Blitz **WS 2**, 55

flat [flæt] Wohnung; Apartment OT 1

flea [fliː] Floh **WS 4**, 135

fleet [fliːt] Flotte **WS 1**, 17

flexible [ˈfleksəbl] flexibel **WS 4**, 136

flight [flaɪt] Flug; Fliegen OT 1

to **flip** [flɪp] umdrehen OT 3

flood [flʌd] Hochwasser; Flut OT 2

to **flood** [flʌd] überfluten **WS 3**, 108

floor [flɔː] Boden; Fußboden; Stockwerk OT 1

flour [ˈflaʊə] Mehl OT 3

to **flourish** [ˈflʌrɪʃ] blühen OT 3

flower [ˈflaʊə] Blume OT 1

fluent [ˈfluːənt] fließend OT 3

fluffy [ˈflʌfi] flauschig OT 2

flute [fluːt] Querflöte OT 1

to **fly** [flaɪ] fliegen; steigen lassen OT 1

focus [ˈfəʊkəs] Fokus; Brennpunkt **WS 1**, 27

to **focus** [ˈfəʊkəs] fokussieren OT 2

foggy [ˈfɒgi] nebelig OT 3

foliage [ˈfəʊliɪdʒ] Blätter OT 3

folk [fəʊk] Volks... OT 2

folklore [ˈfəʊklɔː] Folklore **WS 1**, 26

to **follow** [ˈfɒləʊ] folgen OT 2

food [fuːd] Essen; Nahrungsmittel OT 1

food poisoning [ˈfuːd pɔɪzənɪŋ] Lebensmittelvergiftung OT 2

food supplement [ˈfuːd ˌsʌplɪmənt] Nahrungsergänzungsmittel **WS 2**, 68

foot [fʊt] Fuß; Fußende OT 1

footage [ˈfʊtɪdʒ] Filmmaterial; Filmaufnahmen **WS 2**, 73

football [ˈfʊtbɔːl] Fußball; Football OT 1

footprint [ˈfʊtprɪnt] Fußabdruck OT 2

footstep [ˈfʊtstep] Schritt OT 2

for [ˈfə] für; dafür OT 1

to **force** [fɔːs] zwingen OT 3

forecast [ˈfɔːkɑːst] Prognose OT 2

forefather [ˈfɔːfɑːðə] Ahne; Urvater OT 3

foreground [ˈfɔːgraʊnd] Vordergrund **WS 2**, 53

foreign [ˈfɒrən] ausländisch; fremd OT 1

forest [ˈfɒrɪst] Wald OT 1

forever [fərˈevə] für immer OT 3

to **forget** [fəˈget] vergessen OT 1

to **forgive** [fəˈgɪv] vergeben OT 2

to **form** [fɔːm] gründen; bilden **WS 1**, 13

formal [ˈfɔːml] förmlich; formell OT 3

format [ˈfɔːmæt] Format **WS 2**, 63

formation [fɔːˈmeɪʃn] Formation **WS 1**, 26

former [ˈfɔːmə] frühere(r) **WS 2**, 67

formula [ˈfɔːmjələ] Formel OT 2

fort [fɔːt] Festung OT 2

fortunately [ˈfɔːtʃənətli] glücklicherweise **WS 2**, 63

forty [ˈfɔːti] vierzig OT 1

forum [ˈfɔːrəm] Forum OT 2

forwards [ˈfɔːwədz] vorwärts OT 2

fossil [ˈfɒsl] fossil OT 3

to **foul** [faʊl] foulen (Sport) OT 3

to **found** [faʊnd] gründen OT 2

foundational [faʊnˈdeɪʃnl] Gründer... OT 3

founder [ˈfaʊndə] Gründer(in) **WS 4**, 143

fountain [ˈfaʊntən] Springbrunnen; Fontäne OT 1

four [fɔː] vier OT 1

fourteen [ˌfɔːˈtiːn] vierzehn OT 1

fox [fɒks] Fuchs OT 1

to **frack** [fræk] fracken **WS 1**, 28
fragile [ˈfrædʒaɪl] zerbrechlich OT 3
frame [freɪm] Rahmen OT 3
framework [ˈfreɪmwɜːk] Rahmen
  WS 3, 90
frantic [ˈfræntɪk] hektisch; aufgeregt
  OT 3
freckles [ˈfrekelz] Sommersprossen
  OT 3
free [friː] frei; kostenlos OT 1
freelance [ˈfriːlɑːns] freiberuflich OT 3
freeze-dried [ˈfriːz draɪ]
  gefriergetrocknet OT 3
freezer [ˈfriːzə] Gefrierschrank OT 3
freight [freɪt] Fracht OT 2
French fries [ˌfrentʃˈfraɪz] Pommes
  frites OT 2
frequency [ˈfriːkwənsi] Häufigkeit
  WS 1, 34
frequent [ˈfriːkwənt] häufig **WS 1**, 28
frequently [ˈfriːkwəntli] häufig OT 3
fresh [freʃ] frisch OT 3
freshman [ˈfreʃmən] Student im ersten
  Jahr; Studienanfänger OT 3
Friday [ˈfraɪdeɪ] Freitag OT 1
fridge [frɪdʒ] Kühlschrank OT 1
friend [frend] Freund(in); Bekannte(r)
  OT 1
friendliness [ˈfrendlinəs] Freundlichkeit
  WS 2, 53
friendly [ˈfrendli] freundlich;
  freundschaftlich OT 1
friendship [ˈfrendʃɪp] Freundschaft
  OT 3
to **frighten** [ˈfraɪtn] erschrecken OT 3
frightening [ˈfraɪtnɪŋ] erschreckend
  OT 1
from [frəm] von; aus OT 1
front [frʌnt] Vorderseite; Bauch OT 1
to **frown** [fraʊn] die Stirn runzeln OT 3
frozen [ˈfrəʊzn] gefroren OT 3
fruit [fruːt] Obst; Frucht OT 1
frustrated [frʌˈstreɪtɪd] frustriert
  WS 2, 60
fuel [ˈfjuːəl] Brennstoff OT 2
full [fʊl] voll; komplett OT 1
  full time [ˌfʊlˈtaɪm] vollzeit OT 2
fun [fʌn] Spaß OT 1
function [ˈfʌŋkʃn] Funktion **WS 1**, 32
fund [fʌnd] Geldmittel; Fond **WS 1**, 15
fundraiser [ˈfʌndreɪzə]
  Wohltätigkeitsveranstaltung OT 2
fundraising [ˈfʌndreɪzɪŋ]
  Spendensammlung OT 2
funeral [ˈfjuːnərəl] Beerdigung **WS 3**, 106

funny [ˈfʌni] lustig; witzig; merkwürdig
  OT 1
fur [fɜː] Fell OT 3
furniture [ˈfɜːnɪtʃə] Möbel OT 1
further [ˈfɜːðə] weiter OT 3
future [ˈfjuːtʃə] Zukunft OT 2

G
to **gain** [geɪn] bekommen; erreichen
  WW, 11
gallery [ˈgæləri] Galerie; Empore OT 1
gallon [ˈgælən] Gallone OT 3
game [geɪm] Videospiel OT 1
gang [gæŋ] Bande OT 2
gap [gæp] Lücke; Pause OT 1
garbage [ˈgɑːbɪdʒ] Abfall OT 2
garden [ˈgɑːdn] Garten OT 1
gardening [ˈgɑːdnɪŋ] Gartenarbeit OT 1
gas [gæs] Gas OT 3
gateway [ˈgeɪtweɪ] Zugang; Gateway
  WS 1, 39
gay [geɪ] schwul **WS 4**, 120
to **gaze** [geɪz] blicken; starren **WS 1**, 29
geared: to be geared towards [bi gɪəd
  təˈwɔːdz] auf etw. ausgerichtet sein
  WS 4, 126
geek [giːk] Geek; Spezialist(in) **WS 2**, 66
gel [dʒel] Gel OT 2
gender [ˈdʒendə] (soziales) Geschlecht;
  Gender **WS 4**, 122
gendered [ˈdʒendəd]
  geschlechtsspezifisch **WS 4**, 124
genderless [ˈdʒendələs] geschlechtslos
  WS 4, 124
genderneutral [ˌdʒendəˈnjuːtrəl]
  geschlechtsneutral **WS 4**, 124
general [ˈdʒenrəl] generell; allgemein
  OT 2
generalization [ˌdʒenrəlaɪˈzeɪʃn]
  Generalisierung **WS 4**, 126
to **generate** [ˈdʒenəreɪt] bilden;
  erzeugen OT 2
generation [ˌdʒenəˈreɪʃn] Generation
  OT 3
genetic [dʒəˈnetɪk] genetisch **WS 4**, 131
gently [ˈdʒentli] sachte OT 3
geocache [ˈdʒiːəʊkæʃ] Geocache OT 2
geocaching [ˈdʒiːəʊkæʃɪŋ] Geocaching
  OT 2
geographical [ˌdʒiːəˈgræfɪkl]
  geografisch **WS 3**, 85
geography [dʒiˈɒgrəfi] Erdkunde;
  Geografie OT 1
geology [dʒiˈɒlədʒi] Geologie OT 2
gesture [ˈdʒestə] Geste **WS 4**, 137
to **get** [get] bekommen; holen OT 1

to **get in** [get ɪn] einsteigen OT 1
to **get on** [get ɒn] zusteigen OT 2
to **get out** [ˈget aʊt] aussteigen OT 1
to **get rid** [get rɪd] loswerden OT 3
to **get up** [get ʌp] aufstehen OT 1
gherkin [ˈgɜːkɪn] Gurke **WS 2**, 48
gifted [ˈgɪftɪd] begabt **WS 4**, 121
gig [gɪg] Gig; Auftritt **WS 2**, 65
ginger [ˈdʒɪndʒə] Ingwer; rötlich braun
  OT 1
giraffe [dʒəˈrɑːf] Giraffe OT 1
girl [gɜːl] Mädchen OT 1
to **give** [gɪv] geben; schenken OT 1
to **give up** [gɪv ʌp] aufgeben OT 2
glacier [ˈglæsiə] Gletscher OT 3
glad [glæd] froh OT 2
gladiator [ˈglædieɪtə] Gladiator(in) OT 2
glam [glæm] schick **WS 3**, 103
glamorous [ˈglæmərəs] glamourös
  WS 3, 103
glamping [ˈglæmpɪŋ] glamouröses
  Zelten **WS 3**, 103
glass [glɑːs] Glas OT 1
global [ˈgləʊbl] global; weltweit OT 3
global warming [ˌgləʊbl ˈwɔːmɪŋ]
  Erderwärmung **WS 1**, 28
globe [gləʊb] Erdball; Globus OT 3
glory [ˈglɔːri] Ehre OT 3
glove [glʌv] Handschuh OT 1
glue [gluː] Klebstoff; Leim OT 1
to **go** [gəʊ] gehen; fahren OT 1
to **go to sleep** [ˌgəʊ tə ˈsliːp] einschlafen
  OT 1
goal [gəʊl] Tor; Ziel OT 1
goalkeeper [ˈgəʊlkiːpə] Torwart(in)
  OT 3
goat [gəʊt] Ziege OT 3
godmother [ˈgɒdmʌðə] Patentante
  WS 1, 15
gold [gəʊld] Gold OT 2
golden [ˈgəʊldən] golden OT 2
golf [gɒlf] Golf **WW**, 11
to **gongoozle** [gɒŋˈguːzl] gaffen OT 3
gongoozler [gɒŋˈguːzlə] Gaffer OT 3
good [gʊd] gut; gut (geeignet) OT 1
goods [gʊdz] Güter OT 3
gorgeous [ˈgɔːdʒəs] großartig OT 3
gosh [gɒʃ] großer Gott (Ausruf) OT 3
to **govern** [ˈgʌvn] regieren OT 3
government [ˈgʌvənmənt] Regierung
  OT 2
governmental [ˌgʌvnˈmentl]
  Regierungs... **WS 3**, 86
GPS (global positioning system) [ˌdʒiː
  piːˈes] Navigationssystem; Globales
  Positionsbestimmungssystem OT 2

to **grab** [græb] greifen OT 3

grade [greɪd] Klassenstufe OT 2

  sixth grader [ˈsɪksθ ˌgreɪdə] Sechstklässler(in) OT 2

to **grade** [ˈgreɪdɪŋ] bewerten **WS 4**, 129

to **graduate** [ˈgrædʒuət] den Schulabschluss machen **WS 3**, 106

graffiti [grəˈfiːti] Graffiti OT 3

grain [greɪn] Getreide **WS 2**, 68

gram [græm] Gramm OT 2

grammar [ˈgræmə] Grammatik OT 1

granddaughter [ˈgræntʃaɪld] Enkel(in OT 1

grandfather [ˈgrænfɑːðə] Großvater OT 1

grandma [ˈgrænmɑː] Oma OT 1

grandmother [ˈgrænmʌðə] Großmutter OT 1

grandpa [ˈgrænpɑː] Opa OT 1

grandparents [ˈgrænpeərənts] Großeltern OT 1

grandson [ˈgrænsʌn] Enkel OT 1

graph [grɑːf] Diagramm **WS 4**, 129

graphic [ˈgræfɪk] Grafik **WS 2**, 79

to **grasp** [grɑːsp] greifen; festhalten **WS 4**, 131

grass [grɑːs] Gras; Rasen OT 1

grateful [ˈgreɪtfl] dankbar OT 3

gravy [ˈgreɪvi] Bratensoße OT 1

great [greɪt] groß; beträchtlich; toll OT 1

greatness [ˈgreɪtnəs] Großartigkeit **WS 3**, 105

green [griːn] grün; Grünfläche OT 1

greenhouse [ˈgriːnhaʊs] Treibhaus **WS 2**, 69

to **greet** [griːt] grüßen **WS 2**, 53

greeting [ˈgriːtɪŋ] Gruß OT 2

grey [greɪ] grau; trüb OT 1

to **grill** [grɪl] grillen OT 3

to **grin** [grɪn] grinsen OT 2

grizzly [ˈgrɪzli] Grizzlybär OT 2

grocery [ˈgrəʊsəri] Lebensmittel **WS 4**, 124

grouchy [ˈgraʊtʃi] griesgrämig OT 2

group [gruːp] Gruppe OT 1

to **group** [gruːp] gruppieren **WS 3**, 85

to **grow** [grəʊ] wachsen; anbauen OT 1

grown up [ˈgrəʊn ʌp] erwachsen OT 2

growth [grəʊθ] Wachstum **WS 2**, 68

gruesome [ˈgruːsəm] grauenvoll; abscheulich **WS 3**, 98

to **guarantee** [ˌgærənˈtiː] garantieren **WS 3**, 90

guard [gɑːd] Wächter(in); Sicherheitsbeamte(r) **WS 4**, 151

to **guard** [gɑːd] bewachen **WS 2**, 59

guardian [ˈgɑːdiən] Betreuer(in) OT 2

guess [ges] Schätzung OT 1

to **guess** [ges] schätzen OT 1

guest [gest] Gast OT 2

guestbook [ˈgestbʊk] Gästebuch OT 2

guidance [ˈgaɪdns] Anleitung OT 3

to **guide** [gaɪd] führen; leiten OT 1

guide [gaɪd] Führer(in); Leitfaden OT 1

guidebook [ˈgaɪdbʊk] Reiseführer OT 3

guide dog [ˈgaɪd dɒg] Blindenführhund OT 2

guideline [ˈgaɪdlaɪn] Richtlinie OT 3

guilty [ˈgɪlti] schuldig **WS 3**, 90

guitar [gɪˈtɑː] Gitarre OT 1

gun [gʌn] Schusswaffe OT 3

guy [gaɪ] Kerl; Typ **WS 1**, 30

gym [dʒɪm] Turnen; Turnhalle OT 1

gymnasium [dʒɪmˈneɪziəm] Sporthalle; Turnhalle OT 3

gymnastics [dʒɪmˈnæstɪks] Gymnastik OT 1

H

habit [ˈhæbɪt] Angewohnheit; Verhalten **WS 2**, 51

habitat [ˈhæbɪtæt] Habitat **WS 1**, 34

to **hail** [heɪl] grüßen OT 2

hair [heə] Haare; Haar OT 1

haircut [ˈheəkʌt] Haarschnitt OT 2

half [hɑːf] halbe(r, -s); halb OT 1

halfpast [ˈhɑːf pɑːst] eine halbe Stunde nach OT 1

halfway [ˌhɑːfˈweɪ] halbwegs; halb OT 3

hall [hɔːl] Diele; Flur; Halle OT 1

halt [hɔːlt] Haltestelle OT 2

ham [hæm] Schinken OT 1

hamster [ˈhæmstə] Hamster OT 1

hand [hænd] Hand; Hilfe OT 1

to **hand (in)** [hændɪn] (ein)reichen OT 2

handbag [ˈhændbæg] Handtasche OT 3

handbook [ˈhændbʊk] Handbuch OT 3

handicraft [ˈhændikrɑːft] Handwerk OT 3

handle [ˈhændl] Griff OT 2

to **handle** [ˈhændl] handhaben **WS 4**, 131

handset [ˈhændset] Handapparat OT 2

handsome [ˈhænsəm] gut aussehend; attraktiv OT 1

handwriting [ˈhændraɪtɪŋ] Handschrift OT 2

to **hang** [hæŋ] hängen OT 3

  to **hang out** [hæŋ aʊt] herumhängen OT 3

to **happen** [ˈhæpən] geschehen; passieren OT 1

happy [ˈhæpi] glücklich; herzlich OT 1

hard [hɑːd] hart OT 2

hardly [ˈhɑːdli] kaum **WS 3**, 88

harm [hɑːm] Schaden OT 3

harmful [ˈhɑːmfl] schädlich **WS 2**, 65

harpoon [hɑːˈpuːn] Harpune OT 3

harsh [hɑːʃ] rau **WS 1**, 27

harvest [ˈhɑːvɪst] Ernte OT 3

hat [hæt] Hut; Mütze OT 1

to **hate** [heɪt] hassen OT 1

have got [ˈhæv gɒt] haben OT 1

hazel [ˈheɪzl] Haselnussstrauch OT 3

head [hed] Kopf; Verstand OT 1

  head of state [ˌhed əv ˈsteɪt] Staatsoberhaupt OT 2

headache [ˈhedeɪk] Kopfschmerzen OT 1

header [ˈhedə] Kopfball OT 3

heading [ˈhedɪŋ] Überschrift OT 3

to **headline** [ˈhedlaɪn] publizieren OT 3

headline [ˈhedlaɪn] Schlagzeile OT 2

headquarters [ˌhedˈkwɔːtəz] Hauptquartier **WS 3**, 110

headset [ˈhedset] Headset; Kopfhörer **WS 4**, 128

headphones [ˈhedfəʊnz] Kopfhörer OT 2

head teacher [ˌhed ˈtiːtʃə] Schulleiter(in); Rektor(in) OT 1

headword [ˈhedwɜːd] Stichwort OT 2

health [helθ] Gesundheit OT 3

healthcare [ˈhelθkeə] Gesundheitsfürsorge **WS 3**, 84

healthy [ˈhelθi] gesund OT 2

heap [hiːp] Haufen **WS 1**, 16

to **hear** [hɪə] hören; erfahren OT 1

heart [hɑːt] Herz OT 2

to **heat** [hiːt] heizen OT 2

heater [ˈhiːtə] Ofen OT 2

heatwave [ˈhiːtweɪv] Hitzewelle **WS 1**, 28

heavy [ˈhevi] schwer OT 1

hedgehog [ˈhedʒhɒg] Igel OT 1

height [haɪt] Höhe; Größe OT 1

helicopter [ˈhelɪkɒptə] Hubschrauber OT 3

hello [həˈləʊ] Hallo! OT 1

helmet [ˈhelmɪt] Helm OT 1

to **help** [help] helfen OT 1

helpful [ˈhelpfl] hilfreich; hilfsbereit OT 1

helpline [ˈhelplaɪn] Hotline OT 2

hemisphere [ˈhemɪsfɪə] Hemisphäre **WS 1**, 13

heptathlon [hep'tæθlən] Siebenkampf OT 2

to herd [hɜːd] treiben OT 2

herder ['hɜːdə] Hirte, Hirtin OT 3

here [hɪə] hier; hierher OT 1

hereditary [hə'redɪtri] vererblich **WS 3**, 98

heritage ['herɪtɪdʒ] Erbe; Tradition OT 3

hero ['hɪərəʊ] Held(in) OT 3

to hesitate ['hezɪteɪt] zögern OT 3

hesitation [ˌhezɪ'teɪʃn] Zögern OT 3

heterosexual [ˌhetərə'sekʃuəl] heterosexuell **WS 4**, 125

to hide [haɪd] sich verstecken OT 3

high [haɪ] Höhepunkt; Höchststand; hoch OT 1

highest ['haɪest] höchste(r, -s) OT 1

highlight ['haɪlaɪt] Höhepunkt OT 3

highway ['haɪweɪ] Highway; Landstraße OT 3

to hike [haɪk] wandern OT 1

hiker ['haɪkə] Wanderer, Wanderin OT 3

hill [hɪl] Hügel OT 1

him [hɪm] ihn; ihm OT 1

to hint [hɪnt] andeuten **WS 4**, 138

hip [hɪp] Hüfte OT 1

historian [hɪ'stɔːriən] Historiker(in) OT 2

historic [hɪ'stɒrɪk] historisch OT 2

historical [hɪ'stɒrɪkl] geschichtlich OT 2

history ['hɪstri] Geschichte; Geschichtswissenschaft OT 1

to hit [hɪt] schlagen; treffen OT 1

hob [hɒb] Kochfeld OT 3

hobby ['hɒbi] Hobby OT 1

hockey ['hɒki] Hockey; Eishockey OT 1

to hold [həʊld] halten OT 1

hole [həʊl] Loch; Bau OT 1

holiday ['hɒlədeɪ] Urlaub OT 1

hollow ['hɒləʊ] Senke OT 3

hologram ['hɒləgræm] Hologramm OT 2

home [həʊm] Zuhause; Haus OT 1

homecoming ['həʊmkʌmɪŋ] traditionelles Event in Highschool **WS 4**, 130

homeland ['həʊmlænd] Heimat **WS 1**, 28

homeless ['həʊmləs] obdachlos; Obdachlose(r) **WS 3**, 101

homepage ['həʊmpeɪdʒ] Homepage OT 3

homesickness ['həʊmsɪknəs] Heimweh **WS 1**, 30

homework ['həʊmwɜːk] Hausaufgaben OT 1

honest ['ɒnɪst] ehrlich OT 2

honey ['hʌni] Honig; Schatz (als Kosename) OT 2

to honour ['ɒnə] ehren OT 3

hoodie ['hʊdi] Kapuzenpullover; Kapuzenjacke OT 1

to hope [həʊp] hoffen OT 1

hopeful ['həʊpfl] hoffnungsvoll OT 3

hopefully ['həʊpfəli] hoffentlich OT 3

hopeless ['həʊpləs] hoffnungslos **WS 4**, 138

horizon [hə'raɪzn] Horizont **WS 1**, 38

hormone ['hɔːməʊn] Hormon **WS 4**, 125

horn [hɔːn] Horn; Hupe OT 3

horrible ['hɒrəbl] furchtbar OT 2

horrified ['hɒrɪfaɪd] entsetzt **WW**, 11

horse [hɔːs] Pferd OT 1

horse riding ['raɪdɪŋ] Reiten OT 1

hospital ['hɒspɪtl] Krankenhaus OT 1

hospitality [ˌhɒspɪ'tæləti] Gastfreundlichkeit OT 2

to host [həʊst] ausrichten OT 3

hostel ['hɒstl] Hostel **WS 3**, 89

hot [hɒt] heiß; warm; scharf OT 1

hotel [həʊ'tel] Hotel OT 1

hound [haʊnd] Spürhund OT 2

hour ['aʊə] Stunde OT 1

house [haʊs] Haus OT 1

household ['haʊshəʊld] Haushalt **WS 3**, 101

housekeeper ['haʊskiːpə] Haushälter(in) OT 3

housework ['haʊswɜːk] Hausarbeit OT 1

how [haʊ] wie OT 1

howl [haʊl] Geheul **WS 1**, 25

hug [hʌg] Umarmung OT 1

human ['hjuːmən] menschlich OT 2

humour ['hjuːmə] Humor **WS 1**, 30

hundred ['hʌndrəd] hundert OT 1

hungry ['hʌŋgri] hungrig OT 1

to hunt [hʌnt] jagen OT 2

hunter ['hʌntə] Jäger(in) OT 3

hunter-gatherer [ˌhʌntə 'gæðərə] Jäger und Sammler **WS 1**, 24

hurricane ['hʌrɪkən] Hurrikan; Orkan **WS 1**, 28

to hurry ['hʌri] sich beeilen; antreiben OT 1

hurt [hɜːt] verletzt; gekränkt OT 1

to hurt [hɜːt] schmerzen; wehtun OT 1

husband ['hʌzbənd] Ehemann; Mann OT 2

hybrid ['haɪbrɪd] Hybrid... OT 3

hyperactive [ˌhaɪpər'æktɪv] hyperaktiv **WS 4**, 127

hypothermia [ˌhaɪpə'θɜːmiə] Unterkühlung OT 2

I

ice [aɪs] Eis; Eiscreme OT 1

iconic [aɪ'kɒnɪk] ikonisch; Kult... OT 3

ICT (information and communications technology) [ˌaɪ siː'tiː] Informations- und Kommunikationstechnologie; Informatikunterricht OT 1

idea [aɪ'dɪə] Idee; Ansicht OT 1

ideal [aɪ'diːəl] ideal **WS 1**, 28

to idealize [aɪ'diːəlaɪz] idealisieren OT 3

to identify [aɪ'dentɪfaɪ] identifizieren **WW**, 11

identity [aɪ'dentəti] Identität OT 3

idol ['aɪdl] Idol **WS 2**, 68

if [ɪf] falls; immer, wenn OT 1

igloo ['ɪgluː] Iglu OT 3

to ignore [ɪg'nɔː] ignorieren OT 3

to illustrate ['ɪləstreɪt] verdeutlichen; illustrieren OT 3

illustration [ˌɪlə'streɪʃn] Illustration OT 2

imaginary [ɪ'mædʒɪnəri] erfunden; fiktiv **WS 3**, 89

to imagine [ɪ'mædʒɪn] sich etwas vorstellen; sich einbilden OT 1

immediate [ɪ'miːdiət] unmittelbar; umgehend **WS 1**, 24

immigrant ['ɪmɪgrənt] Einwanderer, Einwanderin OT 3

to immigrate ['ɪmɪgreɪt] einwandern **WS 4**, 123

immigration [ˌɪmɪ'greɪʃn] Einwanderung OT 2

impact ['ɪmpækt] Auswirkung OT 3

impaired [ɪm'peəd] beeinträchtigt **WS 4**, 131

to impart [ɪm'pɑːt] vermitteln OT 3

imperative [ɪm'perətɪv] Imperativ; Befehlsform OT 1

importance [ɪm'pɔːtns] Wichtigkeit; Bedeutung OT 3

important [ɪm'pɔːtnt] wichtig; einflussreich OT 1

impossible [ɪm'pɒsəbl] unmöglich OT 2

to impress [ɪm'pres] beeindrucken OT 3

impression [ɪm'preʃn] Eindruck OT 3

to improve [ɪm'pruːv] sich verbessern OT 3

improvement [ɪm'pruːvmənt] Verbesserung OT 3

inaccessible [ˌɪnækˈsesəbl] unzugänglich OT 3

incentive [ɪnˈsentɪv] Anreiz; Antrieb **WS 4**, 142

inch [ɪntʃ] Zoll (2,54 cm) OT 2

to **include** [ɪnˈkluːd] einschließen OT 2

including [ɪnˈkluːdɪŋ] einschließlich; inklusive OT 1

inclusive [ɪnˈkluːsɪv] integrativ **WS 2**, 60

income [ˈɪnkʌm] Einkommen **WS 1**, 27

incomplete [ˌɪnkəmˈpliːt] unvollständig **WS 4**, 123

increase [ˈɪnkriːs] Zunahme OT 3

increasingly [ɪnˈkriːsɪŋli] zunehmend **WS 2**, 62

incredible [ɪnˈkredəbl] unglaublich OT 2

incubator [ˈɪŋkjubeɪtə] Inkubator; Unterstützer von Start-ups **WS 4**, 134

independence [ˌɪndɪˈpendəns] Unabhängigkeit OT 2

independent [ˌɪndɪˈpendənt] unabhängig OT 3

to **indicate** [ˈɪndɪkeɪt] angeben; zeigen **WS 2**, 65

individual [ˌɪndɪˈvɪdʒuəl] individuell OT 3

indoor [ˈɪndɔː] Innen... OT 2

indoors [ˌɪnˈdɔːz] drinnen OT 3

industry [ˈɪndəstri] Industrie OT 2

infection [ɪnˈfekʃn] Entzündung OT 2

infinitive [ɪnˈfɪnətɪv] Infinitiv OT 1

to **influence** [ˈɪnfluəns] beeinflussen OT 3

influencer [ˈɪnfluənsə] Influencer(in) **WS 2**, 62

influential [ˌɪnfluˈenʃl] einflussreich **WS 3**, 99

influenza [ˌɪnfluˈenzə] Grippe; Influenza **WS 1**, 24

infographic [ˌɪnfəʊˈgræfɪk] Infografik OT 3

infomercial [ˌɪnfəʊˈmɜːʃl] Infomercial **WS 3**, 93

to **inform** [ɪnˈfɔːm] informieren OT 3

informal [ɪnˈfɔːml] informell **WS 1**, 16

information [ˌɪnfəˈmeɪʃn] Informationen; Auskunft OT 1

informative [ɪnˈfɔːmətɪv] informativ **WS 1**, 36

ingredient [ɪnˈgriːdiənt] Zutat OT 2

to **inherit** [ɪnˈherɪt] erben **WS 3**, 92

to **injure** [ˈɪndʒə] verletzen OT 2

injury [ˈɪndʒəri] Verletzung OT 2

inn [ɪn] Gasthaus OT 2

inner [ˈɪnə] innere(r, -s) **WS 3**, 110

innovation [ˌɪnəˈveɪʃn] Innovation; Neuheit OT 3

innovative [ˈɪnəveɪtɪv] innovativ **WS 4**, 146

insect [ˈɪnsekt] Insekt OT 2

insecure [ˌɪnsɪˈkjʊə] unsicher; instabil **WS 4**, 142

insecurity [ˌɪnsɪˈkjʊərəti] Unsicherheit **WS 4**, 146

inside [ˌɪnˈsaɪd] in; innerhalb OT 1

inspiration [ˌɪnspəˈreɪʃn] Inspiration; Eingebung OT 3

to **inspire** [ɪnˈspaɪə] begeistern; inspirieren OT 2

to **install** [ɪnˈstɔːl] installieren OT 3

for **instance** [fəˈɪnstəns] zum Beispiel OT 3

instead [ɪnˈsted] stattdessen OT 2

institution [ˌɪnstɪˈtjuːʃn] Einrichtung OT 3

instruction [ɪnˈstrʌkʃn] Anweisung; Anleitung OT 1

instructive [ɪnˈstrʌktɪv] instruktiv; lehrreich **WS 1**, 29

instrument [ˈɪnstrəmənt] Instrument; Gerät OT 1

to **insult** [ˈɪnsʌlt] beleidigen OT 3

insurance [ɪnˈʃʊərəns] Versicherung **WS 3**, 84

intact [ɪnˈtækt] unversehrt; intakt OT 3

to **integrate** [ˈɪntɪgreɪt] integrieren; einbinden OT 3

intellectual [ˌɪntəˈlektʃuəl] intellektuell OT 3

intelligent [ɪnˈtelɪdʒənt] intelligent OT 2

to **intend** [ɪnˈtend] beabsichtigen OT 3

intense [ɪnˈtens] stark; ernsthaft **WS 1**, 32

to **interact** [ˌɪntərˈækt] interagieren **WS 3**, 93

interaction [ˌɪntərˈækʃn] Interaktion **WS 2**, 53

interactive [ˌɪntərˈæktɪv] interaktiv OT 3

interest [ˈɪntrəst] Interesse; Reiz OT 1

interested [ˈɪntrəstɪd] interessiert OT 1

interesting [ˈɪntrəstɪŋ] interessant OT 1

interface [ˈɪntəfeɪs] Interface OT 3

interior [ɪnˈtɪəriə] Binnenland; das Innere **WS 1**, 13

internal [ɪnˈtɜːnl] innen; inner... **WS 3**, 86

international [ˌɪntəˈnæʃnəl] international OT 1

internet [ˈɪntənet] Internet OT 3

internship [ˈɪntɜːnʃɪp] Praktikum OT 3

to **interpret** [ɪnˈtɜːprət] interpretieren **WS 2**, 55

to **interrupt** [ˌɪntəˈrʌpt] unterbrechen OT 2

intersex [ˈɪntəseks] intersex **WS 4**, 125

interview [ˈɪntəvjuː] Vorstellungsgespräch; Interview OT 1

to **interview** [ˈɪntəvjuː] ein Vorstellungsgespräch führen mit; interviewen OT 1

interviewee [ˌɪntəvjuˈiː] Interviewte(r) OT 3

interviewer [ˈɪntəvjuːə] Interviewer(in) OT 3

intriguing [ɪnˈtriːgɪŋ] faszinierend **WS 2**, 70

to **introduce** [ˌɪntrəˈdjuːs] vorstellen OT 2

introduction [ˌɪntrəˈdʌkʃn] Vorstellung; Einführung OT 2

to **invade** [ɪnˈveɪd] einmarschieren OT 3

invasive [ɪnˈveɪsɪv] invasiv **WS 1**, 25

to **invent** [ɪnˈvent] erfinden OT 2

invention [ɪnˈvenʃn] Erfindung OT 2

inventor [ɪnˈventə] Erfinder(in) OT 2

to **invert** [ɪnˈvɜːt] umkehren; umstellen **WS 1**, 31

to **invest** [ɪnˈvest] investieren **WS 2**, 75

to **investigate** [ɪnˈvestɪgeɪt] untersuchen OT 3

investment [ɪnˈvestmənt] Investition **WS 2**, 75

invitation [ˌɪnvɪˈteɪʃn] Einladung; Aufforderung OT 1

to **invite** [ɪnˈvaɪt] einladen OT 2

to **involve** [ɪnˈvɒlv] einbeziehen; umfassen OT 3

involved [ɪnˈvɒlvd] involviert OT 2

iron [ˈaɪən] aus Eisen OT 3

ironing [ˈaɪənɪŋ] Bügeln **WS 4**, 124

irregular [ɪˈregjələ] unregelmäßig; uneben OT 1

irresponsible [ˌɪrɪˈspɒnsəbl] unverantwortlich OT 2

island [ˈaɪlənd] Insel OT 1

islander [ˈaɪləndə] Insulaner(in); Inselbewohner(in) **WS 1**, 12

to **itch** [ɪtʃ] jucken OT 2

itchy [ˈɪtʃi] juckend OT 2

item [ˈaɪtəm] Gegenstand; Punkt OT 3

its [ɪts] sein; ihr OT 1

ivory [ˈaɪvəri] Elfenbein OT 3

J

jacket ['dʒækɪt] Jacke; Jackett OT 1

jam [dʒæm] Marmelade; Stau OT 1

jar [dʒɑː] Einweckglas OT 2

jazz [dʒæz] Jazz OT 2

jealous ['dʒeləs] eifersüchtig OT 2

jeep [dʒiːp] Jeep OT 3

jerk chicken [dʒɜːk 'tʃɪkɪn] in Gewürzen mariniertes und gegrilltes Hühnchen **WS 2**, 48

jewel ['dʒuːəl] Edelstein; Schmuckstück OT 3

jewelry ['dʒuːəlri] Schmuck OT 2

job [dʒɒb] Stelle; Arbeitsplatz; Job; Aufgabe OT 1

to join [dʒɔɪn] Mitglied werden in; eintreten in OT 1

   to join up [dʒɔɪn ʌp] verbinden OT 2

joke [dʒəʊk] Witz OT 2

   to take a joke [teɪk ə dʒəʊk] Spaß verstehen OT 2

to joke [dʒəʊk] Witze machen OT 2

journal ['dʒɜːnl] Journal; Fachzeitschrift OT 3

journalist ['dʒɜːnəlɪst] Journalist(in) OT 2

journey ['dʒɜːni] Reise; Fahrt OT 1

joust [dʒaʊst] Turnier OT 2

judge [dʒʌdʒ] Richter(in) OT 2

to judge [dʒʌdʒ] einschätzen OT 2

judicial [dʒuː'dɪʃl] Justiz- **WS 3**, 91

judo ['dʒuːdəʊ] Judo OT 1

juice [dʒuːs] Saft OT 1

July [dʒu'laɪ] Juli OT 1

to jump [dʒʌmp] springen OT 2

jumper ['dʒʌmpə] Pullover OT 1

June ['dʒuːn] Juni OT 1

junior ['dʒuːniə] Junior(in) OT 2

junk food ['dʒʌŋk ˌfuːd] Junk Food **WS 2**, 52

just [dʒʌst] genau; nur OT 1

to justify ['dʒʌstɪfaɪ] rechtfertigen **WS 3**, 102

K

kangaroo [ˌkæŋgə'ruː] Känguru **WS 1**, 13

kayak ['kaɪæk] Kajak OT 3

kayaking ['kaɪækɪŋ] Kajakfahren OT 2

keen [kiːn] leidenschaftlich OT 2

to keep [kiːp] behalten OT 1

to keep calm [kiːp kɑːm] Ruhe bewahren OT 2

   to keep fit [kiːp 'fɪt] sich fit halten OT 2

keeper ['kiːpə] Hüter(in) OT 3

ketchup ['ketʃəp] Ketchup OT 3

kettle ['ketl] Kessel OT 2

key [kiː] Schlüssel; Taste OT 1

to key [kiː] tippen OT 2

keyboard ['kiːbɔːd] Tastatur; Klaviatur; Keyboard OT 1

to kick [kɪk] treten; einen Tritt versetzen OT 1

kidnapper ['kɪdnæpə] Entführer(in) OT 2

kidney bean ['kɪdni biːn] Kidneybohne OT 2

to kill [kɪl] töten; umbringen OT 1

kilo ['kiːləʊ] Kilo OT 2

kilometre ['kɪləmiːtə] Kilometer OT 1

kilt [kɪlt] Schottenrock; Kilt OT 2

kind [kaɪnd] Art; Sorte OT 1

kindling ['kɪndlɪŋ] Kleinholz OT 2

king [kɪŋ] König; Dame OT 1

kinsman ['kɪnzmən] Angehöriger OT 3

kiss [kɪs] Kuss OT 2

kitchen ['kɪtʃɪn] Küche OT 1

kiwi ['kiːwiː] Kiwi; Neuseeländer(in) OT 1

knee [niː] Knie OT 1

knife [naɪf] Messer OT 2

to knight [naɪt] zum Ritter schlagen OT 3

knight [naɪt] Ritter OT 3

to knock [nɒk] klopfen; stoßen OT 2

   to knock over [nɒk əʊvə] umstoßen OT 2

knot [nɒt] Knoten OT 3

to know [nəʊ] wissen; kennen OT 1

knowledge ['nɒlɪdʒ] Wissen **WS 2**, 64

knowledgeable ['nɒlɪdʒəbl] kenntnisreich OT 3

koala [kəʊ'ɑːlə] Koala **WS 1**, 13

L

to label ['leɪbl] beschriften; etikettieren OT 1

labour ['leɪbə] Arbeit OT 3

labour force ['leɪbə fɔːs] Arbeitskräfte; Arbeitnehmerschaft **WS 4**, 133

lack [læk] Mangel OT 3

lacrosse [lə'krɒs] Lacrosse OT 3

ladder ['lædə] Leiter OT 3

lady ['leɪdi] Dame OT 2

lake [leɪk] See OT 1

lamb [læm] Lamm OT 2

lamp [læmp] Lampe; Laterne OT 1

land [lænd] Land OT 1

to land [lænd] landen **WW**, 11

landfill ['lændfɪl] Mülldeponie OT 3

landmark ['lændmɑːk] Wahrzeichen OT 3

landscape ['lændskeɪp] Landschaft OT 2

lane [leɪn] Fahrbahn; Gasse **WS 1**, 29

laneway ['leɪnweɪ] Sträßchen **WS 1**, 29

language ['læŋgwɪdʒ] Sprache OT 1

lantern ['læntən] Laterne OT 2

laptop ['læptɒp] Laptop OT 3

large [lɑːdʒ] groß OT 1

last [lɑːst] letzte(r, -s) OT 1

   at last [ət 'lɑːst] endlich OT 2

to last [lɑːst] dauern; anhalten OT 2

late [leɪt] spät; zu spät OT 1

Latin ['lætɪn] Latein OT 2

to laugh [lɑːf] lachen OT 1

   to laugh at [lɑːf ət] auslachen OT 2

laundry ['lɔːndri] Wäsche; Wäscherei OT 3

lava ['lɑːvə] Lava OT 3

lawn [lɔːn] Rasen **WS 4**, 124

lawyer ['lɔɪə] Rechtsanwalt **WS 4**, 134

lazy ['leɪzi] faul OT 2

lead [led] Blei OT 3

to lead ['liːd] führen OT 2

leadership ['liːdəʃɪp] Führung OT 2

leaflet ['liːflət] Reklamezettel OT 2

league [liːg] Liga OT 2

to lean [liːn] lehnen OT 3

to learn [lɜːn] lernen; erfahren OT 1

least: at least [ət 'liːst] mindestens OT 1

leather ['leðə] Leder OT 3

to leave [liːv] verlassen; lassen OT 1

   to leave alone [liːv ə'ləʊn] in Ruhe lassen OT 2

   to leave behind [ˌliːv bɪ'haɪnd] hinterlassen OT 2

leaving ['liːvɪŋ] Abschieds... OT 2

leek [liːk] Lauch OT 3

leftover ['leftəʊvə] übriggeblieben **WS 3**, 88

leg [leg] Bein; Keule OT 1

legal ['liːgl] rechtlich; legal OT 3

to legalize ['liːgəlaɪz] legalisieren **WS 4**, 122

legend ['ledʒənd] Legende; Sage OT 3

legion ['liːdʒən] Legion OT 2

legislative ['ledʒɪslətɪv] Legislative; gesetzgebend **WS 3**, 91

leisure ['leʒə] Freizeit **WS 1**, 34

lemonade [ˌlemə'neɪd] Zitronenlimonade OT 1

to lend [lend] leihen OT 2

length [leŋθ] Länge OT 3

lens [lenz] Objektiv; Linse OT 2

lesbian [ˈlezbɪən] lesbisch; Lesbe **WS 4**, 121

lesson [ˈlesn] Unterricht; Lektion OT 1

to **let** [let] lassen; vermieten OT 1

letter [ˈletə] Brief; Buchstabe OT 1

letterbox [ˈletəbɒks] Briefkasten OT 1

lettuce [ˈletɪs] Kopfsalat OT 2

levee [ˈlevi] Deich **WS 3**, 108

to **level off** [ˈlevl ɒf] sich ebnen; abflachen **WS 4**, 132

lexicon [ˈleksɪkən] Wortschatz **WW**, 11

LGBT (lesbian, gay, bisexual, transgender) LGBT **WS 4**, 121

liberty [ˈlɪbəti] Freiheit OT 2

library [ˈlaɪbrəri] Bücherei; Bibliothek OT 1

license [ˈlaɪsns] Genehmigung OT 3

lid [lɪd] Deckel OT 2

to **lie** [laɪ] liegen; gelegen sein OT 1

life [laɪf] Leben; Lebensdauer OT 1

lifeguard [ˈlaɪfɡɑːd] Rettungsschwimmer(in) **WS 4**, 138

lifesaving [ˈlaɪfseɪvɪŋ] lebensrettend **WS 3**, 95

lifestyle [ˈlaɪfstaɪl] Lebensstil; Lifestyle OT 3

life-threatening [ˈlaɪf θretnɪŋ] lebensbedrohlich OT 2

lifetime [ˈlaɪftaɪm] Lebenszeit; Lebensdauer OT 3

to **lift** [lɪft] heben **WS 4**, 140

light [laɪt] Licht; Lampe OT 1

to **light** [laɪt] anzünden OT 2

to **like** [laɪk] gernhaben; mögen OT 1

limit [ˈlɪmɪt] Grenze **WS 1**, 26

limited [ˈlɪmɪtɪd] begrenzt OT 3

line [laɪn] Linie; Falte; Text (eines Schauspielers) OT 1

linked [lɪŋkt] verbunden OT 2

lion [ˈlaɪən] Löwe(-in) OT 1

lip [lɪp] Lippe OT 2

liquid [ˈlɪkwɪd] flüssig OT 2

list [lɪst] Liste OT 1

listener [ˈlɪsnə] Hörer(in) **WS 1**, 28

litter [ˈlɪtə] herumliegende Abfälle OT 2

litter bin [ˈlɪtə bɪn] Abfalleimer OT 2

to **live** [lɪv] leben; wohnen OT 1

lively [ˈlaɪvli] lebhaft OT 3

liver [ˈlɪvə] Leber **WS 2**, 68

livestock [ˈlaɪvstɒk] Viehbestand **WS 1**, 28

living room [ˈlɪvɪŋ ruːm] Wohnzimmer OT 1

to **load** [ləʊd] (be)laden **WS 2**, 67

loads [ləʊds əv] eine Menge OT 3

loaf [ləʊf] Brotlaib; Brot OT 1

to **loathe** [ləʊð] hassen; verabscheuen **WS 1**, 25

lobby [ˈlɒbi] Eingangshalle; Lobby **WS 2**, 56

local [ˈləʊkl] einheimisch OT 2

located [ləʊˈkeɪtɪd] gelegen OT 3

location [ləʊˈkeɪʃn] Standort **WS 1**, 26

lock [lɒk] Schleuse OT 3

locker [ˈlɒkə] Spind; Schließfach OT 2

lodge [lɒdʒ] Pension OT 2

log [lɒɡ] Holzscheit OT 3

to **log on** [lɒɡ ɒn] sich einloggen OT 3

logical [ˈlɒdʒɪkl] logisch; folgerichtig **WS 1**, 36

logline [lɒɡlaɪn] Logline; kurzer Text, der das Wesentliche zusammenfasst **WS 2**, 60

logo [ˈləʊɡəʊ] Logo; Firmenzeichen OT 1

lonely [ˈləʊnli] einsam OT 3

long [lɒŋ] lang; weit OT 1

loo [luː] Klo OT 2

look [lʊk] Blick OT 2

  to **take a look** [ˌteɪk ə ˈlʊk] einen Blick werfen OT 2

  to **look forward to** [ˌlʊk ˈfɔːwəd tə] (sich) auf etwas freuen OT 21

to **look** [lʊk] sehen; blicken; ansehen OT 1

  to **look after** [lʊk ˈɑːftə] auf jdn. aufpassen; sich um jdn. kümmern OT 1

to **lose** [luːz] verlieren OT 1

loser [ˈluːzə] Verlierer(in) OT 3

loss [lɒs] Verlust **WS 1**, 39

loudspeaker [ˌlaʊdˈspiːkə] Lautsprecher OT 2

to **love** [lʌv] lieben OT 1

lover [ˈlʌvə] Liebhaber(in) OT 3

loyalty [ˈlɔɪəlti] Loyalität **WS 4**, 142

luck [lʌk] Glück; Schicksal OT 1

luckily [ˈlʌkɪli] glücklicherweise **WS 3**, 89

lunch [lʌntʃ] Mittagessen OT 1

lunch break [ˈlʌntʃ breɪk] Mittagspause OT 1

lunchtime [ˈlʌntʃtaɪm] Mittagszeit OT 1

lung [lʌŋ] Lunge **WS 2**, 59

luxurious [lʌɡˈʒʊəriəs] luxuriös OT 2

lynx [lɪŋks] Luchs OT 2

M

machete [məˈʃeti] Machete OT 3

machine [məˈʃiːn] Maschine OT 2

madam [ˈmædəm] gnädige Frau OT 1

magazine [ˌmæɡəˈziːn] Zeitschrift; Illustrierte OT 1

magic [ˈmædʒɪk] Zauber; fantastisch OT 1

magical [ˈmædʒɪkl] magisch OT 2

magician [məˈdʒɪʃn] Zauberer, Zauberin OT 1

magnet [ˈmæɡnət] Magnet **WS 1**, 32

magnetic [mæɡˈnetɪk] magnetisch OT 2

magnificent [mæɡˈnɪfɪsnt] großartig; herrlich **WS 1**, 29

magnifying glass [ˈmæɡnɪfaɪɪŋ ɡlɑːs] Lupe OT 2

magpie [ˈmæɡpaɪ] Elster OT 1

main [meɪn] Haupt... OT 1

main course [ˈmeɪn kɔːs] Hauptgang OT 1

mainland [ˈmeɪnlænd] Festland OT 3

to **maintain** [meɪnˈteɪn] pflegen; aufrechterhalten **WS 2**, 53

maintenance [ˈmeɪntənəns] Wartung OT 3

majority [məˈdʒɒrəti] Mehrheit **WS 2**, 69

to **make** [meɪk] kochen; machen OT 1

makeup [ˈmeɪk ʌp] Schminke **WS 2**, 66

malaria [məˈleəriə] Malaria **WS 1**, 34

male [meɪl] männlich OT 2

mammal [ˈmæml] Säugetier OT 2

man [mæn] Mann; Mensch OT 1

to **man** [mæn] bemannen OT 3

to **manage** [ˈmænɪdʒ] leiten; führen; managen OT 1

mandatory [ˈmændətəri] verpflichtend **WS 3**, 108

manifesto [ˌmænɪˈfestəʊ] Manifest **WS 3**, 92

manure [məˈnjʊə] Dung OT 3

many [ˈmeni] viele OT 1

map [mæp] Landkarte; Stadtplan OT 1

to **map** [mæp] aufzeichnen; in eine Karte eintragen OT 3

marathon [ˈmærəθən] Marathon OT 2

March [mɑːtʃ] März OT 1

march [mɑːtʃ] Marsch; Demonstration **WS 1**, 42

marching band [ˈmɑːtʃɪŋ bænd] Marschkapelle OT 3

marine [məˈriːn] Meeres... OT 3

marker [ˈmɑːkə] Markierung; Lesezeichen; Filzstift OT 1

market [ˈmɑːkɪt] Markt; Börse OT 1

marketing [ˈmɑːkɪtɪŋ] Marketing OT 3

marketplace [ˈmɑːkɪtpleɪs] Markt; Marktplatz **WS 2**, 65

marquee [mɑːˈkiː] Festzelt OT 2

marriage [ˈmærɪdʒ] Ehe OT 3

to **marry** [ˈmæri] heiraten; trauen OT 1

marshmallow [ˌmɑːʃˈmæləʊ]
Marshmallow OT 2

mascot [ˈmæskət] Maskottchen OT 2

mashed potato [ˌmæʃt pəˈteɪtəʊ]
Kartoffelbrei OT 1

mask [mɑːsk] Maske OT 3

mass [mæs] Masse **WW**, 11

mass shooting [mæs ˈʃuːtɪŋ]
Massenerschießung **WS 1**, 24

massacre [ˈprɒvɪns] Massaker OT 2

massage [ˈmæsɑːʒ] Massage OT 2

match [mætʃ] Spiel; Match; Wettkampf
OT 1

match [mætʃ] Streichholz OT 2

mate [meɪt] Kumpel **WW**, 10

material [məˈtɪəriəl] Material OT 3

maths [mæθs] Mathematik OT 1

matter [ˈmætə] Angelegenheit;
Problem OT 2

mattress [ˈmætrəs] Matratze **WS 3**, 102

maximum [ˈmæksɪməm] Maximum OT 2

maybe [ˈmeɪbi] vielleicht;
möglicherweise OT 1

mayo [ˌmeɪə] Majonnaise OT 3

mayonnaise [ˌmeɪəˈneɪz] Mayonnaise
OT 1

mayor [meə] Bürgermeister(in) OT 3

maze [meɪz] Irrgarten OT 3

me [miː] mich; mir; ich OT 1

meadow [ˈmedəʊ] Wiese OT 2

meal [miːl] Mahlzeit; Essen OT 1

to mean [miːn] bedeuten; meinen OT 1

meaning [ˈmiːnɪŋ] Sinn; Bedeutung
OT 1

measles [ˈmiːzlz] Masern **WS 1**, 24

to measure [ˈmeʒə] messen;
ausmessen OT 1

measurement [ˈmeʒəmənt] Maß;
Maßeinheit OT 2

meat [miːt] Fleisch OT 1

meatball [ˈmiːtbɔːl] Fleischklößchen;
Hackfleischbällchen OT 1

meat-eater [miːt iːtə] Fleischesser(in)
WS 2, 69

medal [ˈmedl] Medaille OT 2

medical [ˈmedɪkl] ärztliche
Untersuchung; medizinisch OT 2

medicine [ˈmedsn] Medizin **WS 3**, 95

medieval [ˌmediˈiːvl] mittelalterlich
OT 2

medium [ˈmiːdiəm] Mittel; Medium OT 2

medium-sized [ˈmiːdiəm saɪzd]
mittelgroß OT 2

to meet [miːt] treffen; begegnen OT 1

meeting [ˈmiːtɪŋ] Besprechung;
Sitzung; Treffen OT 1

to melt [melt] schmelzen OT 3

member [ˈmembə] Mitglied OT 1

memorable [ˈmemərəbl] unvergesslich
OT 3

memorial [məˈmɔːriəl] Denkmal
WS 3, 89

memory [ˈmeməri] Gedächtnis OT 2

to mend [mend] reparieren OT 3

mental [ˈmentl] geistig; psychisch OT 2

mentally [ˈmentəli] geistig OT 3

to mention [ˈmenʃn] erwähnen OT 3

menu [ˈmenjuː] Speisekarte; Menü OT 1

mess [mes] Unordnung OT 2

message [ˈmesɪdʒ] Nachricht; Aussage
OT 1

to mess up [ˌmesˈʌp] in Unordnung
bringen; vergeigen OT 2

metal [ˈmetl] Metall; Heavy Metal OT 1

method [ˈmeθəd] Methode OT 1

metre [ˈmiːtə] Meter; Versmaß OT 1

midday [ˌmɪdˈdeɪ] Mittag **WS 3**, 99

midfielder [ˌmɪdˈfiːldə]
Mittelfeldspieler(in) OT 3

midnight [ˈmɪdnaɪt] Mitternacht OT 1

mighty [ˈmaɪti] sehr OT 3

to migrate [maɪˈgreɪt] migrieren OT 3

mile [maɪl] Meile (etwa 1,6 km) OT 1

milestone [ˈmaɪlstəʊn] Meilenstein OT 3

military [ˈmɪlətri] Militär OT 3

milk [mɪlk] Milch OT 1

millennial [mɪˈleniəl] zur Millennium-
Generation gehörig **WS 4**, 142

million [ˈmɪljən] Million OT 1

minced [mɪnst] fein gehackt OT 2

mind [maɪnd] Verstand; Meinung OT 1

mind map [ˈmaɪnd mæp]
Gedankenkarte; Mindmap OT 1

mine [maɪn] Bergwerk OT 2

mine [maɪn] meine(r,-s) OT 1

miniature [ˈmɪnətʃə] Miniatur OT 2

minibus [ˈmɪnibʌs] Kleinbus OT 2

minimum [ˈmɪnɪməm] Mindest...;
Minimal... OT 1

mining [ˈmaɪnɪŋ] Bergbau... OT 3

minister [ˈmɪnɪstə] Minister(in) OT 3

minor [ˈmaɪnə] Minderjährige(r) OT 2

minority [maɪˈnɒrəti] Minderheit
WS 4, 132

mint [mɪnt] Minze; Pfefferminzbonbon
OT 1

minute [ˈmɪnɪt] Minute; Moment OT 1

mirror [ˈmɪrə] Spiegel OT 1

to miss [mɪs] vermissen OT 2

missing [ˈmɪsɪŋ] fehlend;
verschwunden OT 1

missionary [ˈmɪʃənri] Missionar(in)
OT 3

mistake [mɪˈsteɪk] Fehler OT 1

to misunderstand [ˌmɪsʌndəˈstænd]
missverstehen **WS 4**, 131

misunderstanding [ˌmɪsʌndəˈstændɪŋ]
Missverständnis OT 3

mitten [ˈmɪtn] Fausthandschuh OT 3

to mix [mɪks] mischen OT 2

mixed up [ˌmɪkstˈʌp] durcheinander
OT 2

mixture [ˈmɪkstʃə] Mischung OT 2

mob [mɒb] Meute **WS 1**, 28

mobile [ˈməʊbaɪl] mobil OT 3

mobile phone [məʊbaɪl ˈfəʊn] Handy;
Mobiltelefon OT 1

model [ˈmɒdl] Modell OT 1

modern [ˈmɒdn] modern OT 1

modest [ˈmɒdɪst] bescheiden OT 2

moment [ˈməʊmənt] Moment;
Augenblick OT 1

monarch [ˈmɒnək] Monarch(in);
Herrscher(in) **WS 3**, 92

monarchy [ˈmɒnəki] Monarchie
WS 3, 92

Monday [ˈmʌndeɪ] Montag OT 1

money [ˈmʌni] Geld OT 1

monk [mʌŋk] Mönch OT 3

monolingual [ˌmɒnəˈlɪŋgwəl]
einsprachig **WS 1**, 24

monopoly [məˈnɒpəli] Monopol OT 3

monotone [ˈmɒnətəʊn] monoton
WS 4, 137

monster [ˈmɒnstə] Monster; Ungeheuer
OT 1

month [mʌnθ] Monat OT 1

monument [ˈmɒnjumənt] Monument;
Denkmal **WS 3**, 89

moon [muːn] Mond OT 1

to moor [mɔː] vertäuen; anlegen OT 3

moor [mɔː] Moor; Heide OT 3

mooring [ˈmɔːrɪŋ] Anlegeplatz OT 3

moral [ˈmɒrəl] Moral OT 2

morally [ˈmɒrəli] moralisch OT 3

more [mɔː] mehr OT 1

morning [ˈmɔːnɪŋ] Morgen; Vormittag
OT 1

mosaic [məʊˈzeɪɪk] Mosaik OT 2

mosquito [məˈskiːtəʊ] Stechmücke
OT 2

most [məʊst] der/die/das meiste;
die meisten OT 1

motel [məʊˈtel] Motel OT 3

mother [ˈmʌðə] Mutter OT 1

to motivate [ˈməʊtɪveɪt] motivieren;
anregen **WS 2**, 70

motivation [ˌməʊtɪ'veɪʃn] Motivation; Begründung **WS 4**, 135

motivational [ˌməʊtɪ'veɪʃənl] anregend; Motivations... **WS 4**, 143

motorized ['məʊtəraɪzd] motorisiert OT 3

mountain ['maʊntən] Berg OT 1

mountain biking ['maʊntən baɪkɪŋ] Mountainbiken OT 2

mouse [maʊs] Maus OT 1

mouth [maʊθ] Mund OT 1

mouthguard [maʊθgɑːd] Mundschutz OT 2

to **move** [muːv] bewegen; woanders hinstellen; umziehen OT 1

movement ['muːvmənt] Bewegung OT 3

to **mow** [məʊ] mähen **WS 4**, 124

Mr ['mɪstə] Herr OT 1

to **muck around** [mʌk ə'raʊnd] Spaß haben **WS 4**, 125

mud [mʌd] Schlamm OT 3

muddy ['mʌdi] schlammig; matschig **WS 3**, 102

mudslide ['mʌdslaɪd] Schlammlawine **WS 1**, 34

muffin ['mʌfɪn] Muffin; Hefegebäck, das getoastet und mit Butter gegessen wird OT 1

mule [mjuːl] Maultier OT 3

multi [mʌlti] multi...; mehr.. OT 3

multicultural [ˌmʌlti'kʌltʃərəl] multikulturell **WS 1**, 33

multiculturalism [ˌmʌlti'kʌltʃərəlɪzəm] Multikulturalismus **WS 2**, 52

multilingual [ˌmʌlti'lɪŋgwəl] mehrsprachig OT 3

multinational [ˌmʌlti'næʃnəl] multinational **WS 2**, 48

multiple ['mʌltɪpl] vielfach OT 2

mum [mʌm] Mutti; Mama OT 1

to **mumble** ['mʌmbl] murmeln **WS 2**, 59

mural ['mjʊərəl] Wandgemälde OT 2

to **murder** ['mɜːdə] ermorden OT 2

muscle ['mʌsl] Muskel OT 2

museum [mjuː'ziːəm] Museum OT 1

mushroom ['mʌʃrʊm] Pilz OT 2

music ['mjuːzɪk] Musik; Noten OT 1

musician [mjuː'zɪʃn] Musiker(in) OT 2

must [mʌst] müssen OT 1

mustard ['mʌstəd] Senf OT 1

my [maɪ] mein OT 1

myth [mɪθ] Mythos; Märchen OT 3

mythology [mɪ'θɒlədʒi] Mythologie OT 2

N

name [neɪm] Name; Ruf OT 1

narrator [nə'reɪtə] Erzähler(in) OT 2

narrow ['nærəʊ] eng OT 2

nasty ['nɑːsti] unangenehm OT 2

nation ['neɪʃn] Nation OT 2

national ['næʃnəl] national OT 1

nationality [ˌnæʃə'næləti] Staatsangehörigkeit OT 2

naturalist ['nætʃrəlɪst] Naturforscher(in) OT 2

nature ['neɪtʃə] Natur OT 2

naughty ['nɔːti] ungezogen OT 2

to **navigate** ['nævɪgeɪt] navigieren; lenken **WS 2**, 57

navy ['neɪvi] Marine OT 3

near [nɪə] nahe; in der Nähe von OT 1

nearby [ˌnɪə'baɪ] in der Nähe **WS 4**, 129

nearly ['nɪəli] fast; beinahe OT 2

neat [niːt] ordentlich OT 3

necessary ['nesəsəri] notwendig OT 3

necessity [nə'sesəti] Notwendigkeit **WS 4**, 139

neck [nek] Hals; Nacken OT 1

to **need** [niːd] brauchen; nötig haben OT 1

negative ['negətɪv] Verneinung; Negativ; negativ OT 1

to **negotiate** [nɪ'gəʊʃieɪt] verhandeln **WS 3**, 99

neighbour ['neɪbə] Nachbar **WS 1**, 13

neighbourhood ['neɪbəhʊd] Nachbarschaft **WS 1**, 19

nephew ['nefjuː] Neffe **WS 4**, 136

nerve [nɜːv] Nerv OT 3

nervous ['nɜːvəs] nervös OT 2

nest [nest] Nest OT 3

net [net] Netz OT 3

netball ['netbɔːl] Netzball **WS 1**, 15

network ['netwɜːk] Netzwerk OT 3

neurological [ˌnjʊərə'lɒdʒɪkl] neurologisch **WS 4**, 131

neutral ['njuːtrəl] neutral OT 3

never ['nevə] nie; niemals OT 1

new [njuː] neu OT 1

news [njuːz] Neuigkeit(en); Nachricht(en) OT 1

newsletter ['njuːzletə] Newsletter OT 3

newspaper ['njuːzpeɪpə] Zeitung; Zeitungspapier OT 1

next ['nekst] nächste(r, -s) OT 1

next to ['nekst tuː] neben OT 1

nice [naɪs] schön; nett OT 1

nickname ['nɪkneɪm] Spitzname **WS 1**, 12

to **nickname** ['nɪkneɪm] Spitznamen geben; nennen **WS 1**, 13

niece [niːs] Nichte **WS 4**, 138

night [naɪt] Nacht; Abend OT 1

nil [nɪl] null OT 3

nine [naɪn] neun OT 1

ninety ['naɪnti] neunzig OT 1

nobility [nəʊ'bɪləti] Adel OT 2

nobleman ['nəʊblmən] Adliger OT 3

nobody ['nəʊbədi] niemand; keiner OT 1

to **nod** [nɒd] nicken OT 3

noisy ['nɔɪzi] laut; lärmend OT 1

nomadic [nəʊ'mædɪk] nomadisch OT 3

nomination [ˌnɒmɪ'neɪʃn] Ernennung **WS 3**, 115

non-native [ˌnɒn 'neɪtɪv] zugewandert **WS 1**, 25

nonsense ['nɒnsns] Unsinn; Quatsch OT 1

noodle ['nuːdl] Nudel OT 2

normal ['nɔːml] normal; üblich OT 1

Norman ['nɔːmən] normannisch OT 2

north [nɔːθ] Nord- OT 1

north-east ['nɔːθ iːst] Nordosten OT 1

northern [nɔːðən] nördlich OT 2

nose [nəʊz] Nase OT 2

nostalgia [nɒ'stældʒə] Nostalgie OT 3

notable ['nəʊtəbl] bemerkenswert OT 3

note [nəʊt] Notiz; Nachricht; Geldschein OT 1

notebook ['nəʊtbʊk] Notizbuch OT 2

nothing ['nʌθɪŋ] nichts OT 1

notice ['nəʊtɪs] Schild; Aushang OT 1

to **notice** ['nəʊtɪs] bemerken **WS 2**, 48

noticeboard ['nəʊtɪsbɔːd] Anschlagbrett; Schwarzes Brett OT 1

noun [naʊn] Substantiv; Nomen; Hauptwort OT 1

novel ['nɒvl] Roman OT 2

novelist ['nɒvəlɪst] Schriftsteller(in) **WS 2**, 52

now [naʊ] jetzt; sofort OT 1

nowadays ['naʊədeɪz] heutzutage OT 3

nowhere ['nəʊweə] nirgendwo OT 2

nuclear ['njuːkliə] Atom...; Nuklear... **WS 4**, 122

number ['nʌmbə] Zahl; Nummer OT 1

numerical [njuː'merɪkl] numerisch **WS 3**, 87

nun [nʌn] Nonne OT 3

nurse [nɜːs] Krankenschwester, -pfleger OT 1

nut [nʌt] Nuss **WS 1**, 14

nutritional [njuː'trɪʃənl] ernährungs- **WS 2**, 63

O

obese [əʊ'biːs] fettleibig **WS 2**, 69

obesity [əʊ'biːsəti] Adipositas; Fettleibigkeit **WS 2**, 69

object ['ɒbdʒɪkt] Gegenstand; Ding; Objekt OT 1

objection [əb'dʒekʃn] Einwand OT 3

obliged: to be obliged (to) [bi 'ɒblɪgeɪtɪd] müssen; verpflichtet sein **WS 4**, 146

observation [ˌɒbzə'veɪʃn] Beobachtung OT 3

obsession [əb'seʃn] Obsession; Besessenheit **WS 4**, 120

obvious ['ɒbviəs] offensichtlich OT 3

ocean ['əʊʃn] Ozean OT 2

odd [ɒd] eigenartig OT 2

of [ɒf] von OT 1

offer ['ɒfə] Angebot OT 2

to **offer** ['ɒfə] anbieten OT 2

office ['ɒfɪs] Büro; Amt OT 2

officer ['ɒfɪsə] Offizier(in) OT 2

official [ə'fɪʃl] Beamter, Beamtin OT 2

official [ə'fɪʃl] offiziell OT 2

off-road ['ɒf rəʊd] geländetauglich OT 2

offstage [ˌɒf'steɪdʒ] aus dem Off OT 2

often ['ɒfn] oft; häufig OT 1

oil [ɔɪl] Öl OT 3

old [əʊld] alt; ehemalig OT 1

old-fashioned [ˌəʊld'fæʃnd] altmodisch OT 2

Olympic [ə'lɪmpɪk] olympisch; Olympia… OT 2

on [ɒn] auf; an; in OT 1

once [wʌns] einmal OT 2

one [wʌn] eins; ein(e, -r, -s) OT 1

oneself [ðəm'selvz] sich OT 2

one-sided [ˌwʌn 'saɪdɪd] einseitig OT 3

onion ['ʌnjən] Zwiebel OT 2

online [ˌɒn'laɪn] online OT 3

onscreen [ˌɒn 'skriːn] auf dem Bildschirm; auf der Leinwand OT 2

open ['əʊpən] offen; auf OT 1

to **open** ['əʊpən] aufmachen; öffnen OT 1

opening times ['əʊpnɪŋ taɪmz] Öffnungszeiten OT 1

open-minded [ˌəʊpən 'maɪndɪd] aufgeschlossen **WS 3**, 100

operation [ˌɒpə'reɪʃn] Verfahren; Vorgang OT 3

opinion [ə'pɪnjən] Meinung OT 3

opponent [ə'pəʊnənt] Gegner(in) OT 2

opportunity [ˌɒpə'tjuːnəti] Gelegenheit OT 2

to **oppose** [ə'pəʊz] gegen etw. sein OT 3

opposite ['ɒpəzɪt] Gegenteil; Gegensatz OT 1

opposition [ˌɒpə'zɪʃn] Opposition **WS 3**, 92

optimistic [ˌɒptɪ'mɪstɪk] optimistisch OT 3

or [ɔː] oder; noch OT 1

oral ['ɔːrəl] mündlich OT 1

orange ['ɒrɪndʒ] Apfelsine; Orange OT 1

orange ['ɒrɪndʒ] orange; orangefarben OT 1

orchard ['ɔːtʃəd] Obstgarten **WS 4**, 140

orchestra ['ɔːkɪstrə] Orchester OT 1

order ['ɔːdə] Bestellung; Auftrag; Reihenfolge OT 1

to **order** ['ɔːdə] befehlen; anordnen; bestellen OT 1

organ ['ɔːgən] Organ **WS 4**, 125

organic [ɔː'gænɪk] biologisch **WS 1**, 30

organization [ˌɔːgənaɪ'zeɪʃn] Organisation; Gesellschaft OT 3

organizational [ˌɔːgənaɪ'zeɪʃənl] organisatorisch **WS 4**, 139

to **organize** ['ɔːgənaɪz] organisieren OT 1

organizer ['ɔːgənaɪzə] Organisator(in) **WS 3**, 102

orientated ['ɔːrɪənteɪt] orientiert **WS 4**, 126

origin ['ɒrɪdʒɪn] Ursprung OT 3

original [ə'rɪdʒənl] ursprünglich; Original… OT 3

originally [ə'rɪdʒənəli] ursprünglich OT 2

to **originate** [ə'rɪdʒɪneɪt] stammen aus OT 3

orphan ['ɔːfn] Waise OT 2

other ['ʌðə] andere(r, -s) OT 1

ounce [aʊns] Unze OT 3

our ['aʊə] unser OT 1

out [aʊt] heraus; draußen; aus OT 1

outdoor ['aʊtdɔː] im Freien OT 2

outfit ['aʊtfɪt] Outfit; Kleidung **WS 3**, 100

outgoing [ˌaʊt'gəʊɪŋ] kontaktfreudig **WS 4**, 139

outlet ['aʊtlet] Markt **WS 2**, 64

to **outline** ['aʊtlaɪn] umreißen; zusammenfassen OT 3

outside [ˌaʊt'saɪd] draußen OT 1

outstanding [aʊt'stændɪŋ] herausragend OT 3

oven ['ʌvn] Ofen OT 2

over ['əʊvə] drüben OT 2

over there [ˌəʊvə ˌðeə] dort drüben OT 2

overall [ˌəʊvər'ɔːl] allgemein; im Allgemeinen **WS 3**, 98

overboard ['əʊvəbɔːd] über Bord OT 3

to **overdo** [ˌəʊvə'duː] übertreiben **WS 2**, 68

to **overflow** [ˌəʊvə'fləʊ] überlaufen **WS 3**, 88

overnight [ˌəʊvə'naɪt] über Nacht OT 2

to **oversee** [ˌəʊvə'siː] überwachen; beaufsichtigen **WS 3**, 92

to **overshadow** [ˌəʊvə'ʃædəʊ] überschatten **WS 3**, 99

overview ['əʊvəvjuː] Überblick; Übersicht **WS 2**, 61

overweight [ˌəʊvə'weɪt] übergewichtig **WS 2**, 69

to **own** [əʊn] besitzen OT 2

own [əʊn] eigene(r, -s) OT 1

owner ['əʊnə] Besitzer(in) OT 2

oxygen ['ɒksɪdʒən] Sauerstoff **WS 1**, 39

P

PA (public address) system [ˌpiː 'eɪ sɪstɪm] Beschallungsanlage OT 2

packed lunch ['pækt lʌntʃ] Lunchpaket OT 1

package ['pækɪdʒ] Paket **WS 4**, 121

packaging ['pækɪdʒɪŋ] Verpackung OT 3

packet ['pækɪt] Paket OT 2

to **pack** [pæk] packen OT 2

to **paddle** ['pædl] paddeln OT 3

pad [pæd] Polster OT 2

page [peɪdʒ] Seite; Webseite OT 1

pain [peɪn] Schmerz; Nervensäge OT 2

painkiller ['peɪnkɪlə] Schmerzmittel OT 2

to **paint** [peɪnt] malen; streichen OT 1

painter ['peɪntə] Maler(in) OT 3

painting ['peɪntɪŋ] Malen; Gemälde OT 1

pair [peə] Paar OT 2

palace ['pæləs] Palast; Schloss OT 1

pale [peɪl] blass OT 3

palm [pɑːm] Palme **WS 2**, 62

pan [pæn] Pfanne OT 2

pancake ['pænkeɪk] Pfannkuchen OT 3

pandemic [pæn'demɪk] Pandemie **WS 3**, 99

panel ['pænl] Gremium; Forum **WS 2**, 70

panel discussion ['pænl dɪ'skʌʃn] Podiumsdiskussion OT 3

to **panic** ['pænɪk] in Panik geraten OT 2

panoramic [ˌpænə'ræmɪk] Panorama… OT 3

panther ['pænθə] Panther OT 2

pants [pænts] Hose **WW**, 11

paper [ˈpeɪpə] Papier; Zeitung OT 1

to **parachute** [ˈpærəʃuːt] Fallschirm springen **WS 2**, 53

parade [pəˈreɪd] Umzug; Parade OT 2

paradise [ˈpærədaɪs] Paradies **WS 1**, 21

paragraph [ˈpærəɡrɑːf] Absatz; Abschnitt OT 1

parallel [ˈpærəlel] parallel OT 2

paramedic [ˌpærəˈmedɪk] Rettungssanitäter(in) OT 1

to **paraphrase** [ˈpærəfreɪz] umschreiben OT 3

parent [ˈpeərənt] Elternteil OT 1

park [pɑːk] Park OT 1

to **park** [pɑːk] parken OT 2

park ranger [ˈpɑːk ˌreɪndʒə] Forstbeamter, -beamtin OT 2

parliament [ˈpɑːləmənt] Parliament; Abgeordnetenhaus OT 3

parson [ˈpɑːsn] Pfarrer(in) OT 3

part [pɑːt] Teil; Einzelteil OT 1

to **take part** [teɪk ˈpɑːt] teilnehmen OT 2

participant [pɑːˈtɪsɪpənt] Teilnehmer(in) **WS 2**, 72

to **participate** [pɑːˈtɪsɪpeɪt] teilnehmen **WS 2**, 60

participation [pɑːˌtɪsɪˈpeɪʃn] Beteiligung **WS 4**, 128

participle [pɑːˈtɪsɪpl] Partizip OT 2

partly [ˈpɑːtli] teilweise **WS 3**, 93

partner [ˈpɑːtnə] Partner(in) OT 1

partnership [ˈpɑːtnəʃɪp] Partnerschaft; Kooperation **WS 2**, 50

party [ˈpɑːti] Party; Feier OT 1

party [ˈpɑːti] Partei OT 2

to **pass** [pɑːs] zuspielen; an etw. vorbeifahren OT 2

passenger [ˈpæsɪndʒə] Passagier(in) OT 2

passion [ˈpæʃn] Leidenschaft **WS 2**, 63

passionate [ˈpæʃənət] leidenschaftlich **WS 2**, 70

passport [ˈpɑːspɔːt] Pass OT 2

pasta [ˈpæstə] Nudeln; Teigwaren OT 1

patch [pætʃ] Fleck; Flicken **WS 4**, 135

patient [ˈpeɪʃnt] Patient(in) OT 1

patriot [ˈpeɪtriət] Patriot(in) OT 2

patriotism [ˈpætriətɪzəm] Patriotismus OT 3

pattern [ˈpætn] Muster **WS 1**, 37

to **pause** [pɔːz] eine Pause machen OT 3

to **pay** [ˈpeɪ] bezahlen; zahlen OT 1

PE (physical education) [ˌpiːˈiː] Sport; Sportunterricht OT 1

pea [piː] Erbse OT 1

peace [piːs] Frieden **WS 4**, 125

peaceful [ˈpiːsfl] friedlich OT 3

peak [piːk] Gipfel; Höhepunkt **WS 4**, 132

pear [peə] Birne OT 1

pedigree [ˈpedɪɡriː] Rasse... OT 3

peer [pɪə] Peer; Gleichrangige(r) **WS 2**, 70

pen [pen] Stift OT 1

penal [ˈpiːnl] strafrechtlich **WS 1**, 22

penalty [ˈpenəlti] Strafe; Strafstoß OT 3

pencil [ˈpensl] Bleistift OT 1

pencil case [ˈpensl ˌkeɪs] Federtasche OT 1

penguin [ˈpeŋɡwɪn] Pinguin OT 2

peninsula [pəˈnɪnsjələ] Halbinsel **WS 1**, 32

penny [ˈpeni] Penny OT 1

people [ˈpiːpl] Leute; Menschen OT 1

pepper [ˈpepə] Pfeffer; Paprika OT 2

percent [pəˈsent] Prozent OT 3

percentage [pəˈsentɪdʒ] Prozentsatz; Anteil **WS 4**, 128

perfect [ˈpɜːfɪkt] perfekt OT 2

to **perform** [pəˈfɔːm] auftreten OT 2

performance [pəˈfɔːməns] Aufführung OT 2

performer [pəˈfɔːmə] Künstler(in) OT 3

permanent [ˈpɜːmənənt] permanent; dauerhaft OT 3

permission [pəˈmɪʃn] Erlaubnis OT 2

to **permit** [pəˈmɪt] erlauben **WS 2**, 54

to **persecute** [ˈpɜːsɪkjuːt] verfolgen OT 3

person [ˈpɜːsn] Mensch; Person OT 1

personal [ˈpɜːsənl] persönlich; privat OT 1

personality [ˌpɜːsəˈnæləti] Persönlichkeit; Prominente **WS 1**, 30

to **personalize** [ˈpɜːsənəlaɪz] personalisieren **WS 2**, 66

perspective [pəˈspektɪv] Aussicht; Perspektive **WS 1**, 35

to **persuade** [pəˈsweɪd] überreden; überzeugen OT 3

persuasive [pəˈsweɪsɪv] überzeugend **WS 1**, 37

pest [pest] Plage; Schädling **WS 1**, 25

pet [pet] Haustier; Liebling OT 1

petrochemical [ˌpetrəʊˈkemɪkl] Petrochemikalie **WS 3**, 108

petrol [ˈpetrəl] Benzin OT 1

pharmacist [ˈfɑːməsɪst] Apotheker(in) OT 2

pharmacy [ˈfɑːməsi] Apotheke OT 2

phenomenon [fəˈnɒmɪnən] Phänomen **WS 1**, 32

philosopher [fəˈlɒsəfə] Philosoph(in) OT 3

philosophical [ˌfɪləˈsɒfɪkl] philosophisch OT 3

phone [fəʊn] Telefon OT 1

photograph [ˈfəʊtəɡrɑːf] Foto OT 1

photographer [fəˈtɒɡrəfə] Fotograf(in) OT 2

phrase [freɪz] Wendung; Ausdruck OT 1

physical [ˈfɪzɪkl] körperlich OT 2

pianist [ˈpɪənɪst] Pianist(in) OT 2

piano [piˈænəʊ] Klavier OT 1

to **pick** [pɪk] auswählen **WS 3**, 100

to **pick up** [pɪk ʌp] aufheben; abholen OT 2

picker [ˈpɪkə] Pflücker(in) **WS 4**, 140

pickle [ˈpɪkl] Essiggemüse; Pickels OT 3

picnic [ˈpɪknɪk] Picknick OT 1

picture [ˈpɪktʃə] Bild OT 1

pie [paɪ] gedeckter Obstkuchen; Pastete OT 1

piece [piːs] Stück; Teil OT 1

in one piece [ɪn ˈwʌn ˌpiːs] heil OT 2

pier [pɪə] Kai **WS 1**, 29

pierced [pɪəst] durchstochen OT 3

pig [pɪɡ] Schwein; Sau OT 1

to **pile** [paɪl] auftürmen OT 3

pill [pɪl] Tablette **WS 2**, 68

pillow [ˈpɪləʊ] Kopfkissen OT 2

pillowcase [ˈpɪləʊkeɪs] Kopfkissenbezug OT 3

pin [pɪn] Stecknadel; Reißnagel OT 1

to **pin** [pɪn] heften; hängen OT 1

pinch [pɪntʃ] Prise OT 3

pineapple [ˈpaɪnæpl] Ananas OT 2

pink [pɪŋk] rosa; rosafarben OT 1

pioneer [ˌpaɪəˈnɪə] Pionier(in) OT 3

pipeline [ˈpaɪplaɪn] Pipeline OT 3

pitch [pɪtʃ] Spielfeld OT 3

pivotal [ˈpɪvətl] entscheidend OT 3

place [pleɪs] Ort; Stelle OT 1

placement [ˈpleɪsmənt] Platzierung **WS 2**, 66

plagiarism [ˈpleɪdʒərɪzəm] Plagiat OT 2

to **plagiarize** [ˈpleɪdʒəraɪz] plagiieren OT 2

plague [pleɪɡ] Pest OT 3

plain [pleɪn] Ebene; Flachland OT 3

plan [plæn] Plan OT 1

to **plan** [plæn] planen; vorhaben OT 1

plane [pleɪn] Flugzeug; Ebene OT 1

planet [ˈplænɪt] Planet OT 2

plant [plɑːnt] Pflanze OT 2

to **plant** [plɑːnt] pflanzen OT 3

plantain [ˈplæntɪn] Kochbanane **WS 2**, 48

plaster [ˈplɑːstə] Verputz; Putz; Gips; Pflaster OT 1

plate [pleɪt] Teller; Platte OT 1

platform [ˈplætfɔːm] Bahnsteig; Podium OT 1

platypus [ˈplætɪpəs] Schnabeltier WS 1, 13

play [pleɪ] Theaterstück; Aufführung OT 1

to play [pleɪ] spielen; spielen gegen OT 1

player [ˈpleɪə] Spieler(in); Spieler OT 1

playground [ˈpleɪgraʊnd] Spielplatz; Schulhof OT 1

playwright [ˈpleɪraɪt] Dramatiker(in) WS 2, 52

please [pliːz] bitte OT 1

pleased [pliːzd] zufrieden OT 1

pleasure [ˈpleʒə] Freude; Vergnügen OT 1

plenty [ˈplenti] reichlich; viel OT 2

to plug in [plʌg] einstecken; einstöpseln OT 1

plum [plʌm] Pflaume; Zwetsche OT 1

plural [ˈplʊərəl] Plural; Mehrzahl OT 1

pocketknife [ˈpɒkɪtnaɪf] Taschenmesser OT 2

podcast [ˈpɒdkɑːst] Podcast OT 3

poem [ˈpəʊɪm] Gedicht OT 1

poet [ˈpəʊɪt] Dichter(in); Poet(in) OT 1

poetry [ˈpəʊətri] Dichtung OT 3

point [pɔɪnt] Punkt; Argument OT 1

poisonous [ˈpɔɪzənəs] giftig WS 1, 35

polar bear [ˈpəʊlə beə] Eisbär OT 3

pole [pəʊl] Stange; Pol OT 3

police [pəˈliːs] Polizei; Polizisten OT 1

policy [ˈpɒləsi] Politik; politische Linie WS 3, 111

polite [pəˈlaɪt] höflich OT 1

political [pəˈlɪtɪkl] politisch OT 2

politician [ˌpɒləˈtɪʃn] Politiker(in) OT 3

politics [ˈpɒlətɪks] Politik OT 3

poll [pəʊl] Umfrage WS 4, 142

to pollute [pəˈluːt] verschmutzen; verseuchen WS 1, 25

pollution [pəˈluːʃn] Verschmutzung OT 3

polo shirt [ˈpəʊləʊ ʃɜːt] Polohemd WS 4, 130

polyp [ˈpɒlɪp] Polyp WS 1, 28

pond [pɒnd] Teich OT 1

pool [puːl] Lache; Pfütze; Schwimmbecken OT 1

poor [pʊə] arm; schlecht OT 1

pop [pɒp] Pop- OT 2

popcorn [ˈpɒpkɔːn] Popcorn OT 2

pope [pəʊp] Papst OT 2

popular [ˈpɒpjələ] beliebt; populär OT 1

popularity [ˌpɒpjuˈlærəti] Popularität WS 3, 98

populated [ˈpɒpjuleɪt] bevölkert; besiedelt WS 1, 28

population [ˌpɒpjuˈleɪʃn] Bevölkerung OT 2

pop-up ad [ˈpɒp ʌp] Popup-Anzeige WS 2, 67

pork [pɔːk] Schweinefleisch OT 2

port [pɔːt] Hafen OT 2

portal [ˈpɔːtl] Portalseite WS 2, 67

portrait [ˈpɔːtreɪt] Porträt OT 3

position [pəˈzɪʃn] Position WS 1, 27

positive [ˈpɒzətɪv] Positiv; positiv OT 1

possession [pəˈzeʃn] Besitz WS 2, 54

possible [ˈpɒsəbl] möglich OT 2

post [pəʊst] Post OT 2

to post [pəʊst] posten WS 1, 29

postage [ˈpəʊstɪdʒ] Post... OT 3

postcard [ˈpəʊstkɑːd] Postkarte; Ansichtskarte OT 1

poster [ˈpəʊstə] Plakat; Poster OT 1

postman [ˈpəʊstmən] Briefträger(in) OT 2

posture [ˈpɒstʃə] Körperhaltung WS 2, 53

pot [pɒt] Topf OT 2

potato [pəˈteɪtəʊ] Kartoffel OT 1

potential [pəˈtenʃl] möglich; potentiell WS 2, 64

pottery [ˈpɒtəri] Töpfern; Töpferwaren OT 3

poultry [ˈpəʊltri] Geflügel OT 2

pound [paʊnd] Pfund OT 1

to pour [pɔː] gießen; schütten OT 1

poverty [ˈpɒvəti] Armut WS 3, 101

to power [ˈpaʊə] antreiben WS 1, 25

power [ˈpaʊə] Macht OT 3

powerful [ˈpaʊəfl] mächtig OT 2

powerless [ˈpaʊələs] kraftlos; machtlos WS 3, 101

practical [ˈpræktɪkl] praktisch OT 2

to practise [ˈpræktɪs] üben; trainieren OT 1

to praise [preɪz] loben WS 2, 75

to pray [preɪ] beten OT 3

prayer [preə] Gebet OT 3

predator [ˈpredətə] Raubtier; Räuber WS 1, 25

to predict [prɪˈdɪkt] vorhersagen OT 2

predictable [prɪˈdɪktəbl] vorhersehbar WS 1, 24

prediction [prɪˈdɪkʃn] Vorhersage OT 2

to prefer [prɪˈfɜː] vorziehen; etwas lieber tun OT 1

pregnant [ˈpregnənt] schwanger OT 3

preparation [ˌprepəˈreɪʃn] Vorbereitung OT 2

to prepare [prɪˈpeə] vorbereiten; sich vorbereiten OT 1

preschool [ˈpriːskuːl] vorschulisch WS 4, 133

to prescribe [prɪˈskraɪb] vorschreiben; festsetzen WS 4, 126

presence [ˈprezns] Präsenz WS 2, 64

present [ˈpreznt] Geschenk; Gegenwart OT 1

presentation [ˌpreznˈteɪʃn] Präsentation; Vortrag OT 1

preservation [ˌprezəˈveɪʃn] Haltbarmachung; Erhaltung OT 3

presidency [ˈprezɪdənsi] Präsidentschaft; Vorsitz WS 3, 115

president [ˈprezɪdənt] Präsident(in) OT 2

presidential [ˌprezɪˈdenʃl] präsidentiell OT 2

to press [pres] drücken; pressen OT 1

pressure [ˈpreʃə] Druck OT 3

to pretend [prɪˈtend] vorgeben; so tun, als ob OT 1

pretty [ˈprɪti] hübsch OT 1

to prevent [prɪˈvent] verhindern; abhalten WS 3, 101

prevention [prɪˈvenʃn] Verhütung OT 2

previous [ˈpriːviəs] vorhergehend OT 3

price [praɪs] Preis OT 1

pride [praɪd] Stolz WS 1, 32

primary [ˈpraɪməri] Haupt...; wichtigste(r,-s); primär OT 1

primary school [ˈpraɪməri ˌskuːl] Primärschule; Grundschule OT 1

Prime Minister [ˌpraɪm ˈmɪnɪstə] Premierminister(in) OT 2

prince [prɪns] Prinz OT 1

principal [ˈprɪnsəpl] Rektor(in) OT 2

principle [ˈprɪnsəpl] Prinzip OT 3

to print [prɪnt] drucken OT 3

priority [praɪˈɒrəti] Priorität OT 3

prison [ˈprɪzn] Gefängnis WS 1, 17

private [ˈpraɪvət] privat OT 3

privilege [ˈprɪvəlɪdʒ] Privileg; Recht OT 3

probably [ˈprɒbəbli] wahrscheinlich OT 2

problem [ˈprɒbləm] Problem; Aufgabe OT 1

procedure [prəˈsiːdʒə] Prozedur; Verfahren WS 2, 56

process [ˈprəʊses] Prozess WS 2, 70

product [ˈprɒdʌkt] Produkt OT 2
production [prəˈdʌkʃn] Produktion; Inszenierung **WS 4**, 130
profession [prəˈfeʃn] Profession; Beruf **WS 4**, 136
professional [prəˈfeʃənl] Fachfrau; Fachmann **WS 2**, 70
professor [prəˈfesə] Professor(in) OT 3
profile [ˈprəʊfaɪl] Profil **WS 4**, 137
profit [ˈprɒfɪt] Profit; Gewinn **WS 1**, 27
program [ˈprəʊɡræm] Programm; Kurs OT 3
to **programme** [ˈprəʊɡræm] programmieren OT 2
programming [ˈprəʊɡræmɪŋ] Programmierung OT 2
progress [ˈprəʊɡres] Fortschritt OT 3
progressive [prəˈɡresɪv] fortschrittlich; progressiv OT 1
project [ˈprɒdʒekt] Projekt; Vorhaben OT 1
projector [prəˈdʒektə] Projektor; Beamer OT 1
prolonged [prəˈlɒŋd] anhaltend; verlängert **WS 1**, 25
prom [prɒm] Schulball OT 3
promenade [ˌprɒməˈnɑːd] Promenade **WS 1**, 29
prominent [ˈprɒmɪnənt] bedeutend **WS 3**, 106
promise [ˈprɒmɪs] Versprechen OT 2
to **promise** [ˈprɒmɪs] versprechen OT 2
to **promote** [prəˈməʊt] fördern **WS 2**, 64
to **provide** [prəˈvaɪd] bereitstellen; liefern OT 3
pronoun [ˈprəʊnaʊn] Pronomen; Fürwort OT 1
to **pronounce** [prəˈnaʊns] aussprechen OT 3
pronunciation [prəˌnʌnsiˈeɪʃn] Aussprache OT 2
proof [pruːf] ...sicher; undurchdringlich **WS 1**, 12
prop [prɒp] Stütze; Requisite OT 1
proper [ˈprɒpə] richtig; anständig OT 1
property [ˈprɒpəti] Eigentum; Immobilie **WS 1**, 25
proportion [prəˈpɔːʃn] Anteil; Proportion **WS 2**, 69
pro [prəʊ] Vorteil OT 2
prospect [ˈprɒspekt] Aussicht; Möglichkeit **WS 3**, 100
to **prosper** [ˈprɒspə] florieren OT 2
to **protect** [prəˈtekt] schützen OT 2
protein [ˈprəʊtiːn] Protein **WS 2**, 68

to **protest** [ˈprəʊtest] protestieren; demonstrieren OT 3
protester [ˈprəʊtestə] Demonstrant(in) OT 2
proud [praʊd] stolz OT 2
to **prove** [pruːv] beweisen **WS 1**, 17
to **provide** [prəˈvaɪd] zur Verfügung stellen; versorgen (mit) **WS 1**, 36
province [ˈprɒvɪns] Provinz OT 2
provision [prəˈvɪʒn] Maßnahme **WS 4**, 127
pub [pʌb] Kneipe OT 2
puberty [ˈpjuːbəti] Pubertät **WS 4**, 125
public [ˈpʌblɪk] Öffentlichkeit OT 3
publication [ˌpʌblɪˈkeɪʃn] Veröffentlichung **WS 2**, 63
to **publish** [ˈpʌblɪʃ] veröffentlichen **WW**, 11
publisher [ˈpʌblɪʃə] Verleger(in); Verlag **WS 4**, 135
puck [pʌk] Puck OT 3
pueblo [ˈpwebləʊ] Pueblo OT 3
to **pull** [pʊl] ziehen; ziehen an OT 1
pumpkin [ˈpʌmpkɪn] Kürbis OT 2
to **punch** [pʌntʃ] schlagen **WS 4**, 151
punctual [ˈpʌŋktʃuəl] pünktlich **WS 4**, 140
punctuation [ˌpʌŋktʃuˈeɪʃn] Zeichensetzung OT 3
to **punish** [ˈpʌnɪʃ] bestrafen OT 3
puppy [ˈpʌpi] Welpe OT 2
purely [ˈpjʊəli] rein; völlig **WS 2**, 64
purpose [ˈpɜːpəs] Zweck **WS 1**, 36
   on purpose [ɒn ˈpɜːpəs] absichtlich OT 2
to **pursue** [pəˈsjuː] verfolgen **WS 2**, 70
to **put** [pʊt] tun; legen; stellen OT 1
   to **put on** [ˈpʌt ɒn] sich anziehen; veranstalten OT 1
   to **put up** [ˈpʊt ʌp] errichten OT 1
puzzled [ˈpʌzld] verblüfft; verwirrt **WS 1**, 14
pyjamas [pəˈdʒɑːməz] Schlafanzug OT 3

Q
qualification [ˌkwɒlɪfɪˈkeɪʃn] Qualifikation; Fähigkeit OT 2
quality [ˈkwɒləti] Eigenschaft; Qualität OT 3
to **quarrel** [ˈkwɒrəl] (sich) streiten OT 2
quarter [ˈkwɔːtə] Viertel; Quartal OT 1
quarter to [ˈkwɔːtə tə] viertel vor OT 1
quarterback [ˈkwɔːtəbæk] Quarterback OT 2
queen [kwiːn] Königin OT 1
queer [kwɪə] schwul; queer **WS 4**, 125

question [ˈkwestʃən] Frage OT 1
questionnaire [ˌkwestʃəˈneə] Fragebogen OT 1
queue [kjuː] Schlange; Warteschlange OT 1
quiet [ˈkwaɪət] still; ruhig OT 1
to **quit** [kwɪt] kündigen **WS 4**, 142
quiz [kwɪz] Quiz OT 2
quotation [kwəʊˈteɪʃn] Zitat OT 2
quotation mark [kwəʊˈteɪʃn mɑːk] Anführungszeichen OT 2
quote [kwəʊt] Zitat **WS 2**, 52
to **quote** [kwəʊt] zitieren OT 2

R
rabbit [ˈræbɪt] Kaninchen OT 1
race [reɪs] Rennen OT 2
racing [ˈreɪsɪŋ] Rennsport OT 2
radical [ˈrædɪkl] radikal; grundlegend **WS 3**, 102
radio [ˈreɪdiəʊ] Radio; Rundfunk OT 1
railway [ˈreɪlweɪ] Bahn; Eisenbahn OT 2
to **rain** [reɪn] regnen OT 1
rainbow [ˈreɪnbəʊ] Regenbogen **WS 1**, 13
rainforest [ˈreɪnfɒrɪst] Regenwald OT 2
rainstorm [ˈreɪnstɔːm] Regenschauer; Gewitter **WS 1**, 38
to **raise** [reɪz] einwerben; erheben; erhöhen OT 2
rally [ˈræli] Kundgebung OT 2
to **ramble** [ˈræmbl] weitschweifend reden **WS 2**, 59
ramp [ræmp] Rampe OT 2
ranching [ˈrɑːntʃ] Viehwirtschaft; Viehhaltung **WS 2**, 69
random [ˈrændəm] zufällig **WS 1**, 24
range [reɪndʒ] Angebot; Palette **WS 4**, 126
rank [ræŋk] Reihenfolge; Rank **WS 2**, 53
to **rank** [ræŋk] einordnen; in eine Reihenfolge bringen **WS 1**, 32
rare [reə] selten OT 2
raspberry [ˈrɑːzbəri] Himbeere OT 1
rat [ræt] Ratte OT 3
rate [reɪt] Rate; Anteil **WS 4**, 133
rather [ˈrɑːðə] ziemlich OT 3
ratter [ˈrætə] Rattenfänger OT 3
raven [ˈreɪvn] Rabe OT 2
raw [rɔː] roh OT 3
to **reach** [riːtʃ] erreichen OT 3
to **react** [riˈækt] reagieren OT 3
reaction [riˈækʃn] Reaktion **WS 1**, 14
to **read** [riːd] lesen; ablesen OT 1
reader [ˈriːdə] Leser(in) OT 2
ready [ˈredi] bereit OT 1
real [rɪəl] echt OT 1

realistic [ˌriːəˈlɪstɪk] realistisch **WS 2**, 68

reality [riˈæləti] Realität **WS 1**, 28

realization [ˌriːəlaɪˈzeɪʃn] Erkenntnis **WS 2**, 62

to **realize** [ˈriːəlaɪz] erkennen OT 2

really [ˈriːəli] wirklich; eigentlich; sehr OT 1

to **rearrange** [ˌriːəˈreɪndʒ] umstellen OT 2

reason [ˈriːzn] Grund; Vernunft OT 1

reasonable [ˈriːznəbl] angemessen; vernünftig **WS 2**, 64

rebel [ˈrebl] Rebell(in) OT 3

rebellion [rɪˈbeljən] Aufstand OT 3

to **receive** [rɪˈsiːv] erhalten OT 2

recent [ˈriːsnt] neueste(r) OT 3

recently [ˈriːsntli] neulich OT 3

reception [rɪˈsepʃn] Rezeption; Empfang OT 1

receptionist [rɪˈsepʃənɪst] Empfangschef(in); Sprechstundenhilfe; Rezeptionist(in) OT 1

recipe [ˈresəpi] Rezept OT 2

to **recite** [rɪˈsaɪt] aufsagen **WS 4**, 146

recognizable [ˈrekəgnaɪzəbl] erkennbar **WS 2**, 48

to **recommend** [ˌrekəˈmend] empfehlen OT 3

to **record** [rɪˈkɔːd] aufnehmen; aufzeichnen OT 1

to **recover** [rɪˈkʌvə] (sich) erholen **WS 3**, 108

recovery [rɪˈkʌvəri] Erholung; Genesung OT 2

rectangular [rekˈtæŋgjələ] rechteckig OT 2

to **recycle** [ˌriːˈsaɪkl] wiederverwerten OT 2

recycler [ˌriːˈsaɪklə] Wiederverwerter(in) OT 3

red [red] rot; Rotwein OT 1

reef [riːf] Riff **WS 1**, 26

to **re-enact** [ˌriː ɪˈnækt] nachspielen OT 3

re-enactment [ˌriː ɪˈnæktmənt] Nachspielen OT 3

to **refer** [rɪˈfɜː] sich beziehen OT 3

referee [ˌrefəˈriː] Schiedsrichter(in) OT 3

reference [ˈrefrəns] Empfehlung **WS 4**, 138

referendum [ˌrefəˈrendəm] Volksentscheid; Referendum **WS 3**, 99

to **refine** [rɪˈfaɪn] verfeinern **WS 3**, 97

to **reflect** [rɪˈflekt] spiegeln OT 2

reformation [ˌrefəˈmeɪʃn] Reformation OT 3

refund [ˈriːfʌnd] Erstattung; Ersatz **WS 2**, 64

to **regard** [rɪˈgɑːd] betrachten; ansehen OT 3

reggae [ˈregeɪ] Reggae OT 2

region [ˈriːdʒən] Region OT 3

regional [ˈriːdʒənl] regional **WS 1**, 32

register [ˈredʒɪstə] Kasse OT 2

to **regret** [rɪˈgret] bereuen OT 2

to **regroup** [ˌriːˈgruːp] (sich) neu gruppieren OT 2

regular [ˈregjələ] regelmäßig; normal OT 1

rehabilitation [ˌriːəˌbɪlɪˈteɪʃn] Rehabilitierung; Wiederherstellung OT 2

rehearsal [rɪˈhɜːsl] Probe OT 2

to **rehearse** [rɪˈhɜːs] proben OT 3

reindeer [ˈreɪndɪə] Rentier OT 3

to **reinforce** [ˌriːɪnˈfɔːs] verstärken; bekräftigen **WS 4**, 124

to **rejoin** [ˌriːˈdʒɔɪn] wieder beitreten **WS 3**, 99

to **relate to** [rɪˈleɪt tə] sich beziehen auf **WS 1**, 34

related [rɪˈleɪtɪd] verwandt OT 3

relation [rɪˈleɪʃn] Beziehung; Verhältnis **WS 1**, 30

relationship [rɪˈleɪʃnʃɪp] Beziehung OT 3

relative [ˈrelətɪv] Verwandte(r) OT 3

relatively [ˈrelətɪvli] relativ OT 2

to **relax** [rɪˈlæks] sich entspannen OT 3

relaxation [ˌriːlækˈseɪʃn] Erholung OT 3

relaxing [rɪˈlæksɪŋ] erholsam OT 2

to **release** [rɪˈliːs] veröffentlichen; auf den Markt bringen **WS 1**, 25

relevant [ˈreləvənt] wichtig **WS 2**, 65

reliable [rɪˈlaɪəbl] verlässlich **WS 3**, 96

reliance [rɪˈlaɪəns] Abhängigkeit **WS 3**, 95

relief [rɪˈliːf] Erleichterung; Hilfe OT 2

relieved [rɪˈliːvd] erleichtert OT 3

religion [rɪˈlɪdʒən] Religion OT 3

religious [rɪˈlɪdʒəs] religiös OT 2

to **relocate** [ˌriːləʊˈkeɪt] umziehen **WS 3**, 87

to **rely on** [rɪˈlaɪ ɒn] sich verlassen auf **WS 3**, 93

remarriage [ˌriːˈmærɪdʒ] Wiederverheiratung **WS 4**, 132

to **remember** [rɪˈmembə] sich erinnern an OT 1

to **remind** [rɪˈmaɪnd] erinnern OT 2

remote [rɪˈməʊt] entfernt; abgelegen **WS 1**, 13

removal [rɪˈmuːvl] Wegnahme; Entfernung **WS 1**, 22

to **remove** [rɪˈmuːv] entfernen OT 2

to **rename** [ˌriːˈneɪm] neu benennen **WS 2**, 59

renewable [rɪˈnjuːəbl] erneuerbar **WS 1**, 28

to **rent** [rent] mieten OT 3

repair [rɪˈpeə] Reparatur OT 2

to **repeat** [rɪˈpiːt] wiederholen; weitererzählen OT 1

repetitive [rɪˈpetətɪv] repetitiv; sich wiederholend **WS 4**, 127

to **replace** [rɪˈpleɪs] ersetzen OT 2

replacement [rɪˈpleɪsmənt] Ersatz; Austausch **WS 2**, 64

replica [ˈreplɪkə] Kopie OT 3

to **reply** [rɪˈplaɪ] antworten; erwidern OT 1

reporter [rɪˈpɔːtə] Reporter(in) OT 1

to **represent** [ˌreprɪˈzent] vertreten **WW**, 10

representative [ˌreprɪˈzentətɪv] Vertreter(in); Abgeordnete(r) **WS 3**, 90

reptile [ˈreptaɪl] Reptil OT 2

republic [rɪˈpʌblɪk] Republik **WS 3**, 90

republican [rɪˈpʌblɪkən] republikanisch **WS 3**, 90

request [rɪˈkwest] Bitte OT 1

to **require** [rɪˈkwaɪə] erfordern; verlangen **WS 4**, 127

requirement [rɪˈkwaɪəmənt] Voraussetzung; Bedingung **WS 1**, 37

rescue [ˈreskjuː] Rettung OT 2

research [rɪˈsɜːtʃ] Forschung OT 2

researcher [rɪˈsɜːtʃə] Forscher(in) OT 2

reservation [ˌrezəˈveɪʃn] Reservierung; Vorbehalt OT 1

to **reserve** [rɪˈzɜːv] reservieren OT 3

reservoir [ˈrezəvwɑː] Reservoir; Behälter **WS 1**, 34

residence [ˈrezɪdəns] Residenz; Wohnsitz **WS 3**, 110

resident [ˈrezɪdənt] Bewohner(in) OT 3

to **resign** [rɪˈzaɪn] zurücktreten **WS 3**, 99

resignation [ˌrezɪgˈneɪʃn] Amtsniederlegung; Rücktritt **WS 3**, 99

resistance [rɪˈzɪstəns] Widerstand; hier: Resistenz **WS 1**, 24

resistant [rɪˈzɪstənt] resistent **WS 2**, 69

resort [rɪˈzɔːt] Urlaubsort OT 3

to **respect** [rɪˈspekt] achten OT 3

respectful [rɪˈspektfl] respektvoll OT 3

respondent [rɪˈspɒndənt] Befragte(r) **WS 4**, 122

response [rɪˈspɒns] Reaktion; Antwort **WS 3**, 108

responsibility [rɪˌspɒnsəˈbɪləti] Verantwortung OT 3

responsible [rɪˈspɒnsəbl] verantwortlich **WS 3**, 90

restaurant [ˈrestrɒnt] Restaurant; Gaststätte OT 1

to **restore** [rɪˈstɔː] wiederherstellen **WS 3**, 98

restriction [rɪˈstrɪkʃn] Einschränkung **WS 3**, 100

result [rɪˈzʌlt] Ergebnis OT 2

to **resume** [rɪˈzjuːm] übernehmen **WS 1**, 26

retailer [ˈriːteɪlə] Einzelhändler(in) **WS 2**, 62

to **return** [rɪˈtɜːn] zurückkehren OT 2

reusable [ˌriːˈjuːzəbl] wiederverwendbar OT 3

to **reuse** [ˌriːˈjuːz] wiederverwenden **WS 3**, 102

to **reveal** [rɪˈviːl] zeigen **WS 2**, 53

review [rɪˈvjuː] Review OT 3

to **revise** [rɪˈvaɪz] revidieren OT 2

revival [rɪˈvaɪvl] Wiederbelebung **WS 4**, 128

revolting [rɪˈvəʊltɪŋ] abstoßend OT 2

revolution [ˌrevəˈluːʃn] Revolution OT 2

revolutionary [ˌrevəˈluːʃənəri] revolutionär OT 3

reward [rɪˈwɔːd] Belohnung; Preis **WS 4**, 129

rhyme [ˈraɪm] Reim OT 2

rice [raɪs] Reis OT 1

rich [rɪtʃ] reich; gehaltvoll OT 1

ride [raɪd] Ritt; Fahrt OT 1

to **ride** [raɪd] fahren **WS 1**, 29

right [raɪt] rechte(r, -s); rechts; richtig OT 1

rigid [ˈrɪdʒɪd] starr; rigide **WS 4**, 131

to **ring** [rɪŋ] klingeln; klingen OT 1

to **rise** [raɪz] aufsteigen OT 3

risk [rɪsk] Risiko; Gefahr **WS 1**, 28

ritual [ˈrɪtʃuəl] Ritual **WS 1**, 31

rival [ˈraɪvl] Rivale, Rivalin OT 2

rivalry [ˈraɪvlri] Konkurrenz **WS 1**, 30

river [ˈrɪvə] Fluss OT 1

river rafting [ˈrɪvər ˈrɑːftɪŋ] River-Rafting **WS 1**, 31

road [rəʊd] Straße OT 1

to **roam** [rəʊm] herumschweifen; durchschweifen **WS 1**, 25

roast [rəʊst] gebraten OT 1

rockstar [ˈrɒkstɑː] Rockstar OT 3

role [rəʊl] Rolle OT 1

to **roll** [ˈrəʊl] rollen OT 3

roof [ruːf] Dach OT 1

room [ˈruːm] Raum; Zimmer OT 1

root [ruːt] Wurzel OT 3

rope [rəʊp] Seil OT 3

to **rot** [ˈrəʊtə] verfaulen **WS 1**, 25

rough [rʌf] rau OT 3

round [raʊnd] rund OT 1

route [ruːt] Strecke OT 2

routine [ruːˈtiːn] Routine **WS 4**, 131

rover [ˈrəʊvə] Fahrzeug **WS 2**, 57

row [rəʊ] Reihe OT 2

rowing boat [ˈrəʊɪŋ bəʊt] Ruderboot OT 1

royal [ˈrɔɪəl] königlich; Königs... OT 1

to **rub** [rʌb] reiben OT 3

rubber [ˈrʌbə] Gummi; Radiergummi OT 1

rubbish [ˈrʌbɪʃ] Müll OT 3

rucksack [ˈrʌksæk] Rucksack OT 1

rude [ruːd] unhöflich OT 2

rugby [ˈrʌgbi] Rugby OT 1

ruin [ˈruːɪn] Ruine OT 2

to **rule** [ruːl] herrschen OT 2

rule [ruːl] Regel; Herrschaft OT 1

rulebook [ˈruːl bʊk] Regelwerk OT 2

ruler [ˈruːlə] Lineal; Herrscher(in) OT 1

to **run** [rʌn] laufen; rennen; leiten OT 1

to **run for office** [rʌn fɔː ˈɒfɪs] für ein Amt kandidieren OT 2

to **run out** [rʌn aʊt] zu Ende gehen OT 2

rundown [ˈrʌndaʊn] heruntergekommen; verwahrlost **WS 2**, 52

runner [ˈrʌnə] Läufer(in) OT 2

rural [ˈrʊərəl] ländlich OT 3

to **rush** [rʌʃ] eilen OT 2

to **rush off** [rʌʃ ɒf] loshasten OT 2

rush hour [ˈrʌʃ aʊə] Hauptverkehrszeit OT 1

S

sack [sæk] Sack OT 2

sack race [ˈsæk reɪs] Sackhüpfen OT 2

sacred [ˈseɪkrɪd] heilig OT 3

sad [sæd] traurig OT 1

saddened [ˈsædnd] betrübt **WS 1**, 26

safari [səˈfɑːri] Safari OT 2

safety [ˈseɪfti] Sicherheit OT 2

to **sail** [seɪl] (mit dem Schiff) fahren OT 2

sailboat [ˈseɪlbəʊt] Segelboot OT 3

sailing [ˈseɪlɪŋ] Segeln OT 1

sailor [ˈseɪlə] Seemann OT 3

saint [seɪnt] Heilige(r) OT 3

salad [ˈsæləd] Salat OT 1

sales [seɪlz] Verkäufe OT 2

sales assistant [ˌseɪlzəˈsɪstənt] Verkäufer(in) OT 2

salmon [ˈsæmən] Lachs OT 1

salt [sɔːlt] Salz OT 2

to **salvage** [ˈsælvɪdʒ] geborgen OT 3

salvage ship [ˈsælvɪdʒ ʃɪp] Bergungsschiff OT 3

same [seɪm] gleich OT 1

sample [ˈsɑːmpl] Stichprobe **WS 4**, 144

sanctuary [ˈsæŋktʃuəri] Schutzgebiet **WS 1**, 29

sand [sænd] Sand OT 1

sandstone [ˈsændstəʊn] Sandstein OT 3

sandwich [ˈsænwɪtʃ] Sandwich OT 1

sandy [ˈsændi] sandig **WS 1**, 29

sash [sæʃ] Schärpe OT 3

Saturday [ˈsætədeɪ] Samstag OT 1

sauce [sɔːs] Soße OT 1

sauna [ˈsɔːnə] Sauna OT 2

sausage [ˈsɒsɪdʒ] Wurst; Würstchen OT 1

to **save** [seɪv] retten; sparen OT 2

savvy [ˈsævi] klug; schlau **WS 2**, 62

saxophone [ˈsæksəfəʊn] Saxofon OT 2

to **say** [seɪ] sagen; aussprechen OT 1

scale [skeɪl] Maßstab OT 2

large scale [ˈlɑːdʒ skeɪl] großskalig OT 2

small scale [ˈsmɔːl skeɪl] kleinskalig OT 2

to **scan** [skæn] überfliegen; scannen OT 2

to **scare** [skeə] Angst machen OT 2

scared [skeəd] verängstigt; erschrecken OT 1

scarf [skɑːf] Schal; Halstuch OT 1

scary [ˈskeəri] unheimlich; beängstigend OT 2

scene [siːn] Szene OT 2

scenic [ˈsiːnɪk] malerisch OT 3

scholarship [ˈskɒləʃɪp] Stipendium **WS 4**, 126

school [skuːl] Schule; College OT 1

school bag [ˈskuːl bæg] Schultasche; Schulranzen OT 1

school day [skuːl deɪ] Schultag OT 1

schoolmate [ˈskuːlmeɪt] Schulkamerad(in) **WS 1**, 28

science [ˈsaɪəns] Wissen; Wissenschaft; Naturwissenschaften OT 1

scientist [ˈsaɪəntɪst] Naturwissenschaftler(in) OT 1

scissors [ˈsɪzəz] Schere OT 1

scorching [ˈskɔːtʃɪŋ] glühend **WS 1**, 21

to **score** [skɔː] punkten; ein Tor schießen OT 1

to **scrape** [skreɪp] kratzen; schrubben OT 2

to **scratch** [skrætʃ] kratzen OT 2

to **scream** [skriːm] schreien OT 3

screen [skriːn] Bildschirm; Leinwand OT 1

script [skrɪpt] Drehbuch OT 2

scroll [skrəʊl] Schriftrolle OT 2

sculpture [ˈskʌlptʃə] Skulptur OT 2

sea [siː] Meer; See OT 1

seabed [ˈsiːbed] Meeresboden OT 3

seabird [ˈsiːbɜːd] Seevogel **WS 1**, 26

seafaring [ˈsiːfeərɪŋ] seefahrend OT 3

seal [siːl] Robbe; Seehund OT 1

search [sɜːtʃ] Suche OT 2

seasick [ˈsiːsɪk] seekrank OT 3

seaside [ˈsiːsaɪd] Meeresküste OT 3

season [ˈsiːzn] Jahreszeit OT 2

seat [siːt] Sitzplatz OT 2

second [ˈsekənd] Sekunde; Augenblick; Zweite(r, -s) OT 1

secondary [ˈsekəndri] weiterführend; zweitrangig; sekundär OT 1

secondary school [ˈsekəndri ˌskuːl] Sekundarschule; weiterführende Schule OT 1

secondly [ˈsekəndli] zweitens OT 2

secret [ˈsiːkrət] Geheimnis OT 2

secretary [ˈsekrətri] Sekretär(in); Minister(in) OT 1

secure [sɪˈkjʊə] sicher OT 3

security [sɪˈkjʊərəti] Sicherheit **WS 1**, 28

seed [siːd] Samen OT 2

to **seek** [siːk] suchen **WS 1**, 16

segment [ˈsegmənt] Segment; Abschnitt **WS 1**, 32

seldom [ˈseldəm] selten **WS 2**, 67

to **select** [sɪˈlekt] wählen; auswählen OT 3

selection [sɪˈlekʃn] Auswahl **WS 2**, 72

selective [sɪˈlektɪv] getrennt **WS 2**, 63

self [self] selbst... **WS 4**, 120

self-employed [ˌself ɪmˈplɔɪd] selbständig **WS 4**, 136

selfie [ˈselfi] Selfie **WS 1**, 16

selfish [ˈselfɪʃ] egoistisch OT 3

to **sell** [sel] verkaufen OT 1

semi-final [ˌsemi ˈfaɪnl] Halbfinale OT 3

senator [ˈsenətə] Senator(in) **WS 3**, 91

to **send** [send] schicken; verschicken OT 1

senior citizen [ˌsiːniəˈsɪtɪzn] Senior(in) OT 2

sense [sens] Sinn OT 2

sensible [ˈsensəbl] vernünftig OT 2

sensitive [ˈsensətɪv] einfühlsam **WS 4**, 140

sensory [ˈsensəri] sensorisch **WS 4**, 131

sentence [ˈsentəns] Satz OT 1; Strafe **WS 4**, 144

to **sentence** [ˈsentəns] verurteilen **WS 4**, 144

separate [ˈseprət] getrennt OT 2

to **separate** [ˈseprət] trennen OT 3

sequence [ˈsiːkwəns] Reihenfolge **WS 2**, 59

to **sequence** [ˈsiːkwəns] in eine Reihenfolge bringen OT 3

sequentially [sɪˈkwenʃəli] der Reihe nach **WS 4**, 126

serious [ˈsɪəriəs] ernst OT 2

serpent [ˈsɜːpənt] Schlange **WS 1**, 13

to **serve** [sɜːv] servieren; bedienen; dienen OT 1

service [ˈsɜːvɪs] Dienst OT 2

session [ˈseʃn] Session; Sitzung **WS 2**, 56

to **set** [set] setzen OT 1

to **set fire to** [set faɪər] in Brand stecken **WS 2**, 69

to **set off** [ˌsetˈɒf] aufbrechen OT 2

to **set the table** [set ðə teɪbl] den Tisch decken OT 2

setting [ˈsetɪŋ] Szene; Umgebung **WS 2**, 53

to **settle** [ˈsetl] sich ansiedeln OT 3

to **settle down** [ˈsetl daʊn] sich beruhigen OT 2

to **settle in** [ˈsetl] sich eingewöhnen **WS 1**, 21

settlement [ˈsetlmənt] Besiedelung; Siedlung OT 3

settler [ˈsetlə] Siedler(in) OT 3

seven [ˈsevn] sieben OT 1

seventeen [ˌsevnˈtiːn] siebzehn OT 1

seventy [ˈsevnti] siebzig OT 1

severe [sɪˈvɪə] schwer; stark **WS 1**, 28

to **sew** [səʊ] nähen **WS 2**, 52

sex [seks] Geschlecht; Sex **WS 4**, 122

shade [ʃeɪd] Schatten **WS 1**, 16

to **shake** [ʃeɪk] schütteln OT 2

shaky [ˈʃeɪki] wackelig OT 3

shame: it's a shame [ɪts ə ʃeɪm] das ist schade OT 2

shampoo [ʃæmˈpuː] Shampoo OT 3

shape [ʃeɪp] Form; Gestalt OT 1

to **shape** [ʃeɪp] formen; gestalten **WS 1**, 38

shard [ʃɑːd] Scherbe **WS 2**, 48

to **share** [ʃeə] (sich) teilen OT 2

shark [ʃɑːk] Hai OT 2

she [ʃi] sie OT 1

shed [ʃed] Schuppen; Stall OT 1

sheep [ʃiːp] Schaf OT 1

sheepdog [ˈʃiːpdɒg] Hütehund OT 2

sheet [ʃiːt] Betttuch; Bettlaken; Blatt OT 1

shelter [ˈʃeltə] Unterschlupf OT 2

shepherd [ˈʃepəd] Schäfer OT 2

shift [ʃɪft] Veränderung **WS 4**, 128

to **shine** [ʃaɪn] scheinen; leuchten OT 1

ship [ʃɪp] Schiff OT 1

shipwreck [ˈʃɪprek] Schiffswrack OT 3

shirt [ʃɜːt] Hemd; Oberhemd OT 1

to **shiver** [ˈʃɪvə] zittern OT 3

shocked [ʃɒkt] schockiert OT 3

shoe [ʃuː] Schuh; Hufeisen OT 1

to **shoot** [ʃuːt] schießen OT 3

shop [ʃɒp] Laden; Geschäft OT 1

to **shop** [ʃɒp] kaufen; einkaufen OT 1

shoplifting [ˈʃɒplɪftɪŋ] Ladendiebstahl **WS 4**, 120

shopper [ˈʃɒpə] Käufer(in) **WS 2**, 49

shopping [ˈʃɒpɪŋ] Einkaufen OT 1

shopping centre [ˈʃɒpɪŋ sentə] Einkaufszentrum OT 1

shoreline [ˈʃɔːlaɪn] Küste **WS 3**, 108

short [ʃɔːt] kurz; klein OT 1

shortage [ˈʃɔːtɪdʒ] Mangel **WS 1**, 34

to **shorten** [ˈʃɔːtn] kürzen; abkürzen **WS 2**, 63

shortlist [ˈʃɔːtlɪst] Auswahlliste OT 2

shorts [ʃɔːts] kurze Hosen OT 3

shot [ʃɒt] Schuss; Schnappschuss OT 2

shoulder [ˈʃəʊldə] Schulter OT 1

to **shout** [ʃaʊt] laut rufen OT 1

to **show** [ʃəʊ] zeigen; vorzeigen OT 1

show-and-tell [ˌʃəʊ ən ˈtel] Kurzvortrag über einen mitgebrachten Gegenstand OT 2

shower [ˈʃaʊə] Dusche; Schauer OT 1

showground [ˈʃəʊgraʊnd] Ausstellungsgelände OT 2

to **shred** [ʃred] zerfetzen OT 2

to **shut** [ʃʌt] schließen OT 1

to **shut up** [ʃʌt ʌp] den Mund halten OT 2

shuttle [ˈʃʌtl] Shuttle OT 3

shy [ʃaɪ] schüchtern OT 2

sibling [ˈsɪblɪŋ] Geschwister **WS 1**, 27

sick [sɪk] krank; übel OT 1

to **sigh** [saɪ] seufzen **WS 1**, 15

sight [saɪt] Sehvermögen; Sicht; Sehenswürdigkeit OT 1

sightseeing ['saɪtsiːɪŋ] Besichtigungen; Sightseeing OT 1

sign [saɪn] Schild; Zeichen OT 1

to **sign up** [saɪn ʌp] sich anmelden OT 2

to **sign** [saɪn] unterschreiben OT 2

signal ['sɪɡnəl] Signal OT 2

significance [sɪɡ'nɪfɪkəns] Bedeutung; Wichtigkeit WS 1, 32

significant [sɪɡ'nɪfɪkənt] bedeutend; erheblich OT 2

silence ['saɪləns] Schweigen; Ruhe WS 1, 14

silly ['sɪli] dumm; doof; albern OT 1

silver ['sɪlvə] Silber...; silbern OT 1

similar ['sɪmələ] ähnlich OT 1

similarity [ˌsɪmə'lærəti] Ähnlichkeit OT 3

to **simmer** ['sɪmə] köcheln OT 2

simple ['sɪmpl] einfach; schlicht OT 1

simultaneous [ˌsɪml'teɪnɪəs] gleichzeitig; simultan WS 2, 63

since [sɪns] seit OT 2

sincerely [sɪn'sɪəli] aufrichtig; mit freundlichen Grüßen OT 3

to **sing** [sɪŋ] singen OT 1

singer ['sɪŋə] Sänger(in) OT 1

single ['sɪŋɡl] Einzel... OT 3

sink [sɪŋk] Spülbecken OT 3

sir [sɜː] (mein) Herr OT 1

siren ['saɪrən] Sirene OT 3

sister ['sɪstə] Schwester OT 1

to **sit** [sɪt] sitzen; liegen OT 1

situated ['sɪtʃueɪtɪd] gelegen WS 3, 108

situation [ˌsɪtʃu'eɪʃn] Lage; Situation OT 1

six [sɪks] sechs OT 1

sixteen [ˌsɪks'tiːn] sechzehn OT 1

sixty ['sɪksti] sechzig OT 1

size [saɪz] Größe OT 2

to **skate** [skeɪt] Schlittschuh laufen OT 2

skateboard ['skeɪtbɔːd] Skateboard OT 1

to **skateboard** ['skeɪtbɔːd] Skateboard fahren OT 3

skeleton ['skelɪtn] Skelett; Gerippe OT 2

sketch [sketʃ] Skizze; Sketch OT 2

to **ski** [skiː] Ski laufen OT 3

skiing ['skiːɪŋ] Skifahren OT 3

skill [skɪl] Geschick; Fähigkeit OT 1

skilled [skɪld] geschickt; ausgebildet OT 3

to **skim** [skɪm] querlesen OT 2

skin [skɪn] Haut OT 2

to **skip** [skɪp] auslassen OT 3

skirt [skɜːt] Rock OT 1

skull [skʌl] Schädel OT 2

sky [skaɪ] Himmel OT 1

skydiver ['skaɪdaɪvə] Fallschirmspringer(in) WS 1, 29

skyline ['skaɪlaɪn] Skyline WS 1, 29

skyscraper ['skaɪskreɪpə] Wolkenkratzer OT 3

slang [slæŋ] Slang WW, 11

to **slap on** [slæp ɒn] aufsetzen WS 1, 16

slave [sleɪv] Sklave(-in) OT 3

slavery ['sleɪvəri] Sklaverei OT 3

sled [sled] Schlitten OT 3

to **sleep** [sliːp] schlafen OT 1

sleepover ['sliːpoʊvə] Pyjama-Party OT 1

slice [slaɪs] Scheibe; Stück OT 1

slide ['slaɪd] Folie OT 1

to **slide on** [slaɪd ɒn] hier: aufsetzen WS 1, 16

slideshow ['slaɪdʃoʊ] Diaschau WW, 11

to **slip on** [slɪp ɒn] rasch anziehen WS 1, 16

slippery ['slɪpəri] glatt OT 3

slogan ['sloʊɡən] Slogan OT 2

to **slop on** [slɒp ɒn] auftragen WS 1, 16

slow [sloʊ] langsam OT 2

to **slow down** [sloʊ'daʊn] verlangsamen OT 3

slum [slʌm] Slum; Getto WS 3, 101

to **slump** [slʌmp] abrutschen; zusammensacken WS 4, 137

small [smɔːl] klein OT 1

smallpox ['smɔːlpɒks] Pocken WS 1, 24

smartphone ['smɑːtfoʊn] Smartphone OT 3

to **smell** [smel] riechen; stinken OT 1

smelly ['smeli] übel riechend OT 3

to **smile** [smaɪl] lächeln OT 1

smoke [smoʊk] Rauch OT 2

snack [snæk] Snack; Imbiss OT 1

snake [sneɪk] Schlange OT 1

to **snap** [snæp] zerbrechen OT 3

sneaker ['sniːkə] Turnschuh WS 2, 66

snow [snoʊ] Schnee OT 1

snowboarding ['snoʊbɔːdɪŋ] Snowboardfahren OT 3

snowmobile ['snoʊməbiːl] Schneemobil OT 3

snowy ['snoʊi] verschneit OT 3

so [soʊ] also; folglich OT 1

to **soak** [soʊk] durchnässen OT 3

soap [soʊp] Seife OT 2

to **soar** [sɔː] schweben OT 3

social ['soʊʃl] gesellschaftlich OT 3

to **socialize** ['soʊʃəlaɪz] Kontakte pflegen WS 2, 65

social media [ˌsoʊʃl 'miːdiə] soziale Medien OT 2

society [sə'saɪəti] Gesellschaft OT 3

sock [sɒk] Socke OT 1

soda ['soʊdə] Limo; Sprudel WS 2, 68

sofa ['soʊfə] Sofa OT 1

soft [sɒft] weich; gedämpft OT 1

solar ['soʊlə] Sonnen... OT 3

soldier ['soʊldʒə] Soldat(in) OT 1

solo ['soʊloʊ] solo OT 2

solution [sə'luːʃn] Lösung OT 3

to **solve** [sɒlv] lösen OT 3

some [sʌm] etwas; einige OT 1

somehow ['sʌmhaʊ] irgendwie WS 3, 106

someone ['sʌmwʌn] jemand; irgendjemand OT 1

something ['sʌmθɪŋ] etwas OT 1

sometime ['sʌmtaɪm] irgendwann OT 3

sometimes ['sʌmtaɪmz] manchmal OT 1

somewhere ['sʌmweə] irgendwo; irgendwohin OT 1

son [sʌn] Sohn OT 1

song [sɒŋ] Lied; Gesang OT 1

songwriter ['sɒŋraɪtər] Texter(in); Liederkomponist(in) WS 4, 120

soon [suːn] bald OT 1

soul [soʊl] Seele OT 2

sound [saʊnd] Geräusch; Ton OT 1

to **sound** [saʊnd] klingen OT 3

soup [suːp] Suppe OT 1

south [saʊθ] Süd- OT 2

southern ['sʌðən] südlich WS 1, 13

southwest [ˌsaʊθ'west] südwestlich OT 3

souvenir [ˌsuːvə'nɪə] Andenken OT 3

spaghetti [spə'ɡeti] Spaghetti OT 1

spaniel ['spænjəl] Spaniel OT 2

spark [spɑːk] Funke OT 2

sparkler ['spɑːklə] Wunderkerze OT 3

to **speak** [spiːk] sprechen; reden OT 1

speaker ['spiːkə] Redner(in) OT 2

spear [spɪə] Speer OT 3

special ['speʃl] besondere(r, -s); speziell OT 1

special effects [ˌspeʃlɪ'fekts] Spezialeffekte OT 2

specialist ['speʃəlɪst] Spezialist(in); Expert(in) WS 4, 131

to **specialize** ['speʃəlaɪz] sich spezialisieren OT 3

species ['spiːʃiːz] Spezies; Art WS 1, 21

spectacular [spekˈtækjələ] spektakulär OT 2

spectator [spekˈteɪtə] Zuschauer(in) OT 2

speech [spiːtʃ] Rede OT 2

speed [spiːd] Geschwindigkeit OT 2

to **spell** [spel] buchstabieren OT 1

spelling [ˈspelɪŋ] Rechtschreibung; Schreibweise OT 1

to **spend** [spend] ausgeben; verbringen OT 1

spice [spaɪs] Gewürz OT 2

spicy [ˈspaɪsi] scharf; würzig **WS 2**, 79

spider [ˈspaɪdə] Spinne OT 1

to **spill** [spɪl] verschütten OT 2

spirit [ˈspɪrɪt] Geist OT 2

spite: in spite of [ɪn spaɪt] trotz **WS 1**, 25

to **split** [ˌsplɪt] trennen OT 2

to **split up** [ˌsplɪtˈʌp] sich trennen **WS 2**, 54

sponsor [ˈspɒnsə] Sponsor(in) OT 2

to **sponsor** [ˈspɒnsə] finanziell unterstützen OT 2

sponsorship [ˈspɒnsəʃɪp] finanzielle Unterstützung OT 2

spoon [spuːn] Löffel OT 2

sport [spɔːt] Sport; Sportart OT 1

sporting [ˈspɔːtɪŋ] sportlich; Sport... **WS 1**, 15

sportswoman, sportsman [ˈspɔːtswʊmən, ˈspɔːtsmən] Sportler(in) OT 2

sporty [ˈspɔːti] sportlich **WS 4**, 130

to **spot** [spɒt] erspähen OT 1

sprain [spreɪn] Verstauchung OT 2

to **sprain** [spreɪn] verstauchen OT 2

spray [spreɪ] Spray OT 3

to **spray** [spreɪ] sprühen OT 3

to **spread** [spred] verbreiten **WW**, 10

spring [sprɪŋ] Frühling; Quelle OT 2

hot spring [ˈhɒt sprɪŋ] Thermalquelle OT 2

to **sprinkle** [ˈsprɪŋkl] streuen OT 2

square [skweə] Quadrat; Feld; Platz OT 1

squirrel [ˈskwɪrəl] Eichhörnchen OT 1

stability [stəˈbɪləti] Stabilität OT 3

stable [ˈsteɪbl] Stall **WS 4**, 138

stadium [ˈsteɪdiəm] Stadion OT 1

staff [stɑːf] Personal OT 1

stage [steɪdʒ] Phase; Bühne OT 2

stairs [ˈsteəz] Treppe; Treppenstufen OT 1

stall [stɔːl] Stand **WS 2**, 49

stamp [stæmp] Briefmarke OT 1

to **stand** [stænd] stehen; stellen OT 1

to **stand for sth.** [stænd] für etwas stehen OT 2

standard [ˈstændəd] Standard; normal **WS 1**, 16

standard [ˈstændəd] standardmäßig; normal **WS 1**, 16

star [stɑː] Stern; Sternchen; Star OT 1

to **stare** [steə] starren OT 2

start [stɑːt] Anfang OT 1

to **start** [stɑːt] anfangen; beginnen OT 1

starter [ˈstɑːtə] Vorspeise; Starter(in) OT 1

to **starve** [stɑːv] hungern (lassen); verhungern OT 1

state [steɪt] Staat; Bundesstaat OT 1

statement [ˈsteɪtmənt] Aussage; Erklärung OT 1

station [ˈsteɪʃn] Station; Bahnhof OT 1

statistic [stəˈtɪstɪk] Statistik OT 3

statue [ˈstætʃuː] Statue; Standbild OT 1

status [ˈsteɪtəs] Status **WW**, 11

to **stay** [steɪ] bleiben; wohnen OT 1

steadily [ˈstedəli] stetig; ununterbrochen **WS 2**, 75

steak [steɪk] Steak; Rindfleisch OT 1

to **steal** [stiːl] klauen OT 2

steam [stiːm] Dampf OT 2

steel [stiːl] Stahl OT 2

steep [stiːp] steil OT 2

to **steer** [stɪə] steuern OT 3

step [step] Schritt; Stufe OT 1

to **step up** [step ʌp] vortreten **WS 4**, 123

stereotype [ˈsteriətaɪp] Stereotype; Klischee **WS 2**, 65

stereotypical [ˌsteriəˈtɪpɪkl] stereotypisch **WS 4**, 124

steroid [ˈsterɔɪd] Steroid **WS 2**, 68

stick [stɪk] Stock OT 2

to **stick** [stɪk] stecken; stechen; kleben OT 1

sticky [ˈstɪki] selbstklebend; klebrig **WS 2**, 60

stiff [stɪf] steif; starr **WS 4**, 131

stigma [ˈstɪgmə] Stigma **WS 2**, 70

still [stɪl] immer noch; noch immer OT 1

still [stɪl] still OT 1

to **sting** [stɪŋ] stechen OT 2

stingray [ˈstɪŋreɪ] Stachelrochen **WS 1**, 21

to **stir** [stɜː] rühren OT 2

stomach [ˈstʌmək] Magen; Bauch OT 1

stone [stəʊn] Stein; britische Gewichtseinheit (6,35 kg) OT 1

stop [stɒp] Halt; Aufenthalt OT 1

storage [ˈstɔːrɪdʒ] Lagerung OT 3

to **store** [stɔː] aufbewahren OT 2

storm [stɔːm] Sturm OT 2

storyboard [ˈstɔːribɔːd] Storyboard; Szenenbuch **WS 2**, 61

storybook [ˈstɔːribʊk] Geschichtenbuch OT 2

storyteller [ˈstɔːritelə] Geschichtenerzähler(in) OT 2

storytelling [ˈstɔːritelɪŋ] Geschichtenerzählen OT 3

stove [stəʊv] Ofen OT 3

straight [streɪt] gerade; direkt OT 3

straight away [ˈstreɪt əˌweɪ] sofort OT 2

strange [streɪndʒ] seltsam; merkwürdig OT 1

stranger [ˈstreɪndʒə] Fremde(r) OT 3

strategy [ˈstrætədʒi] Strategie OT 3

straw [strɔː] Trinkhalm; Strohhalm; Stroh **WS 3**, 98

strawberry [ˈstrɔːbəri] Erdbeere OT 1

stream [striːm] Bach OT 2

streaming [ˈstriːmɪŋ] Streaming **WS 4**, 128

strength [streŋθ] Stärke OT 3

to **strengthen** [ˈstreŋkθn] stärker werden; stärker machen **WS 3**, 108

stress [stres] Stress; Betonung OT 1

stressed [strest] gestresst; angestrengt OT 2

stressful [ˈstresfl] stressig **WS 4**, 142

to **stretch** [stretʃ] sich erstrecken OT 3

strict [strɪkt] streng OT 2

strike [straɪk] Streik **WS 3**, 106

striker [ˈstraɪkə] Stürmer(in) OT 3

string [strɪŋ] Schnur; Saite OT 2

strip [strɪp] Streifen OT 2

strong [strɒŋ] stark OT 2

structure [ˈstrʌktʃə] Struktur; Aufbau OT 1

to **structure** [ˈstrʌktʃə] strukturieren; aufbauen **WS 1**, 29

to **struggle** [ˈstrʌgl] sich anstrengen; sich bemühen **WS 4**, 123

student [ˈstjuːdnt] Student(in); Schüler(in) OT 1

studies [ˈstʌdiz] Studium; Wissenschaft OT 1

religious studies [rɪˈlɪdʒəs stʌdiz] Religionsunterricht OT 1

studio [ˈstjuːdiəʊ] Studio OT 3

to **study** [ˈstʌdi] studieren; lernen OT 1

study [ˈstʌdi] Studie; Untersuchung OT 1

stuff [stʌf] Zeug OT 2

stunning ['stʌnɪŋ] toll; atemberaubend
WS 1, 28

stupid ['stju:pɪd] dumm OT 2

style [staɪl] Stil OT 2

stylish ['staɪlɪʃ] schick **WS 2**, 66

sub-heading [ˌsʌb 'hedɪŋ]
Unterüberschrift OT 2

subject ['sʌbdʒɪkt] Thema; Fach OT 1

to **subscribe** [səb'skraɪb] abonnieren
OT 3

substance ['sʌbstəns] Substanz OT 3

substitution [ˌsʌbstɪ'tju:ʃn] Ersatz;
Ersetzen OT 3

subway ['sʌbweɪ] U-Bahn;
Unterführung OT 1

to **succeed** [sək'si:d] Erfolg haben OT 2

success [sək'ses] Erfolg OT 3

successful [sək'sesfl] erfolgreich OT 2

such [sʌtʃ] so OT 2

suddenly ['sʌdənli] plötzlich;
auf einmal OT 2

to **suffer** ['sʌfə] leiden **WS 1**, 34

sugar ['ʃʊgə] Zucker OT 1

to **suggest** [sə'dʒest] vorschlagen;
hindeuten auf OT 1

suggestion [sə'dʒestʃən] Vorschlag;
Andeutung OT 1

suit [su:t] Anzug; Kostüm OT 1

sum [sʌm] Rechenaufgabe OT 2

to **summarize** ['sʌməraɪz]
zusammenfassen OT 2

summary ['sʌməri] Zusammenfassung
OT 1

summer ['sʌmə] Sommer OT 1

summit ['sʌmɪt] Gipfel OT 3

sun [sʌn] Sonne OT 1

sunburn ['sʌnbɜ:n] Sonnenbrand OT 2

Sunday ['sʌndeɪ] Sonntag OT 1

sundial ['sʌndaɪəl] Sonnenuhr OT 3

sunny ['sʌni] sonnig; fröhlich OT 1

sunscreen ['sʌnskri:n]
Sonnenschutzmittel OT 2

sunset ['sʌnset] Sonnenuntergang OT 3

sunshine ['sʌnʃaɪn] Sonnenschein OT 3

sunstroke ['sʌnstrəʊk] Sonnenstich
OT 2

superhero ['su:pəhɪərəʊ] Superheld
WS 2, 68

superlative [su'pɜ:lətɪv] unübertrefflich
OT 2

supermarket ['su:pəmɑːkɪt]
Supermarkt OT 1

to **supervise** ['su:pəvaɪz] beaufsichtigen
OT 3

supply [sə'plaɪ] Vorrat OT 3

to **supply** [sə'plaɪ] versorgen mit OT 3

support [sə'pɔ:t] Unterstützung OT 2

to **support** [sə'pɔ:t] unterstützen OT 1

supporter [sə'pɔ:tə] Anhänger(in) OT 3

supportive [sə'pɔ:tɪv] unterstützend
WS 1, 14

to **suppose** [sə'pəʊz] vermuten;
annehmen OT 1

supreme [su'pri:m] oberste(r, -s)
WS 3, 90

sure [ʃʊə] sicher; klar OT 1

surface ['sɜ:fɪs] Oberfläche OT 3

surfing ['sɜ:fɪŋ] Surfen; Wellenreiten
OT 1

surgeon ['sɜ:dʒən] Chirurg(in) OT 3

surgery ['sɜ:dʒəri] Praxis; Sprechstunde
WS 3, 110

surprise [sə'praɪz] Überraschung OT 1

surprised [sə'praɪzd] überrascht OT 2

surprising [sə'praɪzɪŋ] überraschend
OT 2

to **surrender** [sə'rendə] aufgeben;
übergeben **WS 3**, 106

to **surround** [sə'raʊnd] umgeben OT 3

survey ['sɜ:veɪ] Umfrage; Untersuchung
OT 1

survival [sə'vaɪvl] Überleben OT 2

to **survive** [sə'vaɪv] überleben OT 3

survivor [sə'vaɪvə] Überlebende(r) OT 3

sustainability [səˌsteɪnə'bɪləti]
Nachhaltigkeit OT 3

sustainable [sə'steɪnəbl] nachhaltig
OT 3

to **swap** [swɒp] tauschen OT 3

to **sweat** [swet] schwitzen OT 2

sweatshirt ['swetʃɜ:t] Sweatshirt OT 1

to **sweep** [swi:p] fegen OT 3

sweet [swi:t] Bonbon OT 1

swelling ['swelɪŋ] Schwellung OT 2

swift ['swɪft] zügig; rasch OT 3

to **swim** [swɪm] schwimmen;
durchschwimmen OT 1

swimmer ['swɪmə] Schwimmer(in) OT 3

swimwear ['swɪmweə] Badebekleidung
WW, 11

switch [swɪtʃ] Schalter OT 3

swollen ['swəʊln] geschwollen OT 2

sword [sɔ:d] Schwert OT 1

symbol ['sɪmbl] Symbol; Zeichen OT 1

sympathetic [ˌsɪmpə'θetɪk] mitfühlend
OT 2

synaesthesia [ˌsɪnəs'θi:ziə] Synästhesie
OT 2

synonymous [sɪ'nɒnɪməs]
gleichbedeutend OT 3

synonym ['sɪnənɪm] Synonym OT 2

synthetic [sɪn'θetɪk] synthetisch
WS 3, 95

system ['sɪstəm] System OT 2

systematically [ˌsɪstə'mætɪkli]
systematisch **WS 1**, 24

T

table ['teɪbl] Tisch; Tabelle OT 1

tablespoon ['teɪblspu:n] Esslöffel OT 2

to **tackle** ['tækl] tackeln; angreifen OT 2

tag [tæg] Etikett; kurze Schnur, die
gelochte Blätter zusammenhält OT 2

tail [teɪl] Schwanz OT 2

to **tailor** ['teɪlə] zuschneiden; anpassen
WS 3, 93

to **take** [teɪk] nehmen; machen OT 1
to **take for granted** [teɪk fə 'grɑ:ntɪd]
als selbstverständlich ansehen
WS 3, 101

talent ['tælənt] Talent OT 3

talented ['tæləntɪd] begabt; talentiert
WS 1, 32

to **talk** [tɔ:k] reden; sprechen OT 1

tank [tæŋk] Tank OT 3

tap [tæp] Wasserhahn OT 3

to **target** ['tɑ:gɪt] ins Visier nehmen;
zielen auf **WS 4**, 150

to **taste** [teɪst] schmecken; kosten OT 1

taster ['teɪstə] Prüfer(in) OT 3

tasty ['teɪsti] schmackhaft OT 2

tattoo [tə'tu:] Tätowierung OT 3

tax [tæks] Steuer OT 3

tea [ti:] Tee; Abendessen OT 1

to **teach** [ti:tʃ] unterrichten; lehren OT 1

teacher ['ti:tʃə] Lehrer(in) OT 1

team [ti:m] Mannschaft; Team OT 1

teammate ['ti:mmeɪt]
Manschaftskollege, -kollegin OT 2

tear [tɪə] Träne OT 2

to **tease** [ti:z] ärgern OT 2

technical ['teknɪkl] technisch OT 2

technique [tek'ni:k] Technik **WS 1**, 29

technological [ˌteknə'lɒdʒɪkl]
technologisch **WS 2**, 62

technology [tek'nɒlədʒi] Technologie
OT 1

teen [ti:n] Teenager OT 2

teenage ['ti:neɪdʒ] Teenager... OT 3

teepee ['ti:pi:] Teepee OT 3

television ['telɪvɪʒn] Fernseher OT 2

to **tell** [tel] erzählen; sagen OT 1
to **tell off** [tel ɒf] ausschimpfen OT 2

temperature ['temprətʃə] Temperatur
OT 2

template ['templeɪt] Vorlage OT 3

temple ['templ] Tempel OT 1

tempted: to be tempted by [bi 'temptɪd baɪ] in Versuchung sein **WS 2**, 79

ten [ten] zehn OT 1

to **tend to** ['tend tə] zu etw. neigen **WS 4**, 124

tennis ['tenɪs] Tennis OT 1

tense [tens] Zeitform; Tempus OT 1

tent [tent] Zelt OT 1

term [tɜːm] Semester OT 2

terrible ['terəbl] schrecklich; furchtbar OT 1

terrier ['teriə] Terrier OT 2

territory ['terətri] Gebiet OT 3

test [test] Test; Untersuchung OT 1

text [tekst] SMS; Text OT 2

to **text** [tekst] texten OT 2

textbook ['tekstbʊk] Lehrbuch OT 3

to **thank** [θæŋk] danken; sich bedanken OT 3

thanks [θæŋks] Danke! OT 1

theatre ['θɪətə] Theater OT 1

their [ðeə] ihr OT 1

then [ðen] dann; damals OT 1

theoretical [ˌθɪə'retɪkl] theoretisch **WS 2**, 50

therapy ['θerəpi] Therapie **WS 4**, 131

there [ðeə] da; dort OT 1

therefore ['ðeəfɔː] daher; deshalb; darum **WS 1**, 13

these [ðiːz] diese; die (hier) OT 1

thick [θɪk] dick; dicht OT 1

thigh [θaɪ] Oberschenkel; Schenkel OT 1

thin [θɪn] dünn; schwach OT 1

thing [θɪŋ] Ding; Sache OT 1

to **think** [θɪŋk] denken; glauben OT 1

to **think about, of** ['θɪŋk əbaʊt] denken an; nachdenken über OT 1

thinker ['θɪŋkə] Denker(in) OT 3

third [θɜːd] Dritte(r, -s); Drittel OT 1

thirsty ['θɜːsti] durstig OT 1

thirteen [ˌθɜː'tiːn] dreizehn OT 1

thirty ['θɜːti] dreißig OT 1

this [ðɪs] diese(r, -s) OT 1

those [ðəʊz] diese; die da; jene dort OT 1

though [ðəʊ] obwohl; jedoch OT 2

thought [θɔːt] Gedanke OT 3

threat [θret] Gefahr **WS 1**, 17

to **threaten** ['θretn] gefährden **WS 1**, 25

three [θriː] drei OT 1

threefold ['θriːfəʊld] dreifach **WS 2**, 69

throat [θrəʊt] Kehle; Hals OT 3

throne [θrəʊn] Thron OT 2

through [θruː] durch; hindurch OT 1

to **throw** [θrəʊ] werfen OT 1

to **throw up** [θrəʊ ʌp] sich übergeben OT 2

thunderstorm ['θʌndəstɔːm] Gewitter OT 2

Thursday ['θɜːzdeɪ] Donnerstag OT 1

tick [tɪk] Haken; Häkchen OT 1

ticket ['tɪkɪt] Eintrittskarte; Fahrschein OT 1

to **tidy** ['taɪdi] aufräumen OT 1

tie [taɪ] Krawatte; Band OT 1

to **tie** [taɪ] binden; zubinden **WS 4**, 131

tiger ['taɪgə] Tiger OT 1

tightly ['taɪtli] fest OT 3

tights [taɪts] Strumpfhose OT 2

tile [taɪl] Fliese OT 2

till [tɪl] bis OT 2

to **tilt** [tɪlt] sich neigen OT 3

time [taɪm] Zeit; Zeitpunkt OT 1

for the first time [fɔː ðə 'fɜːst taɪm] zum ersten Mal OT 2

timeline ['taɪmlaɪn] Zeitachse OT 2

timely ['taɪmli] rechtzeitig; passend OT 3

times [taɪmz] mal **WS 1**, 12

timing ['taɪmɪŋ] Zeitpunkt OT 3

tin [tɪn] Zinn; Dose OT 2

tinder ['tɪndə] Zunder OT 2

tinned [tɪnd] Dosen-; in Dosen **WS 2**, 74

tiny ['taɪni] winzig OT 1

tip [tɪp] Spitze; Tipp; Hinweis OT 1

tipping point ['tɪpɪŋ pɔɪnt] Kipppunkt; Trendwende **WS 1**, 28

tired ['taɪəd] müde OT 1

title ['taɪtl] Titel OT 1

to [tuː] zu OT 1

toast [təʊst] Toast; Trinkspruch OT 2

tobacco [tə'bækəʊ] Tabak **WS 3**, 84

today [tə'deɪ] heute OT 1

toe [təʊ] Zeh; Spitze OT 1

together [tə'geðə] zusammen OT 1

toilet ['tɔɪlət] Toilette OT 2

tolerance ['tɒlərəns] Toleranz **WS 4**, 120

tolerant ['tɒlərənt] tolerant OT 3

tomato [tə'mɑːtəʊ] Tomate OT 1

tomboy ['tɒmbɔɪ] burschikoses Mädchen; Wildfang **WS 4**, 125

tomorrow [tə'mɒrəʊ] morgen OT 1

ton [tʌn] Tonne **WS 2**, 66

tone [təʊn] Ton **WS 4**, 137

tongue [tʌŋ] Zunge OT 3

tonight [tə'naɪt] heute Abend; heute Nacht OT 1

too [tuː] zu; auch OT 1

tool [tuːl] Werkzeug OT 2

tooth [tuːθ] Zahn OT 2

top [tɒp] obere(r, -s) OT 1

top [tɒp] oberes Ende; Spitze; oberster Teil OT 1

topic ['tɒpɪk] Thema OT 1

torch [tɔːtʃ] Taschenlampe; Fackel OT 1

tortoise ['tɔːtəs] Schildkröte OT 1

total ['təʊtl] Gesamtmenge OT 3

totally ['təʊtəli] völlig OT 3

touchdown ['tʌtʃdaʊn] Touchdown OT 2

tough [tʌf] zäh; hart OT 2

tour [tʊə] Reise; Tour; Rundgang OT 1

tourism ['tʊərɪzm,'tɔːrɪzm] Tourismus OT 3

tourist ['tʊərɪst] Tourist(in) OT 1

toward [tə'wɔːd] in Richtung OT 2

towel ['taʊəl] Handtuch OT 2

tower ['taʊə] Turm OT 1

town [taʊn] Stadt OT 1

townspeople ['taʊnzpiːpl] Stadtbewohner(innen) OT 3

towpath ['təʊpɑːθ] Treidelpfad OT 3

toy [tɔɪ] Spielzeug OT 3

tractor ['træktə] Traktor OT 2

trade [treɪd] Handel **WW**, 11

trader ['treɪdə] Händler(in) OT 3

traditional [trə'dɪʃənl] traditionell; konservativ OT 2

traffic ['træfɪk] Verkehr OT 1

tragedy ['trædʒədi] Tragödie **WS 3**, 100

trail [treɪl] Pfad; Spur OT 2

trailer ['treɪlə] Trailer **WS 1**, 27

to **train** [treɪn] ausbilden; trainieren OT 2

train [treɪn] Zug; Folge OT 1

traineeship [ˌtreɪ'niːʃɪp] Praktikumsplatz **WS 4**, 136

training ['treɪnɪŋ] Ausbildung OT 2

tram ['træm] Straßenbahn OT 2

trans [trænz] trans... **WS 4**, 121

transatlantic [ˌtrænzət'læntɪk] transatlantisch OT 3

transcript ['trænskrɪpt] Transkript OT 3

transferable [træns'fɜːrəbl] übertragbar **WS 4**, 142

transformation [ˌtrænsfə'meɪʃn] Veränderung; Verwandlung **WS 3**, 110

transgender [trænz'dʒendə] transgender **WS 4**, 125

transition [træn'zɪʃn] Wechsel; Übergang **WS 3**, 99

translation [træns'leɪʃn] Übersetzung OT 2

transport ['trænspɔːt] Transport; Verkehr OT 3

to **transport** [trænˈspɔːt] transportieren OT 3

trap [træp] Falle OT 3

to **travel** [ˈtrævl] reisen; fahren OT 1

traveller [ˈtrævələ] Reisende(r) OT 3

tray [treɪ] Tablett OT 2

treason [ˈtriːzn] Verrat WS 3, 98

treasure [ˈtreʒə] Schatz WS 1, 32

treasurer [ˈtreʒərə] Schatzmeister(in) OT 3

treat [triːt] behandeln OT 3

treatment [ˈtriːtmənt] Behandlung OT 3

tree [triː] Baum OT 1

trend [trend] Trend WS 2, 62

trial [ˈtraɪəl] Prozess OT 2

tribal [ˈtraɪbl] Stammes... OT 3

tribe [traɪb] Stamm OT 2

trick [trɪk] Trick WS 2, 66

to **trickle** [ˈtrɪkl] rinnen OT 3

tricky [ˈtrɪki] kompliziert WS 1, 21

trilogy [ˈtrɪlədʒi] Trilogie WS 1, 31

to **trip** [trɪp] stolpern OT 2

triumphant [traɪˈʌmfənt] triumphierend OT 3

trolley [ˈtrɒli] Wagen OT 1

 shopping trolley [ˈʃɒpɪŋ trɒli] Einkaufswagen OT 1

trophy [ˈtrəʊfi] Pokal OT 2

tropical [ˈtrɒpɪkl] Tropen- WS 1, 13

trough [trɒf] Trog OT 3

trousers [ˈtraʊzəz] Hose OT 2

truck [trʌk] LKW OT 1

true [truː] wahr; richtig OT 1

truly [ˈtruːli] wirklich WS 1, 29

trunk [trʌŋk] Kofferraum OT 2

to **trust** [trʌst] vertrauen OT 2

truth [truːθ] Wahrheit OT 3

to **try** [traɪ] versuchen; ausprobieren OT 1

T-shirt [ˈtiːʃɜːt] Hemd; T-Shirt OT 1

tube [tjuːb] Schlauch; Rohr; Londoner U-Bahn OT 1

to **tuck in** [tʌk ˈɪn] einstecken WS 4, 139

tuck shop [tʌk ʃɒp] Laden; Geschäft WS 4, 130

Tuesday [ˈtjuːzdeɪ] Dienstag OT 1

tuition [tjuːˈɪʃn] Studiengebühr(en) WS 4, 126

to **stay tuned** [tjuːnd] dranbleiben OT 3

tunic [ˈtjuːnɪk] Tunika OT 2

tunnel [ˈtʌnl] Tunnel OT 3

tup [tʌp] Widder OT 2

turbine [ˈtɜːbaɪn] Turbine WS 2, 52

turn [tɜːn] Wende; Drehung OT 1

It's your turn! [tɜːn] Du bist dran! OT 1

to **take turns** [ˈteɪk tɜːnz] sich abwechseln OT 1

to **turn** [tɜːn] drehen; sich drehen OT 2

turntable [ˈtɜːnteɪbl] Drehscheibe OT 2

turtle [ˈtɜːtl] Wasserschildkröte OT 2

tusk [tʌsk] Stoßzahn OT 3

tutor [ˈtjuːtə] Tutor(in) OT 2

TV [ˌtiːˈviː] Fernsehen; Fernseher OT 1

twelve [twelv] zwölf OT 1

twenty [ˈtwenti] zwanzig OT 1

twice [twaɪs] zweimal OT 2

twin [twɪn] Zwilling OT 1

to **twist** [twɪst] Drehung OT 3

two [tuː] zwei OT 1

typical [ˈtɪpɪkl] typisch OT 2

U

ugly [ˈʌgli] hässlich OT 1

ukulele [ˌjuːkəˈleɪli] Ukulele OT 3

umbrella [ʌmˈbrelə] Regenschirm OT 1

unable [ʌnˈeɪbl] unfähig; nicht imstande WS 3, 93

unacceptable [ˌʌnəkˈseptəbl] inakzeptabel WS 1, 27

unaccompanied [ˌʌnəˈkʌmpənid] unbegleitet OT 2

unattended [ˌʌnəˈtendɪd] unbeaufsichtigt WS 3, 88

uncertainty [ʌnˈsɜːtnti] Unsicherheit WS 4, 142

uncle [ˈʌŋkl] Onkel OT 1

uncomfortable [ʌnˈkʌmftəbl] unbequem OT 2

uncommon [ʌnˈkɒmən] ungewöhnlich; selten WS 1, 17

unconquered [ʌnˈkɒŋkərəd] unbesiegt OT 2

unconventional [ˌʌnkənˈvenʃənl] unkonventionell WS 4, 150

undecided [ˌʌndɪˈsaɪdɪd] unentschieden; unentschlossen WS 1, 19

under [ˈʌndə] unter; darunter OT 1

to **underestimate** [ˌʌndərˈestɪmeɪt] unterschätzen WS 2, 59

undergraduate [ˌʌndəˈgrædʒuət] Student(in) (ohne Abschluss) WS 4, 134

underneath [ˌʌndəˈniːθ] darunter; unter OT 3

to **understand** [ˌʌndəˈstænd] verstehen OT 1

understanding [ˌʌndəˈstændɪŋ] Verständnis OT 2

underwater [ˌʌndəˈwɔːtə] unter Wasser OT 3

undoubtedly [ʌnˈdaʊtɪdli] zweifellos WS 3, 110

undrained [ˌʌnˈdreɪnd] nicht abgetropft OT 2

unelected [ˌʌnɪˈlektɪd] nicht gewählt WS 3, 92

unemployed [ˌʌnɪmˈplɔɪd] arbeitslos OT 2

unemployment [ˌʌnɪmˈplɔɪmənt] Arbeitslosigkeit OT 3

unexpectedly [ˌʌnɪkˈspektɪdli] unerwarteterweise OT 3

unfamiliar [ˌʌnfəˈmɪliə] unbekannt OT 2

unfit [ʌnˈfɪt] ungeeignet; nicht in Form OT 2

unforgettable [ˌʌnfəˈgetəbl] unvergesslich WS 1, 29

unfortunately [ʌnˈfɔːtʃənətli] leider OT 2

unhappy [ʌnˈhæpi] unglücklich; traurig OT 1

uniform [ˈjuːnɪfɔːm] Uniform OT 1

to **unify** [ˈjuːnɪfaɪ] vereinigen OT 3

union [ˈjuːniən] Union; Bund OT 3

unique [juːˈniːk] einzigartig OT 2

unisex [ˈjuːnɪseks] Unisex...; nicht geschlechtsspezifisch WS 4, 124

unit [ˈjuːnɪt] Einheit WS 4, 122

to **unite** [juːˈnaɪt] (sich) vereinigen WS 1, 13

unity [ˈjuːnəti] Einheit WS 1, 17

universal [ˌjuːnɪˈvɜːsəli] allgemein WS 3, 99

universe [ˈjuːnɪvɜːs] Universum OT 3

university [ˌjuːnɪˈvɜːsəti] Universität; Hochschule OT 1

unless [ənˈles] außer wenn OT 3

unlikely [ʌnˈlaɪkli] unwahrscheinlich OT 3

unlimited [ʌnˈlɪmɪtɪd] unbegrenzt; unbeschränkt WS 3, 98

unnatural [ʌnˈnætʃrəl] unnatürlich WS 4, 146

unoccupied [ˌʌnˈɒkjupaɪd] unbewohnt WS 3, 110

unpopular [ʌnˈpɒpjələ] unbeliebt OT 3

unspoilt [ˌʌnˈspɔɪlt] unberührt OT 3

unsurprisingly [ˌʌnsəˈpraɪzɪŋli] erwartungsgemäß OT 3

unusual [ʌnˈjuːʒuəl] ungewöhnlich OT 2

to **unwrap** [ʌnˈræp] auspacken WS 4, 121

up [ʌp] hinauf; hoch; nach oben OT 1

to **update** [ˈʌpdeɪt] aktualisieren OT 3

to **upload** [ˈʌpləʊd] hochladen OT 3

upper [ˈʌpə] obere(r) **WS 3**, 90

upstairs [ˌʌpˈsteəz] oben; im oberen Stockwerk OT 1

upstream [ˌʌpˈstriːm] flussaufwärts OT 3

uptight [ˌʌpˈtaɪt] verklemmt **WS 4**, 122

upwards [ˈʊpwədz] aufwärts; nach oben OT 3

urban [ˈɜːbən] städtisch; urban **WS 2**, 52

to **urge** [ɜːdʒ] dringend bitten **WS 3**, 102

urgently [ˈɜːdʒəntli] dringend **WS 1**, 28

us [ʌs] uns; wir OT 1

to **use** [juːz] benutzen; verwenden OT 1

useful [ˈjuːsfl] nützlich; hilfreich OT 1

user [ˈjuːzə] Benutzer(in) OT 2

usual [ˈjuːʒuəl] üblich OT 2

 usually [ˈjuːʒuəli] normalerweise; gewöhnlich OT 1

V

to **vacuum** [ˈvækjuːm] staubsaugen **WS 4**, 124

vague [veɪg] unbestimmt; vage **WS 1**, 27

valley [ˈvæli] Tal OT 1

valuable [ˈvæljuəbl] wertvoll OT 2

to **value** [ˈvæljuː] wertschätzen **WS 4**, 143

value [ˈvælju] Wert OT 3

vampire [ˈvæmpaɪə] Vampir(in) OT 2

van [væn] Lieferwagen OT 2

vanilla [vəˈnɪlə] Vanille OT 1

variation [ˌveəriˈeɪʃn] Variante; Variation **WS 1**, 33

variety [vəˈraɪəti] Vielfalt; Auswahl **WS 1**, 26

various [ˈveəriəs] verschiedene OT 3

to **vary** [ˈveəri] variieren **WS 4**, 126

vast [vɑːst] enorm; groß OT 3

vegan [ˈviːgən] vegan; Veganer(in) **WS 2**, 52

veganism [ˈviːgənɪzəm] Veganismus **WS 2**, 62

vegetable [ˈvedʒtəbl] Gemüse OT 1

vegetation [ˌvedʒəˈteɪʃn] Vegetation; Pflanzenwelt OT 3

veggie [ˈvedʒi] Gemüse **WS 1**, 30

veggie [ˈvedʒi] vegetarisch OT 2

vehicle [ˈviːəkl] Fahrzeug OT 2

velvety [ˈvelvəti] samtartig OT 2

vending machine [ˈvendɪŋ məʃiːn] Automat OT 1

verbal [ˈvɜːbl] verbal; mündlich **WS 2**, 53

verse [vɜːs] Vers OT 3

version [ˈvɜːʒn] Version OT 2

very [ˈveri] sehr OT 1

vibrant [ˈvaɪbrənt] dynamisch; lebhaft **WS 1**, 19

vice [vaɪs] Vize- OT 2

victory [ˈvɪktəri] Sieg **WS 3**, 106

video [ˈvɪdiəʊ] Videokassette; Video OT 1

video game [ˈvɪdiəʊ geɪm] Videospiel OT 2

view [vjuː] Sicht; Blick; Aussicht OT 1

viewpoint [ˈvjuːpɔɪnt] Aussichtspunkt; Standpunkt OT 3

village [ˈvɪlɪdʒ] Dorf OT 1

vintage [ˈvɪntɪdʒ] alt; klassisch; Vintage **WS 4**, 134

violation [ˌvaɪəˈleɪʃn] Verletzung; Verstoß gegen etw. **WS 3**, 101

violence [ˈvaɪələns] Gewalt OT 2

violet [ˈvaɪələt] violett OT 2

violin [ˌvaɪəˈlɪn] Geige OT 1

viral [ˈvaɪrəl] viral **WS 3**, 93

virtual [ˈvɜːtʃuəl] virtuell **WS 1**, 29

virtue [ˈvɜːtʃuː] Tugend OT 3

virtuous [ˈvɜːtʃuəs] tugendhaft OT 3

visible [ˈvɪzəbl] sichtbar **WS 2**, 56

to **visit** [ˈvɪzɪt] besuchen; Besuch abstatten OT 1

visitor [ˈvɪzɪtə] Besucher(in) OT 1

visitor package [ˈvɪzɪtə ˈpækɪdʒ] Besucherpaket OT 3

visual [ˈvɪʒuəl] visuell OT 2

to **visualize** [ˈvɪʒuəlaɪz] veranschaulichen **WS 2**, 61

vlog [ˈvlɒg] Vlog; Video-Blog OT 3

vlogger [ˈvlɒgə] Vlogger(in) OT 3

vocals [ˈvəʊklz] Gesang OT 2

voice [vɔɪs] Stimme OT 2

voicemail [ˈvɔɪsmeɪl] Voicemail OT 3

volcano [vɒlˈkeɪnəʊ] Vulkan OT 2

volleyball [ˈvɒlibɔːl] Volleyball OT 2

voluntary [ˈvɒləntri] freiwillig **WS 4**, 141

to **volunteer** [ˌvɒlənˈtɪə] sich freiwillig melden; ein Ehrenamt haben OT 2

to **vote** [vəʊt] wählen; abstimmen OT 1

voter [ˈvəʊtə] Wähler(in) OT 3

vowel [ˈvaʊəl] Vokal; Selbstlaut OT 1

W

wage [weɪdʒ] Gehalt OT 3

to **wait** [weɪt] warten OT 1

waiter [ˈweɪtə] Kellner(in) OT 1

to **wake up** [ˈweɪk ʌp] aufwachen OT 1

to **walk** [wɔːk] laufen; gehen (zu Fuß) OT 1

walkway [ˈwɔːkweɪ] Gehweg OT 3

wall [wɔːl] Wand; Mauer OT 1

wallet [ˈwɒlɪt] Brieftasche OT 1

walrus [ˈwɔːlrəs] Walross OT 3

to **want** [wɒnt] wollen; mögen OT 1

war [wɔː] Krieg OT 2

wardrobe [ˈwɔːdrəʊb] Kleiderschrank; Garderobe OT 1

warm [wɔːm] warm; herzlich OT 1

warmth [wɔːmθ] Wärme OT 3

to **warn** [wɔːn] warnen OT 2

warning [ˈwɔːnɪŋ] Warnung OT 2

warrior [ˈwɒriə] Krieger(in) OT 2

warship [ˈwɔːʃɪp] Kriegsschiff OT 3

wartime [ˈwɔːtaɪm] Kriegszeit; im Krieg OT 3

to **wash** [wɒʃ] waschen OT 2

washing up [ˌwɒʃɪŋ ˈʌp] Geschirrspülen OT 2

wasp [wɒsp] Wespe OT 3

to **waste** [weɪst] verschwenden OT 3

to **watch** [wɒtʃ] beobachten; zuschauen OT 1

water [ˈwɔːtə] Wasser OT 1

waterfall [ˈwɔːtəfɔːl] Wasserfall OT 1

water flow [ˈwɔːtə fləʊ] Wasserfluss OT 3

waterhole [ˈwɔːtəhəʊl] Wasserstelle **WS 1**, 38

watering hole [ˈwɔːtərɪŋ həʊl] Wasserstelle **WS 1**, 25

watermelon [ˈwɔːtəmelən] Wassermelone OT 3

waterproof [ˈwɔːtəpruːf] wasserdicht OT 2

wave [weɪv] Welle OT 1

way [weɪ] Weg; Richtung OT 1

waypoint [ˈweɪpɔɪnt] Zwischenstation OT 2

to **weaken** [ˈwiːkən] schwächer werden; schwächen **WS 3**, 108

weakness [ˈwiːknəs] Schwäche **WS 2**, 60

wealthy [ˈwelθi] reich OT 3

weapon [ˈwepən] Waffe OT 3

to **wear** [weə] tragen; sich abnutzen OT 1

weather [ˈweðə] Wetter OT 1

weather vane [ˈweðə veɪn] Wetterfahne OT 3

wedded [ˈwedɪd] verheiratet OT 3

wedding [ˈwedɪŋ] Hochzeit OT 3

Wednesday [ˈwenzdeɪ] Mittwoch OT 1

weed [wiːd] Unkraut **WS 1**, 30

week [wiːk] Woche OT 1

weekend [ˈwiːkˌend] Wochenende OT 1

weekly [ˈwiːkli] wöchentlich **WS 1**, 32

weight [weɪt] Gewicht OT 2

weir [wɪə] Wehr OT 3

welcome ['welkəm] Willkommen! OT 1

to **welcome** ['welkəm] begrüßen; willkommen heißen OT 1

welfare ['welfeə] Wohl; Sozialhilfe **WS 3**, 100

well [wel] also; nun OT 1

    well done [wel 'dʌn] gut gemacht OT 1

wellness ['welnəs] Wellness OT 3

west [west] West; westlich OT 1

wet [wet] nass; feucht OT 1

wetsuit ['wetsuːt] Taucheranzug; Neoprenanzug OT 1

whale [weɪl] Wal OT 2

whaling ['weɪlɪŋ] Walfang OT 2

wharf [wɔːf] Werft; Anlegeplatz **WS 2**, 48

what [wɒt] was OT 1

whatever [wɒ'tevə] Was auch immer. OT 2

wheat [wiːt] Weizen **WS 1**, 28

wheel [wiːl] Rad OT 1

wheelchair ['wiːltʃeə] Rollstuhl OT 2

wheelchair user ['wiːltʃeə ˌjuːzə] Rollstuhlfahrer(in) OT 2

when [wen] wann; wenn OT 1

where [weə] wo; wenn OT 1

wherever [weər'evə] wo (auch) immer OT 3

whether ['weðə] ob OT 2

which [wɪtʃ] welche(r, -s) OT 1

while [waɪl] während OT 2

whirlpool ['wɜːlpuːl] Strudel OT 3

whistle [wɪsl] Pfeife OT 2

white [waɪt] weiß; blass OT 1

whiteboard ['waɪtbɔːd] Weißwandtafel; Whiteboard OT 1

to **whizz** [wɪz] zischen OT 2

who [huː] wer, wen, wem; der, die, das OT 1

whoever [huː'evə] egal wer OT 3

whole [həʊl] ganz OT 1

whose [huːz] wessen; dessen, deren OT 1

why [waɪ] warum; weshalb OT 1

wife [waɪf] Frau; Ehefrau OT 1

wild [waɪld] wild OT 2

wilderness ['wɪldənəs] Wildnis OT 2

wildfire ['waɪldfaɪə] Großfeuer OT 2

wildlife ['waɪldlaɪf] Tierwelt OT 2

to **win** [wɪn] gewinnen OT 1

wind [wɪnd] Wind OT 2

to **wind** [wɪnd] sich winden OT 3

window ['wɪndəʊ] Fenster; Schaufenster OT 1

to **windsurf** ['wɪndsɜːf] windsurfen OT 1

windy ['wɪndi] windig OT 2

wing [wɪŋ] Flügel OT 2

winner ['wɪnə] Gewinner(in); Sieger(in) OT 1

winter ['wɪntə] Winter OT 1

to **wipe out** [waɪp aʊt] auslöschen **WS 1**, 39

to **wish** [wɪʃ] wünschen OT 2

witch [wɪtʃ] Hexe OT 2

with [wɪð] mit; bei OT 1

within [wɪ'ðɪn] innerhalb OT 3

without [wɪ'ðaʊt] ohne OT 1

woman ['wʊmən] Frau OT 1

wombat ['wɒmbæt] Wombat **WS 1**, 28

wonder ['wʌndə] Wunder OT 3

wonderful ['wʌndəfl] wunderbar OT 1

wood [wʊd] Holz OT 2

wood cutting [wʊd 'kʌtɪŋ] Holzhacken OT 2

wooden ['wʊdn] hölzern; Holz... OT 2

woods [wʊdz] Wald OT 2

woodwork ['wʊdwɜːk] Holzarbeit; Tischlern OT 3

wool [wʊl] Wolle OT 3

woolly ['wʊli] wollig OT 2

word [wɜːd] Wort; Nachricht OT 1

wordlist ['wɜːdlɪst] Wortliste OT 2

work [wɜːk] Arbeit OT 1

    at work [ət wɜːk] bei der Arbeit OT 2

to **work** [wɜːk] arbeiten; funktionieren OT 1

worker ['wɜːkə] Arbeiter(in) OT 2

workout ['wɜːkaʊt] Fitnesstraining **WS 1**, 14

workplace ['wɜːkpleɪs] Arbeitsplatz OT 3

worksheet ['wɜːkʃiːt] Arbeitsblatt OT 2

workshop ['wɜːkʃɒp] Werkstatt; Workshop OT 1

world [wɜːld] Welt OT 1

worldwide [ˌwɜːld'waɪd] weltweit **WS 3**, 100

worm [wɜːm] Wurm OT 1

worried ['wʌrid] besorgt; beunruhigt OT 1

to **worry** ['wʌri] sich Sorgen machen OT 1

worth [wɜːθ] wert OT 3

worthwhile [ˌwɜːθ'waɪl] lohnend OT 2

wounded ['wuːndɪd] verwundet OT 2

to **wrap** [ræp] einwickeln OT 2

wrap: bad wrap [ræp] Wortspiel, hier: schlechter Ruf **WS 3**, 95

wreck [rek] Wrack OT 3

to **wrestle** ['resl] ringen OT 2

wrist [rɪst] Handgelenk OT 1

wristband ['rɪstbænd] Armband **WS 3**, 105

to **write** [raɪt] schreiben OT 1

writer ['raɪtə] Schriftsteller(in); Verfasser(in) OT 1

wrong [rɒŋ] falsch OT 1

X

X-ray ['eks reɪ] Röntgen OT 1

Y

yacht [jɒt] Jacht **WS 1**, 43

yard [jɑːd] Yard (91,44 cm) OT 2

yawn [jɔːn] Gähnen OT 2

to **yawn** [jɔːn] gähnen OT 3

year [jɪə] Jahr; Jahrgang OT 1

yellow ['jeləʊ] gelb OT 1

yesterday ['jestədeɪ] gestern OT 1

yet [jet] noch; schon OT 2

yoghurt ['jɒgət] Joghurt OT 1

yolk [jəʊk] Eigelb OT 3

you [juː] du / Sie; dir / Ihnen; man OT 1

young [jʌŋ] jung OT 1

youngster ['jʌŋstə] Jugendliche(r) **WS 4**, 142

your [jɔː] dein / Ihr; Ihr(e); euer / Ihr OT 1

yourself [jɔː'self] dich; euch OT 2

yourselves [jɔː'selvz] euch (selbst) OT 3

youth [juːθ] Jugend OT 2

youth hostel ['juːθ hɒstl] Jugendherberge OT 2

Z

zebra ['zebrə] Zebra OT 1

zip line ['zɪp laɪn] Seilrutsche OT 1

zone [zəʊn] Zone OT 2

zoo [zuː] Zoo OT 1

to **zoom** [zuːm] einzoomen OT 2

Dictionary: German – English

A

abdecken to cover OT 2

Abend evening OT 1
  heute Abend tonight OT 1

Abendessen dinner OT 1; tea OT 1

Abenteuer adventure OT 1

abenteuerlustig adventurous OT 2

Abenteurer(in) adventurer OT 3

Abfahrt exit OT 2; issue OT 2

Abfall garbage OT 2; trash OT 2
  herumliegende Abfälle litter OT 2

Abfalleimer litter bin OT 2

abfeuern to fire OT 2; to shoot OT 3

abflachen to level off WS 4, 132

abgelegen remote WS 1, 13

Abgeordnetenhaus parliament OT 3

Abgeordnete(r) delegate OT 3;
  representative WS 3, 90

abgeschieden distanced WS 3, 93

abgießen to drain OT 2

abhalten to prevent WS 3, 101

abhängen to depend OT 2

abhängig dependent OT 3

Abhängigkeit reliance WS 3, 95

abholen to pick up OT 2

Abholzung deforestation WS 1, 39

Abklärung clarification WS 4, 139

abkürzen to shorten WS 2, 63

Abkürzung abbreviation OT 2

ablesen to read OT 1

Abmessung dimension OT 2

(sich) abnutzen to wear OT 1; to carry
  OT 1

Abolitionist(in) abolitionist OT 3

abonnieren to subscribe OT 3

abreißen to demolish WS 1, 25

abrutschen to slump WS 4, 137

Absatz paragraph OT 1

abscheulich gruesome WS 3, 98

Abschieds... leaving OT 2

abschließen to finish OT 1; to conclude
  OT 3

Abschnitt paragraph OT 1; segment
  WS 1, 34

(sich) abseilen to abseil OT 2

absichtlich on purpose OT 2

absolut absolutely OT 2

abstammen to descend WS 4, 123

Abstammung descent WS 1, 33

abstimmen to vote OT 1; to elect OT 2;
  to dial OT 2

abstoßend revolting OT 2

abstürzen (lassen) to crash WS 3, 106

Abtei abbey OT 3

Abteilung department WS 3, 92

Abwasch: den Abwasch machen to do
  the dishes OT 2

(sich) abwechseln to take turns OT 1

Abzeichen badge WS 4, 130

abziehen to copy OT 1

acht eight OT 1

achten to respect OT 3

achtzehn eighteen OT 1

achtzig eighty OT 1

Acker field OT 1; square OT 1; space OT 1

Ackerland farmland WS 3, 85

addieren to add OT 1

Adel nobility OT 2

Adipositas obesity WS 2, 69

Adler eagle OT 2

Adliger nobleman OT 3

administrativ administrative WS 3, 110

Adresse address OT 1

Affäre affair WS 3, 86

Agentur agency WS 1, 22

agrarisch agrarian WS 1, 24

Ahne forefather OT 3

ähnlich similar OT 1

Ähnlichkeit similarity OT 3

Akkordeon accordion OT 2

Aktion action OT 2

aktiv energetic OT 2

Aktivität activity OT 1

aktualisieren to update OT 3

aktuell current OT 2

akustisch acoustic OT 2

Akzent accent WS 1, 21

Akzeptanz acceptance WS 1, 33

Alarm alarm OT 2

alarmieren to alert OT 2

albern silly OT 1

Album album OT 3

Alien alien OT 2

Alkohol alcohol OT 3

alle all OT 1; everybody OT 1; everyone
  OT 1

alles anything OT 1; everything OT 1

allein alone OT 2; on one's own OT2

allergisch allergic WS 2, 64

allgemein general OT 2; overall WS 3,
  98; universal WS 3, 99
  im allgemeinen overall WS 3, 98

alltäglich everyday OT 3

Alpaka alpaca OT 2

Alphabet alphabet OT 1

alphabetisch alphabetical OT 2

als as OT 1; than OT 1

also so OT 1; well OT 1

alt old OT 1; vintage WS 3, 134

Alter age OT 1

älter elderly WS 1, 34

alternativ alternative WS 1, 27

Älteste(r) elder WS 1, 26

altmodisch old-fashioned OT 2

Amsel blackbird OT 1

Amt office OT 2

Amtsniederlegung resignation
  WS 3, 99

an at OT 1; ononto OT 1; upon OT 3

Analyse analysis WS 4, 144

analysieren to analyse OT 3

Analytiker(in) analyst WS 4, 143

Ananas pineapple OT 2

anbauen to grow OT 1

anbeten to adore WS 4, 138

anbieten to offer OT 2

Andenken souvenir OT 3

andere(r, -s) other OT 1; else OT 1
  ein(e) andere(r, -s) another OT 1

ändern to change OT 1

anders different OT 1

andeuten to hint WS 4, 138

Andeutung suggestion OT 1

Anekdote anecdote WS 1, 29

anerkennen to acknowledge WS 2, 75

Anfang start OT 1; beginning OT 1

anfangen to start OT 1; to begin OT 2

anfangs at first OT 2; firstly OT 3

anfassen to feel OT 1

anführen to cite OT 2

Anführungszeichen quotation mark
  OT 2; inverted commas OT 3

angeben to indicate WS 2, 65

Angebot offer OT 2; range WS 4, 126

Angehöriger kinsman OT 3

Angelegenheit matter OT 2; deal
  WS 1, 21; affair WS 3, 86

angemessen appropriate WS 1, 28;
  reasonable WS 2, 64

angenehm enjoyable OT 2; pleasant
  OT 3

Angestellte(r) employee WS 4, 136

angestrengt stressed OT 2

angewidert disgusted WS 4, 125

Angewohnheit habit WS 2, 51

angreifen to tackle OT 2

Angriff attack OT 2

Angst fear OT 3
  Angst machen to scare OT 2

ängstlich afraid OT 2; anxious **WS 3**, 114
Ängstlichkeit anxiety **WS 1**, 34
anhalten to last OT 2
anhaltend prolonged **WS 1**, 25
Anhänger(in) supporter OT 3; follower OT 3
animiert animated **WS 2**, 53
ankern to anchor OT 3
anklagen to accuse **WS 4**, 151
ankommen to arrive OT 1; to get to (a place) OT 2
Ankunft arrival OT 2
Anlage facility OT 3
anlegen to moor OT 3
Anlegeplatz mooring OT 3; wharf **WS 2**, 48
Anleitung instruction OT 1; direction OT 2; guidance OT 3
(sich) anmelden to sign up OT 2
annehmen to suppose OT 1; to accept OT 2; to adopt OT 3
anordnen to order OT 1
anpassen to tailor **WS 3**, 93
Anpassung assimilation OT 3
anregen to motivate **WS 2**, 70
anregend motivational **WS 4**, 143
Anreiz incentive **WS 4**, 142
Anruf call OT 2
  einen Anruf entgegennehmen to take a call OT 2
anrufen to call OT 1
Anrufer(in) caller OT 2
Ansage announcement OT 2
ansagen to announce OT 2
Ansager(in) announcer OT 2
anscheinend apparently OT 3
Anschlagbrett noticeboard OT 1
Anschrift address OT 1
ansehen to look at OT 1; to regard OT 3
Ansicht idea OT 1; attitude **WS 2**, 65
Ansichtskarte postcard OT 1
(sich) ansiedeln to settle OT 3
ansprechend engaging OT 3
anspruchsvoll demanding **WS 1**, 27
anständig proper OT 1
anstoßen to bump into OT 2
sich anstrengen to struggle **WS 4**, 123
anstregend exhausting OT 2; tiring OT 1
Anstrengung effort OT 3
Anteil proportion **WS 2**, 69; percentage **WS 4**, 128; rate **WS 4**, 133
Antibiotikum antibiotic **WS 2**, 69
antik ancient OT 2
antreiben to hurry OT 1; to hurry up OT 2; to power **WS 1**, 25
Antrieb incentive **WS 4**, 142

Antwort answer OT 1; reply OT 1; response **WS 3**, 108
antworten to reply OT 1; to respond OT 1
Anweisung instruction OT 1; direction OT 2
(sich) anziehen to put on OT 1; to dress OT 1; to attract OT 3
Anzug suit OT 1
anzünden to light OT 2
Apartment flat OT 1; apartment OT 1
Apfel apple OT 1
Apfelsine orange OT 1
Apostroph apostrophe OT 3
Apotheke pharmacy OT 2
Apotheker(in) pharmacist OT 2
applaudieren to applaud OT 2
Applaus applause OT 2
Aquädukt aqueduct OT 3
Aquarium aquarium OT 2
Äquator equator **WS 1**, 13
Arbeit work OT 1; labour OT 3; employment **WS 4**, 133
arbeiten to work OT 1
Arbeiter(in) worker OT 2
Arbeitgeber(in) employer **WS 4**, 142
Arbeitnehmerschaft labour force **WS 4**, 133
Arbeitsblatt worksheet OT 2
Arbeitskräfte labour force **WS 4**, 133
arbeitslos unemployed OT 2
Arbeitslosigkeit unemployment OT 3
Arbeitsplatz workplace OT 3
Archäologe, login archaeologist OT 2
Archäologie archeology OT 3
archäologisch archaeological OT 2
Architekt(in) architect **WS 2**, 48
Architektur architecture OT 3
Archiv archive **WS 2**, 66
Arena arena OT 1
ärgerlich annoying OT 2
ärgern to tease OT 2; to annoy **WS 2**, 66
Argument point OT 1; item **WS 1**
Arktis arctic OT 3
arktisch arctic OT 3
Arm arm OT 1
arm poor OT 1
Armband wristband **WS 3**, 105
Armee army OT 2
Ärmel arm OT 1
Armut poverty **WS 3**, 101
Art kind OT 1; type OT 2; sort OT2; species **WS 1**, 21
Artefakt artefact OT 2
Artikel article OT 1
Arzt / Ärztin doctor OT 1
Asche ash OT 2

asexuell asexual **WS 4**, 125
Aspekt aspect OT 3
Assimilation assimilation OT 3
Ast branch OT 2
atemberaubend stunning **WS 1**, 28
atemlos breathless OT 3
Atem(zug) breath OT 2
atmen to breathe OT 2
Atmosphäre atmosphere OT 3; vibe OT 3
Atom... nuclear **WS 4**, 122
attraktiv handsome OT 1
auch too OT 1; also OT 1
  auch nicht either OT 2; neither OT 3
Audio... audio OT 2
auf on OT 1; onto OT 1; upon OT 3
Aufbau structure OT 1
aufbauen to build OT 1; to structure **WS 1**, 29
aufbewahren to store OT 2
aufbrechen to set off OT 2
Aufdeckung exposure OT 3
Aufenthalt stop OT 1
Auffahrt driveway OT 3
Aufforderung invitation OT 1
Aufführung play OT 1; performance OT 2
Aufgabe job OT 1
aufgeben to give up OT 2; to surrender **WS 3**, 106
aufgeregt excited OT 1; frantic OT 3
aufgeschlossen open-minded **WS 3**, 100; approachable **WS 4**, 139
aufheben to pick up OT 2
aufhören to finish OT 1; to conclude OT 3
aufladen to charge OT 2
aufmachen to open OT 1
Aufmerksamkeit attention OT 2
aufmuntern to cheer up OT 1
aufnehmen to record OT 1
aufpassen to pay attention OT 2
  auf jdn. aufpassen to look after OT 1
aufräumen to tidy OT 1
aufrechterhalten to maintain **WS 2**, 53
aufregen to excite OT 3; to annoy **WS 2**, 66
aufregend exciting OT 1
aufrichtig sincerely OT 3
Aufruf appeal OT 2
aufsagen to recite **WS 4**, 146
Aufsatz essay OT 3
Aufseher(in) attendant OT 2; ranger OT 3
aufsetzen to slap on **WS 1**, 16; to slide on **WS 1**, 16
Aufstand rebellion OT 3

aufstehen to get up OT 1
aufsteigen to rise OT 3
Auftrag order OT 1
auftragen to slop on **WS 1**, 16
auftreten to perform OT 2
Auftritt gig **WS 2**, 65
auftürmen to pile OT 3
aufwachen to wake up OT 1
aufwärts upwards OT 3
aufzeichnen to record OT 1; to map OT 3
Auge eye OT 1
Augenblick second OT 1; moment OT 1
Augenbraue eyebrow **WS 4**, 137
Augenlid eyelid OT 2
August August OT 1
Aula assembly hall OT 1
aus from OT 1; of OT 1; off OT 1
ausbeuten to exploit OT 3
ausbilden to train OT 2
Ausbildung training OT 2; education OT 3; apprenticeship **WS 4**, 134
ausbrechen to erupt OT 2
ausdörren to bake OT 1
Ausdruck phrase OT 1; expression OT 1
ausdrücken to express **WS 1**, 14
auseinander apart **WW**, 11
Auseinandersetzung argument OT 1
ausführend executive **WS 3**, 91
ausführlich detailed **WS 2**, 72
Ausgaben expenditure **WS 2**, 65
Ausgang exit OT 2; issue OT 2
ausgeben to spend OT 1
ausgebildet skilled OT 3
ausgeprägt distinctive **WS 1**, 32
ausgerichtet geared **WS 4**, 126
ausgestorben extinct OT 2
ausgezeichnet excellent OT 2
ausgleichen to balance **WS 1**, 13
ausgraben to excavate OT 2
Ausgrabung excavation OT 2
Ausgrenzung discrimination **WS 4**, 134
Aushang notice OT 1
Auskunft information OT 1
auslachen to laugh at OT 2
im Ausland abroad OT 2
ausländisch foreign OT 1; overseas OT 2
auslassen to skip OT 3
(aus)leihen to borrow OT 2
auslöschen to wipe out **WS 1**, 39
ausmachen to amount to **WS 3**, 110; to account for **WS 4**, 128
ausmessen to measure OT 1
Ausnahme exception **WS 4**, 126
auspacken to unwrap **WS 4**, 121
ausprobieren to try OT 1
ausrichten to host OT 3

Ausruf exclamation OT 3
ausrufen to declare **WS 1**, 42
Ausrüstung equipment OT 2; kit OT 2
Aussage statement OT 1; message OT 1
ausschimpfen to tell off OT 2
ausschließen to exclude **WS 3**, 103
Ausschnitt clip OT 2
Aussehen appearance OT 2
außer except OT 2
  außer wenn unless OT 3
Außerirdische(r) alien OT 2
äußern to express **WS 1**, 14
Äußerung expression OT 1
Aussicht view OT 1; perspective **WS 1**, 35; prospect **WS 3**, 100
Aussichtspunkt viewpoint OT 3
ausspielen to act out OT 2
Aussprache pronunciation OT 2
aussprechen to say OT 1; to pronounce OT 3
aussteigen to get out OT 1
ausstellen to exhibit OT 2
Ausstellung exhibition OT 1; display OT 2
Ausstellungsgelände showground OT 2
Aussterben extinction **WS 1**, 39
Ausstoss emission OT 3
aussuchen to choose OT 1; to select OT 3
Austausch exchange OT 1; replacement **WS 2**, 64
Auswahl choice OT 1; option OT 2; election OT 3; variety **WS 1**, 26; selection **WS 2**, 72
auswählen to choose OT 1; to select OT 3; to pick **WS 3**, 100
Auswahlfach elective **WS 4**, 130
Auswahlliste shortlist OT 2
sich auswirken auf to affect OT 3
Auswirkung impact OT 3
Auszeichnung award OT 2
Auszubildende(r) apprentice **WS 4**, 134
Auszug extract OT 3; abstract OT 3
authentisch authentic OT 3
Autismus autism **WS 4**, 127
Auto car OT 1
Automat vending machine OT 1
Autor(in) author OT 2
autorisieren to authorize **WS 3**, 110
Autorität authority OT 3
Avatar avatar OT 3
Avocado avocado **WS 1**, 34
B
Baby baby OT 1
Bach stream OT 2
backen to bake OT 1
Bäckerei bakery OT 3

Bad bath OT 1
Badebekleidung swimwear **WW**, 11
Badehaus bathhouse OT 2
Badewanne bath OT 1
Badezimmer bathroom OT 1
Badminton badminton OT 1
Bahn railway OT 2; rink OT 3
Bahnhof station OT 1
Bahnsteig platform OT 1
Bakterie bacteria **WS 2**, 69
Balance balance OT 3
bald soon OT 1
Balkendiagramm bar chart **WS 4**, 144
Balkon balcony **WS 3**, 110
Ball ball OT 1
Banane banana OT 1
Band, das tie OT 1
Band, die band OT 1
Bande gang OT 2
Bank bank OT 3
Bar bar OT 1
Bär bear OT 1
Bargeld cash OT 1
Barriere barrier OT 3
barrierefrei accessible OT 2
Bart beard OT 1
Baseball baseball OT 1
basierend (auf) based (on) OT 3
Basis base **WS 1**, 27; basis **WS 2**, 49
Basketball basketball OT 3
Bass bass OT 2
Batterie battery OT 2
Bau building OT 1; hole OT 1; construction OT 3
Bauch stomach OT 1
bauen to build OT 1; to construct **WS 3**, 108
Bauer farmer OT 2
Bauernhaus farmhouse OT 2
Bauernhof farm OT 1
Baum tree OT 1
Baumwolle cotton **WS 3**, 84
beabsichtigen to intend OT 3
Beamer projector OT 1
Beamter, Beamtin official OT 2
beängstigend scary OT 2
beaufsichtigen to supervise OT 3; to oversee **WS 3**, 92
beauftragen to commission **WS 3**, 110
Becken basin OT 3
sich bedanken to thank OT 3
bedeckt covered OT 2
Bedenken concern **WS 1**, 37
bedeuten to mean OT 1; to signify OT 3
bedeutend considerable OT 2; significant OT 2; prominent **WS 3**, 106

Bedeutung meaning OT 1; importance OT 3; significance **WS 1**, 32

bedienen to serve OT 1; to cater **WS 4**, 147

Bedingung requirement **WS 1**, 37; condition OT 2

sich beeilen to hurry OT 1; to hurry up OT 2

beeindrucken to impress OT 3

beeinflussen to influence OT 3; to impress OT 3

beeinträchtigt impaired **WS 4**, 131

beenden to finish OT 1; to end OT 1; to conclude OT 3

beengt cramped OT 3

beerdigen to bury **WS 2**, 59

Beerdigung funeral **WS 3**, 106

Beet bed OT 1

befehlen to order OT 1

befehlshabend commanding OT 2

befestigen to attach OT 3

Beförderung carriage OT 2; trolley OT 2; wagon OT 3

Befragte(r) respondent **WS 4**, 122

begabt talented **WS 1**, 32; gifted **WS 4**, 121

begegnen to meet OT 1

begeistern to inspire OT 2

begeistert excited OT 1; enthusiastic OT 3

Beginn advent **WS 1**, 25

beginnen to start OT 1; to begin OT 2

begleiten to accompany OT 3; to escort **WS 2**, 53

begrenzt limited OT 3

Begriff concept **WS 2**, 60

begrüßen to welcome OT 1

behalten keep OT 1

Behälter reservoir **WS 1**, 34; container **WS 3**, 102

behandeln treat OT 3

Behandlung treatment OT 3

behaupten to claim **WS 1**, 21

Behausung dwelling OT 3

beherrschen to dominate **WS 2**, 52

Behinderte(r) disabled **WS 2**, 56

Behinderung disability OT 2

Behörde authority OT 3

bei with OT 1

beide both OT 1

Bein leg OT 1

beinahe nearly OT 2

beiseite aside **WS 4**, 142

Beispiel example OT 1

    zum Beispiel for instance OT 3

beitragen to contribute **WS 1**, 29

bekannt famous OT 1; familiar OT 2; famed OT 3

    bekannt geben to announce OT 2

Bekannte(r) friend OT 1

Bekanntgabe announcement OT 2

sich beklagen to complain OT 3

bekommen to get OT 1; to gain **WW**, 11

bekräftigen to reinforce **WS 4**, 124

beladen to load **WS 2**, 67

beleidigen to insult OT 3; to offend OT 3

beliebt popular OT 1

bellen to bark OT 2

Belohnung reward **WS 4**, 129

bemängeln to fault OT 2

bemerken to comment OT 3; to notice **WS 2**, 48

bemerkenswert notable OT 3

sich bemühen to struggle **WS 4**, 123

benachteiligt disadvantaged **WS 3**, 105

Benehmen behaviour OT 2

sich benehmen to behave OT 2

beneiden to envy **WS 4**, 123

benutzen to use OT 1

Benutzer(in) user OT 2

Benzin petrol OT 1

beobachten to watch OT 1

Beobachtung observation OT 3

bequem comfortable OT 1

Bequemlichkeit convenience **WS 2**, 62

Berater(in) consultant **WS 4**, 121; advisor **WS 4**, 135

berechtigt entitled **WS 2**, 64

bereit ready OT 1

bereitstellen to provide OT 3

bereuen to regret OT 2

Berg mountain OT 1

bergab downhill **WS 1**, 13

Bergbau... mining OT 3

bergen to salvage OT 3

Bergsteigen climbing OT 1

Bergungsschiff salvage ship OT 3

Bergwerk mine OT 2

Beruf profession **WS 4**, 136

beruhigen to calm down OT 2

berühmt famous OT 1; famed OT 3

Berührung contact OT 1

beschädigen to damage OT 3

Beschädigung damage **WS 1**, 25

beschäftigt busy OT 1

Beschäftigung activity OT 1; occupation **WS 3**, 107; employment **WS 4**, 133

beschämt ashamed OT 3

bescheiden modest OT 2

beschließen to decide OT 1

beschreiben to describe OT 1

beschreibend descriptive OT 3

Beschreibung description OT 1

beschriften to label OT 1

beschuldigen to accuse **WS 4**, 151

Beschwerde complaint OT 2

sich beschweren to complain OT 3

Besessenheit obsession **WS 4**, 120

Besichtigungen sightseeing OT 1

besiedelt populated **WS 1**, 28

Besiedelung settlement OT 3

besiegen to defeat OT 2

Besitz possession **WS 2**, 54

besitzen to own OT 2

Besitzer(in) owner OT 2

besondere(r, -s) special OT 1

besonders extra OT 1; particulary OT 2; especially OT 2; specifically **WS 3**, 95

besonnen cool OT 1

besorgt worried OT 1; concerned **WS 1**, 28; anxious **WS 3**, 140

    besorgt sein to care OT 2

Besorgung errand **WS 4**, 140

besprechen to discuss OT 1

Besprechung discussion OT 1; meeting OT 1

besser better OT 1

bestätigen to acknowledge **WS 2**, 75; to confirm **WS 3**, 91

Besteck cutlery OT 3

bestehen (aus) to consist OT 3

bestellen to order OT 1

Bestellung order OT 1

beste(r, -s) best OT 1

bestimmen to define OT 3; to dictate **WS 4**, 124; to determine **WS 4**, 143

bestimmt definitely OT 2; specific OT 2; particular OT 3

bestrafen to punish OT 3

Besuch visit OT 1

besuchen to visit OT 1; to attend OT 2

Besucher(in) visitor OT 1

Beteiligung participation **WS 4**, 128

beten to pray OT 3

Beton concrete OT 2

betonen to emphasize OT 3

betrachten to regard OT 3

Betrag amount OT 2

betragen to amount to **WS 3**, 110

Betreuer(in) guardian OT 2; carer **WS 4**, 124

Betreuung care OT 2; mentoring OT 2

betrübt saddened **WS 1**, 26

Bett bed OT 1

Bettdecke duvet OT 2

Bettlaken sheet OT 1; leaf OT 2

Betttuch sheet OT 1; leaf OT 2

beunruhigt worried OT 1

beurteilen to assess OT 3; to review OT 3
Beutel bag OT 1
bevölkert populated **WS 1**, 28
Bevölkerung population OT 2
bevorstehen to come OT 1
bewachen to guard **WS 2**, 59
bewegen to move OT 1
beweglich agile OT 3
Bewegung movement OT 3
   körperliche Bewegung exercise OT 1; practice OT 1
Beweis evidence **WS 3**, 90
beweisen to prove **WS 1**, 17
sich bewerben to apply **WS 1**, 37
Bewerbung application **WS 4**, 136
bewerten to evaluate **WS 1**, 36; to grade **WS 4**, 129
Bewohner(in) resident OT 3
bewölkt cloudy OT 1
bewundern to admire **WS 3**, 98; to adore **WS 4**, 138
bewusst conscious **WS 2**, 52; aware **WS 2**, 64
bezahlen to pay OT 1
sich beziehen auf to refer to OT 3; to relate to **WS 1**, 34
Beziehung relationship OT 3; relation **WS 1**, 30
Bezirk district **WS 4**, 126
Bibliothek library OT 1
Biene bee OT 1
Bier beer OT 1
Bild picture OT 1; image OT 3
bilden to generate OT 2; : to produce OT 3; to form **WS 1**, 13
Bildschirm screen OT 1
   auf dem Bildschirm onscreen OT 2
Bildtext caption OT 2
Bildungs- educational OT 3
Bildunterschrift caption OT 2
Billardkugel billiard ball **WS 3**, 95
billig cheap OT 2
binden to tie **WS 4**, 131
Binnenland interior **WS 1**, 13
Biografie biography OT 3
Biograf(in) biographer OT 3
Biokraftstoff biofuel OT 3
Biologie biology OT 1
biologisch organic **WS 1**, 30; biological **WS 1**, 32
   biologisch abbaubar biodegradable **WS 3**, 95
Birne pear OT 1
bis till OT 2; until OT 2
bisexuell bisexual **WS 4**, 121

Bison bison OT 3
Biss bite OT 2
bisschen: ein bisschen a bit OT 1; slightly OT 3
Bitte request OT 1
bitte please OT 1
bitten to ask OT 1
bitterlich bitterly **WS 1**, 26
Blase bubble OT 2; bladder OT 3
blasen to blow OT 2
blass pale OT 3
Blatt sheet OT 1; leaf OT 2
Blazer blazer **WS 4**, 130
Blei lead OT 3
bleiben to stay OT 1; to keep OT 2; to remain OT 2
Bleistift pencil OT 1
Blick view OT 1; look OT 2
   einen Blick werfen to take a look OT 2
blicken to look OT 1; to see OT 1; to gaze **WS 1**, 34
Blindenführhund guide dog OT 2
Blitz flash **WS 2**, 55
Block block OT 3
Blocker blocker **WS 4**, 125
blockieren to block **WS 2**, 67
Blog blog OT 1
bloggen to blog OT 3
Blogger(in) blogger OT 3
blond blonde OT 1
Blues blues OT 3
blühen to flourish OT 3
Blume flower OT 1
Blut blood OT 2
Blutvergießen bloodshed **WS 1**, 26
Boden bottom OT 1; floor OT 1; ground OT 2
Bogen bow OT 2; arch OT 3
Bohne bean OT 1
Bonbon sweet OT 1
Boot boat OT 1
Bootfahren boating OT 3
Bootsfahrer(in) boater OT 3
Bord board OT 3
Bordkarte boarding pass OT 2
Börse market OT 1
böse angry OT 1; mad OT 2; wicked OT 2
Boygroup boyband OT 2
Brachvogel curlew OT 2
brainstormen to brainstorm OT 2
Brandbekämpfung firefighting OT 2
brandneu brand new OT 2
Bratensoße gravy OT 1
Brauch custom OT 3
brauchen to need OT 1

braun brown OT 1
brechen to break OT 1
breit broad OT 3
brennen to burn **WS 1**, 28
Brennpunkt focus **WS 1**, 27
Brennstoff fuel OT 2
Brett board OT 2
Brief letter OT 1
Briefkasten letterbox OT 1
Briefmarke stamp OT 1
Brieftasche wallet OT 1
Briefträger(in) postman, postwoman OT 2
Briefumschlag envelope OT 2
bringen to bring OT 1
Brise breeze OT 3
Brokkoli broccoli OT 1
Brombeere blackberry OT 1
Broschüre brochure OT 1; booklet OT 2
Brot bread OT 1
Brötchen bread roll OT 1; bun OT 3
Brotlaib loaf OT 1
Brücke bridge OT 1
Bruder brother OT 1
Buch book OT 1
Bücherei library OT 1
Bücherregal bookcase OT 1
Bücherschrank bookcase OT 1
Buchstabe letter OT 1
buchstabieren to spell OT 1
Bucht bay OT 2
Buchung booking OT 2
Büffel buffalo OT 3
Buffet buffet **WS 2**, 61
bügeln to iron **WS 4**, 124
Bühne arena OT 1; stage OT 2
Bund union OT 3
Bündel bundle OT 2
Bundes... federal **WS 1**, 28
Bundesstaat state OT 1
bunt coloured OT 1
Burg castle OT 1
Bürgermeister(in) mayor OT 3
Büro office OT 2
Bürste brush OT 2
Bus bus OT 1
Busch bush **WS 1**, 13
Buschfeuer bushfire **WS 1**, 28
Buschland bushland **WS 1**, 28
Busladung busload **WS 1**, 27
Bussard buzzard OT 2
Butter butter OT 1

C

Café café OT 1
Cafeteria cafeteria OT 2

campen to camp OT 1
Camper(in) camper OT 2
Campingplatz campsite OT 2
Campus campus OT 2
Cello cello OT 1
Champion champion OT 3
chaotisch disorganized OT 2
Charakter character OT 2
charmant charming OT 3
Checkliste checklist OT 2
Chef(in) boss OT 2
Chemikalie chemical OT 3
Chili chili OT 2
Chirurg(in) surgeon OT 3
Cholera cholera OT 3
Chor choir OT 1
Chromosom chromosome WS 4, 131
chronologisch chronological OT 3
College school OT 1
Comicheft comic OT 1
Computerraum computer lab OT 2
Cornflakes cereal OT 1
Cousin(e) cousin OT 1
Curriculum curriculum WS 4, 126
Currygericht curry OT 1
Cyber-Mobbing cyberbullying WS 4, 144

D
da there OT 1
Dach roof OT 1
Dachboden attic OT 2
dafür for OT 1
daher therefore WS 1, 13
dahin along OT 2
dahinter beyond OT 3
damals then OT 1
Dame lady OT 2
Dampf steam OT 2
danach afterwards WS 3, 88
daneben alongside WS 3, 100
dankbar grateful OT 3
Danke! thanks OT 1
danken to thank OT 3
dann then OT 1
darum therefore WS 1, 13
darunter under OT 1; below OT 2; among OT 3; underneath OT 3
Datei file OT 2
Daten data OT 3
dauerhaft permanent OT 3
dauern to last OT 2
Deck deck OT 3
Decke ceiling OT 2; blanket OT 2
Deckel lid OT 2
definieren to define OT 3
Definition definition OT 1

definitiv definitely OT 2; specific OT 2; particular OT 3
dehydriert dehydrated OT 2
Deich levee WS 3, 108
dein / Ihr your OT 1
Dekade decade OT 3
dekorieren to decorate OT 2
Delfin dolphin OT 1
delikat delicate OT 3
Demokratie democracy OT 3
demokratisch democratic WS 3, 115
demolieren to demolish WS 1, 25
Demonstrant(in) protester OT 2
Demonstration demonstration WS 1, 28; march WS 1, 42
demonstrieren to protest OT 3
denken to think OT 1
  denken an to think about, of OT 1
Denker(in) thinker OT 3
Denkmal memorial WS 3, 89; monument WS 3, 89
Depression depression WS 2, 70
der / die / das who OT 1; the OT 1
derzeit currently WS 4, 125
deshalb therefore WS 1, 13
Designer(in) designer OT 3
Desinfektionsmittel disinfectant OT 3
dessen / deren whose OT 1
Dessert dessert OT 1
Detail detail OT 2
detailliert detailed WS 2, 72
deutlich clearly OT 3
Diabetes diabetes WS 2, 69
Diagramm graph WS 4, 129
Dialekt dialect OT 3
Dialog dialogue OT 1
Diaschau slideshow WW, 11
Diät halten to diet WS 2, 68
dich yourself OT 2
Dichter(in) poet OT 1
Dichtung poetry OT 3
dick thick OT 1
Didgeridoo didgeridoo WS 1, 23
Diele hall OT 1
Diener(in) attendant OT 2; ranger OT 3
Dienst service OT 2
Dienstag Tuesday OT 1
diese(r, -s) this, these OT 1
Diesel diesel OT 3
digital digital OT 1
diktieren to dictate WS 4, 124
Dilemma dilemma WS 1, 14
Ding thing OT 1; object OT 1
Dingo dingo WS 1, 25
Dinosaurier dinosaur OT 1
Diplom diploma WS 4, 126

dir/Ihnen you OT 1
direkt direct OT 2; straight OT 3
Diskriminierung discrimination WS 4, 134
Diskussion discussion OT 1; debate OT 2
diskutieren to discuss OT 1
distanziert distanced WS 3, 93
Doktor doctor OT 1
Dokument document OT 3
Dokumentation documentary OT 2
Dom cathedral OT 1
dominieren to dominate WS 2, 52
Donnerstag Thursday OT 1
doof silly OT 1
doppelt double OT 1
Dorf village OT 1
Dorfbewohner village OT 1
dort there OT 1
  dort drüben over there OT 2
Dose can OT 2; tin OT 2
  in Dosen canned OT 2; tinned WS 2, 74
Dosen... canned OT 2
Downsyndrom down syndrome WS 4, 131
Drache(n) dragon OT 3
Drama drama OT 1
Dramatik drama OT 1
Dramatiker(in) playwright WS 2, 52
dramatisch dramatic WS 4, 132
dranbleiben to stay tuned OT 3
drastisch drastic WS 1, 24
draußen outside OT 1; outdoors OT 3
Dreck dirt WS 4, 125
dreckig dirty OT 1
Drehbuch script OT 2
drehen to turn OT 2
Drehscheibe turntable OT 2
Drehung turn OT 1; twist OT 3
drei three OT 1
dreifach threefold WS 2, 69
dreißig thirty OT 1
dreizehn thirteen OT 1
dringend urgently WS 1, 28
drinnen indoors OT 3
Drittel third OT 1
Dritte(r, -s) third OT 1
drüben over OT 2
Druck pressure OT 3
drucken to print OT 3
drücken to press OT 1
du / Sie you OT 1
dumm silly OT 1; stupid OT 2
Dung manure OT 3
Dünger fertilizer OT 3
dunkel dark OT 1
dunkelhaarig dark-haired OT 3

dünn thin OT 1
durch through OT 1
Durchbruch breakthrough WS 4, 127
durcheinander mixed up OT 2
durchfallen to fail WS 4, 129
durchführen to conduct OT 3
durchnässen to soak OT 3
durchschnittlich average WS 1, 21
durchschweifen to roam WS 1, 25
durchsetzen to enforce WS 3, 90
dürfen can OT 1; to be able OT 2
Dürre drought WS 1, 25
durstig thirsty OT 1
Dusche shower OT 1
düster bleak WS 3, 106
dynamisch vibrant WS 1, 19
Dyskalkulie dyscalculia WS 4, 127

E
Ebene plain OT 3
(sich) ebnen to level off WS 4, 132
echt real OT 1; authentic OT 3
Ecke corner OT 1
Edelstein jewel OT 3
effizient efficiently OT 3; efficient
 WS 4, 129
egal: Das ist mir egal! I don't care! OT 2
egoistisch selfish OT 3
Ehe marriage OT 3
Ehefrau wife OT 1
ehemalig old OT 1
Ehemann husband OT 2
Ehre glory OT 3
ehren to honour OT 3
ehrgeizig ambitious OT 3
ehrlich honest OT 2
Ei egg OT 1
Eichhörnchen squirrel OT 1
eifersüchtig jealous OT 2
eifrig eager OT 2
Eigelb yolk OT 3
eigenartig odd OT 2
eigene(r, -s) own OT 1
Eigenschaft quality OT 3
eigenständig distinct WS 1, 24
eigentlich really OT 1; absolutely OT 2;
 indeed OT 3; actually OT 3
Eigentum property WS 1, 25
eilen to rush OT 2
eine(r, -s) one OT 1
einbeziehen to involve OT 3
sich einbilden to imagine OT 1
einbinden to integrate OT 3
eindeutig definite OT 1; distinct
 WS 1, 24
Eindruck impression OT 3

einfach simple OT 1; basic WS 2, 61
einfangen to capture WS 1, 39
einflussreich important OT 1; influential
 WS 3, 99,
einfühlsam sensitive WS 4, 140
einführen to establish OT 3
Einführung introduction OT 2; advant
 WS 1, 25
Eingang entrance OT 1
Eingangsbereich entrance hall OT 1
Eingangshalle entrance hall OT 1; lobby
 WS 2, 56
Eingebung inspiration OT 3
eingehen to die OT 1
sich eingewöhnen to settle in WS 1, 21
eingravieren to engrave OT 3
einheimisch local OT 2; native OT 3;
 indigenous OT 3
Einheit unity WS 1, 17
einige some OT 1; several OT 1
sich einigen to agree OT 1
einkaufen to shop OT 1
Einkaufswagen shopping trolley OT 1
Einkaufszentrum shopping centre OT 1;
 mall OT 3
Einkommen income WS 1, 27
einladen to invite OT 2
Einladung invitation OT 1
einloggen to log on OT 3
einmal once OT 2
 auf einmal suddenly OT 2; sudden
 OT 3
einmarschieren to invade OT 3
einnehmen to engage WS 1, 36
einordnen to rank WS 1, 32; to class
 WS 2, 69
einplanen to budget OT 3
einreichen to hand (in) OT 2
Einrichtung institution OT 3; amenity
 WS 3, 88
eins one OT 1
einsam lonely OT 3
Einsatz engagement WS 3, 100
 im Einsatz in action OT 2
einschätzen to judge OT 2
einschlafen to go to sleep OT 1
einschließen to include OT 2
einschließlich including OT 1
sich einschränken to downsize OT 3;
 to reduce OT 3
Einschränkung restriction WS 3, 100
einseitig one-sided OT 3
einsprachig monolingual WS 1, 24
einstecken to plug in OT 1; to tuck in
 WS 4, 139
einsteigen to get in OT 1; to board OT 3

Einstellung attitude WS 2, 65
einstufen to classify WS 3, 108
Eintrag entry OT 2; post OT 3
eintreten to enter OT 2
 eintreten in to join OT 1
Eintritt admission OT 2
Eintrittskarte ticket OT 1
Einwand objection OT 3
Einwanderer, -wanderin immigrant
 OT 3
einwandern to immigrate WS 4, 123
Einwanderung immigration OT 2
Einweckglas jar OT 2
einwickeln to wrap OT 2
Einwohner(in) citizen OT 2
Einzel… single OT 3
Einzelhändler(in) retailer WS 2, 62
einzigartig unique OT 2
Eis ice OT 1; ice cream OT 1
Eisbär polar bear OT 3
Eisen iron OT 3
Eisenbahn railway OT 2,
Eisenbahnwagen coach OT 1
Eishockey hockey OT 1
ekelhaft disgusting OT 2
Elefant elephant OT 1
Elektriker(in) electrician WS 1, 20
elektrisch electric OT 1
elektronisch electronic OT 2
Element element WS 1, 17
elf eleven OT 1
Elfenbein ivory OT 3
Ellbogen elbow OT 1
Elster magpie OT 1
Elternteil parent OT 1
Emission emission OT 3
Emotion emotion OT 3
emotional emotional OT 3
Empfang reception OT 1
empfehlen to recommend OT 3
Empfehlung reference WS 4, 138
empfindlich delicate OT 3
emphatisch emphatic WS 2, 69
Empore gallery OT 1
empört disgusted WS 4, 125
Ende end OT 1
 zu Ende gehen to run out OT 2
enden to end OT 1
endgültig final OT 2
endlich finally OT 1; at last OT 2;
 eventually OT 3
endlos endless WS 2, 52
Energie energy OT 3
eng narrow OT 2; closely OT 3
Engagement engagement WS 3, 100
engagiert dedicated WS 4, 147

Enkel grandson OT 1

Enkelin granddaughter OT 1

Enkelkind grandchild OT 1

enorm vast OT 3

entdecken to discover OT 2

Ente duck OT 3

entfernen to remove OT 2

Entfernung distance OT 2

Entführer(in) kidnapper OT 2

enthalten to contain OT 3

entkommen to escape OT 2

entlang along OT 2

Entschädigung compensation **WS 2**, 64

entscheiden to decide OT 1

entscheidend pivotal OT 3

Entscheidung decision OT 1

entschlossen determined **WS 4**, 134

Entschluss decision OT 1

entschuldigen to excuse OT 1

   sich entschuldigen to apologize OT 2

Entschuldigung apology OT 3

entsetzt horrified **WW**, 11

entsorgen to dispose OT 3

sich entspannen to relax OT 3

enttäuscht disappointed OT 2

entwickeln to develop OT 2

   sich entwickeln to evolve OT 3

Entwickler(in) developer **WS 4**, 134

Entwicklung development OT 3

Entwurf draft OT 2; design OT 3

Entzündung infection OT 2

Enzyklopädie encyclopedia OT 3

Epidemie epidemic OT 2

Erbe heritage OT 3

erben to inherit **WS 3**, 92

Erbse pea OT 1

Erdball globe OT 3

Erdbeben earthquake OT 2

Erdbeere strawberry OT 1

Erde earth OT 1; ground OT 2; soil OT 3

Erderwärmung global warming **WS 1**, 28

Erdkunde geography OT 1

Ereignis event OT 1

erfahren experienced **WS 1**, 27

erfahren to learn OT 1; to hear OT 1; to experience **WS 4**, 130

Erfahrung experience OT 2

erfassen to catalogue OT 3

erfinden to invent OT 2

Erfinder(in) inventor OT 2

Erfindung invention OT 2

Erfolg success OT 3

   Erfolg haben to succeed OT 2

erfolgreich successful OT 2

erfordern to require **WS 4**, 127

erforschen to explore OT 1

Erforschung exploration OT 3

erfunden fictional OT 2; imaginary **WS 3**, 89

ergänzend additional **WS 4**, 127

Ergänzung addition **WS 2**, 56; amendment **WS 3**, 90

Ergebnis result OT 2

erhalten to receive OT 2; to preserve OT 3

erhältlich available **WS 2**, 54

Erhaltung preservation OT 3

erheben to raise OT 2

erheblich considerable OT 2; significant OT 2

erhöhen to raise OT 2

sich erholen to recover **WS 3**, 108

erholsam relaxing OT 2

Erholung recovery OT 2; relaxation OT 3

erinnern to remind OT 2

   sich erinnern an to remember OT 1; to think of OT 1

erkennbar apparent OT 3; recognizable **WS 2**, 48

erkennen to realize OT 2; recognize OT 3

Erkenntnis realization **WS 2**, 62

erklären to explain OT 1

Erklärung statement OT 1; explanation OT 1

erkunden to explore OT 1

erlauben to allow OT 3; to permit **WS 2**, 54

Erlaubnis permission OT 2; permit OT 3

erlaubt be allowed to OT 2

Erläuterung explanation OT 1

erleben to experience **WS 4**, 130

erleichtert relieved OT 3

Erleichterung relief OT 2

ermorden to murder OT 2

ermüdend tiring OT 1; exhausting OT 2

ermutigen to encourage OT 3

ernährungs… nutritional **WS 2**, 63

ernennen to appoint **WS 3**, 91

Ernennung nomination **WS 3**, 115

erneuerbar renewable **WS 1**, 28

ernst serious OT 2

Ernte harvest OT 3

erobern to conquer OT 2

Eroberung conquest OT 2

erreichen to reach OT 3; to gain **WW**, 11; to achieve **WS 1**, 25

errichten to put up OT 1; to erect OT 3; to construct **WS 3**, 108

Ersatz substitution OT 3; substitute OT 3; replacement **WS 2**, 64

Erschaffer(in) creator **WS 1**, 26

erscheinen to appear OT 2

erschöpft exhausted OT 3

erschrecken to frighten OT 3

erschreckend frightening OT 1

erschreckt scared OT 1; frightened OT 1; terrified OT 3

ersetzen to replace OT 2

erspähen to spot OT 1

Erstattung refund **WS 2**, 64

erstaunlich amazing OT 1

erstaunt amazed OT 3

erste(r, -s) first OT 1; premier OT 2

sich erstrecken to stretch OT 3

ertrinken to drown OT 3

erwachsen grown up OT 2

Erwachsene(r) adult OT 1

erwähnen to mention OT 3

erwarten to expect OT 2

Erwartung expectation OT 3

erwartungsgemäß unsurprisingly OT 3

erweitert extended **WS 4**, 123

erwidern to reply OT 1; to respond OT 1

erzählen to tell OT 1

Erzähler(in) narrator OT 2

erzeugen to generate OT 2; to produce OT 3

Esel donkey **WS 3**, 91

Essen food OT 1; meal OT 1

essen to eat OT 1

Esslöffel tablespoon OT 2

Esszimmer dining room OT 1

etablieren to establish OT 3

ethisch ethical OT 3

ethnisch ethnic **WS 1**, 33

Etikett tag OT 2; label OT 3

etikettieren to label OT 1

etwa approximately **WW**, 10

etwas some OT 1; something OT 1

evakuieren to evacuate **WS 3**, 108

Evakuierung evacuation **WS 3**, 108

Examen exam OT 1

Exekutive executive **WS 3**, 91

Existenz existence **WS 1**, 42

existieren to exist OT 3

Expedition expedition OT 2

Experiment experiment OT 2

Experte, Expertin expert OT 3; specialist **WS 4**, 131

explodieren to explode **WS 1**, 25

Exporteur(in) exporter **WS 1**, 28

extrem extreme **WS 1**, 28

F

fabelhaft fabulous OT 2

Fabrik factory OT 3

Fach subject OT 1

Facharbeit coursework **WS 2**, 50

Fachfrau, -mann professional **WS 2**, 70

Fachzeitschrift journal OT 3

Fackel torch OT 1; flashlight OT 2

fähig capable **WS 2**, 55

   fähig sein be able OT 2

Fähigkeit capacity **WS 2**, 70

Fahne flag OT 3

Fahrbahn lane **WS 1**, 29

Fähre ferry OT 3

fahren to drive OT 1; to ride **WS 1**, 29

Fahrer(in) driver OT 2

Fahrerkabine cab OT 1

Fahrrad bike OT 1; bicycle OT 3

   mit dem Fahrrad fahren to cycle OT 1

Fahrschein ticket OT 1

Fahrt trip OT 1; journey OT 1; drive **WS 1**, 19

Fahrzeug vehicle OT 2; rover **WS 2**, 57

fair fair OT 1

Fakt fact OT 1

Faktor factor OT 3

Fall case OT 1; pocket OT 2

Falle trap OT 3

fallen to fall OT 1; to decrease **WS 4**, 132

   fallen lassen to drop OT 1

falls if OT 1

Fallschirm springen to parachute **WS 2**, 53

Fallschirmspringer(in) skydiver **WS 1**, 29

falsch wrong OT 1; false OT 1

Falte line OT 1

Familie family OT 1

Fanatiker(in) fanatic **WS 1**, 15

fanatisch fanatic **WS 1**, 15

fangen to catch OT 1

Fantasie fantasy OT 2

fantastisch fantastic OT 1; terrific OT 3

Farbe colour OT 1

färben to dye OT 3

farbenfroh colourful OT 3

farbig coloured OT 1

fast nearly OT 2

faszinieren to fascinate **WS 2**, 52

faszinierend fascinating **WS 1**, 13; intriguing **WS 2**, 70

faul lazy OT 2

Fausthandschuh mitten OT 3

Feder feather OT 2

Federball badminton OT 1

Federtasche pencil case OT 1

Feedback feedback OT 2

fegen to sweep OT 3

Fehler mistake OT 1; fault OT 2

fehlerhaft faulty **WS 2**, 64

Feier party OT 1

feierlich ceremonial OT 3

feiern to celebrate OT 3

Feind(in) enemy OT 3

Feinkostladen deli **WS 1**, 15

Feld field OT 1; square OT 1; space OT 1

Feldflasche canteen OT 1

Feldfrüchte crop OT 3

Fell fur OT 3

Felsen rock OT 1

Fenster window OT 1

Ferienlager camp OT 1

fern far-off OT 2; faraway **WS 1**, 28

Fernglas binoculars OT 2

Fernsehen TV OT 1

Fernseher TV OT 2

fest tight OT 3

Fest festival OT 1; feast OT 3

festhalten to grasp **WS 4**, 131

Festival festival OT 1; feast OT 3

Festland mainland OT 3

festnehmen to capture **WS 1**, 39

Festspiele festival OT 1; feast OT 3

Festung fort OT 2

Festzelt marquee OT 2

Fett fat OT 2

fettgedruckt bold OT 1

fettleibig obese **WS 2**, 69

Fettleibigkeit obesity **WS 2**, 69

feucht wet OT 1

Feuer fire OT 2

Feuerwerk fireworks OT 3

fiktiv imaginary **WS 3**, 89

Film film OT 1; movie OT 2

Filmaufnahmen footage **WS 2**, 73

Filmemacher(in) filmmaker **WS 1**, 32

Filzstift marker OT 1

Finanzen finances **WS 4**, 142

finanziell financial **WS 3**, 104

   finanziell unterstützen to sponsor OT 2

finden to find OT 1

Finger finger OT 1

Fingernagel fingernail OT 2

finster dark OT 1

Firmenzeichen logo OT 1

Fisch fish OT 1

fischen to fish OT 3

Fischer fisherman OT 2

Fischerei fishing OT 3

Fischstäbchen fish finger OT 1

Fitnesstraining workout **WS 1**, 14

Flachland plain OT 3

Flagge flag OT 3

Flaggschiff flagship OT 3

Flamingo flamingo OT 2

Flasche bottle OT 1

flauschig fluffy OT 2

Fleck patch **WS 4**, 135

Fledermaus bat OT 1

Fleisch meat OT 1

Fleischesser(in) meat-eater **WS 2**, 69

Fleischklößchen meatball OT 1

flexibel flexible **WS 4**, 136

Flicken patch **WS 4**, 135

fliegen to fly OT 1

Fliese tile OT 2

fließend fluent OT 3

Floh flea **WS 4**, 135

florieren to prosper OT 2

Flotte fleet **WS 1**, 17

Flug flight OT 1

Flügel wing OT 2

Flughafen airport OT 1

Flugzeug plane OT 1; airplane OT 2

Flur hall OT 1

Fluss river OT 1

flussaufwärts upstream OT 3

flüssig liquid OT 2

Flut flood OT 2

Fokus focus **WS 1**, 27

fokussieren to focus OT 2

Folge consequence **WS 1**, 24

folgen to follow OT 2

folgerichtig logical **WS 1**, 36

folglich so OT 1

Folie slide OT 1; foil OT 2

Folklore folklore **WS 1**, 26

Fond fund **WS 1**, 15

Fontäne fountain OT 1

fördern to promote **WS 2**, 64

Form shape OT 1; form OT 3

   in Form fit OT 2

Format format **WS 2**, 63

Formation formation **WS 1**, 26

Formel formula OT 2

formell formal OT 3

formen to shape **WS 1**, 38

förmlich formal OT 3

Forscher(in) researcher OT 2; explorer OT 3

Forschung research OT 2

Forstbeamter, -beamtin park ranger OT 2

fortgeschritten advanced OT 3

Fortschritt progress OT 3

fortschrittlich progressive OT 1

Forum forum OT 2; panel **WS 2**, 70

fossil fossil OT 3

Foto photograph OT 1

Fotoapparat camera OT 1

Fotograf(in) photographer OT 2

foulen to foul OT 3

Fracht freight OT 2

fracken to frack **WS 1**, 28
Frage question OT 1
Fragebogen questionnaire OT 1
fragen to ask OT 1
Frau woman OT 1; wife OT 1
frech cheeky OT 3
frei free OT 1
freiberuflich freelance OT 3
Freiheit liberty OT 2; freedom OT 2
Freitag Friday OT 1
freiwillig voluntary **WS 4**, 141
Freizeit leisure **WS 1**, 34
fremd foreign OT 1; overseas OT 2
Fremde(r) stranger OT 3
fressen to eat OT 1
Freude pleasure OT 1
freuen: sich auf etwas freuen to look
    forward to OT 1
Freund(in) friend OT 1
freundlich friendly OT 1
Freundlichkeit friendliness **WS 2**, 53
Freundschaft friendship OT 3
Frieden peace **WS 4**, 125
friedlich peaceful OT 3
frisch fresh OT 3
Fritte chip OT 1
froh glad OT 2
fröhlich cheerful OT 2
Frucht fruit OT 1
früh early OT 1
frühere(r) former **WS 2**, 67
Frühling spring OT 2
Frühstück breakfast OT 1
Frühstücksflocken cereal OT 1
frustriert frustrated **WS 2**, 60
Fuchs fox OT 1
(sich) fühlen to feel OT 1
führen to guide OT 1; to lead OT 3
Führer(in) guide OT 1
Führung leadership OT 2
füllen to fill OT 1
fünf five OT 1
fünfzehn fifteen OT 1
fünfzig fifty OT 1
Funke spark OT 2
Funktion function **WS 1**, 32
funktionieren to work OT 1
für for OT 1; in favour of **WS 3**, 94
Furcht fear OT 3
furchtbar terrible OT 1; awful OT 1;
    dreadful OT 2; horrible OT 2
Fürsprecher(in) advocate **WS 2**, 71
Fuß foot OT 1; base **WS 1**, 27
Fußabdruck footprint OT 2
Fußball football OT 1; soccer OT 2
Fußboden floor OT 1

Fußknöchel ankle OT 1
füttern to feed OT 2

G
gaffen to gongoozle OT 3
Gaffer gongoozler OT 3
gähnen to yawn OT 3
Gähnen yawn OT 2
Galerie gallery OT 1
ganz whole OT 1; entire OT 3; complete
    WW, 11
garantieren to guarantee **WS 3**, 90
Garderobe wardrobe OT 1; cloakroom
    WS 2, 56
Garten garden OT 1
Gartenarbeit gardening OT 1
Gas gas OT 3
Gasse lane **WS 1**, 29
Gast guest OT 2
Gästebuch guestbook OT 2
Gastfreundlichkeit hospitality OT 2
Gasthaus inn OT 2
Gebäude building OT 1
geben to give OT 1
Gebet prayer OT 3
Gebiet area OT 1; territory OT 3
Gebiss dentures OT 3
geboren born OT 2
Gebühr fee OT 3
Geburt birth OT 2
Geburtsdatum date of birth OT 2
Geburtsort birthplace OT 2
Geburtstag birthday OT 1
Gedächtnis memory OT 2
Gedanke thought OT 3
Gedenken commemoration OT 3
gedenken to commemorate OT 3
Gedicht poem OT 1
geeignet fit OT 2
Gefahr danger OT 2; threat **WS 1**, 17;
    risk **WS 1**, 28
gefährden to threaten **WS 1**, 25
gefährlich dangerous OT 1; risky OT 3
Gefängnis prison **WS 1**, 17
Geflügel poultry OT 2
gefriergetrocknet freeze-dried OT 3
Gefrierschrank freezer OT 3
gefroren frozen OT 3
Gefühl feeling OT 2
gegen against OT 1
Gegend area OT 1
Gegensatz opposite OT 1; contrast OT 3
Gegenstand object OT 1; item OT 3
Gegenteil opposite OT 1; contrast OT 3
gegenüber against OT 1
Gegenwart present OT 1

Gegner(in) opponent OT 2
gehackt chopped OT 2; minced OT 2
Gehalt wage OT 3
Geheimnis secret OT 2
gehen to go OT 1
    zu Fuß gehen to walk OT 1
Geheul howl **WS 1**, 25
Gehirn brain OT 2
gehorchen to obey OT 3
gehören to belong OT 2
Gehweg walkway OT 3
Geige violin OT 1
Geist spirit OT 2; ghost OT 2
geistig mental OT 2
Gel gel OT 2
gelangweilt bored OT 1
gelb yellow OT 1
Geld money OT 1
gelegen located OT 3; situated **WS 3**, 108
gelegen sein to lie OT 1
Gelegenheit opportunity OT 2; occasion
    OT 3
gelockt curly OT 3
Gemälde painting OT 1
gemeinsam common **WW**, 11
Gemeinschaft community OT 2
gemischtgeschlechtlich co-ed OT 2;
    co-educational OT 2
Gemüse vegetable OT 1; veggie **WS 1**, 30
gemütlich cozy OT 3
genau exact OT 2; precise OT 3; accurate
    WS 3, 96
Gender gender **WS 4**, 122
genehmigen to approve **WS 3**, 91;
    authorize **WS 3**, 110
Genehmigung license OT 3
Generalisierung generalization
    WS 4, 126
Generation generation OT 3
generell general OT 2
Genesung recovery OT 2
genetisch genetic **WS 4**, 131
genial brilliant OT 1
genießen to enjoy OT 1
genug enough OT 1
Geografie geography OT 1
geografisch geographical **WS 3**, 85
Geologie geology OT 2
gerade straight OT 3
gerade (jetzt) currently **WS 4**, 125
Gerät appliance OT 3; device OT 3
Geräusch sound OT 1; noise OT 1
gerecht fair OT 1
Gericht dish (Essen) OT 2; court **WS 3**, 90
gernhaben to like OT 1
Gesamtmenge total OT 3

Gesang vocals OT 2

Geschäft shop OT 1; tuck shop **WS 4**, 130

Geschäft(e) business OT 3

   geschätzte Ankunftszeit ETA (estimated time of arrival) OT 2

geschehen to happen OT 1

Geschenk present OT 1; gift OT 1

Geschichte history OT 1; story OT 1; tale OT 2

Geschichtenbuch storybook OT 2

Geschichtenerzählen storytelling OT 3

Geschichtenerzähler(in) storyteller OT 2

geschichtlich historical OT 2

Geschick skill OT 1

geschickt skilled OT 3

Geschirr dishes OT 2

Geschlecht gender **WS 4**, 122; sex **WS 4**, 122

geschlechtslos genderless **WS 4**, 124

geschlechtsneutral genderneutral **WS 4**, 124

geschlechtsspezifisch gendered **WS 4**, 124

Geschöpf creature **WS 1**, 26

Geschwindigkeit speed OT 2

Geschwister siblings **WS 1**, 27

geschwollen swollen OT 2

Gesellschaft society OT 3; organization OT 3

Gesellschafter(in) partner OT 1

gesellschaftlich social OT 3

Gesetz bill OT 3; law OT 3; act **WS 1**, 43

gesetzgebend legislative **WS 3**, 91

Gesicht face OT 1

Gespräch conversation OT 1

gesprächig chatty OT 3

Gestalt shape OT 1; form OT 3

gestalten to shape **WS 1**, 38

Geste gesture **WS 4**, 137

gestern yesterday OT 1

gestresst stressed OT 2

gesund healthy OT 2

Gesundheit health OT 3

Gesundheitsfürsorge healthcare **WS 3**, 84

Getränk drink OT 1

Getreide grain **WS 2**, 68

getrennt separate OT 2

Getto slum **WS 3**, 101

Gewalt violence OT 2

gewaltig enormous OT 1; huge OT 2; massive OT 3

Gewicht weight OT 2

Gewinn profit **WS 1**, 27

gewinnen to win OT 1

Gewinner(in) winner OT 1

Gewissheit certainty **WS 4**, 142

Gewitter thunderstorm OT 2; rainstorm **WS 1**, 38

gewöhnlich usually OT 1; commonly **WW**, 10

Gewürz spice OT 2; seasoning OT 2

gießen to pour OT 1

giftig poisonous **WS 1**, 35

Gipfel summit OT 3; peak **WS 4**, 132

Giraffe giraffe OT 1

Gitarre guitar OT 1

Gladiator(in) gladiator OT 2

glamourös glamorous **WS 3**, 103

Glas glass OT 1

glatt slippery OT 3; smooth OT 3

Glaube belief OT 3

glauben to think OT 1; to believe OT 2

gleich same OT 1

gleichbedeutend synonymous OT 3

Gleichberechtigung equality **WS 1**, 43

Gleichrangige(r) peer **WS 2**, 70

gleichzeitig simultaneous **WS 2**, 63

Gletscher glacier OT 3

global global OT 3

Globus globe OT 3

Glocke bell OT 1

Glück luck OT 1; fortune OT 3

glücklich happy OT 1; lucky OT 3

glücklicherweise fortunately **WS 2**, 63; luckily **WS 3**, 89

Glückwünsche congratulations OT 2

glühend scorching **WS 1**, 21

Gold gold OT 2

golden golden OT 2

Golf golf **WW**, 11

Gott god OT 1

graben to dig OT 3

Grad degree OT 3

Graffiti graffiti OT 3

Grafik graphic **WS 2**, 79

Gramm gram OT 2

Grammatik grammar OT 1

Gras grass OT 1

gratulieren to congratulate OT 2

grau grey OT 1

grauenvoll gruesome **WS 3**, 98

grausam cruel OT 3

Grausamkeit cruelty **WS 2**, 62

gravieren to engrave OT 3

Gravur engraving OT 3

greifen to grasp **WS 4**, 131

Gremium panel **WS 2**, 70

Grenze limit **WS 1**, 26; boundary **WS 2**, 48

griesgrämig grouchy OT 2

Griff handle OT 2

grillen to grill OT 3

Grillen barbecue OT 2

grinsen to grin OT 2

Grippe influenza **WS 1**, 24

Grizzlybär grizzly OT 2

groß great OT 1; big OT 1; tall OT 1; large OT 1; vast OT 3

großartig brilliant OT 1; gorgeous OT 3; magnificent **WS 1**, 29

Großartigkeit greatness **WS 3**, 105

Größe height OT 1; size OT 2

Großeltern grandparents OT 1

Großmutter grandmother OT 1

Großvater grandfather OT 1

grün green OT 1

Grund reason OT 1

Grund... basic **WS 2**, 61

gründen to found OT 2; form **WS 1**, 13

Gründer... foundational OT 3

Gründer(in) founder **WS 4**, 143

Grundlage basis **WS 2**, 49

Grundlagen basics OT 2

grundlegend radical **WS 3**, 102

grundsätzlich basic **WS 2**, 61

Grundschule primary school OT 1; elementary school OT 2

Grünfläche green OT 1

Gruppe group OT 1

gruppieren to group **WS 3**, 85

gruselig creepy **WS 1**, 13

Gruß greeting OT 2

   mit freundlichen Grüßen sincerely OT 3

grüßen to hail OT 2; to greet **WS 2**, 53

Gummi rubber OT 1

Gurke cucumber OT 1; gherkin **WS 2**, 48

gut fine OT 1; good OT 1

   gut aussehend handsome OT 1

   gut gemacht well done OT 1

Güter goods OT 3

Gutschein coupon OT 2

Gymnastik gymnastics OT 1

H

Haar hair OT 1

Haarschnitt haircut OT 2

haben have got OT 1; to feature OT 2

Habitat habitat **WS 1**, 34

Hackfleischbällchen meatball OT 1

Hafen port OT 2; harbour OT 3

Hähnchen chicken OT 1

Hai shark OT 2

Häkchen tick OT 1

halb(e, -er, -es) half OT 1

Halbfinale semi-final OT 3

Halbinsel peninsula **WS 1**, 32

halbwegs halfway OT 3
Halle hall OT 1
Hallo! hello OT 1
Hals neck OT 1; throat OT 3
Halsband collar OT 2
Halstuch scarf OT 1
Halt stop OT 1
halten to hold OT 1
Haltestelle halt OT 2
Hamster hamster OT 1
Hand hand OT 1
Handbuch handbook OT 3; manual OT 3
Handel commerce OT 3; trade **WW**, 11
handeln to act OT 1
Handelnde(r) agent **WS 1**, 27
Handgelenk wrist OT 1
handhaben to handle **WS 4**, 131
Händler(in) trader OT 3
Handschrift handwriting OT 2
Handschuh glove OT 1
Handtasche handbag OT 3
Handtuch towel OT 2
Handwerk handicraft OT 3
Handy mobile phone OT 1; cell phone **WS 3**, 87
hängen to hang OT 3
Harpune harpoon OT 3
hart hard OT 2; tough OT 2
Haselnussstrauch hazel OT 3
hassen to hate OT 1; to loath **WS 1**, 25
hässlich ugly OT 1
Haufen heap **WS 1**, 16
häufig often OT 1; frequently OT 3; commonly **WW**, 10
Häufigkeit frequency **WS 1**, 34
Haupt... primary OT 1; main OT 2
Hauptquartier headquarters **WS 3**, 110
Hauptstadt capital OT 1
Hauptverkehrszeit rush hour OT 1
Haus house OT 1
Hausarbeit housework OT 1
Hausaufgaben homework OT 1
Häuschen cottage OT 3
Haushalt household **WS 3**, 101
Haushälter(in) housekeeper OT 3
Hausmeister(in) caretaker OT 1
Haustier pet OT 1
Haut skin OT 2
Headset headset **WS 4**, 128
heben to lift **WS 4**, 140
Heft book, booklet OT 1
heften to pin OT 1
Heide moor OT 3
heilig sacred OT 3
Heilige(r) saint OT 3
Heimat homeland **WS 1**, 28

Heimweh homesickness **WS 1**, 30
heiraten to marry OT 1
heiß hot OT 1
heizen to heat OT 2
hektisch frantic OT 3
Held(in) hero OT 3
helfen to help OT 1
Helm helmet OT 1
Hemd shirt OT 1
Hemisphäre hemisphere **WS 1**, 13
heraus out OT 1; from OT 1; off OT 1
herausfinden to find out OT 2
herausfordern to challenge **WS 4**, 124
Herausforderung challenge OT 3
Herausgeber(in) editor OT 2
herausragend outstanding OT 3
herb bittersweet OT 3
Herbst autumn; fall OT 2
Herd cooker OT 3
Herr Mr OT 1; lord OT 2
herrlich magnificent **WS 1**, 29
Herrschaft rule OT 1; shelf OT 2
herrschen to rule OT 2; to reign OT 3
Herrscher(in) ruler OT 1
herumhängen to hang out OT 3
herumschweifen to roam **WS 1**, 25
herunter down OT 1
heruntergekommen rundown **WS 2**, 52
herunterladen to download OT 3
sich hervortun to excel **WS 4**, 126
Herz heart OT 2
herzlich warm OT 1
Herzog duke OT 2
Herzogin duchess OT 2
heterosexuell heterosexual **WS 4**, 125
heute today OT 1
heutzutage nowadays OT 3
Hexe witch OT 2
hier here OT 1
hierher here OT 1
Hilfe help OT 1; relief OT 3; aid **WS 2**, 59
  Erste Hilfe first aid OT 2
hilfreich useful OT 1; helpful OT 1
hilfsbereit helpful OT 1
Himbeere raspberry OT 1
Himmel sky OT 1
hinauf up OT 1
hindurch through OT 1
hinfallen to fall over OT 2
hinrichten to execute OT 3
hinter after OT 1; behind OT 1
Hintergrund... background OT 3
hinterher behind OT 1
Hinterland backcountry OT 3
hinterlassen to leave behind OT 2
hinüber across OT 1

hinunter down OT 1
Hinweis tip OT 1; clue OT 1; prompt OT 3; cue **WS 4**, 131
hinzufügen to add OT 1
Hirsch deer OT 1
Hirte, Hirtin shepherd OT 1; herder OT 3
Historiker(in) historian OT 2
historisch historic OT 2
Hitparade chart OT 3
Hitzewelle heatwave **WS 1**, 28
Hobby hobby OT 1
hoch high OT 1; up OT 1
hochladen to upload OT 3
Hochschule university OT 1; college OT 2
Höchststand high OT 1
Hochzeit wedding OT 3
Hof farmyard OT 2
hoffen to hope OT 1
hoffentlich hopefully OT 3
hoffnungslos hopeless **WS 4**, 138
hoffnungsvoll hopeful OT 3
höflich polite OT 1
Höhe height OT 1
Höhepunkt highlight OT 3
Höhle cave OT 3
holen to get OT 1
Hologramm hologram OT 2
holperig bumpy OT 3
Holz wood OT 2
Holz... wooden OT 2
Holzarbeit woodwork OT 3
hölzern wooden OT 2
Holzhacken wood cutting OT 2
Holzscheit log OT 3
Honig honey OT 2
hören to hear OT 1; to listen OT 1
Hörer(in) listener **WS 1**, 28
Horizont horizon **WS 1**, 38
Hormon hormone **WS 4**, 125
Horn horn OT 3
Hose trousers OT 2; pants **WW**, 11
Hotel hotel OT 1
Hotline helpline OT 2
hübsch pretty OT 1
Hubschrauber helicopter OT 3
Hufeisen horseshoe OT 1
Hüfte hip OT 1
Hügel hill OT 1
Huhn chicken OT 1
Humor humour **WS 1**, 30
Hund dog OT 1
hundert hundred OT 1
hungern (lassen) to starve OT 1
Hungersnot famine OT 2
hungrig hungry OT 1
Hupe horn OT 3

Hurrikan hurricane **WS 1**, 28
Hut hat OT 1
Hütehund sheepdog OT 2
Hüter(in) keeper OT 3
Hybrid… hybrid OT 3
Hymne anthem OT 3
hyperaktiv hyperactive **WS 4**, 127

I

ich I, me OT 1
ideal ideal **WS 1**, 28
idealisieren to idealize OT 3
Idee idea OT 1
identifizieren to identify **WW**, 11
Identität identity OT 3
Idol idol **WS 2**, 68
Igel hedgehog OT 1
Iglu igloo OT 3
ignorieren to ignore OT 3
ikonisch iconic OT 3
Illustration illustration OT 2
illustrieren to illustrate OT 3
Imbiss snack OT 1
immer always OT 1
  für immer forever OT 3
  immer noch still OT 1
Immobilie property **WS 1**, 25
in in, at OT 1; on, onto OT 1; upon OT 3
inakzeptabel unacceptable **WS 1**, 27
individuell individual OT 3
Industrie industry OT 2
Influencer(in) influencer **WS 2**, 62
Influenza influenza **WS 1**, 24
Infografik infographic OT 3
Infomercial infomercial **WS 3**, 93
Informatikunterricht ICT (information and communications technology) OT 1
informativ informative **WS 1**, 36
informell informal **WS 1**, 16
informieren to inform OT 3
Ingenieur(in) engineer OT 2
Ingenieurwesen engineering OT 2
Ingwer ginger OT 1
Inhalt contents OT 2; content **WS 2**, 64
inklusive including OT 1
Inkubator incubator **WS 4**, 134
innen internal **WS 3**, 86
Innen… indoor OT 2
Innenhof courtyard **WS 3**, 110
Innenstadt downtown **WS 1**, 43
inner… internal **WS 3**, 86
innere(r, -s) inner **WS 3**, 110
innerhalb inside OT 1; within OT 3
Innovation innovation OT 3
innovativ innovative **WS 4**, 146
Insekt insect OT 2

Insel island OT 1
Inselbewohner(in) islander **WS 1**, 12
Inspiration inspiration OT 3
inspirieren to inspire OT 2
installieren to install OT 3
instruktiv instructive **WS 1**, 29
Instrument instrument OT 1
Insulaner(in) islander **WS 1**, 12
intakt intact OT 3
integrativ inclusive **WS 2**, 60
integrieren to integrate OT 3
intellektuell intellectual OT 3
intelligent intelligent OT 2; clever OT 2
interagieren to interact **WS 3**, 93
Interaktion interaction **WS 2**, 53
interaktiv interactive OT 3
interessant interesting OT 1
Interesse interest OT 1
interessiert interested OT 1
Interface interface OT 3
international international OT 1
Internet internet OT 3
interpretieren to interpret **WS 2**, 55
Intersex intersex **WS 4**, 125
Interview interview OT 1
interviewen to interview OT 1
Interviewer(in) interviewer OT 3
Interviewte(r) interviewee OT 3
invasiv invasive **WS 1**, 25
investieren to invest **WS 2**, 75
Investition investment **WS 2**, 75
involviert involved OT 2
irgendein(e) any OT 1
irgendjemand someone OT 1; somebody OT 1
irgendwann sometime OT 3
irgendwie somehow **WS 3**, 106
irgendwo somewhere OT 1; anywhere OT 2
irgendwohin somewhere OT 1; anywhere OT 2
Irrgarten maze OT 3

J

Jacht yacht **WS 1**, 43
Jacke jacket OT 1
Jackett jacket OT 1
jagen to hunt OT 2; to chase OT 2
Jäger(in) hunter OT 3
  Jäger und Sammler hunter-gatherer **WS 1**, 24
Jahr year OT 1
Jahreszeit season OT 2
Jahrgang year OT 1
Jahrhundert century OT 2
jährlich annual OT 3

Jahrmarkt fairground OT 2; fair OT 2
Jahrzehnt decade OT 3
Jazz jazz OT 2
je ever OT 1
jede(r, -s) every OT 1; each OT 2
jeder everyone OT 1; anyone OT 2
jederzeit anytime OT 3
jedoch though OT 2; although OT 2
jemals ever OT 1
jemand someone OT 1; somebody OT 1
jene those OT 1
jetzt now OT 1
Job job OT 1
Joghurt yoghurt OT 1
Journal journal OT 3
Journalist(in) journalist OT 2
jubeln to cheer OT 1
jucken to itch OT 2
juckend itchy OT 2
Judo judo OT 1
Jugend youth OT 2
Jugendherberge youth hostel OT 2
Jugendliche(r) youngster **WS 4**, 142
Juli July OT 1
jung young OT 1
Junge boy OT 1
Junge(s) cub OT 2
Juni June OT 1
Junior(in) junior OT 2
Justiz… judicial **WS 3**, 91

K

Kabel cable OT 3
Kabine cabin OT 2
Kabinett cabinet **WS 3**, 92
Kaffee coffee OT 1
kahl bald OT 3
Kai pier **WS 1**, 29
Kaiser emperor OT 2
Kajak kayak OT 3
Kajakfahren kayaking OT 2
Kaktus cactus **WS 1**, 21
Kalender calendar OT 1
Kalorie calorie **WS 2**, 68
kalt cold OT 1; freezing OT 2
Kamel camel **WS 1**, 25
Kamera camera OT 1
Kamin fireplace OT 1
Kamm comb OT 2
Kammer chamber OT 2
Kampagne campaign OT 2
Kampf fight OT 1
kämpfen to fight OT 1
Kämpfer(in) fighter OT 2
Kanal canal OT 3; channel OT 3
Kanarienvogel canary OT 2

Kandidat(in) candidate OT 2
Känguru kangaroo **WS 1**, 13
Kaninchen rabbit OT 1
Kanone cannon OT 3
Kantine canteen OT 1
Kanu canoe OT 2
Kanufahren canoeing OT 2
Kapitän(in) captain OT 3
Kapitel chapter OT 1
Kappe cap OT 1
kaputt busted OT 3
Kapuzenjacke hoodie OT 1
Kapuzenpullover hoodie OT 1
Karbon carbon OT 3
Karibu caribou OT 3
Karneval carnival **WS 2**, 49
Karotte carrot OT 1
Karriere career OT 3
Karte card OT 1; map OT 1
Karteikarte file card OT 2
Kartoffel potato OT 1
Kartoffelbrei mashed potato OT 1
Kartoffelchip crisp OT 1
Karton cardboard OT 1; box OT 1
Käse cheese OT 1
Kasse register OT 2; cash desk OT 2
katalogisieren to catalogue OT 3
Katastrophe disaster OT 2
Kategorie category OT 3
Kathedrale cathedral OT 1
Katze cat OT 1
kaufen to shop OT 1; to buy OT 1
Käufer(in) shopper **WS 2**, 49
kaum hardly **WS 3**, 88
Kehle throat OT 3
keiner nobody OT 1
Keks biscuit OT 1; cookie OT 3
Keller cellar **WS 3**, 98
Kellner(in) waiter OT 1; server OT 3
kennen to know OT 1
kenntnisreich knowledgeable OT 3
Kerl guy **WS 1**, 30
Kerze candle OT 2
Kessel kettle OT 2
Ketchup ketchup OT 3
Kette chain OT 3
Keulen cull **WS 1**, 25
keulen to cull **WS 1**, 25
Keyboard keyboard OT 1
Kidneybohne kidney bean OT 2
Kilo kilo OT 2
Kilometer kilometre OT 1
Kilt kilt OT 2
Kind child OT 1; kid OT 1
Kindheit childhood OT 3
Kino cinema OT 1

Kirche church OT 1
Kirsche cherry OT 3
Kissen cushion OT 1
Kiste box OT 1; crate OT 3
Kiwi kiwi OT 1
Klammer bracket OT 2
klar clear OT 2; certainly OT 2
klären to clarify **WS 3**, 92
Klarinette clarinet OT 2
Klasse class OT 1
klasse ace **WS 1**, 16
Klassenkamerad(in) classmate OT 3
Klassenstufe grade OT 2
Klassenzimmer classroom OT 1
klassifizieren to class **WS 2**, 69
klassisch classic OT 2; classical OT 2;
    vintage **WS 4**, 134
klatschen to clap OT 1
klauen to steal OT 2
Klavier piano OT 1
kleben to stick OT 1; to paste OT 2
klebrig sticky **WS 2**, 60
Klebstoff glue OT 1
Kleid dress OT 1
Kleiderschrank wardrobe OT 1
Kleidung clothes OT 1; clothing OT 3;
    outfit **WS 3**, 100
klein small OT 1; little OT 1; short OT 1
Kleinbus minibus OT 2
Kleingeld cash OT 1
Kleinholz kindling OT 2
Kletterer(in) climber OT 2
klettern to climb OT 1
klicken to click OT 3
Klima climate OT 2
Klingel bell OT 1; doorbell OT 2
klingeln to ring OT 1
klingen to ring OT 1; to sound OT 3
Klippe cliff **WS 1**, 24
Klischee stereotype **WS 2**, 65
Klo loo OT 2
klopfen to knock OT 2
Kloster abbey OT 3
Klub club OT 1
klug clever OT 1; savvy **WS 2**, 62
Kneipe pub OT 2
Knie knee OT 1
Knöchel ankle OT 1
Knochen bone OT 1
Knopf button OT 1
Knoten knot OT 3
knuddelig cuddly OT 3
Koala koala **WS 1**, 13
Koch, Köchin chef OT 1
Kochbuch cookbook **WS 2**, 79
köcheln to simmer OT 2

kochen to cook OT 1; to boil OT 1;
    to make OT 1
Kochfeld hob OT 3
Koffein caffeine **WS 2**, 68
Koffer case OT 1; pocket OT 2
Kofferraum boot OT 1; trunl OT 2
Kohl cabbage OT 1
Kohle coal OT 2
Kohlendioxid carbon dioxide OT 3
Kohlenhydrat carbohydrate **WS 2**, 68
kohlensäurehaltig fizzy OT 2
Koje berth OT 3
Kollege, Kollegin colleague **WS 3**, 90
kolonial colonial OT 3
Kolonialisierung colonization **WS 1**, 24
Kolonialismus colonialism **WW**, 10
Kolonie colony OT 2
kolonisieren to colonize OT 3
Kolonist(in) colonist OT 3
Kombination combination OT 3
kombinieren to combine **WS 2**, 67
Komiker(in) comic OT 1
Komitee committee OT 3
Kommandant(in) commander OT 2
kommen to come OT 1
kommentieren to comment OT 3
kommerziell commercial **WS 3**, 96
Kommission committee OT 3
Kommode chest of drawers OT 1
Kommunikation communication OT 1
kommunizieren to communicate **WW**, 11
Kompass compass OT 2
kompatibel compatible **WS 4**, 126
komplett complete **WW**, 11
kompliziert complicated OT 3; tricky
    WS 1, 21
komponieren to compose OT 3
Komponist(in) composer OT 2
Kompost compost OT 3
Kompostierungs... composting OT 3
Konferenz conference **WS 2**, 70
Konflikt conflict **WS 1**, 15
König king OT 1
Königin queen OT 1
königlich royal OT 1
Königs... royal OT 1
Konkurrent(in) competitor OT 3
Konkurrenz competition OT 1; rivalry
    WS 1, 30
konkurrenzorientiert competitive OT 3
konkurrieren to compete OT 2
können can OT 1; to be able OT 2
Könner artist OT 1
konsequent consistent **WS 4**, 129
Konsequenz consequence **WS 1**, 24
konstitutionell constitutional OT 2

Konsumverhalten consumerism **WS 2**, 62

Kontakt contact OT 1

Kontakte pflegen to socialize **WS 2**, 65

kontaktfreudig outgoing **WS 4**, 139

kontaktieren to contact OT 2

Kontext context **WS 1**, 16

Kontinent continent **WS 1**, 12

Konto account OT 3

Kontrabass double bass OT 2

Kontrolle control OT 2

kontrollieren to check OT 1; to review OT 3; to control OT 3

Kontroverse controversy **WS 3**, 91

konzentrieren to concentrate OT 3

Konzept concept **WS 2**, 60

Konzert concert OT 1

Koordinierung coordination **WS 4**, 131

Kopf head OT 1

Kopfball header OT 3

köpfen to behead OT 3

Kopfhörer headphones OT 2; headset **WS 4**, 128

Kopfkissen pillow OT 2

Kopfkissenbezug pillowcase OT 3

Kopfsalat lettuce OT 2

Kopfschmerzen headache OT 1

Kopfsteinpflaster cobblestones OT 3

Kopie copy OT 1; replica OT 3

kopieren to copy OT 1

Korb basket OT 3

Körper body OT 1

Körperhaltung posture **WS 2**, 53

körperlich physical OT 2

korrekt correct OT 1; right OT 1; true OT 1

Korrektur correction **WS 2**, 61

Korrespondent(in) correspondent **WS 3**, 106

Korridor corridor OT 2

korrigieren to correct OT 1; to fix OT 2; to mark OT 2

Korsett corset OT 3

Kosmetik cosmetics **WS 2**, 62

kosmopolitisch cosmopolitan **WS 1**, 19

Kosten cost OT 1

kosten to cost OT 1

kostenlos free OT 1

köstlich delicious OT 1

Kostüm costume OT 2

krabbeln to crawl **WS 1**, 38

Krabbeltier creepy-crawly OT 2

kraftlos powerless **WS 3**, 101

Krampf cramp OT 2

Kran crane OT 3

krank sick OT 1; ill OT 2

Krankenhaus hospital OT 1

Krankenschwester, -pfleger nurse OT 1

Krankenwagen ambulance OT 1

Krankheit disease OT 2; illness OT 2

Krapfen doughnut OT 2

kratzen to scrape OT 2; to scratch OT 2

Krawatte tie OT 1

kreativ creative OT 2

Kreativität creativity OT 3

Krebs cancer **WS 2**, 69

Kreditkarte credit card OT 1

kreieren to create OT 2

Kreis circle OT 2

Kreuzfahrtschiff cruise ship OT 2

Kreuzzug crusade **WS 3**, 98

Kricket cricket OT 1

kriechen to crawl **WS 1**, 38

Krieg war OT 2

Krieger(in) warrior OT 2

Kriegsschiff warship OT 3

Kriegszeit wartime OT 3

Krise crisis **WS 1**, 28

Kriterium criterion **WS 4**, 126

kritisch critical **WS 1**, 25

kritisieren to criticize OT 3

Krone crown OT 1

krönen to crown OT 1

Krönung coronation **WS 2**, 74

Krücke crutch OT 2

Küche kitchen OT 1; cuisine OT 3

Kuchen cake OT 1

Küchenchef(in) chef OT 1

Kugel ball OT 1; bullet OT 2

Kuh cow OT 1

kühl cool OT 1

kühlen to cool OT 3

Kühlschrank fridge OT 1

Kühlsystem cooling system OT 3

kühn bold OT 1

Kult... iconic OT 3

kultiviert civilized **WS 1**, 27

Kultur culture OT 1

kulturell cultural OT 3

Kumpel buddy OT 2; mate **WW**, 10

Kunde, Kundin customer OT 2

Kundgebung rally OT 2

kündigen to quit **WS 4**, 142

Kunst art OT 1

Künstler(in) artist OT 1; performer OT 3

künstlich artificial OT 3

Kuppel dome OT 3

Kürbis pumpkin OT 2

Kurier(in) courier OT 2

Kurs program, programme OT 3

kurz short OT 1; brief OT 3

kürzen to shorten **WS 2**, 63

Kuss kiss OT 2

Küste coast OT 1; shore OT 2; coastline **WS 1**, 36; seaside OT 3; shoreline OT 3

Küsten... coastal **WS 3**, 108

Küstenwache coastguard OT 2

L

Lache pool OT 1

lächeln to smile OT 1

lachen to laugh OT 1

Lachs salmon OT 1

Laden shop OT 1

Ladendiebstahl shoplifting **WS 4**, 120

Lage situation OT 1

Lager camp OT 1

Lagerfeuer campfire OT 2; bonfire OT 3

Lagerung storage OT 3

Lamm lamb OT 2

Lampe lamp OT 1

Land country OT 1; countryside OT 1; land OT 1

landen to land **WW**, 11

Landkarte map OT 1

ländlich rural OT 3

Landschaft landscape OT 2; scenery OT 2

Landstraße highway OT 3

Landwirtschaft farming OT 2; agriculture OT 2

lang long OT 1

Länge length OT 3

langsam slow OT 2

langweilig boring OT 1

lassen to let OT 1

lässig casual **WS 2**, 66

Latein Latin OT 2

Laterne lamp OT 1; lantern OT 2

Lauch leek OT 3

laufen to run OT 1

Läufer(in) runner OT 2

laut noisy OT 1; loud OT 1; aloud OT 2

laut according to **WS 1**, 26

Lautsprecher loudspeaker OT 2

Lava lava OT 3

Leben life OT 1

leben to live OT 1

lebendig alive OT 2

lebensbedrohlich life-threatening OT 2

Lebensdauer lifetime OT 3

Lebensmittel groceries **WS 4**, 124

Lebensmittelvergiftung food poisoning OT 2

Lebensstil lifestyle OT 3

Lebenszeit lifetime OT 3

Leber liver **WS 2**, 68
Lebewesen creature **WS 1**, 26
lebhaft lively OT 3; vibrant **WS 1**, 19
lecker delicious OT 1
Leder leather OT 3
leer empty OT 1; blank **WS 2**, 61
legal legal OT 3
legalisieren to legalize **WS 4**, 122
Legasthenie dyslexia **WS 4**, 127
legasthenisch dyslexic **WS 4**, 128
legen to put OT 1; to set OT 2
Legende legend OT 3
Legion legion OT 2
Legislative legislative **WS 3**, 91
lehnen to lean OT 3
Lehrbuch textbook OT 3
lehren to teach OT 1
Lehrer(in) teacher OT 1; instructor OT 2
Lehrling apprentice **WS 4**, 134
Lehrplan curriculum **WS 4**, 126
lehrreich instructive **WS 1**, 29
Lehrstelle apprenticeship **WS 4**, 134
leicht easy OT 1
Leichtathletik athletics OT 1
leiden to suffer **WS 1**, 34
Leidenschaft passion **WS 2**, 63
leidenschaftlich keen OT 2; passionate **WS 2**, 70
leider unfortunately OT 2
leihen to lend OT 2
Leinen canvas OT 3; linen OT 3
Leinwand screen OT 1
sich leisten to afford OT 2
Leistungen attainment **WS 4**, 128
leiten to guide OT 1; to manage OT 1; to lead OT 3
Leiter ladder OT 3
Leitfaden guide OT 1
Lektion lesson OT 1
lernen to learn OT 1; to study OT 1
Lesbe lesbian **WS 4**, 121
lesbisch lesbian **WS 4**, 121
lesen to read OT 1
Leser(in) reader OT 2
Lesezeichen marker OT 1
letzte(r, -s) last OT 1; final OT 2
leuchten to shine OT 1; to seem OT 2
leuchtend bright OT 1
leugnen to deny **WS 2**, 56
Leute people OT 1; folks OT 2; guys 60
Lexikon encyclopedia OT 3
Licht light OT 1
lieben to love OT 1
Liebhaber(in) lover OT 3
Lieblings... favourite OT 1
Lied song OT 1

liefern to deliver OT 3
Lieferwagen van OT 2
liegen to lie OT 1
Liga league OT 2
Limo soda **WS 2**, 68
Lineal ruler OT 1
Linie line OT 1
Linse lens OT 2
Lippe lip OT 2
Liste list OT 1
LKW truck OT 1
loben to praise **WS 2**, 75
Loch hole OT 1
locker casual **WS 2**, 66
Löffel spoon OT 2
logisch logical **WS 1**, 36
Logo logo OT 1
lohnend worthwhile OT 2
Lokomotive engine OT 2
lösen to solve OT 3
Lösung answer OT 1; solution OT 3
loswerden to get rid OT 3
Löwe, Löwin lion OT 1
Loyalität loyalty **WS 4**, 142
Luchs lynx OT 2
Lücke gap OT 1
Luft air OT 2
Luftfahrt aerospace **WS 3**, 108
Lunchpaket packed lunch OT 1
Lunge lung **WS 2**, 59
Lupe magnifying glass OT 2
lustig funny OT 1
luxuriös luxurious OT 2

M
machen to make OT 1; to do OT 1
Machete machete OT 3
Macht power OT 3
mächtig powerful OT 2
machtlos powerless **WS 3**, 101
Mädchen girl OT 1
Magen stomach OT 1
magisch magical OT 2
Magnet magnet **WS 1**, 32
magnetisch magnetic OT 2
mähen to mow **WS 4**, 124
Mahlzeit meal OT 1
mal times **WS 1**, 12
Malaria malaria **WS 1**, 34
malen to paint OT 1
Maler(in) painter OT 3
malerisch scenic OT 3; picturesque OT 3
Mama mum OT 1
man you OT 1
managen to manage OT 1

manchmal sometimes OT 1; some of the time OT 2
Mangel lack OT 3; shortage **WS 1**, 34
Manifest manifesto **WS 3**, 92
Mann man OT 1; husband OT 2
männlich male OT 2
Mannschaft team OT 1; crew OT 2
Mantel coat OT 2
Marathon marathon OT 2
Märchen fairy tale OT 1; myth OT 3
Marine navy OT 3
Marke brand **WS 2**, 62
Marketing marketing OT 3
markieren to bookmark **WS 1**, 36
Markt market OT 1
Marktplatz marketplace **WS 2**, 65
Marmelade jam OT 1
Marsch march **WS 4**, 120
marschieren to march **WS 1**, 42
Marschkapelle marching band OT 3
März March OT 1
Maschine machine OT 2
Masern measles **WS 1**, 24
Maske mask OT 3
Maskottchen mascot OT 2
Maß measurement OT 2
Massage massage OT 2
Massaker massacre OT 2
Masse mass **WW**, 11
Maßeinheit measurement OT 2
Maßnahme provision **WS 4**, 127
Maßstab scale OT 2
Match match OT 1; game OT 1
Material material OT 3
Mathematik math, maths OT 1
Matratze mattress **WS 3**, 102
matschig muddy **WS 3**, 102
Mauer wall OT 1
Maultier mule OT 3
Maus mouse OT 1
Maximum maximum OT 2
Mayonnaise mayonnaise OT 1
Medaille medal OT 2
Medium medium OT 2
   soziale Medien social media OT 2
Medizin medicine **WS 3**, 95
medizinisch medical OT 2
Meer sea OT 1
Meeres... marine OT 3
Meeresboden seabed OT 3
Mehl flour OT 3
mehr more OT 1
mehr... multi OT 3
Mehrheit majority **WS 2**, 69
mehrsprachig multilingual OT 3
Mehrzahl plural OT 1

Meilenstein milestone OT 3
mein my OT 1
meine(r, -s) mine OT 1
meinen to mean OT 1; to signify OT 3
Meinung opinion OT 3
   anderer Meinung sein to disagree OT 1
Meisterleistung feat OT 2
Meisterschaft championship OT 3
Menge crowd OT 1
   eine Menge a lot, lots OT 1; much OT 1; plenty OT 2; loads OT 3
Mensch person OT 1; human being OT 2
   Menschen people OT 1; folks OT 2; guys 60
Menschenmenge crowd OT 1; throng OT 2
menschlich human OT 2
Menü menu OT 1
merkwürdig strange OT 1; weird OT 1
Messe exhibition OT 1; mass OT 2
messen to measure OT 1
Messer knife OT 2
Metall metal OT 1
Meter metre OT 1
Methode method OT 1
Meute mob WS 1, 28
mich me OT 1
mieten to rent OT 3
migrieren to migrate OT 3
Milch milk OT 1
Militär military OT 3
Milliarde billion WS 2, 66
Million million OT 1
Minderheit minority WS 4, 132
Minderjährige(r) minor OT 2
Mindest... minimum OT 1
mindestens at least OT 1
Mindmap mind map OT 1
Miniatur miniature OT 2
Minimal... minimum OT 1
Minister(in) minister OT 3
Minute minute OT 1
Minze mint OT 1
mir me OT 1
mischen to mix OT 2; to combine WS 2, 66
Mischung mixture OT 2; mix OT 2
Missbilligung disapproval WS 2, 71
Misserfolg failure WS 4, 146
Missfallen disapproval WS 2, 71
Missgeschick accident OT 1
Missionar(in) missionary OT 3
Missverständnis misunderstanding OT 3

missverstehen to misunderstand WS 4, 131
mit with OT 1
mitarbeiten to contribute WS 1, 29
mitfühlend sympathetic OT 2
Mitglied member OT 1
   Mitglied werden to join OT 1
Mittag midday WS 3, 99
Mittagessen lunch OT 1; dinner OT 1
Mittagspause lunch break OT 1
Mittagszeit lunchtime OT 1
Mitte centre OT 1; middle OT 1
Mittel medium OT 2
mittelalterlich medieval OT 2
Mittelfeldspieler(in) midfielder OT 3
mittelgroß medium-sized OT 2
Mitternacht midnight OT 1
Mittwoch Wednesday OT 1
mobben to bully WS 4, 120
Möbel furniture OT 1
mobil mobile OT 3
Mode fashion OT 1
Modell model OT 1
modern modern OT 1
modisch fashionable WS 4, 135
mögen to like OT 1; to want OT 1
   nicht mögen to dislike OT 2
möglich possible OT 2; potential WS 2, 64
Möglichkeit possibility OT 1; prospect WS 3, 100
Möhre carrot OT 1
Moment moment OT 1
Monarchie monarchy WS 3, 92
Monarch(in) monarch WS 3, 92
Monat month OT 1
Mönch monk OT 3
Mond moon OT 1
Monopol monopoly OT 3
monoton monotone WS 4, 137
Monster monster OT 1
Montag Monday OT 1
Monument monument WS 3, 89
Moor moor OT 3
Moral moral OT 2
moralisch morally OT 3
   moralisch vertretbar ethical OT 3
Morgen morning OT 1
morgen tomorrow OT 1
Mosaik mosaic OT 2
Motivation motivation WS 4, 135
Motivations... motivational WS 4, 143
motivieren to motivate WS 2, 70
Motor engine OT 2
motorisiert motorized OT 3
Motorrad motorbike OT 1,

müde tired OT 1
Mühe effort OT 3
Müll rubbish OT 3
Müllcontainer dumpster WS 3, 88
Mülldeponie landfill OT 3
multi... multi OT 3
Mund mouth OT 1
   den Mund halten to shut up OT 2
mündlich oral OT 1; verbal WS 2, 53
Mundschutz mouthguard OT 2
Münze coin OT 1
murmeln to mumble WS 2, 59
Museum museum OT 1
Musik music OT 1
Musiker(in) musician OT 2
Muskel muscle OT 2
Müsli cereal OT 1
müssen must OT 1; to have to OT 1; to be obliged WS 4, 146
Muster pattern WS 1, 37
Mut bravery OT 2
mutig brave OT 1; bold OT 1
Mutter mother OT 1
Mutti mum OT 1
Mütze cap OT 1; hat OT 1
Mythologie mythology OT 2
Mythos myth OT 3

N

nach after OT 1; past OT 1
   nach links to the left OT 3
   nach oben up OT 1
Nachbar neighbour WS 1, 13
Nachbarschaft neighbourhood WS 1, 19
nachdenken (über) to think (about, of) OT 1
nachgehen to lose OT 1
nachhallen to echo WS 1, 14
nachhaltig sustainable OT 3
Nachhaltigkeit sustainability OT 3
Nachkomme descendant OT 3
Nachlass discount WS 3, 103
Nachmittag afternoon OT 1
Nachricht note OT 1; message OT 1
   Nachrichten news OT 1
Nachspielen re-enactment OT 3
nachspielen to re-enact OT 3
nächste(r, -s) next OT 1; by OT 1; beside OT 2
Nacht night OT 1
   heute Nacht tonight OT 1
   über Nacht overnight OT 2
Nachteil con OT 2; downside OT 3; disadvantage WS 1, 26
Nachtisch dessert OT 1
Nacken neck OT 1; throat OT 3

nah close OT 1
Nähe: in der Nähe near OT 1; nearby OT 3
nähen to sew **WS 2**, 52
Nahrungsergänzungsmittel food supplement **WS 2**, 68
Nahrungsmittel food OT 1
Name name OT 1
namens called OT 1
Narzisse daffodil OT 3
Nase nose OT 2
nass wet OT 1
Nation nation OT 2
national national OT 1
Natur nature OT 2
natürlich of course OT 1; natural OT 1
natürlich natural OT 1
Naturwissenschaften science OT 1
Naturwissenschaftler(in) scientist OT 1
Navigationssystem GPS (global positioning system) OT 2
navigieren to navigate **WS 2**, 57
nebelig foggy OT 3
neben next to OT 1; by OT 1; beside OT 2
Neffe nephew **WS 4**, 136
nehmen to take OT 1
neigen: zu etwas neigen to tend to **WS 4**, 124
    sich neigen to tilt OT 3
nennen to call OT 1
Neoprenanzug wetsuit OT 1
Nerv nerve OT 3
nervös nervous OT 2
Nest nest OT 3
nett nice OT 1; beautiful OT 1; lovely OT 1
Netz net OT 3
Netzball netball **WS 1**, 15
Netzwerk network OT 3
neu new OT 1
neueste(r, -s) recent OT 3
neugierig curious OT 3
Neuheit innovation OT 3
neulich recently OT 3
neun nine OT 1
neunzig ninety OT 1
neurologisch neurological **WS 4**, 131
Neuseeländer(in) kiwi OT 1
neutral neutral OT 3
Newsletter newsletter OT 3
nicht not OT 1
Nichte niece **WS 4**, 138
nichts nothing OT 1
nicken to nod OT 3
Nickerchen: ein Nickerchen machen to doze OT 2; to nap OT 2
nie never OT 1

niedlich cute OT 3
niemals never OT 1
niemand nobody OT 1
nirgendwo nowhere OT 2
noch still OT 1; yet OT 2
    noch ein(e, -er, -es) another OT 1
nomadisch nomadic OT 3
Nonne nun OT 3
Norden north OT 1
nördlich northern OT 2
Nordosten north-east OT 1
normal normal OT 1; ordinary OT 2; standard **WS 1**, 16
normalerweise usually OT 1
normannisch Norman OT 2
Nostalgie nostalgia OT 3
Not... emergency OT 1
Notaufnahme Accident and Emergency OT 1
Noten music OT 1
Notfall emergency OT 1
Notiz note OT 1
Notizbuch notebook OT 2
notwendig necessary OT 3
Notwendigkeit necessity **WS 4**, 139
Nudel noodle OT 2
    Nudeln pasta OT 1
Nuklear... nuclear **WS 4**, 122
null nil OT 3
numerisch numerical **WS 3**, 87
Nummer number OT 1; figure OT 3
nun well OT 1; now OT 1
nur just OT 1; only OT 1; solely OT 3
Nuss nut **WS 1**, 14
nützlich useful OT 1

O

ob whether OT 2; if OT 2
obdachlos homeless **WS 3**, 101
oben upstairs OT 1; above OT 2
Oberbefehlshaber(in) commander-in-chief OT 2
obere(r, -s) top OT 1; upper **WS 3**, 90
Oberfläche surface OT 3
oberhalb above OT 2
Oberhemd shirt OT 1
Oberschenkel thigh OT 1
Objekt object OT 1
Objektiv lens OT 2
Obst fruit OT 1
Obstgarten orchard **WS 4**, 140
obwohl though OT 2; although OT 2; despite **WS 3**, 106
oder or OT 1
Ofen heater OT 2; oven OT 2; stove OT 3

Off: aus dem Off offstage OT 2
offen open OT 1
offensichtlich obvious OT 3
Öffentlichkeit public OT 3
offiziell official OT 2
öffnen to open OT 1
oft often OT 1
ohne without OT 1
ohnmächtig werden to faint OT 2
Ohr ear OT 1
Ökologie ecology OT 3
ökologisch environmental OT 3; ecological **WS 1**, 25
Ökonomie economy **WS 3**, 84
Ökotourismus ecotourism OT 3
Okular eyepiece OT 2
Öl oil OT 3
olympisch Olympic OT 2
Oma grandma OT 1
Onkel uncle OT 1
Opa grandpa OT 1
Opposition opposition **WS 3**, 92
optimistisch optimistic OT 3
Orange orange OT 1
orange orange OT 1
Orchester orchestra OT 1
ordentlich neat OT 3
Organ organ **WS 4**, 125
Organisation organization OT 3; agency **WS 1**, 22
Organisator(in) organizer **WS 3**, 102
organisatorisch organizational **WS 4**, 139
organisieren to organize OT 1
orientiert orientated **WS 4**, 126
Original... original OT 3
Orkan hurricane **WS 1**, 28
Ort place OT 1
Osten east OT 2
Osterglocke daffodil OT 3
östlich eastern OT 2
Outfit outfit **WS 3**, 100
Ozean ocean OT 2

P

Paar pair OT 2; couple OT 3
paar: ein paar a few OT 1; a couple OT 3
packen to pack OT 2
paddeln to paddle OT 3
Paket packet OT 2; parcel OT 2; package **WS 4**, 121
Palast palace OT 1
Palette range **WS 4**, 126
Palme palm **WS 2**, 62
Pandemie pandemic **WS 3**, 99
Panik: in Panik geraten to panic OT 2
Panorama... panoramic OT 3

Panther panther OT 2
Papa dad OT 1
Papier paper OT 1
Paprika pepper OT 2
Papst pope OT 2
Parade parade OT 2; procession OT 2
Paradies paradise **WS 1**, 21
parallel parallel OT 2
Park park OT 1
parken to park OT 2
Parkplatz car park OT 2
Parlament parliament OT 3
Partei party OT 2
parteiisch biased **WS 2**, 70
Partner(in) partner OT 1
Partnerschaft partnership **WS 2**, 50
Party party OT 1
Pass passport OT 2
Passagier(in) passenger OT 2
passieren to happen OT 1
Pastete pie OT 1
Patentante godmother **WS 1**, 15
Patient(in) patient OT 1
Patriot(in) patriot OT 2
Patriotismus patriotism OT 3
Pause break OT 1; rest OT 1
　eine Pause machen to pause OT 3
peinlich embarrassing OT 2
Pendler(in) commuter OT 2
Pension bed and breakfast OT 2
perfekt perfect OT 2
Person person OT 1; human being OT 2
Personal staff OT 1; crew OT 2
personalisieren to personalize **WS 2**, 66
persönlich personal OT 1
Persönlichkeit personality **WS 1**, 30
Perspektive perspective **WS 1**, 35
Pest plague OT 3
Petrochemikalie petrochemical
　WS 3, 108
Pfad trail OT 2
Pfanne pan OT 2
Pfannkuchen pancake OT 3
Pfarrer(in) parson OT 3
Pfeffer pepper OT 2
Pfefferminzbonbon mint OT 1
Pfeife whistle OT 2
pfeifen to blow OT 2
Pfeil arrow OT 3
Pferd horse OT 1
Pflanze plant OT 2
pflanzen to plant OT 3
Pflanzenwelt vegetation OT 3
Pflaster plaster OT 1
Pflaume plum OT 1

pflegen to care for OT 2; to maintain
　WS 2, 53
Pflicht chore OT 3
Pflücker(in) picker **WS 4**, 140
Pfund pound OT 1
Pfütze pool OT 1
Phänomen phenomenon **WS 1**, 32
Phase stage OT 2; phase OT 3
Philosoph(in) philosopher OT 3
philosophisch philosophical OT 3
Pianist(in) pianist OT 2
Picknick picnic OT 1
Pilz mushroom OT 2
Pinguin penguin OT 2
Pinsel brush OT 2
Pionier(in) pioneer OT 3
Pipeline pipeline OT 3
Plage pest **WS 1**, 25
Plagiat plagiarism OT 2
plagiieren to plagiarize OT 2
Plakat poster OT 1
Plakette badge **WS 4**, 130
Plan plan OT 1
planen to plan OT 1
Planet planet OT 2
Platte plate OT 1
Platz square OT 1; place OT 1
　den ersten Platz belegen to come
　　first OT 2
Plätzchen biscuit OT 1; cookie OT 3
Platzierung placement **WS 2**, 66
plaudern to chatter OT 2; to chat OT 3
plötzlich suddenly OT 2; sudden OT 3
Pocken smallpox **WS 1**, 24
Podcast podcast OT 3
Podiumsdiskussion panel discussion
　OT 3
Poet poet OT 1
Pokal cup OT 1; trophy OT 2
Pol pole OT 3
Politik politics OT 3
Politiker(in) politician OT 3
politisch political OT 2
Polizei police OT 1
Polizeibeamter, -beamtin officer OT 2
Polohemd polo shirt **WS 4**, 130
Polster pad OT 2
Polyp polyp **WS 1**, 28
Pommes frites French fries OT 2
Popcorn popcorn OT 2
populär popular OT 1
Popularität popularity **WS 3**, 98
Porträt portrait OT 3
Position position **WS 1**, 27
Post post OT 2; post office OT 3; mail
　OT 2

Post... postage OT 3
posten to post **WS 1**, 29
Poster poster OT 1
Postkarte postcard OT 1
potentiell potential **WS 2**, 64
Praktikum internship OT 3; traineeship
　WS 4, 136
praktisch practical OT 2
Praline chocolate OT 1
Präsentation presentation OT 1
Präsenz presence **WS 2**, 64
präsidentiell presidential OT 2
Präsident(in) president OT 2
Präsidentschaft presidency **WS 3**, 115
Praxis surgery **WS 3**, 110
präzise accurate **WS 3**, 96
Preis price OT 1; (Gewinn) prize OT 1;
　reward **WS 4**, 129
Premierminister(in) Prime Minister
　OT 2
pressen to press OT 1
prima fine OT 1
primär primary OT 1
Prinz prince OT 1
Prinzip principle OT 3
Priorität priority OT 3
Prise pinch OT 3
privat private OT 3
Privileg privilege OT 3
pro pro **WS 3**, 94
Probe rehearsal OT 2
proben to rehearse OT 3
probieren to taste OT 1
Problem problem OT 1; matter OT 2
Produkt product OT 2
Produktion production **WS 4**, 130
Professor(in) professor OT 3
Profil profile **WS 4**, 137
Profit profit **WS 1**, 27
profitieren to benefit **WS 3**, 103
Prognose forecast OT 2
Programm program, programme OT 3
programmieren to programme OT 2
Programmierung programming OT 2
Projekt project OT 1
Projektor projector OT 1
Promenade promenade **WS 1**, 29
Prominente(r) personality **WS 1**, 30;
　celebrity **WS 1**, 30
Proportion proportion **WS 2**, 69
Prospekt brochure OT 1; booklet OT 2
Protein protein **WS 2**, 68
protestieren to protest OT 3
Provinz province OT 2
Prozedur procedure **WS 2**, 56
Prozent percent OT 3

Prozentsatz percentage **WS 4**, 128
Prozess trial OT 2; process **WS 2**, 70
Prüfung exam OT 1
psychisch mental OT 2
Pubertät puberty **WS 4**, 125
Publikum audience OT 1
publizieren to publish OT 3
Puck puck OT 3
Pullover jumper OT 1
Puma cougar OT 2
Punkt point OT 1; full stop OT 1; item
OT 3; dot **WS 3**, 115
punkten to score OT 1
pünktlich punctual **WS 4**, 140
Puppe doll OT 2
putzen to clean OT 1
Pyjama-Party sleepover OT 1

Q
Quadrat square OT 1
Qualifikation qualification OT 2
Qualität quality OT 3
Quartal quarter OT 1
Quatsch nonsense OT 1
Quelle spring OT 2
querfeldein cross-country OT 2
Querflöte flute OT 1
querlesen to skim OT 2
Quiz quiz OT 2

R
Rabatt discount **WS 3**, 103
Rabe raven OT 2
Rad bike OT 1; wheel OT 1
Rad fahren to bike OT 3
Radfahrer(in) cyclist OT 3
Radiergummi rubber OT 1
radikal radical **WS 3**, 102
Radio radio OT 1
Rahmen frame OT 3; framework
WS 3, 90
Rampe ramp OT 2
Rand edge OT 3; rim OT 3
Rank rank **WS 2**, 53
rasch swift OT 3
Rasen grass OT 1; lawn **WS 4**, 124
Rasse... pedigree OT 3
Rat advice OT 2; council OT 3
Rate rate **WS 4**, 133
raten to guess OT 1; to advise OT 3
Ratte rat OT 3
rau rough OT 3; harsh **WS 1**, 27
Raubtier predator **WS 1**, 25
Rauch smoke OT 2
Raum room OT 1
reagieren to react OT 3

Reaktion reaction **WS 1**, 14; response
WS 3, 108
realistisch realistic **WS 2**, 68
Realität reality **WS 1**, 28
Rebell(in) rebel OT 3
Rechnung bill OT 3
Recht privilege OT 3
rechteckig rectangular OT 2
rechte(r, -s) right OT 1
rechtfertigen to justify **WS 3**, 102
rechts right OT 1
Rechtsanspruch title OT 1
Rechtsanwalt, -anwältin lawyer
WS 4, 134
Rechtschreibung spelling OT 1
rechtzeitig timely OT 3
Redakteur(in) editor OT 2
Rede speech OT 2
reden to speak OT 1; to talk OT 1
Redner(in) speaker OT 2
reduzieren to downsize OT 3; to reduce
OT 3
Referendum referendum **WS 3**, 99
Reformation reformation OT 3
Regel rule OT 1; shelf OT 2
regelmäßig regular OT 1
Regelwerk rulebook OT 2
Regenbogen rainbow **WS 1**, 13
Regenschauer rainstorm **WS 1**, 38
Regenschirm umbrella OT 1
Regenwald rainforest OT 2
Reggae reggae OT 2
regieren to govern OT 3
Regierung government OT 2;
reign OT 3
Regierungs... governmental **WS 3**, 86
Region region OT 3
regional regional **WS 1**, 32
regnen to rain OT 1
Rehabilitierung rehabilitation OT 2
reiben to rub OT 3
Reich empire OT 2
reich rich OT 1; wealthy OT 3
reichlich plenty OT 2
Reihe line OT 1; row OT 2
der Reihe nach sequentially **WS 4**, 126
Reihenfolge order OT 1; rank **WS 2**, 53;
sequence **WS 2**, 59
in eine Reihenfolge bringen
to sequence OT 3; to rank **WS 1**, 32
Reim rhyme OT 2
reinigen to clean OT 1
Reinigungsmittel cleaner OT 3
Reis rice OT 1
Reise journey OT 1; trip OT 1; voyage
OT 3

Reisebus coach OT 1
Reiseführer guidebook OT 3
reisen to travel OT 1; to tour OT 2
Reisende(r) traveller OT 3
Reiseziel destination **WS 1**, 27
reiten to ride OT 1
Reiz interest OT 1
reizvoll attractive **WS 1**, 32
Reklame advertisement OT 1; ad, advert
OT 2; advertising OT 2
Rektor(in) head teacher OT 1; principal
OT 2
Religion religion OT 3
Religionsunterricht religious studies
OT 1
religiös religious OT 2
Rennen race OT 2
rennen to run OT 1
Rennsport racing OT 2
Rentier reindeer OT 3
Reparatur repair OT 2
reparieren to mend OT 3; to repair OT 3
repetitiv repetitive **WS 4**, 127
Reporter(in) reporter OT 1;
correspondent **WS 3**, 106
Reptil reptile OT 2
Republik republic **WS 3**, 90
republikanisch republican **WS 3**, 90
Requisite prop OT 1
reservieren to reserve OT 3
Reservierung reservation OT 1
Reservoir reservoir **WS 1**, 34
resistent resistant **WS 2**, 69
Resistenz resistance **WS 1**, 24
respektlos disrespectful OT 3
respektvoll respectful OT 3
Restaurant restaurant OT 1
retten to save OT 2
Rettung rescue OT 2
Rettungssanitäter(in) paramedic OT 1
Rettungsschwimmer(in) lifeguard
WS 4, 138
revidieren to revise OT 2
Revolution revolution OT 2
revolutionär revolutionary OT 3
Rezept recipe OT 2
Rezeption reception OT 1
Rezeptionist(in) receptionist OT 1
Richter(in) judge OT 2
richtig correct OT 1; right OT 1; true OT 1
Richtlinie guideline OT 3
Richtung direction OT 1
in Richtung toward OT 2; toward(s)
OT 2
riechen to smell OT 1
Riegel bar OT 1

riesig enormous OT 1; huge OT 2; massive OT 3

Riff reef **WS 1**, 26

rigide rigid **WS 4**, 131

Rinder cattle **WS 2**, 69

Rindfleisch steak OT 1; beef OT 2

ringen to wrestle OT 2

rinnen to trickle OT 3

Risiko risk **WS 1**, 28

Ritt ride OT 1; journey OT 1

Ritter knight OT 3

   zum Ritter schlagen to knight OT 3

Rivale, Rivalin rival OT 2

Robbe seal OT 1

Rock skirt OT 1

Rockstar rockstar OT 3

roh raw OT 3

Rohr tube OT 1

Rolle role OT 1; roll OT 2

rollen to roll OT 3

Rollstuhl wheelchair OT 2

Rollstuhlfahrer(in) wheelchair user OT 2

Rolltreppe escalator OT 1

Roman novel OT 2

Röntgen X-ray OT 1

rosa pink OT 1

rot red OT 1

Routine routine **WS 4**, 131

Rücken back OT 1

Rückgang decline **WW**, 11

Rückgrat backbone OT 2

Rucksack rucksack OT 1; backpack OT 2

Rücktritt resignation **WS 3**, 99

Ruderboot rowing boat OT 1

Ruf call OT 1; name OT 1

Ruhe silence **WS 1**, 14

   Ruhe bewahren to keep calm OT 2

   in Ruhe lassen to leave alone OT 2

ruhig quiet OT 1; calm OT 2; steady OT 3

rühren to stir OT 2

Ruine ruin OT 2

rund round OT 1

Rundfunk radio OT 1

Rundgang tour OT 1

S

Sache thing OT 1

sachlich factual **WS 1**, 17

sachte gently OT 3

Sack sack OT 2

Sackhüpfen sack race OT 2

Safari safari OT 2

Saft juice OT 1

Sage legend OT 3

sagen to say OT 1; to tell OT 1

Sahne cream OT 1

Saite string OT 2

Salat salad OT 1

Salatgurke cucumber OT 1

Salz salt OT 2

Samen seed OT 2

sammeln to collect OT 1; to gather OT 3

Sammlung collection OT 2

Samstag Saturday OT 1

Sand sand OT 1

sandig sandy **WS 1**, 29

Sandstein sandstone OT 3

Sandwich sandwich OT 1

Sänger(in) singer OT 1; vocalist OT 2

Sarg coffin **WS 3**, 106

Satz sentence OT 1

sauer acidic **WS 1**, 28

   sauer sein to be angry OT 1

Sauerstoff oxygen **WS 1**, 39

Säugetier mammal OT 2

Säugling baby OT 1

Sauna sauna OT 2

Saxofon saxophone OT 2

scannen to scan OT 2

Schach chess OT 1

Schädel skull OT 2

Schaden damage OT 3; harm OT 3

schädlich harmful **WS 2**, 65

Schaf sheep OT 1

Schäfer(in) shepherd OT 2

schaffen to create OT 2; to achieve **WS 1**, 25

Schal scarf OT 1

Schale dish OT 2

Schalter switch OT 3

Schandfleck eyesore **WS 2**, 52

scharf spicy **WS 2**, 79

Schärpe sash OT 3

Schatten shade **WS 1**, 16

Schatz treasure **WS 1**, 32

schätzen to guess OT 1; to appreciate OT 2; to estimate **WS 1**, 24

Schatzmeister(in) treasurer OT 3

Schätzung guess OT 1

Schauer shower OT 1

Schaufenster window OT 1

Schauspieler(in) actor OT 1

Scheibe slice OT 1; disc OT 3

scheiden: sich scheiden lassen to divorce OT 3

Scheidung divorce OT 3

Schein shine OT 1; note OT 2

scheinen to shine OT 1; to seem OT 2

scheitern to fail **WS 4**, 143

schenken to give OT 1

Scherbe shard **WS 2**, 48

Schere scissors OT 1

Scheune barn OT 2

schick stylish **WS 2**, 66; glam **WS 3**, 103

schicken to send OT 1

Schicksal luck OT 1; fortune OT 3

Schiedsrichter(in) referee OT 3

schießen to fire OT 2; to shoot OT 3

Schiff boat OT 1; ship OT 1

   mit dem Schiff fahren to sail OT 2

Schiffswrack shipwreck OT 3

Schild sign OT 1; notice OT 3

Schilderung description OT 1

Schildkröte tortoise OT 1

Schinken ham OT 1

Schlacht battle OT 3

Schlafanzug pyjamas OT 3

schlafen to sleep OT 1

schlafend asleep OT 2

Schlafenszeit bedtime OT 2

Schlafzimmer bedroom OT 1

Schlag beat OT 3

schlagen to hit OT 1; to batter OT 3; to beat **WS 1**, 14; to punch **WS 4**, 151

Schläger (Sport) bat OT 1

Schlägerei fight OT 1

Schlagzeile headline OT 2

Schlagzeug drums OT 1

Schlagzeuger(in) drummer OT 2

Schlamm mud OT 3

Schlammlawine mudslide **WS 1**, 34

Schlange snake OT 1; queue OT 1; serpent **WS 1**, 13

   Schlange stehen to queue OT 1

schlau savvy **WS 2**, 62

Schlauch tube OT 1

schlecht bad OT 1

Schleuse lock OT 3

schlicht simple OT 1; simple OT 1

schließen to close OT 1; to shut OT 2; to conclude OT 3

Schließfach locker OT 2

schließlich finally OT 1; eventually OT 3

Schlitten sled OT 3

Schlittschuh laufen to skate OT 2

Schloss castle OT 1; palace OT 1

Schlucht canyon OT 3

Schluss end OT 1; conclusion OT 3

Schlüssel key OT 1

schmackhaft tasty OT 2

schmecken to taste OT 1

   sich schmecken lassen to enjoy OT 1

schmelzen to melt OT 3

Schmerz pain OT 2

schmerzen to hurt OT 1

Schmerzmittel painkiller OT 2

Schminke makeup **WS 2**, 66

Schmuck jewelry OT 2

schmücken to decorate OT 2

Schmuckstück jewel OT 3

Schmutz dirt **WS 4**, 125

schmutzig dirty OT 1

Schnabeltier platypus **WS 1**, 13

Schnee snow OT 1

Schneemobil snowmobile OT 3

schneiden to cut OT 2; to chop OT 3

schnell fast OT 1; quick OT 3; rapid OT 3

Schnitt to cut OT 1

schnitzen to carve OT 2

Schnitzerei carving OT 3

Schnitzer(in) carver OT 3

Schnur string OT 2

schockiert shocked OT 3

Schokolade chocolate OT 1

schon already OT 2; yet OT 2

schön nice OT 1; beautiful OT 1; lovely OT 1

Schönheit beauty OT 3

Schöpfer(in) creator **WS 1**, 26

Schöpfung creation **WS 1**, 26

Schornstein chimney OT 3

Schottenrock kilt OT 2

Schrank cupboard OT 1

schrecklich terrible OT 1; awful OT 1; dreadful OT 2

schreiben to write OT 1

Schreibtisch desk OT 1

Schreibweise spelling OT 1

schreien to scream OT 3

Schriftrolle scroll OT 2

Schriftsteller(in) writer OT 1; novelist **WS 2**, 52

Schritt step OT 1; footstep OT 2

Schublade drawer OT 1

schüchtern shy OT 2

Schuh shoe OT 1

Schulabschluss graduation **WS 3**, 106

  den Schulabschluss machen to graduate **WS 3**, 106

Schulausflug field trip OT 2

Schulball prom OT 3

Schuld fault OT 2; blame OT 3

schuldig guilty **WS 3**, 90

Schule school OT 1

Schüler(in) student OT 1

Schulheft exercise book OT 1

Schulhof playground OT 1

Schulkamerad(in) schoolmate **WS 1**, 28

Schulleiter(in) head teacher OT 1; principal OT 2

Schulranzen school bag OT 1

Schultag school day OT 1

Schultasche school bag OT 1

Schulter shoulder OT 1

Schuppen shed OT 1

Schuss shot OT 2

Schüssel bowl OT 1

Schusswaffe gun OT 3

schütteln to shake OT 2

schütten to pour OT 1

schützen to protect OT 2

Schutzgebiet sanctuary **WS 1**, 29

schwach thin OT 1

Schwäche weakness **WS 2**, 60

schwächen to weaken **WS 3**, 108

schwafeln to ramble **WS 2**, 59

schwanger pregnant OT 3

Schwanz tail OT 2

schwarz black OT 1

schweben to soar OT 3

Schweigen silence **WS 1**, 14

Schwein pig OT 1

Schweinefleisch pork OT 2

Schwellung swelling OT 2

schwer heavy OT 1; difficult OT 1; challenging OT 2; severe **WS 1**, 28

Schwert sword OT 1

Schwester sister OT 1

schwierig difficult OT 1; challenging OT 2; complex **WS 1**, 36

Schwierigkeit difficulty OT 2; trouble OT 2

Schwimmbecken pool OT 1

schwimmen to swim OT 1

Schwimmer(in) swimmer OT 3

schwindlig faint OT 2; dizzy OT 3

schwitzen to sweat OT 2

schwul gay **WS 4**, 120; queer **WS 4**, 125

sechs six OT 1

sechzehn sixteen OT 1

sechzig sixty OT 1

See, der lake OT 1

See, die sea OT 1

seefahrend seafaring OT 3

Seehund seal OT 1

seekrank seasick OT 3

Seele soul OT 2

Seemann sailor OT 3

Seevogel seabird **WS 1**, 26

Segelboot sailboat OT 3

segeln to sail OT 1

Segment segment **WS 1**, 32

sehen to look OT 1; to see OT 1

Sehenswürdigkeit sight OT 1; attraction OT 2

sehr very OT 1; really OT 1; extremely OT 2

Sehvermögen sight OT 1; attraction OT 2

Seife soap OT 2

Seil rope OT 3

sein to be OT 1

sein(e, -er, -es) its OT 1

seit since OT 2

Seite page OT 1; side OT 1

Sekretär(in) secretary OT 1

sekundär secondary OT 1

Sekundarschule secondary school OT 1

Sekunde second OT 1

selbst... self **WS 4**, 120

Selbstlaut vowel OT 1

selbstsicher confident OT 3

selbstständig self-employed **WS 4**, 136

Selbstvertrauen confidence OT 2

selten rare OT 2; uncommon **WS 1**, 17; seldom **WS 2**, 67

selten uncommon **WS 1**, 17

Semester term OT 2

Senator(in) senator **WS 3**, 91

Senf mustard OT 1

Senior(in) senior citizen OT 2

Senke hollow OT 3

sensorisch sensory **WS 4**, 131

servieren to serve OT 1

Sessel armchair OT 1

Sessellift chairlift **WS 1**, 31

setzen to set OT 1

  sich setzen to sit down OT 1

seufzen to sigh **WS 1**, 15

Sex sex **WS 4**, 122

Shampoo shampoo OT 3

sich oneself OT 2

sicher sure OT 1; safe OT 1; certain OT 2

Sicherheit safety OT 2; security **WS 1**, 28

sicherstellen to ensure **WS 3**, 90

Sicht view OT 1; sight OT 1

sichtbar apparent OT 3; visible **WS 2**, 56

sie she OT 1; her OT 1

sieben seven OT 1

Siebenkampf heptathlon OT 2

siebzehn seventeen OT 1

siebzig seventy OT 1

Siedler(in) settler OT 3

Siedlung settlement OT 3

Sieg victory **WS 3**, 106

Sieger(in) winner OT 1

Signal signal OT 2

Silber silver OT 1

singen to sing OT 1

Sinn meaning OT 1; sense OT 2,

Sirene siren OT 3

Situation situation OT 1

sitzen to sit OT 1

Sitzplatz seat OT 2

Sitzung meeting OT 1; session **WS 2**, 56

Skateboard skateboard OT 1

Skelett skeleton OT 2
Sketch sketch OT 2
Ski ski OT 3
Skifahren skiing OT 3
Skizze sketch OT 2
Sklave, Sklavin slave OT 3
Sklaverei slavery OT 3
Skulptur sculpture OT 2
Skyline skyline **WS 1**, 29
Slang slang **WW**, 11
Slogan slogan OT 2
Slum slum **WS 3**, 101
Smartphone smartphone OT 3
SMS text OT 2
Snack snack OT 1
Snowboardfahren snowboarding OT 3
so such OT 2
Socke sock OT 1
Sofa sofa OT 1
sofort straight away OT 2; immediately
   OT 3
sogar even OT 1
Sohn son OT 1
Soldat(in) soldier OT 1; serviceman,
   servicewoman OT 2
solo solo OT 2
Sommer summer OT 1
Sommersprossen freckles OT 3
Sonne sun OT 1
Sonnen... solar OT 3
Sonnenbrand sunburn OT 2
Sonnenschein sunshine OT 3
Sonnenschutzmittel sunscreen OT 2
Sonnenstich sunstroke OT 2
Sonnenuhr sundial OT 3
Sonnenuntergang sunset OT 3
sonnig sunny OT 1
Sonntag Sunday OT 1
sonst otherwise **WS 3**, 95
   sonst noch else OT 1
Sorge anxiety **WS 1**, 34; concern **WS 1**, 37
   sich Sorgen machen to worry OT 1
sorgen für to care for OT 3; to cater for
   WS 4, 147
sorgfältig careful OT 1; cautious OT 3
sorglos careless OT 2
Sorte kind OT 1; type OT 2; sort OT2
Soße sauce OT 1
sowieso anyway OT 1
Spaghetti spaghetti OT 1
Spalte column OT 1
Spaniel spaniel OT 2
spannend exciting OT 1
Spaß fun OT 1
   Spaß verstehen to take a joke OT 2
spät late OT 1

später einmal one day OT 2; someday
   OT 3
Speck bacon OT 1
Speer spear OT 3
Speisekarte menu OT 1
spektakulär spectacular OT 2
Spende donation OT 2
spenden to donate OT 2
Spendensammlung fundraising OT 2
Spezialeffekte special effects OT 2
sich spezialisieren to specialize OT 3
Spezialist(in) specialist **WS 4**, 131
Spezies species **WS 1**, 21
Spiegel mirror OT 1
spiegeln to reflect OT 2
Spiel match OT 1; game OT 1
spielen to play OT 1
Spieler(in) player OT 1
Spielfeld pitch OT 3
Spielplatz playground OT 1
Spielzeug toy OT 3
Spind locker OT 2
Spinne spider OT 1
Spitze tip OT 1; top OT 1
Spitzname nickname **WS 1**, 12
Sponsor(in) sponsor OT 2
Sport sport OT 1; athletics OT 1
Sport... sporting **WS 1**, 15
Sportart sport OT 1; athletics OT 1
Sporthalle gymnasium OT 3
Sportler(in) sportswoman, sportsman
   OT 2; athlete OT 2
sportlich sporting **WS 1**, 15; sporty
   WS 4, 130
Sportunterricht PE (physical education)
   OT 1
Sprache language OT 1
Spray spray OT 3
sprechen to speak OT 1; to talk OT 1
Sprechstundenhilfe receptionist OT 1
Springbrunnen fountain OT 1
springen to jump OT 2
Sprudel soda **WS 2**, 68
sprühen to spray OT 3
Spülbecken sink OT 3
Spur trail OT 2
Spürhund hound OT 2
Staat state OT 1
Staatsangehörigkeit nationality OT 2
Staatsoberhaupt head of state OT 2
Stabilität stability OT 3
Stachelrochen stingray **WS 1**, 21
Stadion stadium OT 1
Stadt town OT 1; city OT 1
städtisch urban **WS 2**, 52

Stadtmitte centre OT 1; middle OT 1;
   medium OT 2
Stadtplan map OT 1
Stahl steel OT 2
Stall shed OT 1; stable **WS 4**, 138
Stamm tribe OT 2; clan **WS 1**, 26
stammen aus to originate OT 3
Stammes... tribal OT 3
Stand stall **WS 2**, 49
Standard standard **WS 1**, 16
ständig constant(ly) **WS 2**, 68
Standort location **WS 1**, 26
Standpunkt viewpoint OT 3
Stange pole OT 3
Star star OT 1
stark strong OT 2; severe **WS 1**, 28;
   intense **WS 1**, 32
Stärke strength OT 3
stärken to strengthen **WS 3**, 108
starr rigid **WS 4**, 131; stiff **WS 4**, 131
starren to stare OT 2; to gaze **WS 1**, 29
Station station OT 1
Statistik statistic OT 3
stattdessen instead OT 2
Statue statue OT 1
Status status **WW**, 11
Stau traffic jam OT 2; congestion
   WS 2, 74
Staub dust OT 2
staubsaugen to vacuum **WS 4**, 124
Steak steak OT 1
stechen to sting OT 2
Stechmücke mosquito OT 2
stecken to stick OT 1; to paste OT 2
Stecknadel pin OT 1
stehen to stand OT 1
   auf etwas stehen to be into OT 2
   für etwas stehen to stand for sth.
      OT 2
steif stiff **WS 4**, 131
steigen to climb OT 1
   steigen lassen to fly OT 1
steil steep OT 2
Stein stone OT 1; rock OT 2
Stelle place OT 1
stellen to put OT 1; to set OT 2
sterben to die OT 1
Stereotype stereotype **WS 2**, 65
stereotypisch stereotypical **WS 4**, 124
Stern star OT 1
Sternchen star OT 1
Steroid steroid **WS 2**, 68
stetig steadily **WS 2**, 75
Steuer tax OT 3
steuern to steer OT 3
Stichprobe sample **WS 4**, 144

Stichwort headword OT 2; keyword OT 2

Stichwort cue **WS 4**, 131

Stiefel boot OT 1

Stift pen OT 1

Stigma stigma **WS 2**, 70

Stil style OT 2

still quiet OT 1; still OT 1 OT 2

Stimme voice OT 2

stinken to smell OT 1

Stipendium scholarship **WS 4**, 126

Stirn: die Stirn runzeln to frown OT 3

Stock stick OT 2; twig OT 2

Stockbett bunk bed OT 3

Stockwerk floor OT 1

    im oberen Stockwerk upstairs OT 1

    im unteren Stockwerk downstairs
       OT 1

Stoff cloth OT 2

stolpern to trip OT 2

Stolz pride **WS 1**, 32

stolz proud OT 2

stören to bother OT 3; to disturb
   WS 1, 38

Störung disorder **WS 4**, 131

Storyboard storyboard **WS 2**, 61

stoßen to knock OT 2

Stoßzahn tusk OT 3

Strafe penalty OT 3

strafrechtlich penal **WS 1**, 22

Strafstoß penalty OT 3

Strand beach OT 1

Straße road OT 1; street OT 1

Straßenbahn tram OT 2; trolley OT 2

Straßenmusiker(in) busker **WS 1**, 29

Strategie strategy OT 3

Streaming streaming **WS 4**, 128

Strecke route OT 2

streichen to paint OT 1

Streichholz match OT 2

Streifen strip OT 2

Streik strike **WS 3**, 106

Streit argument OT 1; quarrel OT 2

(sich) streiten to quarrel OT 2; to argue
   OT 3

Streitkräfte armed forces **WS 3**, 92

streng strict OT 2

stressig stressful **WS 4**, 142

streuen to sprinkle OT 2

Stroh straw **WS 3**, 98

Strohhalm straw **WS 3**, 98

Strom electricity OT 2

Struktur structure OT 1

strukturieren to structure **WS 1**, 29

Strumpfhose tights OT 2

Stück piece OT 1; bit OT 2

Student(in) student OT 1

Studie study OT 1

Studiengebühr(en) tuition (fee)
   WS 4, 126

studieren to study OT 1

Studio studio OT 3

Studium studies OT 1

Stufe step OT 1; level OT 1

Stuhl chair OT 1

Stunde hour OT 1

Sturm storm OT 2

Stürmer(in) striker OT 3

stürzen to fall OT 1

Stütze prop OT 1

Substanz substance OT 3

Suche search OT 2

suchen to seek **WS 1**, 16

Süden south OT 2

südlich southern **WS 1**, 13

südwestlich southwest OT 3

Superheld superhero **WS 2**, 68

Supermarkt supermarket OT 1

Suppe soup OT 1

Surfen surfing OT 1

Sweatshirt sweatshirt OT 1

Symbol symbol OT 1

Synästhesie synaesthesia OT 2

Synonym synonym OT 2

synthetisch synthetic **WS 3**, 95

System system OT 2

systematisch systematically **WS 1**, 24

Szene scene OT 2

T

T-Shirt T-shirt OT 1

Tabak tobacco **WS 3**, 84

Tabelle table OT 1

Tablett tray OT 2; tablet OT 3

Tablette pill **WS 2**, 68

Tacho clock OT 1; o'clock OT 1

Tafel blackboard OT 1; tablet OT 2;
   board OT 2

Tag day OT 1

Tagebuch diary OT 1

Tagesausflug day out OT 2

Tagesordnung agenda OT 3

täglich daily OT 2

Takt beat OT 3

Tal valley OT 1

Talent talent OT 3

talentiert talented **WS 1**, 32

Tank tank OT 3

Tante aunt OT 1

Tanz dance OT 3

tanzen to dance OT 1

tapfer brave OT 1

Tasche bag OT 1; pocket OT 2

Taschenlampe torch OT 1; flashlight
   OT 2

Taschenmesser pocketknife OT 2

Tasse cup OT 1

Tastatur keyboard OT 1

Taste key OT 1

Tätowierung tattoo OT 3

Tatsache fact OT 1

taub deaf OT 3

tauchen to dive OT 3

Taucheranzug wetsuit OT 1

Taucher(in) diver OT 3

tauschen to swap OT 3

Taxi cab OT 1; taxi OT 1

Team team OT 1; crew OT 2

Technik technique **WS 1**, 29

technisch technical OT 2

Technologie technology OT 1

technologisch technological **WS 2**, 62

Tee tea OT 1

Teenager teen OT 2; teenager OT 2

Teich pond OT 1

Teil part OT 1; piece OT 1; section OT 2

teilen to divide OT 2

   (sich) teilen to share OT 2

teilnehmen to take part OT 2; to
   participate **WS 2**, 60

Teilnehmer(in) participant **WS 2**, 72;
   contestant **WS 3**, 86

teilweise partly **WS 3**, 93

Telefon phone OT 1

Teller plate OT 1

Tempel temple OT 1

Temperatur temperature OT 2

Tennis tennis OT 1

Termin appointment OT 3

Terminkalender diary OT 1

Terrier terrier OT 2

Test test OT 1; experiment OT 2

teuer expensive OT 1

Text text OT 2

texten to text OT 2

Texter(in) songwriter **WS 4**, 120

Theater theatre OT 1

   Theater spielen to act OT 1

Theaterstück play OT 1

Thema topic OT 1; issue OT 2; theme
   OT 2

theoretisch theoretical **WS 2**, 50

Therapie therapy **WS 4**, 131

Thermalquelle hot spring OT 2

Thron throne OT 2

tief deep OT 1; low OT 2

Tier animal OT 1; beast OT 2

Tierwelt wildlife OT 2

Tiger tiger OT 1
Tipp tip OT 1; clue OT 1; prompt OT 3
tippen to key OT 2; to guess OT 2
Tisch table OT 1
Tischler(in) carpenter OT 3
Titel title OT 1
Toast toast OT 2
Tochter daughter OT 1
Tod death OT 2
tödlich deadly WS 1, 13
Toilette toilet OT 2; restroom OT 3
tolerant tolerant OT 3
Toleranz tolerance WS 4, 120
toll fantastic OT 1; great OT 1; terrific
  OT 3; stunning WS 1, 28
Tomate tomato OT 1
Ton sound OT 1; tone WS 4, 137
Tonne bin OT 3; ton WS 2, 66
Topf pot OT 2
Töpferwaren pottery OT 3
Tor goal OT 1; gate OT 1
  ein Tor schießen to score OT 1
Torte cake OT 1
Torwart(in) goalkeeper OT 3
tot dead OT 1
töten to kill OT 1
Tour tour OT 1
Tourismus tourism OT 3
Tourist(in) tourist OT 1
traditionell traditional OT 2
tragen to wear OT 1; to carry OT 1
Tragödie tragedy WS 3, 100
Trainer(in) coach OT 1
trainieren to practise OT 1; to train OT 2
Traktor tractor OT 2
Träne tear OT 2
trans... trans WS 4, 121
transgender transgender WS 4, 125
Transkript transcript OT 3
Transparent banner WS 2, 66
Transport transport OT 3
transportieren to transport OT 3
trauen to marry OT 1
  sich trauen to dare OT 2
Traum dream OT 2
träumen to dream WS 2, 52
traurig sad OT 1; unhappy OT 1;
  miserable OT 2
Treffen meeting OT 1
treffen to hit OT 1,
  (sich) treffen to meet OT 1
treiben to herd OT 2
Treibhaus greenhouse WS 2, 69
Treidelpfad towpath OT 3
Trend fashion OT 1; trend WS 2, 62
Trendwende tipping point WS 1, 28

(sich) trennen to split OT 2; to split up
  OT 3; to separate OT 3
Treppe stairs OT 1
treten to kick OT 1
Trick trick WS 2, 66
Trilogie trilogy WS 1, 31
trinken to drink OT 1
Trinkhalm straw WS 3, 98
Trinkspruch toast OT 2
triumphierend triumphant OT 3
trocken dry OT 3
Trog trough OT 3
Trommel drum OT 3
Tropen... tropical WS 1, 13
tropfen to drip OT 3
trotz in spite of WS 1, 25; despite
  WS 3, 106
trotzdem anyway OT 1
Tugend virtue OT 3
tugendhaft virtuous OT 3
tun to do OT 1
  so tun, als ob to pretend OT 1
Tunika tunic OT 2
Tunnel tunnel OT 3
Tür door OT 1
Turbine turbine WS 2, 52
Turm tower OT 1
Turnen gymnastics OT 1
Turnhalle gym OT 1; gymnasium OT 3
Turnier joust OT 2; tournament OT 3
Turnschuh sneaker WS 2, 66
Türschwelle doorstep WS 1, 19
Tüte bag OT 1
Tuten blast OT 3
Tutor(in) tutor OT 2
Typ guy WS 1, 30
typisch typical OT 2

U
U-Bahn subway OT 1; underground OT 1;
  metro OT 1
übel sick OT 1
üben to practise OT 1
über about OT 1; above OT 1; via OT 2
überall everywhere OT 1
überarbeiten to edit OT 3
Überblick overview WS 2, 61
übereinstimmen (mit) to conform (to)
  WS 2, 68
Überfahrt sailing OT 1
überfliegen to scan OT 2
überfluten to flood WS 3, 108
überfüllt crowded OT 2
Übergang transition WS 3, 99
übergeben to surrender WS 3, 106
  sich übergeben to throw up OT 2

übergewichtig overweight WS 2, 69
überlaufen to overflow WS 3, 88
überleben to survive OT 3
Überlebende(r) survivor OT 3
übernehmen to take over OT 2;
  to resume WS 1, 26
überprüfen to check OT 1; to review OT 3
überqueren to cross OT 1
überraschen to surprise OT 2
überrascht surprised OT 2; amazed OT 3
Überraschung surprise OT 1
überschatten to overshadow WS 3, 99
Überschrift heading OT 3
Übersetzung translation OT 2
Übersicht overview WS 2, 61
übertragbar transferable WS 4, 142
übertreffen to beat WS 1, 14
übertreiben to exaggerate WS 1, 21;
  to overdo WS 2, 68
Übertreibung exaggeration WS 1, 21
überwachen to oversee WS 3, 92
überzeugen to convince OT 3;
  to persuade OT 3
üblich normal OT 1; usual OT 2
Übung exercise OT 1; practice OT 1
Übungsheft exercise book OT 1
Ufer bank OT 3
Uhr clock OT 1; o'clock OT 1
Ukulele ukulele OT 3
um around OT 1; at OT 1
Umarmung hug OT 1
umbringen to kill OT 1
umdrehen to flip OT 3
umfallen to fall over OT 2
Umfeld environment OT 2
Umfrage survey OT 1; poll WS 4, 142
umgeben to surround OT 3
Umgebung setting WS 2, 53
Umhang cloak OT 2
umkehren to turn around OT 1; to invert
  WS 1, 31
umreißen to outline OT 3
umschreiben to paraphrase OT 3
umstellen to rearrange OT 2; to invert
  WS 1, 31
umstoßen to knock over OT 2
umstritten controversial OT 3;
  contentious WS 3, 99
umwandeln to convert WS 2, 52
Umwelt environment OT 2
Umwelt... environmental OT 3
Umweltschützer(in) environmentalist
  OT 3
Umweltwissenschaft ecology OT 3
umziehen to move OT 1; to relocate
  WS 3, 87

Umzug parade OT 2; procession OT 2
unabhängig independent OT 3
Unabhängigkeit independence OT 2
unangenehm nasty OT 2
unbeaufsichtigt unattended **WS 3**, 88
unbegrenzt unlimited **WS 3**, 98
unbekannt unfamiliar OT 2; unknown OT 3
unbeliebt unpopular OT 3
unbequem uncomfortable OT 2
unberührt unspoilt OT 3
unbeschränkt unlimited **WS 3**, 98
unbesiegt unconquered OT 2
unbestimmt vague **WS 1**, 27
unbewohnt unoccupied **WS 3**, 110
und and OT 1
uneben bumpy OT 3
Uneinigkeit disagreement OT 3
unendlich endless **WS 2**, 52
unentschieden undecided **WS 1**, 19
unentschlossen undecided **WS 1**, 19
unerwarteterweise unexpectedly OT 3
unfähig unable **WS 3**, 93
Unfall accident OT 1
ungefähr about OT 1; approximately **WW**, 10
Ungeheuer monster OT 1
ungeschickt clumsy OT 2
ungewöhnlich unusual OT 2; uncommon **WS 1**, 17
ungezogen naughty OT 2
unglaublich incredible OT 2; unbelievable OT 3
unglücklich unhappy OT 1; miserable OT 2
ungünstig bad OT 1
unheimlich scary OT 2
unhöflich rude OT 2
Uniform uniform OT 1
Union union OT 3
Universität university OT 1
Universum universe OT 3
unkonventionell unconventional **WS 4**, 150
Unkraut weed **WS 1**, 30
unmittelbar immediate **WS 1**, 24
unmöglich impossible OT 2
unnatürlich unnatural **WS 4**, 146
Unordnung mess OT 2
   in Unordnung bringen to mess up OT 2
uns us OT 1; ourselves OT 1
unser(e, -es) our OT 1
unsicher insecure **WS 4**, 142
Unsicherheit uncertainty **WS 4**, 142; insecurity **WS 4**, 146

Unsinn nonsense OT 1
unter under OT 1; below OT 2; among OT 3; underneath OT 3
unterbrechen to interrupt OT 2
Unterführung subway OT 1; underground OT 1; metro OT 1
unterhalten to entertain **WS 2**, 66
Unterhaltung conversation OT 1; entertainment OT 2
Unterkühlung hypothermia OT 2
Unterkunft accommodation OT 3
Unternehmen company OT 1
Unternehmer(in) entrepreneur **WS 4**, 143
Unterricht lesson OT 1
unterrichten to teach OT 1
unterschätzen to underestimate **WS 2**, 59
Unterschied difference OT 1
unterschiedlich different OT 1
Unterschlupf shelter OT 2
unterschreiben to sign OT 2
unterstützen to support OT 1; to endorse **WS 2**, 63; to assist **WS 4**, 139
unterstützend supportive **WS 1**, 14
Unterstützung support OT 2; aid **WS 2**, 59; assistance **WS 4**, 127
untersuchen to investigate OT 3
Untersuchung survey OT 1; analysis **WS 4**, 144
ununterbrochen steadily **WS 2**, 75
unverantwortlich irresponsible OT 2
unvergesslich memorable OT 3; unforgettable **WS 1**, 29
unversehrt intact OT 3
unverwechselbar distinctive **WS 1**, 32
unvollständig incomplete **WS 4**, 123
unwahrscheinlich unlikely OT 3
unzugänglich inaccessible OT 3
urban urban **WS 2**, 52
Urkunde diploma **WS 4**, 126
Urlaub holiday OT 1; vacation OT 2
Ursprung origin OT 3
ursprünglich original OT 3

V

vage vague **WS 1**, 27
Vampir vampire OT 2
Vanille vanilla OT 1
Vanillesoße custard OT 1
Variante variation **WS 1**, 33
Variation variation **WS 1**, 33
variieren to vary **WS 4**, 126
Vater father OT 1
Vati dad OT 1
vegan vegan **WS 2**, 52

Veganer(in) vegan **WS 2**, 52
vegetarisch vegetarian OT 2; vegetarian OT 2
Vegetation vegetation OT 3
Verabredung date OT 3
verabscheuen to loathe **WS 1**, 25
(sich) verändern to change OT 1
Veränderung shift **WS 4**, 128
verängstigt scared OT 1; frightened OT 1; terrified OT 3
veranschaulichen to visualize **WS 2**, 61
veranstalten to put on OT 1; to attract OT 3; to dress **WS 2**
Veranstaltung event OT 1
verantwortlich in charge OT 1; responsible **WS 3**, 90
Verantwortung responsibility OT 3
verärgert cross OT 2; irritated OT 2; annoyed OT 3
Verband bandage OT 2
verbergen to conceal **WS 4**, 125
(sich) verbessern to correct OT 1; to fix OT 2; to mark OT 2; to improve OT 3
Verbesserung improvement OT 3
verbieten to ban OT 3
verbinden to join up OT 2; to connect OT 2
Verbindung connection OT 2; link OT 2
verblüfft puzzled **WS 1**, 14
Verbraucher(in) consumer **WS 2**, 62
Verbrechen crime **WS 3**, 90
verbreiten to spread **WW**, 10
verdeutlichen to illustrate OT 3
verdienen to deserve OT 2; to earn OT 3
(sich) verdoppeln to double **WS 1**, 17
Verein club OT 1
Vereinbarung agreement OT 3; arrangement **WS 4**, 123
vereinigen to unify OT 3
   sich vereinigen to unite **WS 1**, 13
vererblich hereditary **WS 3**, 98
Verfahren procedure **WS 2**, 56
Verfasser(in) writer OT 1
Verfassung constitution OT 3
verfaulen to rot **WS 1**, 25
verfeinern to refine **WS 3**, 97
verfolgen to persecute OT 3; to pursue **WS 2**, 46
verfügbar available **WS 2**, 54
Verfügbarkeit availability **WS 4**, 138
vergeben to forgive OT 2
vergessen to forget OT 1
Vergleich comparison **WS 1**, 29
vergleichbar comparable **WS 4**, 126
vergleichen to compare OT 1
Vergnügen pleasure OT 1

Verhalten habit **WS 2**, 51
Verhältnis relation **WS 1**, 30
verhandeln to negotiate **WS 3**, 99
verheerend devastating **WS 1**, 34
verhindern to prevent **WS 3**, 101
verhungern to starve OT 1
verkaufen to sell OT 1
Verkäufer(in) sales assistant OT 2
Verkehr traffic OT 1; transport OT 3
sich verkleiden to dress up OT 3
verklemmt uptight **WS 4**, 122
verkünden to declare **WS 1**, 42
Verlag publisher **WS 4**, 135
verlangen to require **WS 4**, 127
verlassen to leave OT 1; to desert OT 3;
   to evacuate **WS 3**, 108
   sich verlassen auf to rely on **WS 3**, 93
verlässlich reliable **WS 3**, 96
verlegen embarrassed OT 3
Verleger(in) publisher **WS 4**, 135
verletzen to injure OT 2
verletzt hurt OT 1
Verletzung injury OT 2; violation
   WS 3, 101
verlieren to lose OT 1
Verlierer(in) loser OT 3
Verlust loss **WS 1**, 39
vermeiden to avoid OT 3
vermieten to let OT 1
vermissen to miss OT 2
vermitteln to impart OT 3;
   to communicate **WS 4**, 113
vermuten to suppose OT 1; to accept
   OT 2; to adopt OT 3
Vernetzung connectivity OT 3
Vernunft reason OT 1
vernünftig sensible OT 2; reasonable
   WS 2, 64
veröffentlichen to publish **WW**, 11;
   to release **WS 1**, 25
Veröffentlichung publication **WS 2**, 63
Verpackung packaging OT 3
verpflichtend mandatory **WS 3**, 108
Verrat treason **WS 3**, 98
verrückt crazy OT 2; mad OT 2
Vers verse OT 3
Versammlung assembly OT 1
verschicken to send OT 1
verschieden diverse OT 3
verschlüsselt in code OT 2
verschmutzen to pollute **WS 1**, 25;
   to contaminate **WS 1**, 34
Verschmutzung pollution OT 3
verschütten to spill OT 2
verschwenden to waste OT 3
verschwinden to disappear OT 3

verschwunden missing OT 1
versehentlich by accident OT 2;
   by mistake OT 2; accidentally OT 3
verseuchen to pollute **WS 1**, 25
Versicherung insurance **WS 3**, 84
Version version OT 2
versklaven to enslave OT 3
Versmaß metre OT 1
versorgen mit to supply OT 3;
   to provide **WS 1**, 36
Versprechen promise OT 2
versprechen to promise OT 2
Verstand mind OT 1
Verständnis understanding OT 2
verstärken to reinforce **WS 4**, 124
verstaubt dusty **WS 2**, 55
verstauchen to sprain OT 2
Verstauchung sprain OT 2
(sich) verstecken to hide OT 3
verstehen to understand OT 1
Verstoß violation **WS 3**, 101
Versuch attempt OT 2
versuchen to try OT 1
vertäuen to moor OT 3
verteidigen to defend **WS 1**, 25
Verteidiger(in) defender OT 3
vertrauen to trust OT 2
vertraut familiar OT 2
Vertrautheit familiarity **WS 2**, 53
vertreten to represent **WW**, 10
Vertreter(in) representative **WS 3**, 90
verursachen to cause OT 2
verurteilen to sentence **WS 4**, 144;
   to convict **WS 4**, 144
Verurteilte(r) convict **WS 1**, 17
vervollständigen to complete OT 1
Verwandlung transformation **WS 3**, 110
verwandt related OT 3
Verwandte(r) relative OT 3
verwenden to use OT 1
verwirrend confusing OT 2
verwirrt confused OT 2; puzzled **WS 1**, 14
verwundet wounded OT 2
verzweifelt desperate OT 3
Video video OT 1
Videospiel video game OT 2
Viehbestand livestock **WS 1**, 28
Viehhaltung ranching **WS 2**, 69
viel a lot, lots OT 1; much OT 1; plenty
   OT 2
   viele many OT 1
vielfach multiple OT 2
Vielfalt variety **WS 1**, 26
vielfältig diverse OT 3
Vielfältigkeit diversity **WS 1**, 32
vielleicht maybe OT 1; perhaps OT 3

vier four OT 1
Viertel quarter OT 1
vierzehn fourteen OT 1
vierzig forty OT 1
violett violet OT 2
viral viral **WS 3**, 93
virtuell virtual **WS 1**, 29
visuell visual OT 2
Vize... vice OT 2
Vlog vlog OT 3
Vlogger(in) vlogger OT 3
Vogel bird OT 1
Voicemail voicemail OT 3
Volks... folk OT 2
Volksentscheid referendum **WS 3**, 99
Volkszählung census **WS 4**, 122
voll full OT 1
Volleyball volleyball OT 2
völlig totally OT 3
vollzeit full time OT 2
von from OT 1; of OT 1
vor before OT 1; ago OT 1; prior to OT 3
Voraussetzung requirement **WS 1**, 37
vorbeifahren to pass OT 2
vorbereiten to prepare OT 1; to get
   ready OT 1
Vorbereitung preparation OT 2
Vordergrund foreground **WS 2**, 53
Vorderseite front OT 1
Voreingenommenheit bias **WS 4**, 124
Vorfahr(in) ancestor OT 3
vorführen to demonstrate **WS 4**, 128
Vorgang operation OT 3
vorgesehen designated OT 3
vorhaben to plan OT 1; to arrange OT 2
Vorhaben project OT 1
Vorhang curtain OT 2
vorhergehend previous OT 3
Vorhersage prediction OT 2
vorhersagen to predict OT 2
vorhersehbar predictable **WS 1**, 24
Vorlage template OT 3
Vormittag morning OT 1
vorn at the front OT 1; ahead OT 2
Vorrat supply OT 3
Vorschlag suggestion OT 1
vorschlagen to suggest OT 1; to put
   forward OT 3
vorschreiben to prescribe **WS 4**, 126
vorsichtig careful OT 1; cautious OT 3
Vorsitz chair OT 1; presidency **WS 3**, 115
Vorspeise starter OT 1
vorstellen to introduce OT 2; to present
   OT 1
   sich etwas vorstellen to imagine OT 1
Vorstellung introduction OT 2

Vorstellungsgespräch interview OT 1
Vorteil pro OT 2; advantage OT 3; benefit **WS 1**, 24
vorteilhaft beneficial OT 2
Vortrag presentation OT 1
vortreten to step up **WS 4**, 123
Vorwahl caucus OT 2
vorwärts forwards OT 2
vorziehen to prefer OT 1
Vulkan volcano OT 2

W
wach awake OT 2
wachsen to grow OT 1
Wachstum growth **WS 2**, 68
Wächter(in) guard **WS 4**, 151
wackelig shaky OT 3
Waffe weapon OT 3
Wagen carriage OT 2; trolley OT 2; wagon OT 3
wagen to dare OT 2
Wahl choice OT 1; option OT 2; election OT 3
Wahl... electoral **WS 3**, 91
Wahlbezirk constituency **WS 3**, 92
wählen to vote OT 1; to elect OT 2; to dial OT 2; to select OT 3
Wähler(in) voter OT 3; constituent **WS 3**, 92
wahr true OT 1
während while OT 2; during OT 2; throughout OT 3
Wahrheit truth OT 3
wahrscheinlich probably OT 2; likely OT 2
Wahrzeichen landmark OT 3
Waise orphan OT 2
Wal whale OT 2
Wald forest OT 1; woods OT 2
Walfang whaling OT 2
Walross walrus OT 3
Walspeck blubber OT 2
Wand wall OT 1
Wanderer, Wanderin hiker OT 3
wandern to hike OT 1
Wandgemälde mural OT 2
wann when OT 1
warm warm OT 1
Wärme warmth OT 3
warnen to warn OT 2
Warnung warning OT 2
warten to wait OT 1; to hang on OT 2
Warteschlange queue OT 1
Wartung maintenance OT 3
warum why OT 1
was what OT 1

Wäsche laundry OT 3
Wäscheklammer clothes peg **WS 2**, 74
waschen to wash OT 2
Wasser water OT 1
wasserdicht waterproof OT 2
Wasserfall waterfall OT 1
Wasserhahn tap OT 3
Wassermelone watermelon OT 3
Wasserschildkröte turtle OT 2
Wasserstelle watering hole **WS 1**, 25; waterhole **WS 1**, 38
Webseite webside OT 1; side OT 1
Wechsel change OT 1; transition **WS 3**, 99
Wechselgeld change OT 1
wechseln to change OT 1
Wecker alarm clock OT 2
Weg way OT 1; path OT 1; track OT 2
weg away OT 2
Wegbeschreibungen directions OT 2
wegen because of OT 1; due to **WS 1**, 28
wehen to blow OT 2
Wehr weir OT 3
wehtun to hurt OT 1
weiblich female OT 2
weich soft OT 1
weil because OT 1
weinen to cry OT 1
weiß white OT 1
weit far OT 1; wide OT 2; broad OT 3
weiter further OT 3
weitermachen to continue OT 2; to go ahead OT 2
Weizen wheat **WS 1**, 28
welche(r, -s) which OT 1
Welle wave OT 1
Wellenreiten surfing OT 1
Wellensittich budgie OT 1
Welpe puppy OT 2
Welt world OT 1
weltoffen cosmopolitan **WS 1**, 19
weltweit global OT 3; worldwide **WS 3**, 100
Wende turn OT 1
Wendung phrase OT 1
wenige few OT 1
wenn when OT 1
wer, wen, wem who OT 1
Werbespot commercial **WS 2**, 74
Werbung advertisement OT 1; ad, advert OT 2; advertising OT 2
werden to become OT 2; to get OT 2
werfen to throw OT 1; to toss OT 1
Werft wharf **WS 2**, 48
Werkstatt workshop OT 1
Werkzeug tool OT 2
Wert value OT 3

wert worth OT 3
wertschätzen to value **WS 4**, 143
wertvoll valuable OT 2
Wesen being OT 3
wesentlich essential **WS 1**, 33
weshalb why OT 1
Wespe wasp OT 3
wessen whose OT 1
Westen west OT 1
westlich west OT 1
Wettbewerb competition OT 1
Wettbewerber(in) competitor OT 3
wetten to bet OT 1
Wetter weather OT 1
Wetterfahne weather vane OT 3
Wettkampf match OT 1; game OT 1
Wettkämpfer(in) contestant **WS 3**, 86
wichtig important OT 1; major OT 3; dominant OT 3; essential **WS 1**, 33; relevant **WS 2**, 65
Wichtigkeit importance OT 3; significance **WS 1**, 32
Widerstand resistance **WS 1**, 24
wie how OT 1; as OT 1
wieder again OT 1
Wiederbelebung revival **WS 4**, 128
wiederherstellen to restore **WS 3**, 98
wiederholen to repeat OT 1
wiederverwendbar reusable OT 3
wiederverwenden to reuse **WS 3**, 102
wiederverwerten to recycle OT 2
Wiese meadow OT 2
wild wild OT 2; feral **WS 1**, 25
Wildnis wilderness OT 2
willkommen heißen to welcome OT 1
Wind wind OT 2
Windel diaper OT 3
sich winden to wind OT 3
windig windy OT 2
windsurfen to windsurf OT 1
Winter winter OT 1
winzig tiny OT 1
wir us OT 1; ourselves OT 1; we OT 1
wirklich really OT 1; truly **WS 1**, 29; actually **WS 3**, 98
wirksam effective OT 3
Wirkung effect OT 3
Wissen science OT 1; knowledge **WS 2**, 64
wissen to know OT 1
Wissenschaft science OT 1
Witz joke OT 2; pun OT 3
  Witze machen to joke OT 2
witzig funny OT 1
wo where OT 1
  wo (auch) immer wherever OT 3
Woche week OT 1
Wochenende weekend OT 1

wöchentlich weekly **WS 1**, 32
Wohl welfare **WS 3**, 100
Wohlfahrtsorganisation charity OT 2
Wohltätigkeitsveranstaltung fundraiser OT 2
wohnen to stay OT 1; to live OT 1
Wohnsitz residence **WS 3**, 110
Wohnung flat OT 1; apartment OT 1
Wohnwagen caravan OT 1
Wohnzimmer living room OT 1
Wolke cloud OT 1
Wolkenkratzer skyscraper OT 3
wolkig cloudy OT 1
Wolle wool OT 3
wollen to want OT 1
wollig woolly OT 2
Wort word OT 1
Wörterbuch dictionary OT 2
Wortliste wordlist OT 2
Wortschatz lexicon WW, 11
Wrack wreck OT 3
Wunder wonder OT 3
wunderbar wonderful OT 1
Wunderkerze sparkler OT 3
Wunsch desire **WS 2**, 70
wünschen to wish OT 2
würdigen to appreciate OT 2
Wurm worm OT 1
Wurst sausage OT 1
Würstchen sausage OT 1
Wurzel root OT 3
würzig spicy **WS 2**, 79
Wüste desert OT 3
wütend angry OT 1; mad OT 2; wicked OT 2

Z
zäh tough OT 2
Zahl number OT 1; figure OT 3
zählbar countable OT 1
zahlen to pay OT 1
zählen to count OT 2
Zahn tooth OT 2
Zahnarzt, -ärztin dentist OT 3
Zauber magic OT 1
Zauberer, Zauberin magician OT 1
Zaun fence OT 1
Zebra zebra OT 1
Zeh toe OT 1
zehn ten OT 1
Zeichen sign OT 1; symbol OT 1; notice OT 3
Zeichensetzung punctuation OT 3
zeichnen to draw OT 1; illustrate OT 3
zeigen to show OT 1; to point OT 1; to reveal **WS 2**, 53; to indicate **WS 2**, 65; to demonstrate **WS 4**, 128

Zeit time OT 1; period OT 3
Zeitachse timeline OT 2
zeitgenössisch contemporary **WS 2**, 52
zeitig early OT 1
Zeitschrift magazine OT 1
Zeitung newspaper OT 1
Zelt tent OT 1
zelten to camp OT 1
Zeltplatz campsite OT 2; campground OT 2
Zentimeter centimetre OT 2
Zentral... central OT 1
Zentralheizung central heating OT 2
zerbrechen to break OT 1; to snap OT 3
zerbrechlich fragile OT 3
zerebrale Kinderlähmung cerebral palsy **WS 4**, 127
zeremoniell ceremonial OT 3
zerfetzen to shred OT 2
zerstören to destroy OT 2
Zerstörung destruction **WS 1**, 35
Zertifikat certificate OT 2
Zeug stuff OT 2
Zeugnis certificate OT 2
Ziege goat OT 3
ziehen to pull OT 1
Ziel aim OT 2; target OT 3
zielen to aim **WS 4**, 128
   zielen auf to target **WS 4**, 150
ziellos aimlessly **WS 4**, 125
ziemlich rather OT 3; quite OT 3
Ziffer digit OT 2
Zimmer room OT 1
Zimmermann carpenter OT 3
Zirkus circus **WS 2**, 52
zischen to whizz OT 2
Zitat quotation OT 2; quote **WS 2**, 52
zitieren to quote OT 2
zittern to shiver OT 3
zivilisiert civilized **WS 1**, 27
zögern to hesitate OT 3
Zoll customs OT 2
zollfrei duty free OT 2
Zone zone OT 2
Zoo zoo OT 1
zu to; too OT 1; closed OT 1
Zubehör accessory OT 3
zubinden to tie **WS 4**, 131
züchten to breed **WS 3**, 95
Zucker sugar OT 1
zuerst at first OT 2; firstly OT 3
Zufahrt driveway OT 3
zufällig by chance OT 2; accidentally OT 3; random **WS 1**, 24
zufrieden pleased OT 1
Zug train OT 1

Zugang access OT 2; gateway **WS 1**, 39
zugänglich accessible OT 2
zugeben to admit OT 2
zügig swift OT 3
Zuhause home OT 1
zuhause at home OT 1
Zukunft future OT 2
zumachen to close OT 1; to shut OT 2; to conclude OT 3
Zunahme increase OT 3
Zunder tinder OT 2
Zunge tongue OT 3
zuordnen to allocate **WS 3**, 91
zurechtkommen to cope **WS 4**, 127
zurück back OT 1
zurückgehen to decrease **WS 4**, 132
zurückkehren to return OT 2
zurücktreten to resign **WS 3**, 99
zusammen together OT 1
zusammenfassen to summarize OT 2; to outline OT 3; to sum up OT 3
Zusammenfassung summary OT 1; abstract OT 3
Zusammenhang context **WS 1**, 16
zusammensacken to slump **WS 4**, 137
Zusatz addition **WS 2**, 56
zusätzlich additional **WS 4**, 127
zuschauen to watch OT 1
Zuschauer(in) spectator OT 2; viewer OT 3
zuschneiden to tailor **WS 3**, 93
Zustand condition OT 2
zuständig in charge OT 1
zusteigen to get on OT 2
Zustellung delivery **WS 2**, 64
zustimmen to agree OT 1; to approve **WS 3**, 91
Zutat ingredient OT 2
zuweisen to allocate **WS 3**, 91
zwanzig twenty OT 1
Zweck purpose **WS 1**, 36
zwei two OT 1
Zweifel doubt WW, 11
zweifellos undoubtedly **WS 3**, 110
zweimal twice OT 2
zweisprachig bilingual OT 3
zweitrangig secondary OT 1
Zwiebel onion OT 2
Zwilling twin OT 1
zwingen to force OT 3
zwischen between OT 1; among OT 3
Zwischenstation waypoint OT 2
zwölf twelve OT 1
Zyklon cyclone **WS 1**, 34

Dictionary: Names

A

Abingdon House [ˌæbɪŋtən ˈhaʊs] SEN school in England **WS 2**, 61

Aesha [aɪˈiːʃə] girl's name **WW**, 11

Alain [əˈleɪn] boy's name **WW**, 11

Albuquerque [ˈælbəkɜːkɪ] state in the USA **WS3**, 85

Amelia [əˈmiːliə] girl's name **WS2**, 70

Amir [eˈmɪə] boy's name **WS 3**, 90

Andrew Jackson [ˌændruː ˈdʒæksən] 7th president of the USA and military officer **WS3**, 91

Anne Boleyn [æn bəˈlɪn] Henry VIII's second wife **WS2**, 59

Atlantic Ocean [ətˈlæntɪk ˈoʊʃən] ocean between the Americas in the west and Europe and Africa in the east **WS3**, 84

Auckland [ˈɔːklənd] city in the North Island of New Zealand **WS 1**, 13

Austin [ˈɒstɪn] capital city of the state of Texas, USA **WS3**, 85

Ayers Rock [eɪərs ˈrɒk] former colonial name of Uluru **WS 1**, 26

B

Barkindji [baˈkɪndʒiː] an Australian Aboriginal tribal group in New South Wales, Australia **WS 1**, 15

Ben Ockrent [ben ˈɒkrent] contemporary British writer and theatre director **WS 3**, 122

Blenheim Palace [ˌblɛnɪm ˈpæləs] country house in Oxfordshire, England and birth place of Winston Churchill **WS3**, 107

Boris Johnson [ˌbɒrɪs ˈdʒɒnsn] British Prime Minister since 2019 **WS3**, 111

Boston [ˈbɒstən] capital city of the state of Massachusetts, USA **WS3**, 85

Brad [bræd] boy's name **WW**, 11

Buckingham Palace [ˌbʌkɪŋəm ˈpæləs] the London residence of the British monarch **WS3**, 110

C

Canberra [ˈkænbərə] capital of Australia **WS 1**, 13

Captiol [ˈkæpɪtl] the building in Washington, DC, USA, where Congress meets **WS3**, 87

Cardiff [ˈkɑːdɪf] capital of Wales **WS 3**, 90

Catherine, Duchess of Cambridge [ˌdʌtʃəs əv ˈkeɪmbrɪdʒ] wife of Prince Williams **WS3**, 100

Charles, Prince of Wales [tʃɑːlz ˌprɪns əv ˈweɪlz] eldest son of Queen Elizabeth II and heir to the throne **WS3**, 100

Christchurch [ˈkraɪstʃɜːtʃ] largest city in the South Island of New Zealand **WS 1**, 13

Conny [ˈkɒni] girl's name **WS 2**, 58

D

Donald Trump [ˈdɒnld trʌmp] 45th president of the USA **WS3**, 91

E

Eleni [əˈleɪni] girl's name **WS 1**, 14

F

Fred [fred] boy's name **WS 1**, 18

G

George Washington [ˌdʒɔːdʒ ˈwɒʃɪŋtən] first president of the USA, general during the American Revolution **WS3**, 87

Glastonbury [ˈglæstənbri] town in southwestern England **WS3**, 102

Graham [ˈgreɪəm] boy's name **WS 2**, 58

Grand Canyon [ˌgrænd ˈkænjən] the very deep narrow valley of the Colorado River in Arizona, USA **WS3**, 85

Great Barrier Reef [greɪt ˈbæriə ˌriːf] the world's largest coral reef system, off the coast of Queensland, Australia **WS 1**, 26

Greenpeace [ˈgriːnpiːs] international environmental protection group **WS3**, 102

Greton [ˈgretən] SEN school in England **WS 2**, 61

Gulf of Mexico [ˌgʌlf əv ˈmeksɪkəʊ] an arm of the Atlantic Ocean bordered by the USA, Cuba and Mexico **WS3**, 84

Gunpowder plot [ˈgʌn paʊdə plɒt] a plan in 1605 to blow up the Houses of Parliament and kill King James; it was discovered before the gunpowder was exploded **WS2**, 48

Guy Fawkes [ˌgaɪ ˈfɔːks] man who was part of the Gunpowder plot in 1605 **WS2**, 48

H

Hampton Court Palace [hæmptən kɔːt ˈpælɪs] a castle in London **WS2**, 58

Hillary Clinton [ˈhɪləri ˈklɪntn] wife of former US president Bill Clinton, who also ran for president of the USA, born in 1947 **WS3**, 91

Hosier Lane [ˌhəʊzɪə ˈleɪn] popular street and tourist attraction in Melbourne **WS 1**, 29

I

Iain Murray Rose [ˈiːən mʌri ˈrəʊz] Australian swimmer and six-time Olympic medalist (1939 – 2012) **WS 1**, 22

J

Jacinda Ardern [dʒəˈsɪndə] Prime Minister of New Zealand, born 26th July 1980 **WS 1**, 33

Jamaica [dʒəˈmeɪkə] island in the West Indies in the Caribbean Sea **WS2**, 48

James Cook [dʒeɪmz ˈkʊk] British explorer (1728 – 1799) **WS 1**, 17

Jason [ˈdʒeɪsn] boy's name **WS 1**, 14

Jermaine [dʒəˈmeɪn] boy's name **WS 3**, 107

Joe Biden [ˌdʒəʊ ˈbaɪdən] 46th president of the USA **WS3**, 115

K

Kamala Harris [ˌkɑːmələ ˈhærɪs] 49th vice president of the USA **WS3**, 116

Karen McManus [ˌkærən mækˈmenəs] contemporary American author **WS4**, 152

Keira [ˈkɪərə] girl's name **WS 1**, 18

Kevin Rudd [ˌkevɪn ˈrʌd] Australian Prime Minister (2007 – 2010 and 2013) **WS 1**, 22

Koula [ˈkuːlə] girl's name **WS 1**, 15

Kourakis [kuːˈrɑːkis] surname **WS 1**, 14

L

Lindy [ˈlɪndi] girl's name **WS 2**, 60

M

Margaret Atwood [ˌmɑːgrət ˈætwʊd] Canadian poet and novelist, born 18th November, 1939 **WS 3**, 120

Matthew Flinders [ˌmæθjuː ˈflɪndərz] English explorer and cartographer (1774 – 1814) **WS 1**, 17

Melbourne [ˈmelbən] capital city Victoria, Australia **WS 1** , 13

Milford Sound [ˌmɪlfəd ˈsaʊnd] fjord in the south west of New Zealand's South Island **WS 1**, 32

N

Nasir [nəzˈiə] boy's name **WS 3**, 90

New Guinea [ˌnjuː ˈgɪni] the world's second largest island, located in the southwestern Pacific Ocean **WS 1**, 17

New Holland [ˌnjuː ˈhɑlənd] historical name for mainland Australia in the 17th century **WS 1**, 17

Nick [nɪk] boy's name **WS 1**, 14

Nicole [nɪˈkəʊl] girl's name **WW**, 11

O

Oliver Cromwell [ˌɒlɪvə ˈkrɒmwel] English general and statesman during the English Civil War (1642 – 1651) **WS3**, 98

Oprah Winfrey [ˌɔːprə ˈwɪnfriː] American talk show host **WS 2**, 110

P

Patrick J. Kennedy [ˈpætrɪk dʒeɪ ˈkenədi] American politician and mental health advocate **WS 2**, 73

Paul Theroux [pɔl θəˈruː] American travel writer **WS2**, 52

Philip, Duke of Edinburgh [ˈfɪlɪp ˌdjuːk əv ˈedɪnbrə] husband of Queen Elizabeth II **WS3**, 100

Q

Queenstown [ˈkwiːnztaʊn] city in the South Island of New Zealand **WS 1**, 32

R

Ricky [ˈrɪki] boy's name **WS 1**, 14

S

Sadie [ˈseɪdi] girl's name **WS 2**, 52

San Francisco [ˌsæn frənˈsɪskəʊ] city in California, USA **WS3**, 85

Sanjay [ˈsændʒeɪ] boy's name **WW**, 11

Steven Spielberg [ˈstiːvn ˈspiːlbɜːg] American film director **WS4**, 128

Sydney [ˈsɪdni] capital city of New South Wales and most populous city in Australia **WS 1**, 13

T

Tai [taɪ] boy's name **WS 1**, 30

Tayler [ˈteɪlər] boy's and girl's name **WS 2**, 55

Texas [ˈteksəs] state in the USA **WS3**, 85

Theresa May [ˌtəˈriːzə meɪ] British Prime Minister from 2016 – 2019 **WS3**, 99

Thomas Jefferson [ˌtɒməs ˈdʒefəsən] 3rd president of the USA, main author of the Declaration of Independence **WS3**, 87

Torres Strait Islands [ˌtɔːrəs streɪt ˈaɪlənd] a group of 274 small islands in the Torres Strait **WS 1**, 12

Turner [ˈtɜːnə] surname **WS 1**, 14

Tuscon [ˈtuːsɒn] city in the state of Arizona, USA **WS3**, 85

U

Uluru [ˌuːləˈruː] a rock formation in the Northern Territory, Australia **WS 1**, 26

V

Valerie [ˈvæləri] girl's name **WS 2**, 53

W

Wellington [ˈwelɪŋtən] capital of New Zealand **WS 1**, 32

Wilds Lodge [ˈwaɪldz lɒdʒ] SEN school in England **WS 2**, 61

William the Conqueror [ˈwɪljəm ðə ˈkɑːŋkərər] Duke of Normandy, conquered England in 1066 **WS3**, 98

William, Duke of Cambridge [ˈwɪljəm ˌdjuːk əv ˈkeɪmbrɪdʒ] son of Charles, Prince of Wales and Diana, Princess of Wales **WS3**, 100

Winston Churchill [ˌwɪnstən ˈtʃɜːtʃɪl] British politician who was Prime Minister and Minister of Defence during World War II and Prime Minister from 1951 – 1955 **WS3**, 106

Acknowledgements

Audio credits

Dialogues and words and phrases produced by Anne Rosenfeld for RBA Productions (rbaproductions.co.uk). Recording engineer Mark Smith.
Track 18: "First Nation". Text (OT): Hirst, Rovert George / Tasman, Keith. © SFM Publishing Pty Ltd/Sony/ATV Music Publishing (Germany) GmbH, Berlin
Track 19: "Brown Girl". Text (OT): Silverman, Jeffrey Scott / d'Annunzio, Vincent John jr / Patel, Aaradhna Jayantilal. © Jeffrey Scott Productions LLC/Vincent John Music/Kobalt Music Publishing/Printrechte Hal Leonard Europe GmbH
Track 35 "Waterloo sunset", DAVRAY MUSIC LTD, CARLIN MUSIC CORP
Track 36 "My name is London town", BMG RIGHTS MANAGEMENT (UK) LIMITED

Video credits

Videos 1, 2, 4, 10: produced by Anne Rosenfeld for RBA Productions, Brighton (rbaproductions.co.uk). Editor: David Rafique
Video 1 (picture credits): Anatoly Vartanov / Rozhnovskaya, Tanya; Forster, Stuart; The Print Collector; Long, Suzanne; Delimont, Danita; FLHC Y1; Corbishley, Guy; PA Images; public domain sourced / access rights from PJF Military Collection; McAllister, Neil; Henry Westheim Photography; Horree, Peter; Aflo Co. Ltd.; Mayo, Marcelo; edhar yuralaits
Video 2 (picture credits): structuresxx / iStockphoto.com; Classic Image / Alamy Stock Photo; Rainbird, John / Alamy Stock Photo; Lake Erie Maps and Prints / Alamy Stock Photo; geogphotos / Alamy Stock Photo; Hellier, Chris / Alamy Stock Photo; Swanepoel, Johan / Alamy Stock Photo; simonbradfield / iStockphoto.com; zetter / iStockphoto.com; slowmotiongli / iStockphoto.com; Aristine / iStockphoto.com; Griffiths, Ken / Alamy Stock Photo; Fare, Andrew / Alamy Stock Photo; Totajla / iStockphoto.com; DoraDalton / iStockphoto.com; FiledIMAGE / iStockphoto.com; Crux, John / Alamy Stock Photo; DPK-Photo / Alamy Stock Photo
Video 4 (picture credits): South, David / Alamy Stock Photo; Lesniewski, Rainer / Alamy Stock Photo; World History Archive / Alamy Stock Photo; Granger Historical Picture Archive / Alamy Stock Photo; McLaren, Kirsty / Alamy Stock Photo; Classic Image / Alamy Stock Photo; public domain sourced / access rights from Lakeview Images / Alamy Stock Photo; public domain sourced / access rights from Historic Collection / Alamy Stock Photo; Miceking / Shutterstock.com; Robert Wallace / Wallace Media Network / Alamy Stock Photo
Videos 7-9, 12-14: produced by James Vyner and Luke Vyner for Creative Listening, London (www.creativelistening.co.uk).
Video 10 (picture credits): Discha-AS; Africa Studio; taras.chaban; Paateel, Manoej; SergeBertasiusPhotography; HASPhotos; Aspects and Angles; M-SUR (alle Shutterstock.com)
Video 11: provided courtesy of My Genderation. www.mygenderation.com

Picture credits

|123RF.com, Hong Kong: stefaninahill 22.3. |Alamy Stock Photo, Abingdon/Oxfordshire: Action Plus Sports Images 33.2; AF archive 106.2; agefotostock 22.4, 31.5, 98.3; Allstar Picture Library Ltd 15.1; Arnold, Rob 29.2; Avpics 110.1; Bachman, Bill 23.2, 38.1; Barraud, Martin 130.4; Ben-Ari, Rafael 12.2; Berg, Georg 23.6; Bialasiewicz, Katarzyna 131.2; Black, Ruth 36.1; Blake, Gary 42.4; BluIz60 21.3; Bujdoso, Andor 135.1; Daemmrich, Bob 96.1; Dagnall, Ian 58.4; david a eastley 23.5; Davydov, Aleksandr 137.2; Dorney, Chris 43.1; DPK-Photo 32.2; du Feu, Geoff 134.2; E.D. Torial 131.1; Fremantle 106.1; Fuchslocher, Mike 19.3; Gekko Studios 12.4; Genevieve Vallee 23.3; Gerbino, Silvia 128.5; Gingell, Ben 68.3; Gino's Premium Images 68.4; GL Archive 98.1, 98.2; Haines, Malcolm 107.1; Hasenkopf, Juergen 25.1; Honcharuk, Valerii 68.5; Imagebroker 25.3; imageBROKER 35.3, 36.2; Ison, Chris 25.2; Janine Wiedel Photolibrary 120.3; Jeffrey Isaac Greenberg 17+ 9.1, 130.2; Jeffrey Isaac Greenberg 8+ 23.4; jeremy sutton-hibbert 17.4; Johnson, Mark A. 21.2; Jon Arnold Images Ltd 13.4, 26.1; Jon D 151.1; Kerrison, Mark 111.1; KGPA Ltd 22.2; MacNaughton, Alex 99.2; Marinic, Borislav 130.5; Martin, Paul 58.2; MBI 11.1, 130.3; Michael, Andrew 241.2; Milnes, Richard 22.5; Naoumova, Irina 35.2; New Illustrations by Alfonsodetomas / Alamy Vektorgrafik 66.1; Oeland, Ingo 12.1; Outback Australia 28.2; parkerphotography 52.3, 134.4; paul kennedy 35.6; Pictorial Press Ltd 22.1; Popov, Andriy 137.1; Prisma by Dukas Presseagentur GmbH 13.1; public domain sourced / access rights from History and Art Collection 41.1; public domain sourced / access rights from Lakeview Images 17.1; robertharding 31.4, 74.1; Sally Richards 99.1; Savage, Nick 99.3; Science Photo Library 135.2; Selinger, Andy 42.2; SOPA Images Limited 94.4; Spiers, Nigel 35.5; Sriskandan, Kumar 54.4; Sykes, Homer 143.1; T.M.O.Trave 78.2; Tallec, Tony 142.1; TCC 100.1; Tetra Images 134.5; Thalhofer, Karoline 20.2; tommaso altamura 120.1; Travel Pictures 23.1; travellinglight 32.1; Travelscape Images 42.1, 42.5; Uliasz, Marek 143.3; Urban Napflin 36.3; Vidler, Steve 52.1;

Wall, David 31.1; WDC Photos 116.1; West, Jim 101.4; Wheal, Kevin 35.4; Windsor, Joshua 121.2; Wiskerke, Wim 241.1; Wisniewska, Monika 121.4; World History Archive 17.2; Zoonar GmbH 78.1; ZUMA Press, Inc. 33.1, 94.2. |Alamy Stock Photo (RMB), Abingdon/Oxfordshire: AB Forces News Collection 149.1; Bildagentur-online/Schoening 45.1; Birdsall, John 104.1; Classic Image 17.3; Crandall, Rob 90.2; dabincida 54.2; Douglas Peebles Photography 109.3; Forsberg, Peter 51.2; Green, Duncan Vere 53.1; JLImages 5.2, 57.1; MARKA 90.1; MBI 84.2; MicaUK 113.1; NJphoto 81.1; Pluto 80.1; Stocksolutions 76.2; travellinglight 54.3; Willett, A. T. 35.1. |CartoonStock.com, Bath: 124.1; www.CartoonStock.com/Hardin, Patrick 24.2. |Creative Listening, Newick: 134.1, 137.4. |Diekmann, Udo, Berlin: 48.3, 49.3, 58.1, 58.3. |Domke, Franz-Josef, Hannover: 3.1, 10.1, 258.1, 259.1. |Donnelly, Karen, Brighton: 14.1, 14.2, 16.1, 18.1, 20.1, 30.1, 30.2, 30.3, 31.2, 31.3, 31.6, 50.1, 51.1, 54.1, 55.1, 58.5, 61.1, 61.2, 61.3, 61.4, 61.5, 62.1, 74.2, 87.2, 88.1, 88.2, 89.1, 94.1, 103.1, 126.1, 128.1, 128.2, 128.3, 128.4, 139.1. |fotolia.com, New York: cevahir87 10.3; eyetronic 115.2; totajla 5.1, 44.1. |Hoth, Katharina, Erfurt: 133.2, 145.2. |iStockphoto.com, Calgary: AJ_Watt 11.2; AndreyKrav 57.2; Antonio_Diaz 73.2; anyaivanova 77.1; AurielAki 146.1; bearsky23 62.5; bennymarty 19.1; Brainsil 11.5; Carillet, Joel 97.2; chokkicx 70.3; Damocean 28.3; davidf 11.4; DHuss 56.1; duncan1890 24.1; engabito 151.2; FatCamera 146.2; ferrantraite 120.2; filo 85.4; golibo 64.1; IvelinRadkov 71.1; JackF 148.2; Jan-Otto 95.1; kokkai 13.2; Kyle_Hittner 141.3; lvcandy 92.1; mollypix 21.1; monkeybusinessimages 76.1, 137.3; Moore Media 122.3; MStudioImages 122.2; Muth, Steve 97.1; Patil, Nikhil 11.3; Phooey 52.2; pixelfit 148.5; Plahutar, Ziga 148.3; Ridofranz 68.1; RoBeDeRo 134.3; ROMAOSLO 147.1; ronstik 138.2; Sladic 131.4; South_agency 70.1; stockinasia 49.1; Totajla 19.2; travellinglight 39.1; undefined undefined 148.1; valentinrussanov 70.2; xavierarnau 37.2; xyom 68.2. |My Genderation: 125.1. |Picture-Alliance GmbH, Frankfurt a.M.: AP Photo/Bruce Weaver 109.1; SAKUMA, PAUL 143.2. |Shutterstock. com, New York: Akella Srinivas Ramalingaswami 101.2; antb 105.1; Balasko, Rudy 33.4; bibiphoto 109.4; Bikeworldtravel 49.4; Bluehousestudio 48.1; Bogdan, Serban 13.3; DeawSS 114.4; designer491 138.1; Divizia, Claudio 52.4; dubassy 102.1; Franzi 121.3; Galexia 29.1; Gingell, Ben 94.3; Guillem, Antonio 148.4; HASPhotos 101.3; Huebner, Daniel 33.3; Izzotti, Andrea 7.1, 87.1, 114.1; James, Alexander S 28.1; Keifer, Kenneth 85.5; Kraska 62.3; Luciano Mortula - LGM 85.6; marietta peros 102.3; Markin, Aleksandr 121.1; MaxyM 85.8; mccv 115.1; Melo, Lissandra 109.2; Miceking 10.2; Monkey Business Images 85.2, 131.3; nito 101.1; Nolan, Brian 108.1; Pavone, Sean 97.3; philophoto 85.3; PHOTOCREO Michal Bednarek 48.2; Pickering, Ashley 102.2; PitK 54.5; Pixel-Shot 141.1; polya_olya 85.9; Raggedstone 102.4; Roberts, Lorna 114.3; Shutterstock, Patrick 52.5; sirtravelalot 130.1; SpeedKingz 141.4; stockpexel 42.3; Symchych, Maria 73.1; TheModernCanvas 62.4; Todaro, Massimo 114.2; TongChuwit 62.2; Tupungato 111.2; untitled 49.2; ventdusud 85.1; wavebreakmediaD 141.2; Wildfoto 12.3; YAKOBCHUK VIACHESLAV 66.2; Zaiets, Roman 84.1; Zaskochenko, Olena 85.7. |Shutterstock.com (RM), New York: Moviestore 27.1. |stock.adobe.com, Dublin: Brivio, Marco 26.2; LIGHTFIELD STUDIOS 122.1; Palmer, Matt 37.1. |Williamson, Pete, Kent, Southorough, Tunbridge Wells: 46.1, 46.2, 47.1, 47.2, 82.1, 82.2, 83.1, 118.1, 118.2, 119.1, 119.2, 154.1, 154.2, 155.1, 156.1, 157.1, 157.2, 157.3.

Alaska
(state
of the USA)

Greenland
(Denmark)

Canada

Iceland

Norway
Sweden

Ireland
United
Kingdom
Denmark

France
Germany

Great
Lakes

Ottawa

Portugal
Spain
Italy

Atlantic

United States of America
(USA)

Washington, D.C.

Tunisia

Morocco

Canary Islands

Algeria
Libya

Hawaii
(state
of the USA)

Mexico

Bahamas

Cuba

Haiti
Dominican
Republic

Puerto Rico (USA)

Western
Sahara

Mauritania

Mali

Niger
Chad

Belize
Jamaica

Antigua and Barbuda

Cape Verde
Senegal

Guatemala
Honduras

Saint Kitts
and Nevis
Dominica

Gambia

Burkina
Faso

El Salvador

Saint Lucia
Barbados

Guinea-Bissau

Benin

Nicaragua
Grenada
Saint Vincent
and the Grenadines

Guinea

Côte
d'Ivoire
Togo

Nigeria

Costa Rica

Trinidad and Tobago

Sierra Leone
Ghana

Cameroon

Panama

Venezuela

Liberia

Colombia

Guyana

Suri-
name
French
Guiana

Equatorial Guinea
São Tomé and
Príncipe
Gabon

Equator

Congo

Ecuador

Pacific

Peru

Brazil

Ocean

Angola

Bolivia

Namibia

Ocean

Paraguay

Argentina
Uruguay

Chile

Falkland Islands
(UK)

Antarctica

Abbreviations:

BIH   Bosnia and
      Herzegovina

UK   United Kingdom
USA   United States of America

MNE   Montenegro

RKS   Kosovo

0   500 1,000 1,500 2,000 2,500

km

Atlantic Ocean

Shetland Islands

Orkney Islands

The Hebrides

Scotland

▲ *Ben Nevis*

● **Edinburgh** ●
Glasgow

The United Kingdom
of Great Britain and
Northern Ireland (UK)

North Sea

Hadrian's Wall
Vindolanda ● ● Newcastle upon Tyne
River Wear
● Durham

Northern Ireland

● **Belfast**

The Isle of Man

Irish Sea

Lake District

● Rievaulx

England

● Liverpool
● Manchester

Dublin ■

Bethesda ●
Caernafon ● *River Dee*
Republic of Ireland Llangollen ● Whitchurch ●
Mount Snowdon ▲ ● ● Ellesmere
● Ennis Chirk ●

● Birmingham

● Cambridge

Wales

River Towy

● Oxford
London ■
● Bristol
Cardiff ● *River Thames*
● Bath

● Glastonbury

● Portsmouth ● Brighton
Celtic Sea ● Devon ● ● Hastings
The Solent

● Plymouth

English Channel **France**

■ capital cities of the UK and the Republic of Ireland
● capital cities of the countries
● important cities/places in On Track 1, 2 and 3
● cities in On Track 4

0   50   100 miles
0   100 km